They Were C

MIKLÓS BÁNFFY

Count Miklós Bánffy (1873–1950)

THE WRITING ON THE WALL
(*Erdélyi Tőrtenét*)
The Transylvanian Trilogy
by

MIKLÓS BÁNFFY

BOOK ONE

They Were Counted

Translated by
PATRICK THURSFIELD and KATHY BÁNFFY-JELEN

Foreword by
PATRICK LEIGH FERMOR

ARCADIA BOOKS/UNESCO PUBLISHING

Arcadia Books Ltd
15–16 Nassau Street
London W1N 7RE

First published in Great Britain 1999
Original text © Miklós Bánffy 1934
Translation © Patrick Thursfield and Kathy Bánffy-Jelen 1999
Foreword © Patrick Leigh Fermor 1999
Introduction © Patrick Thursfield 1999

The right of Miklós Bánffy to be identified as
the author of this work has been asserted by his Estate
in accordance with the Copyright, Designs and Patents Act 1988.

All Rights Reserved. No part of this publication
may be reproduced in any form or by any means
without the written permission of the publishers.

A catalogue record for this book is available
from the British Library.

ISBN 1-990850-15-X
UNESCO COLLECTION OF REPRESENTATIVE WORKS
UNESCO ISBN 92-3-103580-0

Typeset in Monotype Baskerville by Discript, London WC2N 4BL

Printed in Finland by WSOY

Arcadia Books distributors are as follows:

in the UK and elsewhere in Europe:
Turnaround Publishers Services
Unit 3, Olympia Trading Estate
Coburg Road
London N22 6TZ

in the USA and Canada:
by Dufour Editions, Inc.
PO Box 7
Chester Springs, PA 19425-0007

in Australia:
Tower Books
PO Box 213
Brookvale, NSW 2100

in New Zealand:
Addenda
Box 78224
Grey Lynn
Auckland

For my dear children, for whom I first started on this translation of their grandfather's greatest work so that they should learn to know him better, he who would have loved them so much.

K. Bánffy-Jelen

FOREWORD
by
PATRICK LEIGH FERMOR

I FIRST DRIFTED into the geographical background of this remarkable book in the spring and summer of 1934, when I was nineteen, half-way through an enormous trudge from Holland to Turkey. Like many travellers, I fell in love with Budapest and the Hungarians, and by the time I got to the old principality of Transylvania, mostly on a borrowed horse, I was even deeper in.

With one interregnum, Hungary and Transylvania, which is three times the size of Wales, had been ruled by the Magyars for a thousand years. After the Great War, in which Hungary was a loser, the peace treaty took Transylvania away from the Hungarian crown and allotted it to the Romanians, who formed most of the population. The whole question was one of hot controversy, which I have tried to sort out and explain in a book called *Between the Woods and the Water*[*] largely to get things clear in my own mind; and, thank heavens, there is no need to go over it again in a short foreword like this. The old Hungarian landowners felt stranded and ill-used by history; nobody likes having a new nationality forced on them, still less, losing estates by expropriation. This, of course, is what happened to the descendants of the old feudal landowners of Transylvania.

By a fluke, and through friends I had made in Budapest and on the Great Hungarian Plain, I found myself wandering from castle to castle in what had been left of these age-old fiefs.

Hardly a trace of this distress was detectable to a stranger. In my case, the chief thing to survive is the memory of unlimited kindness. Though enormously reduced, remnants of these old estates did still exist, and, at moments it almost seemed as though nothing had changed. Charm and *doucer de vivre* was still afloat among the faded décor and the still undiminished libraries, and, out of doors, everything conspired to delight. Islanded in the rustic Romanian multitude, different in race and religious practice – the Hungarians were Catholics or Calvinists, the Romanians

[*] John Murray, 1980.

v

Orthodox or Uniat – and, with the phantoms of their lost ascendency still about them, the prevailing atmosphere conjured up the tumbling demesnes of the Anglo-Irish in Waterford or Galway with all their sadness and their magic. Homesick for the past, seeing nothing but their own congeners on the neighbouring estates and the few peasants who worked there, they lived in a backward-looking, a genealogical, almost a Confucian dream, and many sentences ended in a sigh.

It was in the heart of Transylvania – in the old princely capital then called Kolozsvár (now Cluj-Napoca) that I first came across the name of Bánffy. It was impossible not to. Their palace was the most splendid in the city, just as Bonchida was the pride of the country and both of them triumphs of the baroque style. Ever since the arrival of the Magyars ten centuries ago, the family had been foremost among the magnates who conducted Hungarian and Transylvanian affairs, and their portraits, with their slung dolmens, brocade tunics, jewelled scimitars and fur kalpaks with plumes like escapes of steam – hung on many walls.

For five years of the 1890s, before any of the disasters had smitten, a cousin of Count Miklós Bánffy had led the government of the Austro-Hungarian empire. The period immediately after, from 1905, is the book's setting. The grand world he describes was Edwardian *Mitteleuropa*. The men, however myopic, threw away their spectacles and fixed in monocles. They were the fashionable swells of Spy and late Du Maurier cartoons, and their wives and favourites must have sat for Boldini and Helleu. Life in the capital was a sequence of parties, balls and race-meetings, and, in the country, of *grandes battues* where the guns were all Purdeys. Gossip, cigar-smoke and Anglophilia floated in the air; there were cliques where Monet, d'Annunzio and Rilke were appraised; hundreds of acres of forest were nightly lost at *chemin de fer*; at daybreak lovers stole away from tousled four-posters through secret doors, and duels were fought, as they still were when I was there. The part played by politics suggests Trollope or Disraeli. The plains beyond flicker with mirages and wild horses, ragged processions of stocks migrate across the sky; and even if the woods are full of bears, wolves, caverns, waterfalls, buffalos and wild lilac – the country scenes in Transylvania, oddly enough, remind me of Hardy.

Bánffy is a born story-teller. There are plots, intrigues, a murder, political imbroglios and passionate love-affairs, and though this particular counterpoint of town and country may sound like the stock-in-trade of melodrama, with a fleeting dash of Anthony Hope; it is nothing of the kind. But it is, beyond question, dramatic. Patrick Thursfield and Kathy Bánffy-Jelen have dealt brilliantly with the enormous text; and the author's life and thoughtful cast of mind emerges with growing clarity. The prejudices and the follies of his characters are arranged in proper perspective and only half-censoriously, for humour and a sense of the absurd, come to the rescue. His patriotic feelings are totally free of chauvinism, just as his instinctive promptings of tribal responsibility have not a trace of vanity. They urge him towards what he thought was right, and always with effect. (He was Minister of Foreign Affairs at a critical period in the 1920s.) If a hint of melancholy touches the pages here and there, perhaps this was inevitable in a time full of omens, recounted by such a deeply civilized man.

Chatsworth, Boxing Day, 1998

INTRODUCTION

Miklós Bánffy and the Transylvanian Trilogy

by
PATRICK THURSFIELD

MY ACQUAINTANCE with the works of Miklós Bánffy started one day some years ago when I was motoring from my home in Tangier to Rabat. My fellow passenger was a Hungarian friend, Kathy Jelen, who had lived for many years in Tangier and who was going to Rabat to sign some papers that confirmed her ownership of the copyright to her father's works. All I had known about Kathy's father, Count Miklós Bánffy, was that he had been a wealthy Hungarian magnate and politician; but I had not known before that he had for many years been a Member of Parliament; nor that he had been Foreign Minister in 1921/2; nor anything about his writings or of his directorship of the State theatres in Budapest; nor of his practical support for writers and artists, and indeed all ethnic Hungarians, in the new Romanian Transylvania of the 1920s and '30s; nor anything of his role as a great landowner with a castle near Kolozsvár (once also called Klausenburg and now given the Romanian name of Cluj-Napoca) whose fortune derived from thousands of acres of forest in the mountains of Transylvania. During our leisurely four hour's car ride we talked of little else and when Kathy told me of his great trilogy, *Erdélyi Történet* – in English *A Transylvanian Tale* – which had been a bestseller in Hungary in the 1930s but which had never been translated or published elsewhere as the last volume had not appeared until 1940 when all Europe was in the throes of war, I longed to know more. First of all she told me about the first book of the trilogy, *Megszámláltattál* – *They Were Counted*, which had just been re-issued on its own in Budapest and had been an immediate sell-out; and it had been because of this that Miklós Bánffy's daughter had thought it wise to confirm her ownership of the copyright and so henceforth be entitled to receive some benefit, however modest, from her father's works which was all that remained of her lost inheritance. At that time, of course, no cracks were yet to be seen in the Communist stranglehold over eastern Europe, so there was still no suggestion that dispossessed exiles would ever regain any of their lost possessions.

Kathy then revealed that several years before she had begun an English translation, but that it had not prospered and she had never finished it. I picked up the scent at once and was soon in full pursuit. Could I read what she had written? Of course. As soon as we returned to Tangier she would bring it round to me. A few days later there arrived a tattered brown parcel containing a huge pile of faded typescript in single spacing on flimsy paper. The different chapters were held together with rusty paperclips and the appearance of it all was, to say the least, uninviting. Several pages seemed to have been mauled by cats, as I later found to have been the case. By then Kathy had told me more about her father, a polymath if ever there was one, kind, gentle, a linguist, an artist whose designs were still in use at the Budapest opera, a humanist and a great lover of his country and of women (including, it is said, Elinor Glyn who was thought to have used him as the model for one of her heroes) many of whom had fallen into his arms before he married late in life the actress who had been his great love but whom, because of the shibboleths of that class-ridden world, he had not been able to marry until after his father's death. She also told me of the great baroque castle of Bonczhida, the Bánffy home in Transylvania, which figures in the novel under the name of Dénestornya, much as some years later Lampedusa's Donnafugata was to be a pen portrait of that author's family palace at Santa Margherita Belice in Sicily. Both houses are now ruins, the first through the spoliations of war and official neglect (the mansions of the former Hungarian ruling class were not held in esteem in Communist Romania) and the second destroyed by an earthquake.

I think I had been told that before she became Countess Bánffy, Kathy's mother had been an accomplished and popular actress at the State Theatre in Budapest, but I knew nothing of the story of the aristocrat's love for the actress nor of the many hurdles to be surmounted before their marriage could take place.

Dismayed though I was by the state of the manuscript I tackled it at once and was enthralled. When I started to read to read what Kathy had already translated, the original text and a Hungarian dictionary at my side, I soon discovered that written Hungarian is often a staccato language even when it is at its most elegiac. In consequence a literal translation in English would give none of the quality of the original and would fail completely to give any idea of the idiom and feeling of the first years of this century in central Europe. Besides this the length of the work and its Dickensian range of plot and subplot, as well as the extensive cast-list, meant that anyone tackling it would have to make an English version rather than a literal translation. What a challenge!

I at once asked Kathy if she would let me see what I could do and then, if she agreed and it seemed to go well, I would show what I had done to friends in London and ask their opinion before we embarked on a voyage which would involve much time and effort for us both. Encouraged, we set to work; and now the pages of Kathy's literal translation (on which I could base an English text) arrived in exemplary legible typescript. Of course I must have been a little crazy to tackle anything of that length – particularly a translation of a dead author who, however well-known he may have been in his own country, had never been heard of in the English-speaking world. And not only that, but to tackle, even with the help of a born Hungarian, a book originally written in a language of which I did not then understand a single word (and I confess to not knowing many more now), was sheer folly. But I was caught by the sweep of the story, the range of characters, the heartbreak, the truth and the sheer humanity of it all. I knew that once started I could never stop until it was done for I desperately wanted others to enjoy it as much as I had. Furthermore I did have one unexpected advantage. As a boy I had often spent holidays with Anglo-Austrian cousins in their castle in Tyrol and so I did have some first-hand experience of central-European *vie de château* which in the 1930s had barely changed since the days, thirty years before, that Bánffy had described in the trilogy. A year later the first long draft of our version of *They Were Counted* was completed. The others followed, and six years later it was all done.

Ostensibly a love story, the two principal characters are cousins, one of whom prospers while the other declines into squalor and a lonely death: but the real theme of this extraordinary family saga is the folly and insularity of the Hungarian upper classes, who danced and quarrelled their way to self-destruction in the ten years leading up to the Great War; and the insularity of the politicians who were so pre-occupied with their struggle against Habsburg domination that they saw nothing of the storm-clouds gathering over Europe. Ironically enough I had just arrived at Bánffy's description of the events following the assassination of

Franz-Ferdinand at Sarajevo – and the sad spectacle of the youth of Hungary marching off gaily to war while the hero of the novel reflects that nothing will come of it all but the destruction and dismembering of his beloved country – when bombs started exploding once again in that sad and much disputed city.

At this time a symposium devoted to the life and works of Miklós Bánffy was held in the great hall of the Ráday Institute in Budapest. This was presided over by the then Foreign Minister, Jeszenszky Géza. The guest of honour was Miklós Bánffy's daughter Katalin (my friend Kathy), and in addition to Mr Jeszenszky's opening address there were speeches and reminiscences covering all aspects of Bánffy's distinguished career from no less than eleven speakers, seven of whom had travelled from the former Hungarian province of Transylvania (Romanian only since 1920). These proceedings, which took from 9 a.m. in the morning until 1 p.m. were followed by a buffet lunch, a visit to the opera house where a bust of Bánffy by his friend the great Hungarian sculptor Strobl was unveiled. This had been preserved in the storerooms of the National Museum and had now been loaned to the Opera House by Bánffy's daughter. The celebrations ended with the pinning of wreaths and bunches of spring flowers to the still battle-scarred façade of the former Bánffy house in Pest. All through the proceedings strobe lights were switched on and off, television cameras whirled and repeated flashlights showed the determination of the media photographers not to miss a second of what was going on. Afterwards Kathy, a grey-haired lady married to an American former naval officer, was interviewed for two different television cultural programmes. Now, I asked myself, why was Miklós Bánffy, a name hitherto unknown in England, so highly honoured in his native land?

Count Miklós Bánffy was, as we have seen, Hungarian by birth, but a very special sort of Hungarian in that his family sprang from Transylvania; and Transylvania, Hungary's greatest lost province, conjures up for Hungarians a totally different picture from that of the Dracula country of Bram Stoker's novel and innumerable horror films made in England and America.

After a turbulent history of domination by marauding hordes from Asia and the Turkish empire, and a period of semi-independence, Transylvania had settled down by the seventeenth century into a largely autonomous Hungarian province, a prosperous if turbulent land of mountains and forests and castles and historic towns. It was called Erdély in Hungarian, and Siebenbürgen – 'seven cities' – in German. Its capital, Kolozsvár, renamed Cluj-Napoca by the Romanians after Transylvania had been ceded to Romania by the Treaty of Trianon in 1922, was a university town with a diffuse culture where the dominant Hungarian landowning families all had town houses, and which was proud of its status as an alternative capital to Budapest. The people of Transylvania were partly of Romanian origin, and partly Hungarian. There were also Jewish, Szekler, gypsy and German-speaking communities – the last known as 'Saxons' who formed a solid largely Protestant middle-class that did not take sides either with the Hungarian aristocrats who were the landowners or with the Romanian peasantry. Some of the noble families, like the Bánffy's, were Protestant (though if a wife were Catholic, like Kathy's mother, the sons would be brought up as Protestants while the daughters followed their mother's faith), others Catholic, while the Romanian-speaking minority was Orthodox. It was from the ranks of the Bánffy's, Bethlens, Telekis and other great landowners, that the princes and governors and chancellors of that once autonomous province had been chosen.

Count Miklós Bánffy was born in 1873 and lived most of his life either at the castle of Bonczhida near Kolozsvár, or in the family's town house in Pest a few minutes' walk from the town palaces of his western Hungarian relations, the immensely wealthy Károlyi family. Mihály Károlyi, the country's first republican president after the fall of the Habsburgs, was Miklós Bánffy's second cousin, childhood playmate and once a devoted friend – a friendship which, after Károlyi's marriage and conversion to radical politics, would be destroyed by mutual distrust and hostility. Bánffy, who like many of his class was educated at the Theresianum in Vienna, later studied painting in Budapest with Bartalan Szekely and then law and mathematics at the Hungarian University at Kolozsvár, first became a diplomat and then took up politics as an independent MP for his home province of Kolozs. During the First World War he was intendant of the Budapest Opera House, introducing, despite considerable opposition, the works of Bartok; and in 1916 being responsible for most of the arrangements for the last Habsburg coronation, that of the Emperor Franz-Josef's successor, his nephew King Karl. In 1921 Bánffy became Minister for Foreign Affairs, resigning a year-and-a-half later principally because of ill-health brought about by overwork and the strain of trying to represent his country at the League of Nations (where, despite serious opposition, he had obtained Hungary's admisssion as a full member) while being stabbed in the back by lesser men at home in Budapest. At that time he still had confidence in the régime of Admiral Horthy, who had by now made himself 'Regent' following the short-lived Socialist republic (of which Mihály Károlyi had been the ill-fated President) and the previous few months of the Communist rule of Béla Kun. This early confidence was to wane as Horthy soon showed signs of neo-fascist megalomania.

In 1926 Bánffy retired from public life in Budapest and went back to live at Bonczhida. From then until his death he devoted himself to literature and the arts, partly as a prolific writer whose major work was the now classic trilogy about life in Hungary from 1904 to 1914, and partly in being one of the leading spirits in founding a publishing house to encourage young Transylvanian writers in Hungarian to become better known and so retain their identity in the face of Romanian domination. Bánffy's published works also included novels, short stories, plays and two volumes of autobiography.

On returning to Transylvania he acquired dual Romanian and Hungarian citizenship and, trusted by both sides though holding no official position with either, worked hard to reconcile the mutually suspicious governments in Budapest and Bucharest. His work was made easier for him as, unlike a some of the other Hungarian landowners, he spoke Romanian fluently. Despite the huge success of the Trilogy and widespread public appreciation of Bánffy's cultural work in Transylvania, it is saddening to note that his political aims were not always understood by some of his fellow aristocrats who misinterpreted his efforts at *rapprochement* with Romania as acts of disloyalty to an afflicted and deprived Hungary. Ironically enough the (unpublished) letters of the distinguished Romanian diplomat Virgil Tilea, reveal that he too was subjected to similar criticism from his peers in Bucharest because of his friendship with Bánffy.

The proof of the right-mindedness of both these clearsighted patriots was finally proved in 1943. Early in the war what the Hungarians considered to have been an historic injustice to their country was in part rectified when the so-called Vienna Award restored to Hungary the northern part of Transylvania which included Kolozsvár, the castle and lands of Bonczhida, and the Bánffy forest holdings in the mountains. Romania did not take the same view. On 9 June 1943, Bánffy went to Bucharest to meet the Romanian Foreign Minister, Georges Mironescu, in order to try to persuade the Romanians to sign a separate peace with the Allies and thereby forestall a Russian invasion and the destruction and the Soviet-imposed political revolution this would inevitably bring about. Despite warnings from Hitler that he knew very well what was going on, both sides did agree to abandon the Axis, but there the agreement stopped. Romania, whose claim to historic rights over the whole region had brought about the transfer of sovereignty after the First World War, wanted the immediate return of Northern Transylvania while Bánffy argued that it would be better to leave this question in abeyance until the war was over when the great powers would make a final decision.

Bánffy's private dream, and that of many other Transylvanians at that time, was that this was the opportunity for Transylvania once again to become semi-autonomous as it had been in the seventeenth century. The return to Hungarian rule of the northern part of the province by the 1940 Vienna award had not been greeted by many Transylvanians with quite the same joy that it had been in Budapest. What Bánffy and his friends really wanted was a measure of independence for their beloved country; and though he and the Hungarian Foreign Ministry both wished to postpone a decision on the future of Transylvania, it was not entirely for the same reasons. Neither wanted to offer such a hostage to Fortune as would be a preliminary pledge to return those disputed lands to Romania. It was an agonizing choice, for Bánffy realized that unless both Hungary and Romania agreed to abandon the Axis, this dream would be for ever unobtainable. Nevertheless the negotiations were continued, and there was a further meeting between him and a Romanian delegation, this time headed by Iuliu Maniu. Once again the stumbling block proved to be the Transylvanian question and negotiations were broken off on 23 June 1943. Nevertheless these secret negotiations had one remarkable success. Bánffy was able to arrange that Kolozsvár was declared an open city and so its historic centre was spared the ferocious bombing that devastated much of the surrounding country.

In 1944, as the Russians advanced towards Kolozsvár, the German army looted the castle of Bonczhida, and set it on fire as a spiteful revenge for Bánffy's part in trying to persuade the Romanians to sign a separate peace. The contents of Bonczhida were loaded onto 17 trucks to be taken to Germany and were bombed to smithereens by the allied air forces. The once beautiful medieval and baroque castle is now a largely roofless, windowless, floorless ruin with most of its baroque decoration destroyed. Bánffy himself lived until 1950, dying at the age of 77 in Budapest after staying as long as he could in Kolozsvár (Cluj) trying desperately to save what still remained of his family inheritance. He did not succeed.

A prolific writer, his great work the trilogy *A Transylvanian Tale*, was described in 1980 by Professor István Nemeskurty, one of the speakers at the 1994 symposium, as essential reading for all Hungarians who wished to understand the history and character of their own country. It had been Nemeskurty's article, published in a Budapest literary review when the Communist régime was still in power, that had led to the re-publication in 1982 of the first volume (*Megszámláltattál – They Were Counted*). The English titles of the second and third books are *They Were Found Wanting* and *They Were Divided*. On the fly-leaves of each of the three books is printed a quotation from the Book of Daniel describing Belshazzar's Feast. These are taken from a Hungarian Protestant version of the Old Testament. In December 1993 the whole trilogy was republished in Budapest in one *de luxe* volume, and it was again critically acclaimed.

As we were getting into our stride trying to make a viable English language version of this extraordinary book I reluctantly became only too aware of the leisurely pace of the trilogy, whose first volume – though it can stand on its own as a complete work of art – is much the same length as *Anna Karenina*. I estimated that if we were not careful the full text of our translation of the trilogy would be nearly as long as all four volumes of Paul Scott's *Raj Quartet*. This meant that, as English needed more words than Hungarian to achieve the same effect, we would have to eliminate all textual repetitions (some used for emphasis in the original) and probably sacrifice some inessential details in the many sub-plots as well as some political detail that would be meaningless to anyone not a dedicated scholar of Hungarian political history: that is if any publisher were to look at it twice; and this despite the fact that the recent complete republication in one weighty tome – the original three volumes came out in 1934, 1937 and 1940 – and the symposium held in April 1994, had transformed a dead writer into one very much alive – at least in Hungary.

A Transylvanian Tale is a remarkable work, compulsive and romantic, filled with love and sorrow and bewilderment and sex and action and splendid set-pieces of grand shooting parties, balls in country-houses, gambling for vertiginous stakes, and dramatic scenes in Parliament; as well as benign social comment, which can erupt into indignant condemnation of social folly. It is written by a man of amazingly clear sight, a patriot who loved his country – and women – and who understood, even if he could not wholly forgive, the follies and the political blindness which finally led to its dismemberment and humiliation after the First World War. Bánffy himself was an eye-witness to many of the historical scenes he describes in the book; and his detailed description of the last Habsburg coronation (published as his *Emlékeimböl – From My Memories*, an early book of memoirs now out of print- though we have started doing it into English) forms a sad footnote to the Habsburg domination which had so preoccupied Hungarian politicians from 1848 to the fall of the dynasty in 1918. As the struggle with the Habsburgs was the background theme to the trilogy, my conviction grew that this was a book which, if published in the West, would lead to a far greater understanding not only of present-day Hungary but also of the conflicts now erupting all over the Balkans.

As a pendant to Bánffy's best known work a posthumous book of late memoirs by him was recently published in Budapest. Bánffy wrote these in 1945 when he found himself alone in Cluj (still Kolozsvár to all Hungarians), after his wife and daughter had returned to Budapest to salvage the contents of their town house in Pest, which had all been thrown out into the street by the Russian troops who had requisitioned it. For three years they were separated, for the border between Hungary and Romania was closed by the military; and when Bánffy finally was able to rejoin his family he only had a year or so more to live. After Bánffy's death his widow deposited what remained of the Bánffy papers in the library of the Ráday Institute (the HQ of the Reformed Church in Hungary) in Budapest. These memoirs, which were recently discovered there and edited and published by Zoltan Major, are quite short and deal only with the period when Bánffy's was Foreign Minister to István Bethlen who had succeeded as Prime Minister after the exiled Habsburg monarch, King Karl (who had never formally abdicated), made his first ludicrous attempt at restoration and brought down the government in the process. Karl's second *putsch* (in October 1921) came during Bánffy's time as Foreign Minister, and had more serious repercussions, which included effectively scuttling all Bánffy's efforts to achieve *rapprochement* with the new states of Czechoslovakia and Yugoslavia and the greatly enlarged kingdom of

Romania, as it was now to be spelt. In this work we can see the working-out of much of what Bánffy feared would result from the pre-war fecklessness of his countrymen so graphically described in the trilogy.

I should here mention that in a work filled with unfamiliar names we have thought it better not to further confuse the reader with the many accents which abound in written Hungarian. Similarly, in the course of revising the text it became clear that there were many references, both to actual events and to once well-known public figures, which would mean nothing to an English-language readership, however potently evocative these may have been to Hungarians fifty years and more ago. Rather than inflict footnotes on the reader we decided, where necessary, slightly to amend the text to make the meaning clear.

After much heart-searching we also decided to give our translation of the trilogy the English title of *The Writing on the Wall* rather than *A Transylvanian Tale*. We wanted to get away from the overtones of Dracula now inevitably associated for western readers with any mention of Miklós Bánffy's homeland; and feel that the biblical reference is justified by the author's own choice of titles for his three books – *They Were Counted*, *They Were Found Wanting* and *They Were Divided* and also because he himself placed those quotations from the Book of Daniel before the title pages of each volume.

In a book that includes descriptions of historic events and real characters it is inevitable that some may wonder how much of the work has an identifiable key. The answer is very little. There are descriptions of places which can be identified – for example the library at 'Simonvásár', the fictional Kollonich palace near Lake Balaton, is clearly based on that at the vast Károlyi manor-house at Foth, east of Budapest; while the Kollonich palace in Budapest is equally clearly the Károlyi house just behind the State Museum in Budapest. Similarly there are elements of the Teleki house at Gernyeszeg in the fictional castle of 'Vár-Siklód'. There are many others likenesses of this sort both to people and places but, while incidents in the life of the author have their echoes in what happens to the two heroes of the work, Balint Abády and his cousin László Gyeroffy, the only autobiographical element is that Balint's political views seem to reflect those the author later expressed in his memoirs. There is one notable exception: Abády's family home, the castle of 'Denestornya', is a lovingly described picture of Bánffy's beloved Bonzchida; but even that is situated in a different part of the country. Likenesses abound, but that is the only true portrait, while the family names Bánffy chose for his characters mostly come from those of families who had long ago died out. Even though what has had to be a brief study of the source materials has proved endlessly fascinating, such recondite knowledge is not needed to enjoy the story Bánffy has to tell.

I must now offer grateful thanks to Patrick Leigh Fermor who started by offering me the most helpful advice when we embarked on this project, went on with invaluable textual suggestions, and who has now written such a graceful foreword. Rudi Fischer, of Budapest, was also very helpful and I received much encouragement from Professor István Nemeskurty and also from Professor Mihály Szegedy-Maszák, of Eötvös Loránd University, Budapest, who in 1996 printed extracts from our translation in *Hungarian Studies*, the journal of the International Association of Hungarian Studies (Nemzetkösi Magyar Filológiai Társaság). My thanks are also due to Dr Richard Mullen for publishing my articles on Bánffy and his works in the *Contemporary Review* (which, incidentally, is mentioned in the text of *They Were Counted*).

My deepest thanks are reserved for my co-translator, Kathy Bánffy-Jelen, who has patiently suffered endless questioning from a collaborator largely ignorant of her native language and even accepted with a good grace those textual losses from her beloved father's great work that proved unavoidable if our labours were ever to appear in print.

Tangier, 1998

Patrick Thursfield was born in 1923, educated at Charterhouse and Christ Church, Oxford, and served in the RNVR (combined operations) 1942–6. He joined the staff of *The Times* in 1949 and later wrote scripts for television and articles on literary and other subjects. Since 1971 he has made his home in Morocco.

'And it came to pass that the King commanded a great feast in the Palace and there was feasting and dancing and much drinking of wine. And each man praised his own gods of gold and of silver, of brass, of iron, of wood and of clay, mocking and quarrelling with one another because of them.

'In the same hour came forth the fingers of a man's hand and wrote in letters of fire upon the plaster of the wall of the King's palace, slowly, until there shone brightly the word: MENE – The Lord hath counted thy kingdom...

'But no one could see the writing because they were drunken with wine and wrath with one another, each man praising his own gods made of gold and of silver, of brass, of iron, of wood and of clay.'

PART ONE

Chapter One

THE RADIANT AFTERNOON SUNLIGHT of early September was so brilliant that it still seemed like summer. Two larks were soaring high into the air, pausing a few seconds and then diving to skim the surface of the fields before rising ever higher into the blue sky.

On the ground everything seemed green. Even in the stubble-covered fields the gold was veined with moss, shining like green enamel, with, here and there, a few late poppies glowing crimson. On the soft rolling hills of the Maros valley the fruit trees were still covered with leaves, as were the woods crowning each summit. Between the water-meadows, which bordered the river and the orchards, ran the road to Vasarhely, white with the dust which also coated the late-flowering yellow pimpernels, the wild spinach and the spreading leaves of the burdock which grew so profusely on the sloping verges of the road.

Many carriages and peasant carts had travelled that way in the morning, all hastening to the Sunday races at Vasarhely, raising clouds of dust in their wake. Now in the early afternoon all was still. The dust had settled and the road was empty.

A single vehicle approached slowly from the direction of the town. It was an open hired fiacre drawn by three horses. Sitting back in the passenger seat was a young man, Balint Abady, slim and of medium height, his long silk dustcoat fastened up to his chin. When he took off the wide-brimmed felt hat that had become the fashion throughout Europe after the Boer War, the sunlight caught reddish glints in his wavy hair and made his blue eyes seem even lighter in colour. His features had a faintly oriental cast, with a high forehead, wide cheekbones and unexpectedly slanting eyes. Balint had not been at the races. He had come direct from the station and was heading for Var-Siklod, the country place of Count Laczok who was giving a recepton after the races, which in turn would be followed in the evening by a dinner and dance.

He had come by train direct from Denestornya even though his mother had offered one of her teams of carriage horses. He had refused the offer, warmly as it had been made, because he sensed she had hoped he would. He knew how much she loved the

horses she raised and how she worried over possible hardship for
them. In strange stables they would catch cold or be snagged by
other horses. So, with a smile, he had told her that it would be too
much for them to drive the fifty kilometres from Denestornya to
St George's Meadow beyond Vasarhely, back to the town again
and then out to the Laczoks'. They would have to be put to, un-
harnessed again, fed at an inn . . . no, he would rather go by train.
In that way he would arrive early and maybe have an opportunity to discuss local affairs with the politicians who were sure to
be there.

'All right, my boy, if that is what you prefer – though you know
I would give the horses willingly', his mother had said; but he
knew she was glad he had not accepted. So now he was on his way
to Siklod, travelling slowly in the old fiacre, with its jingling harness and its ancient springs. He enjoyed the leisurely pace along
the lonely road with the dust rising like the lightest of veils carried
by an almost imperceptible breeze over meadows where doe-eyed
cows lazily looked towards the carriage.

How good it was to be back in his own country after so many
years away, to be back home again and to be carried so peacefully
and gently to a place he loved and where he would meet so many
old friends. It was a long time since he had seen them; since, after
his years at the Theresianum in Vienna and afterwards at the
University of Kolozsvar, he had had to go back again to Vienna
to prepare his diplomatic examinations and, after his military service, he had been posted abroad for two years. Now he was back.
How much better this was, he thought, than the diplomatic service where there was no hope of earning money and where the
small allowance, which was all his mother could afford, barely
covered his living expenses. He did not grudge the meagreness of
his allowance. Though her holdings were large – sixteen thousand
acres of pine forest on the slopes of Vlegyasza, three thousand at
Denestornya, rich farmlands between the Aranyos and the
Maros, three-quarters of the great lake at Lelbanya, and smaller
holdings here and there – he knew his mother never had any spare
money, however hard she tried to save.

It was far better to come home, where he could live cheaply,
and where, with his experience and qualifications, he could perhaps make himself useful in his own country.

When, therefore, he was at home on leave in the spring of
1904 and the Prefect of the district had come to Denestornya asking him to stand for the vacant parliamentary seat of Lelbanya,

PART ONE

he had accepted without hesitation. He had only one condition; he would be an Independent, free of party ties. Even when abroad he had read in the newspapers of the fierce parliamentary battles in Budapest which had swept away two governments in as many years and, to Balint, the idea of being tied to a party line and obliged to follow a party whip was infinitely distasteful.

The Prefect, somewhat to Balint's surprise, had raised no objections. He agreed to the Independent label provided that Balint would respect the 1867 Compromise with Vienna, that agreement which ensured the independence of Hungary. What the Prefect did not say was that for him the only important thing was to keep out the opposition and to be sure that Lelbanya should not be represented by some 'foreigner' who had bought his seat from the party leaders in Budapest. Although Lelbanya, once a royal town, had declined until it had become a mere country market town with barely three hundred votes, it still had the right to elect a member of Parliament. For some time the elections had been rigged. Aspiring politicians, with money in their pockets, had come from the capital to win the seat. They would be welcomed, and their pockets emptied, by the Prefect and his friends, to an apparently vicious contest with a loud-mouthed demagogue who, spouting the revolutionary principles of 1848, had been employed to contest the seat. On one occasion the rich candidate from Budapest had tired of paying and retired; and, to the province's shame and embarrassment, the phoney candidate had been elected.

If young Count Abady would stand, the Prefect knew that nothing would go wrong. Since the town's mine had stopped being worked many years before and the soil of the district only offered a poor living, the inhabitants of Lelbanya had lived chiefly by gathering and working the reeds of the lake, which was Abady property. Against the owner of the lake no 'foreign' candidate stood a chance, for if Count Abady decided to sell the reeds elsewhere, the citizens would lose their livelihood.

Of course the Prefect said none of this to the young man. He spoke only in general terms, of the need for a sense of duty, of patriotism and, in Countess Abady's presence, he spoke, with an air of understanding and sympathy, of how she and her people would benefit from the young count's presence in his own country. He spoke too, temptingly, of the salaries earned by Members of Parliament which, though low enough, would be useful. He emphasized that there would be no embarrassing contest and that the election would be almost unanimous. Only when Balint and his mother had been convinced did he visit the countess's agent, Kristof Azbej, and tell him that it would be wise to send a stranger to Lelbanya who would, in a most obvious manner, assess the autumn's reed crop as if Count Abady were considering selling elsewhere. The electors would get a good fright and when, as in previous years, the crop was still made available to the town Count Abady would be elected. And this is what happened; even though Balint had no idea why the electors cheered him so heartily. Balint's innocence stemmed not only from his straightforward nature and an upbringing that had shielded him from dishonesty and greed, but also from the fact that the protected years at the Theresianum college, at the university and even in the diplomatic service, had shown him only the gentler aspects of life. He had lived always in a hothouse atmosphere where the realities of human wickedness wore masks; and Balint did not yet have the experience to see the truth that lay behind.

None of this was in Balint's mind as he travelled slowly towards Siklod in the old hackney carriage. Leaning back in his seat, he thought only of how good it was to be home again and to have the chance to put to good use what he had seen abroad, how he could pass on the benefits of what he had seen in Germany of the new trade unions, of their methods of property administration, of tied-cottages and small holders' rights. Though he had already spoken of such things to the electors, they were still not clearly defined in his mind. In the meantime, the sun was beautiful, the countryside smiling and the sky clear and blue.

A big old-fashioned travelling coach came up behind. A closed carriage with tightly shut windows making a rhythmic jingle of harness drew alongside. It was drawn by two large bay mares, so fat that they were either in foal or had been fed too much hay. On the box was an old coachman wearing a threadbare cherry-red coat – a fashion of the sixties and on his head was a round hat with an ostrich feather now no more than a tuft. He sat, crooked as a folding knife, nodding his head as if answering the horses' silent questions. As the coach passed, Balint saw a little maid sitting on the front seat with a basket on her lap and, in the rear, propped up with cushions, a tiny shrivelled-up old lady. He recognized her at once and bowed, but the old lady never saw him. She gazed directly in front of her, squinting under knitted brows into the distance, into the nothingness over her maid's head, her mouth puckering as if she were whistling.

PART ONE

It was the old Countess Sarmasaghy, in this part of the world Aunt Lizinka to almost everybody. Through her numerous brothers and sisters she really was aunt to two generations of all the families of the district, and the sight of her, silent and alone in her old-fashioned coach, reawakened in Balint the memories of his boyhood in Kolozsvar. Even now he could recall the airless room in which Aunt Lizinka sat in a wing-chair with its back to the tightly closed windows, windows that were never opened for although in perfect health the old lady dreaded catching cold. Between her and the windows were two glass screens as an added protection. She had been huddled into a confused mass of shawls, plaids and scarves, and on her head had been a little lace bonnet under which a small knitted cushion was tied to her forehead. The bonnet was fastened under her chin by a tangle of silken bows. Of her face all that could be seen were her glittering eyes, a sharp eagle-beaked nose and thin colourless lips covered in star-shaped wrinkles. He had been terrified of this shrunken witch-like figure who seemed to have no body at all but only a narrow face and beaky nose, just as he had read in the old fairy books. Balint's mother had pushed him forward. 'Now, Balint, kiss your aunt's hand properly!' and he had kissed the little shrivelled camphor-smelling claw as he was told. He had hated it, but worse was to come. The gnarled little hand had grabbed him and pulled him towards the scarves and shawls with a force that nobody would believe, and then the old lips, unexpectedly moist, had planted a wet kiss on his forehead. For some time after being released from this terrifying embrace he could feel the cold saliva drying on his head; but he had been too strictly brought up to be caught wiping it off.

As the old woman passed in her coach Balint thought that even then she had looked as old she looked now and he remembered, too, many other things things that she had told him about herself or that he had been told about her by his grandfather, old Count Peter Abady, who was her first cousin.

He smiled to himself as he recalled one of her escapades.

In 1848, during the revolution, Countess Sarmasaghy, born Lizinka Kendy, was a young bride. Her husband Mihaly was a major in Gorgey's army (everyone was a major then) fighting for Hungary's independence and she was so much in love with him that, against all tradition, she followed the army everywhere in her carriage. She was at Vilagos when Gorgey surrendered and, ardent patriot that she was, she went immediately up to the Castle of Bohus, burst into the great hall where all the Hungarian and Russian officers were collected, brushed them aside until she faced General Gorgey and yelled at him in her sharp shrill voice 'Governor! Sir, you are a traitor!'

Nothing had ever daunted her, and she was never afraid to say what she thought. She also had a cruel and merciless tongue. She had loathed Kossuth, and every time that his name was mentioned she would tell the story of him at the National Assembly in Debrecen. The Russians were approaching and no one knew what to do. According to Aunt Lizinka, Kossuth rose to speak and said, 'There is no need to panic! Mihaly Sarmasaghy is on his way with thirty thousand soldiers!' And great cheering broke out, even though Mihaly Sarmasaghy, accompanied only by his tiny wife, was actually sitting in the public gallery above. As Aunt Lizinka told the tale she made it seem that everyone knew that her courage alone equalled an untold number of fearless soldiery.

After the revolution, during which her husband had been imprisoned, it was she who handled the appropriations crisis which nearly bankrupted her husband's family. She took their case to every court, she fought against the enforced leasing of their lands, mines and properties, and she got her husband released from his captivity at Kufstein. First she mastered all the legal intricacies of the new decrees, laws and amendments, the complications of Austro-Hungarian imperial patents, and the commercial methods of running the family mines; then she fought their case from Vasarhely to Vienna, and won.

All this Balint recalled as the old lady's coach passed his, and this made him think, too, of his grandfather, her cousin, to whom she paid regular visits every year. He could see the two of them now, sitting together on the open veranda of the mansion at Denestornya where his grandfather had lived. Aunt Lizinka, almost submerged in her shawls and scarves, her knees pulled up, curled like a lapdog in a huge cushioned armchair; Grandfather Abady, facing his cousin in a high-backed chair, smoking cigars, as he did all day long, from a carved meerschaum holder. Aunt Lizinka would, as always, be recounting gossip about their friends, neighbours and cousins. All that Balint would understand, and remember, was his grandfather laughing ironically and saying, 'Lizinka, I don't believe all these evil stories: even half would be too much!' And the old lady would declare: 'It's true. Every word is true. I know it!' But the old count just smiled and shook his head, disbelieving, because even if the old countess said things that were mischievous and untrue at least she was funny when she did so.

At Denestornya Count Peter had not lived in the family castle, but in a large eighteenth-century mansion built by his own grandfather at a time when the two main branches of the Abady family had become separated and the family lands divided. The big castle had been inherited by Balint's mother, together with three-quarters of the family estates, and it had therefore been a great event when she married Peter Abady's son and thus reunited the family domains of Denestornya and the estates in the Upper Szamos mountains.

Count Peter had handed everything over to his son on his marriage. He kept only the mansion on the other side of the hill from the castle at Denestornya and, when his son Tamas died suddenly when still quite young, he insisted that his daughter-in-law kept the properties together and managed them. Though young Countess Abady wanted the old count to move back to the castle, he always refused; and in this he was wise, as Balint came to understand later, because although she seemed offended by his refusal, with her restless nature the good relations existing between the old count and his daughter-in-law would not have withstood the strain of living under the same roof. As it was, they kept up the old custom established when Tamas was still living: on Wednesdays Count Peter lunched at the castle, on Sundays Balint and his mother went to his grandfather's house.

As the young Balint grew up, he often went to see Count Peter on other occasions as well. He would escape from his tutors, which was not difficult, and, as the castle park was separated from the mansion's garden only by two low walls and the Protestant cemetery, he would pretend he was a Red Indian and sneak away silently like 'Leather-Jerkin' over the little wall, pretending it was a high and fearsome tower. When he arrived at his grandfather's, the old man would notice his grubby and dust-covered clothes, but he would never ask him which way he had come or how he had got so dirty. Only if he had torn a hole in his jacket or trousers, and lest trouble should come of it, would he have the damage repaired and send a servant to unlock the park door when the boy went home.

When Balint was small, it was not his grandfather that lured the boy there; it was food. Whenever he arrived he was always given something to eat: fresh rye bread with thick sour cream, cold buffalo milk or a piece of delicious pudding from the larder.

He was always hungry and up at the castle his mother had forbidden him to eat between meals. But when he grew older, it was the old man's company that he sought. Count Peter talked to his grandson with such kindness and understanding, and listened to the tales of his pranks with a smile on his face. And he never told anyone what he had heard.

If Balint came about midday, and the weather was good, he would find Count Peter on the terrace: if it was cold he would be in the library. Though he was always reading he never seemed to mind being disturbed. Mostly he read scientific books and journals and by subscribing to so many he kept up-to-date with all the cultural movements and scientific discoveries of the times; and he would talk to his grandson about his latest enthusiasms, explaining in simple and easily understood words whatever it was that interested him the most. He seemed equally well-informed on an astonishing range of subjects, from the narratives of exploratory expeditions in Asia and Africa to advances in science and mathematics. Especially when he talked of mathematical problems he would expound them with such lucidity that when, later, Balint came to learn algebra at the Theresianum, it seemed already familiar. And these interests, fostered by his grandfather's teaching during Balint's surreptitious visits, remained with him long after childhood.

If he went to his grandfather's in the morning the old count was usually to be found in his garden, where he allowed no one but himself to touch his roses. He tended them with loving care, grafting, crossing and creating new varieties. They were much more beautiful than those in the castle garden where a legion of professional gardeners were constantly at work.

On Sundays, if the boy came over early for the weekly luncheon, he would find his grandfather on the terrace talking to two or three peasants who, hat in hand, would be telling the old landowner about their problems. At such times Count Peter would indicate with a nod of his head that Balint could stay and listen but that he should sit a little to one side. People also came to ask advice from neighbouring villages or even from the mountains. Romanians or Hungarians, they knew him to be wise and just, and so they would come to him, as to their lord, to settle their problems rather than go to lawyers they could not trust. Count Abady never turned anyone away. He would sit motionless on his hard, high-backed cane chair, with his legs crossed and his trousers riding up to show his old-fashioned soft leather boots. With

PART ONE

the familiar meerschaum cigar-holder in his mouth, he would listen in silence to their long explanations. Occasionally, he would ask a question, or intervene with a gentle but authoritative word to calm someone who showed signs of losing his temper with his opponent. This was seldom necessary because in the count's presence everyone was on their best behaviour. He spoke Hungarian and Romanian equally fluently and his verdict was usually accepted by both parties. When all was over, whichever way the count's judgement had gone, they would kiss his hand and go away quietly. They would also go over to Balint and kiss his hand too, as a gesture of respect, and when once Balint tried to prevent this, his grandfather told him in French to let them do it lest they should take offence, thinking he withdrew his hand in disgust.

Other guests would also come to pay their respects: young men to get an introduction or to ask for help in the great world; for though Count Peter seldom moved from home, his influence was known to remain strong and widespread, not only because he was the Protestant church's chief warden and a member of the House of Lords and Royal Standard Bearer for more than fifty years, but above all, because he was known never to support an unworthy cause. It was also believed that he had the ear of the emperor and that Franz-Josef always listened to what Count Abady had to say.

Older visitors would come for friendship's sake – former provincial administrators from the years before the upheavals of 1848, when Count Peter had been the Prefect of Also-Feher, and ex-army officers whom he had protected and saved from imprisonment during the repressive regime of Count von Bach, the Austrian imperial minister imposed on Hungary after the 1848 rebellion.

There were two other regular visitors: Aunt Lizinka, who came for two weeks every year; and Mihaly Gal, always called 'Minya', a great actor of former days, who would come for three days, no more, no less. The young Balint loved Minya Gal, and when he was there he would climb the park walls several times a day just to sit listening to the conversation of the two old friends, to their jokes and reminiscences, to Gal's tales of the theatre and his memories of his old mistress, the once famous actress Célestine Déry, and to stories about many other people whose names meant nothing to the listening boy.

The old actor came on foot and left on foot. He would never accept the offer of a carriage, though it was always made. All Balint knew was that he had kept this habit since his early days as an itinerant actor. Perhaps there was also something of a stubborn puritan pride and perhaps, walking the highways, he fancied he was young again. Minya Gal had been at school with Peter Abady in the 1820s and there, at Vasarhely, they had formed a friendship that had lasted over seventy years.

Although it was twelve years since Balint had last seen Minya Gal – at his grandfather's funeral in 1892 – he recalled that he had come from this region and had told him he still had a small house at Vasarhely. Balint wondered if he was still alive and reflected that if he were he could not be more than five or six years short of a hundred. Balint decided that when he returned from Siklod, he would try to find out what had happened to the old actor, who had such a large part in his most treasured memories of childhood.

The sharp drumming of hoofbeats interrupted young Balint Abady's dreams of the past and brought him back to the present. Two open carriages hurried past in quick succession. The first was driven by Count Istvan Kendy, whom everyone called Pityu; in the carriage Balint recognized one of the younger Alvinczys, who had two young women with him. It was only when they had gone ahead that Balint realized that they were the daughters of Count Laczok, Anna and Ida. When he had last seen them they had still been in the schoolroom wearing pigtails. Now they must be grown up and hurrying home from the races for, as daughters of the family, they would have to be ready to greet their guests when they arrived. They had not even glanced in his direction, but then perhaps it had not occurred to them that they would know anyone in a hired cab.

The second chaise was driven by Farkas, the eldest Alvinczy with, beside him, the third Laczok girl, Liszka. As they sped past, Balint saw that the man behind, sitting with the uniformed coachman, was his cousin Laszlo Gyeroffy. He called out and Laszlo waved and called back, but the chaise kept up its headlong pace. Obviously they were racing each other – all the more wildly as there were girls present – both the young men eager to outdo the other, to stay in front and show who was best. They were so engrossed that the race might have been a matter of life or death.

Balint was pleased and surprised to discover that Laszlo would be at Siklod. It would be good to see again his only real friend

PART ONE

from childhood, from their days together at school and afterwards, before Laszlo had moved to Budapest for his two years at the university. From that time they had not seen each other often. A few times they had been invited at the same time by Laszlo's aunts for partridge or pheasant shoots in Hungary and, sometimes, by chance, they had seen each other in Transylvania. But their bonds of friendship, the stronger for reaching back to their adolescence, had never weakened. It was these, rather than their blood relationship, that were close, since Laszlo's grandmother had been old Peter Abady's sister, which bound them together. There were other ties too, deep and unconscious, similar traits of character and the fact that they were both orphans; for though Balint still had a mother and a home to return to in the summer holidays, Laszlo had lost both his parents when he was only three. His mother, beautiful and talented, a painter and sculptress, bolted with another man, and shortly afterwards Count Gyeroffy was found dead in his woods, shot by his own gun. It was put out that there had been an accident. The family would accept no other explanation, but this vague and uncertain story had cast a dark cloud over young Laszlo's childhood. As he no longer had a home he had been taken by his grandmother, but she in turn died after only a few years and, since then, his school holidays would be spent with his aunts. Until he came of age he would have no home of his own and so he was always a guest, sometimes with cousins in Transylvania, but more often in west Hungary, in Budapest, where his older aunt was married to Prince Kollonich and the younger to Count Antal Szent-Gyorgyi.

Balint leant out of the fiacre to look at the rapidly disappearing chaise. Through the billowing clouds of dust he could just make out the figure of Laszlo waving to him. He waved back, but dust from another passing car soon removed him from sight.

Two men sat in a half-covered victoria. On the right was old Sandor Kendy, who had two nicknames in Transylvania. To his face they called him 'Vajda', after his notorious ancestor, a wilful and violent-tempered nobleman whose misdeeds and arrogance had finally brought him to the scaffold. Behind his back they called him 'Crookface', not out of malice but because whenever he spoke or smiled — which happened seldom — his mouth pulled to one side. An old sabre scar, by no means concealed by a luxuriant moustache, made his expression seem even more ferocious.

Nearly all the Kendys had nicknames, which were needed to distinguish those with the same first name. Apart from Crookface there were two other Sandors: 'Frantic', so-named for his restless, changeable character; and 'Zindi', called after a now-forgotten bandit whom he was thought to resemble.

Next to Crookface in the open two-wheeler sat Ambrus Kendy, ten years younger who, though only a distant cousin, had a marked resemblance to the older man. So it was with all the Kendys. Prolific as the family was, they could be instantly recognized for the family looks, even in the most distant of cousins, had survived generations of separation from the main branch of the family. They were dark, with light eyes and thick bushy eyebrows. All had aggressive belligerent noses, noses like sharp beaks; eagle beaks like Crookface, falcon beaks like Ambrus; all the birds of prey were represented, from buzzards and peregrines down to shrikes. The proof of the enduring hereditary force was this; the family being so numerous, their estates had become smaller and smaller through division between so many heirs; good marriages had to be made, marriages where the dowry was more important than the bride; but no matter what ugly or feeble women they wed – crooked, lame, fat, thin, bulbous or pug-nosed – the Kendy looks endured and they bred handsome boys and pretty girls all with the same aquiline noses, dark hair and light eyes. People said this strength stemmed from heavy pruning. Through the centuries so many wayward Kendys had perished on the battlefield or the scaffold that those who were left sprouted so much the stronger.

Crookface and Ambrus were alike in more than looks. Both were coarse-spoken, irritable, and contrary, given to reply with a single obscene expletive. This was an innovation started by Crookface in Transylvania, where none of his family, even in boundless fury, to which they were much given, had ever been known to use bad language. But though the coarseness of these two Kendys was the same, it was expressed in different ways. Crookface was sombre and stern and was rude in such a commanding way that few ventured to answer back. Ambrus imitated the rough rudeness of his cousin, but he transformed it to his own advantage. When obscenities fell from his mouth they did so, not aggressively like Crookface, but with a sort of natural jolly roughness, as if he couldn't help it, as if it were merely uncouth honesty. It was as if he were saying, 'Of course I am foul-mouthed, but I was born that way, coarse and rough maybe, but sincere, straight and true.' And this impression of honest good-fellowship was heightened by the kindly look in his light-blue eyes, his deep rumbling voice, his heavy stamping tread and the smile that never left his face. Everyone liked this robust, attractive man and many women loved him. When Balint Abady had come to the university of Kolozsvar at the end of the nineties he found that all the students admired 'Uncle' Ambrus and made him their model, everyone imitated him, letting it be known that real men all spoke as he did, using foul language with zest, and that only affected weaklings spoke politely. Ambrus was the students' leader in other ways too. Though married and the father of seven children, he was a great rake and loved drinking and carousing late into the night. He had a strong head, and when he came to Kolozsvar – which was often and always for long visits – there were revelries every night; with heavy drinking and wild gypsy music. The young students loved it and copied him slavishly.

Balint remembered vividly how he too had followed the fashion, entering into the excesses that always started as soon as Uncle Ambrus appeared. Though it was not really to their taste, he and Laszlo had been swept along by the tide. Perhaps he would not have been tempted if he had been older. Perhaps he would have resisted had he not come straight from the seclusion of boarding school. But as it was he did not resist, and neither did Laszlo. Both felt the need to belong, for, in spite of being related to many of their fellow students, they were treated as outsiders, newcomers, to whom few of the others really took, or confided in, as they did among those with whom they had grown up. Nothing of this reserve, this withholding of comradeship, this intangible dislike, showed upon the surface. There was nothing that Balint or Laszlo could get hold of, nothing for which they could seek an explanation; but it was there nevertheless, in the thousand daily trivialities of casual encounter.

Against Laszlo this antagonism, though it never entirely disappeared, soon subsided when they discovered how well he could play the violin. It was a great advantage to be able to stand in for the band-leader and lead the revels with intoxicating gypsy music. And he could also play the oboe, and clarinet and piano. But the latent hostility to Balint did not change. Maybe it was because he never drank himself under the table, never really let himself go. No matter how much he drank, he always knew what he was doing and what everyone else was doing too. It was as if he could never rid himself of that inner critic, ever alert and ironical, who would watch how he would dance in his shirt-sleeves in front of the gypsies and sing and lark about like the others, and who would say to him, 'You are a hypocrite, my boy. Why play the fool?' Still, always hoping that he would get closer to the others, always deluding himself that they would accept him as one of themselves and forget his 'foreign' background, he would throw himself into their drinking parties, shout and break things and try to do everything they did. But that inner voice was never silenced. Even so Balint persevered, trying to merge himself with these companions who despised anyone who didn't get drunk, who didn't go wild at the sound of gypsy music, who didn't know the words of every song, and who didn't have his own tune, at the sound of which one was expected to jump on the table, fall on the floor and break, if not all the furniture, at least a few glasses. Uncle Ambrus did all these things, so everyone else must follow suit; and it was considered a real proof of good fellowship if, towards dawn, one sat crying in the band-leader's lap or kissed the cellist. Much of this was the natural rivalry of young male animals. They had to surpass each other, to show themselves the better man; and one exploit would lead to another, each more exaggerated than the last.

And the next day they would brag about it. To the young girls in their drawing-rooms they would puff themselves up and say, 'God, was I drunk last night!' And the girls, even if they didn't take these tales too seriously, would act duly impressed. For them it was important to please, and thereby to find a husband; and to be told such stories was not only amusing, but meant that they were sufficiently popular to be given such confidences. If they seemed sympathetic and understanding of such behaviour, and seemed to like the gypsy music, it meant also, at the end of such evenings, that it was under their windows that the young men would bring the musicians to play and sing their messages of love and admiration.

Nor were the mothers any more shocked than their daughters. Most of their husbands had grown up before the revolution of 1848, after which a career in public service, previously expected from young men of noble families, had no longer been open to them. Direct rule from Vienna had removed any opportunity for their traditional occupations and many, in their enforced idleness, took to drink instead. Nevertheless they usually remained good husbands even if a few died of dipsomania, and who could say for sure that the wives were not to blame for failing to keep them off the bottle? Mothers, too, had another and more cogent

PART ONE

reason for not looking askance at the young men spending their evenings with the gypsies. Sometimes in Transylvania girls of good family would be invited to the more staid of such evenings, and marriage proposals came more easily when the wine was flowing. And if, as they were more apt to do, the men were getting drunk with the gypsies in all-male groups, they were at least among themselves with no chance of getting entangled with some 'wicked creature'. So, when the young bloods were known to be out spending their time and their money on drink and gypsy music, the matrons would sigh among themselves and be consoled by the thought that otherwise, 'God-knows, dear, where they'd go and catch some nasty disease!'

Reminded by the sight of the two Kendys of those student days of five or six years before, Balint recalled that there was at least one girl who did not feel, or pretend to feel, sympathy for the man who was a notorious rake. He had met only one who, when some young man would start to boast of his exploits, would frown, straightening her well-shaped brows, and lift her chin with disapproval and distaste.

Only one: Adrienne Miloth.

What a strange independent girl she had been, different in almost every way from the others. She preferred a waltz to a csárdás, she scarcely touched champagne and in her glance there was a sort of grave thoughtfulness, sweet and at the same time intelligent. How could she have married such an ugly and gloomy man as Pal Uzdy? Some women seemed to like such grim looks, but then Adrienne Miloth was not 'some women' and, remembering this, Balint felt again the same stab of senseless irritation that he had experienced two years before when he had heard of her betrothal.

Not that this was jealousy; far from it!

He had met Adrienne when she came out in the spring of 1898. He was a senior student then and passionately involved with his first real love affair, with the pretty little Countess Dinora Abonyi. For Balint this was the first adventure that really mattered. He had pursued Dinora for months, and after the sparkling hopes and torturing jealousy of the chase, what a glorious fulfilment! And this was when he had first seen Adrienne, just when all his desires, all his senses, were engaged elsewhere.

He often used to pay visits to the Miloths' town house, but not looking for love. The subject of love never rose with Adrienne and he never raised it. They did not flirt or even talk about flirting. No matter how long they spent together, nor how long they danced, she never aroused him as a woman. And they met almost daily and often sat talking for hours at a time. In their social group there was no gossip if a young man called regularly at a house where there were marriageable daughters. Indeed, at Kolozsvar there was a great deal of social life and, as in all small towns, most people met every day.

The aristocratic families of Transylvania still spent the winters in their town houses in Kolozsvar, and received their friends every afternoon quite informally. Everyone was expected to drop in, from the old ladies, their grandchildren and mothers with marriageable daughters, to cousins, aunts and friends – and all the eligible young men. Invitations were sent out only for luncheons and dinners and it was at tea-time that those who did not make the rounds for some days attracted attention and comment. It did not therefore suggest serious courtship if the same young bachelor came every day and sat with the girls drinking coffee and whipped cream which was then more popular than English tea.

The same groups used to form – three or four girls and five or six young men, brought together by mutual sympathy or family relationship. Together they would drink tea and coffee, play tennis, go to the theatre and organize picnics. In such groups the tie would be friendship and sympathy, above all sympathy, and it was this alone, which existed between Balint and Adrienne Miloth.

Perhaps Adrienne's strange beauty played its part, but Balint's awareness was casual not emotional, and he admired her as he would have admired a fine jewel or an exquisite bronze.

Adrienne's figure was slender and still very girlish, yet her walk, light but in some way determined, reminded him always of a painting of Diana the Huntress he had once seen in the Louvre. She seemed to have the same elongated proportions, the same small head and supple flexible waist that the artist had given the goddess when she reached over her shoulder to take an arrow from its quiver. And when she walked she had the same long stride. Her colouring, too, recalled the Diana of his memory, the clear ivory skin with slight golden tints which never varied from her softly shining face to her neck, and the arms and shoulders that emerged from the silken *décolleté* of her ball-dress. Only her hair was different, and her eyes, for whereas Diana was blonde

PART ONE

and blue-eyed, Adrienne's hair was dark and wavy and alive – and her eyes were onyx, flecked with golden amber.

Not only was Adrienne beautiful, but she was always interesting to talk to. Her ideas were her own, very individual for a young woman of her background. And she had ideas about everything. She was well-read and cultivated, and with her one didn't have to avoid subjects such as foreign affairs, history or literature as one did with so many young girls who would otherwise take offence thinking one was trying to show off superior knowledge. She spoke several languages and she loved to read, but not the romantic novels which were all that most other girls read. Against these she rebelled, for in the finishing school at Lausanne to which she had been sent she had been introduced to Flaubert, Balzac, Ibsen and Tolstoy, and ever since the trivial had no longer appealed to her.

The first time they had supper together, at Adrienne's coming-out party, they had talked about books and ideas, and so they did again, each time that Balint would visit the Miloths, which he now started to do regularly. At this time Balint was reading Spencer's *Principles of Sociology* and it had made a deep impression on him, especially the first volume which discussed the basic ideas about God and the origins of spiritual belief in primitive man. Carried away by his own enthusiasm he spoke impulsively on these subjects to Adrienne and found himself taken by surprise by the depth of her response and by her thirst for knowledge. This is how they began; but of course they did not stop at one subject but touched on numerous others, words flowing in an ever-guessing, probing search for the truth as is the way with the young. Balint told Adrienne about his grandfather, of his wise appreciation and understanding, of his unerring judgement and how it was only now after so many years that he realized how clearly and cogently the old man had explained life to a twelve-year-old boy. As he talked to Adrienne, ever more fluently and enthusiastically, it seemed to him that he could express himself better and more vividly to this girl who always listened with such intensity and whose answers were always so interesting. It seemed that her presence, with those amber eyes fixed on his, increased his power and his eloquence. They had spent many such hours together, and even when the days grew longer it was often dark before he left. Sometimes a late visitor interrupted them, but usually their talks were brought to an end in a different way. From beyond the double-doors which connected the two drawing-rooms would come the sour voice of Countess Miloth, stern and disapproving: 'Why are you sitting there in the dark, Addy? You know I don't like it. Have the lamps lit at once!', and Adrienne would get up in silence, pausing to get control of herself, forcing herself not to answer back. She would stand for a moment, defiant, her head held high, gazing straight in front of her into the darkness. And then, still silent, she would cross the room with her long strides to the high standard lamp and light it. Before she returned to Balint she would remain there, motionless, gazing into the light with narrowing pupils.

All these memories crowded into Balint's mind, not in order, not in words or sentences, but in pictures vivid with every detail, time and place rediscovered, recaptured without the need for connected thought or conscious recall, the images of an instant, and as fleeting.

Another carriage passed Balint's: more acquaintances. As he waved to them the previous vision vanished, like the reflections on the smooth surface of a lake wiped off by the slightest breath of wind over the surface. Other carriages passed, more and more, hastening to Var-Siklod to bring guests after the races and, after each, billows of dust coating the verges and the meadow beyond them. Two large greys, drawing a grand open landau drew alongside. The Prefect sat alone in the rear seat. He called out a friendly greeting to Balint and then his carriage too disappeared in a cloud of dust.

Soon Balint's old fiacre, moving slowly, was overtaken by all sorts of other vehicles, some driving so fast that he could only occasionally recognize a face or two before they too were swallowed up in the dust. He caught a glimpse of Zoltan Alvinczy alone in a one-horse gig. Then two elegant carriages, in one of which he saw the widowed Countess Gyalakuthy with her daughter, Dodo. An American racing four-wheeler hurtled by with a fearsome rattle of harness and pounding of hoofs and quickly vanished. It was Tihamer Abonyi, driving his finely-matched pair of black Russian trotters. He drove with style and elegance, his elbows out and his hands pressed to his chest, and next to him was his wife, the fascinating Dinora, who turned and waved and smiled back at him with her open, white-toothed, sensual mouth.

The dust had hardly settled when another carriage appeared beside him, a carriage drawn by four heavy strong bays, trotting unhurriedly in steady unison together. Clearly, like all the horses of the plains, they were used to long distances. They were the opposite of Abonyi's Russians, who would make ten kilometres in as many minutes but then could do no more. These bays could travel a hundred kilometres a day but, though in high spirits, they never altered their even steady trot. Abady loved these old-fashioned Transylvanian carriage horses and gazed at them with the eye of a connoisseur. So intent was he on admiring the team that it was only when the carriage was almost past that he saw who the passengers were. At first Balint only saw a man unknown to him, then beside him with her back to the coachman he recognized Margit, the youngest Miloth girl. In the rear seat there were two ladies. Though he couldn't see the face of the one on the left he assumed that it must be Judith, because on her right sat Adrienne, her profile turned towards her neighbour. A moment passed before he was sure, because her distinctive flaring hair, her most recognizable characteristic, was concealed in a turban, which in turn was swathed in a voluminous dust-wrap which covered her neck and shoulders in thick coils, and a fine veil caught under the chin. It had to be her, with her fine slightly aquiline nose and chiselled lips. So Adrienne would also be at the ball.

Balint realized that, as a married woman, she had come to escort her younger sisters, replacing their sour-faced mama who had made such heavy weather of Addy's coming-out. He wondered how old the younger girls were now. When he had last seen them they were still in the schoolroom. Even so they must still be rather young to come out. Perhaps Judith was already seventeen but Margit could hardly be more than sixteen at the most. But then he remembered how closely related they were to the Laczoks – Countess Miloth and Countess Laczok were sisters, Kendys from Bozsva – and young girls could always attend family parties.

Though Balint realized that he would see Adrienne that evening the thought had little effect on him. It caused neither joy nor that slight irritation he had felt previously when he had thought of her marriage. He felt only indifference and soon his mind was occupied with other things. Other carriages passed, some with single carriage-horses, some with teams of two and occasionally a four-in-hand. One-horse farm wagons started to appear, filled with farmers and their wives, and those who had had a drink at the races would be yodelling and singing in high good humour as they raced each other home. These were the Szeklers, who loved their little grey and bay horses with the same passion as the young aristocrats loved their thoroughbred teams. The Szekler farmers would let no one pass; they drove to the right, to the left, or weaving in the middle of the road so as not to be overtaken, jangling their bridles and shouting encouragements to the horses.

Some middle-class townsfolk, each trim little carriage driven by their single servant, were also on the road. They were the parish clerk, the vicar, the orthodox priest, but however loud they shouted the Szeklers would not give way.

The dust became so thick one could not see five yards ahead.

A single rider, unimpeded by the carriages, rode briskly up. It was Gaspar Kadacsay, known to everyone as Crazy Baron Gazsi. He was still wearing his white racing breeches and brown-cuffed boots. On his head was a soldier's red field cap and over his shoulders the light blue cape of an officer of the 2nd Hussars. He had ridden four hurdle races that afternoon and now, as if that were not enough, he was riding to Siklod on a fresh young piebald. He galloped in silence, weaving between the trundling one-horse farm carts, pulling up when a lumbering wagon appeared out of the dust clouds, spurring on, reining in, zig-zagging through the carts and carriages as if they were obstacles in a slalom race. No sooner had Gazsi disappeared than the sound of cracking whips was hear from behind, whips cracking like gunfire coming ever closer, a tremendous clatter of hoofs, bells and harness coming up like thunder. A high, shrill commanding voice could be heard, 'God damn it! Out of the way! Make way there!' The Szeklers, who had paid no attention before, pulled their wagons off the road in great speed, only with seconds to spare before a team of five horses drew level with Balint's fiacre. First the three leaders, their nostrils flaring, their mouths foaming and their harness covered with ribbons and rosettes, and then the two shaft-horses, all so close to Balint they almost brushed against the old carriage. Behind the rushing team of five dappled greys was a long, low wagon, skidding to and fro as the speed brought the hind wheels off the ground.

In the deep leather driving seat, swinging on its straps like a spring, sat Joska Kendy, proudly erect, his legs spread wide, his body rigid and a pipe between his teeth. In his left hand, tied in a wreath, he held the reins of the five horses tight as cables, while in his right he wielded the fourheaded driving whip, cracking incessantly and rhythmically and making figures of eight in the air.

In front of him the road cleared as if by magic, for everyone knew that delay would be fatal when Joska Kendy had the whip in his hand and cried out for room on the road. With his strong wagon he could tear a wheel off any cart and send everyone into the ditch. It was wiser to let that one go by! And so they gave way, letting the racing team of five vanish swiftly into the distance.

At last, through the dust, Balint began to make out the long avenue of Lombardy poplars which led to the Laczoks' place. The old fiacre turned in on to the straight pebble-paved drive and the clatter of wagons which had become so deafening during the last half hour, began to die away behind him, leaving only the slight tinkling of the harness bells and the soft hiss of the wheels on the ground.

Chapter Two

THE CASTLE OF SIKLOD, the home of the Laczoks for many hundreds of years, was a typically Transylvanian fortress erected on a slight rectangular platform that jutted out from the side of the hill behind. Hardly more than ten metres above the surrounding country it had been built during the Middle Ages on the site of an old Roman fort, open on three sides and backed on the fourth by the rolling hills of the Maros valley, now covered in vineyards. The first Laczok to make his home on the edge of this smiling valley, which now lay between the main road and the village where the peasants lived, seems to have chosen the site as a strategic point between the counties of Maros and Torda, where he could best protect his lands and serfs from marauding bands of Szekler huns.

Even in those early days Var-Siklod can never have inspired the same awe as those great frowning fortresses of stone that we know from drawings in medieval French and German monastic manuscripts. The four square walls, following the lines of the Roman camp, were joined at each corner by stout little towers. Over the entrance gates was another small castellated tower and in the centre of the wide courtyard stood the keep, where the lord and his family lived, and which, in those days was merely a two-storey building standing by itself, with massive walls and tiny windows set in deep stone embrasures. Useless against cannon and sophisticated siege machinery, the little fort had been all that was needed to hold the land against the fierce raids of Tartars, armed only with their courage and primitive weapons, and, later, against the bands of brigands and free Szeklers. If the raiding party was large, and enough warning had been given, the livestock for miles around could be herded into the great courtyard around the keep.

Var-Siklod had not changed until the middle of the eighteenth century when the then head of the Laczok family, Count Adam – Vice-Chancellor of Transylvania and Governor of the province – decided that he must have a residence more worthy of his great position. It was just when the massive elegance of baroque was being transformed in Vienna, Munich and Brandenburg, into the fantasies of rococo; and it was this last that appealed to the taste of Count Adam.

First he removed the battlements from the fortified keep and replaced them with a soaring roof of shingle, made in three sections like a pagoda, the first ascending steeple, and the second and third mounting in an elaborate S-bend to form a mushroom-shaped roof that was taller even than the building beneath. He did not enlarge the windows but surrounded them with carved stone cornices decorated with garlands of flowers and fruit. Stone pilasters with elaborate capitals were grafted on to each corner of the building and, over the main entrance, he built out a new doorway, surmounted by vaulting, which in turn supported a balcony whose parapet of carved stone reflected the wildest and most fantastic intricacies of rococo taste. Above the balcony, supported on thin iron poles, was another roof made of copper, separate from that of the main house but also mushroom-shaped in two elaborate and unexpected curves. As the supporting poles were barely visible it seemed as if the heavy shining roof hung in the air unsupported from below. In Count Adam's time rich curtains had been hung between the iron poles, thus giving him the appearance he wanted, the fashionable Chinese style that had inspired the Pagodenburg at Munich. That this was the effect intended was clear from the upturned edges of the different sections of the roof above, and from the oriental detail of the drainpipes which, in times of rain, shot spouts of water in arcs of ten metres out of their dragon-shaped mouths.

The eastern fancies of Count Adam, however, did not long remain unchallenged. As the nineteenth century brought added riches to the family so the Laczok of those later days, inspired by the same building mania as his predecessor, decided to enlarge

PART ONE

and as he thought, improve the castle. As a modern and up-to-date magnate, his contribution was in the then fashionable Empire style that had come in at the end of the eighteenth century and spread throughout Europe at the time of Napoleon. The wide courtyard behind the house was quickly transformed into new kitchens and stable-yards. Then, leaving the entire rococo mansion untouched, two classical wings were added and embellished with a wide colonnade, which reached out each side of the house to the old outer walls. These two wings were then brought forward at right angles to form a symmetrical U-shape. And as defensive walls were no longer needed to keep out marauding tartars, that part of the battlements that lay in front of the house was demolished and replaced by a broad terrace which overlooked the spreading Laczok lands.

This was the aspect that the old fortress of Siklod presented to the arriving guests as their carriages passed from the long poplar avenue and through the great entrance gates which were bordered by the ancient spreading oaks that marked the boundaries of the park. The drive swept past the main façade of the house and climbed gently to the huge iron-studded doors under the eastern tower of the precinct. Beyond these doors the carriages passed through the stable court and, turning left again under an arch formed in the eastern wing, found themselves beneath the columned portico that gave onto the great terrace in front of the house.

When Balint arrived he found that the portico steps were lined with waiting servants. On the lowest rung was the butler, Janos Kadar, grey and stooping, dressed in the long braided coat of the Laczok livery. It seemed as if he were so frail that he could barely support the work and worry that would be his lot that day. Behind him stood the hired footmen, and with them the odd-job boy, Ferko, who rushed forward to take Balint's coat and bag.

As he walked up the steps Balint told the old butler that before greeting the family he would like to wash off the dust in which he had been covered during the drive from Vasarhely.

'Of course, my lord!' he replied, and turning to the boy, 'Ferko, show Count Balint to the corner room. And see that there is water ... and clean towels!' But thinking the boy too inexperienced he went on impatiently, 'No! No! I'll go myself' and, taking Balint's things from him, he hurried ahead, showing the latest visitor the way through the vast entrance hall to a door at the back. The room set aside for visitors had clearly already been used. A few soiled towels were scattered here and there, some on the floor, some on the washstand. The tin bucket was full of dirty water and the jug was empty.

'I beg the Count's pardon,' said the old man, hurrying out through a door at the far end of the room. From the court behind the house his voice could be heard querulously chiding, 'Aniko! Mali! Where are you ... Hurry now ... clean towels and water to the guest-room ... quickly now! Must I do everything myself?' And a door was slammed somewhere.

In a few moments a young servant girl bustled in, curtsyed to Balint and sighing deeply replaced the sodden towels with fresh ones, changed the water jug and hurried out with the tin bucket, her bare feet slapping softly on the scrubbed pine floorboards.

In a small drawing-room on the first floor the older ladies were gathering in a group round their hostess. Aunt Lizinka was already there, sitting as she always did with her knees drawn up in a large armchair, with the widowed Countess Gyalakuthy, the rich Adelma, and two or three other mothers who had brought their daughters to the dance. With them were some other ladies, among them Countess Bartokfay, who lived nearby, and the wife of the family lawyer, Beno Balogh-Peter, had come in merely to greet Countess Laczok on her name-day. Their husbands had already made a brief appearance upstairs, kissed their hostess' hand, and then gone down to the garden where Count Laczok received the male guests. Only the ladies remained. They had been offered tea and coffee, plumcake, cold ham, sugared biscuits and lemonade, and the room was still littered with empty cups and crumb-filled plates, for the servants had more important things to do than clear away.

The little room soon filled up, the guests sitting on small chairs in a semi-circle round their hostess who, as she always did, had placed herself on a small sofa with its back to the wall near the door. Countess Ida chose this narrow boudoir to receive her guests because from there she could remain in close contact with the running of the house. Every so often the door beside her would be slightly opened and one of the maids or other servants would put their head in, whisper something in the countess's ear and disappear discreetly as soon as they had received her equally discreet and softly-spoken order. The ladies' conversation would then go on as if there had been no interruption.

Countess Ida always received on her saint's day and for her it

PART ONE

was always the most difficult day in the entire year. Invited or not there were masses of callers in the afternoon, and in the evening there was always a large dinner followed by a dance. Rooms had to be chosen and prepared for the guests who stayed overnight, the great reception rooms prepared and polished, the reputation of the famous Siklod cooking had to be maintained and every detail, including the baking, needed her personal attention. Something always went wrong if she didn't see to it herself. On her last saint's day she had nearly died of shame when it was discovered that salt had found its way into the iced puddings; and the year before, at the very last moment, a most peculiar smell had been identified as coming from the potted veal tongues, and a carriage had had to be sent post-haste to Vasarhely to find some more. Alice Laczok, her sister-in-law who should have helped her, was so vague that she needed more supervision than the servants. In recent years her daughters had begun to be useful, running errands, checking the larder and the cold store, but today they had gone to those idiotic races, disappearing at midday and not returning until it was almost dark. They had left their mother to see to everything herself. And so she had, until the guests started arriving and she found herself nailed to the sofa and making polite conversation while her whole mind was on the thousand details of the preparations for the evening. She could hardly wait to get rid of all those who had dropped in, knowing that there was little time left before she would have to go and dress.

Not that any of the ladies would have guessed that they did not have her full attention. With a sweet smile on her still beautiful if rather full face, she would turn from one to another with every sign of sympathetic interest, 'Yes, indeed, my dear. How well you put it, I do agree!' And all the while she was thinking: Did they put the champagne on ice? Have they let the cream curdle? Did someone remember to shut up the ice pit? Was there enough beef for the guests' coachmen's dinner? Was Alice actually checking all these things or not? Despite the fact that her husband's sister was so unreliable she had been forced to entrust it all to her; and until the girls got back there was nothing else she could do. But though reconciled to the inevitable, she still worried.

It was a mercy that Aunt Lizinka was there and that she never drew breath. In her high, piping, and surprisingly penetrating voice, she held all the country ladies spellbound with her version of the latest scandals. No one ever interrupted her: neither the mothers of marriageable daughters who feared her evil tongue and what she might say if she were offended, nor the country ladies who had come to pay their respects, for they knew that however frail and ancient she might seem she was still a power to be reckoned with in Maros-Torda. Only two years before she had used this power, to the whole province's rage, to ensure the election to Parliament of its first peasant member, the demagogue Makkai, simply because she had been angered by the choice of a candidate she did not approve. People said that even Makkai's election speeches had been dictated by Aunt Lizinka.

Her latest tirade concerned her old enemy, Miklos Absolon, who, although he hardly ever left his estates in the northern part of the province, still wielded great influence, usually in direct opposition to whatever Aunt Lizinka was trying to achieve. She never lost an opportunity of discrediting Miklos Absolon, who for many years had lived with his housekeeper, a fact well-known to everybody, and who according to Lizinka was nothing more than a 'crack-heeled servant'. 'And now, my dears – I know it for a fact – she's cheating on him with every Tom, Dick and Harry! It's true! I know it because it is so!'

All this was happening while Balint was washing in the guest cloak room. As he stepped out into the hall he met again the butler Kadar carrying a large tray of glasses.

'Where can I find Countess Laczok?' he asked.

'The Count should leave her be,' replied the old man testily, 'and go on out into the garden. That's where all the gentlemen are.' And without waiting for an answer, he marched on breathing heavily.

So Balint went out through the front door again. About a hundred yards away on the edge of the old moat was a gaunt old lime tree under which the men were gathered. Some of them had come from the races, while others were husbands of the ladies upstairs who had come from Vasarhely and the country around Var-Siklod to call upon the hostess. Under the tree was a round table made from an ancient mill-stone, on which had been placed decanters of wine, bottles of lemonade and mineral waters and several trays of glasses. Directly under the tree sat the host, Count Jeno Laczok. The visitors, on benches and garden chairs – and some standing – had grouped themselves according to their political allegiance; one party on his left, the other on his right.

Next to the host, on his right, sat Crookface, who had been

PART ONE

Prefect for fifteen years during the Kalman Tisza régime, and beside him the present Prefect, Peter Kis, with Soma Weissfeld, the banker who was also a State Counsellor. This last honorary title had been obtained for Weissfeld by Jeno Laczok as a reward for having helped him run the private company which had been formed to manage the combined forestry interests of the different branches of the Laczok family. Nearby sat Beno Balogh Peter, the ambitious notary who was always being wooed by the opposition; Uncle Ambrus who, though he secretly inclined away from the party in power, gave outward allegiance to whichever policy was supported by his cousin Crookface; Adam and Zoltan Alvinczy, who followed Uncle Ambrus in everything; and, finally, Joska Kendy, who sat silently smoking his pipe. Joska never discussed politics but he had placed himself there because he had two horses to sell and planned to palm them off on the Prefect.

Here the party line was broken by a large and hairy man with a black beard, Zoltan Varju, a neighbour of the Laczoks, who was generally regarded as an irresponsible and dangerous demagogue, and who sat facing the host.

On Count Laczok's other side sat Ordung, the County Sheriff, whose dealings with the opposition were by no means as discreet as he believed; his friend the Deputy Sheriff Gaalffy, and an elderly man, Count Peter Bartokfay, in Hungarian dress and boots, who had been Member for Maros-Torda for many years in the past. Beside the old politician sat Zsigmond Boros, an eminent lawyer in the district and one of the leading political figures in Vasarhely; and a round-faced, puffy young man, Isti Kamuthy, who was politically ambitious and so liked to keep in with anyone important.

Between Kamuthy and Varju sat old Daniel Kendy who had no political ideas of any sort, but who had chosen that place because there he was nearest to the wine. He never spoke, but just sat quietly drinking, refilling his glass the moment it was empty.

A little further away, outside the main circle, stood and sat the young men who had been asked to the ball, together with a few others who had not found places nearer the host. Among these last was Tihamer Abonyi who had placed himself beside Laszlo Gyeroffy, partly because they came from the same district and partly because of Laszlo's grand Hungarian connections. Balint went at once towards Laszlo, his friend and cousin, rejoicing to see a kindred spirit. As he did so he recalled the words of Schiller *'Unter Larven die einzig' fühlende Brust* – in all these grubs just one faithful heart', but even as he quoted the words to himself he was seized by the Prefect, Peter Kis, who greeted him with as much warmth as if he had been the prodigal son.

Balint, who had met only the Countess Laczok, asked him: 'Which is the host?'

'I'll introduce you at once, my dear friend,' replied the Prefect, putting an arm round Balint's shoulders and propelling him forward as if Balint were his special responsibility. They had to stoop to pass under the low spreading branches of the tree to reach the wide pine bench on which Count Jeno was sitting.

The host was a heavy-set man, fat and almost completely bald. A single lock of hair was combed over his forehead, like a small brown island in the yellow sea of his smooth shining hairless skull. There were two ridges of fat at the nape of his neck and he had three double chins, and his large pale face was given distinction only by an impressive black drooping moustache and the upward sweeping eyebrows that peered out from the layers of fat. Count Laczok sat rigidly upright, neither leaning on the arms of the bench nor against the tree behind him. One of his short legs reached the ground, the other was drawn up under him, and he held his hands spread on his knees. Balint at once thought of those squat Chinese soapstone figures displayed in oriental bazaars. The Lord of Siklod, sitting hieratically under the old lime tree, seemed a reincarnation of some Szekler-hun ancestor from the distant past.

'May I present Count Balint Abady, my latest and dearest Member?' said Peter Kis, pushing Balint forward with a special squeeze on his shoulder as if he were thus sealing their friendship.

'Welcome, my boy! Welcome!' said Count Jeno, extending his hand but not otherwise moving, as neither rising nor turning was easy for him.

After greeting his host, Balint introduced himself to the guests he did not already know and went to sit down beside Laszlo Gyeroffy.

'*Your* Member, my dear prefect?' quietly asked Sheriff Ordung from the other side of the table, in a mocking tone that barely concealed his underlying animosity. Ordung had two reasons to resent the Prefect: firstly because, unlike Peter Kis whose father was a middle-class merchant from far-away Gyergyo, the sheriff came from an ancient noble family of Maros-Torda and secondly, because they belonged to different political parties. As a result they were on worse terms than were usual between elected sheriffs – who could hold office for as long as they retained the confidence of the voters – and the prefects who, as appointees of the government, were apt to come and go with every political upheaval in the capital.'

'Well, Lelbanya *is* in my country,' the Prefect replied heartily, but somewhat on the defensive.

'Elected members belong to the people who have elected them,' cried Zoltan Varju.

'... or to the town or country,' added old Count Bartokfay.

The Prefect, finding himself cornered, took refuge in evasion. 'I only said "my" because I like him so much!'

Even this did not satisfy the demagogue Varju.

'Sheer absolutism! Just as if he were appointed by the government,' went on Varju. 'It's not as if it hasn't happened before.'

'But he supports the '67 Compromise.'

'He's not a member of any party ... and this means he disapproves of the government and the Tisza party,' intervened Peter Varju who, turning to Balint, went on: 'Am I right, Count?'

'I am far too much of a beginner to give an opinion,' answered Balint, who was not at all sure what to say and felt he was getting into rather deep water.

Now the host thought it was time he intervened.

'Well spoken, son! That's the way to defend yourself. I keep clear of opinions too and keep my mouth shut. It's the only way not to be torn to pieces either by the dogs,' and he waved at the politicians on his right, '... or by the wolves,' indicating their opponents. 'Frankly, gentlemen, I don't see why you all growl at each other so much. The peace has been made by old Thaly, the Hungarian curse has been laid to rest, and all should be friends!'

While saying this, Count Laczok spread his arms wide and then brought them together again, hugging his own huge bulk as if it were the whole world. 'Be friends, my good fellows, be friends!' And bursting into loud derisive laughter, he reached for his wine-glass, refilled it to the brim, and raising it high, said:

'Long life to this clever and excellent peace! Drink up, my friends. *Vivat! Vivat!*'

And with this ironic toast to the uneasy parliamentary truce, the floodgates of party discussion were opened again.

The bitter battle in Parliament about responsibility for national defence, which had begun a year and a half before and which had brought into the open many old grievances about the complicated legal relationship between Hungary and Austria, had dwindled into an uneasy peace in the previous spring. Though the party leaders in power had managed to overcome some of the technical objections to the integration of the Austrian and Hungarian armies – and indeed had isolated the small group of those politicians who clung to the 1848 policy of complete independence – they still needed, so as not to lose votes, to brandish patriotic slogans that demanded, if not the separation into two of the monarchy's armies, at least the appointment of Hungarian senior officers. Without such token signs of resistance – and some even thought the national colours woven into Hungarian officers' insignia would be enough – they were defenceless against the persistent stubbornness of the little group headed by Ugron and Samuel Barra which, though in the minority, took every advantage of the absurd anomalies in the old Hungarian parliamentary rules of procedure to block the passing of budgets, and the approval of foreign contracts, all essential if the business of government was to continue.

By forced votes, all-night sittings, by referring all important issues to rediscussion in closed committees, this little group had done its utmost to outlaw the government itself. To anyone outside politics it seemed inconceivable that such a tiny minority could even attempt to force its will not only on the large majority in Parliament who supported the government but also on the entire monarchy including the Emperor himself. Only those students of history who knew how effectively the Hungarians had used this sort of legalistic quibbling in their centuries-old struggle with the Habsburgs could see what the minority were up to and where they had learned their methods. To this dissident minority, whose heads and hearts were always ruled by patriotic resistance, the achievements of 1790 and 1867 owed nothing to historic circumstances and everything to this sort of delaying tactic.

The precarious armistice between the government and the opposition that had been agreed six months before had only come about because old Kalman Thaly intervened to support the Minister President, Istvan Tisza, when he threatened to reform the Standing Orders by force but let it be known that if peace were made concessions would follow. And both contending parties had become so impatient of the stalemate, and so bored, that they had reluctantly agreed.

Many greeted the parliamentary peace with relief and joy; but there were still those who, sitting at home smoking their pipes, brooded in rebellious discontent and accused even the extremists of being fainthearted and infirm of purpose.

PART ONE

One of those armchair politicians was the elderly Count Bartokfay who, at Var-Siklod that afternoon, had ensconced himself comfortably close to the wine table.

'That wicked old Master Tisza wouldn't have got away with it if I'd still been in the House,' said Bartokfay in his old fashioned country drawl. 'I'd have had him impeached for breaking the law!'

'What law? You can't say he broke any law.' The prefect Kis was always on the side of authority.

'He collected taxes that hadn't been voted!'

'Come, come! Voluntary contributions aren't taxes,' said the notary, who was also known for supporting the government. 'No one had to pay. Those aren't taxes!'

But nothing would stop Bartokfay. 'I'll keep off the army question then. Maybe that was necessary. But the government started discussing international commercial contracts – and that is a constitutional offence! Yes, a con-sti-tu-tional offence! Even according to the Compromise!'

'I beg your pardon!' parried the Prefect, 'but there's nothing illegal about discussion. The matter had to be discussed and they were free to do so. Now I agree that a settlement would have to have been stopped ... I say it myself, but ...'

'Then all discussion is pointless! Absurd!'

'All *this* discussion is absurd!' shouted Peter Kis, completely losing his temper.

For a moment there was silence. Then a rich deep baritone voice, with melodious depths to it like organ notes, spoke up from the background: it was Zsigmond Boros, the lawyer whom everyone respected.

'You must excuse me, Prefect, but our old friend is quite right. Allow me to clarify the problem ...'

The lawyer's calm and lucid explanation smoothed down the rising tempers of the others. He paused for an instant and then the puffy young Isti Kamuthy spoke up, his lisp all the more pronounced as he tried to get his word in before anyone else.

'Thatth just what I thought, at home in Burgozthd. Then I thought I was thtupid. Now I thee I am not tho thtupid!'

'You were right the first time, in Burgozthd!' Old Crookface shouted. Everyone laughed, even young Isti, though he did not know why.

Then, as the laughter died down and everyone seemed calmer,

the banker Weissfeld started again. Balint rose quietly, touched Gyeroffy on the shoulder and unobtrusively moved out from under the tree. All this narrow-minded, prejudiced, dogmatic talk got on his nerves. Even the prefect, whom he admired, brought only clichés and worn-out legalistic quibbles to the discussion. Laszlo joined him as they walked away.

Slowly they made their way back to the terrace. It was growing dark. Between the small corner tower and the library a small door opened onto steps that led down to the rose garden. They went this way but did not speak until they had left the terrace. It was as if they both felt the need for the quiet privacy of the garden before starting to talk, so many months had passed since their last meeting. Balint still felt dazed by the useless clamour of the politicians and he reflected ruefully on the very different experiences he had had while abroad on mission. He thought of the methodic logical work that had gone into the preparations for the commercial treaty with Italy, and of the barely disguised contempt expressed by foreigners, especially by the Austrians and Germans, for the fuss that Hungary was making about Austrian control of the united armies. To them the security of the Dual Monarchy depended on the unification of the armed forces, and this was being foolishly undermined by the Hungarians. In the context of world politics the Hungarian attitude was short-sighted and meaningless. Of course foreigners knew nothing of Hungary's past and they could not understand why the Hungarians loathed and resented the integration of their army with that of Austria. Balint's ardent national feelings had been outraged every time he had heard his countrymen laughed at and misunderstood.

Laszlo's thoughts were very different. He had barely listened to the argument under the lime tree. Politics were not for him, and in any case his mind was far away, on matters more important to him.

The meeting with all these friends and relations today at the races, and again at Var-Siklod, had reawakened in Laszlo that old feeling of being an outsider. It was odd how even in Transylvania he did not feel a part of the group. This sense of not belonging went everywhere with him. Here, as at his aunt's place in Budapest, everywhere, it was the same. The grown man still carried with him the aura of his orphaned childhood. He was alien, a foreigner; politely welcomed perhaps, but never completely accepted.

PART ONE

How he yearned to be loved – and loved for himself, not just for what he could do to amuse and entertain, not for his excellent dancing, not because he could play the piano so well, providing waltzes and foxtrots that all could dance to; not because he was a good shot and an excellent fourth at tennis. When he visited his Kollonich or Szent-Gyorgyi relations in West Hungary, all his cousins seemed overjoyed when he came, tried to make him prolong his stay and were sad when he left. But still Laszlo sensed that it was only for these superficial reasons and not because they really understood and liked him.

Of all these cousins there was only Klara, who was about his own age – and she was not really a cousin at all as she was the daughter of Prince Kollonich's first marriage – who seemed to see more in him than the others. Only she was interested in what he thought rather than what he did. Even when they were still very young they would pair off in team games, the two of them against the others. Klara was different; but her half-brother, his aunt's sons, and the two Szent-Gyorgyi boys? He doubted very much if they saw anything more in him than an amusing cousin who was good at tennis.

This was why he was so pleased to see Balint again, why he had squeezed his arm in friendly greeting when Balint had sat down next to him under the lime tree. Since they had both been young, since as long as he could remember, Balint had been his only true friend, who understood him and from whom he hid nothing, and so when, as the twentieth century approached, they talked of their futures it was only to Balint that Laszlo confessed his determination to be a musician.

To Balint he poured out his seemingly fantastic hopes of writing great operas and symphonies that would seduce the whole world. And to Balint too he had recounted all his difficulties with his Uncle Stanizlo Gyeroffy who the court had appointed to be his legal guardian until he came of age. Uncle Stanizlo, who was no real uncle but only a distant relation, had absolutely vetoed Laszlo's musical studies and forced him instead into the law school. There had been a stormy scene between them when he had left school, and Laszlo had then recounted to Balint his deep resentment when the old man had said: 'While I am your guardian I won't allow anything so idiotic. When you're of age you can do any foolishness you like!' Laszlo was recalling all this as he stepped down into the rose garden. Balint turned to him, as if in answer to his thoughts, and asked:

'You came of age last March. What are you going to do?'

'I'm entering the Academy of Music in Budapest. I'm going back in a few days.'

'And the university exams?'

Laszlo laughed. 'Devil take them! What do I care? I'm going to do what I want at long last. I only came here to take over the estate. And that's a nasty business I can tell you ... and very complicated if you have to deal with old Carrots...' This was Laszlo's nickname for his guardian who always wore an obvious red-blond wig.

'Why complicated?'

'Oh, Lord! He says he's invested a lot of his own money in the property and he wants to be paid back before he'll hand it over! Not that I've got any money ... none at all. All I've got is debts! Don't worry. I'll sort it out somehow,' said Laszlo, laughing ...

'Debts?'

'Not many. A few thousand crowns ... to a money-lender, of course. I couldn't live on what old Carrots allowed me.'

'Well, you'll have to settle them. There's nothing worse than owing money.'

'Oh, I will. Somehow. Everything would be quite simple if I could sell the wood from my part of the Gyeroffy forests. The problem is that I only have a one-third share with Uncle Staniszlo ... and he's got other plans, some sort of industrial project he's dead keen on, the stubborn old fool! Oh! For heaven's sake let's not talk about anything so boring! I'm so glad to see you, Balint!'

And taking him by the arm, he started to tell him how he had been received by the music professors, what they thought about his playing and what they had said about his compositions, some of which Balint had heard. Carried away by his enthusiasm Laszlo talked and talked as they walked up and down between the long-stemmed roses. It was almost dark. Only in the western sky was there still a rose-red glow, while in the east the moon rose, so full and bright that deep shadows were cast by the castle walls, enveloping the garden where they talked.

As Laszlo and Balint passed the entrance to the castle they met a group of guests descending the steps. They were already dressed for the evening, the women in low-cut gowns and the men in stiff shirts which shone white in the moonlight like shooting targets. Though they were silhouetted against the sunset Balint saw at once that among them was Adrienne Miloth. Her face was in shadow, but he could not fail to recognize her Diana-like stride

PART ONE

and the outline of her head with the wavy dark hair weaving wild arabesques around the perfect oval of her face. She had her two sisters with her and they were accompanied by two young men.

Balint's first reaction was to move away, to avoid them – an inexplicable subconscious reflex that lasted but a moment. Adrienne came calmly towards him, without quickening her pace, her beautifully formed mouth in a wide and generous smile. She put out her hand, saying:

'How marvellous to find you here, AB!' This was what he had always been called in Transylvania: 'Look! I've dwindled into a chaperon! I'm responsible for these two now!' and she put her arms round the shoulders of her two younger sisters, who were both extremely pretty and slightly shorter than Adrienne.

The two young men came up to join them. One was Akos, the youngest Alvinczy boy. Balint did not know the other, who turned to him and clicked his heels in a formal soldierly manner.

'Egon Wickwitz,' he said, and bowed. He was the unknown man Balint had seen in the Miloths' carriage. Shaking hands, Balint looked him over, trying rapidly to assess him.

Baron Wickwitz was tall and good-looking, with the wide shoulders and narrow hips of an athlete. The impression of an inverted triangle was emphasized by the line of the stiff white dress shirt and outlined by the sloping lapels of his black tailcoat. He was dressed with meticulous care, as if he were not entirely at ease in such garb. Balint did not like this, and though he could not deny that Wickwitz was a handsome man, he did not like his face either. He had sad brown eyes, a long, narrow jaw and black hair that grew low on his forehead.

For a few moments they exchanged polite courtesies and then started to walk along the paths between the rose beds. Balint was in front with Adrienne, behind them Margit Miloth with Alvinczy and finally Judith with Laszlo and the Austrian.

'Who is this nitwit?' Balint asked Adrienne. She laughed.

'It's funny you should call him that. Everyone does, though you can't have heard it anywhere. It's very apt,' and she added seriously, 'but it shows how good-natured he is because he never seems to mind.'

'Well then, who is this good-natured gentleman?'

'He's really very nice. Amateur rider – good all-round sportsman – a *Haupt-Leutnant* in the Hussars and stationed at Brasso.'

'Shouldn't he be in uniform?' Balint could not help sounding somewhat hostile.

'He's on long leave.'

As they walked on in silence Balint found himself more and more in the same groundless, aggressive mood that he had felt each time he had met Adrienne since her marriage.

'And he's your latest flirt, is he?' he asked offensively.

'Not actually mine ... though they do say he's paying a lot of attention to your old flame, the pretty Dinora!'

Coming from Adrienne this was most unexpected. In the old days she had never given any sign that she even knew of his passion for the little Countess Abonyi. Balint veered away from the subject.

'He seems to speak Hungarian quite well.'

'That's because his mother came from Hungary; from Bihar, I fancy.'

'He's got cow's eyes!'

Adrienne laughed again, lightly.

'Does it matter? He's not overburdened with brains!'

Suddenly the peace of the garden was shattered by a shrill peal of bells from inside the castle. Cling! Clang! Clang! Cling-Clang! The rhythmic carillon announced that dinner would be served in half-an-hour's time. Balint and Laszlo ran, because they still had to change. The others walked slowly towards the house.

Chapter Three

IN THE GREAT HALL on the first floor, which stretched right from the facade to the rear of the building, a large table was laid for forty guests. Countess Laczok sat with her back to the balcony at one end of the great table; Count Jeno sat opposite her at the other.

The older guests, with one exception were all seated in order of precedence on each side of the host and hostess. The exception was the Prefect, who was seated on Countess Ida's right, in the place of honour which by right should have been accorded to Crookface Kendy, who was not only older than Peter Kis but also a Privy Counsellor. So Crookface found himself on his hostess's left. The reason was simple. The Prefect was not a man of their class; and this was underlined by giving him precedence.

Of course Peter Kis did not himself grasp the reason for this distinction. He was already flattered and grateful that he alone of

PART ONE

the politicians had been asked to stay to dinner and he decided that, in appreciation, he would make a speech which would show these aristocrats that he, too, was a man of the world and knew how to behave in grand company. Accordingly he sat in silence, trying to work out a play of words on his hostess's Christian name.

On the Prefect's right sat Alice Laczok, a skinny version of her brother; after her was Joska Kendy, who just managed to pocket his pipe while dinner lasted, and then young Ida Laczok, named after her mother, and Balint.

Next to Crookface on the other side sat the pretty little Dinora, Countess Abonyi, and after her Uncle Ambrus and Adrienne. Countess Laczok had put Uncle Ambrus between the two young women because she thought they would have more fun being next to someone so popular.

At the centre of the table, on both sides, were seated all the young people, boy next to girl but in no special order. They sat where they chose. Only three seats were reserved, furthest away from the places of honour. These were for the two young Laczok boys who were seated at the centre of the long table with their tutor between them. At the far end of the table Count Jeno had Aunt Lizinka on his right and Countess Gyalakuthy, the rich Adelma, on his left. From where the hostess sat that end of the table seemed unbalanced. Aunt Lizinka's tiny shrunken head was only just visible above the table cloth while Adelma, though a woman of only medium height, seemed to tower a head above her neighbours. Countess Ida, thinking someone had made a mistake, called down the table to her husband:

'Jeno! Change chairs with Adelma! Someone's given her too high a chair.'

Countess Gyalakuthy protested: 'I'm perfectly all right!'

But the hostess insisted: 'Not at all! Come along, change the chairs!'

Count Jeno looked up but did not move, so Tihamer Abonyi, who was sitting on Adelma's left, jumped up, eager to please, and gave up his chair. Somewhat unwillingly Adelma rose and accepted the other chair ... but when she sat down she was just as tall as before. There was a painful silence and a few artificial coughs – and some barely suppressed giggles from the young. Then Lizinka spoke up, her voice shrill and malicious as ever:

'Dear Adelma, no matter where you sit you will always be a queen upon her throne!'

The embarrassed widow said nothing but the whole table rocked wirth mirth. The loudest laughter came from the two young Laczoks who, quite without manners, laughed so hard that one lolled forward until his head was in his plate and the other doubled up and disappeared under the table. Between them their tutor sat tight-faced and serious, upright in his high-buttoned Franz-Josef tunic, his face expressionless.

Balint, sitting opposite the tutor, noticed his non-committal expression and wondered where he had seen his hard wooden face before. Between jutting cheekbones a smallish pug-shaped nose divided slanting black eyes. Above his rather fleshy face there was a huge dome skull whose shape was emphasized by the closely shaven hair – every division of the cranium was defined by faint grey lines as in an anatomy model.

I know that face, thought Balint, Where? Where? And, as the laughter subsided, he turned to his neighbour, the young Ida Laczok.

'Who is he, your brothers' tutor?'

'Oh! He's only here for the summer. Papa hired him as those rascals failed their exams. He's preparing them to take the maths again at the end of the holidays. He's called Andras Jopal and he's very good even if he isn't qualified,' she said. Then, confidentially; 'You know he's quite crazy! Imagine, he thinks he's going to invent a flying machine!' She laughed softly.

Then Balint remembered. They had met in Kolozsvar when Balint had attended Professor Martin's lectures on higher mathematics. It was during his third year when he had no examination. Andras Jopal had been by far the best student and though they had only exchanged a few words, Balint had found him intelligent and full of interesting ideas.

The first course was served. Janos Kadar entered the great hall at the head of three footmen, all carrying huge dishes. The old butler, breathing noisily, carried a tray on which reposed two giant pike whose white eyes gleamed in the candlelight. He looked round at the footmen, nodding his head to show where they should start serving. Behind each of them was a young maid carrying trays with sauce-boats and, behind Kadar, was the little apprentice Ferko.

Countess Laczok watched anxiously to be sure that the service was properly carried out and then turned to her neighbour, the Prefect, and said proudly:

PART ONE

'Do take some more! Don't be afraid, there aren't any bones in my pike!' She served pike to her guests whenever she could, and she always said this when it was offered. It was one of the treasured secrets of Var-Siklod how this delicious but exceptionally bony fish could be presented apparently completely whole, head, tail, fins and skin in place, and yet without a bone in its body! It was a real mystery, and a great surprise to those to whom it was offered for the first time. Not a bone ... not one. It was indeed remarkable, and it was Countess Ida's special pride.

The Prefect was suitably impressed at this marvel and the hostess smiled with pleasure and gratification when all the older ladies started exclaiming that it simply wasn't possible!

The plates were changed with much clatter as soon as the first course was finished. Then in came the main dish of the dinner, the classical *pièce de résistance* at all Transylvanian banquets; cold Richelieu turkey with truffles, huge birds bulging with a variety of delicious stuffings.

The guests fell to heartily, hardly noticing the arrival of the gypsy orchestra, who tiptoed silently into the hall, along the table, edging their way between the guests and the great tiled stove, trying not to trip over the legs of the chairs or crash their instruments against the wall or over the guests' heads. Even the cymbalist managed it somehow, though he once almost dropped the great brass plates as he stumbled over the chair legs. Gathered behind the hostess and led by the famous Laji Pongracz who had played for the Archduke Rudolf, the band, gently at first and then louder, struck up the old tune 'Blue Forget-me-not', which Countess Ida had chosen for her own when she was still very young and when, like so many girls of her generation, she had been half in love with its composer, Gyurka Banffy.

The hostess looked round, as if in surprise – though of course, as nothing escaped her, she had been perfectly aware of the band's arrival. She smiled a welcome to Laji, who bowed low directly to her, his arms outstretched on either side of him, the violin in one hand, the bow in the other, thus silently offering his homage on her name day. Then he straightened up and went on playing, his bow caressing the strings, the well-known melody that everyone associated with Countess Ida.

When he had finished he looked down the table at Count Jeno and, with a playful smile that said much he started to play the host's favourite: 'Long, long ago when I drove the carriage for beautiful ladies...'

Suddenly, as the tune was being played, the Prefect got up. He cleared his throat and tapped his glass with a knife. The music stopped as if cut by scissors.

'Ladies and gentlemen! Ladies and gentlemen!' Then, to Sandor Kendy who went on talking, 'I beg the Count's pardon, but I would like to say a few words!' Crookface scowled and muttered half under his breath, 'Go fu...', but the words were almost inaudible through the thick moustache, and no one noticed. The Prefect had already begun his toast.

He started with an elegant reference to Greek mythology, to the Judgement of Paris, slipped from that to Mount Ida and a play on the hostess's name, drew a far-fetched parallel (which no one understood) between the Trojan Wars and the hospitality of Var-Siklod, returned to the beauty of the three goddesses, and, declaring that Countess Ida outshone them all, ended with calling for three cheers for the hostess. The gypsy band, by now quite ready, played a swift fanfare, a mere flourish on the strings.

When the cheering and clinking of glasses had somewhat abated old Daniel Kendy, from beyond Aunt Lizinka, rose and turned, his big bulbous nose facing the prefect. Everyone noticed and waited, on tenterhooks because they all knew how mischievous Uncle Daniel could be. 'Wait for it! It's Uncle Dani!' They all wondered what would come out. Then he opened his mouth, stuttering more than usual as he was already not a little drunk.

'M-M-Mister Prefect! You are a m-m-monumental f-f-fraud!' and he sat down, with a self-satisfied smile on his face, and emptied his champagne glass, his swollen shining face creased into ridges of pleasure.

General laughter followed, though some of it seemed a little artificial and a few people muttered that Uncle Dani had gone a bit far this time. Even the prefect forced a smile. But the situation was saved by the quick wit of Laji Pongracz who raised his violin and after a few loud chords, led the band into such a tearing, rippling csárdás that everyone was silenced and all emotions forgotten as the company was swept along by the well-known rhythm which seemed to make even the glasses dance upon the table.

The dinner went on: ices were served and monumental cakes, quince jellies, fruit and fine liqueurs in tiny Bohemian glasses. But like all good things, it had to end. The company rose from the table and left the hall, the older men to the library where they were served with more liqueurs – the family's pride as they were made at Var-Siklod – the hostess and the matrons to her small sitting-

PART ONE

room – while the young people went out onto the large copper-roofed balcony. This was necessary so that the servants could dismantle the great table and prepare the hall for dancing.

In Countess Laczok's little sitting-room the conversation was sluggish. Everyone had eaten well and occasionally some lady would congratulate the hostess on the excellence of the feast. The room was lit only by one small lamp, for, although there were hundreds of lamps in the castle, they had all been needed to light the many rooms that had had to be brought into use that evening. After the brilliance of the great hall the semi-darkness of the small room brought on a sleepy mood that was occasionally interrupted by the arrival of the guests from the neighbourhood who had been asked to come to the ball after dinner. And, for not a few of the older ladies, the prospect of having to stay awake until dawn was infinitely oppressive.

Only Aunt Lizinka seemed as lively as ever, titillating the ladies, as always, with poisonous stories and gossip which was as often as not left half-told as the wife, husband or daughter of the person about whom she was talking entered the room. Whenever this happened Lizinka, in the sweetest, most sympathetic voice, and as if she were deeply concerned, would ask the latest arrival some simple question relating to the subject of the gossip. And she could not conceal her glee if the answers seemed to confirm what she had just been recounting.

Countess Laczok, however, did not remain for long among her guests. As soon as she had greeted the new arrivals she left the room to supervise the preparation of the buffet which was to be served later. Her departure was the signal for Aunt Lizinka to start talking about the Laczoks, for her a subject of perennial interest.

'My dears!' she began: 'I do feel so much for darling Ida and my dear nephew Jeno...' And she embarked with great relish on the subject of the family black sheep, Jeno's elder brother, Tamas, the 'ne'er-do-well' who, after several years' absence, had recently returned to Transylvania as, of all things, a railway engineer! This had surprised everybody since, for the first forty-odd years of his life, Tamas had lived entirely for pleasure, never giving a thought to anything more serious than drinking and making love. When he was young he was continually getting into debt, for which his family was always expected to pay up, and he had lived openly with a succession of gypsy girls. Largely as a result of this last offence he had been disowned by the family and one day he had disappeared, apparently abroad. For six or seven years nothing had been heard of him, until quite recently he had suddenly returned, qualified as an engineer. And now here he was, building the new railroad not far from Var-Siklod.

'But don't think he's changed, my dears. Oh, no! It's the same story all over again. He's got a little gypsy with him. She can't be more than fourteen! Oh, yes, I know it for sure! Isn't it dreadful? My poor niece. Why, he could even go to prison ... debauching a minor. There's a law against it – what a shame for the family! Who would have thought it when he was little?' and added, pointing at a portrait on the wall depicting a lady in a crinoline with two small boys, 'What a beautiful child he was! The one on the right is Jeno, and the other is that monster Tamas!' And so she went on, her little piping voice spreading poison nonstop.

While Aunt Lizinka was at her usual mischief-making upstairs, the smoking-room was ringing with the laughter and loud talk of the men. Count Jeno sat on a green velvet sofa smoking a pipe while most of the others lit cigars. Though the main subject of conversation was politics, it was not the bitter, passionate politics of the discussions under the lime tree. Those discussions had concerned serious matters, Hungarian matters and Hungarian politics. Now they talked about happenings in the great outside world, happenings that were for them only a comedy, subject for fun and mockery, for entertainment and ribaldry, not to be taken seriously nor talked about with passion or real fury. The Russo-Japanese War had just reached a crucial point. So, discussing it, the men split into two groups, dividing those who thought the Russians would win and those who were convinced it would be the Japanese. No one took it too seriously; they would even retract and change sides if there was an opportunity for a good pun or a joke.

To start with, the very names of the admirals and generals sounded funny and so they would twist them, purposely mispronouncing the unfamiliar sounds to give ribald or coarse interpretations: the pro-Russians trying to ridicule the Japanese and the pro-Japanese doing the same with the Russian names.

Anything went if it sounded rude enough. This light-hearted chaff continued for some time until Tihamer Abonyi, Dinora's husband who always took himself seriously, tried to raise the level of the conversation. Coming from Hungary he felt he was in a position to show these provincial Transylvanians that he had superior knowledge of world politics. Also he had had far too much champagne and several tumblers of brandy, with the result that this normally retiring and modestly-spoken man became unusually bold and talkative.

'One moment, please! If you don't mind?' And everyone fell silent because they all realized they would soon have an opportunity to tease somebody – and teasing was the Transylvanians' greatest pleasure.

And so the poor man started. Clichés fell, one after another, from his lips: 'Well-informed circles', 'in regard to this', 'in regard to that', 'all serious students of world affairs know that if the Russians, etc., etc., etc., then the English and the Americans will be obliged', 'all this must be reckoned with', 'and as for us, the Tripartite Agreement'. The pompous voice droned on and on...

But not for long. As soon as one hackneyed phrase was uttered it would be taken up by someone else, distorted, laughed at, thrown to another, who would take the joke further with a new twist. A third would then turn the meaning inside out and offer it back to the speaker, who, still completely serious, would try to explain what he meant. And while he did so, another of his sayings would be taken up and teased and dissected in the same way until it sounded a ridiculous confirmation that these provincial Transylvanians understood nothing.

Everyone took part in the game. Old Crookface interjected only short obscenities; Jeno Laczok, with a straight face and dry humour, would pose seemingly irrelevant questions; while Uncle Ambrus kept to the subject, but, in his deep rumbling voice, gave every phrase a grossly sexual meaning. Abonyi, his eyes bulging in astonishment as he found himself mocked by the country bumpkins, could not conceive why his superiority was not universally respected. He battled on, and finally tried to explain that the war would never end because neither side had the necessary weapons...

'Because then comes the great big Kaiser with his great big tool...' roared Uncle Ambrus.

Abonyi jumped up, furious: 'And as for you, Ambrus, you know nothing of – politics. All you care about is sex...' Offended, he ran to the door, fumbled with the handle, and rushed out. He was followed by roars of mocking laughter.

On the wide balcony above the porch the young were also enjoying themselves. Some sat on the rococo stone balustrade and some on chairs that the footmen had brought out from the hall.

Gazsi Kadacsay was making a good story of his ride to Var-Siklod, and it seemed even funnier because his slanting eyebrows, raised high, gave his face the expression of someone begging for mercy.

It had started on the rrrace-course, he said, rolling his r's. Just as he was about to start, Joska Kendy had come up to him and said, cigar-holder in mouth:

'What can you do with that nag of yours? I'll get my lumbering old wagon to Siklod before you've even got that hay-bellied hack into a canter!' and he imitated Joska's grating voice so well that everyone laughed. 'Well, you know me! I'm such a sucker I bet on it – ten bottles of bubbly. How could I be such a moron? We'd start late, Joska said, shrewd old beast that he is, and the road'd be clear. What happened? I got among all those cursed Szekler carts – they were all over the road – nearly fell into one, nearly snagged my poor beast's legs on the axle-pins, was blinded with dust; and Joska, crafty old thing, just drove them all off the road! He got through easily, driving like Jehu, and I only caught up with him once . . . once, I tell you. It was just as we turned off the main road – and when I tried to get past that team-of five of his, he nearly ran me down. After that I had no chance in the narrow drive!'

'You certainly fooled me that time, you dreadful man,' went on Gazsi plaintively but grinning at Joska as he spoke. Kendy just looked at him ironically and said, dryly:

'That piebald isn't a horse, it's just a louse with four legs!'

Gazsi cringed in mock horror at the insult, holding his head as if recovering from a blow.

'Vulgar abuse, on top of it all! I'll kill this man, you'll see! One of these days I'll get him!'

But it was all good-humoured fun. The anger was mock-anger, and the despair mock-despair. To Gazsi, Joska was a hero and he knew he could never get the better of him, let alone surpass him, either riding or driving. He did not mind losing the bet, in fact he was rather pleased because if Joska had not won Gazsi's whole world would have collapsed. So he rejoiced and was glad, and all his clowning was really just an expression of his happiness.

As with the older men in the library the conversation ended in general laughter interrupted by the music starting again in the

PART ONE

great hall. Laji had begun with an old Transylvanian waltz that everyone knew. Everyone went inside.

The band looked happy and relaxed, and Laji's face shone. Obviously they had been given a good supper and no doubt a good few bottles of champagne had come their way.

Farkas Alvinczy grabbed young Ida Laczok and swept her off to start the others dancing. Down the long hall they went, turning and gliding to the beat of the music. Other couples soon joined them.

In a few moments the room was filled with dancers; the girls, in many-coloured gowns that swept the ground, holding their heads high and gazing at their partners as they skimmed swiftly over the polished floor.

❦

Dances... Dances... Dances...

Two French quadrilles, two typical exciting csárdáses lasting an hour, many waltzes slow and fast and even a polka, though not many cared for this.

At about half-past-one the big double doors of the hall were opened and Countess Laczok, round and smiling, made her appearance just as they were finishing the last figure of 'The Lancers', which was still popular in Transylvania though in Vienna it had disappeared at the end of the Biedermeier period half a century before. The countess stood in the doorway until the dance was over and then made a sign to Farkas Alvinczy, who had been leading the dance. He signalled to the band leader, and the music stopped.

The young people flowed out into the great drawing-room of the castle where the supper was laid. The gypsy musicians vanished to their by now third meal of the evening, and Janos Kadar, helped by a maid, started changing the candles in the Venetian chandeliers. As he did so, young Ferko and the footmen rushed to remove spots of candle-grease from the floor and polish the parquet.

In the drawing-room the long dinner-table had been re-erected to form a buffet and on it was displayed a capercaillie, haunches of venison, all from the Laczoks' mountain estates in Czik; and home-cured hams, hare and guinea-fowl patés and other specialities of Var-Siklod, the recipes of which remained Countess Ida's closely guarded secret (all that she would ever admit, and then only to a few intimate friends, was: 'My dear, it's quite impossible without sweet Tokay!').

At one end of the table were grouped all the desserts – mountainous cakes with intricate sugar decorations, compotes of fruit, fresh fruit arranged elaborately on silver dishes, and tarts of all descriptions served with bowls of snowy whipped cream. As well as champagne there were other wines, both red and white. An innovation, following the recent fashion for imitating English ways, was a large copper samovar from which the Laczok girls served tea.

As the guests were finishing their supper and beginning to leave the table replete with delicious food and many glasses of wine, the gypsy musicians filed into the room and took up their places to play the traditional interval music. On these occasions Laji Pongracz would play, in turn, all the young girls' special tunes. At the winter serenades he had made sure that he knew exactly who had chosen which melody as their own and now, each time he started a new tune, he would look directly at the girl whose song it was and smile at her with a discreet but still knowing air.

The guests had all seated themselves on the chairs and sofas pushed back against the wall and Balint, looking round the room for a place, found nearly every seat taken. At the far end of the room, near the door, he saw a free chair beside Dodo Gyalakuthy, who was the only girl present not to be escorted by a partner.

'Aren't you afraid to sit with me, Abady?' she said quietly as Balint took his place beside her.

'Is it so dangerous then?'

'Oh, very! No one dares sit with me. All the young men are afraid they'll get a bad name if they're seen paying me any attention!' She laughed, her long eyes and round face smiling. 'Yes! Yes! It's true. I'm too good a *parti*, and they don't want to be thought fortune hunters! I promise you it's true. You've been away so long you don't know, but I've known it for two years now, ever since I first came out. Even for square dances and cotillions I'd never get a partner if the organizers didn't take pity on me. I'm a wallflower. And as for waltzes and csárdás I'm only asked by boys too young to be accused of looking for a wife!'

Dodo said all this humorously, smiling sweetly as if she did not care; and Balint realized that he had hardly ever seen her on the dance floor; she was always sitting apart, by the wall. He looked at her more closely. She was very pretty, with a small rather pert nose. She was intelligent and her kind smiling mouth was full and naturally red. Her round, white neck and smooth full shoulders seemed infinitely desirable, like ripe fruit. She had

PART ONE

beautiful hands and small shapely feet, and was in every way a most attractive girl.

'I've thought about it a lot, and there can't be any other reason why no one asks me. And I certainly don't dance any worse than the other girls. Hasn't anyone warned you?' she asked, in playful reproach. She went on: 'Nobody even talks to me. You wouldn't know, of course. The girls don't because they're jealous that I'm so rich, and the boys are frightened people will gossip about them. You're the only one that's safe. The Heir to Denestornya is above suspicion.' She laughed with light irony. Then she continued, more seriously: 'Only that Nitwit talks to me. He doesn't seem to care, but then he's Austrian, not Transylvanian!'

'I saw you had supper with him.'

'Of course! He's the only one who dares come near me. Perhaps I'll decide to marry him, but I don't like him much. You know something?' and she leant confidentially towards Balint, as if taking him into a great secret, and went on: 'I don't like stupid men! Nitwit's quite nice, and very good-looking, but he can't string two words together!'

Balint looked round, searching for Egon Wickwitz. He was standing in the embrasure of a window, talking to a woman half-hidden by the curtains. For a moment Balint thought that it was Adrienne, but only for a moment for, as the woman leaned forward, he saw that it was Dinora Abonyi. The couple in the window seemed to be arguing, Dinora's face looked unusually serious, her fine eyebrows drawn together almost into a scowl, while her normally smiling mouth was set in anger.

Balint looked away as the musicians were suddenly silent. Laszlo Gyeroffy had crossed over to the band-leader and asked for his violin and, by way of prelude, plucked a few pizzicato notes. Then he raised his bow. Everyone waited, excited and pleased. What would he play? Those who had heard him in Kolozsvar, playing at the late-night gypsy revels, started calling out: 'It's Laszlo! How marvellous! Listen everybody!'

So Laszlo started to play, but not the sentimental little ballads that the gypsies had just been playing for the girls. He played tunes that were sharper, full of rhythm, but witty and playful. When he played a song, he would not sing the words but would speak them mockingly, ironically, even scornfully. Sometimes he would imitate the famous Lorant Frater, but in the manner of a French *diseuse*. His technique was extraordinary. The violin itself seemed to chuckle as if it were being tickled, and then suddenly

Laszlo would pluck the G-string sharply, so that the instrument itself seemed to be scandalized with shock; and a pause would follow as if a question had been asked, and it was waiting for an answer. And, after the pause, again a sudden rush of melody which seemed to bubble with merriment.

The guests loved it. They applauded, cheered, and their laughter and appreciation spurred him to give them more. Perhaps because Laszlo was already a little drunk he began to clown, searching for broader and funnier effects. Without for a moment ceasing to play he would run round the room, jumping and whirling and leaping between the chairs before returning to the band-leader's place beside the cymbalist. Sometimes he would play with the fiddle on his knee or hold it above his head while he crouched on the floor, slithering from side to side, his legs flung out as in a Russian dance, his toes twinkling, until once more he leapt in the air like a goat. Whatever he did the sound remained perfect, flawlessly beautiful, the melodies unbroken by his antics, the rhythm impeccable. The poor band-leader, Pongracz, watched anxiously, worried about his beloved violin. It was as good as any turn in the music hall, and so funny that the guests rocked with laughter.

Balint himself was embarrassed by the clownishness of Laszlo's performance. It annoyed him to see his friend debase himself. Edging up to him he said, in a low voice:

'Play us something of your own!'

Gyeroffy stopped, suddenly serious: 'I have nothing to suit these people...'

'The Valse Macabre?' suggested Balint, remembering one of Laszlo's earlier and milder works.

'Well, yes. That one, perhaps...' Laszlo turned to the gypsies and, so as to give them a lead, played a few notes in the key of G-minor. Then he straightened up and stepped forward in front of the little band. Suddenly he was no longer a clown but a figure whose demeanour and presence sent a wave of surprise among the guests. A frown furrowed his wide clear brow which was surrounded by thick wavy brown hair, features that more strongly than ever recalled his Tartar ancestry, and his mouth was set in a hard line, severe and implacable – a straight, calm and elegant figure that would not have been out of place on the stage of a famous concert hall. He paused for a moment and then, drawing his brows together in still more of a frown, he began to play.

PART ONE

First he held a deep long-drawn note for about four beats – the gypsies hesitant, not quite knowing what to expect – and then, almost imperceptibly the rhythm of a slow, unusual waltz began to emerge. The beat was unconventional, strange, not the usual three-four beat, but modified, transformed, modern, harsh, with unexpected passages which seemed sadder than anything anyone had ever heard before. The bewildered gypsies could not follow him; more and more confused they stopped playing, one by one. Pongracz shook his head with disapproval; this was not at all his kind of music. But Laszlo played on, unperturbed by the gypsies' defection until he was playing quite alone.

There was silence. Then Farkas Alvinczy jumped up, waved to the disconcerted gypsies and led them back into the ballroom. In a few moments the latest popular waltz from Vienna could be heard and soon the hall was filled up dancing couples.

Laszlo Gyeroffy stood alone in the middle of the almost empty drawing-room. Dodo Gyalakuthy came up to him, looking up with admiration in her large doe-eyes.

'It was beautiful, what you played! I don't think many people understood it, but I did. I liked it very much. It was lovely, so unusual, so new and interesting.'

Laszlo looked down at her, resignedly.

'It was silly even to try!' he said. Then, encouraged that he had at least one listener who sympathized with him and understood his music, he started to explain how difficult it was for a band to follow his unfamiliar harmonies.

As Laszlo and Dodo talked in the middle of the room, the little Countess Abonyi emerged from the window embrasure, followed by Egon Wickwitz. She walked towards the ballroom and, seeing Balint still by the door, called to him, her spirits visibly improved by the slght of her old friend: 'Dance with me!' It was an order and, when Balint complied, she nestled into his arms and whispered her old endearment for him: 'Little Boy – Little Boy!' in her once-familiar caressing voice as they danced away into the great hall. Balint pressed her hand in recognition of the memory, but his eyes remained cold and unmoved.

'Don't worry,' she went on, 'I don't expect anything of you. I'm just pleased to see you again, Little Boy!'

They danced in silence, Balint's arm tightly round the well-remembered slim waist that pressed against him with such careless abandon. They danced for a long time until, at the far end of the room where no one was standing, Dinora suddenly stopped.

Looking at Balint with something of the old feeling in her eyes, she said:

'Look, Balint, you'll be back at Denestornya in a day or two. Do come over to Maros-Szilvas soon. I'd love to see you. And I'm sure you remember the way,' she added flirtatiously, 'but seriously, I want to ask your advice about something important. We are still friends, aren't we?'

'Something important? A serious matter? Of course I'll come.'

'A very serious matter!' Dinora smiled sweetly, but she looked worried. Then she seemed to recover and her little white teeth gleamed between the voluptuous lips. Suddenly she passed her hand over Balint's cheek in the lightest of caresses. She laughed at her own audacity and turned away. 'Goodbye,' she murmured over her shoulder as she glided away, to be swept up at once by another dancer; and in a flash she was gone.

Balint pondered what Dodo had told him in the drawing-room, and looked around to find her. Once again she was sitting alone on one of the chairs ranged along the wall, and so he walked over and asked her to dance. As they floated round the floor he thought how well she danced, indeed she followed instinctively everything that her partner wanted to do, and when he reversed and danced anti-clockwise round the hall in a complicated new step that had just been introduced in the capital, she followed perfectly. She was like an ideal pupil who divines every unspoken instruction. He was so pleased that they went on waltzing for a long time.

It was hot in the hall when they finally parted. The windows had been kept shut as the slightest breeze sent a shower of wax from the candles. Balint decided he would like a breath of fresh air, and stepped out onto the terrace.

———

The unexpected beauty of the moonlight made Balint catch his breath as he might have had he been startled by a sudden cry of fear. Coming from the hothouse atmosphere of the ballroom it was like emerging into a wonderland as unreal and full of magic as a fairy tale. The azure sky merged into the far horizon; distance and nearness did not exist. The terrace was all in dark mysterious shadow, limited only by the faint horizontal line of the balustrade where here and there a carved stone arabesque gleamed faintly.

Glancing round he saw a woman near the right hand corner. It was Adrienne Miloth. She stood motionless against the glow of the night sky and the light behind her was so strong that her face,

PART ONE

bare arms and shoulders seemed scarcely lighter in hue than the deep-green silk of her dress.

Adrienne stood quite still, erect and alone, gazing out into the distance. Balint was reminded of the days when she would stand beside the newly lit lamp, her chin up, her arms clasped behind her back, her stillness recalling the half-repressed rebelliousness of her youth. It was perhaps because of this surge of memory within him that Balint, instead of avoiding her, approached softly and leaned on the balustrade beside her.

She moved slightly, tacitly acknowledging Balint's presence and seeming to approve of his coming, as if she had said aloud that she needed sympathy, kinship and spiritual understanding. Relaxing from the unbending pose she had adopted, Adrienne leaned forward, slowly and quietly resting her hands on the balustrade. Balint thought of the silent movements of a panther, solitary and dark in the blackness of the night. Like Adrienne, panthers moved in slow harmonious symmetry and grace. And, like Adrienne, they gazed into the distance with their golden eyes.

For some time neither of them spoke. The faint sound of the dance music from the castle behind them barely disturbed the silence of the night, indeed its muted tones and faintly heard rhythm deepened the infinite stillness. Occasionally they could hear a dog barking far in the distance.

Balint began to feel with increasing urgency that he must say something common-place that would break the silence between them and release Adrienne from whatever sorrow or disappointment it was that seemed to hold her so firmly. In a low voice, almost a whisper, as if he were afraid to break the magic by a harsh note, he murmured:

'What a lovely night it is!'

'Yes. Yes indeed. It's lovely.' She too spoke quietly, not daring to raise her voice, '... but what a lie it all is!'

'What do you mean, a lie?'

Adrienne remained motionless, looking away into the distance. Then, very slowly, choosing her words hesitantly and carefully, she started:

'It's all untrue. A lie. Everything beautiful is a lie, a deception. Everything one believes in, or wants. Everything one does because one believes it to be helpful, or useful. It's all a snare, a well-baited trap. That's what life is,' and we are stupid enough to be taken in, to be duped. We swallow the bait, and "click!" – the trap is sprung.' She gave a little half-uttered laugh, but her eyes remained serious, gazing ahead. Then she turned to Balint and said: 'What are you going to do now that you've come home? What are your plans?'

But Balint was thinking only of what she had said previously:

'I don't believe that, that in our lives everything beautiful must be a lie. No! No! The opposite is true. Beauty is the only eternal truth there is! Beauty of purpose, of deed, of achievement. That is the only thing worth seeking for, what we must all try to find. Other ethical arguments are false, this is the only real one. Why? Because you can't define it or classify it, put it down in black and white. We've talked about this before. Do you remember, back at Kolozsvar?'

'Oh yes, I remember, I remember it well. And then I think I believed it.'

Balint wanted to ask, why only then, why no longer? But he felt she would say no more if he dared approach whatever secret pain lay behind her words.

For a few moments they spoke no more. Then Adrienne started again.

'People *say* nice things, nice words and so on, but . . .' She narrowed her eyes in a search for the right words to express what she wanted to say but her instinct told her should remain hidden. She took refuge in parable.

'Look how beautiful that distant hillside looks, soft, undefined, lovely but uncertain. We don't know what it's made of, what it's really like. Is it mist, or cloud, or is it just a dream? Pure beauty, as you were saying? It looks as if one could dive into it and become a part of it, vanish inside it as into a fog; but only now, and from here in the deceitful moonlight. It's really just an ordinary hillside, made of hard yellow clay, poor grass and dead thistles. It's not even a real mountain of clefts and rocks. When dawn breaks we can see it's land fit only for sheep and goats. Useful, of course, but all we can say then is how many ewes and lambs can graze there. She laughed again and added: 'You see what a dull dour farmer I've become!'

Balint went on, in the same low voice as before but in more fervent tones.

'Maybe it's no more than a farmer's stock-in-trade. Perhaps tomorrow we will see it for what it really is, a common pasture with dumb sheep bleating and aimlessly leading their lambs from place to place. But tonight it isn't! *Now* it isn't! I don't care about

PART ONE

tomorrow. Tonight, tomorrow does not exist! Tonight, everything is beautiful and that beauty which fills our eyes, your eyes, mine, remains ours for ever. Nobody, nothing can take it away from us. We can lock it in the steel tower of our memory where no one can touch it, and there it will remain, like the Sleeping Beauty in her magic castle, until we – and we alone, – can bring it back to life again. You and I. No one else.'

'Not all memories can be wished back. There are others too, unwanted ones, but no Sleeping Beauties!'

'How we feel ourselves is all that matters. Nothing outside can touch us. Hurt and joy come from inside. Conscience is our only judge. That is our secret, and we can neither change nor control it.'

'Maybe...' Adrienne spoke so low he could hardly hear her. Resting her head in her hands, she still looked away from him, away from the world. It seemed that she could not find the words to define what it was she found so hard to express. Balint waited. She must speak first or he would never know what was in her mind. He hardly dared look at her lest she should be disturbed, so he kept his eyes fixed on the garden.

The walls of the courtyard and the wings of the great house were in deep shadow, a shadow whose outline was a sharp as if drawn by a ruler. Outside this shadow the parterre shone with a blue light, and the paved circle in the centre gleamed with a myriad little points of light, each pebble seeming to sparkle like hoar-frost or snow and at its heart the grass lawn too seemed to shine, each blade distinct and separate. Only the lilies remained dark and velvety, the deep red flowers black in the moonlight and the russet leaves like ink-stains spreading on the ground.

Balint looked up at the right-hand wing of the house. Lamps burned behind the long french windows, etching long strips of yellow light between the grey vertical lines of the columns. Looking further round, past the seemingly ethereal little tower at the corner of the walls, Balint's gaze came to rest on the steps under the ramparts, where he could just make out a sitting figure. In spite of the darkness he recognized him at once. It was Andras Jopal, the tutor. He had changed his evening coat for a pale linen jacket.

The young mathematician was seated, almost crouched, on one of the bottom steps, his legs pulled up under him. He seemed to be gazing fixedly at the moon oblivious of the beauty of the night, lonelier now and even more solitary than he had seemed at dinner when, of all those present, he had been the least affected by the general high spirits. Balint decided to seek him out later. Now he turned back to Adrienne wondering when she would decide to speak again.

She was still leaning on the balustrade. The silk wrapper that had been round her shoulders had slipped down, showing that she had become even thinner, almost gaunt, with hollows under her collar-bones. Her long neck was as firm as ever, but her early leanness was more pronounced with her chin joined to her neck in the stylized angle of an old Greek statue. She was still the girl he had known before, but marriage had not given her the soft roundness that often comes with motherhood. The bud was still a bud, unopened; the flower was still a promise, and Balint was surprised for he knew that her little daughter was already two. The unresolved conflict between her girlish appearance and the experience of motherhood was perhaps the reason for the faintly bitter note he thought he detected when she spoke.

Adrienne pulled the silk wrap up around her shoulders, perhaps sensing Balint's eyes upon her bare skin. It was a shy, almost girlish movement and, after wrapping herself still more firmly she turned, leaning back against the parapet, and said: 'I love to hear you talk, AB. You're so confident about life. It's good for me, perhaps even necessary. Please go on. Tell me more.'

So Balint went on, with renewed confidence, in a low dreamlike voice, as if someone else were speaking through him. He spoke long and intensely, and Adrienne listened, only occasionally interposing a word or a question. And when she spoke, 'Oh, Yes! Yes! It's possible. Perhaps, but you really believe then...?' she no longer looked into the night but gazed deeply into his eyes. Her eyes were the colour and depth of yellow onyx.

Balint could have continued for ever, but all at once the door of the ballroom burst open and a stream of dancers flowed out onto the terrace, the rushing melody of a popular galop filling the air with its gaiety and rhythm.

Farkas Alvinczy, who had been leading the dancing all evening, was the first. Bent almost double in his haste and dragging his partner after him, he ran, followed by the others, all holding hands, stumbling, tumbling and whirling round the terrace in giddy speed, the men in their black tail-suits, the girls in silks and satins of every colour, down the paths, round the stone balusters, rushing with careless abandon until they all vanished once more into the house.

PART ONE

The last in the chain was young Kamuthy, his feet scarcely touching the ground as if he were a child's top at the mercy of a whip. He bumped into the columns and into the stone balusters and stretched out his hand to Adrienne as he swept by. She stepped back, and on he flew, in a tremendous arc of movement, crashing into anything and anybody in his way, twice into the stone balustrade and finally into the door-post. Then he too was swallowed up once more into the vortex of the ballroom.

It only lasted a few moments, and then Balint and Adrienne were suddenly alone again. From inside they could hear the music change from the madness of the galop to a slow waltz and, through the great doors they could see the chain of dancers break up and dissolve and divide once more into pairs, each couple swaying gently to the music, turning and gliding in each other's arms.

The magic that had made Balint and Adrienne forget time and place, everything but their own existence and thoughts, was broken. Without speaking they moved slowly back to the castle. As she went in someone asked Adrienne to dance; and she turned and disappeared into the crowd with all the others.

⁕

Balint did not dance. He stood near the wall for a few moments, needing time to come back to reality after the dream-world created by his talk with Adrienne. He thought of Jopal sitting alone beneath the tower and he decided to go and seek him out and talk. It would be better than returning to the ball for which he was no longer in the mood.

He left the ballroom and went slowly down the great staircase into the entrance hall where the bar had been placed, out through the entrance doors and down the few steps to the moonlit garden, and on towards the corner tower; but there was no longer anyone there. He paused and listened in case he should hear the sound of footsteps. Maybe Andras Jopal would come into sight; but no one moved.

Towards the east a faint strip of light heralded the dawn. Balint walked slowly along the path in front of the castle wing where lamplight steamed out from the library windows.

Inside the long narrow room two card tables had been set, one at each end, and at the smaller of these, Crookface, gruff as ever, was playing tarot with his host, the prefect and Tihamer Abonyi. Their table was lit by four candles and they played in a silence which was only occasionally interrupted by Abonyi who as always liked to show off his superior knowledge, and so remarked from time to time that things were done differently at the National Casino Club in Budapest and in Vienna. As no one paid any attention, he was soon forced to give up and play on in silence.

The other table was much noisier. Uncle Ambrus had got a poker game together. He had gone round the ballroom slapping the young men on the back and crying heartily, 'Come and have a shifty at the Hungarian Bible, sonny' or, 'You can't hide behind skirts all the evening,' or even 'A man needs some good Hungarian games, my boy, not *German* waltzes,' adding, for good measure, 'They serve some damned good wine downstairs!' He had gathered together quite a number of the brighter, more dashing young sparks, to whom he was still a hero and who looked to him as their leader, even if he always did prefer a poker game to a ball.

Not that they guessed the whole truth, which was that the older man was no longer spry enough for dancing and preferred to rest his feet under the card-table. This was also profitable, as he usually took quite a lot of money from younger players less experienced than himself.

At Uncle Ambrus' table, next to which trays of tall glasses and delicate Bohemian crystal decanters had been placed on a side-table, sat the two middle young Alvinczys, Adam and Zoltan, together with Pityu Kendy and Gazsi Kadacsay. This was a family party, since Ambrus's mother had been an Alvinczy, while Pityu was his second cousin and Kadacsay was Uncle Ambrus's brother-in-law's son. But Ambrus never let kinship stand in the way of his winning a little money and, sometimes, more than a little. No one was a better player than Ambrus. He was a great gambler and the younger players could never guess what he was up to. Sometimes he would bet high on a single ace or throw in a winning hand. Sometimes he would act coy and complaisant, as if he were holding good cards, and then egg the others on with loud-mouthed hints that he held nothing – but no one ever knew whether he really had a good hand or not. He would complain to the heavens of his bad luck and swear obscenely and then tease them, saying: 'Don't go on, son, I'll have the pants off you!' And his resounding laugh and avuncular good humour made the young almost glad to lose to him.

As Balint stepped into the library Uncle Ambrus was in full flood.

'Oh, my God! What shall I do? I'll bet one of you has a pair

PART ONE

of these! Jesus! And the other'll have these. You Alvinczys'll skin me, I know it!' and he leaned back, banged the table, struck his head and turned in mute appeal to Daniel Kendy who was sitting behind him already far gone in drink, and then, as if risking his all in mad despair, he pushed a pile of coins into the centre of the table, and cried: 'Devil take it! Might as well lose the lot! Here, I'll stake four hundred more and don't you dare give it back!'

One of the Alvinczys threw his hand in at once. The others followed suit . . . and the game was over.

'Don't you want your revenge? I would! I'm terrified of you all Well, don't you want to see what beat you?' and, dealing out his hand, card by card, he showed a straight flush, better than anything the others could possibly have held. And he still pretend to be astonished that he'd won, though he'd known it ever since the cards had been dealt.

'What luck! What fucking luck! Lucky at cards, unlucky in love! The girls don't love me any more, poor old man that I am!' And he reached out with his great hairy hands and scooped up all the money with a gesture of pure grief.

Balint remained standing near Ambrus' table. He felt faintly disgusted by this shameless display of feigned disingenuousness and ashamed too of his own generation who drank too much and fawned on the old vulture with servile admiration.

Lost in these thoughts he did not notice that the dawn was breaking. The candles and lamps began to lose their brilliance and the library, which had been like a huge cavern lit only by pools of light, was now revealed in its true size. The carved pillars between the bookshelves and the golden-green columns of light cherry-wood, began to define themselves, and between them one could again make out the thousands of beautifully bound books that were arranged in no order but placed on the shelves regardless of size. They all had ribbed and gold-embossed spines. Some had been collected by the Vice-Chancellor Laczok when he had first transformed the medieval castle into a nobleman's mansion. His were the thick volumes of *Compilatums* and *Tripartitums*, lawbooks bound in ivory-coloured vellum, and the volumes of the French *Encyclopédie* and the works of Voltaire. Most, however, had been collected by his grandson who had added the wings and the library. When Balint looked up at the shelves he saw there many rare architectural works of the late eighteenth century, huge volumes which included the whole of Palladio, whose reissue had so influenced the neo-classical movement, the *Ornamentisme* of Percier and Fontaine, and a complete collection of the Ecole de Rome competitions dating from the first decade of the nineteenth century.

How cultivated Transylvania had been in those days, reflected Balint, as he saw what had been collected on those shelves. He was just passing the next pair of columns when he found his way was blocked. Old Daniel Kendy was swaying from side to side, clutching at one of the pillars for support. He had an unfamiliar look in his watery old eyes, a look of nostalgic sorrow quite different from his usual air of cynical mockery.

'*Mon p-p-prince!* Though he stuttered his pronunciation was excellent: '... *dieses sind w-wunderbare w-Werke!*' and going on in English, 'Quite w-wonderful!' He stroked the backs of those magnificent books, shining with golden blazons and embossed lettering. Perhaps he was reminded of his own golden youth when everyone thought him to be a young man who would go far, before he began to drink and had run through all his money, when he had travelled all over Europe and moved always in the highest circles. He reached out again to caress these magic symbols, as if reminded, by this treasure-house of learning, of lost memories and the great career he had himself destroyed. It was his last gesture, for as he put out his hand he collapsed and slid to the ground like a puppet without strings and half-sat, half-lay on the floor, with his legs stretched out in front of him, and immediately started to be sick. Wine and vomit poured from him without effort or retching, in jets, as from a water pistol, and spread in a pool over the parquet in front of him.

Everyone jumped up from the card-tables, and gathered round him, everyone except old Crookface, who said 'Filthy old swine!' several times before throwing down down his cards and stalking out of the room.

The poker players looked at the old man on the floor and just laughed. This was nothing unusual. Pityu and Gazsi edged behind him – as no one could go near in front – put their arms under his shoulders and dragged him like some huge wooden doll on to one of the sofas; and there they left him. No one could have remained in that dreadful sour-smelling room.

In the growing light of day many carriages had gathered in front of the castle entrance. Cocks were crowing in the village and the ball was drawing to a close. Already some of the mothers, tired and thankful, were coming down the steps with their dancing daughters in tow, huddled into silken wraps to hide their sweating faces from the daylight. Quickly they mounted the folding steps and disappeared into the dark interiors of the carriages. A few young men had come out to wave to the girls they had flirted with, and perhaps even to snatch a hasty hand-kiss.

Kadar the butler, alone this time, bustled about calling for one carriage after another and opening the doors with his left hand. His right hand was held in such a way that tips he seemed to find their way there as if by chance.

Balint found Laszlo Gyeroffy waiting in the hall. They arranged to go back to their hotel in Vasarhely together and so went into the guests' cloakroom to find their bags and coats. The hall was filled with departing guests, but Balint could not see Adrienne among them. For a moment he thought of going back upstairs to say goodbye, but then thought better of it. What was the use of a few commonplace words in the sober light of day? He and Laszlo followed the stream of guests out into the courtyard, where several ladies stood shivering in the cold air, and started to search for their hired fiacre. Passed a waiting group they sensed that something unusual was happening. A wave of excitement flowed through the crowd and a booming stammer could be heard:

'*M-m-mesdames, m-m-messieurs! Il v-v-vostro umilissimo s-s-servitore! g-g-gehorsamster D-D-Diener!*'

Old Dani had somehow roused himself and stumbled out on to the terrace. He stood there, embracing one of the pillars, his shirt hanging out and covered in vomit-stains, his beard matted with wine. He bowed right and left, waving his free arm in a sort of semaphore. Some of the younger men jumped up and dragged him away; and the waiting ladies, pretending that they had noticed nothing, piled into their carriages.

Once old Kadar had shut a carriage's doors, the coachman would whip the horses up into a brisk canter. They turned towards the inner door and swept through the outer courtyard which was lined with the stable-boys and peasant girls and other servants who had danced all night under the balcony. Now they stood in line to speed the parting guests and every now and again, without any apparent reason, a small girl or two would dash out and run screaming across the court in front of the cantering horses, and then burst into fits of laughter because they hadn't been run over.

As the long line of carriages bowled down the drive the sun was already shining brightly. It was morning.

Chapter Four

BACK IN THE HOTEL BALINT and Laszlo were only able to catch a couple of hours of sleep. The sun was shining through the slits in the torn curtains when they woke at eleven. They rang for the maid, but when she realized that all they wanted from her was hot water she went away sulking and kept them waiting so long that it was nearly midday before they were ready.

Balint was anxious to find out if his grandfather's friend, the old actor Minya Gal, was still alive, so Laszlo and he went to look for him and discovered that although he was known to be still living in his old home no one seemed to know exactly where that was. Then they saw a notice on an old and dilapidated peasant's dwelling. It read 'IZAK SCHWARTZ: Fine Tailoring for Ladies and Gentlemen' in big lettering. Underneath, in small letters, were the words, 'Mending Done'.

'Let's ask here,' said Laszlo, 'these little Jewish shopkeepers know everyone.'

The man who did fine tailoring for ladies and gentlemen came to the door. He was a tiny dwarf of a fellow with a long grey beard and trousers so worn and tattered that they were no advertisement for his skills.

'Yes, masters, if it is Mr Gal you vant, I know him vell. Ze third house it is, if it pleases my masters, down zere . . .' and he came out and showed them the way. They thanked him and entered the little garden by the gate that he had pointed out.

The house was in the old Transylvanian style, broad and whitewashed, with a shingle roof and a portico in front. Three windows overlooked the street across a small flower garden. On the left were a cowshed and pigsties. Behind the house beyond a heap of manure were apple trees laden with ripening fruit. In the yard a barefoot young girl was cutting up vegetables for the pig swill.

'Is Mr Mihaly Gal at home?' asked Balint.

The girl looked at him suspiciously. 'What do you want him for?'

'We just came call.'

The girl still looked uncertain. 'Are you selling something?' she asked, her hostility unconcealed.

PART ONE

'No!' Balint smiled. 'We've just come to see him.' To dispel her suspicions, he gave their full names and titles. The girl did not seem at all impressed. She went on with her work, crouched over the pig pail and just indicated the direction of the apple trees with her chin. 'Over there!' she said without ceasing to chop at the giant marrows with her knife, the slices falling messily into the swill.

Behind the little orchard and a kitchen garden, an acre and a half of vineyard climbed the hillside behind. They found the old man digging in the deep loam at the foot of the hill, shovelling and scattering the loose earth. He still had the same tall straight figure that Balint recalled from the day of his grandfather's funeral ten years before. Though now well over ninety his bristling moustaches were still pepper and salt, darkened with wax. He was working in his shirtsleeves, boots and well-worn trousers. Balint went up and waited until the old man saw him.

'Don't you recognize me, Uncle Minya? It's Balint Abady, from Denestornya.'

The patriarchal figure looked at him with eyes grown pale with age. After a brief struggle with half-forgotten memories, he seemed to recognize the grandchild of his oldest friend.

'So you are little Balint! How you've grown!' He stuck his spade in the soft earth, wiped his hands on the threadbare trousers, and clasped the young man by the shoulders. 'How nice of you to come and see an old man! Let's go inside.'

Balint introduced his cousin and they walked slowly back towards the house, slowly but strongly, for the old man moved with assurance and held himself erect. As they passed the yard he called to the girl: 'Julis, my dear! Bring plum brandy and glasses for the gentlemen!'

'At once, Uncle!' she replied and ran indoors.

'She is my sister's great-granddaughter,' Minya explained, and made his visitors go before him into the living-room. It was a wide cool place whose door gave onto the portico and which was lit by the three windows overlooking the road and the flower-garden. The walls were whitewashed and it was sparsely furnished with an old rocking chair near one of the windows, a long, painted chest against one wall and in the centre of the room there was a pine-wood table with an oil lamp on it and two wooden chairs. There were simple bookshelves in one corner, with a thick black Bible among twenty or thirty tattered volumes. At the other end the bed was piled high with pillows covered in homespun

61

cloth. The walls were bare except for an old violin, darkened with age, hanging on a nail near the foot of the bed, its bow threaded through the strings. Over a chair hung a single print in a narrow gilt frame showing a Roman knight in full armour who seemed to be making a speech.

Minya showed his guests to the table, where they sat down, and then pointed to the picture.

'That was me,' he said. 'Miklos Barabas made the drawing from life. It was my last appearance.'

Balint read the inscription. 'MIHALY GAL, illustrious member of the National Theatre, Kolozsvar, in the role of Manlius Sinister, 17 May, 1862'

'Where did you go, after your last performance?'

'Nowhere. I realized I couldn't do it any more so I retired. I was no longer any good, and one shouldn't try to force something one can't do properly. That's when I bought this house. I didn't spend all my money like most actors. Perhaps if I had been more like them I'd have been better. As it was I was rotten! So I took to gardening and tending the vineyards. This I do well! Julis!' he called to his young niece, who had just put the plum brandy on the table, 'Bring some bunches of the ripe Burgundy grapes, you know – the ones on the left!' Julis bustled out, and the old actor went on:

'Anyone who tries to do what he can't do is mad!' Balint caught a bitter note he had never heard before. To change the subject Laszlo asked about the violin. He had noticed it as soon as they came in.

'That old fiddle?' answered Minya. 'I only keep it as a souvenir. It was His Excellency Count Abady, your grandfather,' he said, looking at Balint, 'who gave it to me, oh, so many years ago. It must have been '37 or '38 – I think it was '37. He asked me me look after it for him; but later, whenever I tried to give it back he refused. He never played again'.

Balint was astonished. He had never known that Count Peter even liked music, let alone could play. He had never spoken of it.

'Oh, yes!' said Minya, 'he played beautifully. Not light stuff or gypsy music. He played Bach, Mozart and suchlike ... and all from the music. He could read beautifully.'

Laszlo asked if he might look at the instrument.

'May I take it down?' he asked.

'Of course!'

'But this is a marvellous violin! It's beautiful! Look what noble lines it has!' He brought it to the table to inspect it more closely.

'Yes, that is the Count's violin. He really did play very well. He started when still at school, and I sang. I was a baritone. Oh, Lord, where did it all go? He must have studied very hard; he was a real artist. I remember when I got back to Kolozsvar – in '37 it was because I was with Szerdahelyi then. Yes, that's when it was. Every evening that winter, when there wasn't a party or something, he always went to – oh, she was so lovely – he went quite secretly, and sometimes they asked me to join them, no one else, mark you, just me. They knew they could trust me not to tell.'

The old man said nothing for a moment. He bent forward, his open shirt showing the grey hairs thick as moss on his powerful chest. He reached a gnarled hand towards the violin and caressed it lightly.

Balint longed to know more about his grandfather's past, but somehow it seemed indiscreet to ask. However Laszlo went on: 'Did he play with a piano accompaniment?'

'Yes, of course, with a piano, always with a piano.'

'Who played for him?'

The dignified old actor lifted his hand in protest. He would not reveal the lady's name then, or ever, the gesture seemed to say. Then he started to reminisce in half sentences and broken phrases, as if his tired mind and faded eyes could only catch glimpses of the past in uncertain fragments. Following his memory's lead he was talking more to himself than to his listeners. Everything he said was confused and mixed up, complicated by a thousand seemingly irrelevant, and to the young men, incomprehensible details. He talked of other old actors, of plays and dates and though most of it meant nothing to Laszlo and Balint, it was clear that to old Minya it was all still as real as if everyone he mentioned were still alive. Throughout the scattered monologue, they sensed that he was recalling a personal drama which had nothing to do with the theatre, a real-life drama that had taken place seven decades before. But however alive this memory was, the old man never once spoke the name of the woman who had meant so much to his friend, nor even a hint as to whether she were an aristocrat or an actress. Though everyone he spoke of had been dead for many years, he still guarded the secret entrusted to him so long ago.

As he spoke they felt that he was getting near to the climax. His voice was very low:

'How beautiful they both were! And how young – she was even younger than he, so young, so young. And then it ended. There was a concert in the Assembly Rooms ... Beethoven, Chopin ... Was it the music? What was it? I can see them now, they were so beautiful, a wonderful shining couple. Everybody felt it, everybody saw it! Through their playing, you could tell they belonged together. The trouble was that, everyone saw it, everyone ...' The old man frowned, 'And, three days later it was over. I was given a letter for him – a goodbye note, though I didn't know it then – and I had to give it to my best friend, me – of all people.'

He was silent. Laszlo had listened politely, untouched by the rambling tale, but Balint had been deeply moved. Mysterious though it all was, a memory had been stirred by the incoherent story. Once, sitting beside his grandfather's writing desk, he had seen a tiny ancient pair of lady's dancing slippers inside an open drawer. They were old-fashioned party shoes of white satin and, though old, they looked almost new; even the little satin ribbons which tied like the strings on Greek sandals, were smooth and fresh. The tiny heel-less slippers were shaped like ladies-finger biscuits and were thin as paper. When Balint asked his grandfather about them the old Count had taken them out of the drawer and shown him how worn the soles were. 'Look,' he had said, smiling, 'see how much that little charmer danced!' and he had tied the ribbons together again and dropped the slippers back into the drawer where he had kept them for so many years.

Only now, as the memory of old Count Peter came back to him, did Balint understand the regret and nostalgia that lay behind his grandfather's always kind and welcoming smile. Was the heroine of old Minya's story the owner of the little dancing shoes?

'What happened then?' asked Balint, with a catch in his throat.

'Count Peter went abroad. He didn't come back for a long time, not for years. He travelled to countries few people visited then; perhaps few go today. He once wrote to me from Spain just a brief word, and later from Portugal. Once he went on a walking tour in Scotland, just as I did as an itinerant actor. He wrote to me then that there were many lakes and the country was wild and bare, just like the hills of Mezöses ...'

Balint had known nothing about all this. Old Abady had never mentioned his travels. Looking back, Balint realized, though he had never given it a thought at the time, that no matter what part

PART ONE

of Europe was mentioned, his grandfather had known it well. Had he been impelled to travel by sorrow, or had there been some other reason, some irrepressible wanderlust? Now, hearing the old story that revealed so much and yet kept its essential secret, Balint looked once more at the old violin on the table. How beautiful if was, lying there on the bare planks. What melodies still slept behind the myriad golden lights reflected in the dark patina of its varnish? What enchanting melodies and ancient passions? And would those melodies, poured forth by two young people alive only to their love and to their music, ever be heard again, or would the old violin be forever silent, the tomb of their secret love?

Young Julis brought in the grapes and, as she put them down, a cart, drawn by an old horse with harness tinkling with bells, drew up in front of the house. The girl looked out of the window.

'Look! Uncle Minya, Andras has arrived!' She ran out, beaming with pleasure.

Steps were heard outside and in a moment the door was opened and Andras Jopal came in. He seemed disconcerted to see who the old man's visitors were, but made them a stiff formal bow. Then he turned to Minya and started whispering to him. The old man looked up at Jopal's face, murmured something, shook his head and then slowly took a ten-crown note from his wallet and handed it to the newcomer. Jopal went out, and they could hear the cart drive into the yard.

'You must excuse me, gentlemen,' said Minya. 'That was Andras Jopal, my nephew. He's a very clever, learned fellow!' But there was a note of annoyance in his voice, despite the words of praise. 'He could have been a professor by now, but he wouldn't take his finals. He's got a crazy idea he can build a flying machine. He's so stubborn. Now he's out of a job again.'

'We saw him yesterday, at the Laczoks'.'

'That's where he's just come from. It seems they've just thrown him out. He didn't even have any money for his fare and he pretends left on his own accord. Bah! He's crazy!' The old man got up and looked angrily out of the window.

On the little cart was a jumble of fine wooden laths, rolls of paper, tangled wire and great sheets of stretched canvas like the wings of a gigantic dead moth.

'Well, there it is, the precious model! He spends every penny of the little money I give him on it!' Old Minya strode across the room, and then turned back to them, 'And even if he succeeds, what's the use, I ask you? What purpose would it have? People would still kill each other, even from the air!'

Balint wanted to say it wasn't true, but the old man went on: 'If human beings invent something new, they always use it first for killing. Iron was made into clubs and swords, bronze into cannon. And what did they do with gunpowder? Split rocks and build something? No! They destroyed each other more than ever!' He waved his arms about and stumbled to a chair where he sat down heavily, tired, exhausted and disillusioned, and the weight of his many years seemed to overcome him.

'It's time I left this world,' he murmured, oblivious of his visitors. 'High time!' The two young men stole away, but the old actor hardly noticed.

Balint and Laszlo walked together back up the hill. Then Balint decided he must go back to Minya's house and talk to Jopal. He wanted to help the unhappy young mathematician, as was always his impulse when he found someone in trouble. While still in school at the Theresianum he had helped half the class with their examination papers and sometimes this had got him into trouble. He might have been inherited this from his grandfather, who always did his best to help and protect others, or it might have been an unconscious reversion to the *noblesse oblige* habits of his more distant ancestors who had voluntarily served their people, their church or their country. Back at Minya's little house, Balint found that Jopal had taken the broken model off the cart. The ex-tutor was annoyed with himself because, however much he told himself that he was right to have acted as he did, an inner voice constantly reminded him that, if he hadn't let his temper run away with him, things would not have ended as they had, up in the tower room at Var-Siklod.

This is what had happened.

Count Jeno Laczok had gone to bed at five, but by nine o'clock he was wide awake and unable to go back to sleep. Tired and cross, he had got up. No one was about. After much shouting he had roused a cook to get him some breakfast; but when it arrived the coffee was cold and his egg almost raw. Although normally good-tempered, a bad breakfast always irritated him and put him in a bad temper. He went to the stables, but found all the lads and the coachmen were asleep, lying like corpses in the straw. In the kitchens even the cook had gone back to bed: in the gardens, not a gardener, not a sweeper, not a handyman.

PART ONE

Count Jeno could find no one on whom to vent his ill-humour until it occurred to him that, as his sons had not stayed up all night, they would be up and about. So he walked over to the corner tower where the boys' work room was on the ground floor, with Andras Jopal's lodging above it.

When he entered the room the boys were already dressed. Dezso was lying on a couch reading an adventure story while Erno was sharpening a pencil. Their tutor was nowhere to be seen.

'Is this how you work, you rascals?' shouted Count Jeno. 'Where is your teacher?'

'He's just gone up to his room.' The boys lied to protect Jopal who, always busy with his invention, never made them work hard. One of them jumped up to go and find him, but their father barred the way with his walking stick. 'You stay here! I'll go myself!' he shouted, and made for the steep wooden stairs.

The boys were dismayed. They realized that this meant serious trouble, because Jopal always bolted the door when he was in the room, and when he went out, he locked it and took the key with him.

The boys knew what was in the room. Hanging from the roof-rafters was a huge dragonfly-shaped contraption, whose wings were made of canvas stretched over wooden laths. A big designer's desk near the window was spread with gigantic drawings which meant nothing to them. But there the answer was, for all to see in large letters on each plan: 'Blueprint for Jopal's Flying Machine'. They had discovered it one day when the tutor had gone into the village and they had climbed in through a window that gave on to the ramparts. It had been a dare-devil adventure. Taking care that it did not break under their weight they had had to climb up the centuries-old ivy that grew up from the edge of the moat and, slipping through the battlements, clung to the inside of the walls. Then had come the most difficult part. After edging their way along the side of the wall, hanging on only with their hands, they had had to bridge a two-metre gap between the wall and the open window. This they had managed by stepping, one by one, on the old stone supports of a former wooden defence platform that jutted at intervals from the wall like chipped teeth over the abyss below. They had made it without mishap, being experienced nest-robbers who were used to scaling sixty-foot high poplars to get at the doves' eggs in the spring.

They had never told anyone what they had found in the room. By anyone, they meant grown-ups. Under great oaths of secrecy

67

they did tell their sisters and with them, and them alone, they laughed at the Mad Professor who was their tutor.

When Count Jeno had heaved his heavy bulk up the rickety wooden steps with considerable difficulty, he leaned, out of breath, against the door of Jopal's room. It did not yield.

'Who's there?' cried an angry voice from inside.

'It's me! Open at once!' cried Count Jeno, rapping on the door with his stick.

The bolt rattled and the door swung open under the weight of the irate count, sweeping Jopal, who tried to stop him, out of the way.

At first the master of the house stood dumb with surprise at what he saw. Then he started shouting: 'What the Devil's going on here? What's this contraption? Instead of doing your job you waste your time making toys for children?'

The inventor, whose quick temper always landed him in trouble, was cut to the quick. Full of his own self-importance, and conscious that his so-called 'toy' could be of world-shattering importance, he stepped in front of the model machine and spread out his arms dramatically.

'This! This! This! Do you know what this is? It's the most important invention ... the Flying Machine!' He was sure this staggering answer would confute all criticism, but it had quite the reverse effect. At another time Count Jeno might have found the situation absurd and laughable, but now, angry already, he growled deeply and then shouted:

'So you're spending my time on this ... this idiotic contraption? That's not what I pay you for. You ought to be locked up in an asylum!' and he went on in the same vein, working himself up into a towering rage.

For a while Jopal listened, his face stony, his lips tight over clenched teeth, and only his blazing eyes revealed the extent of his hurt and anger. Suddenly he screamed at the count: 'Shut up!'

Surprised, Count Jeno fell silent, and now it was Jopal's turn to pour forth a torrent of words. He went at it with all the fanaticism of someone bent on a single goal. All the bitterness of years of privation and frustration erupted at this moment. Blind to everything but his own unrecognized genius he became defiant, praising his lonely struggle and his importance and reviling the blindness, ignorance and lack of imagination of people like Count Laczok. Finally he spat out: 'It's I! I ... who would have brought everlasting fame to this stinking, rotten owl's nest, this God-forsaken rat-hole. *My* name would have made Siklod go down in history!'

This was too much for the count. Slashing at the machine with his stick until it spun on the cords from which it hung, he cried, 'What? This idiocy? This crazy rubbish! This is what I think of it!' and he struck out again, breaking the slender laths and tearing the canvas.

'I won't stay here another minute!' screamed Jopal, from behind the swinging remains of the broken model.

Count Jeno did not answer. He turned on his heel and clumsily, with difficulty, descended the rickety wooden stair. By the time he had reached the bottom his anger had evaporated; and if he had not had the last word at least it was his action that had brought the confrontation to an end. It flashed through his mind, too, that it was all the same if Jopal left now or later. If the tutor broke his contract and left at once he would not have to be paid and, as the boys' examinations were only two days away, they would not be able to learn much more anyway. This thought put him back in a good humour and he had left the tower and gone for a walk, smiling and quite pleased with himself.

When Balint got back to old Minya's house, the girl Julis and the wagoner were still unloading the broken parts of the model and carrying them piece by piece into a little room next to the kitchen. The mathematician stood beside the cart collecting his papers. Defiant and self-righteous, he looked at Balint with open hostility. Balint took no notice but walked over and introduced himself.

'I think we've met before,' he said, 'at Kolozsvar, at the university. I was in the Law School.'

'Possibly. I don't remember. What do you want with me?'

'Your uncle told me of your work.' Balint pointed to a fragment of the broken model. He spoke hesitantly, embarrassed by the fact that he was about to do someone a favour. 'He also told me what's just happened. In our place, at Denestornya, there's a big empty room. I know my mother would be happy for you to use it. You could work there in peace, without any interruption. If you needed anything – materials, wood – I'm sure we could find it for you. *I* believe a Flying Machine is possible.'

Jopal's eyes sparkled.

'Possible? It's already done. I've created it. Yes I really have! The Wright Brothers' experiments were all very well in their way, but their construction was all wrong.'

He started to explain what he meant. Previously every attempt to build a flying machine had been based on the mathematical formulæ worked out by Lilienthal, but these, though sound as far as they went, neglected certain important mechanical and practical factors. It was this aspect of the problem that he had been studying, for until these things were solved the theory could never be put into practice. Everything up until now had been nothing more than elementary children's stuff, scientists' toys, he said bitterly, thinking of Count Laczok's insulting words.

He spoke of natural flight, of birds and their movements and proportions. At first he spoke only in general terms, as one does in popular lectures, but soon he was so carried away by his own enthusiasm that he sat down on the ground beside Balint and began to draw in the sand. With one of the broken laths he drew diagrams of the wing-spans of cranes, falcons and swallows, showing the relationship between size and weight. Alongside, still in the sand, he wrote the apposite algebraic formulæ. Soon the whole space was filled with traced shapes and figures.

Jopal's eyes were bright with excitement and his bulging forehead was creased with perpendicular furrows. Until now, he said, no one had discovered the right coefficient to settle the problem of air-resistance. The solution was this: the formula must be based on a fifteen degree sinus-angle – and he stood up and scraped a line with the heel of his boot.

Then he stopped, and looking at Balint with a shy smile, he said, 'But I'm afraid that I must be boring the Count with higher mathematics that are beyond the range of his studies?'

'Not at all. I'm very interested. Though I studied law, mathematics was my second subject. That's why I went to Martin's lectures at Kolozsvar. So you see I do know enough to follow and appreciate...'

'Oh! Oh!' Jopal's face clouded and he looked at Balint reflectively. 'So you studied mathematics, did you?'

'Not very much! Just the elementary aspects of these problems ... Eiffel's and Langley's theories. Just enough to know that this problem can be solved. That's why I would like to support your work.'

Balint was trying to be encouraging, but the effect was just the opposite.

Jopal strode up and down a few times, hurriedly stamping out the designs and formulae in the sand, looking more and more pensive and muttering to himself, 'So! So!' Then he stopped and turned to Balint.

'Thank you for your offer, but I can't accept. No! I'm sorry, but I can't accept.' He hesitated for a moment and then added, 'I've already promised to go to a friend. I'll go to him.'

It was obviously a lie. Clearly he didn't want to come. Perhaps he thought that Balint planned to rob him of his secret.

For a moment they looked each other straight in the eye.

'Then you are not coming to Denestornya?'

'Ah! If you hadn't admitted that you too are a mathematician. You too!' The ideas that were crowding into his head made the arteries on his forehead swell and his lips draw back tight as if he were getting ready to bite. He bent forward and shouted in a fury of passion: 'It's monstrous! Unfair! You sneak back and cunningly make me talk, and all the time you only want to spy on me!'

'I just wanted to help. Really! I had no other motive.'

Jopal interrupted him, still shouting: 'Help me? Help me? That's what every spy says. You think I don't know?' And he paced up and down pouring out more and more violent abuse and working himself up until he was completely out of control. Balint had no idea how to react. It was so absurd that he almost found himself laughing, and his initial anger faded away.

The girl Julis, hearing the noise, came to the kitchen door and looked out bewildered. Her surprise was obvious when Balint turned to her, lifted his hat and began to walk away with an ironic smile on his face. Andras was still jumping about in his rage and shouting. As Balint walked up the hill he could still hear the inventor hurling ever ruder insults after him.

Balint reflected that this was altogether too much to bear. But if he had hit him perhaps the poor man would have called for seconds and demanded satisfaction. And the idea of a duel with someone of the middle class who had never held a sword would have been too absurd. And how could he, Balint Count Abady, fight a man he had only tried to help? Why, even the seconds would have laughed. Wiser to take no notice as if it were not worth another thought. He walked quickly away and soon crested the little hill.

Still, as he walked down into the town, he could not quite shake off his vexation that his good intentions had been taken so ill.

Chapter Five

BALINT AND LASZLO left Vasarhely early the next morning. While Laszlo went to visit his land up the Szamos river beyond Kolozsvar, Balint left the train at Maros-Ludas, He had sent a telegram to his mother asking for a carriage to be sent to Ludas to meet the morning train as he intended to visit the district for a few days.

Why had he said 'a few days'? He had nothing important to do in the Lelbanya district, but the real reason was that he did not want to feel bound to return as he would have done had his mother expected him. Without fully admitting this, Balint tried to convince himself that it was necessary for him to visit Lelbanya to start the co-operative he had always promised himself would be one of the first improvements he would inaugurate. This ought to be discussed with the people on the spot; and then there was the scheme for a cultural centre. These useful projects would justify his being their Member of Parliament.

But, deep inside himself, though he would not acknowledge the fact, he knew that this was not the real reason why he wanted 'a few days'. During the week, in the middle of the autumn work in the fields, few of the people he wanted to see would be at home. One afternoon would be enough. The truth was that from Lelbanya he would be within an hour's ride of Mezo-Varjas, the Miloths' place. Adrienne had not invited him to go, but she had said that she would be there for a few weeks. She had said it: so he would go.

Uneasily aware of his own hypocrisy he made a point of visiting the mayor and the two clergymen of the district. He explained his plans to them; and very convincing they seemed, for when he started to expound his ideas the details seemed to spring to his lips as complete and detailed as if he had studied them for months. But later, when he was eating in the little restaurant, it was as if the co-operative and the cultural centre had never existed: his mind was filled with other things.

He was worried about Adrienne. What was troubling her? Why did she seem so disillusioned? She had married Pal Uzdy of her own free will – she had chosen him herself. No one had forced her. Presumably she had been in love and so she had married him: why else? But, if that were so, whence came that inner revolt, that tension, the bitter tone in her voice when she spoke of the purpose of life and its aims? Perhaps her husband had turned out to be cruel. Perhaps he even struck her. Balint would not have put it past that evil-faced satanic man. As the thought came to him, he involuntarily clenched his hand into a fist on the tablecloth.

And why did she still retain that girlish, maidenly appearance? She did not have either the assurance or the mature look that came to most girls with marriage and motherhood. The oddly shy movement on the terrace when she pulled the stole up round her bare shoulders was not the normal assured gesture of a fulfilled woman.

Something was wrong and he must find out what it was. Perhaps he would be able to help; he would deeply like to. Perhaps Adrienne would tell him, and then he would be able to advise and reassure her, or his unselfish understanding might find a realistic solution to her problem, whatever it was. Obviously he must try to help – and the best way would be to go over to the Miloths' place that afternoon.

The two glossy bay horses that the Countess Roza had sent from Denestornya trotted along the smooth well-worn road. The lake, edged by reeds, was on the right of the road and in the distance lay the village of Varjas, a group of thatch-roofed houses surrounded by plum trees. On one side of the valley was the outcrop of rock on which stood the Romanian church with its toothpick spire, and on the other, above the village, were the gardens of the Miloth estate. All around to the west hills rolled towards the sunset as soft as waves. The carriage rounded the last turn in the road by the lake. Ahead on the left the boundary to the Miloth property, a thick hedge of acacia trees planted in a straight line up the hillside completely obscured the view ahead. All at once, as the carriage approached the acacia thickets, there was the sound of galloping horses. Five riders, bare-back and masked like bandits, suddenly appeared from behind the trees.

The riders were all dressed in extravagant and peculiar clothes. The leader wore a Turkish turban, the others had wide-brimmed Boer felt hats or fur caps with ear muffs and one had a red fez. They wore odd coats: dressing gowns and rubber macintoshes. This most awe-inspiring sight was somewhat diminished by the fact that three of the bandits wore silk stockings and high heels.

Galloping towards the carriage they cried out 'Your money or your life!' in high girlish voices, while the last, who was perhaps, after all, a man, sounded a blast on a hunting horn.

The first two jumped off their horses and ran to the carriage shouting 'Hand over your money! Your jewellery!' as they menaced Balint with a broomstick and a squash racket. In an instant their ferocity was overcome by merriment as Balint knelt on the carriage floor and with clasped hands begged for mercy, no resistance being possible in the face of such power.

Laughing, the bandits took off their masks. The turbanned leader was Adrienne, her brother Zoltan the warrior with the squash racket cudgel and two of the others were Adrienne's sisters, Judith and Margit, who almost fell off their horses they were laughing so much. Everyone started to talk at once:

'We heard you were coming...'

'The man from the stables told us...'

'Did we frighten you?'

'...and when he came out from Lelbanya this morning, he said you'd asked him the way.'

'Why are you so late?'

'How long can you stay?'

'It's marvellous you're here!'

With all the talk no one noticed that Adrienne's mount, which was only a draught-horse usually employed drawing a plough, had turned away and begun to amble homewards. He was fifty paces away before they noticed and then all was excitement as they realized that here was another chance for a chase.

Wickwitz, the rider with the horn who had remained behind the others, immediately rushed after the riderless charger. The others followed, while Adrienne jumped into the carriage beside Balint and urged the coachman to give chase: 'After him! After him! Faster! Faster!' and she leant forward passionately beating the front seat with her fists. Her turban unwound and her wavy hair streamed in the wind. It was not long but very thick like a rich dark mane. With her laughing mouth, her eyes wide with excitement, her chin jutting forward and the short windswept hair, she looked almost boyish. Adrienne's whole being was filled with the excitement of the pursuit. She seemed unaware of her tousled hair, of the bodice slipping from her shoulders or the skirt that pulled up over her knees as she jumped into the carriage. Nothing mattered but the excitement of the moment.

Balint looked at her. How beautiful she was, how different

and how passionately alive compared with the Addy of two days before, with whom he had stood on the dark terrace of the Castle of Siklod; the Addy with whom, in whispers, he had discussed the problems of the world at such length, the Addy who had spoken only in short broken phrases broken by long eloquent silences. Today she was a young huntress, an Amazon, her whole being alive with energy and passion. She cared for nothing but the exhilaration of the chase; nothing in the world was important but the need to catch the runaway.

The farm-horse, normally so quiet and calm, was disturbed to find himself alone and free and soon became frightened. And his fright was increased by the shouts of his pursuers and the thunder of the hoofs on the road. He broke into a canter and then a gallop, and the loose reins slipped until they flapped against his forelegs like the touch of a whip. He raised his head and went off at a speed no one would have believed possible from such an old big-bellied animal.

Down the road to the village they went, the old farm-horse in front, neighing fiercely, the four riders in hot pursuit and the carriage team from Denestornya bringing up the rear in a swift racing trot. They sped through the village and up the steep slope to the Miloths' house, cantering straight into the farm yard where the old horse made directly towards the stables just managing to enter without skinning himself against the yard gates. He was lucky not to have been hurt. Everyone thronged after him, relieved to find that he had got back unharmed into his own stall. He was already calmer by the time they reached him and, after snorting a couple of times in their direction, turned calmly to munch the hay in its rack at the back of the loose-box.

The little group walked up through the farm buildings to the garden of the manor house whose white walls could be glimpsed through a thick grove of ancient elms. As they approached they could hear the noise of someone shouting in apparent rage. Balint stopped, but the others went on quite unconcerned. Young Zoltan turned to Balint.

'Don't worry! It's nothing! It's only Papa!' he said, not in the least worried.

As they reached the long vine-covered veranda they could see Count Akos Miloth standing at the top of the steps. He was a stocky, elderly man with a wide moustache and a large mouth. He was shouting furiously:

'How dare they! Galloping off with the farm horses! They

could all be crippled! Who did it? And my fur cap, my raincoat, my dressing-gown? I'll teach them all a lesson and a half, stealing my things!' and he went on in the same vein, repeating himself and working himself up into a rage.

Neither his daughters nor young Zoltan seemed to take the smallest notice but walked quietly up to the veranda. Their father, old Rattle, went on shouting, his voice as loud as any bull bison's, each new oath emphasized by wild gestures.

As he paused for breath, Adrienne said quickly: 'Dear Papa. Look! AB is here!'

'My dear friend, welcome!' bellowed Count Akos in the same loud tones but the expression on his large mouth had changed in an instant from one of deadly wrath to a wide smile. He hurried down the steps to Balint and took his arm.

'Welcome! Welcome!' He shook Balint's hand warmly and, as he did so, noticed young Zoltan at his side. His face darkening, he struck out to give him a cuff on the head. The boy dodged the blow but stood where he was as if nothing had happened.

'You see!' the count said to Balint, 'look how cheeky they are!' By now he was smiling again. 'They steal all my clothes just for a bit of fun! But from tomorrow things will change. Just you look out!' he went on to his children. Turning again to Balint, he said:

'Did they offer you tea, my boy? I thought not. Really, these people!' Then turning, he shouted over his shoulder, 'Miska, Jozsi! Where the devil are you? Idiots!' and, back to Balint again, he said warmly, 'Tea or coffee?'

A tall footman appeared at the door.

'Where have you been hiding, you ass? You should be here when guests arrive. Bring tea at once!'

The footman did not move.

'Where does the Count want it served?' he asked.

'Here, on the veranda, you dolt! Can't you see? That's where we are!'

'Soon it will be dark, sir. Perhaps it would be better in the drawing-room. The lamps have already been lit.'

'Very well then. Take it there, you idiot. But hurry! Run! I want it at once.'

The man turned away with dignity and went unhurriedly back into the house.

During all this Egon Wickwitz, who had been seeing that the horses were stabled, rejoined the others. He came to take his leave

PART ONE

as he had to return to Maros-Szilvas whence he had come that afternoon to play tennis with the Miloths. As Maros-Szilvas – which was the property Dinora Abonyi had inherited from the Malhuysens – was more than twenty kilometres away in the valley of the Maros, Wickwitz explained that he would have to start at once or he would be late for dinner.

'Dine with us, my boy,' said Count Miloth. 'The moon rises about eleven.'

But Wickwitz did not accept. He told them that Count Abonyi had gone to Budapest and left him in charge of the racehorses. He would have to be up at dawn to exercise them.

'Are you on your own then, at Szilvas?'

'No, Countess Dinora is at home. She'll expect me for dinner and I couldn't leave her alone. It's almost seven already.'

Old Rattle laughed deeply. 'Ah ha!' he said, 'what an idiot that Abonyi must be to leave you alone with the little Countess, eh?' And he dug Wickwitz sharply in the ribs.

Adrienne and the girls smiled but Balint didn't like it. He didn't like the joke and didn't like, either, the way that the Austrian's face froze for an instant while his straight athlete's body stiffened before he relaxed, grinned sheepishly and shrugged his shoulders. Wickwitz's handsome, calm face and dreamy brown eyes had taken on a cynical expression which Balint found inexpressibly repellent.

Wickwitz's chariot, drawn by Count Abonyi's pair of beautiful black Russian trotters, was already at the veranda steps brought round by the Miloth's coachman and a stable boy. Wickwitz clicked his heels, saluted, and hurried down the steps and jumped into the open carriage. In a flash he was in the driver's seat between the big front wheels and when his hosts leaned over the veranda railings to wave goodbye, he was halfway down the drive

'Are you coming back tomorrow for tennis?' they called after him, and from behind the lilac bushes that concealed a bend in the road Wickwitz's voice came back: 'The day after tomorrow.'

The carriage brakes screeched as he started down the slope to the village. After that they could hear the Russians' hoofbeats die away in an ever faster and more mettlesome pace.

'Come and have tea at once, AB,' said Adrienne, 'and then we can all go out again.'

'How restless you are, Addy!' Countess Miloth sounded as sour as ever as she sat knitting on the sofa. She looked very much like her sister, Ida Laczok. She had the same Kendy profile, the same plumpness; but while Countess Laczok's chubby limbs seemed to radiate good humour, Countess Miloth seemed made of more ill-tempered material. And while her sister was always busy with household tasks, she herself was prone to migraine and nervous headaches and would remain idle for days, resting in a darkened room. She went on, speaking to her eldest daughter in a complaining tone, '... and you make everyone quite mad when you're here. *Elle les rend folles quand elle est ici*,' she added, turning to Mlle Morin, the desiccated old French spinster who sat beside her on the sofa, and pointing to her younger daughters.

Mlle Morin had been governess to the two Kendy sisters when they were young and had stayed on in Transylvania after they had both married. Now she was governess to the Miloth girls thus tackling a second generation even though she was really past doing the job properly.

'*Oh, mon dieu, ces enfants!*' replied the old Frenchwoman, noticing that Judith and Margit could hardly wait for their guest to finish his tea.

Adrienne took no notice of her mother or the governess but turned to Balint with sparkling eye:

'A hedgehog comes out in the kitchen garden at about this time. We want to catch him!'

Countess Miloth, who seemed to be having difficulty with her knitting needles – she was very shortsighted – gestured to the children that they could leave the table.

Balint accompanied them as they all ran out into the garden. They slowed down in the orchard and started to move quietly so as not to disturb the hedgehog if he were there. When they arrived at the entrance to the kitchen garden they crept silently along a path between a cabbage patch and the potato beds, pausing from time to time to hide behind the blackcurrant and gooseberry bushes from where they could spy out the land.

They waited for a long time in the damp kitchen garden. Up from the village, deep in the valley below them floated wisps of sweetish smoke, that characteristic smell of the high moorland which came from burning dried cow-dung instead of the wood which was scarce in those parts.

Adrienne knelt patiently on the right of the weed-covered path and Balint, on her left, found his good humour gradually evaporating. During the long silent wait he began to ponder consciously on a theme that had hitherto lurked only in his subconscious.

PART ONE

What was that Nitwit doing at Varjas? Why did he ride more than forty kilometres a day leaving his mistress, Dinora Abonyi, all alone? Surely not just to play tennis? He was convinced that it was a pretext to cover up a much more sinister purpose.

Balint's instinct was not wrong. But he was not right in thinking that the Austrian lieutenant was chasing Adrienne. Wickwitz came to Varjas, not for Adrienne's sake but to pay court to Judith. He was so good at concealing his intentions that no one, except Judith herself, noticed anything out of the usual; and even she was not sure, because Egon Wickwitz was very careful, very silent and very shrewd.

His request for long leave had been granted immediately. He had not wanted to ask for it but he had had no alternative. He had serious debts which he could not meet, and unless these were settled he would automatically be dismissed from the army in disgrace. His colonel had sent for him and said that, out of respect for Egon's father who had commanded the same regiment, he would take no action for the moment. But he had also said that he could not avoid taking notice of the situation if Wickwitz were to remain with the regiment at Brasso. He must therefore go on leave at once and find a solution to the problem and, until he had found it, he should not return. The next day Wickwitz applied for six months' leave. He had to find something . . . but what?

Baron Wickwitz was penniless. His mother lived in Graz and gave him a small allowance out of the meagre pension she received as a field marshal's widow. She gave as much as she could, but even if she were to mortgage part of her pension – as she had once before when Egon got himself into trouble at the military academy (and that, too, had been overlooked for the sake of his father) – it would not be enough. Even Egon himself could not bear the thought of troubling her further, good-hearted though she was. He had to find some other solution.

Marriage? A rich wife? There seemed no other way.

His first thought was young Dodo Gyalakuthy. She was perfect. An only child who had inherited from her father five thousand acres at Radnotfalva and two other estates in the high prairie-land, she was the ideal candidate to get him out of a tight spot. Later she would inherit more from her rich mother. No one could be better.

It was lucky that Radnotfalva was not far from Maros-Szilvas where the Abonyis lived. He could easily propose himself there, to pretty little Dinora who had been so sweet to him the previous winter. At Maros-Szilvas he would have no expenses, he would be close to the field of action. And as for that good old Tihamer Abonyi, he would be delighted. Had he not asked him several times before to come and train his horses? He ought to thank him – he might even win some races for him!

Wickwitz worked all this out sitting at a marble-topped table in a cafe in Brasso after the disagreeable interview with the colonel. His thinking was slow, with the plodding logic of a limited intelligence. And when he thought of Count Abonyi's gratitude he chuckled to himself, pleased with his own quick-wittedness. His spirits rose and he walked over to the pretty little cashier-girl, with whom he had already spent several agreeable evenings, and started to whisper to her. She agreed to meet him after closing hours and, in high good humour in spite of his miserable situation, he ordered a bottle of champagne. After all it was his last night in Brasso . . . and one only lives once.

He had arrived at Szilvas the following day and been warmly welcomed by the Abonyis. Almost at once they went to look at the racing stables and Wickwitz commented contemptuously on the condition of Tihamer's horses. Weren't they given any oats, he asked? And when Abonyi said that they had twelve pounds a day, Wickwitz laughed as if he didn't believe it but said nothing.

That afternoon Abonyi asked him to stay and take charge of the stables. And the little countess was pleased because it meant she would have her friend with her. All this had happened at the beginning of June.

Wickwitz soon took Dinora into his confidence and told her some of his plans. He said that he loved only her but he had to marry; there was no other way.

At Radnotfalva he was welcomed equally warmly. The widowed Countess Gyalakuthy was a kind good-natured woman, and she had noticed what a difficult time her daughter had. It would be good for her to be with someone who entertained her. And if it led to anything, if Dodo fell in love with him – though, as a foreigner and coming from a family of which she knew little, he was hardly the ideal son-in-law that she had had in mind – did it really matter? The widowed Countess suspected that this strong silent young man was really rather stupid, but he seemed to be a good boy who would appreciate her daughter and, after all, Dodo had enough brains for two.

PART ONE

Wickwitz had met Judith Miloth at the Gyalakuthys' and, with the keen sense of the totally self-centred, he had felt that the young girl was attracted to him, something of which he had seen no sign in Dodo. Thinking in sporting terms, as he was apt to do, he had said to himself that one should not put all one's money on the favourite but hedge the bet with a wager on a hopeful outsider. As there were three girls and a boy in the Miloth family it was clear the Judith's dowry would not be large but, if the worst came to the worst and Dodo would not have him, it would surely be enough to clear the debts if he married her. Time was running out. One way or another he had to find the means to pay before his leave ended in December.

Something made a slight movement between Balint and Adrienne; it was the hedgehog who had come out from under the leaves of a big plantain weed that covered the ground just beside the path on which they waited.

The little animal moved with quiet confidence a few inches away from the place where Adrienne had rested her suede-gloved hand. Something must have struck him as strange as he sniffed warily to catch its unfamiliar smell, the little snout covered with fine hairs quivering with concentration. He looked around with little bright button eyes and his needle-sharp quills, sleekly at rest, seemed as smooth as a soft fur coat. Such a strange little animal, he did not hurry, but moved deliberately down the path, sniffing to right and to left as he went, for all the world like a miniature bear. Suddenly he was no longer there. Without any noise and moving surprisingly swiftly he disappeared off the path; and even the grass did not move in his wake.

As he finally vanished from their sight, young Zoltan and the girls cried out: 'Why didn't you catch him, Addy? He was right there, beside you. What a shame! You ought to have caught him!'

For a moment Adrienne did not answer. Then she said: 'I couldn't! We shouldn't do it! Poor thing, we must let him live his own life. He must be free.'

Her voice sounded faint, remote...

After dinner they all sat in the countess's sitting-room and listened to Akos Miloth's stories of his days with Garibaldi. He was happy to have someone there to whom he could recount all over again the tales his family had heard so many times already. He loved to recall those days and the stories had been well polished with retelling. He had fought in Sicily with the Thousand and had had many adventures which were fascinating to anyone who had not heard them before. Count Miloth told them well, with humour and without conceit.

His daughters grew impatient and soon fled back to the dining-room where they had laid out a jigsaw puzzle, which was then all the rage and which they had brought back from the party at Siklod. Soon they became completely absorbed.

'Come on, AB, come and help us,' they called after a while. But Balint, out of politeness to his host and because he was so interested in the tales he was hearing, did not obey until Adrienne came back into the sitting-room and, laughing, took his hand, dragged him up from the sofa and led him into the adjoining room.

The next morning Balint was woken by voices calling to him. Someone knocked on the shutters of his room and called out: 'Come on, lazy-bones, get up! We've been up for hours!'

In fifteen minutes he had joined them on the long veranda where they were having breakfast. The girls and young Zoltan had already finished and could hardly wait for Balint to drink his coffee and buffalo milk. Then they all walked up through the garden, laughing and talking until they found a small meadow with a haystack, up which young Zoltan immediately climbed and started pretending to be an Indian chief doing a war-dance.

'Come down, you idiot, you'll spoil the hay!' they shouted at him, but the boy just jumped about all the more, hooting war-cries.

At once the others joined the game and started besieging young Zoltan in his fort. Not that they took the war seriously, for as soon as Adrienne succeeded in getting to the top she changed sides and joined the enemy. Now the battle became more equal, two against three, and the outcome less sure; but suddenly one side of the haystack collapsed and Zoltan came tumbling to the ground, leaving only Adrienne on top clinging precariously to the stackpole. For a moment she hesitated, high above the ground, but, as Balint extended his arms towards her, Addy cried 'Catch me!' and flung herself into the air laughing. Somehow Balint did so, and for a moment she clung to him, her arms round his neck, knees bent, like a little girl hanging round her grandfather's neck.

Her warm, shapely body pressed against Balint's, her bare arms encircling his neck in a cool embrace, or at least what would have been an embrace if it had not been a game and their closeness unintentional. In those few moments, before she moved, while her slender female body was pressed to his, Balint felt desire welling up inside him, all his being crying out to go on holding her close, to kiss her warm naked shoulder, to make her his. He wanted to stay like that for ever, oblivious to everything and everyone around them; but Adrienne just laughed unconcernedly, and put her feet to the ground, apparently unconscious of anything but the merriment of their game.

They continued their walk all talking at once, teasing each other in easy comradeship, though Balint found it difficult to fit into their mood.

One of the maids ran up with a telegram for Adrienne. 'Excuse me, it was the Countess who opened it,' she explained as she handed the envelope to Adrienne.

Adrienne read the telegram. 'Thank you,' she said, 'you can go back to the house now.' Her expression showed only that she was controlling herself with a certain effort. She tucked the folded telegram into her waistband and turned to the others.

'Where shall we go now?' she queried. Zoltan suggested that they visit the cowsheds where there were some newborn calves. Everyone agreed and off they went, petted a few cows, stroked the heads of the farm dogs, teased the turkeys and chased the ducks into the pond. But however light-hearted they seemed, a cloud had come over their merriment. Even though only Adrienne knew what was in the telegram, its arrival had spoilt their mood and everyone seemed depressed. At long last it was time to return for lunch and they all went back to the manor house with dampened spirits.

The weather was still so fine that they had coffee on the veranda. Shafts of sunlight penetrated the vine-leaves overhead and scattered tiny spots of light which sparkled on the chairs, the tablecloth and the paved floor, almost like glow-worms did at night. Some of the vine leaves were already turning red and they glowed like hot embers in the strong sunlight.

Adrienne touched Balint on the shoulder. 'Come with me,' she said, and led him in silence until they reached the end of the garden, where a simple wooden seat, lilac-coloured with age, overlooked the slope of the valley below. They sat down.

'This is my favourite place,' she said. 'When I was a child I always took refuge here.'

From where they sat they could see the outlines of bare mountains receding into the distance. The view was beautiful, but it was not at all the sort of romantic landscape usually considered so. Here was no picture postcard beauty of forests, mountains and soaring rocky cliffs. Strangers unused to this bare Transylvanian upland country might find it too unusual, perhaps even ugly in its austerity and wildness. Yet it was beautiful, with a grandeur of its own, chain upon chain of bare woodless mountains, rising behind each other as far as eye could see, each range seemingly identical to the last.

Everywhere there was silence.

In front of where Balint and Adrienne sat there was an old burial ground with ancient neglected headstones standing among untended grass and nettles. It was the remains of a Protestant cemetery, abandoned when the community died out. Farther down the slope of the hill, on a small ridge, could be seen the races of old walls where once a small chapel had stood.

Adrienne sat with legs crossed, motionless, with her head resting on her right hand. She looked straight ahead of her without speaking.

After some time she took out the telegram and handed it to Balint. It read, 'COME HOME AT ONCE – UZDY'.

'What does it mean?' he asked

'Nothing. Nothing that means anything. They wouldn't send for me if the baby was ill: they wouldn't need me. Neither then nor any other time. Six months ago when the child had a fever they locked me out of the nursery. My husband's mother takes charge of everything. When the baby was born they took her away at once – You don't know anything about babies! they said. They don't believe I know anything about anything. No matter how hard I try, no matter what I do. They don't want anything from me, anything at all. I'm only an ornament – a living toy who has only one use . . . that's why I'm there.'

She was silent for a while. Then she went on in a different tone:

'When I married him I believed I could be useful by helping him with his work, that I would be the companion, the friend he needed. He often spoke about it. He would tell me how lonely he had been with no one close to him, in whom he could confide, with whom he could work. But afterwards, the day after we were married, the very next day, he was quite different. Everything he had said . . . what was it? Moonshine, just moonshine!'

PART ONE

Adrienne was silent again. She looked away, into the far distance, thinking back to the days when she was a young girl full of rebellion. She thought about all the conventions that ruled her life at home and which, after the years of freedom in a foreign boarding-school, had seemed so unbearable, so humiliating. There had been the prohibition of any book, any play more serious than musical comedy, the impossibility of escaping alone, away from the ever-present chaperon; and never, ever, had she been able to escape from being watched. She, a grown girl, was still treated as a small child who needed constant supervision and control. She remembered one small incident that had weighed heavily with her when she was deciding to accept Pal Uzdy. Adrienne had been invited to tea with the Laczoks. After lunch Countess Miloth, who always took a siesta, fell asleep. The old governess, Mlle Morin, had been ill and Adrienne, left on her own and not liking to disturb her mother, had climbed into the waiting family carriage and accompanied only by a footman had had herself driven to her aunt's house. It had taken a bare five minutes.

The awful boldness of this adventure had unexpectedly serious results.

Her mother had accused her of all kinds of depravity, accusations that remained partly veiled only because in front of an unmarried daughter, she could not bring herself to say the word 'whore'. Her father, too, had shouted at her, echoing her mother's wild and hysterical accusations; not because he believed them, but because he loved to shout whenever he could. It was then that she had finally decided to marry Uzdy. She knew him to be a serious man who worked hard and who did not often come to town to carouse with the gypsies like the other young men. She had not been in love with him, but she had yearned to be free of the tyranny of her old-fashioned home, to be her own mistress, to carry some responsibility and to have duties of her own.

Recalling this, she said to Balint:

'I know you never understood why I married Pali! Don't deny it! I felt it whenever we met. But I couldn't go on living at home, I couldn't stand it. And I really did feel that I was needed, that I could help. I believed that I had found a vocation.' She paused for a moment, and then spoke again. 'I soon found that I was nobody there either, but at least I can read when I please, and I can go for walks alone in the woods! Do you know the country where we live, the woods beside the Almas? It's beautiful there.'

'Poor Addy!' said Balint softly. He picked up the hand that lay beside him and slowly caressed the long fingers, the palm, the wrist. Adrienne did not resist. She was like a trusting child whose hurt could be comforted by being petted.

With her hand still in his, Adrienne went on: 'I'll have to go. I could refuse but it wouldn't be worth it! Mama knows they've called me home. She wouldn't give me a moment's peace. Oh, it's so good to be here with the girls! I can forget how lonely I am.' Balint could hardly hear the last words which Adrienne had whispered almost to herself.

She looked steadily and calmly into the distance. Though she did not break down, Balint could see that her eyes and thick lashes were clouded with tears.

Deeply moved, Balint started to tell her everything that he had always felt for her. He told her how unique she was, how unlike anyone else he had ever known, how even when she was still a girl how different he had found her from all the others. And, as he spoke, many new feelings, hitherto unrecognized even by himself, pushed themselves forward demanding to be put into words, the heralds of an emotion which he did not even try to analyse.

He spoke for a long time, his hands still caressing Adrienne's in slow rhythm with his low-spoken words, moving along the arm up to the elbow and down again to the hand and the fingertips. At first he spoke only as a good friend, understanding, consoling but, as he poured out his love and sympathy and as his fingers moved over her flower-petal skin, even though she offered no noticeable response to his caresses, he became increasingly aware of what was really in his heart. His words meant more than friendship, and the movement of his hands was no longer merely soothing. Both voice and hands became the instruments of a new passion, the words became words of love and homage and, as he spoke, they were punctuated by kisses, on the fingers, on the wrist, on her palm and slowly up her unresisting passive arm. As he spoke the meaning of his words changed; sympathy became desire and friendship demanded its reward. Of all the feelings that had poured forth from him only passion remained as he spoke of her beauty, of her lips, her hair, her skin . . . of death, and of redemption and fulfilment.

For how long did Balint pour out his feelings? Neither of them could have said. Adrienne listened, silent and motionless, seeming to respond to the music of the words rather than to their meaning. But when the man's lips pressed deeper into the curve of her elbow, she suddenly came alive again. She pulled her arm away violently and jumped up.

'So! Even you! You want only that! You, of all people, only that! I thought I had a friend, but I have no one, no one!'

She looked at him with hatred and, straightening her slim back, started to walk stiffly away.

'Addy! Please, Addy! Forgive me!'

But she just went on, her head held high, her whole body rigid with anger and hurt. They walked back to the house in silence, side by side but worlds apart. Abady left that afternoon.

Trying not to show his hurt, he said lengthy goodbyes to all the family. He shook hands warmly with Adrienne's father, with the girls, the old French governess and with Zoltan; and he tried hard to have a few words with Adrienne herself. His eyes followed her wherever she went, meek with humility, silently begging forgiveness. But she avoided all contact until, just before he was due to enter his carriage and she could no longer remain completely aloof, she allowed him merely to kiss her fingertips. Then she swiftly pulled her hand away and turned back into the house without looking at him.

As the carriage moved off, he looked back to the veranda. Judith and Margit waved back gaily; but Adrienne was nowhere to be seen.

They drove slowly down the steep slope to the road by the lake, the same road by which, gay, carefree and full of hope, he had arrived only the day before. Today his heart seemed to beat in his throat.

He felt that he had lost Adrienne for ever.

PART TWO

Chapter One

WHEN LASZLO GYEROFFY returned to his two-roomed furnished flat in Budapest he started to work in earnest and hardly ever went out. It was a modest little apartment that his guardian, old Carrots, had found for him when he had transferred from the University of Kolozsvar to the Academy of Budapest a few months before. There was just a small living-room with two windows giving onto the garden of the Museum and an even smaller bedroom that looked into the dark courtyard behind. The furniture was worn and shabby, typical of that to be found in the sort of small furnished flats whose rents could be afforded by students. Laszlo had brought with him only two things of his own; a photograph of his father in Hungarian costume taken when he was an usher in the Coronation in 1867, and his guns in a fine leather case which had been placed on the chest of drawers. A drawing board placed on one of the window-sills served as a writing desk.

Laszlo had taken his cousin Balint's advice to heart. While they had been together in Vasarhely, and in the train until they separated at Maros-Ludas, Balint had tried hard to make Laszlo understand the problems he would have to face now that he had chosen music as a career, problems that would never be solved unless Laszlo contrived to be freed of his debts. Balint advised and, because he loved and admired his cousin, Laszlo had listened and was now trying hard to put that advice into practice. He worked hard, he cut himself off from all social life and he was determined as soon as possible to catch up with the other students who had entered the Academy of Music immediately they had received their baccalaureate.

The experience of the last year had had an important effect on Laszlo, who, deeply ambitious, had resented finding himself no longer among the leading students. To be second-best was hateful to him.

The few weeks he had stayed in Transylvania before returning to Budapest had been spent in raising money. As his guardian refused point-blank to accept Laszlo's ideas about the forests, and because he had only a short time available before he had to be

PART TWO

back in Budapest to register at the Academy, he had mortgaged the property along the banks of the Szamos river that he had inherited from his father. He had only been able to raise a few thousand florins more than he owed to the money-lenders, but at least he now had something in hand and could live, without worrying and without having always to apply cap-in-hand to his guardian for every penny he needed.

He told nobody of his return to Budapest, not even his Kollonich or Szent-Gyorgyi relations. He did not go near the Casino, of which he had become a member in the spring, in case the news of his presence in Budapest would get around the town; and when he went to concerts in the evening he sat in the gallery so as to be sure he would not be seen by anyone who knew him. In the daytime he studied, went to classes and ate his meals in the sort of small eating houses only frequented by students.

If the mornings were beautiful, so were the evenings. Sometimes, when Laszlo returned to his little flat after supper, and before his newfound discipline sent him to bed so as to be ready to rise early the next morning, he would go to the window and gaze out over the tranquil gardens of the museum. He did not do this often because, he knew not why, it reminded him of the carefree, frivolous life he had led as a law student. It made him hanker after the life to be led in the country. But it was not of Transylvania that he thought, nor of the little country house of Szamos-Kozard that his father had started to build but never finished and which he had never known. Nor was it for the Transylvania of his barely-remembered childhood that he longed; rather it was for Nyitra, the Szent-Gyorgyis' country place, where the sugar-beet fields were rich in coveys of pheasants waiting to be shot, and the woods of the lower Carpathians filled with wild boar to be stalked. Even better, how wonderful it would be to find oneself at Simonvasar, the Kollonich place in Veszprem. That would be the best. How marvellous to ride over the soft Veszprem hills with his Kollonich cousins, with Klara, to play tennis with her and the boys and, in the evenings, to play the piano to her in the long dark music-room, weaving long romantic fantasias to which she would listen in silence with dilated eyes, drinking in every sound of the music he was creating just for her. That would be the most wonderful of all.

One Sunday, completely immersed in his studies, Laszlo worked from midday until it was almost dark and even in the light of the window embrasure it became hard to see clearly enough to read. Still Laszlo did not break his concentration until, all at once, the doorbell rang ... and rang again and again, four or five times. Laszlo, angry at being interrupted, got up at last to open the door. Two of his Kollonich cousins, Peter and Niki, erupted into the little room.

'So here you are! Why have you been hiding like this! When did you get back! Anyhow, we've caught you now!' Shaking his hand, slapping his shoulders, and both talking at once, they filled the little room with their high spirits and good fellowship. With their English-made clothes, their well-brushed hair and general air of ease and elegance, Laszlo felt that his cousins put to shame the shabbiness of his little student's lodging. He was glad it was so dark that they could hardly see it, and he weakly resolved to move and have his own furniture brought to Budapest. Why should he feel ashamed when his relations dropped in unexpectedly?

'This is preposterous,' said the oldest, Peter, a chubby young man with very fair hair. 'We've been looking for you all over Transylvania, sending wires everywhere, and here you are all the time!'

While Peter was a full brother to Klara, being the son of Prince Kollonich by his first, Trautenbach, wife; his half-brother Niki was so much a Gyeroffy in looks that he could have been Laszlo's brother. Peter went on: 'Even at the Casino no one had heard of you. We wired to Balint, who told us you'd left ages ago. What's this all about. What's the big secret?'

'You see, I was right! I said he'd gone to ground and we'd have to dig him out,' said Niki, who loved to use old Hungarian hunting language since the rest of his family, in his view, had become too Germanized.

'I'm working hard, that's all. I'm studying.'

'Nonsense! That's no excuse! One always passes examinations one way or another,' said Peter, who then, to show off his use of fashionable English, continued, 'besides, that's no reason to "cut" us. Anyhow now we've caught you, I'll tell you why we've been looking for you. Our first shoot's next week. The guests arrive on the 20th, for three days as usual. You've got to come!'

Laszlo demurred. He used all the arguments that Balint had rehearsed for him; he couldn't leave his studies, he said, and he started going into lengthy detail about his work, but his cousins remained unimpressed. To their way of thinking music or any other studies were only of secondary importance. You could pass the time studying, and maybe you could learn something useful, after a fashion, but a pheasant shoot, one of the best in the country and which only lasted three days – to miss that was incomprehensible. Unless there were some other, unspoken reason. It was Niki who gave voice to the only plausible explanation, 'To be sure, there's a woman behind this! Don't deny it, Laszlo. Give us a week and we'll find out who she is!'

'You just have to come,' insisted Peter. 'It's unthinkable that you shouldn't be with us for the first shoot of the season. Papa would be very hurt if you let us down, especially this year when all the important guests are terrible shots! What's more, with Louis up at Oxford with Toni Szent-Gyorgyi, there'll be no good shots from the family except for us and Uncle Antal. Balint's coming but he's not much use with a gun. The bags will be a disaster without you. We've got to net at least two thousand brace, or Father will blame us for a rotten shoot. It's unthinkable that you should let us down.'

They argued for a long time, the Kollonich cousins asking what sort of a friend and cousin he was who could abandon them just when they needed him most? And in the end Laszlo yielded, as much to his own secret desires as to the entreaties of his cousins. But he insisted that he couldn't stay a minute more than three days.

As Peter and Niki took their leave they tried to tempt Laszlo into going with them, but Gyeroffy remained firm. He absolutely had to get up in the morning and so, defeated but content, the two cousins took themselves off happy that Laszlo had agreed to come.

When they had gone Laszlo lit the lamps and tried once again to settle to his studies, but the theories of point and counterpoint blurred before his eyes. No matter how hard he tried, he could not concentrate: serious study eluded him. At last he gave up and went over to the gun-case on the chest of drawers. It was a long, smooth case of fine leather with brass corner-guards and a patent lock. The case, with its fine pair of triggerless Purdys inside, had been the unexpectedly lavish Christmas present from his two aunts three years before. On the butt of each gun was a small golden disk engraved with the Gyeroffy arms, and on the outside of the case, embossed on the leather, was his name, with a small spelling mistake: 'Count Ladislas Gieroffy'.

Laszlo took out one of the guns and, as he put it together, he thought how easily it handled, how beautifully it was made, like a fine clock. He peered through the long gleaming barrels, cocked the gun for the pleasure of hearing that easy, precise click. What a clean sound! After gently handling the gun for some time he dismantled it and put it lovingly back in its case.

Then he went for a long solitary walk along the banks of the Danube.

On the 19th Laszlo travelled to Simonvasar with Balint Abady, who had come to the capital for some political meetings.

They arrived in the late afternoon, after a slow carriage drive which seemed even longer than the ten kilometres from the station to the castle because the road was so bad. The reason for this was that Prince Kollonich was always on such bad terms with whatever government was in power in the county that he rarely ever communicated with the authorities in the county town and then only through his land agent.

The carriage finally entered the forecourt of the castle, turned a half circle round the horseshoe-shaped carriage way, and drew up under the columned entrance. As they entered the house two statuesque footmen helped them out of their fur coats and a third, dressed in the blue tailcoat of the Kollonich livery, led them through the huge library, with its tall cupola-shaped roof, through the vast red drawing-room with its five windows, where some of the younger guests were already assembled, and finally through double doors into the corner saloon where the Princess Agnes always received her guests. This salon was one and a half floors high, like the library through which they had just passed but, unlike the library which was lined with tier upon tier of beautifully bound books, it was decorated with coloured stucco in light relief: all pastel colours, butter-yellow, pale lilac and a mint green simulated marble, all in the purest Empire style, even though the castle, designed by the great architect, Pollak, creator of the National Museum, had only been finished at the end of the sixties.

The princess received the new arrivals with her usual warmth and kindliness. She stroked Laszlo's head as he bent to kiss her hand. Though she was as ever, extremely gracious, she never made it easy to forget that she was, after all, a very great lady whose every kind word was a gift and to kiss whose hand was a privilege.

She was tall and still beautiful, even though her dark hair was

PART TWO

streaked with grey and her once radiantly pink complexion was now touched here and there with tiny dark-brown liver spots. She wore a tea-gown in the English fashion, the neck and sleeves sewn with festoons of old lace which set off her still beautiful hands and arms. Although the garment was loose and flowing she sat so erect that it was obvious that she also wore a tightly-laced corset.

At the princess's side sat one of the principal guests, Field Marshal Count Kanizsay, who commanded the national cavalry regiments, a heavy old man who had been a hero of the Bosnian occupation. He came from an ancient Hungarian family and was descended from the Kanizsay who fell with Zrinyi at the siege of Szigetvar. His ancestors had played a great part in the wars against the Turks, always serving the Habsburg interests, and in recognition of this service the Kanizsay coat of arms bore the motto *Perpetuus in Komarvar* and the head of the family was made hereditary military governor of that little Bosnian fortress. In spite of his family's great national past the old soldier only spoke broken Hungarian, having spent all his life in German-speaking regiments of the Austro-Hungarian army. Although the field marshal had long retired from active service he always wore uniform, a grey tunic with a collar of gold braid, countless medal ribbons and one order, the Maria Theresia Cross, gleaming white on his still powerful chest.

Sitting on the silken sofa on her hostess's left was the wife of the field marshal, a massive, boring old German lady who was very conscious of her own importance in being related to the Wittelsbachs by a morganatic marriage; and the Countess Lubianszky, who had brought her two pretty daughters with her from Somogy. Opposite them sat the young and beautiful Countess Beredy, the lovely Fanny, who was obliged by her rank to seat herself with the old ladies even though she longed to be in the red salon with the young.

The hostess and her principal guests sat in a circle round the tea table, where everything from the silver to the hot muffins and thin sandwiches was arranged in the fashionable English style. Beside the door to the adjoining salon the butler, Szabo, stood motionless with the face of a Roman emperor, together with a bearded man in the livery of a Kollonich *Jäger*. Two tall footmen in tailcoats served the guests, moving from one to another as silently as shadows.

At a second table sat Klara and her two brothers, her cousins

Stefi and Magda Szent-Gyorgyi, the two Lubianszky girls and a somewhat older young man, Fredi Wülffenstein, who was Fanny Beredy's younger brother.

As Laszlo and Balint had passed through the red salon, and again as they had greeted their hostess and the others present, Laszlo could not help noticing his cousin's calm assurance. Though every bit as polite and deferential as the occasion demanded, every movement, every word showed that he belonged to these circles; that he knew himself to be in every way their equal and in no way an intruder. Laszlo watched him with envy, wondering if he had acquired this air of smooth distinction while *en poste* abroad, and wondering too if he could ever attain the same ease, he to whom every greeting, every nod and handshake seemed fraught with condescension, as if he were no more than a humble serf tolerated by consciously superior beings.

He knew he had no reason for this sense of inferiority; no one present was better born than he, indeed his own family was older than theirs, the Gyeroffys having been noble in the Middle Ages; and his own estate, though small and only bringing him a modest measure of independence, was an ancient freehold rather than a modern donation from the crown. He knew, too, that the grandeur of the Kollonich family dated only from the end of the seventeenth century when one of them had become a cardinal, while the great wealth they now displayed, indeed everything they owned – the great castle and estate, the palaces in Budapest and Vienna – had all been purchased by his cousins' grandmother, the daughter of a banker called Sina, a Greek who had spent his life polishing the seat of his office desk. Why then, he wondered, did he, the descendant of conquering Magyar warlords, feel that his relations were grander, better, more distinguished, than he?

All these thoughts vanished the instant that he held Klara's soft hand in his and when he looked into her wide-open greenish-grey eyes and saw her warm smile of happiness and welcome.

After exchanging a few words of polite conversation with everyone in the room, Balint Abady, who had not been at Simonvasar for several years, asked where he could find his host. Uncle Louis was in the smoking-room, replied Stefi, as their aunt did not allow cigars in her drawing-room. Indeed since the state rooms had been redecorated, Stefi went on in a low voice, Aunt Agnes hardly tolerated even cigarettes.

Passing through a side door Balint and Laszlo went down a

long, wide carpeted corridor which followed the horseshoe curve of one of the castle's side wings. At last, at the far end, they reached the smoking-room, a vast tobacco-coloured apartment whose walls were covered with hunting trophies, stuffed heads of deer, chamois, wild boar, bear and buffalo, and countless sets of antlers on shield-shaped plaques of polished mahogany. The furniture, in contrast to that of his wife's rooms, was heavy, comfortable, even shabby, with plenty of deep leather-covered chairs and ancient sofas.

Uncle Louis cared nothing for fashion and when the Princess Agnes had spent a fortune in redecorating every other room in the castle he had allowed her her way providing that his own comfortable room was left untouched.

Three men sat at ease in a corner of the vast, barely lit apartment. They were the host, a chubby man of middle height dressed in Austrian hunting clothes with a pair of carpet slippers on his feet; his brother-in-law, Antal Szent-Gyorgyi, beside him; and, sprawled in an ancient armchair facing them, the huge form of Pali Lubianszky. The prince was telling a seemingly endless and complicated story about an incident during the last deer stalk, and Pali Lubianszky was having difficulty in concealing his impatience.

With every turn and twist of the story the host made sweeping gestures, imitating now the spread of the great antlers of the red deer, now the warning snorts and nervous movements of the fawns; and with every gesture he heaved himself from side to side so that the springs creaked under him, and with every sound it made it seemed as if the chair would collapse, as indeed it often had. Antal Szent-Gyorgyi looked silently on with a faint ironic smile as if that were what he was hoping would happen.

The two brothers-in-law were extreme opposites — a greyhound and a pug. Szent-Gyorgyi was tall and thin, with a long narrow face and bluish-grey hair; Kollonich was fair with a round face, a tiny nose and small eyes almost buried in the fat of his cheeks, and he wore a moustache and a short round beard like the Emperor's. Beneath Szent-Gyorgyi's acquiline beak was a thin moustache clipped in the English style.

Lubianszky did not conceal his pleasure when Balint and Laszlo came in, partly because it put an end to Prince Louis' stalking tale — and sportsmen are rarely interested in any stories but their own — but principally because he was deeply interested in politics and wanted to hear from Balint the truth about the recent developments in Budapest, of which until now he knew only what he had read in the newspapers. Szent-Gyorgyi was also interested, but from a less nationalistic point-of-view, being a court official, Master of the Horse to the Emperor, and a natural courtier.

The prince lit a new cigar as the others started to ply Balint with questions about what had happened in Parliament. Had he been present? What was the real truth? Who had said what? He must stay with them, sit down and recount all he knew.

Laszlo took his leave and went to rejoin the girls, and Balint began his tale.

The session of Parliament on the 18th of November was all that interested the four men in the smoking room.

In Budapest things had been far from calm.

When the House reassembled in November it was in an atmosphere of such tension that it was clear to all that a real storm was brewing. The Minister-President, Count Tisza, immediately submitted proposals for the reform of the House of Representatives and asked for the appointment of a committee to study them and, if necessary, submit amendments. Even this moderate suggestion met with fierce obstruction from the demagogues, who tried every trick, every subterfuge to block agreement and talked out the Government's proposals so as to prevent any progress toward their acceptance. In this mood of obstruction and artificially engendered resentment, the Leader of the Opposition announced his total rejection of the Tisza proposals.

Then came the 18th of November.

Since the previous day, a series of simultaneous though parallel meetings had been in session and on the afternoon of the fatal 18th, the opposition met behind closed doors. Late in the evening session of the House, members of the Government party started appearing in force and when Tisza finished speaking, with only occasional interruptions from the thirty-odd opposition members present, some Government supporters stood calling for an immediate vote. 'Put it to the vote!' they cried in increasing numbers. 'A vote! A vote! Put it to the vote now!' they cried from every corner of the Chamber; and in the bedlam the Speaker rose, waving a paper and mouthing words that no one could hear above the uproar.

Balint told the story coldly, recounting what he had seen and heard that day as briefly as he could, suppressing all his personal impressions, keeping to himself much of the detail and all his own outraged feelings. But he had heard and seen everything that had happened and he would never forget it.

What had really happened was this. After the closed meeting had ended, Balint went into the dark Chamber and stood behind the last row of benches facing the Speaker's raised desk. Suddenly the supporters of the Government party started flooding in; they had all been in the bar waiting for the closed meeting to come to an end. They had rarely been present in such numbers and never in such a belligerent mood.

Tisza rose to speak. His tall virile figure seemed etched in black before the upturned well-lit faces of the deputies seated behind him. In a firm voice, with strength and power and passion he warned the House what would happen if order was not restored to their debates. Speaking like one of the prophets of old his words became ever more impassioned, as once again he foretold the catastrophe that Hungary would face if all progress were to be blocked by petty party politics. Would only a great national upheaval, he asked, disastrous to everything they held dear, fatal to the greatness of the Hungarian nation, bring them to their senses? He begged, exhorted, commanded them to listen before it was too late. The left-wing members listened in silence, stone-faced. They stopped their interruptions and their clamour: it was as if they were under a spell.

From time to time some members on the right jumped up and cried, 'Put it to the vote! Vote!' and started stamping their feet, but Tisza waved them back, determined to be heard to the end. And he went on despite the increasing noise and confusion, only barely keeping order by the authority or his voice and gesture, an authority increasingly challenged until, at his last ringing words, 'Let the comedy end!', his party rose in a body all crying out, 'Vote! Vote! Vote!' If any members of the opposition had shouted back no one could hear them; they were drowned in the roar of several hundred government voices.

The Speaker stood up on his platform, waving a folded order-paper in a vain attempt to restore order. His mouth could be seen to move but not a sound could be heard above the uproar. Finally he had tottered down from his seat of authority apparently completely overcome.

A crowd of members poured down to the floor of the Chamber and filled the wide space where the 'Table of the House' was covered with the law books and State papers. There they argued, shouted, gesticulated – a rabble out of control – and as the argument became more heated so a leaf of paper was thrown upwards, then a book or two, then more, not thrown in aggression, only upwards, apparently without reason.

At this point Abady had left, weak with nausea, his head sick with a bitter sense of the deepest disillusion.

Only Tisza's speech had seemed real; only that had been honest, truly felt, sincere. The rest had been mere play-acting. All that jumping about and shouting, those apparently zealous members rising and calling for a vote, inciting the other members of their party, all that had been thought out and rehearsed in advance, as was the opposition's attitude of shock and surprise: it was all a fake. Balint had turned away and walked swiftly down the corridor, his footsteps deadened by the soft carpeting.

The silence was now so great that the huge building seemed dead. Turning a corner Balint found himself face to face with the old Speaker of the House, supported on one side by the Secretary of the House and on the other side by the Keeper. What happened? Balint had asked. What ruling had he given? But the old gentleman had been so overcome that he could only stammer: 'Everything, everything is ... ov ...' and helped by his two faithful supporters he tottered away to the Speaker's room.

The National Casino Club, when Balint arrived, was swarming with people, like an ant-hill accidentally disturbed. The Deak Room was the headquarters of the opposition led by Andrassy and it was filled with his supporters, while every corner of the club was occupied by groups of four or five, all arguing, protesting, worrying and either outraged or triumphant according to their political allegiances. Only the card-rooms were unaffected; the bridge and tarot players engrossed only by such problems as whether they shouid try a finesse or whether their double would be successful.

<hr />

Balint did not reveal all this in the smoking-room of Simonvasar. He neither mentioned what he had felt nor what his feellngs had been. He answered the questions put to him but he did not elaborate, even though it was obvious that they wanted to hear more. He could not explain his reluctance, he only knew that he must keep his feelings and his opinions to himself.

Antal Szent-Gyorgyi's reactions were predictable. He saw everything from the Olympian height of the Hofburg in Vienna.

He was delighted that those who 'ignored His Majesty's wishes' had been taught a lesson. He was glad, without thinking for a moment of any individual's personal involvement, because to him all politics were a sordid business not fit for the attention of a gentleman, a necessary evil, like muck-spreading on the farms. He managed to overlook the fact that Balint was a Member of Parliament only because, as a learned genealogist, he knew too that the Abadys' first ancestor had been a Bessenyo chief from the Tomai clan, who had settled in Hungary as long ago as the reign of Prince Geza, and that Abadys had been princes, governors and palatines in Transylvania under the Arpad dynasty. With antecedents like those it was perhaps permissible, if one felt like it, once in a while, to indulge a taste for the gutter.

Lubianszky's views were not so clear-cut. He had been Lord Lieutenant in Tolna during the time of the Szell regime and now, after his resignation, he had joined the dissident group that supported Andrassy. He had a horror of the revolutionaries of 1848 but, as he loathed Tisza, he had hoped that if the demagogues could be broken they would take him with them in their fall.

Though these two attitudes could hardly be reconciled, Kollonich was not really interested in either. Like every other catholic magnate, he felt obliged to contribute to the National Front each time there was an election. Therefore, in so far as they existed at all, his sympathies lay with the official government party. At the same time, he distrusted all governments, no matter which party might find itself in power. The only matters Prince Kollonich took seriously were hunting and shooting, and he could hardly wait to get back to his deer-stalking story which had been so unnecessarily interrupted by the arrival of Abady. Now that the political tale had been told he felt he could return to more important matters.

'Well, as I was saying, I had just about reached the cover of the beech hedge when a roebuck started calling from the left! What was I to do? I thought it would be best if carefully I were to . . .'

Balint rose and made his way back to the ladies in the red salon.

⁂

Most of the guests had now arrived at the castle. Only two were still missing: the guests of honour, Count Slawata, Counsellor to the Foreign Office and Prince Montorio-Visconti. It was known that they had set off by motor from Vienna that morning but, although it was now long past six o'clock, they had still not arrived.

The hostess's face had begun to show traces of anxiety carefully suppressed. In spite of this she continued her insipid social conversation with the guests gathered around her. As she did so she glanced from time to time at the great clock on the chimney-piece, a massive affair of bronze and green enamel adorned with gilded baroque figures representing Kronos and Psyche. It was a famous piece by Pradier but the princess, taking its beauty for granted, was only interested in the hands of the clock which moved inexorably round without seeming to bring nearer the arrival of these important guests from whom she expected so much. At last, with a barely perceptible gesture she summoned one of the tall silent footmen.

'Call Duke Peter,' she murmured. And when her stepson bent over her, she murmured, 'A carriage should be sent to the highway'. Then, even lower, she added in English, 'Your father never thinks of anything!'

Hardly had the young man reached the far end of the big drawing-room when the double doors from the library were flung open and two men entered, one tall and one short with broad shoulders; they were Montorio and Siawata, arrived at last.

The prince, Italian in name and title only, was Austrian with vast properties in Carinthia. He was a nice-looking young man, dark-complexioned and slightly balding, with light blue eyes that startled with their brilliance. His fashionable moustaches were so narrow that they could have been stuck on with glue, and he moved with the gliding step of one used to highly waxed floors. Count Slawata, in contrast, was fair-haired and short-nosed, with broad cheekbones. He was clean-shaven and wore thick horn-rimmed spectacles, an eccentricity in those days when only monocles or rimless pince-nez were the accepted form. His glasses seemed in some way ostentatious, as if the wearer wished to stress a more serious and thrifty view of life than that of the others. Slawata's way of moving, with heavy peasant-like tread, underlined this same impression. His clothes were dark blue in colour and unexceptional in cut.

After greeting their hostess, the latest arrivals were conducted to the smoking-room to meet their host, whose stalking story, still not completed, was destined never to reach its end, as no sooner had the newcomers greeted him than the dinner gong sounded announcing that it was time to go and dress.

The house guests who had arrived that afternoon then gathered in the great entrance hall, whence they were conducted by

PART TWO

servants to the rooms allocated to them and where their luggage had already been taken and unpacked and their evening clothes laid out.

Peter Kollonich stepped over to Laszio. 'I hope you don't mind but we've had to put you in the kitchen wing! There are so many women and married couples this year that there seemed no other way. We thought you, as the nearest relation...' and he waved to a footman to show Laszlo the way.

The footman went to a door in the opposite side of the hall from the great State rooms where the guests had gathered. Here there was no carpet, only great stone slabs which formed the floor of the corridor. They passed the silver vaults and the butler's pantry and along the whole length of the castle's kitchens. Here was none of the majestic silence that had seemed to rule the other parts of the huge building. From inside the kitchen came the clatter of copper pans, the sound of the chef's voice raised in anger at some underling and all the multifarious rhythms and drumbeats that made up the symphony of sound that accompanied the creation of a great formal dinner. A door flew open, and then slammed shut after a kitchen boy had shouted something back before running off down the passage in front of them. A scullery maid, her face flushed, ran in the opposite direction and disappeared through another door which she too banged behind her. A bevy of chambermaids, giggling, emerged from a narrow staircase and hurried past, across the courtyard, towards the guest wing.

No one paused respectfully as a guest passed. It was as if they had not even seen him.

After two turns in the long corridor they eventually reached a large room at the end of the wing opposite that where Laszlo had found his host. It was a good room, spacious and high ceilinged, differing only from the guest-rooms in the other part of the house in its old-fashioned decoration and cheap, worn furniture. Even so, it was incomparably better than Laszlo's flat in Budapest.

Once again Laszlo felt a surge of bitter resentment that he, and only he, had been exiled to the servants' wing – to a room which he knew was usually used to lodge visiting valets or artisans called to work in the castle. Even Peter's friendly words of reassurance – 'our nearest relation' – did not soothe him. After all, Stefi Szent-Gyorgyi was a first cousin too, and he was with the other guests. Why just me? Laszlo wondered as he sat down in front of the old-fashioned dressing-table.

Old impressions flooded back to him as he sat gazing unseeingly at his ivory hairbrushes laid out in front of him. There was nothing new in the discrimination made between him and his cousins. When he had been a child he had hardly noticed, and when he did he put it down to his being an orphan, with neither father nor mother to protect him. At that time, too, he had romanticized the situation and imagined himself, perhaps after reading some children's book like 'The Little Lord', as a hero of mystery, the young heir to a great position unrecognized in youth only to be triumphantly re-established after years of obscurity. This impression of a mysterious secret was accentuated by the fact that in his presence his father and mother were never mentioned.

His grown-up relations were invariably kind and attentive. At Christmas, and on birthdays, he received the same presents as they gave to their own children; at first the same toys, later there were books, riding whips, 4.10 shotguns or .22 rifles. While at school in Vienna at the Theresianum, when one of his aunts came to take the Kollonich and Szent-Gyorgyi boys for a Sunday outing, or to the opera, or to eat cakes at Demmel's, he was always one of the party and, during the holidays, either here at Simonvasar or with the Szent-Gyorgyis, there was nothing to remind him that he was after all, here, there and everywhere, in the last analysis, a guest.

Only gradually, as he began to grow out of adolescence towards adulthood, did the real truth begin to dawn on him. Little things, minor pinpricks that wounded self-esteem and his pride – noticed perhaps only by one who had been made extra sensitive as a result of being an orphan – revealed the reality of the discrimination against him.

Some of these incidents came back to Laszlo as he sat unhappily at the table in the room usuaily given to visiting guests' servants. One year, when he was about fifteen, the Kollonich children had been bought ponies which were ridden by Laszlo whenever he was at Simonvasar. On one occasion when the Moravian riding master was teaching them how to take their fences (though these were only low bars and hedges) the horse that Laszlo was riding came in badly, fell and strained a shoulder. The next day Niki, then an ill-behaved little brat four years younger than Laszlo, said to him:

'You lamed my horse! I shan't let you ride him again!' Maybe it had only been said to tease, or perhaps it had just been a piece of childish arrogance, since the ponies were ridden by all the

PART TWO

children and only nominally attributed to any one child; for it was the riding master who decided who rode which mount. But to Laszlo, to whom no pony had been allocated, these remarks, uttered thoughtlessly, suddenly brought home to him that he did not really belong and that even his cousins still thought of him more as a dependent than as one of themselves.

Another, more painful memory came to his mind. They were having a boxing lesson and it was an unwritten law that even when they boxed in play, heads shouid not be touched. Laszlo was sparring with his cousin Louis who, though a year and a half younger than he, was a large and strapping youth, headstrong and self-willed. From the start Louis had ignored the rule about blows to the head and Laszlo had begun to lose his temper. By chance he had hit Laszlo on the mouth, loosening one of his teeth and splitting a lip from which blood spurted copiously. The fuss had been appalling: not that Louis minded at all but the princess, told at once by one of the girls' governesses, had been cold and angry and had made Louis apologize publicly to his cousin – even though the bruises on his own face were clear evidence that it was not he who had started their rough play.

Even now he could recall the menace behind his aunt's icy forgiveness. The meaning was clear enough: any repetition of such behaviour would entail automatic banishment. That had been eight or ten years before.

With the passing years he became more and more aware of the gulf that divided him from his cousins, of the financial and social differences that set him apart. And though this awareness never provoked his envy, nevertheless it gnawed upon his consciousness and made him increasingly ill at ease in his cousins' presence. It was, perhaps, the unjustness that had most upset him. Why should he be the one to be exposed to the cruelty of being treated with undisguised contempt by visitors who spent half a day at Simonvasar without noticing his presence, to the disdain of the servants who, with an arrogance they would never dare show to their masters, would, finding themselves along with Laszlo, relax from their obligatory immobility, lounge about and even chat together, something they would never permit themselves if they could be seen by even the smallest Kollonich or Szent-Gyorgyi child?

The second gong, announcing that dinner would be served in five minutes, broke into Laszlo's reverie and sent him in haste to scramble into his evening clothes.

Chapter Two

L ASZLO REACHED THE LIBRARY just as the guests were starting to move towards the dining-room.

At the head of the formal procession the princess was escorted with old-fashioned courtesy by the field marshal, resplendent in dress uniform. Behind him in order of precedence followed other couples, the ladies' hands resting lightly on the arms of the gentlemen who accompanied them. Laszlo joined in at the rear with his cousins for whom no more ladies remained to be escorted. Slowly they progressed through the long music-room to the formal dining hall beyond it. This was an exact duplicate of the marble salon on the other side of the house. It was one and a half stories high and its walls were covered in stucco decorations painted in a butter yellow colour. As the room had been completed at the end of the 1830s, after the great days of the classical revival, the marbleized panels were edged with multi-coloured garlands of roses in high relief, the corners softened and curved. In the centre of the panels were escutcheons of flowers and great wreathes of roses which seemed full of movement and warmth, and gave an air of lightness and festivity to the huge high formal apartment.

In the middle of the hall stood a vast wide table covered with a white starched linen table-cloth which was in turn almost concealed by the profusion of silver objects covering its surface. Down the centre of the table stood eight giant candelabra decorated with sculptured goats' heads and standing on tripods imitating the legs of roe-deer. Between them were ranged several tall oval urn-shaped vases with lids representing swirling acanthus leaves and, placed between the larger objects, a multitude of other high and low covered dishes crowned with pine-cones and pineapples in massive silver. Though the intention had been to reproduce what was thought to be the Greek style, here there was none of the severity of the Empire period. All these objects were elaborately decorated with curves, domes, lattices, bunches of grapes, entwined branches of vine leaves and pearls, so highly polished, so rich and complicated, that the general impression would have been irretrievably restless had not the brilliance of the light from the electric chandelier above dissolved the detail of

PART TWO

over-rich craftsmanship into a unity of glitter. It was the famous Sina service, a treasure in itself which had been made for the imperial banker by silversmiths from Vienna.

The host and hostess took their places opposite each other at the centre of the table, and the other guests ranged on each side of them in diminishing order of precedence.

The dinner started in the usual silence that marks a fashionable gathering. It was as if a devout atmosphere was obligatory, with the guests playing the part of the congregation and the frozen-faced hieratic butler and lesser servants that of the officiating clergy. These last moved round the table in ceremonial silence and intimidating efficiency. Not a plate clattered, not a glass tinkled: the solemn hush was broken only as the butler or head footman poured wines with a soft murmur of mysterious words 'Château Margot '82? . . . Liebfraumilch '56?'

Slowly, under the influence of fine wines and excellent food, most of which appeared in unrecognizable magic disguises, conversation began and a general hum of talk could be heard as the guests bent towards each other, nodding, smiling and beginning to relax and enjoy themselves.

Magda Szent-Gyorgyi turned towards Laszlo. 'Nice things we hear about you!' she said roguishly, looking away from him as she spoke with a quick bird-like twist of the head.

Laszlo had no idea what she meant.

'Oh, don't deny it!' Her tiny rose-red mouth pouted and she went on in a whisper, 'We all know why you've been hiding in Budapest all these months!' Her little pointed tongue darted in a swift movement over her lips as if she were tasting something sweet and she glanced at her left-hand neighbour, Lubianszky. Seeing that he was busy talking to Countess Kanizsay she turned back to Laszlo and with more assurance said boldly: 'Tell me, is she very beautiful?' and then with wide-open eyes, '. . . your little cocotte?'

'What on earth are you talking about?' asked Laszlo, sincerely puzzled.

'Oh, you, you poodle-faker!' Her low voice gurgled with pleasure as she used the slang word a young girl should not have known. 'They had to ring three times before you opened the door and you didn't turn on the light for fear they'd see something of hers, right?'

Then it dawned on him. She was talking about the evening when Peter and Niki had come to his little flat in the evening. He turned angrily to Niki who sat next to him around the corner of the table.

'Did you invent this nonsense?'

But Niki only hung his head in mock shame and, grinning wickedly back, did not answer. He was sitting too far away for Laszlo to go on without attracting attention so, ignoring Niki, he turned back to Magda and was about to speak when the thought flooded through him that if Niki had told this pack of lies to Magda he had surely related them to Klara. Angry as never before that the sweet Klara, so pure and innocent, should have been exposed to the frivolous Niki's thoughtless slanders, the blood rushed to his face.

'You're blushing! See how you're blushing!' Magda whispered triumphantly. 'What a bad fibber you are!'

Before Laszlo could reply a long serving dish floated between them. Like a silver ship carrying on its deck a pile of little grass-green and white striped white hearts, a wonderful and famous dish, the fifth course that evening, was called *Chaud-froid de bécasses panaché à la Norvégienne*. When this battleship sailed away its place was at once taken by two destroyers in the shape of oval silver sauce-boats. The conversation which had been interrupted by the arrival of the woodcock, was finally killed when an arm stretched out towards Laszlo's glass and an unctuous voice murmured in his ear, softly and mysteriously, '*Merle blanc '91*?'

Laszlo looked across the table to where, farther up, Klara sat between Wülffenstein and the Principe. And so low were the *décolletages* that year that all he could glimpse of the girl over the mass of silver ornaments on the table were her head and bare shoulders.

He had not seen her in evening dress for at least a year and it struck him how she had filled out in the intervening months and how much more beautiful she had become. When he had last seen Klara she had been somewhat skinny and undeveloped, almost anæmic, still with the body of an adolescent though she was nearly twenty-two. When he had thought about her, which was often, he had not thought so much about her body but always about her expressive grey eyes. And now, suddenly, she was all woman, radiant with femininity. Her face had a higher colour, her mouth was fuller and redder, her neck and shoulders and the curve of her breasts were all rounded out with the fullness of a baby's flesh and the bloom of ripe apricots, and her pale smooth skin shone with an inner glow, not the glow of alabaster or marble but rather that of some ripe and living fruit. As the sea reflected the sun's rays on the arms and bare flesh of a bather, so the light of the electric chandeliers reflected through the prism of the multifaceted silver touched the pale salmon-colour of Klara's skin with a myriad tiny lights, glowing green and mother-of-pearl on her shoulders, dancing at the corners of her mouth as she spoke and under her chin, moving back and forth with every slight movement she made. A modern Venus Anadyomene, thought Laszlo, gliding above waves of frozen silver. And in his delight he forgot all his previous annoyance.

Klara felt his eyes upon her and from across the table she looked up at him with a smile in her eyes.

He wondered if she sensed how beautiful he thought she was.

By the time the dinner was coming to an end everyone was talking at once and the conversation at the centre of the table was all about the latest political events in the capital. The prince, a member of the Austrian *Herrenhaus* in Vienna, had begun the subject.

'Is it true that the two-year Military Service Bill has been passed? We don't seem to have heard anything about it!' His manner implied that he took it almost as a personal insult that the news had been made public in Budapest before it was known in the capital of the Empire.

Old Kanizsay overheard the prince's words. He could hardly believe his ears. '*Nah, so was!*' He was shocked, for to someone who had started his career in the army when military service had been twelve years, this seemed hardly credible. 'Two years to make a peasant into a soldier! Absurd! Have they announced it in the House? Has His Majesty agreed?'

'Surely His Majesty knows best!' said Szent-Gyorgyi in faint reproval.

'It was forced on the Government by pressure of public opinion,' explained Lubianszky, who never lost an opportunity of putting the blame on the Minister-President. 'Tisza thought that it would help to get the Defence Bill passed. Of course he was wrong, and it's all been for nothing!' And he started to retell the story of the uproar in Parliament on November 18th, stressing how all the Standing Orders had been cynically ignored.

Kanizsay seemed to like this. '*Diese Tintenschlecker! Diese Bagage!* – these penpushers! What rubbish!' he said, referring to the Hungarian opposition, and when Lubianszky turned towards Abady for confirmation, the old field marshal looked in Balint's direction and said:

'*Kennst Du diesen Tisza? Was ist der für ein Kerl? Ist es ein guter Kerl?* – Do you know this Tisza? What sort of a fellow is he? Is he a good fellow?' he asked in a loud nasal hectoring voice.

Balint had to laugh. 'Oh, yes! He is quite a good *Kerl*!'

But Lubianszky was not content to leave it at that. He started to explain at some length what a mistake this show of strength had been, how there was nothing left now for the Government to do but to resign and thereby make legal the disputed amendment. Lubianszky did not have an easy time with his political dissertation as almost every sentence was interrupted when a servant offered him the dessert: a mountainous ice-cream – '*Bombe frappée à la Sumatra?*' – or dishes of whipped cream, biscuits and *petit fours*. Then, as he started again, a liveried arm extended in front of his face and a sepulchral voice murmured in his ear: '*Moët & Chandon Réserve? Tokay '22?*'"

All the older men present – Kollonich, Szent-Gyorgyi, and even Wülffenstein, though he was sitting some way away beside Klara, began to join in the discussion. Only Count Slawata said nothing, though he seemed to listen intently despite the fact that as the talk became more heated the others mostly spoke in Hungarian. With his eyes screwed-up behind the thick glasses in the manner of so many shortsighted people, he listened and observed.

'Are you interested in all this?' asked his neighbour, the beautiful Countess Beredy, her voice tinged with contempt for the nonsense that men seemed to think important. Slawata turned towards her and gazed short-sightedly into her deep *décolletage* which was made all the more provocative because her dress only appeared to touch her arms, shoulders and body here and there, thus affording most tempting glimpses of her body.

'For me,' answered the diplomat, 'they might as well be talking Chinese!'

Fanny laughed, a deep-throated sensual sound that suggested she was recalling some voluptuous memory. At such moments she resembled a languorous cat, her long eyes narrowed to slits, her well-shaped, fine-drawn mouth curved in a feline smile of satisfaction, as if she had just feasted off several canaries.

The host, who tended to lose his temper in all arguments unless everyone agreed with him, was becoming flushed and cross even though his views were almost identical to those of Lubianszky. Both of them hoped for the fall of Tisza, but Kollonich thought it should come later, after he had had an opportunity of clearing

PART TWO

up the present mess, while Lubianszky was for his immediate dismissal. At this moment, thought the prince, everyone should back him up in his role of 'chucker-out'.

'Of course we should support him,' he shouted. 'What does it matter if he's a Protestant! It's a dirty job and he's just the man for it!'

The princess glanced swiftly at Balint, who was the only Protestant among them, and then, perhaps to cover up her husband's tactlessness, she started to get up. Everyone immediately followed suit and the hostess led them out of the great dining hall. Now there was no ceremony and no order of precedence, and so the guests left the room talking animatedly and noisily. Only the servants maintained their stony calm.

Coffee, whisky and soda and liqueurs were served in the drawing-room and in the library.

Talk! Talk! Talk! Later, the young people drifted into the music-room where they danced to the music of a gramophone just brought from England.

Fanny Beredy whirled in Laszlo's arms.

'You dance well,' she said 'You have a marvellous sense of rhythm.'

'I am a musician.'

'How interesting! The piano?'

'Yes! And the violin.'

Laszlo was only replying mechanically. He was watching Montorio waltzing with Klara, leaning closely towards her. It was too much, he thought. It shouldn't be allowed! It was almost indecent.

'And I am a singer, a mezzo,' said Fanny. 'Could you accompany me?'

'Perhaps. I've never tried!'

'Well then,' said Fanny, laughing and looking up into his face, 'Let's try!' And her hand tightened on his shoulder.

Laszlo did not answer: all his attention was taken by Klara and Montorio.

Really, it was indecent how that man danced, he thought. And what an unhealthy colour his skin was; perhaps he had some disease. With hatred in his heart he saw the prince bending close to Klara's ear, his pencil-slim moustache just brushing her skin as he whispered something to her. The girl laughed and turned her head away, and when her eyes found Laszlo's she smiled fondly.

'Tomorrow I'll send over for my music!' said Fanny.

'I'd like that,' replied Gyeroffy; but he was thinking how sweet and good Klara was, how beautiful, how kind...

They danced on, and it was well past midnight when the company dispersed.

Laszlo found his way alone to the servants' wing. The long stone-flagged corridor was lit only by a few bare bulbs here and there.

As he passed the narrow back stair he saw Szabo the butler, who had changed out of his tailcoat into a light grey jacket, standing on one of the lower steps, leaning against the wall. He seemed to be waiting for someone.

Back in his room Laszlo undressed quickly and went to bed, but he soon discovered that the room was so hot that sleep would be impossible. He got up and went to the window, but search as he might he could find no way of opening the huge panes. Instead he went to the door and, leaving it ajar, returned to his bed and turned out the light.

He was almost asleep when the glass door from the courtyard to the corridor clanged shut. A woman's quick steps could be heard on the stone slabs, and then some whispered words, low and urgent: a man and a woman were talking, but Laszlo could only catch a word or two.

'No, no! Mr Szabo! No! Please? I am not...'

And a deep commanding baritone replied: 'Don't play the fool with me. You know damn well...'

Sleep overcame him and he heard no more.

Chapter Three

AT NINE O'CLOCK the men of the shooting party gathered for breakfast in the dining-room.

They came in one by one, twelve of them, most of them sleepy and in a bad temper, and sat down at the large table.

Everyone was dressed in shooting clothes and though no one was dressed exactly alike it was clear that they followed two distinct fashions. The first was the traditional Austrian *Waldmann* style which with one exception was followed by all the older men, including the host, Kanizsay and Lubianszky: the exception was

PART TWO

Szent-Gyorgyi. These all wore jackets of grey loden cloth with green lapels, deerhorn buttons, green waistcoats, all old and patched with leather. So ancient and worn were their clothes that they might have been taken for superior *Jäger*, or forest guards, which indeed would have pleased them immensely as it would have given the impression that they had spent all their lives in the woods, that being their only occupation. Among the young, Duke Peter belonged to this school, though he was by no means orthodox, being in shades of slate-grey and moss-green and everything he wore was new, in itself a heresy.

The other fashion was for everything imported from England – Scottish homespuns in a variety of design and cut, and an even greater variety of colour. Szent-Gyorgyi and all the younger men had adopted this fashion which gave infinite opportunity for individual taste and imagination. As a result even their characters were reflected by their clothes.

There was nothing ostentatious about Antal Szent-Gyorgyi. Everything he wore seemed simple, modest, unstudied. Yet a close look at the deep and perfect harmony shown by everything he wore revealed a high sophistication of taste. His clothes were so discreet, with no false notes, that without any attempt to draw attention to himself, his tall greyhound-slim figure dressed in exquisite harmony was clearly the most elegant of them all. In contrast, Fredi Wülffenstein, in a confusion of multi-coloured checks, looked like a walking chessboard. Even his socks, for which he had searched London, were of Shetland with huge tassels of red, blue, green and orange. Perhaps Count Slawata belonged to the English faction, but his grey cloth suit buttoned to the chin was so unassuming that it was impossible to define. Walking behind him the irrepressible Wülffenstein, conscious of his own glory, and making no attempt to lower his voice, said: 'That bugger looks like a cheap chauffeur!'

'... or a mechanic in his Sunday best!' added the mischievous Niki, just as loudly as they followed after him, laughing together. After all what foreigner understood Hungarian?

On the well-swept sandy drive of the castle courtyard twelve carriages were drawn up ready for the guests. Ten of them were high old-fashioned yellow coaches, pulled by heavy-boned horses and driven by peasant coachmen with handlebar moustaches who seemed ill-at-ease in the Kollonich livery which, obviously, they only wore on grand occasions. Two other vehicles clearly came from the castle stables. Drawn by fine-bred horses with noble heads and driven by two assured clean-shaven coachmen, one was a long-slung open landau, provided for the field marshal so that he would not have too far to heave his heavy body, and the other was the host's light wicker-work chaise which he also used in the summer for the deer shoots.

Two men stood by each carriage, one an estate worker to carry the heavy cartridge cases, the other either the guest's own loader or one of the estate foresters provided by the host. These last carried the guns and, on their jackets, a number – the same number was borne on the carriage, attached to the lantern. These numbers would be used throughout the day to show the guest where he should take his place. Although the guests never changed their numbers, they were never placed in the same order, but varied from one stand to another according to the difficulty of the shoot and the guest's skill and social position. It was a system introduced by the Archduke Josef and because it simplified the problem for all the guns to find their places without search or discussion, it had been adopted at most of the important shoots. Indeed the organization of a great shoot, with twelve guns, several teams of beaters, game carts, carriages for the guests, keepers, head keepers and uniformed heralds, needed almost as much planning as an imperial manoeuvre.

The carriages set out along a seemingly endless avenue of poplars that traversed the great estate. It rose over the slight eminence of the low hills, dipped into valleys where the road was covered by a thin film of sand, rose again over the next hillock, and in the distance was veiled by the mists that rose each morning from Lake Balaton far to the west. On each side were fields, each of several hundred acres bordered by well-trimmed thorn hedges, and here and there were farmhouses and barns and clusters of small farm-workers' cottages surrounded by smaller fields, brown when fallow and green when in cultivation. Between every second or third field were stands of timber, L-shaped with a wide gap at their centre. At these places, already prepared, were the numbered stands for the guns, ten in the middle and one each at the outer edges.

The carriages stopped at the first stand, and the guests descended and placed themselves according to the numbers accorded them. As soon as they were in place one of the heralds sounded his horn to signal the first team of beaters to start their

PART TWO

work. At once could be heard the sound of whistling, the beaters never shouted, and a strange sound of rattles, made by two wooden balls chained to a small plank of wood, which when shaken did not panic the pheasants so that they flew back over the line beaters but instead drove them forward towards the gaps between the trees and the line of guns already in place. The faint sound of rattles grew louder as the beaters approached.

And so it continued the whole morning. The only change was in the order of the guns, and this had been cunningly arranged so that the old field marshal, Szent-Gyorgyi, Prince Montorio and the host were always placed where the birds were most abundant. Why one place should be better than another was a mystery to the uninitiated, for the wooded plantations all seemed the same.

And yet it was so. For every place where the important guests had been placed there were clouds of pheasants, whereas beside them the gun had only the choice of those birds his neighbour failed to kill. The secret was that in front of the main line of beaters three or four more specialized men, like advance scouts of an advancing column, would herd the running birds in the right direction while in the wooded thickets, low hedges of broom had been planted which, like funnels, directed the pheasants to rise in front of the most honoured guests.

This was justified by the necessity to make the guests of honour feel gratified by the quantity of game provided for them to shoot. However, the most honoured guests were not always the best shots, as was the case with Montorio, and even more so with old Kanizsay, whose natural clumsiness was not helped by his pair of old-fashioned smoking shotguns to which he had remained faithful for more than thirty years.

Consequently, if the most important guests failed to kill many of the birds that came their way, the bag would suffer and the honour of the host would suffer too. To correct this the best young shots would be placed on either side and young Duke Peter would whisper instructions: 'You'll have to help 'em, especially the old one!'. Laszlo Gyeroffy, Stefi Szent-Gyorgyi and Niki, as the best of the young shots, took turns in standing beside the field marshal.

Laszlo and Stefi followed their cousin's instructions discreetly. They stood slightly back and only shot the birds he had missed or let pass. Niki, on the other hand, had no such scruples – he shot swiftly and accurately before the old man had had a chance even to lift his gun to his shoulder, and when he did, he not infrequently saw the bird at which he was aiming already falling to the ground at his feet... and he was the guest of honour!

The old soldier began to get angry, and the angrier he became so the thick smoke from his guns curled round him like a symbol of his wrath. During the first beats he merely grumbled, but later, as Niki took no notice, he called out, though to no avail: '*Nicht vorschiessen!* – Don't poach!'

It was during the last beat before lunch that the storm broke.

This time old Kanizsay had been placed at the corner of the woods, with only Niki beyond him. Lots of birds came his way, and at first he tried a few shots, but every time he was too late. Niki got in before him and each bird fell before he could let off his gun.

The old man gave up the unequal struggle. Scowling, he wedged his gun between his large chest and even larger belly and refused to raise it no matter how many shouts of 'Cock to the left! Cock to the right!' would reach him. He was like Jupiter Tonans, hurling thunderbolts of anger and swearing like a trooper. Niki, disregarding the old gentleman, continued to pick off every bird that came his way.

When the beaters appeared Kanizsay exploded.

'*So ein Lausbub! So ein Rötziger!*' In his anger he used the choice vocabulary of the parade ground, the words with which he would castigate the stupidity of raw recruits. Niki, by now thoroughly alarmed, tried to excuse and justify himself, but nothing would pacify the enraged old man. Even when Kollonich tried to calm him by scolding his son, Kanizsay went on until he had run out of breath – and even then he went on panting and roaring like an old buffalo run berserk.

Only Szent-Gyorgyi remained aloof, a faint ironic smile on his lean aquiline face; nothing would draw him into other people's quarrels just as he would never, following English etiquette, poach anyone else's birds. In this, as in everything else, he was indomitably correct.

Still unmollified, the field marshal marched off to lunch with the others. Only when the meal was served and he found himself surrounded by young ladies did his natural sense of gallantry allow him to relent.

Tactfully, Duke Peter placed him between the beautiful Fanny and Magda Szent-Gyorgyi and, after a few glasses of wine, the old field marshal started to chat merrily with them. Then he remembered the terrible words he had used to Niki, smiled, and reached across the table touching his glass to Niki's.

After luncheon a long carriage ride was to take the guests to stands in a more distant part of the estate.

Just as Balint was getting into his carriage, Slawata called to him.

'Let's go together. I would enjoy a talk with you,' and he turned to the two loaders, his and Balint's, and said in fluent Hungarian: 'You two go in my carriage.'

As they carriage moved off, Balint turned to Slawata.

'I didn't know you spoke Hungarian?'

'Really very little. I once served in the 7th Hussars and I try to keep up what I learned then. Sometimes one hears interesting things.' And he smiled a little maliciously behind his thick spectacles, no doubt recalling the previous day's political discussions or even the mockery of Wülffenstein and Niki when they had laughed at him behind his back. 'I haven't seen you for some time,' he went on, 'How are you? What are you doing now? I always thought it was a pity you left the Diplomatic Service.' This was, perhaps, just a piece of social politeness as he continued 'Yet perhaps not! Perhaps it is better so. You should know what is happening in Hungary. Observe, study. With your experience abroad it should prove useful, even invaluable, in the future. You don't belong to any party?'

'No.'

'Quite right. Much the best policy. Don't take an active part, don't involve yourself. Just observe and, above all, don't join anything! This world won't last long!'

Balint's interest was aroused. He recalled that he had heard people say that Slawata was intimate with the Archduke Franz Ferdinand, and he felt a sudden conviction that the reason why the Counsellor to the Foreign Office now wanted to talk to him was to sound him out and possibly recruit him to the party that was gathering around the Heir. He answered cautiously and vaguely, while encouraging the other to continue. At the least he might get some idea of what was being talked about in the private discussions in the Belvedere Palais, for here in Hungary all was rumour and gossip, for no one knew the truth.

'The Old Man can't last for ever, and then it will be the Heir's turn,' Slawata went on in the lowered voice used when dangerous matters are discussed. 'A few years, maybe? How many? Four?

Five? And then it will be His Highness! This is a certainty. This is what we have to plan for! Franz Ferdinand! When he rules, things will begin to change. Then we'll see the end of this worthless "Dualism" so dear to the Old Man's heart. Of course it's dear to *him*; he took his coronation oath on it. But the next ruler hasn't promised anything, nor will he! He'll rule on new principles; his plans for the Empire are all ready. But he'll need some new men, men who haven't compromised themselves by getting too involved with this old and useless system.' He went on explaining speculating how 'Dualism' would be replaced by centralization, constitutional certainly, but based on the real up-to-date statistics. Numbers were important. Provinces should be re-formed according to nationalities; and all should be represented in one grand central council which would control everything; economy, army and navy. There might be a trial agreement with the Catholic Slavs of the south. Everything was possible. Only one thing was sure: today's order would change. If Tisza succeeded in discrediting the loud-mouthed Hungarian opposition it would be all for the better. What was needed was a belief in the future and recruits to the principle of change. In the meantime the main thing was to build up the army. With a strong army His Highness would impose order everywhere.

Balint listened, petrified in growing horror. He barely spoke, but occasionally put in some slight query, or offered a mild disagreement as Slawata talked on in the confidential manner of one to whom service in the Ballplatz must be an everlasting bond, like Freemasonry, as if, even after leaving the service, the fact of having been initiated into the secrets of Foreign Office coding meant an eternal and confidential link. He drew an enthusiastic picture of a shining future in which they could share, in which the Austria-Hungary of today would no longer be the second Sick Man of Europe but the Master of the Balkans, a real power, with the dynasty's second sons placed in the positions of importance and the rule of Vienna extended to the Sea of Marmora!

Their carriage neared its first stop.

'Think over what I've said, Abady! There can be a great role for you if you play your cards properly!' As they got down from the carriage, Slawata clapped Balint on the shoulder and said: '*Unter uns, naturlich!* – just between us, of course.' With these ritual words, he winked behind his thick glasses and moved over to join a newly arrived group of ladies.

The loaders and cartridge carriers had taken up their places at the numbered stands and were waiting for the signal that the beaters had started. In the meantime the guns chatted in pairs until it was time to take up their new places.

Wülffenstein, who loved explaining, especially to those younger than he, was busy laying down the law on everything to do with codes of honour, fashion, and shooting – even politics, though that was of secondary importance to him. His judgements, which he thought infallible, were based on only two criteria: it was done or it was not done – by gentlemen of course.

He was busy putting Niki to rights when the ladies arrived.

'Oh, what darling little yellow cartridges!' cried Mici Lubianszky, pointing to Wülffenstein's elegant fitted case.

'English, of course!' said Wulffenstein carelessly. 'You can't use anything else. Impossible! These German and Austrian makes are just rubbish!' He stamped his English brogues until the tassels on his socks bounced. 'All they can do is ruffle the birds' feathers!'

If he had noticed that Antal Szent-Gyorgyi was standing behind him it is possible that he would not have risked such a remark.

'Really? How interesting!' said Szent-Gyorgyi. 'Would you mind lending me some? I've only been using Austrian ones today and yours might improve my aim!' He spoke quietly and seriously, with no sign of mockery in his voice and a completely straight face. Nevertheless the mockery was there for all to hear, for Szent-Gyorgyi was well known to be the most skilful among them all. He shot calmly, with style and elegance and all his birds – he never missed – were shot cleanly through the head. No matter how high they flew, no bird that came within reach of Szent-Gyorgyi's gun was ever wounded or fluttered writhing and broken to earth, but rather fell, wings folded, head bowed, diving to oblivion in a graceful arch; and when picked up there was only occasionally to be seen a small drop or two of blood on its beak.

'Of course. Help yourself!' said Wülffenstein, a trifle restrainedly. Niki turned away to hide his laughter and quickly moved over to join his Uncle Szent-Gyorgyi who took up his station quietly holding two of the English cartridges in front of him with as much reverence as if they were blessed saints' relics.

When the ladies arrived Laszlo was already in his place at the end of the row on Montorio's right. He watched as they got down from their carriages and gradually made their way towards him.

The two Lubianszky girls and Magda joined some of the guns farther along the line but Klara and Fanny Beredy continued on their way, passing Antal Szent-Gyorgyi, Wülffenstein and Duke Peter. I'll bet Klara stops beside Montorio, thought Laszlo bitterly; but both girls came right along the line until they stopped beside him.

'Is it a good day?' asked Klara.

Almost simultaneously Fanny said, 'I've sent for my music; it'll probably be here by tonight.'

Klara said 'You might even get partridges at this end!' just as Fanny was saying: 'Will you accompany me as you promised?'

This antiphonal conversation continued for a few minutes as both girls gave the impression that they were expecting the other to move away. However the beaters' horn sounded and the soft rattling began to be heard in the distance.

Klara closed the lid of the wooden cartridge case and sat on it. Laszlo offered her his shooting stick.

'No!' said the girl, 'I won't take it away from you. This,' she went on with unconcealed emphasis, 'is my place!'

Fanny Beredy turned away with a faint smile and moved slowly, her hips swaying gently, towards Montorio. Laszlo, watching her involuntarily, thought how beautifully she was dressed, in softly draped tweeds that clung to her supple body showing off the curves of her figure as if she were wearing only a light wrap over her naked flesh.

The beaters were still far off. In the distance a hare or two dashed out from the cover of the trees and fled into a field of clover. Once or twice one would stop, sit up and look round before moving off at a light comfortable trot, the white spot on its tail bobbing rhythmically up above the green leaves. Occasionally a gun would go off. Otherwise there was silence but for the faint distant sounds of the approaching beaters.

'It wasn't very nice of you to be in Budapest so long without letting us know,' started Klara, smiling at him.

The young man, seated on his shooting stick, tried to explain that as he had begun his course at the Academy so long after the others he had to work extra hard to catch up, and that this would not have been possible if he'd allowed anything to distract him from his work. He talked too much, over-justified himself, always conscious that that mischievous Niki had spread the rumour that he had only hidden himself for the sake of some woman. Several times, uneasy about Niki's lies, he repeated that he had seen no

PART TWO

one, not a soul, since he had returned to the capital. Why hadn't he written? No! That would have been impossible. If he'd written they would have answered and invited him, and if he'd been invited he couldn't have resisted the temptation to accept. And he needed to study, study, study.

Klara listened, the same secretive smile on her face, and he could not tell if she believed him or if she smiled because she did not. But she was sweet and kind and seemed to understand, even to share, his hopes, enthusiasms and ambitions. What she really thought he was not then to discover because just as Laszlo started to ask if she thought he was doing the right thing they were startled to hear Peter's stentorious voice calling out: 'Laszlo! What are you up to? *Tiro! Tiro!* You've already let by three cocks!' And he had to jump up, reach for his gun and get to work to 'help' Montorio. He was only able to speak to Klara again when the second band of beaters began their work.

'Do stay on a few days when the others go,' said Klara, speaking generally, but showing by her glance that she was referring to Montorio.

'I can't! It'll be difficult enough to catch up these three days. I promised myself to be back by Wednesday night.'

'One day more? Just one! There's such a mob here now. and besides,' she went on flirtatiously, 'you must play to me. Wasn't I your first audience?'

Laszlo remained silent, torn but inflexible.

'You must remember. It was your *Valse Macabre*? I was the first to hear it, and I was still at school.'

'Yes, the *Valse Macabre*.' They looked deep into each other's eyes, a long, long look.

A shrill whirring rose in the air and cries of 'Partridge! Partridge!'

Laszlo jumped up again, his gun to his shoulder. He emptied both barrels, changed guns and emptied two more at the swift-flying covey above him. Three birds fell, rolling as they hit the ground from the speed of their flight. One fell at Klara's feet. She bent down and picked it up and holding it in one elegantly gloved hand she caressed it with the other.

'Look, how beautiful he is! He might be asleep. There's not a spot of blood on him!' She lifted the bird to her lips and again and again gently kissed the soft grey feathered breast and, tenderly smiling, looked up into Laszlo's face.

'Do look! It's so strange!' She blew into the downy feathers that fluttered around her mouth and there was something essentially voluptuous both in the way she parted her lips and in her questioning look.

Once again they were interrupted. A mass of pheasants flew over them and Laszlo had his work cut out to bring down the cocks and do the job for which he had been invited.

When the beat was over the girl walked away quietly and joined a group of other ladies. Laszlo remained at his place, his loader and cartridge-carrier busy with the beaters picking up the fallen birds, jealously ensuring, for the honour of their master, that everyone knew what a good shot he was and how many birds had fallen to his gun. So they shouted to each other: 'There's another cock over there! That one's ours! There are two more beyond those bushes!' each man showing as much pride as if he had shot them himself.

Gyeroffy stood silently at his place. The men thought that he was counting how many brace they were laying at his feet; but he did not even see them, his heart was beating too fast.

To Laszlo it seemed that the late afternoon was filled with a mysterious scent.

It was dark before the shooting party reached the castle. In the drawing-room a lavish tea was served, but no one stayed long. Excuses were made that they must dress for dinner, and so they all retired to their rooms. But the truth was that after such a tiring day everyone was exhausted.

Chapter Four

THE PRINCESS WAS READY FOR DINNER long before the ladies who had gone out with the guns. She had had her hair dressed for the evening before she came into the drawing-room for tea so that when she returned to her own rooms she only had to change her dress.

'Ask the Duchess Klara to come to me when she is dressed,' she said to her German maid as soon as the finishing touches had beeen put to her gown and jewellery. The maid hurried away leaving the princess alone at her dressing table. When the woman had left the room she rose and moved over to the sofa that stood at the foot of the great State bed. It was from this sofa that

PART TWO

Princess Agnes ruled the family. She always sat there when either her husband or children gave trouble or needed advising as to their conduct. She would issue a summons to this spot and they would come to it. No one knew whether she had chosen the place by chance or whether she realized quite consciously that her authority was underlined by the fact that sitting there in the centre of a vast expanse of formal satin upholstery she had a hieratic advantage over her visitor who must either stand submissively before her, or walk up and down, or take a seat on one of the small chairs with which the room abounded. It was a strategic position and it was generally felt that she knew it.

The princess waited, and, as she did so, she recalled just how much planning and hard work she had devoted to arranging a marriage between Montorio and her stepdaughter. Early in the spring, before they moved to Vienna for the Derby and the racing season, she had persuaded a mutual friend to mention the idea to the Prince's mother. When she arrived in Vienna she had immediately given a lavish garden party at the Kollonich Palais to which were invited only those guests whose presence would prove to Princess Montorio – who had been born a Bourbon-Modena – that both families had equal standing in Viennese high society, the 'Olympus', as the inner circle of ruling families was known and to which only those to be found in Part Two of the *Almanach de Gotha*, and not all of them, were accepted. The party, which had been a great success, had also been extremely expensive, as the princess had thought it necessary to redecorate certain State rooms which had not been used since the death of the Sina grandmother, to re-lay the elaborate parquet floors, to install a quantity of modern plumbing and to wire the huge gardens with electric light. She had also filled the whole place with displays of imported tropical flowers. Not that the princess minded this lavish expenditure – though Louis Kollonich had not stopped nagging her about it for months afterwards – for it had certainly achieved the desired effect of strengthening the social position of the Kollonich family to the point at which the ladies of the Olympus seemed to greet her with added deference. Soon after the party Princess Montorio herself mentioned the idea of a marriage between her son and Klara.

Since then the two ladies had corresponded and met frequently. Each praised the qualities of their candidate and the Princess Kollonich had indirectly let the Princess Montorio know that even though Klara's portion from her mother was only modest the 'good' Louis Kollonich would provide an ample dowry to be paid over in full on the day of her marriage. Naturally none of this had been discussed openly – it had been conveyed discreetly by the good offices of their mutual friends, as God forbid that anything so vulgar as money should be mentioned between them – and this left the ladies free to dwell only on such subjects as praise of character, kindness, good manners, health, love beauty and, of course, breeding.

The inevitable understanding had been reached and the Prince Montorio had been asked to shoot at Simonvasar. Although the young man was no sportsman, this would give him unrivalled opportunities to make the formal proposal his mother had made clear he was now ready to do.

And what had happened? Quite ostentatiously Klara had seemed to ignore his presence! Not once during the first day's shoot had she visited him at his stand; indeed she had joined everyone but him, and this despite the fact that Klara had been told distinctly that this handsome, elegant and eligible young man had been invited for her sake alone. Such contrary behaviour could spoil everything and undo all that hard work and expense! If it were allowed to go on, this most desirable suitor would go away feeling he was not wanted; and then his ancient name, his title, his immense fortune and acceptable good looks would soon get scooped up by some worthless girl and all their plans would be for nothing.

With this passing through her mind Princess Agnes waited for her stepdaughter. She wanted to warn and admonish her before it was too late. Not, of course, that she would mention all the planning that had led up to the present moment – no young girl would take kindly to the idea that her happiness had needed planning – but she would have to be told how thoughtless it was for her to behave in this way and so jeopardize the best offer she was ever likely to get!

<hr />

The princess knew she was right. She was conscious that she wished only the best and most suitable and splendid future for Klara, whom she loved every bit as much as she did her own children. This made it even more important for her to intervene.

The door opened, and Klara came in, freshly bathed, in deep *décolleté*, all pink and sweet-smelling.

'You have asked for me, Mama?' she said, and sat down opposite her.

PART TWO

Klara was very fond of her stepmother, who was the only mother she had ever known, her own dying at her birth. She had been two years old when her father had married again and this handsome dark-haired lady, 'Mama' in her earliest memories, though she could be severe, had always been kind to her, perhaps even more so than she had been to her own children.

'My sweet!' When she was angry the princess invariably began with this endearment. 'Why are you neglecting Montorio? Oh, yes you have! You've been avoiding him all the afternoon.'

'Mama, I didn't avoid him. It just happened, really! Anyway I did spend some time at his stand.'

She hesitated; then seeing her stepmother's stern look, she faltered and gave herself away. 'I . . . Anyway I'll be sitting next to him at dinner tonight. I thought that would be enough!'

'You will sit next to him at dinner because I arranged it like that, even though your Uncle Antal could take offence as it should really be Magda's place, not yours. Montorio knows this perfectly well, so it makes it worse that you neglect him and don't even seem to notice his presence. Don't deny it! You made a point of avoiding him at the shoot, and that's a fact!' She paused, and then went on: 'You avoided him most conspicuously. You went to everyone else, even to Laci! This is absurd! To Laci, throughout the whole of the last beat and that a double one, and Montorio was next to him. It couldn't have been more obvious and more insulting! You cold-shouldered the man who only came here for your sake and who had even asked your father for an invitation so that he could meet you.'

The girl's ocean-grey eyes darkened. That scoundrel Niki must have sneaked, she thought, and she remembered all her grievances against him throughout her childhood, how he had invariably told tales about her to the governesses and to her stepmother. All these old sadnesses now rose up to reinforce her present distress and she replied, her voice hardening:

'Every move I make,' but here she paused as she did not want to go on 'your spies report to you', so she changed it to 'Every move I make is difficult to explain.'

Just for a moment storm clouds had seemed to gather between the two women; but these were dispelled when Klara changed what she had been going to say.

Princess Agnes said drily: 'That's why I have to think for both of us!' Now she changed her tone. The time for harshness was past. The girl had realized that she could not pull the wool over her stepmother's eyes and that was enough. Now was the time for frankness and common-sense. In a friendly and down-to-earth manner the princess started to explain what an eminently satisfactory choice Montorio would be. She enumerated his virtues, how nice he was, how he had no vices like drink or gambling, how he worked hard managing his family's vast estates in Carinthia. She spoke of his great town house in Vienna on the Herrenstrasse, of his close relationship to the most important families, how his mother was a real Bourbon and not one of those trumped-up morganatic branches that gave themselves such airs. Their ages were right, too, Montorio being only thirty-two. It was rare in life to find, just at the right moment, a *parti* so suitable in every way. She ended up:

'Your father will give you an ample dowry so you wouldn't be dependent on your husband. Really, Klara, everything would be for the best! Why you'd be the first lady of Vienna!'

Klara got up, turned away slightly and walked a few steps. She was searching for an answer that would sound convincing.

'Yes, Mama. Everything you say is true, of course, but somehow... well, I don't know.'

'What do you mean, you don't know?'

'Somehow, in spite of all that... I don't want it!'

'Why ever not?'

'Somehow...' and she spread out her arms in a wide gesture, wiggling her fingers in the air as if trying to clutch at the right word to express the confusion of her thoughts, 'Somehow I'm just not interested.'

The princess moved her still beautiful if somewhat massive shoulders in a little shrug of disdain. 'Not interested? Why not, may I ask? He is very elegant and very handsome. What's more, he's in love with you!'

'Perhaps... but I'm not interested,' repeated the girl, happy to have found even this inadequate reply.

'Strange! Almost unnatural in the young healthy girl!' Then, as a new suspicion crossed her mind, 'You're not in love with anyone else, are you? Then I'd understand.'

'Oh, no, Mama. How could you?' replied Klara, a little too quickly, and then, to correct the impression such a swift denial might have, she went on, 'but I could never decide... I wouldn't want to decide, not so quickly and so suddenly. It's such a great decision!'

'But you don't have to decide yet! Of course not! But in the

PART TWO

mean time do show just a little interest. Keep him warm. I don't have to tell you that he'll only propose when you want him to. That always depends on us women!' And she laughed softly, with feminine superiority. Then she rose and went to her stepdaughter, put her arms round her and kissed her. Her voice became warm and cajoling:

'My darling little Klara! I only want the best for you when I tell you these things. You must remember that such a chance as this doesn't come twice. Young men today don't seem to think much of marriage; they're getting almost cunning, and if you miss this chance? You're past twenty-three, don't forget, and it's high time you were married. Isn't it so, my little Klara?'

Her last words were spoken softly and lightly, but they were meant to tell. And her laugh, equally light, was as full of warning as it was of practical feminine wisdom.

Klara blushed but did not answer.

'You promise you'll be nice to him?'

'All right! I promise! Only that! Nothing more.' Her hand turned the knob and as she went out the princess called after her:

'Your father wants this very much too!'

Klara went out and closed the door. The older woman's last words had spoiled in an instant any effect that their talk might have had, because Klara knew from long experience that her father only did what his wife wanted and that everything always happened in the way the princess had decided; though by that time the prince had usually decided it was what he had always wanted. What worried Klara was that if her father did not get what he had come to believe was his own will he could become very angry indeed.

Why must she menace me with Papa? thought Klara mutinously as she descended the stairs, though by the time she reached the bottom step she had consoled herself with the thought that she had only promised to tolerate Montorio's courting. She had not bound herself to anything that might affect... No! She could not harm anyone by that!

And so that evening, she flirted lightly with Montorio at dinner and afterwards: and on the last two days of the shoot she often went to stand beside him.

But she did not allow things to go any further.

Chapter Five

ON THE AFTERNOON OF THE THIRD DAY Balint found himself at the end of the line. It was a quiet stand with few birds coming his way, and it was where he nearly always found himself for, as a comparatively near relation, second cousin to the hostess, and an indifferent shot, he had no claims to a better place and he was not needed to 'help' the guests of honour.

Although the beaters were rattling away furiously in the distance the birds were all being directed to the far end of the line where guns were going off as rapidly as in battle. Where Balint stood only a few wise old cocks moved quietly about in the brush having discovered that they should never run in the direction they were being herded and, above all, that they should never leave the ground. They strutted in two's and three's not far from Balint, only occasionally putting out their emerald-green necks, waiting for a good moment to run to the next block of cover.

Balint had never been an ambitious or even very eager shot and now he welcomed his quiet corner as it gave him time to think.

He was still troubled by the talk he had had with Slawata. Whenever he had been alone in the two days that had followed, the Counsellor's indiscreet confidences came constantly to his mind insisting that he decide where he stood. That much was clear: the whispers about the Heir were true; he was planning the breakup of the old Hungarian constitution.

Balint pondered the programme outlined by Slawata: centralization, rule by an Imperial Council, the ancient kingdom of Hungary reduced to an Austrian province, and national boundaries to be re-arranged statistically according to the ethnic origin of the inhabitants! Why all this? To what purpose? Slawata had given him the answer: Imperial expansion in the Balkans so that feudal kingdoms for the Habsburgs reached the Sea of Marmora; and it was all to be achieved with the blood of Hungarian soldiers and paid for by Hungarian tax-money! So it was merely to help Vienna spread Austrian hegemony over the nations of the Balkans that Tisza was to be helped to build up the Hungarian national armed forces.

It seemed now to Balint that both parties in Parliament were fighting instinctively, but without a clear understanding either of their motives or of the inevitable results of their policies and strategy. While Tisza battled to strengthen the army, he could have no inkling that, once strengthened, it would be used to suppress the very independence it was designed to assure – and when the opposition delayed the implementation of Tisza's policy by petty arguments about shoulder-flashes and army commands, they were unaware that, inadvertently, they were providing ammunition for those very arguments that in the near future would threaten the integrity of the constitution.

How simple everything could seem if one looked only at the figures, those cold statistics that took no account of people's feelings and traditions. How much would be destroyed if men were to be treated as robots! What of the myriad individual characteristics, passions, aspirations, triumphs and disappointments that together made one people different from another? How could anyone ignore all the different threads of experience that, over the centuries, had formed and deepened the differences that distinguished each nation?

How would anyone believe that any good was to be obtained by adding the Balkan states to the already unwieldy Dual Monarchy and so increasing the Empire to a hundred million souls with differing traditions and cultures? Of course armies could be recruited and young men could die, but great States evolved only through centuries of social tradition and mutual self-interest; they were not imposed by bayonets. To believe the contrary would be as mad as the folly which had put the Archduke Maximilien on the throne of Mexico.

Balint had been taken so unawares by Slawata's disclosures that he had not known how to reply to the the diplomat's proposals. This distressed him because it revealed to him his own chronic failure ever to know the right answers. He needed deep reflection before he could make up his mind what to say.

Seated on his shooting stick at the end of a quiet shoot, everything became clear to him, not in any ordered sequence of words or arguments that like tiny pieces of mosaic gradually revealed a finished picture, but rather as a painter, before he put paint to canvas, envisages the finished effect.

⁂

'Why, you look just like Rodin's *Penseur*!' The mocking voice came from Fanny Beredy who, a smile on her beautiful face, had come up and stood beside him. Balint offered her his seat.

'What deep, interesting thoughts am I disturbing? I hope you're not cross!' she said, accepting the stick.

'Very!' laughed Abady, who only now realized that the first beat was finished and that he must wait for the second line to start. He sat on the ground at Fanny's feet.

'I have to ask. With you Transylvanians it's so difficult to know where you are! One's never sure of one's welcome!' She laughed, and when Balint protested, she went on, quite seriously: 'But it's true! *You* can't see it, but I can. You're quite different from the rest of us here. You're an individual, not moulded out of one pattern as we are – the group here that is. One can never be sure what your reaction will be, or why!'

'Perhaps from living with bears?'

'Oh, they are sweet! Nice clumsy bumbling little bears. Oh, no, it isn't that. The only two I know are you and Gyeroffy, and you two are much more amusing animals.'

'Monkeys, perhaps? They can be amusing!'

'Oh, no! More like birds of prey, hawks, always gazing into the far distance, to the horizon, and never noticing what lies at their feet, what is close at hand.'

'And what is close at hand?'

Fanny gave him a rapid sideways glance, and then looked away. 'Oh, I don't know. I just said it not meaning anything in particular,' she continued, chatting lightly and jumping from one subject to another, perhaps so as to deflect his attention from what she had just said.

'Cocks to the right! Cocks to the right!' The beaters' cries brought Balint back to his feet, shooting what he could of the sudden rush of birds in the sky above. He also bagged a few hares on the ground.

As suddenly as it had begun the beat was over. While the fallen birds were being collected, most of the guns went back to the waiting carriage. Balint waited until only he and Fanny, the two Lubianszky girls and Laszlo remained behind.

'Gyeroffy's a cousin of yours, isn't he?' asked Fanny. 'He said he'd accompany me and I had my music sent over yesterday, but somehow he seems to have forgotten.'

'How boorish of him! I'll remind him.'

'No! Don't say anything about it! It's not important. It was just seeing him there in front of us...' She quickened her pace and moved forward between the rows of beaters carrying the bag to the game carts.

PART TWO

Abady, following behind her, noticed her strange swaying walk. Fanny placed one foot precisely in front of the other and Balint realized that if she were walking through snow she would make a single line of tracks like a wild cat.

As the guests gathered in the red drawing-room Balint turned to Laszlo and asked: 'Are you going back tonight?'

'I think so. If I start at half past nine I can catch the midnight milk train.' Laszlo spoke somewhat uncertainly. He did not look at his cousin as his eyes were fixed the end of the room where Montorio and Klara were sitting on a sofa and sipping tea.

Klara had chosen this place so that her stepmother, from her chair in the next room, could see how well she was obeying orders.

'I asked because Countess Fanny mentioned her singing. I think that she's a trifle hurt that you didn't play for her yesterday. Perhaps you should say something to her?'

'Oh, Lord! I completely forgot. Well, maybe I'll stay on; it would be churlish not to. One night more or less won't make all that difference.'

Balint looked sharply at his cousin. He regretted immediately that he had given him a reason for staying on as he sensed that Laszlo had taken advantage of this pretext even though his real reason was something quite different. Noticing how tense and tormented his cousin looked, and how his gaze always returned to the sofa at the end of the room, Balint realized that what he had always assumed was a mere cousinly flirtation had taken on for Laszlo a fatal seriousness: fatal for Laszlo, for Balint grasped what apparently his cousin had not, that there would be a thousand obstacles standing in the way of any happy fulfilment to such a dream. He wondered if Klara returned Laszlo's love and, if she did, whether she had the determination and stamina to overcome what lay ahead. Dismissing these thoughts from his mind, he said: 'We can leave together if you like, tomorrow morning?'

'Why not? We came together, we go together,' and his look made the words into a promise. Then, to justify what he was doing, Laszlo went over to the chair where Fanny was sitting and started to talk about what she would like to sing that evening.

The long Bösendorfer grand stood at one end of the music-room and in its curve, leaning back against the mellow walnut sheen of the piano, stood Fanny Beredy, conscious that her pose showed her supple figure at its best and that her salmon-pink dress and golden honey-coloured hair stood out advantageously against the apple-green of the walls and the ivory and dove-grey of the panelling. Apart from Fanny herself, everything in the room was in pastel shades, even the furniture standing around the walls and the cherry-wood parquet floor. High above, only the stucco swags of flowers that bordered the ceiling were in stronger shades of angry blue and gold.

Candles burned in two three-branched candelabra on the piano for, when electric light had been installed, no one had thought to put a point nearby.

Laszlo was playing soft roulades while the other guests came in and sat down. Several armchairs had been placed in front of the doors into the library and here the princess and the older ladies were seated. Behind them were their husbands, who had most unwillingly been induced to abandon their cards, all except the field marshal who had chosen a sofa near the piano either because he was a little deaf or else to be closer to the beautiful Fanny.

When everyone had taken their places Fanny moved round to Laszlo and gave him a sign that she was ready. He played the first notes and she began to sing – it was Schumann's *Mondnacht*.

She sang beautifully, with the ease of a well-trained voice, which, if not exceptionally powerful, was rich and warm especially in the lower register; and from the moment she started it was clear that she was entirely absorbed by the music. The gay, flirtatious, light-hearted Fanny that everyone knew was changed into a completely different person; simple, sincere, without either artifice or the smallest sign of self-consciousness, a transition as remarkable as it was unexpected. She stood very straight, seemingly mesmerized by the music, and her eyes, normally hooded and watchful like those of a bird of prey, opened wider and wider as if she were hypnotized by some apparition being brought ever closer on the wings of the song and only fading as the last notes died away. Then she closed her eyes with infinite resignation.

At Fanny's first notes Laszlo had looked up in surprise; he had not expected such perfect artistry nor such depth of feeling, and, as she sang, so he played, no longer out of politeness but for sheer love and devotion to the music.

There was applause, the discreet, polite applause to be expected at a society gathering. Fanny bowed her head slightly in acknowledgement, but she seemed far from conscious of her audience, so wrapped up was she in the music that made her so happy. She turned to Gyeroffy and put before him the next song, *Still wie die Nacht, tief wie das Meer*, an old piece by Koestlin.

Laszlo started the prelude and, as he took it slightly faster than she wanted, she placed her hand on his shoulder and with her fingers lightly indicated the slower tempo she felt to be right. Her touch had nothing sensual in it; it did not seek for pleasure, nor was it a caress, rather it underlined their mutual enjoyment of the music, that and nothing else. As Fanny continued to sing her hand remained on Laszlo's shoulder, sometimes signalling emphasis or a change of speed, the physical link ensuring that the two musicians were as one in every detail of their performance. They were bound together by their love of the passionate music they played, and they could have been quite alone, for the candle-light on the piano acted almost as a fire-screen between them and the listeners at the other end of the hall. Other songs followed: Brahms's *Feldeinsamkeit*, a Paladilhe, some more Schumann.

They were so absorbed that they did not notice when some of the men crept quietly away to the card-tables in the library, nor when, a little later, most of the young disappeared too. To Laszlo and Fanny, only the music they made together existed until, after about an hour, the butler appeared silently at the door, like the Ghost in *Hamlet*, and bowed to the hostess to indicate that tea was served.

The princess was immensely relieved after the boredom of sitting so long in silence, and sensing that most of her guests were bored too. As soon as Fanny finished the song she was then singing and started to search among her music for something to follow it, the hostess rose, swept across the room in her most regal manner and asked, with a patronizing smile: 'Are you not tired, my dear?' And though she received a swift denial from Fanny, she went on, 'Tea is served. I am sure you need a cup after so much ... er ... singing!'

'Thank you! Indeed I would,' said Fanny. 'I'll join you as soon as I have collected my music.'

The princess gathered her guests and left the hall. Only old Kanizsay remained, sitting straight upright, his legs spread wide, hands on knees, appearing to see nothing. The field marshal was so deep in thought that he had not noticed the others leave.

'Are you tired?' Fanny asked Laszlo.

'I'm not! But you, Countess. If anyone should be, it should be you? I could willingly go on all night, with the greatest of pleasure.' And he sat down again at the keyboard.

'Then let's try some of these, though I don't know them very well yet.'

She picked out an album of Richard Strauss who was just then beginning to become famous. 'I love these ones, but they're rather difficult. Would you like to look them through before we try?'

Laszlo played a few chords. The harmonies and transitions were unexpected and would need careful playing until he knew them. As he practised, Klara, who had left with the others, came back into the room, gliding silently with her special walk, and stood beside him.

'Oh, Strauss!' she said.'I will turn the pages for you.'

Laszlo gave all his concentration to the music, playing carefully through the accompaniment of the song Fanny had chosen so as to master its complicated harmonies. Then Fanny, her hand still on his shoulder to guide him and sometimes pressing her waist against his shoulder as she leant forward to read the words, sang again. So Laszlo had the beautiful Fanny, rapt in her music, on one side while, on the other, Klara sat close so as to turn the pages of the song. When she reached her white scented hand up to the music stand her arm brushed his sleeve and her firm breast pressed against him; but now Laszlo was so engrossed in the music that he hardly noticed a contact that at any other time would have sent his blood racing. The music absorbed him totally, and yet it did not go smoothly. When they started, Klara was a little late in turning the pages, but from the middle of the song it went wonderfully well.

Then they stopped and stood up and moved towards the drawing-room, in silence for somehow their spirits were strangely dampened.

The field marshal, breathing heavily, heaved himself up and followed them. He bowed to Fanny and kissed her hand. '*Schön, schön, wunderbar schön* – So beautiful, marvellously beautiful!' His old eyes were moist with emotion. '*Dank, Dank, schöne Frau, vielen Dank!* – Thank you, beautiful lady. Many, many thanks!'

As they moved towards the drawing-room he asked Klara who had been the composer of the last song.

'Strauss,' said the girl.

'Strauss? Johann Strauss? *Grossartiger Kerl!* – What a clever fellow!' and putting an arm round Klara's waist he pressed her to him and started humming one of the waltzes of his youth, one of those tunes to which he, a young, dashing and handsome lieutenant of Hussars, had danced and carried all before him in the ballrooms of Lombardy.

In the drawing-room everyone was beginning to say goodbye as most of the guests were leaving early in the morning. Gaily they made plans for meeting again in other country houses or at the next shooting party.

Fanny, who was also leaving early by car with her brother, found Laszlo standing alone:

'Shall I see you again soon? Thank you again, you played marvellously! When we know each other well it will go even better.' She told him that she would probably be in Budapest for Christmas or, at the latest, in the New Year, and that he must come and see her. 'You will come, won't you? And we'll make more music together!'

But Laszlo could only answer with automatic politeness, with a bow and a few words of thanks. He hardly noticed the beautiful woman who was paying him such compliments for every nerve in his body, all his senses, were concentrated on the far end of the room where Klara was sitting with Montorio. He could not see her face, as she was sitting in an armchair with her back to him, but he could clearly see the prince, opposite her, leaning forward in his chair and talking earnestly, his expression deeply serious. He's asking her to marry him, thought Laszlo with agony in his soul, he's doing it now, now!

What if she were accepting him? What could he do about it? The inexorable laws of politeness ensured that he must stay where he was while a cruel Fate decided Klara's happiness ... and his own. And even if he did walk over towards them he could never get near, for Niki and Magda Szent-Gyorgyi had seated themselves close by as sentinels, guards to make sure that Montorio would not be disturbed.

It seemed like an eternity until Klara and Montorio rose and joined the others who were making their farewells, and though he tried to get a word with Klara he was prevented by her leaving the room with a group of other girls to go upstairs to bed.

Laszlo found himself alone. All the others had gone. He waited, though he hardly knew why, without reason, without purpose, without hope.

The footmen started to collect the teacups and glasses and to carry out the trays. They switched out the lights in the salon, in the hall and on the staircase and one of them stood about waiting to finish until Laszlo had left. He could stay no longer and moved slowly to go back to his room at the end of that long dark service passage.

Once again, as he passed the service stair he saw Szabo, the butler, on the first landing. This time he was not alone but held a girl in his arms, one of the maids, very young and very pretty, who was struggling to get free and pleading: 'No! No, Mr Szabo! Please let me go, I beg you! ... Please, Mr Szabo ... please!'

Nauseated, Laszlo moved on quickly but not before, in a shaft of light coming from above, he had recognized the girl's face: it was Klara's personal maid, a country girl who had been with her since she had been in the schoolroom. The little scene accentuated his worry over Klara. It seemed symbolic, as if the butler's treatment of the maid foretold the rape of Klara by Montorio.

Back in his room Laszlo sat down still dressed, distraught and staring at nothing. He was tormented by doubts and unanswered questions. Had that fellow Montorio proposed in the salon? Was that why he seemed so serious? Had he dared? And what had Klara replied? Had she refused him, or what? This 'or what' seemed to place an icy hand round his throat, suffocating him, pushing all the blood to his burning head. Feeling he would die from not knowing, he walked up and down, bumping into anything in his way. It was like pacing a prison cell, airless and confined. The very room seemed filled with terrible thoughts from which he must somehow escape. He opened the door and stepped into the cool spacious corridor where he could breathe and move about, and maybe escape the phantoms that pursued him. Up and down the long corridor he paced...

The movement and the coldness of the air calmed him so that, eventually he could once again think rationally and begin to weigh up the situation, analyse the probabilities, the circumstances. He tried to recall every word, smile, movement and glance that Klara had given him, how she sat with him at the shoot, how she had picked up and caressed the dead partridge, blowing into its feathers and looking all the time at him, how they would exchange almost secret glances over the mass of silver on the great dining table.

Even though she had been seated beside that man at every meal, their eyes had met. If she loved Montorio it was impossible that her eyes should have sought out those of Laszlo and smiled at him in mutual understanding. Even the idea was repulsive! How could he have imagined that she was in love with that loathsome man, had even perhaps accepted him, when it was to Laszlo that she directed her secret glances?

More calmly, and now more slowly, he continued to walk up and down the corridor until, getting tired he returned to his room and went to bed. But although he turned out the light he could not sleep.

From a room above he heard some muffled sounds, then silence, and then some footsteps. He fancied he could hear someone crying. Much later a door slammed which, in the silence of the night or maybe only in Laszlo's keyed-up imagination, sounded like the blast of a cannon.

And again it seemed as if someone were crying...

Most of the guests left early in the morning. Only four remained, the field marshal and his wife who were going over to Fehervar in the evening to catch the night express to Fiume as they were going to spend some weeks in Abbazzia; Magda Szent-Gyorgyi, who was staying on while her father and brother went for a few days' shooting elsewhere; and Laszlo, who, when Balint was already waiting in the carriage, sent word to say he wasn't ready but would follow him to Budapest that afternoon.

Louis Kollonich and Niki would be leaving that evening as they were invited to shoot hares and pheasants on one of the archduke's estates. They planned to leave just as the sun set and in the meantime they had decided to have a little informal shoot in those parts of the Kollonich property where the old cocks had not been properly cleared. The prince loved these quiet days when he could go out with just a few keepers and the dogs, and he was even more pleased when old Kanizsay sent to excuse himself, saying that he had a touch of rheumatism. So much the better, there would be no waiting about for other people and they would all have a relaxed day with just his two sons and his nephew Laszlo. Impatient to set off, the Prince hurried them through breakfast and they had hardly had time to eat before they were hustled out to the waiting carriages.

In the castle courtyard were just two vehicles: the host's low-slung wicker chaise, into which he jumped quickly and drove off alone; and a long *tarantas*, a Russian-style cart with a bench in front and cushioned planks running lengthwise between the front and rear wheels. The young people climbed into this, the men on the front bench and, behind them, Klara and Magda sitting sideways. They did not take a coachman as Peter would drive.

Just as they were setting off a little maid ran out and handed Klara her gloves: 'You left them on the table, my lady!' she said.

Laszlo recognized her as the same girl he had seen struggling in Szabo's grasp the night before, and thought how sad she looked. Peter whipped up the horses so quickly that Klara's 'Thank you!' was lost as they sped down the drive.

They were in such excellent spirits that everything was fun. In the clear pale sunlight the hoar frost glistened silver on the fields and trees, and the boys, even in their father's presence, made a game of everything, shooting in front of each other, poaching the other's birds and behaving in a manner they would never have dared during one of the grand shoots.

Laszlo laughed and joked with the others, but his eyes betrayed him and remained clouded and serious no matter how hard he tried to keep up with the general high spirits. Always he was hoping to have a moment alone with Klara so that he could ask what had happened the night before.

But no chance came. Every time he attempted to get her on her own he seemed to detect a spark of mockery in her eyes. She eluded him, and he became increasingly hurt.

And so it went on the whole morning with Laszlo becoming ever more tortured. At last he just followed Klara in silence, and the dry leaves crackling under his feet were the only accompaniment to the gloom of his thoughts. All his attention was riveted on Klara, so much so that he barely heard when someone spoke to him. Even so he just managed to keep enough self-control to disguise his feelings. Though in agonies of doubt and jealousy, nothing showed in his face when he spoke to Klara or to Magda, and he would reply to their questions as lightly as if he had nothing on his mind.

Even when they got back to the castle and sat down to tea, he could still not get near enough to her to get an answer to that question that never ceased to scream inside his head.

When it was time for Niki and his father to leave they said goodbye to the princess and the Kanizsays in the marble salon and, accompanied by Klara, Peter, and Magda – with Laszlo just behind them – moved through the great hall to the entrance where their large Mercedes was waiting. Passing through the library Laszlo slowed down; what was he doing, going to the door to see his host depart? What business was it of his? He was only another guest and a quite unimportant one at that, only invited to help with the shooting. Why, his cousin Peter had made it quite clear, even if unintentionally, that it was his skill with a gun that was wanted, not he himself, not Laszlo Gyeroffy! Why should he then go to the door as if he were of any importance?

He stopped by one of the long windows of the library. It was growing dark and, as the lights had not yet been switched on, long strips of the dying light of day came through the french windows and covered the polished parquet floor with a glow like that on ice. Outside everything had taken on a bluish grey colour, the lawns, the box hedges, the bare trunks of the trees were all grey, as were the lilacs and other ornamental shrubs which had been planted in avenues to lead the eye in three directions; to the artificial lake, to the miniature Greek temple with its Corinthian columns, and to a vista of the great plain that lay between the castle and Lake Balaton.

Looking at this late autumn landscape, where nature seemed already to have sunk into the sleep of winter, Laszlo felt welling up inside him a great sadness.

The park had been laid out after the best English landscape models. It gave the impression of being a great deal larger than it was in reality, even though here the trees did not grow tall in the sandy soil which itself was burned brown each year by mid-August. But now, in the twilight, the bare trunks and the ground lightly shrouded by the mists of evening looked mysteriously sad, and spoke to Laszlo only of his own sorrow and loneliness.

He said to himself that if Klara were to marry Montorio he would never come to Simonvasar again, never! So he stood there, feeling that he was saying goodbye for the last time and must therefore try to etch the scene on his memory so that, later, recalling the hell he was now going through, he would be able to recapture every detail and, in his unhappiness, recall the scenes where once, so many years before, he had been happy and free of care.

When they were still children they had run about those lawns, played croquet behind the rose gardens – and always he had sided with Klara and hidden among the lilacs with her when they had played hide-and-seek. In every corner of that garden there were a myriad childhood memories.

The sound of chatter behind him brought him back to earth. Quick, running footsteps and laughter told him that Peter and Magda were on their way back to the red drawing-room. Then his heart contracted as he heard light steps behind him: it was Klara.

'I love this view, especially at dusk!' As she reached up to put her hand on the handle of the shutters her arm brushed Laszlo's shoulder. 'I look at it often... when I am alone.'

This was the moment to ask. Now or never he must know if Montorio...? But he did not know what to say. His voice was hoarse with emotion. 'Klara! Tell me?' It was too late; she had already started to speak.

'Don't you remember? There! You rescued me from that poplar! What a coward I was! I didn't dare jump.'

'Of course I remember.' He hesitated. Should he ask his question now? Again it was too late. Before he could open his mouth Klara turned towards him, very slowly, and when they were face to face she looked him straight in the eye. Though she did not speak he knew that she too was asking him something.

Her red lips were slightly parted. She was waiting for something, and somehow her whole face seemed different. This was a Klara he had never seen before. Of course she was the same but something about her was new and mysterious. As she looked at him, Laszlo forgot his misery, his doubts, his loneliness and despair. Everything was wiped away as he knew that he had only one thought, one desire; to take her in his arms and kiss her. But still he hesitated. Would she be annoyed, take offence, if her childhood friend and playmate suddenly abused her confidence, took advantage of her weakness and her vulnerability and forced a kiss on her? How could she know how desperately, how deeply, how fatally and forever, he loved her?

For a moment they stood, neither of them moving; gazing into each other's eyes. Then Klara turned and with gliding steps made her way back to the drawing-room. Laszlo followed despairingly, knowing that he had let another chance escape him. What a fool he was! Why hadn't he kissed her? What an utter, utter fool he was not even to ask!

Laszlo had to find another opportunity to be alone with her, so after dinner he asked if she would like to hear his latest composition. When they went towards the music-room they were joined by Peter and Magda, who were enjoying a light-hearted cousinly flirtation and who accepted Laszlo's suggestion with joy knowing that they could talk in private if Laszlo were at the piano.

While they sat down at the far end of the room Klara joined Laszlo, but instead of sitting beside him as she had the night before, she stood in the curve of the piano facing him. Laszlo played

PART TWO

a few chords and then looked up. 'Go on,' she said and closed her eyes.

'I based this piece on an old Szekler melody,' said Laszlo as he began to play.

It was a strange tune, strange and slow, like a musical sentence endlessly repeated in different keys with unexpected dissonances and harmonies, moody and sad. When the repetition seemed almost unbearably poignant, it broke off with a cry of yearning, a dream-like sob of frustrated desire, and then returned to the little tune with which the piece had begun. At the end an unresolved chord left a question hanging in the air.

'It's beautiful! Please play some more!' said Klara, not moving from where she stood.

Laszlo played two more pieces. One was the half-finished fantasia he had started in Budapest and in which he tried to portray all the sounds of the city. Called *Dawn in Budapest*, it was wild, chaotic music with a profusion of rhythms and contrasting harmony. The other was a low and sensually beautiful Nocturne which in a legato melody gently rising expressed all the agony of desire. And, when it seemed as if the heart must break, it died away in a hopeless pianissimo. It was new music, cruel and full of sorrow, far from the sugar-sweet melodies of the drawing-room.

As each piece came to an end Laszlo would look at Klara, enquiry in his eyes. But she just said: 'Please go on! Please play some more!' standing motionless where she was, leaning against the piano with her bare arms, bare shoulders, and the curve of her breasts swelling the soft material in which she was clad. She stood there with half-closed eyes, her lashes casting a bluish glow on her cheeks. She seemed to be listening to the music in a trance from which she only awoke to say: 'Please go on! Please play some more!'

Now Laszlo started a little Transylvanian peasant song.

> If I could catch a little devil
> I'd put him in a cage
> And shake him up and down until
> He jumped about in rage!

And as he played he'd speak the words, change the rhythm, play it fast and then slow, now in one key now in another, giving the little tune sometimes in a high treble clef sometimes deep in the bass, a helter-skelter medley of bubbling, teasing good humour, interspersing the melody with sudden shrill notes or thundering chromatic scales, imitating the sounds of cymbals, flutes, brass and drums, conjuring up the sound of a whole orchestra out of one piano. It was something Laszlo loved to do and he knew he did it well, and the music released and revealed all the latent violence within him that he could never show in speech or gesture.

While from Laszlo's darting fingers the music still laughed and danced, Klara suddenly straightened up. Deeply sensitive, she had become aware of a slight movement in the salon beyond her: it was the Kanizsays getting ready to leave to catch the night train. Slowly she moved to the centre of the room from where she could see what was going on in the drawing-room and where she too could be seen.

The old Kanizsays were now saying goodbye. The princess went with them to the entrance hall and all the others followed to pay their respects, kiss hands, and say farewell to the guests of honour. After they had gone the princess turned to Laszlo.

'How beautifully you play, Laci!' she said. 'Quite beautifully! I wish I had been able to hear and enjoy it more. You really do play well!' and she touched her nephew's cheek affectionately. 'What a pity it's so late! God knows I'm tired today.' And, giving her hand to be kissed she started upstairs followed by the girls.

As they reached the first landing Klara looked back at Laszlo, lips parted again as they had been at the library window, as if she wanted to tell him something. She stood there just for a moment, and then she too was gone.

The next morning Laszlo slept late and it was already after ten when he awoke. Those few minutes with Klara in the library, and the release he had found in playing his music to her, had given a new turn to the doubts that had tortured him the day before. He was still not entirely happy about Montorio, but his doubts were now alloyed with new thoughts, new ideas, new hopes.

What had been Klara's intention in standing so close to him at the library window? How slowly she had turned towards him! What was the question behind the deep look she had given him? Would she really have been angry if he had kissed her then? And later, at the piano, why had she remained standing, never looking at him, rather than sitting beside him as she had the previous evening? It was impossible that he could have in some way offended her for at the window . . . ? And yet she had never once looked at him as he played! Again, when she gazed down from the stairs, had he imagined that her lips framed an unspoken question?

PART TWO

These thoughts had chased through his mind until he fell asleep, and were still with him when he awoke. Yet the world seemed better after a good night's sleep and, as he lay in bed and stretched, he decided that he would stay on until Sunday evening for by then he would have found time to say so many things.

He dressed quickly, remembering that the girls usually came downstairs about eleven. When he was dressed he went to the library. There it would be the most natural thing in the world to glance through the great albums that lay open on the library tables, and from there, too, one could look out into the garden and hear steps on the stairs and in the entrance hall.

In the library all was silence and peace. On the upper shelves the books glowed mysteriously in the light from the long windows and the parquet floor that had seemed like ice in the twilight shone golden in the winter sun. The gilded titles on the leather-bound books glinted in the light. One side of the great room, that opposite the windows, was brilliantly lit, while the rest of the room which was not directly reached by the sunlight seemed dim in comparison; the doors to the entrance hall and the little spiral stair which led to the upper gallery were deep in shadow. The loveliness of the morning seemed a good omen to Laszlo as he stood there and waited to see what the day would bring.

After about a quarter of an hour Szabo the butler came in and in his ceremonial tones said: 'Her Grace has asked if the noble Count would be so good as to visit Her Grace in her sitting-room upstairs!' He then bowed with all the dignity of a court official and left the room.

'What on earth is all this about?' thought Laszlo. 'What can I have done for Aunt Agnes to issue one of her summonses?' He recalled the many occasions in his youth when regal commands would come from his aunt whenever any of the children were to be scolded into obedience.

Full of apprehension, Laszlo hurried upstairs by way of the little circular stair to the gallery and down the corridor that led to the small sitting-room out of which opened the princess' bedroom. He was relieved to find his aunt, not on the fatal sofa but sitting in an armchair by the window.

'My dear, dear Laci, come in! You've been here for five days and we've had no chance to talk.' She stroked his hair as he bent to kiss her hand and then kissed him lightly on the forehead. She smiled fondly at him.

Nothing in her manner showed how worried she really was. It

had only been the previous evening when her suspicions had been aroused. During the whole shooting party the princess had been disturbed and mystified by Klara's indifference to Montorio's wooing. A word or a glance from her and the prince would have offered marriage at any time during the last three days, but though Klara had entertained him obediently it was clear that she had only done what she had been told to do and that she had skilfully side-stepped any opportunity for the prince to declare himself. Why had she done this? What was the explanation for this behaviour, when everything depended on her, and only on her. It could not be mere caprice, for the princess knew her stepdaughter well enough to know that she was never capricious. Only one other reason was possible – the girl must have a 'crush' on someone else! That was it! *Elle a un béguin!* . . . but who?

Then the princess remembered how she had been told that on the first day of the shoot, before she had had her little talk with Klara, her stepdaughter had been twice with Laci during the afternoon instead of beside Montorio. And after Peter and Magda had rejoined her after saying goodbye to Prince Louis, it had been some time before Klara and Laszlo had come in together. Then there had been that long session at the piano after dinner the previous evening after which she had noticed a peculiar expression on the girl's face, as if she were wrapped in remote dreams. Emotion was not good for young girls; neither was too much music. Young people should not remain alone together for long periods unless there were swarms of guests to occupy them! It was only the faintest of suspicions, barely formulated; nevertheless the princess decided that she must act at once. If it were true, no good would come of it. For this reason that she had sent for her nephew, and she would talk to him very sweetly.

'Peter has told me what a great task you have undertaken at the Academy, how hard you study!' The princess made it clear from her manner and way of speaking that she approved and sympathized with the path he had chosen. 'Why should everyone feel they have to go into politics? It is wonderful if someone has a talent and wants to develop it. Dear Laci, I'm sure you will do great things with your music. You have a great talent! Still, it wasn't very kind of you not to let us know you were back from Transylvania, not to write or send us word. You know how I've always been like a mother to you, don't you! I was rather hurt, you know, but it doesn't matter. At least you have been with us now.' She was carefully to say 'have been' in the past tense, but

PART TWO

Laszlo, starved of affection, was so grateful to her, so appreciative of her kindness to him, that the nuance escaped his attention.

Kissing her hand again to show how touched he was by her kind words he begged forgiveness for his neglect of them in Budapest and began to pour out to her all his plans and ambitions, what the professors had said of his work and, as always when he spoke of music, he became carried away by his enthusiasm, describing his visions of a new kind of music, of daring new forms and harmonies.

Though she hardly understood anything of what he was telling her the princess listened to him with apparent attention only occasionally interjecting an encouraging word: 'Ah, how interesting that would be!' or 'Dear Laci, that's beyond me!'

'I love your enthusiasm, your devotion to your music. You must promise to play for me next time you come!' This time Laszlo noticed what she was saying, the little phrase 'next time you come' tolled in his ears, for was he not planning to stay now, was he not here, ready, and could play for her that afternoon? But his aunt went on, not giving him the chance to speak: 'What a pity, as you're taking the midday train that there won't be another chance today! I've ordered the big carriage for you, so you'll be quite comfortable!'

The princess was still smiling, but her look was implacable, and her words were an order, severe and irreversible.

Laszlo felt suddenly cold, too stunned to find words.

'Of course. Yes . . . the midday train. I don't have much time!'

The princess, having delivered her broadside, continued to speak in the gentle, affectionate tone she had adopted since her nephew had come to her room. But though she talked gently, pouring the ointment of family affection into the wound she had herself just inflicted, she was watching Laszlo's face with close attention. Was he in love with Klara? Was he courting her in secret? Princess Agnes still did not know, and Laszlo, accustomed as an orphan to hide his feelings in public, was careful to keep his face expressionless and not to allow anything in his words or manner to betray him. Blandly, therefore, he talked on for a little while and then rose to say goodbye.

'I really must go and pack!' he said as he bent over his aunt's hand.

He closed the door of his aunt's little sitting-room slowly, with perfect control, and then, though the main stair was closer he went automatically back to the library by the way he had come. After such a heavy, totally unexpected blow only his feet knew where they were leading him; in his mind he could only think: They've thrown me out! They've simply thrown me out! The words drummed in his brain: They've simply thrown me out!

He found himself on the little library stair and there, leaning against the carved railing, stood Klara.

'Good morning, Laci,' she said, coming towards him and holding out her hand. 'I love to look down from here. Everything looks so different, so beautiful!'

Laszlo leaned on the smooth balustrade, with Klara so close that their shoulders touched. 'Look down there,' she went on. 'See how strange it is, it only shines where the sun touches.'

They stood together in silence. Laszlo thought: I should take her in my arms now. Kiss her! One kiss at least before they throw me out! But before he could make a move the girl stirred slightly, straightened up and took a few steps along the library's upper gallery. Then she turned, stood once more against the balustrade, her body leaning back: 'These are all old French novels from the eighteenth century. Poor stuff, all very silly – but look how beautiful the bindings are!'

Again they stood side by side in silence, and again Laszlo thought: If only she'd look at me! If only she'd look at me as she did yesterday and I could be sure she would not be angry, then I would kiss her before they throw me out!

But again the moment passed, and Klara moved away, back across the landing, and stood in front of a door that faced that of the princess's sitting-room. Leaning back against the doorway, she looked once more up into Laszlo's face, her whole expression one of mute questioning, of expectancy. Now! thought Laszlo, Now! Take her in your arms, you ass, and kiss her! It's obvious that's what she wants, what she's yearning for! As these thoughts crossed his mind, he glanced involuntarily at the door to his aunt's room. Would she come out and for ever banish him from the house?

Perhaps Klara sensed what was in his mind, for she drew away and said lightly: 'You've never seen my new little home? Papa's just had this room done up for me.'

She opened the door and went in. It was a small room with just one window, furnished with English furniture upholstered in floral glazed chintz: even the walls were covered in the same material.

'Isn't it pretty? It's so cool and smooth to the touch; I love to touch it!'

Laszlo stepped into the room behind her. They stood together

PART TWO

by a chest of drawers. The girl raised her fingers to the wall. 'It's fresh and cool, just as if it had been iced!' With the movement, her breast touched the young man's arm. They were very close.

Now, at last, he put his arms round her and drew her even closer. Their lips met and for a long time they were sealed together in a long hungry kiss. Klara's hand went up to Laszlo's shoulder, her fingers searching the nape of his neck, caressing. Their kiss could have lasted forever for she seemed to promise herself to him with the last drop of strength in her. Her body was soft, yielding, seemingly without bones, nothing but melting flesh, yearning for fulfilment; and it was his, only his. Only when they had no more breath left did they draw apart.

'You must go!' whispered Klara. 'Leave now, at once!' Her arms held him away from her. 'Go now! They'll be looking for you. The carriage is already waiting.'

All along the bumpy country road to the railway station and in the train compartment itself, Laszlo felt himself to be riding on a soft billowing pink cloud. He felt no movement and saw nothing of the country, though it was bathed in a clear sober light and the fields and meadows stood out clearly in the bright winter sunshine. Everything around him had the unreality of a fairy tale and even when the carriage darkened as the train entered the station at Fehervar, it seemed the effect of magic and not because the carriage was in the shade of the station roof. Sitting looking out of the window as the train moved on, he saw nothing of the lake, bordered with ice, nothing of the reeds on the shore, nothing that passed before his eyes. Everything was a dream-land invisible to all but him.

Even the quite modest speed of the train was like a dizzying vortex. Laszlo felt as if he were borne on wings, being hastened to a blissful unknown paradise. Before his eyes there was the image of Klara looking at him with her mute, appealing gaze before she had lowered her lids over her ocean-coloured eyes in the ecstasy of their kiss.

He arrived at Budapest after what seemed like a journey of a few seconds only, still in the same disordered fever. By now it was night and the lights of the twin cities that were connected by the bridges over the great river were reflected a thousand-fold by the water beneath, a feast of glittering splendour placed there expressly to celebrate his joy.

When Laszlo arrived back at the house near the Museum, the

porter's assistant collected his bags from the fiacre while Laszlo himself ran ahead carrying only his gun-case. Once back in his little flat Laszlo hurriedly unpacked, putting his coats on their hangers and the other things in drawers, helter-skelter, not noticing what he was doing nor how crumpled everything was. And crumpled everything was, for when he had hurried to his room at Simonvasar he had thrown all his things into the suitcases, boots, jackets, evening clothes, shirts, pushing them down in no order, punching them and even stamping on the cases to close them with as much passion as if Montorio, the dead body of the vanquished Montorio, had been inside.

As soon as the cases had been emptied he went into the living-room, no longer minding the shabbiness of his humble little rented room. Now he gloried in it for it it seemed only right and suitable that it should be from here that he should start his road to fame, to dazzling success, to world-wide triumphs – and, above all, to Klara, that angel he would possess for ever and ever. Everything that he might obtain in life, the conquest of music, of society, the fame would only be an ornament, a wreath of gold and silver treasure to pile at her feet, to enhance her beauty, a diadem to crown her radiant head. Everything would be a tribute to Klara.

He paced up and down the little room, clasping his hands, flinging wide his arms, the fever which had mounted in him ever since the kiss in her room increasing in intensity until he could have climbed the walls to embrace the whole world.

He went over to the window and flung it open, the cold evening air rushing in as he gazed out over the darkness of the garden, past the huge block of the Museum to a dark shape in the distance: the Kollonich Palais. Ah! There he would at last be accepted, not as a childhood playmate, not as an amusing fellow who entertained the family and who, like a gramophone, could make music when people were bored, not as an elegant dancing partner or a useful shot; and, above all, not as a poor relation! No! He would be there by right as Klara's fiancé, her bridegroom and finally, though he hardly dared formulate the thought, so radiant did it seem, as her husband!

Laszlo stood for a long time before the open window. Outside the lights shone on the boulevard; streetcars, brakes screeching and bells tinkling, approached and faded away; smoke hung over the houses, opalescent, shimmering. The roof-tops stretched away into an infinite distance and he felt himself floating above the city, a Power, a presence that lorded itself over all before him. Gone for ever was the feeling of inferiority that had subdued and depressed him for so many years. Klara's kiss had absolved him from all previous misery.

And so, oblivious of the menace of the cold night air that swirled around him, Laszlo stood at the open window, arms flung wide in a gesture that embraced the whole universe.

PART THREE

Chapter One

BALINT DID NOT GO BACK to Transylvania until the middle of December. Then he took the night train from Budapest, which was supposed to leave at eleven in the evening and, at six in the morning, arrive at Kolozsvar where he would find his rooms ready for him, with a hot bath, breakfast, and more sleep if he wanted it. However, the winter of 1904-5 was exceptionally severe and Balint's train, which could not leave until the Vienna express had arrived, was late departing.

Waiting for the train to start Balint thought about the events of the previous days and found it impossible to sleep. While all around him trains shunted and clanked in monotonous repetition of the same noises, he felt like a fugitive, as if he were running away, fleeing from the need to decide which side he should take.

After the momentous debate on 18 November, it was some time before the House met again. From the day that Tisza announced the strengthening of the Rules of Order, rumours, many of them mere malicious gossip, began to circulate freely. Every day there was something new, and the following day it would be contradicted. Today the Speaker had resigned, tomorrow he had hired special bodyguards to eject trouble-makers from the House; the day after he had had a stroke, and the day after that he was taking fencing lessons preparing for the inevitable duels that the next session would bring. There were rumours, too, about the government. Tisza had gone to Vienna to resign. Tisza had come back from Vienna more belligerent than ever.

Never before had the newspapers attacked a Hungarian Minister-President with such open venom and personal insult. The cruelest, most outspoken articles were written by Miklos Bartha with such a masterly control of logic that Balint had almost been convinced by him, despite the violence of his views.

The editorials in the conservative newspapers were more moderate, but their verdicts were just the same: Tisza must go, and when his head had fallen a new cabinet would legalize new Rules of Order which in themselves were, of course, both necessary and useful. This two-faced argument, formulated with one eye on the opposition and the other on the Emperor in Vienna, deceived no one.

The views expressed by the newspapers set the tone for discussions in the National Casino Club which was still the capital's political storm centre. Here members of all the parties would collect in groups, in the billiard-room and in the Deak Room, everywhere. The loudest talkers were always the youngest and above the uproar made by patriotic members or party candidates was always to be heard, shouting louder than anyone, the voice of the Austrian-born Fredi Wülffenstein, who declared that his Hungarian blood boiled at such contempt of the Constitution and that he would fight anyone who contradicted him.

Balint had been to the Casino every night during the previous two weeks, but though he had tried to remain impartial he had not been entirely unaffected by the revolutionary atmosphere. Ever since Slawata had spoken to him and given him a glimpse of the secrets of the Heir's political workshop, he had begun to see these party antics in Budapest in a new light. Now he had become more sympathetic to those who attached such importance to maintaining forms and rules that helped to preserve, in whatever way, the integrity and independence of the country.

Parliament was recalled and 13 December was announced as the date of the next session. On the preceding day a small paragraph appeared in the official gazette:

The Parliamentary Guards have been instructed that in no circumstances, even if bodily assaulted, are they to restrain Members by force.

Needless to say this decree had not been inspired by respect for the members, but rather was the Government's reply to the rumours of violence that had been put about by the opposition, and which had done so much to alarm the public.

On 13 December Balint had arrived somewhat late and, seeing the quantity of hats and coats in the cloakroom, realized that most of the other members had got there before him. It only occurred to him later how worried all the doorkeepers and porters had seemed.

No one was to be seen in the corridors leading to the Chamber. All was silence; he could not even hear his own footsteps on the heavily carpeted floor. And any noise from inside was effectively cut off by the heavy curtains that draped all the entrances.

Balint stepped inside totally unprepared for what he would find there.

Only about thirty members were present, all 'Zoltans' – the nickname for those on the extreme left. They were standing on the Speaker's platform, throwing down chairs, ripping out the balustrades, throwing the recording secretaries' equipment about and, in the middle of the floor of the House, where the Table of the Law had already been overturned, they were making piles of the desks and chairs of the ministerial benches.

At one side, surrounded by six or seven of his colleagues, stood Samuel Barra, their leader. When they saw Abady enter the room they swarmed round him, happy to boast of their antics to a newcomer.

All shouting at once they bragged about their behaviour and their misdeeds, roaring and stamping. Balint listened in growing horror and disgust as they shouted:

'We beat the hell out of them.'

'Did you see how I hit him with an inkpot?'

'The coward bent double... did you see?'

'We've had a real battle here, my friend.'

'But the guards couldn't hit back. The Decree forbade it!' shouted Balint when he had a chance to speak.

'Be damned to that! They would have if we'd given them a chance, but we didn't!' cried Barra and he launched into one of his usual rabble-rousing speeches full of slogans like 'Girded with the Nation's Right', 'The Power of the People', 'Irresistible Force', and 'Spurred by the Sacred Flames of Hungary's Freedom' until finally halted by one of his henchmen who, interrupting this flow of self-praising oratory, came up and said: 'Chief! Did you see how I beat them off the platform with this?' He brandished a weapon made from a long piece of oak torn from the platform railings, from which nails protruded unevenly. 'I harpooned the dogs!'

Still bragging, they hardly noticed one of their band who had been sitting at the side and who now moved down to the centre of the floor where they had made a pile of the chairs and desks. He was a tall, skinny, unshaven and swarthy man dressed in a dirty priest's frock. He climbed to the top of the pile of broken furniture and sat down, smiling viciously, his hands on his hips in the stance of a stage conqueror.

'Bravo, Jancsi! Bravo!' they cried.

At this moment a side door opened. Tisza walked in. He stood quite still and just looked at them. There was a sudden silence as everyone present saw who was there. Tisza spoke quietly and coldly.

PART THREE

'Aren't you ashamed of yourselves?' With a gesture of utter contempt, he turned on his heel and left.

To Balint, lying sleepless in the train, the rumble and clatter beneath his carriage – *Choo-choo-choo* . . . *Choo-choo-choo* – recalled the mindless uproar in the Chamber and seemed to mock his own indecision.

How could he ally himself to a crowd who could beat up defenceless public servants? Yet if he remained aloof he would be helping the secret plans of the Belvedere Palais, where the Heir was only waiting to pounce and destroy Hungarian independence once and for all.

It was this dilemma that now chased Balint away from the capital. A sort of nausea overcame him as he lay there seeking, and yet fleeing from a decision. And all the time the monotonous, heartless *Choo-choo-choo* beneath him chased both sleep and a decision from him.

It was late when Balint finally slept and it was late, too, when he awoke the following morning to find the sun glinting through the window blinds. At first he thought that the attendant had forgotten to wake him and that he had passed Kolozsvar in his sleep, but he was soon reassured: his train was now several hours late.

He dressed quickly and went out into the corridor. The weather outside was superb. The snow glistened in the bright sunshine, and ice floated on the Koros river which ran beside the railway track. Everything was blindingly white; even the steep mushroom-like roofs of the peasants' houses were thickly covered by snow. Here and there a dray-cart pulled by a buffalo could be seen on the road, its shivering owner walking alongside.

Both far and near the thick carpet of snow had the fine texture of powdered icing sugar. Without stopping the train sped through Banffy-Hunyad and started the steep climb to the Sztana Tunnel.

Balint moved back into his sleeping compartment to look out the other side of the train. He remembered that surely it was somewhere here that Adrienne's home was to be found, a white house opposite an old ruin that could be seen as the train came out of the tunnel; and when, brakes screaming on the curve, the train did emerge from the darkness, the first thing Balint saw in the distance were the ruins of an old castle and in among a stand of now leafless beech trees, two vertical white shapes which were probably the corner towers of a country house. He wondered if Adrienne were there, perhaps even at this very moment gazing, as he was, at the castle ruins. And if she were, would the knowledge that Balint was doing the same upset her as much as had the touch of his hand the last time they had met? It was many weeks since he had allowed himself to think about Adrienne, for after the scene in the garden he had chased away all thought of her even when his memories had brought her involuntarily to his mind.

⁕

Balint's mother, Roza Abady, was a short, chubby little woman who dressed always in black and whose snow-white hair and old-fashioned clothes made her seem years older than the mere fifty she really was. Since the early death of her husband, which had been a terrible blow to her after barely ten years of marriage, she had braced herself to accept the unwelcome role of a widow and had dressed as such ever since. Though their marriage had been planned by their families, the union of the handsome, talented and charming Tamas Abady with his rich little cousin Roza had been a love-match from the start. Even so, their early years together had been stormy and fraught with tension because their characters had been so different.

The young Roza, an only child whose arrival after her parents had been married for more than twelve years was hailed as some kind of miracle, had been wilful, capricious and spoilt. She tyrannized her parents' house and she had been treated so much like a princess in a fairy tale that, in time, this is what she believed herself to be. The grandeur of her surroundings, the huge castle of Denestornya with its countless servants and seemingly limitless parklands, over which the only child was allowed to believe she had absolute power, all contributed to inflate Roza's sense of her own importance, and made her arrogant and, at times, uncontrollable.

When she first married this had led to terrible quarrels between husband and wife, though, as she had fallen deeply in love with her handsome, understanding husband, these scenes invariably ended with Roza giving in. Soon she was to change and for the later years of their marriage she saw everything through her husband's eyes and his every wish was as faithfully carried out as if it had been an Imperial decree. These had been happy years, and, as it turned out, her only happy years, for suddenly, after barely a decade together, Tamas was struck down by an incurable cancer and died only a few months later.

PART THREE

Tamas Abady, a sensible man blessed with the gift of clear sight, had known what was the matter and how long he had to live. In the few months left to him he had concentrated all his time and declining energies to preparing Roza for their parting and for the tasks she would inherit when he died. Knowing his wife so well he took care that his wishes were expressed as definite instructions to be followed to the letter. Young Balint, as soon as he reached the age of ten, was to be sent to school in Vienna at the Theresianum; he was then to study law and, upon obtaining his degree, was to enter the Diplomatic Service. Tamas, conscious of the dangers to an only child brought up in a household of women, wanted to be sure that his son would grow up independent, travelled and experienced, and so be well equipped, when the time came, to decide his own future.

After discussing his ideas with his father, old Count Peter whose knowledge of the world was of immense help to him, Tamas wrote down in a large notebook everything that his wife was to do for their son and also exactly how she was to run the Abady estates. He had made a great point of Roza promising that she would run the property herself and not put it in the hands of estate managers. He wanted her to make her own decisions. He also wanted to give her something useful to do which would occupy so much of her time that it would help lighten the burden of sorrow after his death.

Count Tamas's instinct had been right. After the first few months of deep mourning the Countess Roza set about her new responsibilities with heroic dedication. She began by reading closely the book of instructions and very soon she had it by heart. This book became her bible, the holy writ which her beloved husband had ordered from the World Beyond. And if her adoration of his memory at times bordered on the morbid, the responsibilities he had imposed upon her saved her reason.

In her great house she led the life of a hermit. At first she would not see even her own close relations. She wanted no guests. She would live only to carry out her husband's sacred orders. Gradually she lost touch with all her friends; and neighbours, knowing they were not welcome, stopped calling. While her father-in-law lived he would bring his guests up to see her at the castle, but after his death she saw no one. This was something which her husband, in all his wisdom had not foreseen, and it had its ill effects. The countess by nature was generous and good-hearted, but she needed the company of people with she could talk and who would, in return, talk to her. She needed, too, people whom she could help and to whom she could be of service and play Lady Bountiful. Soon there appeared those who recognized not only this but also the fact that Countess Roza was susceptible to flattery, and who gradually began to insinuate themselves into the castle's service so that they could take advantage of the solitary countess's weaknesses.

The first was an unscrupulous lawyer, Kristof Azbej, with whom Countess Roza had made contact when she had been to Torda for some trivial lawsuit. He soon discovered how she could best be manipulated. He started by praising her late husband, and went on, apparently reluctantly, to allow the countess to force him to admit that he was poor because he only accepted briefs from the righteous, even if they could not afford to pay him. The widowed countess, impressed, used his services, without noticing that lawyer Azbej gave them even though she could afford to pay. She felt sorry for him and little by little allowed him more and more power and responsibility in the management of her affairs, until in the end, in all but name, the simple Mr Azbej became Agent for the Abady estates – a title he was careful never to use in her presence.

Gradually he made himself indispensable – principally by dint of revealing to her abuses she would never have discovered for herself ('The noble Countess will understand that I would never have mentioned it were it not that...') to the point at which she suggested he should always be near at hand to devote himself to her service. After her father-in-law died, she offered him rooms in the house at Denestornya where Count Peter had lived.

In much the same way, two women insinuated themselves into the countess' confidence and after a while they came permanently to live with her in the castle in the summer and in the town house in Kolozsvar when she moved there in the winter. They were Mrs Tothy, widow of a Protestant sexton, and Mrs Baczo, whose origins were more obscure but who was rumoured once to have been a cook in Des. These two, whether at Denestornya or Kolozsvar, would sit with the countess, take their meals with her and talk to her over their needlework. They also assumed responsibility for certain household tasks – Mrs Tothy supervised the laundries and made lavender water, while Mrs Baczo took charge of the kitchens and made all the preserves; she made them very well.

However their principle function was to listen to everything their mistress said and to agree that she was right. They were also the bearers of gossip on whom their mistress relied for all

PART THREE

information of that sort both from inside and outside the castle walls. This they did faithfully with one reservation; they never gossiped about each other or about Mr Azbej, who in turn always supported the two women. Together they formed a kind of triumvirate who between them shared the rule of the Abady estates. Just as the women controlled everything in the house and in the orchards and kitchen gardens, so Azbej ruled the farms and forests. As might be expected this alliance brought advantages to all three. The one domain over which they had no power and in whose rule the countess never consulted anyone's opinion but her own was the stables and the stud-farm.

The day Balint returned home he had coffee with his mother in her sitting-room. The countess sat on a sofa behind a long table and, one at each end, sat the two ladies on upright chairs which they always chose instead of more comfortable *fauteuils* to show that they knew their place. They were so alike that Balint was never quite sure which was which. Both were thick, fleshy women with olive complexions and dark hair and tiny sharp eyes sunk in the fat of pendulous cheeks. Their appearance showed how they thrived on the rich food of Transylvania. Each time he returned after a long absence Balint had to relearn that the only way to be sure which was which was to remember that the widow Tothy had three double chins while the Baczo had only two. Now, as Balint came into his mother's room he found them both doing crochet work, sitting bolt upright and working at exactly the same speed. In front of his mother, but untouched, was a large Chinese lacquer bowl which served her for a work-basket. The countess made Balint sit beside her on the long sofa. She gazed at him fondly with her slightly bulging eyes and, took his hand in her pudgy little fingers.

'Tell me everything! Where have you been? What have you been doing?'

Balint first told her all about the shooting party at Simonvasar, who was there and who was not there. Then he recounted the political events in Budapest. He tried to tell her everything but she, never talking her eyes off his face and constantly pressing his hands as if to reassure herself that it was really he, never really grasped whether he was talking about his cousins or telling about the rows in the House. That this was so was made perfectly clear as her occasional interjections only concerned his health: 'Are you sure you didn't catch cold? Are you well?'

'You'll stay on a bit now, won't you? You won't leave us too soon. It will soon be Carnival, and there are some very pretty girls around.'

'Very pretty, yes indeed!' echoed the widow Tothy.

'Yes, indeed, very pretty!' said the widow Baczo.

The countess went on: 'You should look around. It would be so nice if you found someone here and settled down. I should like that so much!'

Why did allusion to marriage suddenly make him think of Adrienne? For a moment he saw her face before him.

'Don't worry, Mama, I'm going to stay for a long, long time!' said the young man, raising her hand to his lips as if sealing a pact. 'Anyhow if they have new elections, which seems very likely, I'll probably not stand again.'

'No? Why not?'

'I haven't yet made up my mind, but I hated everything I saw in Budapest. It was very depressing!'

'Far better come home and take the estate in hand. I'm an old woman now and the work and worry are getting to be too much for me. I don't get about as much as I should any more. You're a man, you're young ... and it'll all be yours anyway when I die!' She turned to the two women: 'Aren't I right?'

'Yes, indeed!' said Mrs Tothy.

'Indeed, yes!' echoed Mrs Baczo.

'I'll have a lot to learn,' Balint said, 'I've never had to deal with these things before.' And, as he spoke, he realized how much he really would like to take the estate in hand, all the more so as for some time he had wondered why, with such enormous properties, they always seemed to have so little income. 'I'll need a few months to get the hang of things. Then I'll gladly do as you wish, even if I do decide to remain a Member.'

'That's wonderful!' said Countess Roza, knowing that if he did so Balint would have to spend much more time at home with her. 'Your poor father insisted that I should take it on, me, a woman alone! But I know that he'd want you to take over now that you're grown up. Wouldn't he?' She exacted reinforcement from the two ladies.

'Indeed he would!' They both answered dutifully, concealing their dismay, for though they had neither of them known the late Count Tamas, it was more than their place was worth not to agree.

'I'll tell Azbej to prepare all the accounts and get out the contracts. He'll explain everything.' And, turning again to her two companions, she asked: 'When will he be here next?'

'He said he would be back before Christmas, after the first pig-killing,' replied the two well-informed ladies.

⁕

Azbej arrived a few days later. He received the countess's orders with suitable deference and, bowing very low indeed, he expressed himself overjoyed that he would have the young count for his master. His whole conversation was punctuated with bows, which he made still sitting on the edge of his chair so as to show the depth of his loyalty and respect.

Although Balint had seen him each time he had been at Denestornya he had never before talked to the little lawyer. Until now he had sensed that his mother somehow did not want him to meddle with the management of the estate. When he spoke to her of such matters she had never gone into any detail but had merely complained of the worry and torment it caused her without once explaining what she was talking about. Balint had therefore strictly avoided discussing estate matters with Azbej lest his mother should think he was going behind her back. This was therefore the first time that he had heard the lawyer speak of such matters. Azbej knew how to make a good impression despite an unprepossessing appearance, for he was a dwarfish little man with short arms and a pot-belly, practically no neck and a round head covered in black hair cut the same length as his beard; of all which had the singular effect of suggesting that above his high collar there sat a porcupine. Two clever bulging little eyes projected from the porcupine's quills and, in the centre, there was a very red little mouth from which emitted, when he spoke, a surprisingly educated voice expressing precise and well-phrased thoughts. As to the estate business he had all the figures, details and dates at his finger-tips. He assured his new master that the Noble Count would find everything in good order, all done strictly according to the instructions and wishes of the Gracious Countess. He emphasized the fact that he had at all times acted for the best while never deviating from the orders he had been given. Another phrase emerged from time to time. Should Balint, finding some procedure either surprising or old-fashioned, ask a question, he would find Azbej answer always ended with the words 'as his late Lordship, with the wisdom of his sacred foresight, intended.' This happened whenever Balint asked about the management of the forests, which seemed extremely haphazard to him.

Azbej bowed himself out, swearing strict obedience to Count Balint's orders, which would be carried out with alacrity. His manner oozed eagerness to serve, and nothing revealed his determination to keep the young man in such ignorance that no changes would be made. He had already decided this when he had received a letter from the two ladies, Tothy and Baczo, who had immediately reported to him everything that had passed between the countess and her son.

It was clear to Azbej that two things were of the utmost importance if he were to be able to maintain his control of the Abady properties. The first was that the young count should continue to be a member of the House of Representatives, which would often keep him in Budapest. If he were to remain permanently at home in Denestornya it was inevitable that sooner or later he would stumble upon some of the things Azbej would rather were kept from him. It was not that the agent had ever broken the law, he had never gone quite as far as that; but over the years certain practices had become established which would cease at once if Balint discovered their existence. From the first days when Countess Roza had given him any responsibility Mr Azbej had exacted commissions on every transaction he arranged. Sometimes they were small, almost symbolic such as little 'presents' of turkeys, wine or flour from the miller, innkeeper or fuller, or hay from the smaller farms. Sometimes the benefits were more substantial as when, for example, Mr Azbej's sheep and cattle – and he kept surprisingly large herds on all the Abady farms – grazed in the Abady meadows and fed, in winter, on the feed raized for the Abady livestock. Countess Roza, of course, knew nothing of this. In the beginning, before Azbej had started his operations on a big scale, it so happened that once or twice a discontented servant or angry tenant would try to denounce him, but Azbej would take such swift action to discredit his accusers that they would be forced to contradict themselves and withdraw their complaints. When this lesson had been well learned by everyone who worked under Azbej's control, only anonymous complaints sometimes found their way to the countess's desk – and these she would ignore, having been warned against such things by her late husband. So Azbej, at the time of Balint's return, was getting everything as he wanted it and even those who had cause for complaint kept silent since the agent himself turned a blind eye as long as they followed his example. But if Count Balint were allowed to stay at home with time on his hands it was inevitable that all this would come to light.

PART THREE

Next it was important to find some task, or problem, that he could put in the young count's way that would occupy him so much that he would be deflected from taking too much interest in the running of the farms or the relations with the Denestornya estate tenants. From a hint or two that Azbej had picked up during his first talk with Balint, the lawyer had noticed that the new young master had not seemed entirely convinced by his report on the forestry management. The forests were some way from Denestornya... in the mountains... ah, there lay the solution! From the few objections that Balint had raised he realized that the young man had ideas of his own for introducing modern theories of planting and felling, and installing modern equipment in the saw-mills. Well, let him! Let him get involved in all the petty intrigues going on among the men in the mountain villages! Let him sink his teeth into the lengthy negotiations that would be necessary! Let him find out all the difficulties for himself: he'd have his hands full there all right!

Azbej laid his plans carefully. He sent instructions to Beles for the forest manager to present himself at Denestornya directly after the Christmas holiday. Everything went just as he had hoped, for Kalman Nyiresy was of the old school and, overconscious of his status as a member of the minor country gentry, made no effort to ingratiate himself with the young count. Where Azbej had cunningly disguised his contempt for his employer and thus had made a good first impression, Nyiresy, puffed up with a sense of his own importance, sat down before being invited, lit an evil-smelling meerschaum pipe and, in a patronizing manner, was unwise enough to admit that he had not himself set foot in the Abady forests for over ten years. Why should he? He knew every tree as well as his own hand! Balint realized at once that the old man was incompetent and, worse, arrogant. When, coldly, he stated his intention of making a tour of inspection directly after the New Year, Nyiresy burst into loud derisive laughter.

'You don't know what you're saying, sir! Not even bears go there in winter... or birds either, for that matter!'

Azbej, seeing that the old man had made just the impression he had hoped for, then intervened and made him agree to supply horses and guides as soon as word arrived from the castle.

'Well, sir, you can do as you like, I don't mind! Nothing'll come of it, mark my words! I'll offer your Lordship some good wine and the hospitality of my house, but go up there? Ha, ha! Quite impossible!' and, still laughing at the young Count's folly and ignorance, he took his leave.

As it turned out Balint was prevented from going when he had planned. On 5 January Tisza dissolved Parliament and announced new election for the 28th of the same month. Despite his previous decision to abandon politics, Balint renewed his candidature and postponed his trip to the mountains until February so that he could work on his election speeches.

The election campaign had been carefully engineered by Azbej.

Living at Kuttyfalva was a man of the lesser nobility whose name was Janko Cseresznyes, which meant 'cherry-tree'. He had once been town clerk, though only for a short time before losing the job for reasons that were never made public. Since then he had become a jack of all trades, now selling farm produce, now doing a little horse-coping, now buying and selling cattle or farm machinery. He did not mind what he set his hand to. It was, however, at election time that he really came into his own for his real talent was rabble-rousing. With a huge voice capable of making itself heard above the loudest hubbub and a wicked sense of humour, he was in his element whenever a new election provided a demand for his services. And these services were given to whichever party would pay the best. Though naturally inclined to the left, he usually found that the government side would pay more. Azbej who had previously found his services useful and employed him when certain rather shady deals were in the offing, sent Cseresznyes to Balint's constituency at Lelbanya with instructions to round up an impressive delegation of local notabilities and bring them to Kolozsvar to beg the count, whom they loved so much, not to desert them.

This delegation arrived on 7 January. Headed by Janko Cseresznyes it consisted of about ten people; the chemist and public notary in black morning coats, the judge and a few other prominent citizens in navy-blue Sunday suits, and also some shabbily-dressed peasants, as Janko thought that a group drawn from all social classes would be all the more effective. They brought with them a written petition with some two hundred signatures begging Count Balint Abady to renew his candidature and thus not forsake his faithful friends. The judge, who was also the mayor, made a speech and Janko, who felt it had not been sufficiently forceful, backed it up with another improvised peroration which brought in the thousand-year-old Hungarian Constitution, the wickedness of German-speaking foreigners, the tobacco concessions, Kossuth, taxation, the greatness of the Noble Count's illustrious ancestors and free access to salt deposits! Balint was duly impressed by this show of mass affection and reluctantly agreed to stand again.

On 14 January he addressed the people of Lelbanya from a first floor window of the town hall which overlooked the marketplace. To Balint's surprise he was received with a marked lack of enthusiasm which, despite an occasional cheer to break the general silence, almost amounted to hostility. He thought that maybe this was due to the extreme cold and Azbej, who accompanied him back to Kolozsvar, confirmed that this must be the reason and assured him that all would be well.

But it wasn't.

The political fever that swept Budapest had spread even to the little town of Lelbanya where the atmosphere was no different from that anywhere else. The leading articles in the Budapest papers and the party manifestos, filled as they were with the election slogans and ringing war-cries of party strife, were passed eagerly from hand to hand and provoked as much argument and bad blood among the citizens of Lelbanya as they did among the more sophisticated *habitués* of the Casino Club in the capital. In one sense the discontent aroused in the little country town became even more serious as the date of the election approached. It was such a small constituency that it returned only one member and now, just as the independence of Hungary seemed threatened by the complacency of the ruling party, there was only one serious candidate – and he was no revolutionary vote-buying politician from the capital but only their own Count Abady, the owner of the lake and the industries that depended on it, who relied on his social position to get elected but from whom the locals could expect no other benefit, and certainly no bribes! Unrest mounted to such a point that Abady's prospect of election became far from certain.

Azbej had already sensed what was happening and when Janko Cseresznyes, worried by the seriousness of this unexpected development which threatened both their interests, went to see the little lawyer to explain that money, and quite a lot of it, would be needed if the count were to have any hope of being re-elected. They whispered together, made notes on slips of paper, added up some figures ... and a wad of banknotes disappeared into Janko's pocket.

Three days later Mr Azbej presented himself to Countess Roza, now installed for the winter in her town house at Kolozsvar.

Mysteriously he asked for a private interview. This was so unusual that, for once, the Countess asked the two ladies to leave the room and turned questioningly to the little lawyer who stood, wringing his hands and bowing with an excess of apparent humility and embarrassment.

A long and flowery speech followed. Before reaching the real reason for the interview Azbej dwelt on how long and faithfully he had served her Ladyship's interests, how he had always worked only to maintain the good name of the Counts Abady whose great past had contributed much glory to the nation's history and how he would go to any lengths to shield her Ladyship and His Excellency the Count Balint from any embarrassment or affront.

The countess, thoroughly alarmed, begged him to explain.

With seeming reluctance he recounted the growing unrest at Lelbanya and how Count Balint's re-election was menaced by the growth of revolutionary fervour. So far he told only the truth; there was no need to invent. Now, however, was the time for a little embroidery. In the last few days, he told Countess Roza there had been a new and even more serious development. Another candidate had presented himself, a worthless demagogue who had made himself much beloved by the gullible country folk of Lelbanya, and he, Azbej, felt he could never again hold up his head if such a scoundrel of a popular agitator should set himself up as a rival to the young Count and beat him at the polls! It was terrible, unthinkable! He had not slept all night worrying about this dreadful dilemma they now faced. It was no longer possible for the young master to withdraw his candidature, for he had already made his election address and this had been printed in the newspapers. To withdraw now would be an admission of weakness, of defeat, of lack of courage – a mortifying blow to the prestige of the family. And for the future lord of Denestornya to be defeated by such a low class rascal . . . ! He left the phrase unfinished.

The countess reacted just as he had expected. Aghast at the thought of such humiliation she swallowed her pride, forgot or ignored the fact that it was really to her son that the lawyer should have applied, and turned to Azbej.

'How terrible! This must not be allowed! Is there nothing we can do?'

Now came the opportunity he had been seeking. He told the countess that he must now reveal to her something that he would never normally have dared mention. Always in the past, that is until Count Balint's election, Lelbanya had been bought! The first and only time in the memory of all the electors living that a candidate had been elected cleanly, without corruption, had been the Noble Count's election in the previous year. The people had become accustomed, and now expected, to be paid; and in this time of ferment even the prestige of the Abadys was not enough to overcome the people's greed. He would never have dared mention the matter, let alone propose such a solution if the Gracious Countess had not herself asked. As it was he could see no other way. There was a pause.

'How much?' asked Countess Roza.

The lawyer's carefully phrased speech had made a deep impression on the countess. All her ingrained pride of race rebelled against the very idea that a failed small-town municipal employee should succeed where her son, the descendant of palatine princes and imperial viceroys, had failed, that an obscure town clerk should defeat an Abady. It was not for this that she had been brought up to believe herself all but royal in lineage, that, moving from one great room to another in the castle of Denestornya, she had been told that the portraits of her ancestors that hung upon the walls represented governors, commanders-in-chief, and great national heroes including even Istvan Bathory's famous general. If anything the countess was even prouder of the part played by the family in Hungarian history than she was of its ancient noble status. Living for so many years alone and isolated from the political events of the capital, this pride in the thought that Abadys had always played an important role in the country's affairs had become as ingrained in her way of thinking as had the sense of her own superiority and importance. Since she had been a child no one had contradicted her – except her husband and that was different – and what she had wanted, and commanded, was automatically carried out. And now . . .'

'How much?' she said again.

'It is difficult to say, exactly, but I think we could do it with forty thousand crowns.'

The countess rose and went over to a little rosewood escritoire which stood in the window embrasure. She sat down, opened a drawer and rummaged around for a moment without taking anything out. She liked to think that no one knew where anything was kept nor how much money she had, little dreaming that Azbej, with the help of the two ladies, knew all the details even better than she did: he even managed even to draw commissions from the banks each time that she made deposits. Finally Countess Roza drew out a savings-bank book and carefully re-locked the drawer.

'Take this!' she said, handing it to him. 'The account contains forty thousand, seven hundred crowns, and there's a half year's interest due. Use this!' Then her natural generosity overcome any reservations that good sense might have suggested.

'Don't mention any of this to my son. I wouldn't like him to know that I had made this sacrifice for him!'

Nothing could have suited Azbej better. He pledged himself to the utmost secrecy and bowed himself from the gracious lady's presence. A few days later a telegram arrived for the countess saying: 'Situation promising' and, on the eve of the elections, another which announced: 'Victory certain!'

On the morning of 20 January a third telegram arrived which stated: 'Rival withdrew. Count Abady elected unanimously. Congratulations. Azbej.'

The following day Azbej returned to Kolozsvar and again asked for a private interview with the countess. He brought with him the sum of five thousand, two hundred and twenty-seven crowns and forty-two cents in cash. This amount, he explained as he handed it to Countess Roza, had not been needed; and he proceeded to account for the rest in minute detail. The countess, impressed by this display of meticulous honesty, praised his reliability and expressed her pleasure with him and joy at the success of his mission.

He then went to see Balint.

Here he was not so well received, indeed he met with marked coldness.

'Now I expect to be told what really happened,' said Balint icily.

Azbej hummed and hawed. Naturally the majority of the electors wanted only his Lordship, the other had no chance and when he, Azbej, had persuaded him that his candidature was hopeless of course he had resigned. Balint, unconvinced, then asked why the lawyer had written that it might be 'disadvantageous' for him to appear at Lelbanya? Azbej parried this awkward question by saying that the man had had some adherents and he thought it better not to expose his Lordship to possible insult. Then why, asked Balint relentlessly, had the man withdrawn?

At this point Azbej felt that the moment had come when he would have to admit at least a part of the truth; by no means all of course, not that he already had had the other candidate's resignation in his pocket by 14 January, nor that of the countess's forty thousand crowns he had given fifteen to the fake candidate and kept twenty for himself. He decided to mention only that his Lordship's gracious mother had sent a certain sum of money and that it had had the desired effect and was just about to open the tiny red mouth that lurked in the hedgehog beard when Balint interrupted.

'I warn you that I'll resign at once if I hear that there has been any dirty business!'

The little lawyer now realized that he had better keep his mouth shut; it would not fit his plans at all for Count Balint to stay at home after all the trouble he had taken to get him elected. Quickly he searched for another explanation. Using all his powers of invention Azbej launched into a long and complicated story about the morning of the election.

Balint listened to his rigmarole in silence. Then he dismissed the lawyer as coldly as he had received him. He did not believe what he had been told, but not knowing about his mother's part in the affair, thought that he would have to seek some other explanation. But the good impression that the lawyer had previously made had received its first serious dent.

The result of the national elections was that the party which had governed Hungary since 1878 found itself in the minority. In the shock of surprise with which this news was everywhere greeted no one was more taken aback than the leaders of the former opposition who had now been placed in the uncomfortable position of having to make good their extravagant promises. Everyone was filled with a sense of foreboding, for now a conflict between the Crown and Parliament seemed unavoidable.

The situation was so strange and so exciting that Balint decided not to resign his seat, no matter how it had been gained. He wanted to be there when battle was joined; perhaps after all he would be able to contribute something useful.

Chapter Two

AT THE BEGINNING OF FEBRUARY, soon after the elections, Carnival started in Kolozsvar. All the families with marriageable daughters opened their town houses and prepared, politics or no politics, to go to dances, give dances and generally do everything they could to create the necessary opportunities for the girls to meet the eligible young men.

The Miloth family were among the first to arrive, and Countess Miloth immediately started taking her two unmarried daughters to call on the dowagers. Sometimes they made as many as seven such visits in a day.

One of their first calls was naturally on the widowed Countess Abady who, though she never went out herself, was by rank and breeding the most distinguished lady in their social group. At four o'clock one afternoon therefore a footman entered Countess Roza's sitting-room and announced that Countess Miloth had called, with her daughters.

'Pray bring them up!' said Countess Roza, gesturing to the footman to remove from the table in front of her the needlework with which she and her two companions had been occupying themselves, as well as the empty coffee cup that had remained there after Balint, a few moments before, had left his mother to make arrangements to visit the forests at Beles two days later. Mrs Tothy and Mrs Baczo disappeared silently through a side door as Countess Miloth, with Judith and Margit, was announced. After the usual ceremony of symbolic kisses between the two elder ladies and handkissing and bows on the part of the girls, the visitors seated themselves opposite their hostess, Countess Miloth flanked by her two offspring as was correct. An insipid and formal conversation was begun all about the new débutantes, and what dances and balls were to be given.

Next it was the turn of fashion. They were just wondering if boas or shawls should be worn and whether tulle was more suitable for young girls than muslin when these exciting topics were brought to an end by the unexpected entrance of Balint. It was not the custom for young men to be present during such calls, but from the window of his room he had recognized the big-boned horses he had seen on the road to Var-Siklod, so saying to himself that he really should go and greet the Miloths as he had been their guest in the autumn, he had returned to his mother's sitting-room.

Countess Miloth was agreeably surprised, assuming at once that he must be interested in one of her girls – but was it Judith or Margit? She forced a welcoming smile on her normally sour face and went on talking about the balls to be given. It was lucky for her younger daughters, she said, that Adrienne would be able to chaperone them as she herself could never stay up so late!

'Is Adrienne in town?' asked Countess Roza politely.

'Not yet; I don't expect the Uzdys until the day after tomorrow. But it doesn't matter as there won't be any dances before that.' She went on to explain that Adrienne would be staying with her mother-in-law at the Uzdy house out on the Monostor road, where the old lady had already arrived with Adrienne's child and the English nanny. A ground-floor wing of the house had been put at the Adrienne's disposal for the season.

'What a long way out!' exclaimed Countess Roza who rarely moved and for whom almost any distance seemed too far.

'Not too much, really,' said Countess Miloth. 'Anyhow they're bringing two carriages so they'll manage all right.'

After this exchange, which told Balint all he wanted to know, the talk returned to the absorbing topic of clothes and the young man took his leave, explaining that one of his forest wardens was waiting to see him. As he left Margit looked up with a tiny smile at the corner of her mouth.

The ranger was waiting in the hall.

'What's the road like to Beles?'

'It's quite passable from Hunyad to Kalota, my Lord. That's because it gets a lot of use. From there on there'll be snow drifts. Packed snow'd be better!'

'Why?'

'Well, the runners cut deep into soft snow, 'specially when the road's uphill. But no matter, your Lordship, we'll make it, even if we do go a bit slow, as you might say. The day after tomorrow then, Sir, at midday . . . ?'

Balint thought for a moment. 'Perhaps the road will improve if we wait? What do you think?'

'Next Thursday, my Lord?'

'Oh, I don't know. I'll send word when I'm ready.'

Balint spent the next few days in seeing that he had everything he would needed for a winter trip to the mountains. He was fairly well provided, having spent a year in Stockholm where winter sports were beginning to be all the rage, but some things had to be bought. Three days after the Miloths had visited his mother, he caught sight of Adrienne coming out of one of the shops in the main square. Though she was still far away he recognized her at once from her long swinging stride. She was deep in conversation with two young men, Adam Alvinczy and Pityu Kendy, both of whom carried skates slung over their shoulders. In addition Adam carried a picnic basket and another pair of skates while

Pityu had a fur rug in one hand and a thermos flask in the other. They were chatting gaily.

For a moment Balint wondered if Adrienne were still angry with him but, even as the thought flashed across his mind, she had stopped in front of him and was holding out her hand: 'Here I am!' she said happily, her golden onyx eyes full of light and welcome. It was as if the scene on the bench had never happened.

'We're going skating. The ice must be wonderful.'

'But it'll soon be dark!'

'All the better; nobody'll be there! What's the matter? Do you think it's not "done"?'

'Not at all!'

'We're going to have tea there, on a bench beside the lake. Any nasty suspicions must freeze into nothing at ten below zero, isn't that so, Adam Adamovitch?' She lifted her aquiline nose at Alvinczy, whose father was also called Adam and who was then engrossed in reading Russian authors. She laughed provocatively.

'What a pity you don't skate, AB! It's marvellous!'

'But I do! I learned in Sweden.'

'Come with us then! Do!' said Addy with sudden warmth. 'You won't regret it... and you've never seen me on the ice!'

'All right. but I must go home and get my skates. I'll join you there.'

Balint walked home as quickly as he could, but it took him some time to find his things and when he had finally discovered where his boots, jerseys, trousers and woollen stockings had been hidden it seemed almost too late to go and join the others. Still a promise was a promise, and she did seem to have forgiven him...

―――

It was dark when Balint arrived at the park. The frozen lake was surrounded by a railing over which hung a few lighted lanterns. He bought his ticket and entered the enclosure. There were only few people there apart from one or two beginners who were practising with wicker chairs to hold them up, and who did not venture far from the little pavilion, but he could see Adrienne and the two young men gliding about on the far side of the lake. One of them had paid a man with an barrel organ to play to them and he was grinding out an ancient waltz which had once been the rage of Vienna. On it went, the tune endlessly repeating '*Nur ...für Natur... hegte Sie... Sympathie...*', and to this old melody they waltzed in wide figures of three, leaving behind them faint white furrows cut in the ice.

He should have gone straight over, but instead he stood there watching and thinking how lovely Adrienne was, gliding effortlessly across the ice like a shadow in a dream. She was wearing a dress of brick red which seemed almost black in the half light, the same colour as her hair and the sealskin collar, hat and edging to the hem of the funnel-shaped skirt, which fluttered round her like an ever widening saucer as she turned and twisted in the movements of the dance.

How beautiful she was! She looked weightless and ethereally tall as she danced with both men at once, doing a few turns with one and then, with a double turn, seeming to fly into the arms of the other, spinning arabesques of grace to the rhythm of the old waltz. It was like a ballet with every step lengthened into great sweeps of movement each covering more than thirty feet to a single beat.

As she danced Adrienne seemed more youthful than Balint had ever seen her, her fine elongated silhouette more slender, more alluring, watching her now, passing so lightly from one admirer to another, her lips parted in a dazzling smile of pleasure as each man in turn caught her by the waist and whirled her away with the speed of an eagle taking its prey, Balint knew that he would never again think of Adrienne as the reincarnation of Diana the Huntress who hated men.

In total surrender to the intoxication of the dance, she seemed to be moving in a trance, dazed but ecstatic. This was no virgin goddess performing her hieratic ritual dance; this was a wild young mænad caught in a magic wintery bacchanalia, a prey to every madness of love and abandon, drunk with unrestrained desire and ready for whatever the night might bring. She was the stuff that dreams were made of, impelled by speed, by the rushing strength of her own young body and by the darkness of night in which all desire could be fulfilled and yet remain secret, a nature free of all restraint.

Balint felt like an intruder, a Peeping Tom to whom something forbidden had inadvertently been revealed. This was no longer the Adrienne he knew, neither the moody Addy of his youth nor the bitter Adrienne who escaped from the gaiety of the dance to pour out her disillusion on a moonlight night. Nor was it the playful, childish Adrienne who climbed the haystack with her sisters at Mezo-Varjas, or even the sad woman in flight from the bitterness of a failed marriage who had revealed her soul to him in her father's garden and then rounded on him in anger and disgust when he dared to kiss her arm. This was a different being, someone he did not know, a stranger, flirtatious, without fear, without regrets and free of the constraints with which he had thought his Adrienne to be inexorably hedged.

Suddenly he felt himself a stranger, an intruder who had no right to be granted this forbidden insight. He had no business to be there unless, perhaps, he was just one more young man she was drawn to seduce!

The music of the barrel-organ stopped abruptly. Adrienne and her two young admirers skated smoothly to the side of the lake where, spreading the fur rug on a bench, they took out their picnic and started to eat. Even from where he stood Balint could see what a good time they were having, how they laughed together and joked and chatted, and how the vapour of hot tea curled up from the open thermos beside them.

'What are you doing here?' he asked himself. Spying?'

He turned away, left the frozen lake, and walked slowly home.

The very same evening he sent off a telegram: 'ARRIVE BELES MORNING TRAIN WEDNESDAY. HAVE SLEIGH AND HORSES READY AT NOON.'

Chapter Three

THE SLEIGH BELLS TINKLED MERRILY as they drove up through the pine forests to the ridge of Csonka-Havas which formed the watershed that had to be crossed before they could reach the little settlement of Beles. Andras Zutor, known as 'Honey', the forest ranger who had come to Kolozsvar, and the coachman, 'Clever' Janos Rigo, sat huddled together in the driver's seat. Both wore jackets made of thick flannel embroidered in patterns of red, blue and green. Over these they had old worn sleeveless sheepskin waistcoats, for no one wore new clothes to go to the mountains in the winter. These too were elaborately embroidered with flowers and traditional Hungarian symbols. Both jackets and waistcoats were short and when their wearers bent forward they showed a line of bare tanned skin between them and the tops of their trousers: all Kalotaszeg folk wore short shirts and jackets, for it was said that they did not feel the cold as other mortals did. Both men were of similar build, stocky and so wide of shoulder that there was only just room for the two of them on the narrow driver's seat of the sleigh.

PART THREE

As they turned a bend in the road Andras Zutor turned to Balint. 'That's Beles in front of us now,' he said. On the floor of the valley below, Balint could see a huddle of little shingle-roofed huts where the foresters and workers in the sawmill were lodged. From a distance they looked like rows of blackened wooden coffins. Beyond them could be seen the canteen, the houses of the sawmill manager and clerks and, still farther on, the larger roofs of the sawmill itself surrounded by huge piles of uncut tree-trunks, neat mountains of cut planks and heaps of greying sawdust.

The little settlement was ringed with mountains, the Gyalu Boulini side of the Funcinyeli range, and these, shrouded in greyish mist darkened by wisps of smoke rising from the houses and the sawmill, effectively obscured any more distant view.

The noon siren sounded as they drove between the houses. Here the snow had been trodden into mud. All this, explained Andras, was part of the Abady estate. They passed a group of workers, some of whom raised their hats. Once through the settlement the sleigh turned once towards the mountains passing between snow-covered meadows, bare and white between dark plantations of fir trees. Here and there a rock stood out above the snow. As they passed an old willow tree that leaned over the edge of a deep canyon Andras turned again to Balint and explained that this marked the boundary of the Count's property. Even though the road now started to climb steeply the horses increased their speed knowing that they would soon be home. Behind a fence stood a row of ash trees laden now with bunches of red-brown berries, and behind these again stood the little house of the forest manager. The sleigh turned in through an open gate and drew up before the front door where Kalman Nyiresy, he who had made such a bad impression on Balint when he had come to Denestornya, stood waiting on the steps, pipe in mouth and cap in hand.

'Welcome, your Lordship, welcome!' he cried, taking the meerschaum from his lips and shaking hands heartily. 'I must say I never thought you'd really come in the winter! Come in and have a little something to warm the heart after such a long cold ride. And something to eat too! I'm afraid lunch won't be until two; we never thought you'd get here so soon!'

'I shall not be staying to lunch. I want to arrive before dark so as to set up camp,' replied Balint coldly.

Old Nyiresy was stunned. 'You won't stay? You won't honour my house? But I have invited guests to meet your Lordship; two of my best friends, the notary Gaszton Simo from Gyurkuca and the manager of the State forests. They're fine men both of them, especially Simo who's of a very good family from Bud-Szent-Katolnay. Why his uncle ... If your Lordship's really set on going up there you could start tomorrow morning.'

Balint made a gesture to indicate that none of that would be possible, and they moved into the combined living and dining-room of the forest manager's house. In the middle of the room stood a large square oak table of the style known in the eighties as *Altdeutsch*, and in one corner was a sofa and two armchairs.

They sat down, and in came two young Romanian servant-girls dressed in fine starched linen skirts and cotton blouses, one carrying a tray with glasses and the brandy bottle, the other a plate of biscuits. These they placed on the table, then they made a curtsy to Balint, and said in Romanian: '*Poftyic mariasza* – at your Lordship's command!' and left the room winking at Balint as they went.

Without thinking Balint looked up at them.

'Tasty morsels, eh? Look! If your Lordship will stay I'll send one of them to your bed tonight ... or both if you think you can handle them!' The old man chuckled and then added, with a leer: 'I sample 'em myself from time to time!' and he twisted his moustache with a swagger.

Abady replied coldly: 'No, I'll not be staying. I'll be off just as soon as the horses are ready.'

'Pity! Pity! It's my loss!' The old man gave a great puff of smoke between each exclamation. He was deeply offended that the oriental welcome he had planned to soften up the unwelcome guest had been spurned.

They sat for a few minutes in hostile silence. Then Balint said stiffly: 'Be so good as to give me the estate maps. I want to compare them with the military surveys.'

'No idea where they are!' said the old man gruffly. 'I put them away years ago. I've got no need of such things, it's all in here!' He tapped his head and continued to pull on his pipe in proud, offended immobility.

Outside the house the dogs began barking and firm steps could be heard crossing the wooden veranda. The door was flung open and a tall, rawboned man walked in. He was dressed in a short jacket and corduroy riding breeches cut in the fashion that country tailors thought to be English, box-calf boots, and carried a hunting crop. He did not remove his hat, into which were stuck three large boar bristles, but stood in the doorway with extended hand.

'I'm Gaszton Simo!' He spoke proudly as if everyone should tremble at the sound of his name.

Balint disliked him at once. He appeared not to notice the outstretched hand, and spoke condescendingly: 'Please be seated, Mr... er... Notary.'

Old Nyiresy was deeply hurt. Although he knew that the house and most things in it belonged to the estate, and that he himself was no more than an employee, his pride had suffered a severe blow from the young count's refusal to accept him on equal terms and the disdain shown for their efforts to entertain him. He boiled inwardly that this aristocratic brat should lord it over him in his own house, even to playing the host when Nyiresy's friends appeared. It was too much!

To make up for Balint's coldness he greeted the newcomer with extra warmth. 'How are you, my boy? Come in! Come in! Have a little brandy!' he went on, as he helped the newcomer off with his coat, put hat and whip on the table, and ushered him to an armchair.

'His Lordship won't be staying for lunch,' he complained. 'He's starting at once for the mountains!'

Simo turned towards Balint enquiringly. What a bandit, thought Balint, now that he could see his face properly. Why, he looks like a medieval mercenary who would go anywhere, serve no matter who, kill anyone, so long sas he was properly paid. Gaszton Simo had a hard, resolute face under short hair which grew so low on his forehead that it almost touched his thick black brows. He had small shrewd button-like eyes, and thick black moustaches which joined equally thick black whiskers. He looked both forceful and cunning.

'Madness, going up there in the winter!' growled old Nyiresy. However Simo did not back him up as he had hoped.

'Why not? The weather's beautiful now, even if the nights are cold. This time last year I went shooting with my uncle, the Chamberlain. We went to the foot of the Humpleu and camped on the Prislop. Wonderful weather we had!' He turned to Balint. 'Have you got everything you need, sleeping bags, fur rugs, watertight tent, kettles...? If you need anything I'd be glad to lend it. If you like I could go with you and take care of everything.'

This did not fit in with Balint's plans.

'Thank you, I have all I need. The horses are being loaded up now.'

'When do you return? I'll have a roe-buck for you.'

'A roe-buck? In February?'

'There're no restrictions in the mountains,' laughed Simo scornfully. 'It's better if I order it shot than let it be taken by some common poacher. I just have to say the word!'

Balint was too outraged to reply at once and just as he was about to speak Andras Zutor came in. He clicked his heels to Abady and announced that the horses were ready whenever his Lordship wished to leave.

Balint got up at once and went out. He shook hands on the veranda with Nyiresy, and this time also with Gaszton Simo. Then he ordered Janos Rigo, who was waiting at the foot of the steps, to have the sleigh ready for him in three days' time at Szkrind in the Retyicel Valley as he would not return to Hunyad the way he came but planned to return by way of Mereggyo.

The old forest manager muttered something into his beard but said nothing more to retain the young man who had made so light of the welcome he had planned for him.

In front of the house, standing about in the snow, were eight horses of which three were saddled: two, for Balint and Andras Zutor, with wooden Hungarian saddles covered with sheepskins, while the third, a much more impressive animal, had a military saddle and well-oiled bridle and reins. This was the notary's horse, a fine dapple-grey, sleek and well cared-for. All the others were skinny mountain ponies with shaggy winter coats.

In the centre of the group stood Honey, who had discarded the old hat he had been wearing and replaced it with a splendid affair of sheepskin which he wore only on special occasions. Slung round his shoulders was a Werndl sporting gun and at his side he carried a bulging knapsack on which was displayed a brass plaque engraved with the Abady arms, the symbol of his official status as a *Foleskudt* man, someone who had taken the oath of loyalty and was therefore respected as an officer of the State. With his reddish beard trimmed like the monarch's, erect stance and commanding glance, he had the air and presence of a sergeant-major, and was accorded the same respect.

Around him stood the five *gyorniks* – forest guards – who had been summoned by Andras Zutor. These were Todor Paven, a tall Albanian who had charge of the Intreape forest; Krisan Gyorgye, a big man with a black moustache and huge hands from

PART THREE

Toszerat; the overweight Juanye Vomului, who, with new clothes, a vast sheepskin hat and a copper-studded belt with copious pockets, and who was not an Abady employee but was an independent smallholder from Gyurkuca and liked to underline his special status by the elegance of his appearance; Vaszi Lung from Valea Corbului, known as Zsukuczo or 'Tipstaff' because as a young man he had been the bailiff's runner. He was a small elderly man, blond and chubby with inflamed red eyes who, from having once been a noted poacher was now such an efficient keeper that no one dared set traps or wander with a gun in his part of the forest. Lastly, there was Stefan Lung from Vale Szaka, the youngest of the band, tall and slim, who had inherited his job from his father. Young Stefan was no relation to Vaszi; they bore the same name simply because nearly all the families of the Retyicel district were descended from two brothers who had settled there a hundred and fifty years before. All five guards carried a long-handled axe and knapsacks bearing brass plaques with the Abady arms as symbols of their authority in their respective districts.

Abady mounted swiftly and, as Zutor was adjusting his stirrups, Gaszton Simo, who had been whispering something to old Nyiresy, came up and asked if he could ride some of the way with him.

'I thought that you were going to have lunch with Nyiresy?' said Balint, who was not at all eager for the notary's company.

'I'll be back in time. I would like to ask the Count's opinion on something ... something political, nothing to do with the estate.' As Balint hesitated, he jumped on his horse and was soon riding beside him.

The little caravan got underway with Andras Zutor in the lead, sitting sideways as if kneeling in the saddle but still in full control of his mount. In the rear came the *gyorniks* in single file with the pack animals; and in between rode Balint and the notary.

When they had ridden only about a hundred paces Simo began to talk about the recent elections. Who would have thought that things would have turned out like this with the old ruling party now in the minority? How could it have happened? What would happen next? How would it affect the 1867 Compromise? What did the monarch think? Who would be the next prime minister? With all these questions he was trying to show this little aristocrat who played at politics that he too, Gaszton Simo, was no simple ink-licking notary from the backwoods but an informed man-of-the-world who deserved proper consideration. With each query he looked at Balint, hoping for an answer. The latter was silent for some time, and finally said: 'It's really too early to say definitely, but maybe the only constitutional solution will be a coalition.'

'Hm!' said Simo. 'A coalition? Could that possibly work?' He did not speak for a few moments and seemed worried. Then he went on talking in roundabout terms about how those loyal to the King had had to stand up to the machinations of revolutionary demagogues and finally arrived at what Balint realized was the purpose of this whole conversation. Perhaps, hinted Simo, the new party in power might now seek vengeance on those who had been loyal to the previous government? Did his Lordship believe that those who had given good service to the State in recent years might now find themselves in trouble? It was clear to Balint that the notary was scared that his own skin might be in danger. Reassuringly he said:

'You have nothing to fear, Mr Notary. State legal officers are elected by the community and can only be displaced as a result of disciplinary action.'

'Yes, yes, of course I know that, but...' He looked around him as if to be sure that no one would overhear, then: 'Look, sir, between men of the world, between gentlemen, I don't need to hide the truth. The fact is I fixed the last elections in Hunyad. The government candidate won by nine votes, and that was only because I myself had brought in all the voters from here, all thirty-seven of them. Well, now I hear that some people are saying that the election was rigged and that twenty of those I brought were never on the electoral roll. The rascals! Someone's already been up to spy around. Of course I threw him out.'

'What really did happen?'

The notary, thinking his explanation had been convincing enough, began to bluster: 'Well, the district judge is a good friend of mine. It was he who asked me to bring everyone. There are many bad people here; they hate me because I keep strict order, don't let them get away with anything! Also I'm the only real Hungarian here, in this little outpost. Let them grumble, I'm not afraid! But if we had a new county prefect, named by the government, then perhaps they'd think they could testify against me. False witness, of course, false witness!' He struck the pommel of his saddle to emphasize his point.

There was no need for Balint to reply at once as the road just then descended to a small river and the riders were obliged to go in single file, the sure-footed little ponies wading through the swift running water carefully testing each step for sharp or dangerous stones. When they had made the crossing successfully Simo again advanced to Balint's side.

'I have something else to request of your Lordship. The church at Gyurkuca is very small and ought to be enlarged. Only a small quantity of timber would do the job and it would create an excellent impression if it were to be donated by your Lordship. May I send them word?'

Balint said that he would look into the matter.

'I can vouch for the district *popa*, a most trustworthy man. His son is actively pro-Romanian, but it doesn't matter as he is dying of tuberculosis. But the priest is a good man, reliable; he always lets me know what is going on up there! I help him, of course, and try to keep the son out of trouble with the authorities. So can I tell them they can have the wood?'

'I can't decide now. I'll look into it when I get there.'

'But I'm vouching for him. I, Gaszton Simo!' The notary was incensed not to have his word accepted at once.

'I'll think about it,' said Abady. 'And now, if you don't mind, I would like you to return to Beles. I have things to discuss with the rangers. Good-day to you, Mr Notary!' Balint raised his hat and spurred his horse on ahead to catch up with Zutor.

Simo looked after him, his expression full of hate. 'Damned stuck-up aristocrat!' he said to himself and turning his horse abruptly he started to gallop back the way they had come. Blind with rage he nearly ran down the foresters leading the pack-horses.

Now they started to leave the valley and climb up to the high mountains. Here and there they passed log cabins surrounded by wooden fences. Dogs ran out and barked, but kept their distance as there were too many people for them to attack with safety. Krisan Gyorgye, in his self-appointed role as the young master's body-guard, ran towards them cursing, while the other porters and the men and women of the settlement giggled with amusement.

The valley they rode through was filled with a light mist, a bluish vapour that softened the outlines of everything around them while nevertheless holding a sparkling quality which hinted that the sun above was shining brightly. Almost before Balint was aware, the mist was blown away by the mountain breezes and the little party emerged on to a high ridge from which they could see an endless panorama of mountains and forests stretching into the far distance.

They stopped. There was not a cloud in the sky which arched above them like an ice-blue celestial dome. The mountain ranges in front receded in ever paler shades of cobalt, darkening only in the intervening valleys. On their left the bright sunlight etched the outlines of ridge after ridge of dense forest. As Balint took out his maps, Andras showed him the landmarks in front of them.

'There, on the right, is the Gyalu Boulini! The Szamos river curves round the base of the mountain. That sandy hill there marks the start of the foothills of the Humpleu, but we can't see the summit from here, it's too far away. Our boundary lies on the top of that mountain ridge – there! – and then descends to the river. Beyond lie the Church lands, there, on the fourth ridge, is the Intreapa. The boundary follows that bend, rises to the left and then rises again to the summit. That's the third side. His Lordship's Valko forest meets the State lands at the Pietra Talharalui, those high cliffs there.' He pointed at three rocks rising like giants' tombstones on the horizon.

Far in the distance, about four or five miles away beyond the deep valley of the Szamos river which was shrouded in wisps of low cloud, Balint could just make out some faint black specks on the snow-covered mountainside and, behind them, a patch of grey that seemed to have a toothpick planted upright beside it.

'Is that the church of Gyurkuca? Perhaps we could pass that way tomorrow? I'd like to see it.'

'As your Lordship wishes.'

The road was extremely steep and also, because it was used by the peasants for hauling down the cut tree trunks, very slippery. To Balint it seemed a miracle that the little ponies could manage to climb it at all. As they went on their way they met a few Romanian peasants on the way down, their ox-carts dragging huge trunks after them. Each time a cart appeared, Krisan Gyorgye would run forward ordering them out of the way shouting and waving his arms about to show the *mariasza* – the exalted one – that he was loyal, efficient, and always strict and severe in his master's service. His zeal was such that Balint had occasionally to intervene to prevent him boxing the ears of the poor sandal-shod peasants. Andras Zutor's behaviour was quite different. Always soft-spoken, he opened his mouth only if it were necessary to ask for a receipt or check that no more than the quota had been taken. Then he would ride on without a word.

PART THREE

The little party finally arrived at the highest point of the track which marked the boundary of the Abady forest holdings. Here they rested for a while and Balint dismounted to sit on a rock and enjoy the view before they plunged once more into the darkness of the woods.

Four of the *gyorniks* went ahead so as to prepare the night's camp before their master arrived. With long even strides, they soon crossed the open meadow and disappeared into the dense fir plantations.

Abady decided to follow, but this time he went on foot for, not being used to the high wooden saddle and the steepness of the climb, his legs were beginning to feel cramped. Going was slow on the icy path. The forest was beautiful and mysterious, silent and seemingly full of secrets. The sun's rays, unable to penetrate the dense overhead foliage, cast no shadows and, on each side of the track, dark fir trees stood, majestic in their perfect immobility. As the little party moved slowly onwards the deep silence was broken by the faint sound of knocking in the distance and, as they turned a bend in the track, in a clearing fifty yards below, two men could be seen cutting a great fir with their axes. Wood thieves, obviously, for as soon as they realized that they had been spotted they ran swiftly off downhill, with Krisan Gyorgye after them, using his axe-handle as a rudder as he skidded down the slope on his heels as if they were skis. Fast though he moved the men had long disappeared into the depths of the forest by the time he reached the tree stump. For a moment, until Abady told him to return, Krisan stood there shouting curses after the thieves, and he continued to growl and curse under his breath long after the march had been resumed, thereby still showing the *mariasza* how faithfully he was served.

The camp was well sited, a low stone wall forming a semicircle under an outcrop of rock. In the centre a pillar made of a tree trunk supported a roof thickly covered by fir-boughs. Below, beds of more fir-boughs neatly tied together, were ready for the rugs that would be thrown over them. Firewood, long dry branches, had been laid against the entire length of the stone wall. When lit these would have to be fed all night so that those inside the shelter would not freeze to death.

Even before they had finished unloading the horses and bringing their supplies into the shelter, Zsukuczo, who knew better than the others how to arrange the dry sticks, feed the young flames slowly and intersperse them with strips of resiny bark so that the flames spread evenly, had had the campfire started. In ten minutes it was burning merrily.

It was Zsukuczo, too, who had chosen the site. As a former poacher he knew the whole forest even better than the others and he knew, too, how important was the protection offered by the rock-face and where the nearest spring of sweet water bubbled up among the rocks. No man bred to the mountains would ever camp on an open site or far from water.

Darkness fell and Zutor handed out the bread, bacon and onions that were to be their evening meal. The men, knowing their station in life, settled near the fire a little away from the place accorded to the master; and when Zutor gave out the large tin cups generously filled with brandy, they all drank noisily, with much clearing of throats, which was the way of mountain folk when they wanted to show their appreciation that so little water had been added to the spirit.

As soon as Balint got into his sleeping bag he fell into a deep sleep partly because he was so tired but also because everyone slept well in the sharp mountain air. At about eleven, however, he woke up, conscious that around the campfire his party was entertaining visitors. Three men had joined the group, as is the custom in the mountains where men will walk three hours and more if they see a camp fire where they can come and talk the night away exchanging news and discussing their problems.

As everyone thought that the *mariasza* was asleep they talked freely without restraint. They spoke in Romanian, and one of the visitors, an old shrivelled man squatting on his haunches, who was facing Balint, was recounting a long and mournful tale of injustice concerning a house, money, lambs, loans and interest, and cheese. The words *domnu Notar* occurred frequently and there was some reference to the Romanian priest at Gyurkuca. Even more frequently he repeated a name, Rusz Pantyilimon, and each time he did so he spat contemptuously into the fire.

Balint raised himself on to his elbow trying to hear what was being said, but even though he could remember a few words of Romanian from his childhood, he could not grasp the details of the old man's tale of woe. He understood, all the same, that the others commiserated with him and nodded their heads in sympathy.

At one moment Zsukuczo got up from where he was sitting to stir the dying embers of the fire with his axe-handle. When all was arranged he threw on some new dry branches and, as the flames sprang up, he noticed that Balint was awake. Quickly he turned away and said something to the others who fell silent.

Balint watched as the campfire blazed into life again. The thick logs on which it had been built were already half consumed, and a multitude of tiny white flames glowed round the dark stumps at the heart of the fire. Every now and again, stirred by some internal gust of air there stretched out long tentacles of orange flame, dancing with apparent life, which rose up in moving arabesques only to vanish and die as quickly as they had appeared. He watched for a long time, feeling that he had never before seen such beauty, such a raging desire for life, and as this thought came into his mind he was reminded of Adrienne flying over the ice. Did she not have the same restless thirst for movement, for life? Was it not of a flame that she had then made him think, as she fluttered, bending and gliding from one partner to another, her half-opened mouth red and burning with life?

Thinking now once more of Adrienne, he felt that at last he knew what she was really like and that she, like the fire, was driven by some fatal force of which she herself could barely be aware but which, powerful and uncontrollable, must, in the end, prove fatal.

Balint felt relieved that he had at last understood the truth behind her mystery, and said to himself that he was lucky to have realized this before he was tempted to start an affair with her. Driven by this demonic passion Adrienne was not a woman with whom one could amuse oneself for a few hours, with whom one could have a light-hearted adventure and then part to remain light-hearted friends. Ah, no! It would be wiser not to start anything. Of course it would have been different if he had been in love with her, but he wasn't. Better leave well alone, far better . . .

And then he went back to sleep.

When Balint awoke it was already dawn. It was bitterly cold and he was shivering. He felt better after a mug of hot tea laced with rum, and better still when he had eaten the bacon that Krisan prepared for him, roasting it on a split of wood over the embers of the fire. As he ate the men started loading up the horses and soon they were on their way again.

When the track passed small open meadows Balint could occasionally get glimpses of the distant mountains as they had the day before, but though now all was bathed in the same dazzling clear light, the morning colours were not at all the same. Where yesterday had been in varying shades of cobalt, today the faraway mountain ridges glowed with a lilac tint shaded by patches of pale green, and in the dawn light the snow seemed pink. They reached a place where their route was crossed by another.

'We'll pass by here again tomorrow when we return from Gyurkuca,' said Zutor, and he went on, pointing to the south: 'If your Lordship wishes we can then go on down into the valley of the Retyicel, or perhaps turn by the waterfall at the Burnt Stone and go down to Szkrind.'

The road wound slowly downhill. Coming up along the same track were three buffalo carts but this time Krisan Gyorgye did not run forward and order them out of the way as he had done when they met the woodcutters the previous day. These were men of the Kalotaszeg, people with whom no one trifled.

Balint stared at the buffaloes with interest. He had never seen these animals in the winter when, unlike other wiser beasts, they shed their ragged stringy fur to reveal sleek coats of shiny black hair. Because of this reversal of the normal process buffalo owners would provide their animals with quilted blankets made of sack-cloth and so fitted that they covered the animals from neck to tail and were tied under their chests with a wide girth.

The buffaloes moved slowly, dragging behind them carts laden with cut wood for hut-building, and though their sad, long-lashed eyes had a wary look as they approached Balint's horses, they did not waver in their solemn progress. There were three men and two boys with the carts. All were dressed in the same way as Honey Zutor in leather waistcoats and blue shirts, leggings and boots; except for the boys who wore sandals, even in the deep snow. The men did not speak as they showed their wood-cutting permits to Zutor but, after he had checked that they were in order, the *Kalotaszegi* lifted their hats in polite and dignified greeting and went silently on their way.

Balint had decided that as the air was so cold he would walk rather than ride. The track at this point was an easy one, a far gentler slope than any they had so far encountered. Once again the only sound to be heard was the faint crunch of the horses' hoofs on the snow, until, as before, there came the faint sound of someone cutting wood. At first they could hear only one repeated knocking, but slowly, as they moved forward, this seemed to come from several different directions. Balint asked Zutor why this was, and if the cutters were allowed to fell trees wherever they liked.

'Not exactly, my Lord, but once they have got their permit

from the forestry office they can fell anywhere they like on this side of the mountain.'

'Who decides how much they can fell?'

'They can cut as much as they like, but they can only take out what it says on the permit.'

'What a waste! What disorder!' thought Balint. He turned again to Zutor. 'Haven't they heard of forest planning?'

'Oh, yes, my Lord, but they don't do it.' And he went on to tell Balint how, twenty years before when he was still a boy, he had gone to the forest with one of the estate engineers and spent two months with measuring tapes, signposts, planning how the forest would be developed for years ahead. 'That's when I first learned to love the mountains,' he said, 'and afterwards, in the spring, he took me to Beles when he presented his reports. It was many years ago, just after Count Tamas died. Nobody's worked like that for a long time!'

<hr>

When dusk fell Balint's party left the long watershed and descended to the valley of the river Szamos, where they found a clearing at which feed could be bought for the horses.

The men started to build a shelter on a slope above the river and in front of it a campfire which was already ablaze by the time the shelter was ready.

As on the previous night the food was cooked and shared out, the brandy handed round and, as the little band finished their meal and the *mariasza* retired to his makeshift bed, other men joined them for the company and the news of the outside world. Though somewhat restrained in front of Balint they seemed to relax as soon as they thought he was sleeping; and once again the talk was all about the notary and the priest – the *popa* of Gyurkuca – both of whom they seemed to detest equally, though their real curses, as the night before, were reserved for the man they called Rusz Pantyilimon who should be 'damned to Draku!'

In the morning they struck camp early, and by ten o'clock they came to the outlying cottages of the village of Gyurkuca, the main part of which was built on a low hill surrounded by steep cliffs that rose almost like an island in the centre of a wide bend in the river. Here a makeshift bridge had been thrown across the river. It was supported by two high pillars, one on each side with a third in the middle of the river, and in between were fixed some narrow wooden planks set three to four metres above the level of the water. At each end loose planks that bent with every step were placed to lead up to the bridge itself. These were left loose so that they could be replaced with longer ones should the river rise in the spring floods.

Three men were waiting at the foot of the bridge. In the middle stood the priest Timbus, the *popa*, a fat man with a little black goatee that did nothing to hide his double chins, wearing his clerical frock and a fur coat and, on his head, the wide-brimmed hat that was normally brought out only when the bishop came on a pastoral visit. On each side stood one of the town elders, both in their best clothes with sheepskin hats, their hair tied in braids over their ears. These two took off their hats and all three started bowing obsequiously when Balint was still a hundred yards away. When he approached the priest stepped forward and respectfully requested his Lordship to dismount and honour their church with a visit, saying that the community needed his help.

Balint got off his horse and as he did so the two old men came nearer, knelt before him and kissed the hem of his coat. The priest, too, made a show of deference in trying to kiss the hand that Balint held out to be shaken. This Balint naturally did not allow, knowing that these gestures were symbolic – the ritual greeting of respect traditional in the mountain country – and were not to be taken as a sign of obsequiousness. This done, he moved towards the bridge.

The first to climb up was the *popa*, then came Krisan, holding out his axe-handle to pull his master up the steep planks. The tall Todor Paven and Juanye Vomului stood on either side of Balint until he had reached the pillar, and then walked on with their arms outstretched so as to catch him if he fell. To do this they had somehow to get across the river bed which meant scrambling over snow-covered rocks or plunging their feet in the shallow water that ran between the ice-floes.

Balint then walked up the hill with the priest and the two old men while his travelling companions stayed below. The snow on the hillside had been cut into steps. At the top was the priest's house, standing on stone foundations on the sloping hillside thereby giving the impression from below that it was two stories high, though from higher up it could be seen that the back of the house was sunk into the hillside. A covered veranda ran the length of the house, leading directly from the front door into the family living-room, and, leaning over the balustrade waiting for the distinguished visitor, stood the priest's two beautiful, doe-eyed daughters. Near them Balint's attention was drawn to a thin young man, still barely more than a youth, who was lying in the sun on a long wicker chair covered in cushions. He was wrapped to the chin in a sheepskin coat so that all that could be seen of him was an emaciated face with tell-tale red patches on his cheeks. His mouth was tightly shut and his glance was both curious and hostile as he watched Balint pass in front of him.

Balint lifted his hat in greeting but the boy did not respond. He only watched in silence, hatred and distrust in his eyes.

'He's a foolish boy, very foolish,' said the priest Timbus, apologizing for the rudeness of his son in not returning the master's salute. 'He's not like other people and causes me much trouble! He's very, very sick...'

They had to walk round the church to find the entrance which, since the Orthodox custom demanded it should be on the west, was situated on a narrow shelf that faced the steep abyss below.

They stepped in through a small doorway. The little church was built of wood, and inside the walls had been plastered and were covered from floor to ceiling with mural paintings; scenes from the Old Testament on the right and from the New on the left. The colours were faded but clear. The paintings were naïve and primitively executed in the old Byzantine style by a travelling painter who had come to Gyurkuca some eighty years before. The first thing Balint noticed was the story of Elijah on the right. The prophet was shown ascending to heaven in a Transylvanian peasant's cart surrounded by vivid orange flames; and every detail of the vehicle, even down to the carved cart-pole and the masterpins that held the harness were lovingly and faithfully represented. Turning, Balint saw that the whole wall above the entrance, facing the iconostasis and the altar, was covered by a *Last Judgement* in which huge devils with fearsome faces were busy swallowing mouthfuls of sinners, ten or twenty at a time. Balint was cynically amused to note that the sinners were all Hungarians and clearly distinguished as such by their large moustaches, boots and clothes decorated with elaborate braiding. On the other hand, the saved, who were being transported by angels to the Land of the Just, were dressed in the traditional Romanian belted shirts that hung to their knees.

Balint would have liked more time to examine the paintings but Popa Timbus, anxious for the master's aid, drew him away and started to explain what he wanted. The building was too small, the congregation had doubled in size and there wasn't room for half of them in the church as it was. They wanted to build an extension on the western front. Only forty beams would be needed;

forty beams and twenty rafters, no more; but the community had no funds, no money at all, so if these beams could be found...?

'What will happen to the *Last Judgement* if you enlarge the church? Will it be destroyed?'

The light ironic smile with which Balint had looked at the damnation of the Hungarians had not escaped the *popa*'s notice.

'Oh, that! Never mind that! It's a bad painting anyway, bad, very bad!' And taking Balint by the coat sleeve he led him outside to continue his explanation. 'Here, on the new front, we'll carve an inscription on the wood that the enlargement of the church was made possible by the generous gift of Count Abady. Everyone will see it! It will last for ever!' he said, thinking that this would clinch the matter and be for Balint an irresistible inducement. He smiled slyly, congratulating himself on his own cunning when Balint promised him the wood, little realizing that this is what the Count had already decided to do and had only delayed giving an answer until he was himself at Gyurkuca, and could do it himself without the good offices of the notary.

On their way down the hill they again passed the priest's house where the tubercular youth lay on his cushioned bed. This time the *popa* admonished the boy and told him to greet the Count, who had just given the wood for the church. The boy nodded but did not speak. In his look burned the same hatred as before and his eyes followed Abady as he passed.

Below, at the bridge across the frozen river, Balint took his leave of the *popa* and the two grey-haired elders and, looking back up at the priest's house he saw the sick boy still staring intently at him.

From Gyurkuca the road followed the river Szamos down to Toszerat where Balint owned a sawmill. Krisan Gyorgye lived nearby. From there they continued on their way uphill to the next watershed, but before they arrived at the top they decided to turn off and make a detour to see the famous waterfall.

The valley was narrow but so thickly wooded that no view of the other side was possible from the road until they came to a place where the strong winds had cut a wide swathe in the forest. On the opposite side of the valley a few small peasants' houses could be seen and, about a quarter of a mile above them, a square stone house with a roof of tiles rather than the stone shingles usual in the mountains. The windows were heavily barred and the plot of land on which the house stood was surrounded by high stone walls

PART THREE

now almost submerged by snowdrifts. Even from across the valley Balint could hear the barking of three ferocious guard-dogs.

'What on earth is that strange building?' asked Balint.

Zutor replied: 'It belongs to a man called Rusz Pantyilimon. He decided to move out here.'

Balint remembered the name and looked at the house with renewed interest. 'Why did he build such a fortress?'

'Well, your Lordship, I can't really say. Perhaps he is afraid . . .'

'Afraid? Why?'

'Why? Because . . . well, he's afraid, that's all.'

Balint would have none of these evasions and ordered Zutor to tell the truth. The story was that Rusz, a Romanian, had been a school teacher somewhere in Erdohat and there had been some trouble which cost him his job. Some people said he had tried to corrupt small boys. To get away he had come up here to the mountains in the Retyicel country where his mother had been born. Soon he had set up as a money-lender, and now he was a rich man.

'How did he start if he had no money?'

'People say it was the *popa* who provided the money, and they split the profits!'

'And the *popa*? Where did he get the money?'

Zutor hesitated again. Then he replied: 'Well, your Lordship, it's said that he's an agent of the Unita Bank and funded by them.'

Balint tried to remember the snatches of conversation he had heard round the campfire. 'Does Notary Simo have anything to do with all this?'

Honey Zutor looked around to see if they were overheard. Krisan Gyorgye and young Stefan were some way ahead clearing the way of fallen branches and the others were still far behind them with the pack horses. When sure that no one could hear what he was saying, the forester went on: 'People do say that he writes the loan contracts, and that what he reads out to them is not what is written on the paper! That's what they say, but, your Lordship, you can't believe everything you hear. These are ignorant, foolish people!' He seemed to regret that he had gone so far because he quickly added: 'Your Lordship ordered me to relate what people say . . . it's not me who says all this. I don't believe a word of it.'

Balint understood Honey's fears and, shaking his head at him, said reassuringly:

'Don't worry! Nothing you have said will go any further!'

It was already dusk by the time they arrived in the Valea Arsza under the high peak of *Egett kö* – the Burnt Stone – where they were to make their last camp.

Here in the deeply forested valley the dawn broke later than on the high mountains. Nevertheless the little party was early on its way. The going was hard, for many fallen trees, their trunks deeply buried in snow, blocked the way. Even so it was easier for the men than for the ponies, whose weight made every step hazardous. The calm and dexterity of the animals was extraordinary, impressing Balint with the skill with which they tentatively put down each hoof to be sure it was on solid ground and not in a snowdrift.

Balint, who was anxious to get the best view of the famous waterfall – famous even though it was so difficult to reach – started descending the steep side of the ravine with Stefan, Krisan and Todor Paven. Zutor he sent the long way round to meet them at the lower creek with the horses. To get down the almost vertical thickly wooded side of the canyon the men cut long fir branches which they used as ropes to lower each other over the snow-clad boulders. At last they reached the bed of the ravine which was so narrow that it was like a very deep well. It was almost dark as the sun never reached these depths, and on each side were nearly perpendicular stone cliffs which seemed black against the occasional patches of snow. The vegetation was dense and lush with hanging beards of moss, thick bunches of fern fronds which were now covered with tiny frozen droplets of spray that hung like ice-thorns in the still air. Though the waterfall could still not be seen, they were so close that at every step they were drenched by the spray, while the roar of the falling water echoed round them like thunder. Then, clinging to their long fir boughs and sliding, slipping through the snowdrifts, they rounded one more giant boulder and there it was, right in front of them, a huge arc of water springing clear from the rocks a hundred feet above.

Nothing interrupted the fall of the water: it was like a pillar of liquid bluish-green metal in front of the glistening black of the wet rock cliffsides, and from this dark mass rose white foam-crests of spray, which in turn were transformed into large droplets white as pearls that fell into the boiling swirling mass of water in the basin at the foot of the great fall. Sometimes a thread of water would break away from the central mass and seemed to hang quivering in the air until it too dissolved and merged with the rest. Immediately others would take its place springing out freely over the chasm below, endlessly repeated, endlessly varied, a constant picture of which the details were never the same from one moment to another. Underground springs fed the basin at the foot of the fall and even when in the air it was degrees below zero steam would mingle with the spray to form icicles which hung from every bow and every overhanging rock, so that the fall itself was framed by pillars of ice.

Balint was fascinated by the sight of the great surging energy and apparent will to live that was represented by all this turbulence at the heart of the silent, motionless frozen forest. In its own way it was like the soaring flames of the camp-fires, a force of nature, invincible, unquenchable, dominating all around by the sheer force of its blind progress to unknown but inevitable ends. Once again, as when Balint lay contemplating the fire so now, in front of the waterfall, Adrienne's image was conjured up by the beauty and restless movement of uncontrolled nature. He could only think of the woman as once more he saw in his mind the image of her graceful form, her movements, the arc of her lips, and her impulsive, enchanting smile.

Angry at himself for allowing her image to pursue him, Balint turned away and hurried down to the edge of the basin below him. But the image did not disappear; so clearly did Adrienne remain in his mind that he began to wonder if he were bewitched. Dismayed, he asked himself why of all the women in the world he should have become obsessed by one so complicated and capricious.

Following the path beside the rushing water he decided that until he had freed himself from the torment of thinking of Adrienne he would do everything he could to avoid meeting her.

Chapter Four

A TELEGRAM WAS WAITING for Balint in Kolozsvar. Parliament had been recalled and he would have to leave at once if he were to be there for the formal presentation of credentials before the session opened.

His mother was upset. 'You never spend any time with me,' she complained. 'It's almost worse than when you were a diplomat!' She made him promise to come back at the end of the month no matter what happened in the capital.

The atmosphere in Budapest was just as stormy as it had been the last time Balint had been there. The members of the coalition now in office were still delirious with pleasure at finding themselves in power and clung desperately to their election promises, insisting that no matter how they, and only they, would bring about the independence of the banking and customs systems and the national integrity of the army commands. But it was not to be as easy as the coalitionists imagined. There had been audiences with the monarch in Vienna; and Franz-Josef, in his capacity as King of Hungary, had rejected all their extremist demands. The crisis, therefore, was no longer that of opposing political ideals for now it had become constitutional, a conflict between the government and the crown with the various opposition parties jockeying for position in an undignified and confused scramble.

The first two meetings of the House passed relatively calmly, but at the third a storm broke out. In his opening speech the Minister-President made an outspoken indictment of all that had happened in the past. No party was spared, every word was an accusation, a battle cry. Uproar followed. After two more brief sittings the House was adjourned.

Only one event marked this brief and largely useless session, a sad, absurd, unnecessary and, had it not ended in tragedy, almost ridiculous incident.

One of the newly elected Members was old Istvan Keglevich who would have been Speaker of the House if Tisza's party had won the election and so responsible for implementing the new Rules of Procedure which had been proposed in November. It was for this reason that, for the first time in his long life, he had accepted nomination as a parliamentary candidate.

Tisza himself had selected him for this difficult task because he had a commanding personality, and was forceful, courageous and daring. He also had a first class brain. He could be as merciless as a Renaissance tyrant prince, and as lordly, even though he had lost nearly all his once vast fortune in speculative economic and artistic ventures. The reason for this was simple: Keglevich was way ahead of his time and whether he planned improvements in planting forests, founding theatres or building distilleries, he always spent more than the budget and then met the losses from his private means until he had nothing left. At the time of his election he was Director of the State-owned theatres, an honorary post which he held with such distinction and efficiency that Franz-Josef had accorded him a state pension in lieu of a salary to which, as it was an honorary position, he was not entitled. In this situation the man-eating wolves among the Members of Parliament found a succulent morsel into which they could sink their teeth.

During the verification of the Members' credentials an extreme left-wing member asked to be heard as soon as Keglevich's name was mentioned. He accused him of being disqualified for membership of the House as he was a servant of the crown, a King's man on the payroll of Vienna, and that this was not compatible with being a Member of Parliament. The Opposition went mad with joy. No one stopped to consider that as Keglevich had renounced the pension on his election there was no longer any incompatibility. They had found a whipping boy ... and whip him they would!

From all sides of the House came hoots of derision and Balint was disgusted by the pleasure they seemed to take in sneering at and deriding this distinguished seventy-year-old man who might have been their Speaker.

As the wolves howled the old man sat erect on the front bench, his back straight and his great chest puffed out proudly like a mighty bear surrounded by snapping hounds. His chin stuck out. He sat motionless before the storm, but his eyes searched the room for the first man to insult him personally so that he could challenge him to a duel.

His opportunity came when new young member shouted: 'King's lackey! Hireling swine!' No sooner had the words been uttered than Keglevich had leapt to his feet and challenged the man. Gravely and in measured terms he demanded satisfaction for the insult, which could only be assured by a fight with the weapons of his own choice.

Speaking with cold authority he issued his orders. The duel would be fought with his own swords, old-fashioned weapons with broad rigid blades honed to a knife-edge. No bandages would be permitted; thrusts would be allowed – and this despite the fact that he was a swordsman of the old Hungarian school which used only cutting strokes while his opponent was of the Italian style – the *punto d'arresto* in which the master stroke was a killing thrust. The next day Keglevich was carried out dead from the gymnasium where the encounter had been arranged. At the first 'On guard!' the old man attacked with all the vigour of youth. His opponent backed away and then suddenly countered with a thrust of such force that the old man was run through, the sword point coming out through his back. So a man of no importance took the life of a statesman old enough to be his father.

As soon as the House had been adjourned Balint, after only ten days in Budapest, returned home to Kolozsvar as he had promised his mother to do. He arrived on Shrove Tuesday in time for the Mardi Gras Ball, and though he was not all that keen to attend he realized that as everyone knew he had returned he had no excuse not to go. He decided to put in an appearance but to leave early. After all he had no reason to stay until dawn. After dinner he told his mother he must go and dress.

'Come and see me when you're ready,' said Countess Roza. 'I haven't seen you in tails for such a long time and I like you in your finery. Come and be admired! We don't go to bed early.'

'No, indeed!' said Mrs Tothy.

'We'll be waiting for you!' said Mrs Baczo.

Balint promised to return and went to his room. Laid out on the bed was the tail suit with the stiff white shirt and collar neatly placed between the coat and white waistcoat. The sight of these formal clothes brought back memories of Budapest and especially of his cousin Laszlo. Balint stripped and started to shave before the washstand on which a jug of hot water stood waiting with a towel laid over it. As he did so he remembered how he had only seen Laszlo once or twice, always at the Casino and always dressed in evening clothes. They had only exchanged a few words because there had been dancing every evening in the great ballroom on the ground floor and Laszlo, now the official organizer, had to be present all the time. He had wanted Balint to join him, but Balint had refused as it would mean returning to his hotel to change. Laszlo had not insisted.

Now, lathering his chin, he recalled how Laszlo's manner had somehow seemed subtly different, more assured and distinguished. He had carried his head higher than when they had last met at Simonvasar.

As Balint dipped his razor into the hot water – for if he didn't shave in the evening he would be covered in bristles before morning – he remembered how an English friend had once told him that no gentleman should ever wash without a razor!

A little later, now in trousers and stiff white shirt, Balint returned to the mirror to put on his tie, an operation he did not relish as unless it was perfectly achieved in one single movement the starched white piqué cotton became wrinkled and the whole thing had to be done again. Balint's first effort went wrong and, as he started to thread a second tie through the loop at the back of his collar it came to his mind that Adrienne was sure to be there. He imagined her in the dark green dress she had worn at Var-Siklod – though as no doubt she possessed many dresses there was no reason to think it would be the same one. Still, he could see her in green, her dark hair fluttering as she moved, dancing with one of the young Alvinczys or Pityu Kendy. Let her dance the whole night if she wished! He at any rate would not be there to see because he would only go for a few moments, just long enough to show his face so that no one could say he'd stayed away out of pride.

The second white tie was a success. After glancing approvingly at himself in the looking glass above the dressing table, Balint stepped back to the bed, put on his white waistcoat, checked the pearl buttons, put on his tail coat and was ready to leave. Suddenly he thought of a little cocotte he had met in Budapest. She, he decided, would be better for him. It would not cost him much and would be far better than getting entangled with a married woman. Of course it had been different when he had been abroad *en poste*. Everyone knew that diplomats would move on, that they were not their own masters and that any affair must naturally come to an end. He had had several liaisons with married women who, as the phrase went, 'accorded him their favours', cried a little when the parting came, gave him a last night of passionate lovemaking ('to remember me by!') and then maybe wrote a letter or two or a postcard before the inevitable silence. These affairs, transient though both parties had known they must be, had had their compensations. The first moves were as exhilarating as the beginning of a deer stalk – with the difference that though the prey might have to be pursued for two or three weeks, both knew that the doe wanted, eventually, to be caught.

Now almost ready, Balint started to collect all those small objects without which no gentleman felt properly dressed: a slim gold watch on a chain, keys, cigarette case and lighter, wallet and some small change. Then he selected four fine linen handkerchiefs and sprinkled them with eau-de-cologne as he had been taught by an elegant and accomplished Swedish lady during his stay in Stockholm. It was she who had told him that men should never use scent, which was either vulgar or effeminate: cologne alone was socially acceptable. And she had taught him many other things besides, the fine points of making love, the etiquette of a lady's bedchamber, the details of dressing and undressing. What a charmer she had been and how intelligent! He wondered what she was doing now ... and he tried hard to remember her name.

Checking that he had forgotten nothing, he went down to see his mother.

Chapter Five

THE MARDI GRAS BALL at Kolozsvar was the most important social event of the whole Carnival season. It was held in the Assembly Rooms of the Casino and so strong were the ancient traditions that some men still wore, for this occasion, the mulberry-coloured tailcoats and grey trousers that had been the fashion in the 1830s. The ball, which naturally began on the evening of Shrove Tuesday, went on well into the morning of Ash Wednesday.

It was also the tradition that even the oldest ladies turned out for Mardi Gras, dressed as if for an imperial reception, and wearing all the family jewels they could find a place for. Even those who had kept away from all the other dances turned up on this special night and it was only young girls who did not wear imposing tiaras.

By ten o'clock the rooms were already filling up, carriage after carriage drawing up at the Casino portico to discharge their cargoes of soberly-dressed men and sumptuously-dressed women and girls. Adrienne arrived with her husband and her two sisters and the three women moved slowly up the steps holding their long skirts with one hand and clutching their furs to them with the other.

Pal Uzdy did not wait for them. He hated walking slowly so rather than matching his pace to theirs he hurried up the steps and was already waiting at the door by the time that Adrienne and the others were only halfway up. Uzdy was a tall, thin-shouldered man who stood a head taller than most. He had inherited this feature from his mother, an Absolon, whose brother, whom Uzdy resembled, had been a well-known Asian explorer. But while the uncle had been a large well-proportioned man with massive muscular shoulders, the nephew, long and narrow, seemed more like those emaciated bronze statuettes of Mephistopheles which became popular after Gounod had produced his *Faust*. Pal Uzdy's head, however, had a marked oriental look,

PART THREE

with a high forehead, olive-brown almost green skin, with high cheekbones and hair growing from a widow's peak on his forehead. With a small pointed beard and close-cut moustaches with long drooping waxed points in the Tartar manner, his triangular face had a satanic look, unusual and interesting. Though he dressed with impeccable care his clothes were unfashionably cut as if to underline that their wearer was too distinguished to care about anything so trivial as fashion. Condescendingly he shook hands with Farkas Alvinczy and Gazsi Kadacsay, who were waiting to conduct the ladies to the ballroom; and while he did so stood watching the approach of his wife.

Adrienne came slowly up the steps, a smile on her face, conscious that she was looking her best and knowing that others thought so too. She knew how well the diamond stars set off her for once carefully dressed dark hair. She had put on her newest and most ravishing dress, which was cut princess-style in one flowing line from bust to flaring hem. Of flame-coloured shot silk, its folds glistened with subtly changing shades of colour as she moved; and she knew it would cause a sensation when she removed her cloak.

She was smiling, too, for another reason. She was pleased with a piece of news related to her by her youngest sister Margit – she who always knew everything – namely that Balint Abady had arrived that morning and so she would have someone to talk to who was more than a tailor's dummy and who knew how to dance. At the same time a fleeting thought crossed her mind, a thought which also carried an unanswered question; did she have any reason to be made happy by this news? Did not the fact that he had not joined them at the skating rink show that he was avoiding her? It was only a passing doubt, so transient that she was still smiling when she joined her husband at the top of the steps.

'What are you smiling at?' he asked.

'I'm just happy . . . happy to dance.'

But though this was what she said, her smile faded and she looked at Uzdy with a hostile light in her eyes. Her mouth turned down and her half-opened lips closed tightly as she moved away from him, her head held high, to accept Baron Gazsi's arm.

The dowagers all sat in a line on the sofas ranged along the long wall of the Assembly Room. A few of the older men sat with them, among them the three Kendys – Crookface, Dani and Uncle Ambrus – though the last still occasionally took the floor. The most strategic point, opposite the gypsy band and from where she could watch both the doors to the card-room and to the billiard-room, which tonight had been transformed into a supper-room, had been selected by Aunt Lizinka. Huddled as usual into a large armchair with her feet tucked up under her, a long-handled tortoiseshell lorgnette in her right hand, she chose this place as the best from which she could gather grist for her gossip. Turning her sharp vulture nose in every direction, never missing a detail of who came and went, she kept up a constant stream of malicious stories about everyone she saw.

'My dears, it's a real scandal! She keeps him with her all the time. The scoundrel's actually living in the house at Szilvas, and that idiot of a husband doesn't even seem to mind. Perhaps he can't do it himself!' and she laughed spitefully as she unfolded her version of the story of Baron Wickwitz and the pretty little Countess Abonyi.

Prompted perhaps by her own memories, her old eyes flashed with glee as she said: 'Of course women in our time used to have lovers, but nobody kept them in their own stables, like a stallion at stud!' Then she turned to Countess Kamuthy, who was well-known to have had more than one lover in the past and who even now was rumoured to take an interest in young actors, and went on: 'Isn't that true, my dear?' Countess Kamuthy murmured something noncommittal; she did not mind the insinuation but did not take kindly to the words 'in our time', for although she was now acting as chaperone to one of her granddaughters, she was at least ten years younger than old Lizinka.

'Now, Adelma, you must know all there is to know about it,' continued Lizinka, turning to Countess Gyalakuthy who sat on her right. 'After all, it's going on in your part of the world, under your very nose!

Countess Gyalakuthy, kind and charitable as always, merely replied: 'All I know is that he's training Abonyi's horses this season. That's why he's staying there: Abonyi himself invited him.'

'He! He! He!' Old Lizinka cackled, 'why, he's a regular Chef Pali!'

'Chef Pali? What *do* you mean?'

'It's an old story. My great uncle Teleki had a head cook called Pali who had a pretty young wife. One day someone told my uncle that every night one of the footmen was sleeping with the cook's wife. So my uncle sent for the man and told him this must stop. "But, your lordship," said the footman, "Chef Pali agreed!"

PART THREE

— "Well, if Chef Pali agreed I don't mind either!" said Uncle Teleki; and so it was settled. Therefore I say that Abonyi's a Chef Pali! Then, with mock solicitude she turned again towards Countess Gyalakuthy.

'I do feel for you, dear, I know he used to come over often to see you. Of course men will be men and it would be silly to mind that! And I don't really care what she does either, but then *I* don't have marriageable young daughters to protect. If I did I certainly wouldn't like to let loose such a light-bottomed little thief among them!'

'Light-bottomed thief?' said Countess Gyalakuthy, genuinely puzzled.

'Thief! That's what they call people who steal, don't they? ... and just as some people are light-fingered, other women steal their men by waggling their backsides at them. *That's* why I call her a light-bottomed thief!'

And Aunt Lizinka went on in the same strain for the entire time she stayed at the ball.

By the time that Adrienne and her sisters arrived there was already quite a crowd on the dance floor. Aunt Lizinka watched through her lorgnette as they were immediately surrounded by a band of young men eager to greet them and carry them off to dance. Judith and Margit were soon whirled away, and almost immediately Adrienne moved on to the floor with Adam Alvinczy. They made an impressive pair. Adam, tall and well-built like all the Alvinczys, was a handsome man with a straight somewhat Greek profile, short nose and high forehead. He danced well and his dark blue evening suit brought out the highlights in Adrienne's dress, which glittered like fire as she whirled in his arms.

'Heavens! Look at that!' cackled old Lizinka as loudly as a pea-hen. 'What kind of a dress d'you call that? It ought to be forbidden, it's nothing but a shift! God in Heaven, I don't believe she's wearing a corset. In my time she'd have been run out of town for less! Scandalous!'

Adrienne heard it all and as she turned and glided across the floor in Adam's arms she looked straight at Aunt Lizinka with a smile in her amber eyes, her head held high, conscious that nothing the malevolent old lady could say would dim the radiance of her youth and beauty.

By the time that Balint had taken leave of his mother it was already quite late and when he arrived at the ball they had just finished the second quadrille and were striking up for the last waltz before supper. He entered the great hall of the Assembly Rooms and, slipping past the group of men who clustered round the door, kissed the hands of the old ladies sitting nearby. He did not stay there long – too many couples came bumping into him as they waltzed by – but, glancing round the room until he caught a glimpse of Adrienne, who was now dancing with Pityu Kendy, he moved on to the next room where a group of older men were clustered round the fireplace talking politics while they waited for supper. Balint, fresh from Budapest and presumed to be fully informed as to what was going on, was given a warm welcome. Everyone hoped that he would confirm their own ideas and prophecies, and turned to him to judge who was in the right. The first were Abonyi, who declared that the only hope lay in a Government under Andrassy's leadership; and fat lisping Kamuthy, who cried that 'thith wath treathen and everyone who doth not demand Perthonal Union' ith a traitor to hith country'. Kamuthy's fat cheeks were red with excitement.

'Yeth, yeth, we accept only Perthonal Union!' he shouted as if his was the only voice that mattered. Since running for Parliament, his self-confidence had grown enormously, even though he had lost the seat by a small margin.

'Why didn't you come skating that day?' asked Adrienne.

Balint guessed that she had waited until they were alone before asking this question. They had danced several times, met more than once at the buffet and sat together at one of the large tables with some of the younger dancers. Only now, he noticed, did she ask this question when the csárdás, which was always the first dance after the supper break, had started and most of the others had gone back to the ballroom.

Adrienne asked the question simply, not in anger or resentment, but in much the same tone and with the same smile as when she had sat talking gaily with Adam and Pityu at supper. It was an ironic smile, only mildly provocative, and as the tone of her voice had in no way changed since the light-hearted chatter at supper Balint realized that the real significance of her query lay in the fact that she had waited until then to ask it.

'That afternoon? Before I went out to our forests?'

'Yes. You never came! I waited a long time, and was late getting home, just because of you!'

She was still smiling, but her eyes were grave, with the calm gravity of a lioness in repose.

PART THREE

Bending towards her, and looking deeply into those strange onyx eyes, Balint said, very slowly: 'I was there.'

'You were? But then why...?'

'Why? I watched you for a long time, and you seemed different, a new Addy, someone I'd never seen before. I saw you immediately I passed the entrance, but I couldn't come any closer. I just had to watch. You seemed to be someone I didn't know, a stranger, not my Addy at all, but someone different.'

'Different? In what way someone not myself?' Her smile faltered as she caught the intensity in Balint's voice.

'You showed me something I'd never seen before, a new side to yourself... Besides those others were there. I couldn't intrude, I could only stand and watch. You were so beautiful...' Then, so as not to sound too commonplace, he added: '...so beautiful to watch. Suddenly I felt that I saw many things that I'd never seen before – things about you that I'd sensed and wondered about, but which had never been clear to me. It was the way you moved.'

'While skating?'

'Maybe it was the skating that showed me. But it was in the way you moved that I sensed an Addy driven across the ice, by an uncontrollable force of nature, swept along by a power greater than herself, yearning, searching for something ... something outside herself...' He looked steadily into her face, his whole expression a question.

'Oh no!' said Adrienne lightly, her dark brows contracting somewhat. 'I'm not searching for anything!' Then she smiled again, thinking back to the evening on the ice. 'But, you know, AB, when I'm skating I'm not myself. I go crazy with the movement, I think of nothing else. I just want to go faster and faster, more and more! Oh, how wonderful never to stop!'

'That's what I saw, that's what I sensed, something inside you that had to break out, that needed only the vortex of speed, something from deep down surging from depths you knew nothing of, an unconscious urge that had to be obeyed no matter where it led you. When I was up in the mountains I sat alone by a great fire whose flames erupted into the sky, seemingly impelled by a power that would never be quenched. Was that real, or was it just the effect of the colour and the light? Could it be explained by a chemical formula? Where did the impulse come from which made the fire seem like a volcano, which made the leaping flames seem to reach out for an unknown, infinitely unobtainable goal? Where does it come from, this urge to run, to fly, to strain after achievement without even asking what it is one is seeking to achieve? Nobody can answer this question. You can only feel that it's there, true and eternal in all of us. And look,' he added playfully, 'what a coincidence! You're wearing a flame-coloured dress!'

Adrienne laughed. 'Don't think I was aware of all this; and it isn't just for you, AB!'

'Of course, but I am a part of it all the same. There is a connection, for you as well as for me, even if you weren't thinking of me when you chose the dress, even if you weren't thinking of anybody. You had an impulse that made the choice for you, just as in all nature where natural impulses further nature's own purposes. *That* impulse made you choose this dress, just this one, no other – perhaps because you like it and know it suits your dark hair and white skin. Be honest; didn't you think, when you put it on, that all the men's heads would turn and that all the women would be jealous?'

'And how do you know I didn't think of you when I chose it?'

Adrienne intentionally threw out this flirtatious remark in the same tone with which she had chatted with her other admirers at the ball, consciously trying to diminish the tension that was building up between them, to trivialize a conversation that had by now gone beyond the superficial. It was not so much Balint's words but the intensity with which he spoke that impressed and at the same time confused her. Balint's voice, so warm and passionate, expressing everything that normally she tried to avoid, disturbed her because, for once she felt herself moved and, instead of resenting it, had even felt a kind of warm response when he had dared to speak of something so personal as her skin . . . her *skin*!

Balint refused to notice her change of tone. Once more he looked into her eyes, then asked: 'Have you read Bölsche?'

'Yes! It's a wonderful book. Why?'

'Bölsche has written everything I'm trying to say. In springtime all nature's creatures put on ornament and parade themselves. Members of the same species vie with each other to become the most beautiful, the most desirable. This isn't planned, it's instinctive, emanating from some unconscious inner command from . . . well . . . *Lebensbejahung* if you will. Look at me!' he went on jokingly. 'When I tied my white tie tonight, wasn't I doing the same as the cock pheasant in spring when he grows two extra little feathers on each side of his head?'

'You always refer to animals, but we're not animals!'

PART THREE

'Of course we're not. And more's the pity, because unlike them we add so much extra to what in animals is pure and natural. All the noblest motivation exists in animals; motherhood, defence of the nest, of the young, even of the community. It's all there in nature without having to be taught. It comes from instinct, not from big words and impressive phrases. A kingfisher will risk his life to distract a polecat from the young in the nest; a roebuck confronts a wolf that snaps at the new-born faun; and the young hinds select a stag bull not because he is rich or well born or because their mothers choose for them, but because he is the one, and the only one, they fancy.'

Balint did not look at Adrienne as he spoke. His eyes seemed fixed on the far end of the room, but his words were spoken more softly and more slowly than before. He went on: 'With the animals all is pure and natural. There is no foreign element, no theorizing, no prejudice, no complicated theory ... and above all no speech to spoil everything. The animals all have their emotions, of course, but they're lucky not to be cursed with ideals as well!'

'Don't you think it's odd, you preaching about speech, AB? You, of all people! And what are you doing now? Don't you call all this theorizing?'

'Of course, but then I have to! I don't have a great roar like a roebuck! But if I did,' he said, laughing, 'I assure you this hall would reverberate as from a blast from an organ!'

Adrienne drew back a little and straightened her back. She searched for words, obviously unconvinced even if she did not know how to refute what he said.

'All right. Of course there's some truth in what you say. Put it like that if you must, but it's not the whole truth. There's a plan behind it. Oh, I know there's beauty in birdsong and deer calls and mating instincts in the spring, but you forget something ... or don't choose to mention it. Behind all this natural beauty there's no real free will; it's all programming. I'll tell you a story. We came to Kolozsvar this year by road. On the way we stopped at a village. It was market day and there was a booth in front of which stood a man beating a drum and calling out, "Come along! Come along! Come and see the Sea Lion, the terrible Lion of the ocean! Come along! Only ten copeks to see the terrible Sea Lion!" So we paid and went in, and what did we find? A lonely little seal!' Adrienne laughed bitterly. 'But we'd paid our ten kopecs, and no one would refund us that!'

'I don't see the connection.'

'You don't? It's quite clear to me. Everything you said so eloquently, all your wonderful sonorous beautiful words, spoke of only one thing. You talk of the call of nature, the truth and purity of those unconscious programmes, their seductiveness undefiled by reason or thought or speech. But that's no more than a beginning, a hint, a promise. Only later you can see it for what it really is . . . a baited trap, a swindle. That's what nature consists of, just like the busker taking our ten kopecs with a false promise!'

Balint looked closely at her face, reminded by her words of their talk on the terrace at Var-Siklod and on the bench at her father's house. He realized, suddenly, that he must feel his way carefully, that 'baited trap' was like a warning signal, and he had seen it before.

'That really isn't true, you know. Not at all. On the contrary the more you pay – and you must always pay – the more valuable the prize when you finally get it. Human beings are born to be disappointed. We complicate everything too much. We expect too much, cloak our feelings in too many words, hide behind conventions, pretend . . . always we pretend. Sometimes we know only too well what we are doing, but all too often we don't, not really. We may think that we have noble reasons for our actions, we justify ourselves saying that it is for pity's sake or for the ultimate good of others or some such cliché we've been brought up to believe; but it's all nonsense, excuses or rules dreamed up by philosophers – or priests. This has nothing to do with nature. It's all alien, imposed on ourselves by ourselves, human interference cooked up by old men sitting at desks. What you say is against all reason, it cannot be, it must not be. I was thinking about it up in the mountains.'

'By the camp fire?' asked Adrienne with an attempt at irony.

'Not this time. Beside a waterfall. Think of a deep canyon, dark and narrow like a well. All around is snow and ice. Even the rocks seemed frozen. I looked up and . . .'

He stopped as Pal Uzdy came up to them. Though it was getting late, Uzdy was as immaculate as when he had just left his dressing-room, his collar impeccable, his face cool. Of course he did not dance, indeed he rarely even sat down but stood leaning against a doorpost if people were dancing or against the wall in the supper-room while others ate, always apart, a spectator. He was so tall that his cadaverous diabolic face could be seen over the heads of everyone else. Now he moved slowly and deliberately to where his wife was sitting with Balint. He spoke to Adrienne

PART THREE

as if she were alone. Balint might not have existed for all the sign he gave of noticing his presence.

'I'm going home.'

'You are?'

'What time would you like the carriage?'

'I really don't know. The ball will go on until morning. For the girls' sake it's hard to say...' Adrienne faltered. For a moment she seemed frightened of something.

'Naturally, of course!' Uzdy appeard to agree.

'I could ask the organizers...' suggested Balint, feeling that he should say something.

'There's no call for that,' said Uzdy without turning his head and still looking at his wife. 'Stay as long as they want to, of course!... I'll send the carriage at seven. The horses can wait until you're ready to leave. Enjoy yourselves!' Abruptly he bent his long body in a stiff jack-knife bow and brushed Adrienne's hair with his lips. As he straightened up he glanced for the first time in Abady's direction, and a faint ironic smile seemed to hover under the drooping moustaches. From his great height he waved a limp hand to Balint and repeating 'Enjoy yourselves!' he turned and walked away as slowly and deliberately as he had come.

For a moment neither of them spoke. Then Adrienne turned back to Balint with searching eyes and, gasping slightly like someone who is feeling faint and who needs water, said: 'What were you saying? A waterfall? Go on, tell me! Go on! Go on! Quickly...'

'I was standing beside the rocky pool at the base of the fall. It was very dark down there. Everything around me was covered in ice. Into this lifeless, petrified world there poured a great column of water seemingly from inside the earth, pushing its way through solid rock, breaking through the wall of granite. The water leapt out victorious, triumphant, unstoppable, liberated, unending, throwing out garlands of spray and vapour as it fell and then rushing on over the stones below me, following its fate, going wherever it had to go, wherever it was driven, down the mountain valleys, across the plains, going where nature led until it flowed into the vast waters of the ocean. Before my eyes was the triumph of life and motion over all obstacles... and I thought of you, just as I had by the fire. Of you, who are throbbing with ... I've always felt it. On the terrace at Var-Siklod and when you were skating. Long ago, when you were still a girl in your mother's drawing-room, it was already there, unformed, waiting.

I could feel it, that powerful urge inside you...'

He was silent for a moment, then very faintly, in a whisper, he said very slowly: 'I love you, Addy!'

Adrienne had been listening to him, leaning back in the armchair with her head propped up on one hand, her chin supported by her long supple fingers whose pressure made her lips seem even fuller than usual. Her eyes were half-closed like someone listening to a symphony, and when Balint reached out and touched her right hand which was resting lightly on the arm of her chair, threading his fingers between hers, she accepted the caress with no sign of the alarm she had shown the last time, at Mezo-Varjas.

'It's only now,' he murmured, 'only now that I realized I was in love with you, and always have been ever since we first met though I didn't know it until now. There's never been anyone else. I've always loved you and nobody else, never ever!'

And for a long time he kept murmuring those two words 'never ever' like rain-drops falling in endless repetition, monotonous rhyming little words to replace the passionate phrases of a moment or two before.

Little Dinora Abonyi came into the room with light steps. She had torn a flounce on her dress and was on her way to have it repaired in the ladies' room which could only be reached through the library where Balint sat with Adrienne. Balint heard someone coming and pulled his hand back from her's.

Dinora stopped beside them and, putting her hand on his shoulder, spoke to Adrienne: 'He's very sweet, this Balint! I know him ... and he talks beautifully! Nobody can talk like him! *And* he's kind and good, not like the others. I know! I can recommend him!'

She smiled at Adrienne and moved lightly away. Her words, which could have sounded bitchy coming from anyone else, were not vicious, not from her. From Dinora they came from the heart, a gift for Adrienne who, unlike the others, had gone out of her way to be kind to her all the evening. Dinora's simple, kind heart had been deeply touched when Adrienne had spoken to her at the buffet, taken her by the arm and asked her to eat at her table whereas the other ladies, after listening to Aunt Lizinka's malicious gossip, had seemed to take pleasure in cutting her, ostentatiously turning away if she approached. She had nothing else to give Adrienne so she offered her old friend.

Dinora's coming back had broken the spell that until then had separated Balint and Adrienne from the rest of the world.

PART THREE

Adrienne did not take in what Dinora had said, but the fact that someone else had spoken to her brought her back to reality, to the fact that she was in the Assembly Rooms of the Casino, attending the Mardi Gras Ball and that gypsy music was being played in the ballroom next door. Dream-like she came back from a world of dreams.

When the csárdás came to an end several couples started to drift back to the supper-room. Isti Kamuthy, after seeing that his partner was seated among friends and noticing that Abady was already sitting there with Countess Uzdy, same over to greet them, eager to hear the latest news from the capital.

'Tho you're back from Budapetht? What'th new in Budapetht?'

Balint replied politely but non-committally. Then they got up and moved back to the ballroom, still in a dream of their own ...

As they arrived a waltz was just beginning. They stood for a moment in the doorway, Adrienne looking at Balint with her wide eyes, golden in the candle-light like those of a lioness, looking deeply into his. Then, putting her hand on his shoulder she leaned towards him, her eyes closed. Neither spoke; their movements were natural, inevitable and, as Balint put his arm round Adrienne's waist, they moved out on to the dance floor, gently turning and yielding themselves to the rhythm of the music in mute tenderness, each of them conscious of nothing but the other. Though surrounded by a milling crowd, once again they were alone.

After the waltz they separated and, after agreeing to sup together at the following evening's ball, they each went their separate ways, even trying to keep apart, Adrienne by instinct and Balint consciously, not wishing that they should give any occasion for gossip by the hawk-eyed old ladies. But their efforts were in vain. Wherever they were, on the dance floor, at the buffet, in the drawing-room, every few minutes they seemed to come together again automatically as if an invisible thread bound them always to each other. And, whenever this happened, they would exchange a few banal phrases – 'Isn't it a lovely ball?' – 'How sweet little Dodo looks tonight!' – 'I love this old tune, don't you?' – 'What a good organizer Alvinczy is!' or some such trivial remark that could be overheard by anyone without a malicious interpretation being possible. Yet all the time a secret current flowed between them, isolating them from all others, creating for them a world of their own as private as if they had been alone on a desert island. No matter what words came from their lips, for both

Adrienne and Balint they could have only one meaning: 'You! You! You!' and whenever one caught sight of the other it was with a kind of happy surprise at the discovery of their new-found bliss.

Balint and Adrienne were so wrapped up in this new little world of their own that it was with a shock of surprise that they found it was eight o'clock when the ball came to an end. In the entrance hall a crowd of waiting footmen helped the girls and their chaperones to find their wraps and the young men were busy collecting the cotillion favours and flowers of the girls with whom they had flirted the night away.

Adrienne called for her sisters. Margit came at once but they had to look for Judith, who was found talking to Wickwitz in a dark corner. Their party now left escorted by a whole band of admirers: Wickwitz, the ball's two organizers, Baron Gazsi and Farkas Alvinczy, as well as Adam Alvinczy and Pityu Kendy. Adrienne was on Balint's arm. Well wrapped up against the fierce cold of the morning, they waited just inside at the head of the steps until the noise of the carriages and the hurried entrance of a footman announced that their carriage was at the door.

Balint and Adrienne still moved like figures in a dream, for the fact that in a few hours time there would be another ball at which they would naturally meet again and which would give them the opportunity to pass another whole evening in each other's company, was enough to remove any sting from this morning's parting.

Everyone said goodbye; the men shook hands with the girls and, as with the other married ladies, they bowed to Adrienne and kissed her hand. Balint was the last. Adrienne had not yet put on her gloves and, when he took her hand, the feel of her bare skin went up his arm with the power of an electric shock. He paused, bending over her, holding her hand in his for a fraction longer than was usual. Suddenly, speaking so low that no one else could hear, he said: 'Not where the others did!' and turning her hand quickly over he buried his face in her palm. Adrienne made no resistance, and in a second Balint had straightened up again. No one had noticed.

The ladies climbed into their carriage, the doors slammed and the horses were quickly whipped away in a fast trot.

Most of the young men ran quickly back up the steps to say goodbye to other friends, but Balint stood motionless with closed eyes, suffused with a happiness he had never known before. Then

PART THREE

he pulled himself together and returned to the Casino, bounding up the steps two or three at a time.

Quickly finding his fur coat, he returned and hurried down into the open street. Outside it was a bright sunny morning with a few inches of fresh untouched snow covering everything in sight. He walked slowly home, his narrow patent leather dancing shoes leaving sharp tracks in the virgin snow. It was like walking in cold water, cool, refreshing, somehow wonderful. He was entirely alone in the deserted streets. He was happy.

Chapter Six

ADRIENNE LEANED BACK in her corner of the carriage so absorbed in her own thoughts that she did not notice that Judith also remained totally abstracted. The two of them, wrapped almost to the eyes in their furs and shawls, had the same closed expression on their faces, the same taut line round the mouth, and they both shut their eyes as if they had secrets that must be protected from the outside world. Only Margit, sitting opposite them, was her usual merry self, keeping up a stream of chatter and excitement.

The carriage stopped at the Miloth's town house. Briefly wishing Adrienne goodnight and saying they'd see her again that evening, the girls hurried indoors.

Over the freshly fallen snow Adrienne's carriage moved silently as it made its way along the Monostor road. Even the hoofbeats of the horses were muffled to a mysterious murmur.

Finally they turned into the forecourt of the Uzdy villa, a large two-storeyed house flanked by long low wings which were fronted by glazed galleries to keep out the cold. The carriage stopped at the entrance to the wing on the right, where the young Uzdys lived. Only the old countess, Pal Uzdy's mother, lived in the main house with Adrienne's little daughter and her nanny. At this moment however the old countess and her grandchild were not there; they had left Kolozsvar for Meran ten days before.

The house was an old one dating from the eighteenth century, with tall rooms and long windows. The wing where Adrienne and her husband had their rooms, though the windows had a marvellous view across the park to the river, must originally have been designed as servants' quarters for, with one exception, all the rooms were small and linked by a long narrow vaulted gallery. The exception, right at the end of the wing, was a large room which Adrienne had furnished as a drawing-room. It had once been the kitchen where meals could be prepared for a hundred people.

The entrance to Adrienne's apartment was in the centre of the glassed-in gallery and, as she hurried inside, the carriage turned and drove out again through the entrance gates as the stable-yard and coach-house were reached through a separate gate further along the main road.

As she went towards her room, Adrienne glanced at the windows of her husband's room which also led off the gallery. The door was open and the place was obviously being aired. This surprised her, for Uzdy was not usually an early riser.

'Is the Count already up?' she asked the maid who was carrying the basket of favours and flowers, an elderly grey-haired little woman who had once been her nanny, '... or didn't he go to bed at all?'

'His Lordship didn't go to bed, my lady. He just changed his clothes and left for Almasko before dawn.'

Adrienne was not altogether surprised at this news since Uzdy often came and went unexpectedly without telling anyone of his plans in advance. He kept a post-chaise always ready in town, and a four-horse carriage at his farm in Szentmihaly, halfway to Almasko. By doing so he could make the trip quickly, only stopping long enough to change the horses, without having to make arrangements in advance. He liked to arrive unannounced: it kept everyone on their toes! Adrienne said nothing, but a close observer could have told from the way her body relaxed that she was relieved to hear the news.

'Just put the flowers in water, Jolan, and don't wake me 'til five. I want to sleep. You can go now, I don't want anything.' Adrienne always dressed and undressed herself. She did not like having people hovering round her.

'I'll bring in the breakfast,' said the old nanny.

The big room was bathed in light, sun streaming in through the three long windows which gave over the park, casting over the white painted walls a faintly bluish tinge from the reflection of the snow. It was the same shade as the colour of the shadows on the outside of the house here in Kolozsvar and on the banks of the Szamos.

Adrienne moved over to the tall french doors that looked over

PART THREE

the park and leant against the moulded window-frame, her mind devoid of thought, her eyes narrowed in the blinding morning light. She stood there staring outside but seeing nothing, feeling nothing, thinking nothing. She did not hear her maid come with the breakfast, nor her murmured farewell when she left. For a long time she stood there, weary with a faintly sensuous languor that kept her from thinking of what had happened that evening. Everything was in a hazy confusion in her mind, but a confusion tinged with nameless happiness.

A sudden sound recalled her to herself: it was the crack of a burning log in the fireplace which had fallen into the centre of the fire. Adrienne turned to look and, as she did so, the sight of the flames reminded her of what Balint had said about her dress. Slowly she looked down at her bare arms and shoulders and half-concealed breasts, and at the shimmering panels of silk that flowed from them down to the floor. In the brilliant sunlight she felt naked and exposed. Turning quickly she almost ran through the dark bedroom into the bathroom beyond and undressed. Her movements were automatic and when, a few moments later, she returned to the bedroom and lay down, she thought that she would certainly not be able to sleep. Somehow she did not even want to, for in this unusual feeling of being remote from all thought, all reality, there was a sort of magic which Adrienne would have liked to go on for ever. She lay with her eyes open, the only light in the darkened room coming from narrow spaces where the closed shutters did not quite meet. It was only a few minutes before she sank into a deep dreamless sleep which wiped away every image, thought and memory.

Adrienne awoke as three o'clock struck on the church clock in the town nearby. For a few seconds she stared into the darkness before being gripped by a nameless fear. She did not know why, but she was so terrified that she sat up looking wildly around her and clutching her knees tightly to her chin.

What was it? What had happened at the ball?

And then it all came back to her quite clearly. As she slept the impressions of the evening, which had been so confused and vague when she went to bed, had sorted themselves out in her mind. Everything now fell into place with a clarity that appalled her. Repeating to herself the astonishing words, 'I am in love! In love! In love!', all the consequences of this reared up in her. It wasn't possible. She had a husband, a child. She couldn't. She was tied, bound to the duty that she herself had chose and husband she had accepted. She was no longer free, so what could it all come to? Balint's love was no mere *Schwärmerei*, no little girl's crush, brought on by propinquity and moonshine. In his words rang the deep sincerity of a real emotion not the light cajolery of mere flirtation. He wanted her . . . and there would be no bargaining.

With an aching heart Adrienne realized that she had not only listened to everything that Balint had had to say, but that she had also accepted it. Not in so many words, of course, for she herself had hardly spoken, but with her eyes and her expression as she listened to him, with her body when she danced with him, in her silent acquiescence to his words, her acceptance of his hand twined in hers, and with the pressure of her fingers when he kissed her palm on the steps. She had never for a moment held back, resisted, never protested or rebuked him or even given the smallest indication that his ardent demands were not welcome and might not be accepted.

Adrienne shuddered to think how far she had let him go, she who had never allowed Adam Alvinczy or Pityu Kendy to sit too closely beside her or to hold her tightly when they danced, and who had always frozen anyone into silence if they dared to flirt too outrageously or make even the mildest allusion to sexuality between men and women. Of course it had been easy with the others. Their attentions were all play-acting. Even if Pityu and Adam fancied themselves in love with her, she treated such attentions as a joke, to be shrugged off as lightly. It was easy because it meant nothing. With such friends she did not care, so she played with them as if they were outsize dolls made only for her amusement. If they tried to go further and tell her of their feelings with tears in their eyes, pleading to be taken more seriously, she only joked with them the more and teased them and made fun of them with careless coquetry.

And now?

Last night she had given everything to Balint that she had denied the others. She saw herself listening, captivated by the magic of his words and the strength of his passion. How sweetly what he had said had sounded in her ears, how welcome, how fascinating. And she had not flinched at the passion, the desire, which pulsated through everything he had said. His yearning for her could not be disguised. His meaning was so clear, so direct, that even when they had exchanged nothing but otherwise meaningless banalities, his words had only reflected his desire to love her.

PART THREE

It was obvious what he was speaking of when he told her about the fire or the waterfall and his voice, so low and seemingly devoid of passion, and his look, which gave a new significance to otherwise innocent words, rang with the force of his inner feelings. Finally, when after a long pause he had said, 'I love you, Addy!', had she tried to stop him uttering the words that should never have been said? No! On the contrary she had drunk in his words with silent joy, sitting there with her hand in his, her heart beating; it had been as if they were alone in the world and existed only for each other. Lying now in her darkened room she stretched languorously at the memory of those magic moments until, all at once, she seemed to come to her senses, alert and conscious of a reality which almost made her jump out of bed. Adrienne shuddered as she realized what little Dinora must have seen in her face. What had she said? That Balint was 'sweet and good', that she 'recommended him'! How shameful! And with horror she suddenly grasped the appalling implication.

'How hateful! How mean! How vile I am! Now AB himself must believe that I'd be willing... with him... Oh, that revolting act! He's a right to believe...' Even in thought she couldn't bring herself to put her revulsion into words.

Adrienne was filled with horror. It was not only that the situation was so complicated, that she was a married woman who had given herself irrevocably to a man she did not love and who would never let her go, not only because of their child but also because, in his disgusting way, he loved her. Neither was it the thought of the social consequences, the menace of shame and exposure she would risk by falling in love with him. No! There was something much deeper in her woman's consciousness that tore at her nerves and demanded, loath as she was, to be faced and accepted, a truth from which she recoiled with every fibre of her being. She had married without love, without even thought of love. She had longed to be free of her parents' house; and when Pali Uzdy had courted her even he had not spoken of love but only of his loneliness, his desire for a partner in his work and his life, his longing for someone to help and support him. Their desires met and merged, seemed mutual, compatible. He had kissed her only once before their marriage, a brief passionless embrace under her ear, on her neck, at the moment she had accepted him, and he had released her quickly. Now, knowing him better, Adrienne realized that this was probably because he knew that he could not control himself. When, after the marriage ceremony, they had travelled by carriage to Almasko, and throughout the evening until it had been time to go to bed, he had maintained always his easy, calm, friendly manner though — or was it only afterwards that she had been conscious of it? — in his eyes had lurked the same watchful glitter as that with which a beast of prey would stalk its victim.

The memory of that night still made her sick with fear and disgust. She had gone to bed, nervous and frightened, but nothing had prepared her for the horror that followed. As soon as Uzdy had come to her bed he had flung himself upon her, tearing at her with his hands, his teeth clenched in mindless passion as he assaulted her and, brutally forcing her legs apart, entered her with all the power of a battering ram. He subjugated her, defamed her, taking his pleasure how and when he wished, with never a word of tenderness or thought for his victim — and he went on until morning when he abruptly left her without a word as dawn began to show through the curtains. And every time since it had been the same. Never once did Uzdy make the smallest attempt to arouse in his wife any tenderness, to awaken any response to his passion, to allay her fear. He seemed, on the contrary, to glory in the terror that he must have sensed in her, as if, by some atavistic instinct, he himself was only aroused by resistance in the female. From that very first night, whenever Adrienne had seen that tell-tale glitter in her husband's eye, she had felt as if she were being stalked by hired assassins.

Lying now in her room as the afternoon light was fading the memory of these scenes came back to her so vividly that her soul cringed with disgust. This loathsome memory was all that Adrienne had ever experienced of love, and now she was filled with dread at the thought that this was what Balint would wanted of her and, what was worse, what she herself had allowed him to expect.

How could she have given Balint hope that she, of all people, would ever permit him to do this to her? She must stop it at once. She must not cheat him or lead him on. She must put an end to this terrible situation before this strange love for him that she felt welling up in her drove her unconsciously into his arms. She knew that this would happen, and she knew too that if it did she would hate him for ever. If she were to preserve her love for him she must act at once and, though she had barely realized that this was her real motive, she made a swift decision. Jumping out of bed, she hurried into the drawing-room, stumbling through the

PART THREE

growing darkness to her desk. The clock struck a quarter after four. There was so little time! On a leaf of paper she wrote: '*I have a bad headache and slight fever. Can't take you to the ball. Get someone else. Love. Addy.*' Slipping the note into an envelope, she addressed it to Judith Miloth, marking it 'Urgent. Deliver at once'. Then she went back into her bedroom, lit a candle, got back into bed and rang for her maid.

'Please have this sent at once to my sister Judith,' she said.

'Wouldn't her Ladyship like something to eat? It's ready...'

'No. No, I don't want anything. Wait! A little beef-tea. I think I have a temperature!' Adrienne realized that she had better start playing her part at home if she did not want her servants inadvertently to betray her.

When the soup was brought she drank it swiftly and went to sleep. Soon after seven she was woken again by the arrival of her sisters, both already dressed for the ball, hoping that they could persuade her to go with them.

'Do come, Addy! It will be so boring with Papa, and we can't find anyone else so late. You're not really ill, are you? Not too ill to come with us? Please, Addy!' They both spoke at once and Mlle Morin, who had come with them, added her own plaintive soprano warblings.

Adrienne lay back looking coldly at them from the mountain of lace-edged pillows. She did not reply, thankful that her face could hardly be seen in the faint candle-light. Judith went on: 'Papa is cross as pie, and there really isn't anyone else!' Then, very determinedly, she said, 'I absolutely must go tonight. I'm engaged for supper.'

With a knowing smile Margit asked: 'Have you taken any aspirin?'

Adrienne hated lying, so she just said, rather crossly 'Do go now and leave me alone!'

Margit looked back from the door and asked, 'Who were you having supper with? I'll take him over if you like. I haven't got anyone.'

Adrienne did not answer, but she gave her youngest sister such an angry look that Margit hurriedly left the room and closed the door behind her.

Adrienne counted the chimes as the church clock struck, first eight, then half past, then nine o'clock. Now they must be dining. Half past nine. Ten o'clock. Now they would be striking up the csárdás, and if she had gone to the ball, she would have been alone with him as she had on the previous day. Could it have only been yesterday?

Staring unseeingly at the dark ceiling she conjured up the scene in the deserted supper-room. Balint's face, lean and hard, a young man's face with a thin, straight nose, narrow blond moustache, fairer than his hair which he wore longer than most of the other young men. How shiny it is! she thought, remembering how his head had glowed in the candle-light. How silky it must be! How intently he had gazed at her with those steely grey eyes, and how serious was the curve of his lips as he spoke those magic sentences of love and adoration.

She longed to be with him again and asked herself over and over why she had given up so easily, hidden herself away and pretended she did not long to be with him and sit dreamily with eyes closed as he talked, letting those beautiful words flow deep into her heart. He would be bitter and angry that she had not come, though he could not know – and thank God for it – what her real reasons had been. But why hadn't she gone herself to tell him, to explain the confusion in her heart? Balint Abady would have understood that he must not expect... Now probably he was thinking that she had led him on only to forsake him. There would have been no real harm in seeing him again tonight, for he would soon have to go back to Budapest to attend Parliament, or to the mountains to visit his forests, or ... So why not allow one more meeting, just one, perhaps the only one? Now it was too late! She had given him up and he would know it because she had not come; and she had gone through all this only to throw away the only joy she had ever known. She had never ever... 'Never – ever', his words rang in her head, endlessly repeated, as her throat tightened and the tears gathered in her eyes, slowly running down her cheeks and falling one by one on her breast. When she could bear it no more she turned, strangled with sobs and buried her face in the pillows, her black hair tumbling about her head, and cried, one crying fit following another until sleep came to blot out her sorrows.

The clock tower chimed the passing hours but Adrienne heard nothing.

When she woke in the morning the hair about her face and her pillows were still wet from her tears.

Chapter Seven

THE ASSEMBLY ROOMS of the Casino were full of people waiting for the evening's festivities to begin. Today was the Ash Wednesday Ball. It was already after eight-thirty but, though the dinner had been ordered for eight o'clock, the Miloth party had still not arrived.

Farkas Alvinczy, as official organizer, was looking at his watch every few minutes, for though the caterer had already twice sent word that the dinner would be spoilt if it were not served at once, he was anxious that everything should go right. Five more minutes, he said, but he was not pleased that something seemed to have gone wrong on the last night of the season.

Alvinczy turned to his fellow organizer, Baron Gazsi. 'What shall we do? If we don't start soon the dinner will be ruined!'

'It's very awkward. We could send word, or telephone?'

'They don't have one, but we could send a carriage to meet them. Perhaps something has happened. One of their horses may have fallen and they're stuck somewhere,' said Farkas, again looking at his watch.

'I'll do it,' said Gazsi, turning to give an order to one of the waiting footmen. Hardly had he done so when a stentorian voice could be heard at the entrance.

'What a mess! But it's not my fault. How are you, my boy? They dragged me here by force! Me! An old man at a ball!' The big double doors were flung open and there appeared framed in the doorway Judith and Margit Miloth with old Ratle behind them, keeping up a constant flow of talk in his loud voice. The group of waiting young men, with Adam Alvinczy, Pityu and Balint in the lead, swarmed round them.

'Where's Adrienne? Didn't she come?' Adam asked Margit, who raised her little hawk-like nose and, looking at Abady though replying to Alvinczy, said: 'It seems she has a headache – and a temperature!'

A hint of a smile hovered at the corners of Margit's mouth, which made Balint think that she did not believe a word of it and was making fun of him.

'A headache! Did you ever hear such nonsense?' roared old Rattle. 'Just like her mother, never without a headache or a migraine! Got one tonight too. Ah, women! Women! Never marry, my boy, or you'll get like me, always at their beck and call! Get dressed, they say, without a by-your-leave. What? Sit at a ball 'til dawn, at my age? These old bones ought to be in bed. A coffin! That's where I should be!' He shook hands all round, full of life and good spirits, gesticulating widely as with a huge smile under the walrus moustache he continued to shout over the heads of the company who had now started filing into the dining-room. 'These stupid servants of mine couldn't find my tails! "What the Devil do you think I should wear, you ox!" I said, "I can't go naked! D'you think I'll prance about in front of all the ladies in a fig leaf? I'd be thrown out on my ear! What d'you think I am, a gypsy brat? They can go naked, not me, you ox!"'

Everybody laughed, everybody but Balint who was filled with anger.

Bitch! Flirtatious bitch! he said to himself. Obviously this headache was just an excuse, Margit's secret little smile proved that. Here he was, the victim of the oldest trick in the world. All over you one day, kick you in the teeth the next. What a fool he was to be taken in! Play cat and mouse with him, would she? Tease until you plead, and then let you back until the time to get thrown out again. Oh, but with him this little game would not work, he knew how to have his revenge and he wouldn't spare her, not now! He'd play the same little trick on her. He had hesitated to declare his love because he wanted to spare her the problems such a love would provoke. He had thought that Adrienne was different, sincere, true and straight, not to be played with like the other married women he had known. This was why he had tried not to fall in love with her. Well, no more. His scruples had been ridiculous, for this evening proved that Adrienne was indeed just like all the others; and he knew how to treat them! They were all alike, shallow and untrustworthy.

Balint looked around to find a supper partner so that no one should gossip about his being stood up by Adrienne. Perhaps the little Gyalakuthy girl was free? He would seek her out.

As it happened Dodo was free. No one had asked her and the organizers were just then looking for someone among the young men who were attending their first balls. She was overjoyed when Abady approached her, even though she thought that he had been sent over to rescue her, and putting her hand on his arm she cast a grateful glance at Farkas for having found her such an escort.

PART THREE

They went down to the large Casino dining-room where Abady found two places at the table farthest from the door, sitting diagonally across from where Judith Miloth was sitting with Wickwitz. Their presence reminded Balint of what Dodo had told him at Var-Siklod. When the first course had been served the music began. As at Siklod, it was Laji Pongracz who led the band. Under cover of the popular gypsy music, Balint turned to Dodo and said: 'I didn't dare hope to have supper with you!'

Dodo looked at him, astonished. 'But I told you everybody avoided me, didn't I?'

'There's one who doesn't. Over there!' he said as he glanced at Wickwitz across the table.

The girl shrugged her shoulders. After a little pause she said: 'How is your cousin Laci? What is he doing? I would have thought he'd be here now.'

Balint told her all about Laszlo's work at the Music Academy in Budapest.

He spoke gaily, light-heartedly, for he wanted the whole world to see how merry he was so that it should not guess he was eating his heart out with misery and anger. Exaggerating somewhat he told Dodo everything that Gyeroffy had outlined to him when they had been together at Var-Siklod, all his dreams, ambitions and plans. Dodo listened enthralled, drinking in his words. And when Balint had said all there was to say about Laszlo's ambitions he recounted how they had been together at Simonvasar, though he told the girl nothing about Laszlo's love for his cousin Klara. It had always been against his nature to gossip about such matters, and especially now, when his anger made him despise all things to do with love, he steered well clear of the subject and concentrated on telling Dodo about the pheasant shoot, about his hosts and the guests they had assembled at the castle. Balint did his best to be as amusing and entertaining as possible, but more for the benefit of anyone else sitting near them than for little Dodo herself.

As it happened, no one was watching him except Dodo, and she only wanted to hear about Gyeroffy. When Balint told her Laszlo was now organizer of the Carnival Balls in the capital, she sighed and said: 'Wouldn't it be wonderful if Mama should take me to Budapest! Oh, how marvellous it must be!'

'Don't you believe it! Girls from Transylvania aren't made very welcome there ... or men either, for that matter! Besides you might fall in love with someone, and that would never do!' Balint laughed in sympathetic mockery.

'Yes, it could happen.' Dodo said in a subdued voice.

'Really? That Nitwit is good-looking enough. I could quite understand?'

'Not him!' interrupted Dodo. 'Not at all! He isn't after me any more.'

'Who, then? I thought...'

Dodo burst out laughing: 'You men never notice anything! Why, Judith Miloth, of course!'

'Not possible! I've never seen...'

'Look at them! Do I have to spell it out for you?'

Balint turned slowly so that he could watch Judith with Wickwitz. She was talking to him in a low voice, rather hesitantly it seemed, but Balint saw nothing out of the way in her manner, only that her expression was perhaps a little more serious than usual.

Lieutenant Baron Wickwitz had gone back to his regiment in November. He had paid off those dirty debts – in the army all debts to tradesmen were dirty as opposed to those incurred by gambling which were considered honourable – and so was back in uniform. He had gone to see his colonel and, with a wooden face, had told him that he was now free of 'embarrassment'. The colonel, who knew well that Wickwitz had no means of his own, had wondered where the money had come from but was sufficiently relieved that he would no longer have to expel the young man from the regiment that he did not enquire further. All the same he wondered how he had managed to raise the ten or twelve thousand crowns that he had estimated Wickwitz had owed.

A month later Wickwitz had again asked to see his commanding officer, and once again he had asked for leave, this time for two or three months as he intended to get married and he would need this time to get everything organized.

'*Die kleine Gyalakuthy* – the little Gyalakuthy girl?' asked the colonel, who had heard something of Wickwitz's activities in Transylvania. '*Na, gratuliere* – congratulations!'

Wickwitz did not undeceive him, though he knew that Dodo would not marry him, at least not now. It would take at least two years' hard wooing on his part and it would always depend on whether someone else took her fancy. If no one else came along, then perhaps ... but not now; and Wickwitz could not wait. He did not have enough time.

The reason he could not wait was that the money he had used

to square his debts had been obtained from a dangerous and equivocal source. It was Dinora Abonyi's money and if it were not repaid – and if the means he used to get it became known – then he could not avoid being cashiered. All this had happened at the end of the autumn just when his six months' leave was expiring and when he had to go back to his regiment. He knew that if he returned to Brasso without money to pay his debts he would be forced to resign his commission. And then he'd be on the streets.

Wickwitz had turned to Dinora for help. It was not the first time. On several occasions during the summer and autumn he had touched her for a few hundred, later a few thousand crowns, for 'petty expenses', of course. And she had given them gladly. Now the fatal date for his return to duty approached and with no rich marriage to justify his absence and solve his problems, something drastic had to be done. Dinora was rich, good-hearted, extravagant . . . and she had no idea what words like a 'bank draft' implied. When Wickwitz told her that if she signed some bank drafts for him to cash he would be able to pay her back immediately what he had borrowed from her, she trustingly agreed. It all seemed so simple! You put your signature on a paper and your problems were solved. If Nitwit had asked for cash it would have been different, because Dinora was such an easy spender that she never seemed to have any ready money. And what was more this meant that as soon as Wickwitz had repaid what he had borrowed from her she would be able to settle that bill from the dressmaker who was becoming tiresomely insistent.

So Wickwitz had gone to Weissfeld's bank in Maros-Vasarhely with three drafts for eight thousand crowns each.

Soma Weissfeld received him immediately. However, when he saw Countess Abonyi's signature, he paused for a moment, removed his pince-nez, polished them meticulously and replaced them on his nose with fussy little delaying movements.

'May I ask why . . . why have these drafts not been signed by Count Abonyi. It is usually he who signs and of course we know his signature well. Please understand, the Baron must excuse me, but this is rather awkward, rather delicate.' He looked at Wickwitz with narrowed eyes while a somewhat suspicious smile pulled at the corners of his mouth.

Wickwitz managed not to lose his temper. He explained that the Countess did not want to involve her husband in this matter – she had run up a number of debts (this was true) and he might be angry with her. Of course she was a rich woman but she did not want to sell her crops immediately, he added with quick invention, but when she did she would see that the bank was repaid.

Weissfeld did not believe a word of it, but as he knew that Maros-Szilvas was Dinora's own property inherited from her Malhuysen ancestors, and that it was extremely valuable, he decided that the matter was none of his affair. Accordingly he cashed the drafts, handing over to Wickwitz something over twenty-three thousand crowns. Egon returned to Maros-Szilvas with this sum, giving to Dinora four thousand, one hundred and sixty-two crowns and sixty cents. Dinora did not want to accept the two crowns and sixty cents but Wickwitz insisted, saying that it was a debt of honour and that he would consider himself disgraced if he owed a single cent to a lady. He told her that he had noted down exactly what he had borrowed so as to keep his accounts in order. As it happened this was true. He knew that his debts in Brasso amounted to exactly fifteen thousand, three hundred and seventy-seven crowns, and he would keep the difference as he would now have to find somebody who would pay back Dinora's drafts and, until that person was found, he would need money to live. After all, he would never solve his problems if he didn't go to balls and meet people – and no one could live without a cent in their pockets.

Dodo was given up at once: there was no time for a long-drawn-out pursuit. Only two possibilities remained. The first was Judith Miloth, and the other was a widow of over thirty whom he had met on a train. There had been an answering sparkle in Mme Bogdan Lazar's eyes when he had first made her acquaintance by helping with her luggage, and he had soon learnt that she had a handsome property near Apahida. However it seemed that Judith would be the best bet so he would start with her. If that failed there would be plenty of time to go after the widow.

This was Egon Wickwitz's plan when he came back at Kolozsvar. Without delay he started his pursuit of Judith and sensing that Judith would not be impressed by the more usual tactics of the confident male wooer, he opened his campaign not with words – speech was not his strongest point – but with half suppressed sighs, long covert looks from sad spaniel's eyes and mysterious silences. He played the part of the good-hearted rather stupid man, whose noble heart would perish if it found no mercy, and who was the slave of a passion he hardly dared admit, let alone express. Indeed he played it extremely well, for he was not naturally a bad man and had he been born to a fortune would probably

PART THREE

never have found himself reduced to such a devious course.

By the end of the season he began to feel that he was making progress and that, as any trainer of horses might say, the filly was ready for her first race.

All through the Mardi Gras Ball he waited for the opportunity to present itself, and, finally, as dawn was about to break, he managed to get Judith alone with him in a small room off the drawing-room. For a little while they talked, he hesitantly, pausing as if he did not quite know, or dare to say, what was in his mind. Then suddenly, after he had made quite sure that no one could see them, he took Judith in his arms and kissed her passionately on the mouth.

Everything went as he had planned. Judith made no resistance. It was as if she had expected just this. Then, as suddenly as he had begun the kiss, Wickwitz released her and stepped back.

'I'm sorry! I'm a swine!' he muttered.

'But why? I love you too!' replied the girl, breathless from their kiss.

'But I shouldn't have. I'm a swine – *ein Schwein! Ein miserables Schwein!* – a miserable swine! I can't ask you to marry me!'

'Why not, if we love each other?'

'I can't! It's impossible. I won't even ask you, I'm not worth it... I'm a scoundrel to have gone so far. Anyhow it's the end for me. Tomorrow I'll go away... for ever. I have to go anyway, and I'll not come back. I can't go on. This is the reason why, just once, I allowed myself... I had to tell you I loved you, if only just once!'

'But why, if I love you too?' cried Judith. Then she shrugged and said, smiling: 'I always knew you had no money. Neither have I, now, and won't have until much later. We'll manage somehow. Papa will let me have the marriage portion and then...'

Wickwitz allowed himself a sad smile. 'This is nothing but an impossible dream! It would be wonderful, but you don't understand. You don't know. I'm a doomed man... I can't escape what's coming to me...'

'But you can tell me, Egon. Just tell me what's the matter! What is it that threatens you? Why you are in such despair! You know I'd do anything to help. It would be a joy to me!' And she took his hand and pressed it to her heart.

'How good you are, much too good for me,' said Wickwitz sadly. 'I'm so ashamed. It's so difficult to tell you because you'll despise me.'

At this point Judith had to go as they were calling for her. Seeing that Margit was coming for her Judith had quickly whispered: 'Tomorrow! We'll have supper together and you must tell me everything! Everything, you understand, everything!'

This is what had happened on the previous evening. Now at supper, with the music playing loudly, they did not have to whisper as no one could hear what they were saying. So as to approach the subject slowly, Egon spoke first of his mother, of how poor they were. Then he told Judith of his debts and of the scene with his colonel and how his whole career would be at stake if he couldn't raise some money to clear himself of this burden. Some aspects of the tale he embellished, others he suppressed, but he admitted at once that his first plan had been to try and marry Dodo and that if he had been able to force himself to go through with it he would already be her husband with all his problems solved. This would have changed everything and he would not have found himself placed in the horrible situation he was now in. But he couldn't do it ... Instead he had fallen in love with Judith. That had been his doom, and looked like being his ruin. For him this was the end of the road. Wickwitz spoke slowly, with many pauses, hesitating as if he searched for the right words with which to explain himself, his face expressionless, his large brown eyes full of sad hopelessness. From time to time he broke off a crust of bread and ate a morsel, or sipped at his glass before going on with his tale. Anyone who could not hear his words, would have thought he was speaking of nothing more personal than the last race he had run or the problems of training horses. It was more difficult for Judith.

While taking in every word he said she somehow managed not to show any signs of emotion. She too ate little, and though she often glanced round the room so as to give the impression that she was merely chatting idly while being more interested in what else might be going on around her, her heart was beating ever faster as she became more and more involved in what Wickwitz was telling her.

Finally, explained Egon, in despair lest he lose his commission and with it any chance of seeing Judith again, he had done a most shameful, dishonourable thing: he had persuaded Dinora to guarantee his bank drafts. He had only done it so that, by getting hold of some ready money, he would be able to stay in the army and not dishonour his name. 'Now you despise me, don't you?' he said, looking deeply into her eyes.

PART THREE

'No!' she said. 'No. I understand.'

Wickwitz breathed again; she had passed the first test. When Judith did not seem to react at the mention of Dinora he knew that all was well. It was like the first fence in the competition ring; once over that he was confident he would have no difficulty at the wall or the water-jump. He begged Judith not to tell anyone, not ever to admit that she knew the truth. He was done for, of course. There was no way he could escape the inevitable dishonour that would come to him if his actions became known, as become known they must. And when they did he would kill himself rather than live without honour, a scoundrel rejected by everyone.

'So you see why you can't take such an outcast as a husband!' he said, still with the same wooden expression even though inwardly he was smiling confidently, for he now knew that everything was going to plan.

When dinner was over they all started back to the ballroom. Just as Abady and Dodo were passing through the doorway they heard the church clock strike ten, the same chimes that Adrienne could hear in the silence of her room.

As they reached the foot of the staircase where early that morning Balint had kissed Adrienne's palm and where, for a moment, he had become dazed with happiness, Balint felt a stab at his heart. What a bitch she is, he thought, sitting in her room now, laughing at him, triumphing, rejoicing that she had made him suffer! But he wouldn't give her that satisfaction, he would enjoy himself as never before! He would dance and dance and drink plenty of champagne . . . and someone was sure to tell her so she would know her little plan had not worked! Accordingly he took Dodo straight out on to the dance floor and there executed a csárdás with such abandon and skill that even old Ambrus, who prided himself on his dash and expertise, applauded him as a worthy successor.

The csárdás was followed by a long waltz and that by a quadrille and another waltz. All the time Adrienne's father, Count Akos, was having the time of his life despite his protestations that he had come against his will. The mothers, who usually spent the evening dozing in their chairs or languidly exchanging gossip, listened avidly to his tales of the Garibaldi campaign and the old count, happy to have found a new and eager audience, waxed so eloquent and was so amusing that he had all the older ladies in fits of laughter. They all agreed that he was far better value than

Daniel Kendy, who usually entertained them until he got too tipsy to go on.

Rattle's triumph reached its peak when, towards dawn, they struck up an *écossaise* which, with the Lancers, had been the most popular dance when he was young and had organized the Carnival balls. Becoming very excited, he herded everyone in the drawing-room onto the dance floor and then burst into the card-room where Uncle Ambrus was busily engaged in emptying the younger men's pockets.

'*Ecossaise!*' he roared. 'Come on, my boys, all of you on your feet! This is no time for stupid cards!'

'Still rutting, are you, you old lecher?' said Ambrus, concealing with a roar of laughter his anger at having such a profitable game interrupted. Turning back to the table, he said: 'Well? Who's in the game? All right, I'll raise it a hundred and sixty crowns! What? Nobody wants to see me? What a lousy lot of cowards you are!' And he scooped up all the chips on the table. But, though he immediately dealt another hand, the zest had gone out of the game. The young men had had enough of being bullied into losing money and even Uncle Ambrus was unable to outshout old Rattle, who soon got them all on their feet and back into the ballroom.

Akos Alvinczy, who lost more than most, lingered behind the others. 'Do you mind waiting?' he said to Ambrus. 'I'm a bit short at the moment...'

'Of course, of course!' said Uncle Ambrus, patting the tall young man on the shoulder. 'Take a couple of weeks! I'll wait that long, but no longer, mind! Then you must pay up, young fellow. I don't lay golden eggs, you know!' And, laughing in high good humour, he gave Akos a friendly punch on the arm and stumped off.

Akos stayed where he was for a moment, his handsome face clouded with worry.

Back in the ballroom the dancers had formed up for the *écossaise* and the dance was just starting when Rattle burst into the line, shouting: 'Not like that! That's not how you do it! You, young man! Let me show you!', and seizing little Ida Laczok from Baron Gazsi's arms he whirled her round the floor. 'Right ... Left ... Right ... Left ... !' and, with surprising agility for a man of his age, bounded about like a balloon with his niece on his arm. Then, leaving Ida at the end of a row of girls, he ran back to the two couples at the head of the set, showed them what they ought to be doing, made them do it again, sent them on their way, repeated the manoeuvre with the next two pairs, correcting errors,

PART THREE

pulling, pushing and prancing about until everything was to his satisfaction. Then he made sure that the next figures were done right, now shouting: 'La Coquette! Do the Coquette! Do La Souris!' now clapping and bowing and waving encouragement. It was years since the humorous old dance had been given such life and, when it ended, he embraced his little niece with a huge bear-hug, the sweat from his black moustache dripping on to her cheeks. If little Ida was none too pleased, the same could not be said for old Akos Miloth who was happier than he had been for years. Panting heavily he collapsed into a chair beside Countess Kamuthy and, as soon as he had got his breath back, started again:

'Do you remember, dear Aniko, how in our day . . .'

※

Dinora was standing at the buffet eating compote of oranges from a small glass dish. She stood alone because when she had arrived at the table the other ladies already grouped there all found various reasons why they should be somewhere else, anywhere, provided it was not beside Dinora Abonyi. One lady suddenly felt like sampling a galantine of chicken that sat temptingly on the other side of the table, another a fish salad she had caught sight of some way away, another a particularly luscious cake that was just out of each. So Dinora had eaten her supper by herself and now stood alone, her only companions being her dish of dessert and her glass of wine. Balint saw her and came over.

'You see how people avoid me?' said Dinora, with a smile of mock offence on her generous lips. 'It started yesterday towards dawn, with snide little glances and whispered impertinences. Today they avoid me openly!'

'You must be mistaken,' said Balint consolingly. 'I'm sure it's just coincidence and you're imagining things.' But though he said this he knew that what she said was true as he had heard of the malicious campaign of gossip that Aunt Lizinka had launched the night before.

'No!' she said. 'I'm not imagining anything! But, you know, the funny thing about it is that nobody seemed to care when that Nitwit was with me. Now that I've thrown him out, oh, ages ago, all this happens!'

'You threw him out? Why? Wasn't he any good?' said Balint with a smile.

'Not because of that!' laughed Dinora. 'Though these athletes are overrated! But that's quite unimportant. No! For totally different reasons,' she said seriously. 'Come and sit down. I'd like to tell you about it. Nobody will come near us, never fear!'

They sat down on a sofa by the wall.

'You remember when we met at Siklod I asked you to come over and see me. I wanted to discuss this with you and ask your advice. But you didn't come. Were you very afraid of me? Is that why?' She raised her open fan to hide her face from any observer and whispered in his ear, caressingly, 'Little Boy, Little Boy? I loved you very much once; and you loved me too, didn't you? But don't worry ... that was over long ago!' She paused, lowered the fan, and went on seriously, 'Nitwit was always asking me for money!'

'Not possible! Really?' Balint was amazed.

'Well, you know, I always like to help people, but this was too much! If I didn't do what he asked at once he'd become quite rude ... well, very rude. You know I don't ever have much cash. I always have to ask my husband whenever I need any; and it's not always very ... very convenient. *Ce n'est pas toujours agréable.*'

'But this is very serious!'.

'It wasn't too bad to start with ... they were only little loans. Then he got me to sign some drafts and paid me back what he owed me, every cent!'

'For goodness' sake! How much did you sign for?'

'I don't know ... twenty ... twenty-two thousand. Something like that; I don't remember exactly. Now I'm worried that Tihamer'll get to know about it and then I'll be in trouble! You see, some bank has written to me asking for the matter to be "settled", they say, and I really don't understand because *I* don't owe them anything, do I? Nitwit cashed the money, but if it became known, then my good Tihamer would begin to wonder, wouldn't he?'

Dinora laughed at the thought while looking enquiringly at Balint, who sat silently beside her, his eyes narrowed and an unusually serious expression on his face.

What a vile thing to do! he thought. How base to ask a woman for money, to drag such a bird-brained generous little creature into such a mess!

Balint's natural instinct to help was at once awakened, as always when he encountered the weak and defenceless in trouble. He wondered what he could do to get Dinora out of this muddle. There would be no point in denouncing that scoundrel Nitwit to his regiment; that would only provoke a public scandal and then Dinora would be involved and would suffer as much as he would. No, that was impossible: they would have to find another way.

PART THREE

To gain time he advised her, as she was pressing him for an answer, to find an opportunity of tackling Wickwitz, very seriously and as soon as possible, and asking when he was going to clear up the matter. Balint agreed to meet Dinora again soon to discuss what further moves she should make. Then they went to dance.

Spinning round the room in Balint's strong arms Dinora soon forgot her troubles. She opened her full lips in a smile of contentment; she was so obviously enjoying herself that no one would have thought that only a few moments before she had been obsessed by worry and the possibility of a scandal.

Balint, on the other hand, seethed with inner indignation for a long time until, with dancing, champagne, more dancing and more champagne, his anger began to dissolve and Dinora's worries ceased to upset him. Still he was not entirely untroubled; his suppressed anger at the way he had been treated by Adrienne still welled up from time to time as he, too, sought forgetfulness in the dance.

Chapter Eight

THE LAST BALL of the Carnival season the dancing went on well into the small hours. The older ladies, tired after two nights-out running, urged their daughters to go home, and finally, about six o'clock they all left, though most of the men remained behind. Many of them would soon be going back to their estates in the country, while others would be returning to the county towns where they had official duties. For the men at least this was their last chance for some months of seeing each other all together.

They pulled up chairs around the now devastated supper table and called for more champagne. This was the moment when Laji Pongracz came into his own and he played with renewed fervour, wittily titillating his hearers by subtly juxtaposing the tunes of all those he knew to be involved in courtship or dispute. Laji never forgot anyone's special tune, nor who was or had been in love with which girl and who no longer spoke to who. Now that he was not restrained by the presence of the ladies the tunes he played chronicled the loves and hates of more than a quarter of a century. With a roguish look in his eye he would gaze pointedly at the man to whose past the music referred. Sometimes he would step close to someone, his violin barely audible, just breathing an old tune in their ears and sometimes, with a wild flourish he would make everyone laugh as they recalled a forgotten scandal. Uncle Ambrus, of course, enjoyed the musician's mockery more than anyone. He sat, still drinking heavily, sprawled in an armchair, his waistcoat unbuttoned, his huge bulk the centre of a group of young men. Daniel Kendy, now completely sodden but who could not afford to order bottles himself, sat nearby and held out his glass whenever the champagne was being poured. On a sofa behind him sat Joska Kendy, pipe in mouth, and Isti Kamuthy, who had fallen asleep. Most of the company were pretty drunk.

Balint too had had far more than he usually did but, though he tried hard to get drunk, the effect of the wine was merely to increase his sense of irritation. He sat, cross and out of temper, at one end of the long buffet table while, beside him, Pityu Kendy morosely drank glass after glass from a giant goblet that must have held nearly a litre.

To vary his programme Laji would sometimes break off his chronicle of love and start a rollicking csárdás. Each time he did so Baron Gazsi would jump up and dance unsteadily in his shirtsleeves, waving his arms, snapping his fingers and bawling out the words of the song at the top of his voice. When drunk, as this evening, but only when drunk, he would fancy himself dying of love for the eldest Laczok girl and would sit slightly apart from the others moping. But when he danced he would more often look at Joska Kendy, his long woodpecker nose fixed in Joska's direction like that of his favourite pointer and his eyes filled with a silent plea for pity and understanding. Joska never noticed this any more than did Adam Alvinczy, who sat cross-legged on the floor at the feet of the orchestra, a cigar drooping from his lips, and who was being constantly jostled by Baron Gazsi's antics. Even when Gazsi nearly sent him sprawling across the floor he took no notice but continued to stare fixedly at the window where the morning light was beginning to shine ever more brightly.

Despite the approach of day the electric chandeliers were still it. No one wanted to be reminded that the night's revelries must come to an end. Clouds of cigarette smoke hung in the air and Pongracz was still playing even though few of his listeners were in a state to take much notice. After another csárdás he broke into an Godefrey waltz of the '60s, the 'Gardes de la Reine', which old Dani Kendy had always asked for in the days when he could afford to reward the musicians himself. Pongracz played it specially for the bankrupt old aristocrat, knowing that it would remind him of the days when they called him *le comte Candi* in Paris and when he had been an ever-welcome guest at the Empress Eugénie's court at Biarritz.

The Galahad of former days looked gratefully at the gypsy until suddenly the music was interrupted.

Pityu Kendy jumped up violently and, without any apparent reason, started yelling: 'God damn it! ... God damn it!' and in his anger struck out at the great goblet on the table in front of him. No one ever knew what had provoked this outburst, whether it was because he didn't like the music, or if he had had a flash of intuition that drink would be his ruin, or whether perhaps Laji's waltz-tune had made him think of Adrienne.

The glass flew towards Balint and though he was quick enough to jump out of the way he could not avoid the wine which spilled over his trouser-legs. At any other time he would have laughed off the incident, but tonight his ill-humour was too strong and he shouted at Pityu in a rage:

'Hey! Hey! Hey! Watch out!' Though the words were innocent enough, his manner was unmistakably threatening. Everyone jumped to their feet, including old Dani who stood straight and tall even if he did sway like a reed in the wind.

'*Une affaire d-d-d'honneur! Une affaire d-d-d'honneur!*' he cried, waving his arms, mistakenly believing that the insult had been intended for him and for his past.

Quickly Joska Kendy and Gazsi grabbed the old man from behind. They knew what happened when old Dani suddenly stood up with too much drink inside him so they half dragged half pushed him out through the door. Two footmen silently stepped forward, picked up the broken pieces of the shattered goblet and mopped up the wine on the floor.

Everyone sat down again, Abady a little apart from the others. No one spoke and even though the music started up once again the mood had been shattered. Within less than half an hour it was broad daylight and everyone went home.

―――

The next evening Abady went again to the Casino. As he passed through the big drawing-room it seemed to him that a group of elderly men who were chatting in a corner fell silent at his approach. In another corner he saw Pityu deep in conversation with Adam Alvinczy and two others. He moved on into the card-room where everyone present looked up at him enquiringly as if they were expecting something from him. No one spoke, and he went on into the library to read the day's newspapers. As he was sitting there he was joined by Tihamer Abonyi, who came out of the card-room.

'Excuse my interrupting you,' he said, 'but what are you proposing to do?'

'About what?' said Balint, not knowing what he was talking about.

'About what happened last night, of course! It's my view that you are the offended party, not Pityu Kendy. He threw the glass and that constitutes an Act of Violence according to the Code Duverger. On the other hand, your reply of 'Hey! Hey! Hey! Watch out!' was much less serious. I don't want to meddle, but this is how I see it and, as your friend, I would advise you to look at it from this point of view.'

Abonyi looked at Balint, his protruding light-coloured eyes full of sympathy. He was one of those men, not so rare, who feel involuntarily drawn to the men their wives find attractive.

'But he didn't throw it at me on purpose! In fact he didn't throw it at all. He just struck out at the glass and it came my way by accident, that's all. I'm not in the least offended.'

'You think that because you're a gentleman! The others see it quite differently. Everyone's been talking about it, ever since lunch.'

This was the truth. At lunchtime someone had said that there had been a serious incident after the ball. No one afterwards could recall who had started the gossip, but when more people came into the club – Uncle Ambrus, young Kamuthy and others who had been present – they were cross-questioned as to exactly what had occurred. The eyewitnesses all gave their versions, most of them conflicting and before anyone realized what was happening the whole affair had become a *cause célèbre* with everyone taking sides. The Abady faction was convinced that Pityu had thrown the glass on purpose, while those who decided to support young Kendy declared that though the glass had been hit at random Abady had rushed at Pityu with clenched fists and menaces. There were those who denied the clenched fists and the menace but who declared that the words 'Hey! Hey! Hey! Watch out!' could only have meant 'Watch out, or I'll hit you!' Again another group decided that the 'Watch out!' only referred to the flying glass but that the 'Hey! Hey! Hey!' would have been quite innocent if

PART THREE

said quickly without emphasis, but that 'Hey! Hey! Hey!' broken by pauses and uttered in a stentorian voice constituted an insult because one only spoke to inferiors in such a manner!

When one or two moderate men tried to suggest that the whole affair was a storm in a teacup and that neither party had intended any offence, they were shouted down by the others. Even Daniel Kendy, who had been far too drunk to know what had actually happened, saw the gravity of the insult, and as on the night before cried out: 'It's *une affaire d'honneur . . . une affaire d'honneur!*'

Shortly after Balint had arrived at the Casino, Major Bogacsy came in and the whole complicated issue was immediately laid before him for a decision as to whether insults had been exchanged and, if so, who should demand satisfaction from whom. Bogacsy was a retired officer who for many years had been employed as an assessor at the Court of Chancery and who was considered the greatest expert in affairs of honour in Kolozsvar. In fact he considered this true profession, treating his work for the orphan's welfare as a mere sideline by which he happened to earn a living . . . For a long time not a duel had been fought in the district without Major Bogacsy being involved as arbiter or second. His looks were well suited to his self-appointed role. He was a large man who sported a monocle in his right eye, which gave him a lopsided, sardonic expression; and the impression of ferocity which he liked to display to the world was carefully underlined by the cultivation of a giant moustache of which each side was reinforced by long whiskers from his beard. His face was round, his nose short and snub, and though he would have liked to look like a lion the general effect was more that of a tomcat who had stolen a sausage.

When they appealed to his judgement the Major, with much self-importance, stood with his back to the fireplace, his full belly protruding pompously, and listened carefully to the different versions put forward by the witnesses.

'Well, all I can say is that this affair doesn't seem at all clear to me! Still, my guiding principle is always to seek a peaceful settlement. Kendy must first ask Abady for an explanation of his words. What follows will depend on the reply.'

A small deputation went to find Pityu who was in the billiard-room. Though he had been far too drunk to remember anything at all, he meekly agreed to do what he was told. He asked Adam Alvinczy, who was standing beside him, and young Kamuthy, to act for him.

Accordingly these two went at once to the library and asked Abady to explain the meaning of his words 'Hey! Hey! Hey! Watch out!' Balint replied that now he could not recall exactly what he had meant but that it must have been intended to refer to the glass. Then they asked if the words had had any offensive intent, and Balint replied that he had no reason to offend Pityu Kendy. The seconds seemed to be completely satisfied with this reply and everyone assumed that the matter would end there. But it didn't.

For the rest of the evening no one discussed anything else, the most opinionated being those who were in no way concerned. Bogacsy himself was dissatisfied, perhaps because he had not been asked to be a second. While discussion raged Balint went home to see his mother and did not return to the Casino. Gradually the general opinion was formed that Abady's reply had not been satisfactory and that therefore the matter was not settled. What had he meant, they asked, by 'no reason to offend'? This was circumlocution: it was always possible to mean to offend even if one had no reason. Honour demanded a straight answer. Abady would have to be asked again if he *intended* to offend: and he must answer 'Yes' or 'No'. Everyone agreed, because Abady was not really liked. Some were jealous of his money, others found him conceited and stand-offish, and the general opinion was that he was not really one of them. Well, they would show him that they weren't to be trifled with!

The following morning Abonyi, who surprisingly took Balint's cause very much to heart, went to see him and related that it had been decided that Pityu Kendy should ask for a further explanation before he would agree to be satisfied.

'Really, this is nothing but tomfoolery! You've given a perfectly adequate answer and that should be an end of it! Have his seconds called yet?' asked Tihamer with good-hearted indignation.

He had hardly spoken when Major Bogacsy and Egon Wickwitz were announced. Dressed in black coats they advanced ceremoniously into the room and sat down, side by side like twins, upon a sofa. Then Bogacsy started to speak:

'We are here to represent our good friend Count Peter Kendy. He is not satisfied with the answer you gave him yesterday and demands a precise explanation. Did Count Abady intend to offend him or not?'

'I gave my answer yesterday,' replied Abady with a disdainful gesture, 'and I have no intention of saying anything further.'

'Then I must ask you to name your seconds!' cried the assessor

PART THREE

of the Court of Chancery with all too apparent joy; and he jumped to his feet with all the precision of a toy soldier on springs. Wickwitz followed suit, faithfully copying every move his leader made. Balint looked at them with cold displeasure. He found it derisive that Wickwitz, who had acted so dishonourably with Dinora, should now be setting himself up as a defender of someone else's honour. Too angry to reply, he turned to Tihamer.

'Count Abonyi! I should be honoured if you would accept this challenge on my behalf and choose someone to assist you in the matter.'

Abonyi was delighted. 'Naturally! I'm most gratified. I will do so willingly, but who do you wish me to choose?'

'Oh, I don't care. Perhaps Gazsi ... or anyone else you can find. I leave it all to you.'

Kendy's seconds took their leave, stiffly and formally, and Abonyi hurried out after them, full of zeal. Balint remained alone.

'What an absurd situation!' he said to himself as he walked up and down in his room.

Abonyi returned at midday saying that in his opinion the choice of weapons should be theirs as they were the offended party. Their opponents, however, disagreed, maintaining that as they had issued the challenge, the choice was theirs.

'I won't give in over this,' insisted Abonyi. 'As I said yesterday the most important thing for me is your best interest. I'm determined to establish an "act of violence" on Kendy's part. The glass proves it! Therefore I've insisted on pistols as is clearly prescribed by the Code Duverger. I don't want to speak about swords unless the exchange of pistol shots has no results. They don't want to accept this, so what do you think I've done?'

'What have you done?' asked Balint with a smile, thinking that the whole matter was becoming increasingly absurd.

'I've demanded that a Court of Honour and Arms be convened!' said Tihamer triumphantly. 'They won't decide until lunch-time, or by early afternoon at the latest, so that the duel can take place before dark. Where can I find you after lunch?'

They agreed to meet at the Casino at three o'clock.

Balint had lunch at home with his mother. He kept her amused by recounting many little incidents that had occurred at the ball until Countess Roza was laughing happily, pleased to know what

233

was going on in the world but thankful she had not had to be there in person. After they had drunk their coffee Balint rose and took his leave. When he was sure that his mother could not see him he beckoned to Mrs Baczo to follow him. She put down her knitting needles and got up, but left the room by the little service door that led to the back passages of the house. Balint was just wondering if the old housekeeper had misunderstood him, or had gone that way so as not to arouse her mistress' suspicions, when Mrs Baczo appeared in the hall.

'At your Lordship's service!' she said with a small curtsy.

'Look, Baczone,' he said hesitantly, searching for the right words. 'Everyone gossips so much ... It's possible that ... I wouldn't want my mother to be worried...'

'I know all about it, my Lord! Indeed, the whole town knows, my Lord! A duel! God forbid!'

'I don't think my mother knows yet, and I want to make sure she hears nothing.'

'Your Lordship can set his mind at rest. Naturally! You can be sure of that! We've already warned all the servants to keep their mouths shut, and the porter has been told not to admit any callers to the Gracious Countess. We'll watch over her, never fear!'

Reassured by this Balint went to the Casino. There he found an unusually large number of hats and coats in the hall and realized that many people had come in solely to hear the latest news about the impending duel. Not wishing to run the gauntlet of enquiring glances in the billiard and smoking-rooms, he went by a back way directly to the library and sat down at the end of the long reading table from where he would have a direct view through the adjoining room and would be able to see the arrival of his seconds when they came in search of him. To pass the time he started to glance at an illustrated magazine that lay on the table. After a few moments Pityu Kendy came in, also trying to get away from the impertinent glances of the curious. When he saw Abady already there he paused in slight confusion, and then, not wanting to draw attention to his presence, he sat down at the far end of the table from where Abady was sitting. The latter, engrossed in his magazine, had not noticed Pityu's arrival and so they sat there, for some time, Balint reading, unaware of Pityu's presence and Pityu gazing sadly at him. No one in the smoking-room had noticed.

From where Balint and Pityu sat the noisy group in the smoking-room could be heard but not seen, since all the men who were so eagerly discussing whether pistols or swords should be the choice of weapons were gathered round the fireplace in the far corner of the room. From the library it was only possible to distinguish occasional words when someone got excited and started shouting; old Rattle, forthright as ever telling some young man not to be idiotic, or Uncle Ambrus growling that true Hungarians only fought with swords and that 'if it was my duel I'd cut off his balls', though the obscene end of the sentence was swallowed up by a roar of laughter.

One man took no part in the general discussion. This was Pal Uzdy, who reclined in an armchair well apart from the others and in full view of Balint, his long legs crossed in front of him, appearing to take no notice of what else was going on in the room. He lay back in silence holding his watch-chain in his left hand, the watch itself swinging like a pendulum in front of his face. As the watch swung to and fro he would narrow his right eye and close his left just as he did when taking aim through a gunsight.

As the argument at the fireplace became more heated, young Kamuthy began backing away from the others until he was standing in the centre of the room under the chandelier. He was of the sword party and took great pleasure in insisting on his point of view in a high-pitched voice, lisping out his arguments with unusual vigour.

'What, the thword ithn't a theriouth weapon! I deny thith motht thtrongly! Ethpecially now afther old Keglevich wath killed in Budapetht; he wath killed on the thpot, on the thpot! Ithn't that theriouth enough?' With every phrase he would raise his fat little body on tiptoe in emphasis. Balint could see him and found the sight irresistibly funny. As he watched, he saw Uzdy suddenly leap to his feet his hand reaching for his jacket pocket.

'This only is serious!' said Uzdy in a tone of hard mockery, and raising his right arm towards the ceiling he let off the Browning automatic he had just taken from his pocked. In the chandelier a bulb shattered with an almost simultaneous explosion, and pieces of glass rained down on the head of Isti, who jumped aside in fright.

'God Almighty! – Christ, what an idiot! – That's going too far!' and other such remarks could be heard from some of the fireplace group while others just doubled up with mirth. Uzdy laughed derisively and flung himself back in his chair, his expression one of satanic amusement at a job well done.

Tihamer and Gazsi arrived just as the shot went off. Tihamer was startled but pulled himself together and went up to the others shaking his head gravely, as it was an unwritten law that a second must at all times remain calm and avoid any sign of excitement or distress. He looked around him as if nothing had happened and then, seeing that Abady was in the next room, moved unhurriedly to the library to join him. Only when he had sat down did he say quietly to Balint: 'Uzdy must be mad! What a thing to do, letting off a pistol in the club!' and he wiped his forehead with his handkerchief.

'He always carries a gun. But you must admit he's a good shot!' said Baron Gazsi, laughing as he came up behind Tihamer.

At the far end of the library Major Bogacsy appeared and went straight to where Pityu Kendy was sitting. Abonyi got up and bowed to them ceremoniously and then, turning back to Abady, broached the subject for which he had come.

The Court of Honour and Arms, he explained, had reached a decision. The ruling was that there had been offence on both sides for which satisfaction must depend on a duel with swords, to be fought until one party at least was disabled. As it was too late to fight on that day the seconds had agreed that the meeting would be held on the following morning at eight o'clock precisely.

'You know how to fence, don't you?' asked Tihamer. 'If you're a bit rusty, or need some training, I'd gladly go with you to the gymnasium. It's only a quarter past four, so we've time for a practise session.'

Balint looked at the clock; he had thought it must be much later.

'No, thank you,' he said. 'I think I'll go for a walk!'

'Shall I come with you?' asked Tihamer good-naturedly.

'It's good of you, but no thank you. I really ought to go and see my mother first!'

Abonyi made a slight bow and shook Balint's hand warmly.

'I quite understand. Oh, indeed I do!' He thought that Balint wanted to be alone to say goodbye to his mother; but that was not what Abady had in mind. As soon as he left the Casino he went towards the main square which was in the opposite direction to his mother's house.

Immediately Tihamer had told him that there would be no duel that day he had decided to go to Adrienne. Her husband was still in the Club and her mother-in-law away in Meran and so he was sure that if he went quickly he would be sure to find her at home alone. He was convinced that her illness had only been an excuse, but even so she would not have gone out if she wanted to keep up the deception. Also it was certain that she would have heard something about this idiotic duel as the whole town was talking of nothing else. It was an ideal opportunity for him to see her. Perhaps she was even a little worried on his behalf. He would be foolish not to take advantage of the situation.

When he reached the square he hailed a cab and told the driver to take him quickly to the Uzdy villa on the Monostor road. As Balint sat back in the carriage he started to think out his strategy. He was seized with all the excitement of a hunter at the start of the chase. He would make no direct reference to the duel, he decided, though perhaps it would be as well to let drop some slight allusion, vague but unmistakable in its implications. The most important thing would be, somehow, to kiss her as soon as possible. It would be difficult but once achieved the rest would be easy. With the threat of death hanging over him she could hardly refuse one last embrace. No one could be so heartless. Once they kissed the ice would be broken and then he could ask for more, always a little more until she surrendered completely. And the thought of such ecstasy made him so excited that he quickly tried to banish such fancies, wishing above all to remain calm, collected and in full control of himself.

The cab stopped and Balint quickly paid off the driver and sent him away.

The shutters of the main building were still closed showing that no one was in residence. Balint walked across the snow-covered path to the glazed veranda in front of the entrance to Adrienne's apartment where he found the old maid doing some work.

'Is Countess Adrienne at home?' he asked.

'The Countess is not at home to anyone, my lord,' said the old servant. 'She is indisposed.'

Balint took a visiting card from his case and scribbled on it: '*I shall probably have to go away tomorrow for a long time. Please see me!*' This he gave to Jolan, saying: 'Pray give this card to her Ladyship all the same. I'll wait here for an answer.'

The maid disappeared into the house, leaving Balint on the veranda. He waited for what seemed an eternity though in reality it was only a few minutes before Jolan reappeared.

'If your Lordship pleases,' she said, gesturing to him to follow her to the drawing-room door, which she opened, and then stood aside for him to enter.

The room was at least thirty feet long. It was lit by three large windows through which the last rays of the afternoon sun cast a soft glow over the white walls which were hung with portraits of former Uzdys who looked down with frozen, meaningless smiles. Most of the furniture dated from the late Empire period, as in so many Transylvanian houses. An unusual feature of the room was the wide fireplace sunk deep in the walls between crudely carved limestone columns. This was the only reminder that the room had once been the villa's kitchen. The fireplace was quite large enough to roast a whole calf on the spit of which there were still traces on the stone columns.

In all other respects, except one, the room was just like countless others at Kolozsvar and in the country around. What was unusual and surprising was that on the floor in front of the fireplace lay a large white carpet with a deep pile and on it were strewn a quantity of soft cushions covered in different shades of red silk. In the centre of these cushions Balint could see a deep indentation as if someone had just been lying there. Adrienne, however, got up from a small sofa in the corner of the room.

'I'm glad you've come,' she said smiling. 'I hardly dared hope you would.'

'I had to see you once more, before ... before I leave. I wanted to take with me the memory of your face, as a sort of parting gift.' He spoke seriously but calmly, in a low musical tone. 'There are so few who mean anything, but I wanted to be sure that ... well, that there might be one person who would remember me ...'

Balint went on. He started repeating himself, for he was far less at ease than he had planned and, indeed, as soon as he started speaking his plan of campaign went completely out of his head. There was nothing artificial either in his manner or in the words he spoke; words of resignation and farewell which came directly from his heart. The idea that he would never see her again had so taken hold of him that the elation of the hunter that had so possessed him in the carriage had completely given place to the despair of the rejected lover. He spoke ever more softly: '... so I was sure I'd find you at home, alone. It had to be alone. I had to tell you, just once more, quite soberly, without passion ... you had to know how much I love you. I know I've told you already; but you have to know it's true. I thought if I came and told you now ... now that ... well, perhaps you'd believe it. And I had to hold your hand once more, your beautiful soft hand, just feel your touch in mine, not by force, but humbly, very humbly ...'

Adrienne did not resist. Indeed, on the contrary, she offered him her hand as a gift when, rather tentatively, he put out his own towards her. Gently, rhythmically he caressed her palm, looking deep into her eyes, talking, persuading, cajoling.

As they sat there the room grew darker and darker. Adrienne's golden onyx eyes seemed to Balint to glow with an inner light. He was not sure but he thought he heard a clock chime somewhere. And just at that moment Adrienne leant forward and murmured: 'I love you too!'

'Thank you!' whispered Balint. 'Thank you!'

For a long time they sat together in silence, lost in each other. Their faces were very close and Balint, conscious only of his joy, gave himself up to the ecstasy that flooded his soul. Now he felt only a deep longing that absorbed him almost to the point that had he died then, he would have died happy.

'Give me one kiss, just one, before I go!'

For a brief moment it seemed as if Adrienne's glance faltered. Then she lifted her head and offered him her lips. For a long time they remained in a close embrace, Balint kissing her closed mouth and holding her, very lightly, by the waist. Then, holding her more tightly, he made as if to bring her body more closely to his. Adrienne pushed him gently away.

'Now you must go,' she murmured. 'Please!'

They rose and moved slowly towards the door, their hands entwined like brother and sister. They did not speak. When they reached the door Balint turned to Adrienne and bent over her hand to kiss it.

'If... if... you don't have to go away,' she said in a whisper, a catch in her throat, 'how will I know?'

'Then I'll come at the same time as today!'

───

Balint spent the evening quietly at home with his mother. He tried hard to keep her amused by telling her little jokes and anecdotes about people she knew, but somehow it was not a success, for try as he would he was too absentminded to be convincing. This was not due to thoughts about the next morning's duel: his mind was filled only with Adrienne. Even when he was giving orders to be called early he was thinking of the time he had spent in her drawing-room that afternoon, how she had murmured 'I love you, too!'; how they had gazed silently into each other's eyes without speaking, and how, when they kissed, it had been as if he were embracing a young inexperienced girl who knew nothing of love between a man and a woman.

It was extraordinary that the gay flirtatious woman who he had seen gliding over the ice from one man to another, who had been capable of parrying the overtly sensual advances of Alvinczy and Pityu while continuing to keep them on a string, and who, by enouraging him on Tuesday and failing him on Wednesday, had also reduced Balint to a state of bewildered frustration, could only kiss like a child! After more than three years of marriage and giving birth to a daughter, how was it possible that she would keep her lips tightly closed when kissed by the man she had just said she loved? Something was very wrong!

Balint could think of nothing else the whole time he was with his mother and it was the same back in his own rooms. Even after he had gone to bed he could not sleep but tossed and turned pondering the enigma he had uncovered. When, finally, sleep began to overcome him and the self-questioning that obsessed him started to fade from his mind, Balint became conscious only of a feeling of happiness and wonder. It was as if instead of falling for an experienced woman he had met a virgin who wanted to offer her love but did not know how.

Chapter Nine

BALINT ROSE EARLY and had a bath. Then he dressed with his usual care and was ready and breakfasted well before Tihamer, formally dressed in a black morning coat and carrying a top hat, came to fetch him. Baron Gazsi was waiting for them downstairs and together they went in a closed carriage to the gymnasium, a long barrack-like building which was always used for duels in Kolozsvar.

Abady was led into a small, barely heated dressing-room where he found the physicians and the fencing master awaiting him. On their instructions Balint stripped to the waist and then the physicians bandaged his entire upper body with layers of cotton wool and gauze covered with bands of black silk. When all was ready Balint's seconds led him into the ice-cold fencing hall, and as they went in another door opened at the far end and Pityu Kendy entered flanked by his seconds, Major Bogacsy dressed like Abonyi in top hat and a morning suit which was too tight for his increasing girth, and Baron Wickwitz, who had put on his dress uniform. He hardly recognized Pityu, who was swathed to the chin with black silk bandages exactly like those they had just wound round Balint.

While the antagonists remained where they were the four seconds advanced, greeted each other ceremoniously and drew for choice of swords. At the same time the physicians started arranging their implements on the benches that lined the walls. To Balint they looked like medieval instruments of torture, strange shaped knives, scissors, saws and tweezers. With them were placed big pharmaceutical jars filled with strange liquids, and piles of cotton wool and gauze bandages. When they declared themselves ready they proceeded to disinfect the pair of sabres that had been selected for the fight, soaking them in carbolic solution until the gymnasium began to smell like a public lavatory. When all this had been done Bogacsy stepped forward to perform his role as principal second. With heavy portentous steps he moved to the centre of the hall, carrying a third sword with which he waved the two antagonists to their appointed places with imperious self-important gestures. Then he spoke, his loud voice echoing in the large hall.

'Firstly, according to the accepted Code, I invite the parties concerned to make peace!'

Nobody answered; Balint and Pityu had both been warned that any reply at this stage was strictly forbidden. Bogacsy waited for a few moments, then spoke again.

'For the second time, I invite the parties to make peace!'

This is ridiculous! thought Balint. They bring me here, stand me half-naked in a freezing room with a sword in my hand, and then they start playing charades! And if I said now that I'd make peace, I'd be disqualified!

Both antagonists were shivering with cold, but Bogacsy was not to be hurried. His self-importance demanded that he perform his role to the full, leaving nothing undone that the Code demanded should be done. It was clear that the retired major enjoyed these affairs as he enjoyed nothing else in his otherwise humdrum life.

'For the third time I invite the parties...'

Naturally there was no reply. Balint felt his nose beginning to twitch and was sure he'd catch cold if he stood there any longer.

Bogacsy began again: 'My bounden duty being fulfilled and both parties having refused to be reconciled ... Gentlemen!' he cried at the top of his voice, his chest thrust out and his huge moustaches bristling, '*En garde!*'

Balint and Pityu took up their positions, but they still had to wait for a few moments until Bogacsy ordered: 'Go!'

Four feet stamped the floor, two swords clashed. When Balint touched his opponent it was as if his sword rebounded like a ball on rubber. That he had been touched himself he did not notice.

'Stop!' cried Bogacsy at once. Not to be outdone, Tihamer cried 'Stop!' too and, grabbing a sword stepped up to the other side of the duellists from where Bogacsy stood. Balint and Pityu both stopped in their tracks and the physicians hurried over to them with wads of cotton wool in their hands. They dabbed officiously at Pityu's shoulder and Balint's elbow, though, as the swords had clashed and lost most of their striking power before touching human flesh, the wounds were barely skin deep and only a drop or so of blood was to be seen.

'Disabled?' asked Bogacsy severely.

'Absolutely!' cried one of the physicians.

'Indubitably!' said the other almost simultaneously. And they continued speaking alternately like priests in church.

'Gash near the artery...'

'Deltoid... very nasty!'

'Danger of haemorrhage!'

'... paralysis, cramp...'

'... any sudden movement...'

'... could be fatal!'

'Fatal, certainly...'

The retired major clicked his heels: 'I declare that both parties are disabled!' With his sword he saluted the whole company present. 'Gentlemen! Honour is satisfied!'

While one of the doctors stuck an unnecessarily large plaster on Balint's elbow, Tihamer came up and said in a low voice: 'Excuse me! Do you want to be reconciled?'

'Of course,' said Balint good-humouredly, and walking over to his recent opponent, he shook him by the hand, saying: 'Hello, Pityu!' and adding, 'I really don't know why we had to fight in the first place!'

This should not have been said, and the seconds pulled long faces and pretended not to have heard. As the remark made light of the importance of their functions they should now, according to the Code of Honour, have demanded satisfaction themselves. Among them only the irrepressible Gazsi turned away unable entirely to suppress his amusement.

This awkward moment having passed, everyone shook hands

PART THREE

and, after Balint and Pityu had got back into their own clothes, walked back to the town centre.

'Let's go and have some food,' suggested Bogacsy, who wanted to prolong the occasion as long as he could. Balint did not want to do this as he resented being forced to remain in the company of Wickwitz after what Dinora had told him. The man was clearly a 'bounder' and he wanted to have as little do to with him as possible. However, to refuse would have been churlish, so they went towards a coffee-house on the main square. On their way Wickwitz excused himself, saying in German that there were important matters to which he must attend. He saluted and turned away before anyone could ask him to explain.

The reason he had left them was that as they were on their way to the coffee-house they had been passed by Judith Miloth's young brother, Zoltan, who had surreptitiously touched Egon's sleeve. Wickwitz used young Zoltan as a combination of spy and message-carrier. In return for the occasional gift of otherwise forbidden cigarettes Judith's brother would tell the Austrian where his sisters were going that afternoon, with whom they were taking tea or dinner and what their plans were for the following day. Zoltan felt himself very important and did what Wickwitz asked both well and cheerfully. The job made him feel grown-up, especially as he hero-worshipped the handsome athletic young officer.

While Balint and his companions sat round a marble-topped table and ordered beer, sausages and hot pies, Wickwitz was hurrying with his schoolboy companion toward the Miloth town house.

The Miloths lived in a house in the heart of the medieval part of the town. It was built on a narrow plot that had its front on the Unio street while the back could be reached through one of the narrow little alleys that abounded in the old town. It was to this back entrance that Zoltan led Wickwitz. Leaving the officer outside the boy went in to make sure that the coast was clear. While still on their way he had told Wickwitz that Judith wanted to see him. If she wants to see me, thought Wickwitz, then all is well ... and still a secret! That's a good sign. Wickwitz repeated these words to himself several times: with his limited vocabulary he thought only in short sentences. Despite the success of his plans he was not over excited. The boy had told him to wait, so he waited. He was used to it, for life in the army often entailed waiting for long periods without any apparent reason. In the meantime he

243

walked up and down, slowly and deliberately, and when he saw a pretty maid come out of one of the neighbouring houses and cast admiring glances at the handsome young officer in the street, he automatically took note of the number of the house from which she had emerged.

Zoltan soon returned and beckoned urgently to Wickwitz, who moved quickly inside the house and followed the boy up a dim service stairway leading to the upper floors. Zoltan took the stairs three or four steps at a time. Arriving at the top floor Zoltan showed the officer into what seemed to have been a schoolroom and himself disappeared down a corridor. As he waited, Egon looked for a place to put his cap. The furniture was grubby and obviously rarely used. First he thought of putting it on a bed that stood against the wall, but thought better of it, reflecting that one never knew when a bed might not be useful. Finally he hung it on the corner of a washstand.

He heard light steps in the passage outside. The door opened and Judith entered quickly, holding out her hand with a nervous gesture.

'I sent for you to come because they're sending me away, to Vienna ... perhaps today, perhaps tomorrow!' Judith was excited and out of breath, and sank down into one of the Thonet chairs beside the dusty work table. The young man sat beside her, gazing at her with his great soulful spaniel's eyes. 'It's because I told them,' she went on breathlessly. 'I told them yesterday that we loved each other and that you wanted to marry me!'

Wickwitz shook his head gravely and waited until she spoke again.

'I know that it was only your noble nature that prevented you ... I know that but I love you! I don't care about anything. I love you and I want to save you!'

Wickwitz stretched out his hand and held hers tightly as a sign of gratitude and encouragement. At his touch her face began to soften its expression and tension, and he could see the tears that stained her lashes.

'You can't imagine how awful it was! Papa shouted, of course, as he always does; but Mama, Mama said the most dreadful things...' and she broke off, too ashamed to admit that her mother had slapped her face as if she had been a small girl caught out in some naughtiness. 'It was terrible, terrible! But I didn't give in and I'll hold out whatever they do to me. That's what I had to tell you!' and she put her free hand over the one of his that

PART THREE

already held her in a gesture of one who makes a solemn vow.
  Wickwitz felt that his turn had come to speak, but he could not think of anything better than 'How good you are, Judith!'
  Even he realized that something more was called for and so not knowing what to say, he stood up, pulled the girl towards him and kissed her on the mouth. This, he thought to himself, was better and simpler way than words. When, after a long kiss, he released her, she continued to speak, softly but with great determination.
  'I belong to you! I am yours for ever! I don't mind how long we have to wait, even if it's the two whole years before I'm of age. I'll hold out if you do.' She paused, and then, as if sensing his thoughts, she said, 'Could you ... because of ...?'
  The devil waits for no one, thought Wickwitz. If the matter of Dinora's drafts became known, 'Dishonourably Discharged' was all he could expect. The words burned into him like a flame. Still he could not break the thread that he had spun so successfully. He could not ruin everything by merely saying, 'No! I won't wait!' So, somewhat hesitantly, but still with enough emphasis to keep the girl reassured, he said: 'I'll wait as long as I can! And if, after all, everything comes out and I'm exposed ... well, then, *Schluss* – it's the end, as I told you yesterday. But, as long as it's possible *Treu bis an der Tod!* – True unto death!' and he laughed sadly.
  The choice of the little German phrase was a happy one and had an immediate effect on the girl. She shook herself and clutched convulsively at his arm.
  'No!' she cried. 'Don't even say it! Never that! But how much time do we have? How long can you hold out? I can't do anything now ... but if I have time I'll do it. I promise!'
  'Two months, three at the most. In the meantime I'll do what I can. I'll try to stall it until you come back ... if then ...' he left the phrase unfinished knowing he could hardly say 'If you're my wife then your family will pay my debts!' So he kissed her again, and while doing so he thought that maybe he could get an extension on Dinora's drafts by somehow arranging to pay the interest.
  'I'm sure we won't stay in Vienna more than four weeks – six at the most!' She pressed herself to him: 'Until then! Can I be sure that until then ... you won't ...?'
  'I swear it!' said Wickwitz in a voice as brave and manly as he could make it. 'But where will you be in Vienna?'
  Before Judith could answer Zoltan had put his head round the door and whispered urgently: 'Come quickly, Judith! Margit's

just called to ask if you were with me. Mama's looking for you. You'd better go down quickly!'

As Egon and Judith exchanged another quick embrace, Margit's voice could be heard in the distance calling out: 'Yes, Mama, of course I've called her! She's coming at once!' and her voice faded away at the last words, showing that she had already started to descend the main stairway.

Judith quickly glided along the corridor to the head of the stairs where she looked back, just for an instant, as Zoltan was hurrying Egon back the way he had come.

'Quickly now!' hissed the boy, and Egon, tucking his sword under his arm, ran down the stairs and into the street. Once outside he straightened up, let his sword hang free, and with an unmistakable swagger walked back towards the centre of the town. Catching a glimpse of himself reflected in a shop window, he stopped for a moment to twirl his moustaches and admire the splendour of his own image.

Balint got home just as midday was striking. As he entered the main hall of the house he met one of his mother's housekeepers coming out of the kitchen passage. This time it was not Mrs Baczo but Mrs Tothy, though as they were so alike it made no difference. Balint at once gave orders that no word should ever be uttered about the duel in his mother's presence, even now that it was all over. He explained that everyone should know this lest the Countess should catch an unguarded word and be angry that no one, neither her son nor her servants, had told her what had happened.

'Indeed! Of course!' agreed Mrs Tothy, her chins wobbling. 'God forbid that our Gracious Countess should hear a word of it! We've told the porter to warn all visitors to keep their mouths shut! Not a word, your Lordship, not a word!'

Balint started to go up to his room when the old woman came after him and said, 'Your Lordship's pardon, but is your Lordship wounded? We heard that there was a great gash in your Lordship's arm! Four inches, they say!'

He laughed. 'Look,' he said, 'it's nothing. I don't even need a sling!' and he waved his arm about in proof of what he was saying. Nodding to the old woman, he went on upstairs, feeling rather annoyed that the whole town should know and gossip about this ridiculous affair. How they all loved to blow everything up way beyond its real importance. All he could feel was a slight prickling

PART THREE

on his elbow, no more than a nettle sting; and they thought that worth talking about! Still, as he got nearer to his room he reflected that perhaps, after all, it did not really matter if the rumours about his being wounded were exaggerated, for they would be sure to reach Adrienne who would all the more appreciate his coming to her later that day.

There was a slight thaw in the air as Balint walked along the Monostor road that afternoon. Little rivulets of melting ice ran along the edge of the compacted snow on the road and down into the gutters that bordered the highway. The trees and rooftops were dripping and vapour seemed to hang in the mild air so that the snow-capped peaks of the Gyalu mountains that shone so brilliantly in the winter sunshine could no longer be seen in the milder weather that heralded the arrival of spring.

Balint turned into the villa's entrance gates and went round the court towards the side door in the covered veranda. At the corner of the main house he met Pali Uzdy.

'Well, well! Who do I see?' said Uzdy in his usual dry mocking voice.

'From a distance I thought it was Pityu Kendy! How are you? I hear you got somewhat cut up!'

'Oh, it was nothing, nothing at all!'

'Indeed? And Pityu? Did you leave him churning in blood?'

'No more than me! Nothing to write home about!' said Balint calmly. Uzdy laughed derisively.

'These duels are absurd,' he said. 'All duels are absurd! What would happen if someone really got angry? All that ceremonial! Such rubbish! Nothing more than games for children! If I wanted to kill someone, I'd shoot him without a word! Bah! All that marching up and down, and taking aim, or choosing swords. Old fashioned nonsense!' He pulled mockingly on his long moustache with his left hand while with his right he patted Balint on the shoulder. 'You'd better go in,' he said. 'My wife's at home, but I'm going to the Casino. You'll forgive me? *Au revoir!*' Chuckling to himself he strode off, his head tilted back at its usual angle.

Adrienne's maid was waiting near the door as if she knew that Count Abady was expected. When she saw him she came forward, took his hat and fur coat and galoshes and led him to the drawing-room. Adrienne looked up as he entered the room. This time she was half lying, half sitting on the pile of cushions in front of the blazing fire. As she looked up, only her head and the upper part of her body turned towards him. Her lips were parted and her golden eyes were alive with welcome. Balint stepped quickly across to her, knelt down on the thick rug and drew her to him, his mouth searching for hers. For a moment it seemed as if she might resist; but then she relented and gave him her mouth, though, as on the previous evening, she kept her lips tightly closed.

This time Balint was not prepared to accept so limited a response so with his mouth caressing her cheeks he whispered, 'Not like that. Let me show you,' and with his lips he gently and slowly parted hers until their two mouths clung together in a full embrace. At first he felt like a teacher, coaxing a willing but ignorant pupil, but soon desire so flooded him that all thought was wiped from his mind by the overpowering urge to possess her. The kiss did not last long for Adrienne soon opened her eyes, drew back her face from his and gave him an imploring look. Then she buried her face in his shoulder, as if hiding herself from him. When he started to kiss her neck, his lips moving over the skin below the hairline, she moved again, saying, 'No, no! You mustn't! No! Don't do that!' Then she put up her slim hand between his lips and her neck, as a barrier between them. For a moment she did not move, then she slowly pulled herself away from him. She said again: 'No! Don't! Don't do that!' Balint sat down near her on one of the other cushions trying to regain his calm, but the blood was pulsating so hard in his head that it was a long time before he could clear his thoughts. Finally it was Adrienne who spoke.

'Tell me what happened this morning? I heard you were wounded on the arm! But where, and why don't you have it in a sling?'

'It was nothing! I didn't even need a stitch, only a plaster.'

'Tell me, all the same!' she asked, drawing back timidly when he tried to kiss her again. Balint did not insist, for in her eyes he saw such an imploring look that he knew he must do nothing to break the spell that was being woven between them. It was as if they were just emerging from childhood and discovering for the first time that a game called love was played by grown-ups, a game that was enchanting but which could also be frightening in the revelation of the forces it released. Balint, sensing something of this in Adrienne, forced himself to be playful and lighthearted. In no time at all he had Adrienne laughing delightedly, sharing his fun with comradely amusement, which, if not exactly the effect he was after, at least proved that he had driven the tension from her.

PART THREE

The evening shadows fell and a maid came in to light the lamps. Then she left again to fetch the tea-tray. When she came back, Balint would not let her put it formally on the table but insisted that the tea things were placed beside them on the carpet in front of the fire. With fresh logs blazing in the fireplace, Adrienne smiled with girlish pleasure saying, as she buttered the toast, what fun it was, just like a picnic! Like two children they devoured the hot toast, the sweet fritters and little cakes that the maid had brought in. All feeling of passion had evaporated; they might have been in the nursery.

By now it was quite dark outside and their conversation, formerly so animated, languished until they spoke only in broken phrases. The desire that Balint had suppressed with such determination and self-denial, flared again within him. He wondered how he could kiss her again after being so gently but so firmly pushed away. Of course! It was simple: by saying goodbye! When he heard the church clock strike six, he started to get up, raising himself to his knees.

'I must go now. May I come again tomorrow at the same time?'

'Of course. I never go out in the afternoons.'

Abady put his arm round her waist to draw her to him, but once again she stiffened and tried to put away from his grasp, her hand on his wrist:

'Don't!' she said. 'Please don't!'

'You're holding my bad arm,' he said, 'the wounded one!' He spoke very softly, directly into her ear and at his words, as if melting to the gentle blackmail they implied, she abandoned her resistance and, obediently, like a good pupil, put her open mouth to his, eager to please though he could still sense a hint of resigned acceptance of the inevitable. Adrienne, while not totally surrendering to Balint's embrace, felt herself almost swept away by the reassuring warmth of having his arms round her, and she felt giddy and breathless as when led in an intoxicating waltz by an expert partner.

Balint kissed her for a long time, more sure of himself now and slightly more demanding, though still holding himself back so as not to alarm her. By now the hand that rested on his shoulder did not attempt to push him away ... but it did not draw him to her either. When he finally let her go and straightened up to take his leave, Adrienne gently touched his arm:

'But don't think, or expect ... Don't ask more of me ... ever!'

'Only what you'll allow. I promise! And I'll be grateful, whatever it is.'

At that moment Balint honestly believed his words to be true and spoke with such conviction that Adrienne smiled at him with renewed happiness in her heart.

The next day Balint presented himself at the Uzdy house at the same hour. Once again they started to kiss, but Adrienne seemed preoccupied and worried about something and wanted to talk about it. They sat down side by side and Adrienne at once started to explain:

'Can you imagine it! Judith wants to get married! And to whom? To Nitwit, of all people. Can you conceive anything so mad as to want such a horrid, dull man!' Adrienne then told him that soon after he had left the day before her sisters had come to see her and how she had almost quarrelled with Judith. 'They'll probably come again this afternoon,' said Adrienne. 'It's very disagreeable because for the first time in my life I agree with my mother, and my mother blames me for the whole horrid mess! That's why she sends Judith to see me. It's all my fault, she says, for not looking after her properly at the balls. I've been a bad influence, she says! As if anyone can watch what's happening every minute of the time! That Wickwitz has got a nerve. How dare he! Judith never told me anything, not a word! She never even asked me ... I'm really very annoyed and I'm so sorry for poor Judith who doesn't know what a horrible decision it is!'

Balint recalled indignantly what Dinora had told him of Wickwitz's behaviour and his immediate instinct was to tell Adrienne everything he knew about the Austrian; but then he thought again and checked himself. If he told all he knew it would compromise poor foolish Dinora, and that he could not do. Rather confusedly, therefore, he replied: 'Of course it's a bad choice, unworthy of her. I don't think he's the man for her ... I hardly know him, mind you ... but I should think he's, er, somewhat undesirable. People say he's very reckless.'

'That wouldn't matter! But after all I've told them ... for one of my sisters to make the same ...' She almost said 'the same mistake as I did' but stopped herself, only to go on ever more heatedly: 'It makes my blood boil!'

'Is she very much in love?'

'In love! In love! What does a young girl know about love? She imagines all sorts of things ... believes goodness knows what!

PART THREE

But I've told them, warned them not to rush into marriage like...' Again the 'like me!' was suppressed, although Adrienne could not resist an involuntary shudder as she thought of what marriage had meant to her. Then she pulled herself together and went on in a matter-of-fact voice.

'It'll really be much better for them to go away for a while. The girls are leaving for Vienna tonight; only my brother will stay behind. It's for the best. There'll be theatres, concerts, museums and Judith will have a taste of another world. A little experience of life and she'll soon come to her senses, poor girl! Yes! It'll all be for the best ... though I'll be very lonely, all on my own.'

'Poor Addy!' said Balint, taking her hand and kissing her palm to show his sympathy. He tried to pull her more closely to him, but Adrienne shook her head, she was too preoccupied with the tragedy of her own marriage and the threat that she was sure marriage posed to the happiness of her much-loved sister to respond at the moment. Judith's misfortune weighed heavily on both of them, though for quite different reasons, and so they sat together in silence, bound to each other by loving confidence and trust.

Suddenly the door opened and Judith and Margit entered accompanied by their old governess, Mlle Morin. Balint immediately rose to greet them and take his leave, but before he could open his mouth Judith cried out passionately to Adrienne: 'This is your doing, I know it! It's you who have plotted with Mama to send me away, to separate us! But it won't work, I tell you right now! I love him and I will marry him! You can't keep me in Vienna for ever!'

'*Mais ma chère enfant* – but my dear child!' cried Mlle Morin, shocked by this lack of reticence in front of Abady who, hardly knowing which way to turn, was still standing between Adrienne and her sister.

'*Ça m'est égal* – it's all the same to me. I don't mind if the whole world knows! The more the better! Then you'll all *have* to agree...'

Adrienne jumped up and tried to take her angry sister in her arms: 'Judith, my darling, you're very unjust. I only said...'

Judith brushed her away. 'I know what you said! You told me the same yesterday! But afterwards ... afterwards you took Mama's side against me! Against me!'

'You know I only wanted to spare you.'

'Oh, I know all about that! You've explained many times how loathsome, how disgusting it is! I don't care! It's all the same to me what happens to my body if I can save him! That's what I want – to save him – and I also learned from you that if it wasn't for that...'

Judith's words upset Balint, making him feel he was inadvertently, spying on Adrienne's married life and must put a stop to the conversation or he would hear things that afterwards would distress Addy herself. So he bent over Adrienne's hand, kissed it swiftly and formally, took leave of the girls and the old governess and left the room quickly. As he closed the door behind him he heard Adrienne's voice raised in anger: 'How could you be so shameless? Speaking about me like that in front of Balint Abady! How dare you!'

Pausing for a moment Balint reflected on what he had just heard. Had Judith really said 'how loathsome! how disgusting!' and if she had used such surprising words what had she meant? He set off home and tried to banish this mystery from his thoughts. It was to no avail. As he walked he could think of nothing but those words 'loathsome, disgusting! I don't care what happens to my body!' Had Adrienne really talked like that to her sisters? Did she see love and making love as a frightening, disgusting horror from which her sisters must be shielded? Did she wish to spare them experiences which for her had been so terrible? If all this were true it could explain her girlish unawakened appearance, her withdrawal when he started to kiss her. It would explain too how it was that she did not even know how to kiss. In this could lie the key to everything about her that he had found so mystifying.

Poor, poor Addy! he thought as he walked towards his home. How unhappy she must be! Sudden hatred for Pal Uzdy flooded over him as he realized that it must have been he who had done this to her. Everything would be explained if he had taken her without love, brutally deflowering an inexperienced girl, and so damaging her pure and noble heart that at one stroke he had prevented her from knowing the greatest joy that life had to offer, indeed the only form of bliss those merciless gods had left to mankind!

Chapter Ten

WICKWITZ NOW SET HIMSELF in all earnestness to settle his money problems. He had realized that he could not get hold of Judith without waiting at least three or four months, for even if the girl were ready and willing there would still be trouble ahead before her parents would agree to their marriage. This would be a test of endurance, a cross-country endurance ride rather than a short hurdle race, and so he must prepare himself accordingly, as he did when he trained his horses. Thinking with slow but inexorable logic he finally arrived at the thought that somehow he had to play for time, to find the means to parry any attack that could jeopardize his long-term plans. And what was needed to achieve that? Why, more money, of course! Money was needed, not only to live while he waited but also to pay the interest of Dinora's drafts, and be available to meet any other, unforeseen calls on his purse. He might even want to elope . . . but that would need money too. Reckoning that his best bet was to touch Dinora again, but in a way she would think merely set everything in order, he had prepared prolongation forms, carefully not mentioning the sums involved, and two new drafts of six thousand crowns each. He would get Dinora to sign all these while she was still well disposed to him, though he would only cash the new drafts if it proved vitally necessary. All this he would have to do quickly, before Dinora became difficult and suspicious and turned on him.

He went to see Dinora as soon as the papers were ready. Telling her that he was horrified at the 'impertinence' of the bank in 'daring' to ask anything from her, he explained that if she signed the papers he had brought with him, all would be settled and she would never hear from the bank again. It was monstrous, he said, and explained that with the prolongation papers and the two new six thousand crown drafts, the amortization would be paid off and he would be able to arrange everything for her. Dinora was delighted; she felt a great load had been taken off her mind and even went so far as to show her gratitude by kissing him as soon as she had finished signing the papers. Wickwitz, for all his slowness in some matters, was never behind-hand when he sensed that he had the advantage with a woman, at once gathered the little Countess in his strong athlete's arms and made it abundantly clear that he would like to express his gratitude even more lovingly. Dinora did not resist. It was not bad, she said to herself, even if she did not love her Nitwit any more ... and so, after he left, she sat down at her writing desk and addressed a note to Abady on her oddly-shaped lilac-coloured writing paper:

Little Boy! (Do you remember, darling?)
  Everything I told you of the other day has been arranged. It was all just a muddle, a misunderstanding! Wickwitz has paid in full. Don't think too badly of him. When shall I see you? You know you are always welcome. Tihamer and I are going to Budapest in a few days as everyone here is so beastly to me ... though I don't care!
  Lots of kisses and ... well no! That's enough for now. Dinora

Balint received the letter the following day and though he had no idea how Wickwitz could possibly have raised the money, he was so glad that this unsavoury matter had been settled that he did not look for any further explanation but dismissed the matter from his mind.

As it happened he received another letter by the same post which immediately occupied his entire attention. It was from Count Slawata, and was far more mysterious and absorbing than Dinora's little note. Slawata wrote that it seemed as if matters in Hungary had reached an impasse, with relations between the sovereign and the majority party daily becoming worse. He referred to the government's difficulties, how impossible it was for Tisza's cabinet to rule when powerless in the face of an opposition majority in Parliament, how the cabinet was constantly trying to resign, how there was no question of recalling Parliament until a solution had been found to the major problem, etc., etc. None of what he wrote was new to Balint: he had seen it all for himself when he had last been in Budapest. But now a sentence occurred that aroused Balint's suspicions. 'Since we shall never give in on the army question,' wrote Slawata, 'we will have to find a solution somewhere that these rich demagogues will never think of looking. *Salus populi suprema est lex* – the good of the people is the supreme law.'

After dropping this sinister hint, Slawata went on to say that he believed Abady to share his opinion and he finished his letter by saying that he would be coming to Budapest towards the end of March and would look forward to meeting him again then. '*Ich könnte Dir manches Interessante sagen* – I have something most interesting to tell you,' he wrote.

PART THREE

Balint was annoyed with himself for saying nothing when Slawata had taken him into his confidence at the shooting party at Simonvasar. If he had not wanted it to be assumed that he was in sympathy, he should have said so at once; and now, receiving Slawata's letter which clearly showed that he assumed Balint to belong to the faction that surrounded the Heir, Balint knew he must at once put a stop to any suggestion that he had the smallest sympathy with Slawata's views. It had been useful to have a glimpse of the future ruler's plans, but if he allowed himself further contact with Slawata the plotters in the Belvedere Palais would take it as confirmation that he was on their side.

Balint decided quickly what to do. He sat down without delay and wrote, rather coldly, that as his private affairs would keep him in Transylvania for the present he was obliged to deny himself the pleasure of coming to Budapest at the time of Slawata's visit.

Having written this, Balint had to find some reason to justify his staying on. If he were to remain in Transylvania until Parliament was recalled, and this seemed the only sure way of avoiding even a chance encounter with Slawata, he would have to find some genuine activity that would keep him in the country. In the month of March there was nothing he could do to further his forestry plans on the mountain estate. It would have to be something else. At this point his formerly vague ideas for starting a co-operative at Lelbanya came back to him so clearly that during the course of his visit to Adrienne the next afternoon he settled nearly all the details in his mind. After their first embrace and when they had spent a few precious moments in each other's arms, Balint started to tell Adrienne about his plans and ideas. He was amazed by how interested she was; she seemed as involved as she had always been in the scientific and literary subjects they used to discuss so eagerly together. Now Balint, fired by her enthusiasm, found his ideas coming more swiftly to him, his explanations becoming ever more fluent and more cogent.

That afternoon he stayed at the Uzdy house for longer than usual. As before they lay together, entwined in a brotherly embrace on the cushions in front of the fire, but today he spoke eagerly, though in a completely matter-of-fact manner, about the advantages to the people of different co-operative systems, and Adrienne drank it all in. He had already recalled that his mother owned a small town house and property at Lelbanya which might serve as the nerve centre of this project. Now it was obvious to him how best to use it: two of the rooms would be enough for the Co-operative Centre while the rest would serve for the Farmers' Club and Library. The grounds would be quite adequate for a model market garden.

As Balint explained all his ideas to Adrienne, so did his plans become formed into a cohesive and practicable proposition. Now, in her arms in the darkening room, Balint knew that he had made up his mind what he was going to do. At the same time, however, as his conscious being was apparently totally concentrated on working out the best way of forming a farmers' co-operative, so unconsciously within him his male instincts were becoming gradually awakened and alert as he stroked Adrienne's bare arm, or her foot, ankle or elbow, whichever part of her was closest to him. And all the while he talked without any hesitation of how he could best help the people in his constituency.

When a few days later Kristof Azbej came to report to the countess before he returned to the country, Balint lost no time in asking him about the house at Lelbanya. He needed to know who the tenants were and for how long it was let.

'One is a joiner who doesn't pay the rent, and the other is a tailor to whom I was about to give notice, because he pays so irregularly and does a lot of damage to the property. Your Lordship should know that I had intended to throw them both out on St George's Day. You see, my Lord, I never neglect anything. I watch over your Lordship's interests more than I do my own! My only aim, as always, is...'

'How much rent should we be receiving, from them both?' asked Balint, interrupting the lawyer's flow of loyal protestations.

Azbej looked at his master, his protruding eyes full of suspicion: Why ever does he want to know that? he thought. I'd better go carefully here! So he answered uncertainly: 'I imagine it must be about five or six hundred crowns ... I don't know offhand ... and something more for the land. They don't pay it! If your Lordship wishes it I'll send a detailed report from Denestornya?'

'That's all right, it isn't urgent. I just wanted to know if we could get rid of the tenants. Please don't mention this to anyone until we have spoken about it again!'

'Naturally, my Lord, naturally. Anyhow it was the Gracious Countess who signed all the contracts, as always it is her Ladyship, always her Ladyship, not me!'

As he backed towards the door the little gnome-like lawyer

PART THREE

kept bowing obsequiously and repeating: 'Always at your Lordship's service. Whatever your Lordship commands.'

Abady left for Lelbanya by the morning express train. He arrived with little time to spare and forgot to buy a newspaper.

One other passenger was already seated in the first-class compartment, a broad, heavy-set, elderly man with large grey moustaches and striking blue eyes. His chin was close-shaven though it was obvious that a strong beard grew under the smooth skin. He was rather like Count Miloth, thought Balint, only he was much bigger. He found the stranger sympathetic.

Seeing that his travelling companion had two newspapers – the Budapest *Hirlap* and the Viennese *Reichspost* which he was then reading, Balint asked him if he could borrow the former. Later, when he had read all he wanted, he handed it back and then the stranger offered him the *Reichspost*, saying: 'Take a look at this one! There's an article on the Hungarian situation you might find interesting' and he indicated the leading article.

It dealt with the crisis which faced the Dual Monarchy and pointed out that the present conflict was entirely due to the failure in practise of the concept of Dualism. It was intolerable, therefore, that the Hungarians should be in a position to jeopardize the security of the whole Empire. The article suggested that the Hungarian government, whatever it might pretend, was by no means democratically elected and therefore represented only a limited privileged class. In no way could it be taken as expressing the will of '*die Gesamptheit der Völker* – the totality of the people'. The army, however, must essentially be an integral part of imperial organization, a joint interest with a joint duty, and though this did not imply that Austria had any intention of meddling in Hungary's internal affairs, it did mean that its prime task was to watch over the security of the Empire. The article ended with a vague appeal to the emperor not to forsake his paternal role of keeping in mind the interests of all the peoples he ruled.

'Interesting, don't you think?' said the old man when he saw that Balint had finished reading. 'That's what they think in Vienna, and I must say that there's a lot of truth in it.'

Abady rose and introduced himself. When he held out his hand the other looked at him with an air at once hesitant and faintly mocking, as if the mention of his own name might make Abady withdraw his hand:

'I am Dr Aurel Timisan, one of the defendants in the Memorandum trial!'

'I am very happy to meet you,' said Balint, smiling. 'I hear you're one of our new members?'

'That's why you find me in this compartment. First class is not normally for the likes of me!'

They started to talk. Dr Timisan spoke such excellent Hungarian, and expressed himself so wittily in that language, that no one would have taken him for a Romanian. He was extremely well-informed about world affairs. He talked about the recent revolution in Russia and wondered what would be the effect on the European situation if the proposed Duma were to be established, as now seemed likely. Perhaps he chose these subjects knowing that Abady had formerly been a diplomat, or perhaps because he thought it more tactful to avoid the thorny subject of the minority nationalities in Hungary. In fact it was Balint who broached this subject himself as he was anxious to obtain information and thought he could learn much from a frank discussion with the Romanian lawyer, far more than was to be culled from political speeches or published party programmes.

Timisan spoke reasonably, taking care to choose his words well and forcefully. He discussed the projected Nationality Bill, its faults and the important aspects of the situation that it failed to cover. He emphasized that the minority Members would not oppose it, for it was absurd of Hungarians and Romanians to be at each others' throats when they were surrounded by an ocean of potentially hostile Slavs. Hungarians and Romanians needed each other and should act together in harmony. It was senseless to foster suspicion and hatred between the two peoples, but co-operation was constantly being artificially hampered by the activities of a group of shortsighted chauvinists. Now Timisan allowed himself to get worked up, showing plainly his hatred for the politics of those shallow chauvinists who, he said resentfully, were often not true Hungarians at all but just a bunch of foreign riff-raff! Why, Rakosi himself was nothing more than a German from Szepes, whose name used to be Kremser until he bought a Hungarian name by bribing the registrar. Now he had the nerve to tell other people how to be Hungarians, talking about the Romanians as 'Romanian-Hungarians' and the Moldavians as 'Hungarian-Romanians' as if such important matters could be settled by playing word games with names and terminology. Did they really think that Hungarian public

PART THREE

opinion could be manipulated like that? It was all such nonsense: Romanians were Romanians and would remain so eternally, no matter what new names were invented for them.

'Nobody expects anything else,' said Balint, 'but you must admit that the country in which you live has a right to demand that you learn its language!'

'Naturally, I'm not against that,' said Timisan, and once again a barely perceptible mockery lurked in his smile. 'That's to everyone's advantage. As you see I've learned it myself, even becoming a Doctor of Law at a Hungarian university and serving in the Hungarian army, both with tolerable success, though I say it myself. It's true I've been to prison twice, for political reasons, of course, but all that was most interesting, even enjoyable!' He laughed, remembering the Memorandum trial, which had been the highlight of his career, and the judgements which followed. 'But you must admit, too,' he went on, 'that it is most unjust that the public notaries, high sheriffs, tax-collectors – indeed all public servants – are not obliged to speak the language of the people they serve. It is really absurd that the people cannot explain themselves in court in their own language, but have to use an interpreter. The Nationality Bill was supposed to grant us this ... but of course it's been drawn up by Hungarians without our being consulted!'

Balint did not know enough about this to discuss it in any detail so he decided to change the subject.

'It's my view,' he said, 'that we should try and find the means to draw closer together spiritually and economically. Here in Transylvania we are both at home. It is your country and it is my country. It is common ground to both of us. We could learn a great deal if we paid more attention to what really matters, and did not allow ourselves always to be sucked into the whirlpool of Budapest politics.'

Timisan listened attentively to everything that Abady said.

'I'm most interested that a Hungarian aristocrat should have the perception to see these things. It is most unusual! But very little will be done for there are too many vested interests in Budapest, the bankers and big business will never allow it! Everything you say is true, but it's a mirage all the same, just a *fata Morgana*!'

Balint would have liked to go on with the discussion and talk to his new friend about his ideas for a co-operative. It would have been instructive, too, to hear what he had to say about the best ways of organizing credit, production and marketing, but the train started to slow down for its approach to Ludas and he was obliged to get up and take his leave.

'I'm getting off here so I've no time to convince you,' he said, smiling, 'but, if you're agreeable I'd very much like to see you again and talk some more about these matters. I believe you live in Kolozsvar. Perhaps I could come and see you?'

'I should be delighted!' replied the lawyer.

Abady spent two days at Lelbanya. As soon as he arrived he sent messages to the mayor, the notary and several other leading members of the community, the two parish priests, the doctor, the chemist, the mill-owner and a few others, asking them to meet him in the afternoon. The meeting seemed to Balint to go well for everyone listened to his proposals with rapt attention, nodded their agreement to everything he said, and finally made it clear that they were all lost in admiration for the wonderful plans that their representative had been so good as to work out for them. Later they all dined at the Grand Restaurant Csillag, or 'Star', which was the only restaurant in the town, on excellent paprika-chicken and fried dumplings. A lot of wine was drunk and speeches and toasts were made well into the night.

In the morning Balint found a large group of people waiting to see him. Everyone wanted something, a favour or privilege or concession. One desired a licence to sell alcohol, another tobacco, a third sought a place, and a grant, for his son at the college at Eged; others asked for work on the roads, in the burial ground at Vasarhely, promotion for a brother-in-law who worked on the railways, a word to the bailiff, exemption from military service, or advice on how to cure a sick cow. As might have been expected the majority either had some complaint of injustice or bad treatment that they had received from the judge, sheriff, schoolmaster – indeed from anyone who exercised any authority, while others merely wished for help in fighting the wickedness of their neighbours. They all seemed to think that Abady was all-powerful and they came to him with the same simple confidence that children say their prayers knowing that God is listening and all will be well. And everyone ended their requests with the words: 'It only needs a word from your Lordship.'

Balint listened gravely and patiently took notes of every complaint or petition. He told them all that he would look into the matter but that he could not guarantee anything. Nobody believed this last phrase, for they were all convinced that if the count wished it then it would be done. They also believed that if

PART THREE

it were not done then it was because the count had *not* wished it.

A public meeting had been arranged for ten o'clock in the two-storey house they called the Town Hall. Balint was shown into a large room on the first floor which had four windows overlooking the market-place. At one end a table had been placed. It was covered in oil-cloth and behind it, under a large print of the Emperor Franz-Josef, were three chairs. Balint was shown to the chair in the centre and on each side of him sat the mayor, who was also the chief magistrate, and the notary. Behind them, tacked to the wall beside the gilded frame of the Emperor's portrait, was a large railway timetable. The chairs for the public were placed in rows facing the table.

The room was already full when Balint was shown to his place. Some of the younger of the leading citizens' wives came, dressed in all their finery, and smiled at the young count perhaps hoping that he might find one of them to his liking. These all sat in the front row. Behind the ladies everyone placed themselves in strict order of precedence, the most important in the front rows, the insignificant farther back. At the rear the young men and youths milled about in an unruly throng.

The meeting started and Abady outlined his ideas for a local co-operative. He explained the advantages of everyone's working together, how an organization that united them all could obtain better results and more profit for everyone than if they all worked independently and in competition with each other. He talked about the peasants in Saxony, where these ideas had long been accepted, gave statistics from other countries and tried hard to use simple phrases that everyone would understand. It was not long before he realized that few people understood what he was talking about, so he brought his discourse to an end with a few resounding clichés such as 'God helps those who help themselves!'

There were a few cheers when he sat down – not very many, it is true, but just enough. The Hungarian priest now made a beautiful speech, whose relevance Balint did not entirely follow, and then, as it seemed that no one had anything further to say, the mayor rose and declared that the assembly welcomed the idea and that he was happy therefore to announce the formation of the Lelbanya Co-operative Society. He further announced that, once the co-operative had been organized, a marketing organization would be formed.

Balint now stood up again and made the offer of the use of the Abady house and property in the town as headquarters of the society, which would be swiftly expanded to include a farmers' club, a free public library, and a model market-garden which would be to everybody's advantage.

This announcement brought further applause, though it seemed to Balint to be somewhat less than before, and the mayor rose again and declared that the meeting had unanimously accepted all three suggestions put forward by Count Abady. He then read out the names of those appointed to the preparatory committee, warmly thanked the Member for Lelbanya for his efforts on behalf of the constituency, and declared the meeting at an end.

The whole discussion had lasted no more than an hour and a half, so Balint proposed that they should take a look at the property he had offered for the society's use. Most of the leading citizens who had dined with him the night before, and a few of the younger farmers, agreed to this proposal, so they all left the Town Hall and walked along the rough road that led to the upper end of the town. There, on a small hillock shaped somewhat like a rock-cake, stood a sturdy-looking stone-built farmhouse surrounded by a shrubbery. The building had a two-tiered roof and a large veranda supported by two strong wooden pillars. Directly inside the main door was a long room which had once served as the family living and eating room and which was now the carpenter's workshop. As the party entered they were greeted by the agreeable smell of fresh sawdust. Everywhere around were piles of newly cut laths and boards of pine wood, strewn in such apparent confusion that there was hardly space enough left to open the door properly.

There was only one occupant of the long room, a small boy, about three years old, who sat on the floor dressed in a ragged shirt and nothing else. He was eating an apple but, seeing all these dark-clad strangers, he threw it away and, after staring at them for a moment, got up and ran towards a door at the back of the room. When he was unable to open it he hung on to the door-handle and started to cry. The door opened and a woman in the last stages of pregnancy came in. The child buried its head in her skirts and stopped crying. As it did so the woman saw the strangers who crowded the doorway and, pressing the little boy's head to her legs, she called back to the room from which she had just come: 'Janos! Come here, there are some gentlemen to see you.'

A man looked briefly out through the door and recognizing Abady and his companions, muttered something indistinctly and disappeared again. He had been in the doorway just long enough for the visitors to see that the carpenter was in his shirt-sleeves and that, naturally, they must wait for a moment while, for decency's sake, he put on his jacket so as to be able to greet them properly dressed.

'How can I serve you, gentlemen?' he asked when he came back into the workshop.

'We would like to have a look at the house and see what condition it's in,' said Balint.

The carpenter at once began a litany of complaints: 'By your Lordship's leave, it's in a terrible state! The paintwork's all peeling! There's a crack where one of the cornerstones has moved! The inner room is so damp that everything gets mildew at once! And there's a cracked beam that, by your leave, my Lord,' and he went on, hoping that this way he might obtain a reduction in the rent.

The visitors inspected the dirty and dilapidated rooms where the carpenter and his wife lived in great disorder. Then they went to the tailor's part of the house, which was no better and where unmended windows had been blocked up with paper.

The party then went to look at the outside of the building. It was true that one corner had shifted where the foundation stones were displaced. Water from a nearby pigsty had overflowed and collected at the corner of the house, eating away at the earth until a small lake of dirty water had formed in which a yearling pig was rubbing itself against the loose foundations. The carpenter and the tailor, both surrounded by their broods of children, followed Abady and by their endless complaints tried to distract his attention from the dirt and refuse that was everywhere such damning proof of their own neglect of the property. The carpenter's little son got in everyone's way. Wherever the visitors went the child always managed to stand by Abady's feet, staring up at him and picking his nose with his right forefinger. No matter how much the mother threatened the child would not leave Abady's side.

The little group of farmers who had come on from the meeting stood apart from the others, listening in silence to all that was said but seeming unconcerned as if nothing of it was of any importance to them. Balint expounded his plans: the tailor's apartment would become the co-operative's office, the pantry would be for the society treasurer, the big room that the carpenter used as a workshop would become the library, which could also be used for meetings and lectures, and the rooms where the carpenter now lived would be just the place for the caretaker who, by living on the premises, would be able to act both as watchman and gardener.

After examining the house Balint went to look at the garden where now there were only a few acacia trees and an old lilac bush. A muddy stream of water bordered by some reeds formed a bog at one side, while on the other there was a field still covered with patches of snow which showed signs of once having been planted with potatoes. A few dried-up maize stalks were further evidence that the garden was still in partial cultivation.

'Is there a spring here?' asked Abady, pointing to the boggy patch.

'Indeed there is! And more's the pity!' said the carpenter. 'They tell me it used to run freely in the old days, but it got blocked up years ago. That's why the place is so wet in some places and dried up in others!'

'Why don't you put it in order?' asked Balint. Turning to his companions, he explained how the spring could be made to irrigate the model garden. They would only have to dig out a winding trench with catchments at each corner and the whole area would be properly watered, just as they did in Bulgaria. It was a blessing that there should be a natural water supply at this height above the town.

Balint's companions all agreed, with unqualified enthusiasm, to everything the count suggested. The proposals were magnificent, everything should be carried out just as the count suggested. Of course, they said, there was the question of cost. Repairs would be needed as the property could not be used in its present state. Finance would have to be found.

'If the Co-operative and the Farmers' Club paid a rent then of course my mother would be responsible for the repairs. However, I hope that she will make the property available free of charge as it's for the public good. If that were the case then naturally the society and the club would be expected to pay the repairs ... but very little is involved, just a few hours' work by the mason and some attention to the drainage. All that would be well and truly covered by the profits made on the garden's products, as long as it is properly handled, of course.'

'Of course! Naturally!' echoed his audience. 'It's nothing at all! Hardly worth mentioning! We'll get it done, never fear!'

They walked back to the main square where everyone took their leave and went home to lunch. Balint went alone to the

PART THREE

Grand Restaurant Csillag, which he now realized was no more than the dining-room of the inn where he was staying. He was pleased to be on his own after the morning's work, however successful it appeared to have been. When the innkeeper brought his coffee he brought up a chair, sat down and started to talk.

At first he confined himself to flattering comments, saying how magnificent were his Lordship's plans for their little community, how lucky they were to have a Parliamentary representative who took an interest in them, who was so generous as to offer his property as a gift for the benefit of all. Several times he said how grateful they all were. Afterwards he began, carefully, to ask more detailed questions, into which were woven a few remarks intended to give rather than obtain information. As regards the Farmers' Club, which he supposed would really just be for peasants rather than country gentlefolk; it would not have a licence to sell liquor, would it? His Lordship would realize, of course, that it would not be at all for the public good if the people started doing their drinking anywhere than the inn in the town where he could keep an eye on them. Here he could not only see that no one got too drunk – which was bad for them – but also, by listening to what they said among themselves, he was able to make the inn an unrivalled centre for local 'intelligence'!

The innkeeper looked enquiringly at Abady. He was immediately reassured and looked greatly relieved when Abady said there would be no question of either liquor or cards at the Farmers' Club. The plan was to provide a place for study and serious conversation, not for debauchery and carousing. There would be lectures on agricultural subjects, or modern farming methods and ways of making marketing more profitable. Books and newspapers would be available and, if these did not prove enough, then perhaps they could build a bowling alley where the people could go on Sundays.

'Bowling?' asked the innkeeper, now thoroughly alarmed again. 'Bowling? Oh, no! That wouldn't be a good idea at all! I wouldn't do that!'

'Why ever not?'

The innkeeper stammered a little, looking for arguments that would convince the count without having to reveal what was uppermost in his mind.

'Well ... because, you see, there's always fighting where there's bowling, lots of trouble, arguments, blows! People get hurt. I know, because we've got one here, partly on the chemist's land, partly on mine. Oh, how I wish we hadn't done it! Always trouble, nothing but trouble! But I can't stop it now. It's there. It cost a lot of money ... so you see I have to go on with it. But, of course, they respect me. I've got a certain authority and I can keep them in order. If they went bowling somewhere else, well, you see, your Lordship, that'd lead to trouble!'

Balint saw. The innkeeper's worry was indeed perfectly clear, and Balint, who had no desire to harm anyone's private interests, quickly set his mind at rest.

'I never thought of it like that! Most interesting! Well, we'll have to think it all out most carefully. I'm not even sure there's enough level ground anyway!'

The innkeeper cheered up at this and, growing more voluble than ever, he offered himself to go and measure up the available space, check over the grounds, and send an immediate report as soon as he had discovered whether the idea of a bowling alley was feasible. That it was unlikely to be found to be feasible, though Balint was not to know this, was proved by the fact that as soon as Abady had left, the inn-keeper hurried over to see his friend, the chemist, to whom he expressed his deep distrust of Balint's good faith.

'That Farmers' Club idea, we must do everything to stop it,' he started, and the two of them sat down and began to think hard about the many dangers that menaced their mutually profitable association. It was perhaps appropriate that the room that they chose for this essentially private conversation was the little dispensary where the chemist kept his poison cupboard and the stock of illicit tobacco which had to be hidden from the Customs inspectors.

Balint then went to see the notary. They had agreed that morning to discuss technical and legal aspects of Balint's projects that afternoon before he took the evening train back to Kolozsvar. The notary, Daniel Kovacs, had proposed this himself, saying that he would take care of everything.

The office was on the ground floor of the Town Hall and the notary's wide desk was placed facing the wall. Daniel Kovacs sat at the centre with a pile of documents on each side of him and a pen in his right hand, taking each document in turn from the pile at his right, noting what action was required on the document, entering its number and date in the registers he kept open propped against the wall in front of him, and then placing it face

PART THREE

downwards on the pile at his left.

When Abady entered the office Daniel was busy writing '... *Peter Nagy, Andras and Ilona Nagy, wife of Salaman Szasz, and Vasili Niag, the son of Petre, petitioninq about the division of property are advised that a decree of judgment, No.16–273 1904, has been given under which...*' and he was so engrossed in his work that it was a moment or two before he noticed that Abady was in the room. Then he jumped up, pushed his reading glasses on to his forehead, took off his elbow-guards and pulled up a chair for his visitor.

They started talking about what had happened that morning at the meeting and afterwards at the Abady house.

'Naturally I am entirely at your Lordship's service,' said the notary. 'I think the plans for a co-operative at Lelbanya most practical and helpful. I have some experience of such things,' he went on, smiling, 'as I used to be assistant notary in the Szekler part of the province and we had a co-operative there. I was its secretary, so you see, my Lord, I really do appreciate what your Lordship is doing in trying to help the people here.'

Balint was becoming used to meeting nothing but agreement and obsequious praise, and though as yet he was by no means suspicious of the good faith of those with whom he talked, he was nevertheless unconsciously becoming somewhat cautious. He answered the notary non-committally, while studying his appearance, which he found unusual and interesting. Kovacs was a man of medium height, but he looked taller than he really was as a result of being exceptionally thin. He must have been about forty and had a bald head above a high forehead. Dark bushy eyebrows shaded a pair of brown eyes in which intelligence and goodwill held a fair balance. Indeed it was the notary's eyes that made his face particularly interesting for in them was an unmistakable expression of benevolence which illumined and irradiated a face which would otherwise have seemed tired, disillusioned and careworn. Two deep furrows were etched from each side of his nose until concealed by his moustaches, and the lines on his forehead suggested many years of toil and worry. Above all Daniel Kovacs gave an instant impression of being alert and helpful.

'The peasants, of course, don't understand the idea, not yet,' he said. 'Neither do most of the others, for that matter, but the peasants least of all. Anything new takes them by surprise and they're always suspicious of anything that comes from townsfolk. No matter what is suggested they'll always think people are out to swindle them! Set a trap for them!'

'But what trap could be in this? They're getting the house, garden and library for nothing. They can elect who they like to the co-operative committee. What more do they want?'

'They don't know what they want. They're just naturally suspicious because they don't understand, poor souls. Your Lordship shouldn't forget that they've every reason to distrust people. No matter with whom they have to deal, bailiffs, salesmen, everyone is always out for their own advantage whatever they may say, and a peasant has to be pretty spry not to be cheated. It's true! One day they'll begin to realize that it really is for their own good, but it'll take time. Has your Lordship thought who should be the co-operative's first president?'

'I was going to ask you, Mr Notary. Would you accept?'

'I am afraid that it's not in my power as I have an official position. The best choice, if I may say so, would be the Protestant pastor. He is a good man, and I could do any official business that was needed until he gets to know the ropes.'

Kovacs then pulled down the register of town voters to check what other names he could put forward for the different posts to be filled. 'I'll tackle them one by one, if your Lordship agrees, and explain to them what is involved. Of course, the first priority is to form the co-operative itself. When we've got all the committee members appointed and everything's running smoothly, then perhaps it should be the turn of the Farmers' Club. As for the house, well, perhaps we had better leave that for the moment! When they see how much they need the premises they'll come asking for it themselves.'

'That's funny,' said Balint, 'I thought the offer of the house would be the first thing to attract them!'

Kovacs gave a slight smile as he replied: 'Better this way round. Go slowly, your Lordship, these folk have a lot to learn!' The notary was thinking of what he had heard when they walked round the property that morning. The farmers who had hung back from the main party had been muttering rebelliously among themselves, saying that the only reason the Count offered them this rotten property was that he didn't want to have to pay for the repairs himself. And they asked themselves why they should be expected to fork out money on someone else's decaying old house. As for the proposed model market-garden, all that would do would be to make it impossible for their wives to earn some extra money by selling the produce of their own little plots. If some fancy gardener was raising finer vegetables in the model garden, who would buy the little strings of onions, the few beans and peppers that the farmers' wives used to take to market? And why should they pay good money for a gardener's wages when all he'd do would be to take the bread out of their own mouths? The notary was thinking of all this when he advised Abady to go slowly as regards the house. He recalled, too, the count's disastrous last words at the morning meeting – 'God helps those who help themselves!' Whatever Abady may have intended, the very vagueness of this phrase had made a bad impression on those used to the nonsense spouted by demagogues at election times. They did not have to go to special meetings to hear such phrases as 'God helps those who help themselves!' What they wanted was something real, something tangible.

Bearing all this in mind the notary said: 'They've got to learn how to serve the community themselves, and not to expect that everything is handed to them on a plate! They're all far too used to having things given to them. Of course they were spoiled by getting money at the time of the elections! That's why they've no interest in matters of public welfare, as there is in other small towns.'

Balint thought about the odd circumstances when he had been elected himself. 'Honestly now, tell me, did they get money at the last election? I'd very much like to know!'

Kovacs smiled. 'At the last election, no! I can guarantee that at neither of your Lordship's elections did money pass. You can rest assured of that!'

For the first time in their talk the notary had found himself obliged to go further than merely suppressing part of the truth. These last words were a lie. He knew perfectly well all the details of how Azbej and Cherrytree had rigged the elections between them and how they had been cursed for it by the electorate. However, he felt that the moment had come for discretion and when motives of self-protection must outweigh other considerations. The count must be told what he clearly wanted to hear, whether true or not; because if he were told what everyone had conspired to keep from him, it was certain that sooner or later Azbej would revenge himself on whoever had revealed the truth.

Abady was most relieved. He had been worried about the election and now knew he would have to find some explanation other than that he had feared. Filled with goodwill to the notary, he started to thank him for all his help and co-operation.

'I really am most grateful to you, Mr Notary,' he said. 'I can see how busy you are,' he continued, pointing to the piles of official documents on the desk, 'and I do appreciate all that you have agreed to do!'

Kovacs waved at the evidence of his work in a gesture of dismissal: 'I'm quite used to it! After sixteen years I can carry the burden. That's what the town notary's for! Not many people appreciate just what it involves. Why, there isn't a new law made by a minister, country sheriff, or instruction concerning taxes or building standards, or whatever, that doesn't come through this office and fall on my shoulders. People at the top don't realize, when they make even a quite simple order, that all the burden falls on those on the lowest rung of the ladder. No matter how hard a notary works he's always in arrears ... and not only that, if he makes a mistake, there's the disciplinary commission hanging over his head! But, never fear, what your Lordship has in mind won't add too much to the load. I'll do it gladly!'

'I really am deeply grateful,' said Balint, shaking his hand warmly. 'If I can be of any service, I'd be very happy.'

'Your Lordship is most kind,' said the notary, 'but for the moment I cannot think of anything. Perhaps one day in the future. In the meantime I serve my country!'

Abady then took his leave of the notary and made his way to the pastor's house. As he went he reflected that nothing he had learned during his law studies at the university had given him the smallest insight into the tremendous work-load that a country notary had to shoulder.

Daniel Kovacs stood for a moment on the threshold of his office following Balint with his eyes until he arrived at the front door of the priest's house. Then he returned to his desk and, as it was starting to get dark, lit the paper-shaded paraffin lamp that stood on his desk.

This count isn't a bad fellow, he thought to himself, not a bad fellow at all, but, oh dear, how little he knows about life! He's like a child in some matters, but I won't let them take advantage of him! And he sat pensively for a little while before putting on his glasses, picking up the next document from the pile on his right, and starting to read:

'*I have been informed that Domonkos Kacsa alias Kukui or Bubura, former delinquent and now vagrant, has been seen in Lelbanya. You are therefore ordered to check upon the situation and report to me within forty-eight hours, failing which ...*'

Chapter Eleven

IN THE NEXT FEW WEEKS Balint went back to Lelbanya twice, on the first occasion to bring with him the General Secretary of the Hungarian Co-operative Movement's central office, and on the second to attend a meeting of the preparatory committee. This last went far better than he had expected and Balint was surprised by the degree of serious attention that the townsfolk of Lelbanya devoted to the project, which, of course, was principally due to the notary's discreet and well-thought-out preparations.

Even at this meeting some of those present themselves raised the question of the property, proposing that the tailor's lodging should be immediately taken over so as to allow the co-operative to move its office there. As it happened the majority were opposed to this, which suited Balint as his mother had unexpectedly opposed cancelling the tenants' leases.

'I am very, very surprised', said Countess Roza one night as she drank her after-dinner coffee, 'that you should have seen fit to make plans for the house at Lelbanya without first mentioning the matter to me!' Mrs Tothy and Mrs Baczo had already left the room on a gesture from the countess, who went on, 'You can imagine what I felt when the first I hear about it all is when those poor people feel impelled to write to me themselves from Lelbanya... not from you, but from our poor tenants!'

Balint apologized to his mother. He explained that he had not wanted to bother her until he had first seen the property and checked that the project was feasible and the house convenient for the purpose he had in mind and, when he had seen it, there had not appeared to be any reason to raise the matter as nothing had yet been proposed officially.

Countess Roza was not to be mollified. 'That is not the point! I am saying that you did this behind my back and that I am extremely hurt and upset! The first thing I hear about it is – well, read it for yourself! It's from the tailor and the joiner...' and she fished a letter out of the Chinese lacquer bowl that stood on the table in front of her.

'*Have mercy on us, most Noble and Gracious Countess! On bended knees we beg...*' and so on, one obsequious phrase leading to the next and all of them describing their terrible plight in terms of humble flattery. They related how they and their families had ever been devoted servants to the Noble and Gracious Countess's family, how they were now menaced with losing their livelihood and being thrown out on the streets with their helpless children, how they kept the property in good order, as far as they were able, and paid their rents regularly, when they could, how they were beggared by the expense of maintenance and were already in a state of dire misery and if, now they were to have to take to the roads like vagrant beggars... And so it went on, with many repetitions but only one theme.

'These good people are lying to you, Mama,' said Balint after reading the letter. 'The house and gardens are both in a disgraceful condition because of *their* negligence, no one else's! I've seen it all for myself. Azbej told me that the carpenter hasn't paid a sou in years and he was about to give notice to the tailor for the same reason.'

'This does not concern Azbej! He has no authority in these matters!' said Countess Roza stiffly. 'Azbej does what I tell him to do and I will not have these poor people thrown out on the street for no reason. I have never done such things and I don't intend to start now. When the property is yours you can do what you like! But while I'm alive we'll have none of these new methods, if you please!' And she glared at Balint crossly, her little eyes bulging with anger.

'My dear Mama, I really didn't think...' started Balint, but he was not allowed to continue.

'All right! But let it be clearly understood I don't want to hear anything more about it. And, what's more, you will please remember to speak to me before you raise such things with other people!'

This was the first time that Balint had had a collision with his mother since she had asked him to take more part in the running of their estates.

The experience taught him that he would have to proceed with great caution as it was obvious that his mother was by no means as prepared to relinquish the reins as she had previously suggested. About two weeks later, therefore, when Kalman Nyiresy, the forest supervisor, brought in the report for which Balint had asked, he went immediately to his mother taking with him the old plans of the forests which Nyiresy now admitted he had found among the archives. Countess Roza was delighted and gave Balint a free hand at once.

PART THREE

The weeks and months passed. Spring arrived, and whenever Balint found himself in Kolozsvar he would go, as dusk was falling, to visit Adrienne. He would usually go on foot and, as he walked down the Monostor road he would always ask himself the same questions: What did he want from Adrienne? What was the use of all this? Did he really want to start something that couldn't be stopped and would tie him down, for he certainly did not want to lose his independence to any woman? Life should be lived without that sort of encumbrance. No commitments, that was always best. But if that is what he felt why was he pursuing Adrienne, when there were plenty of other women around with whom he could amuse himself without any problems? Each time he walked up the Monostor road he was assailed by the same confused thoughts and ideas.

Sometimes another voice spoke within him, a voice more cynical, more arrogant, a voice that laughed at his scruples and self-searching, and which accused him of behaving more like a timid schoolboy than a grown man of the world. This was the voice that said Balint was a fool, which scorned his moral reticence and laughed at his failure to end their little game of caresses by a serious and determined onslaught. 'Take her, you timid little college boy!', it said.

And one day, as they were lying close to each other on the cushions in front of the fire, it was to this second voice that Balint listened.

As so often they had been talking about love but, whereas in what Balint said there was always a hidden meaning, a purpose that he felt impelled to conceal from her, when Adrienne spoke her words were cool, impersonal, genuine reflections of what was in her mind. She talked of love as calmly and logically as she might of painting, sculpture or books, and her opinions were radical and modern. Marriage, said Adrienne, was an old-fashioned and meaningless institution. Nobody had the right to limit the freedom of another individual. All women as well as men should be free to act as they chose, as much with their bodies as with their thoughts. This was the only undisputed right that was accorded to mankind. Free will must be paramount. If you wanted to – and, shying away from the subject, she paused before going on to say that of course it was incomprehensible that anyone should want to ruin their lives just for that – then it should be their own affair and no one else's. She herself would never judge anyone for going against the judgment of society. If that's what they wanted, well, let them! It seemed to Balint as if her disappointment in her own marriage echoed through her words and encouraged him to hope that this was the moment for which he had been waiting, the moment when he should press for more. Gently murmuring words of agreement and encouragement, he started his attack by pressing his mouth into the back of her neck and gently covering with kisses that part where the almost invisible hairs are as soft and velvety as the skin of a peach. It was here too that her very individual woman's scent seemed at its strongest.

Finally, when she paused for a moment he pressed her down violently, thrusting forward his shoulder to push her farther down among the cushions, his hands searching, searching, searching ... For a brief moment Adrienne did not react; then she tensed and with the speed of a panther at bay, she jumped up and stood, back to one of the stone columns of the fireplace, tense, angry and defensive. She looked at Balint with hatred and amazement, outraged, unable to find words adequate to express her fury.

'What? What?' She was panting with emotion. 'How dare you!'

Balint bowed his head humbly, without moving from where he sat at her feet. 'Forgive me!' he said. 'Please forgive me!' And he tried to cover up with a lie, saying that he had slipped, that it was an accident, that he hadn't meant anything ... really nothing at all!

Adrienne stood there without speaking, mutinous, looking at him with distrust, in her eyes the look of an animal that feels trapped and unsure of itself. After much pleading and more abject apologies from Balint she agreed once again to sit down beside him on the cushions, but apart, not close as before. This time she sat opposite him, her legs drawn up under her, defiant, coiled like a spring and ready to leap up and flee at his smallest move. Balint felt that she did not believe a word he said to her as she sat there, tense and strained, and so, after about half an hour of halting conversation on totally impersonal subjects, he got up to say goodbye. Adrienne gave him her hand but when he asked if he could call again on the following day, she said that she had some calls to make in the town and would not be at home.

'Perhaps I could walk with you when you go calling? At least that way we could see each other,' said Balint.

'Very well. I suppose you could, though I don't yet know who I'll be visiting or when.'

PART THREE

And so they parted.

※

Balint was very angry. He blamed himself far more than he blamed Adrienne and even now he could not make up his mind exactly where the fault lay nor where he had gone wrong.

Once again two warring voices competed in his brain, the one despising him for being a coward and not following up his advantage by taking her regardless of any resistance. This voice told him that he would never achieve what he wanted by hesitating until the moment had passed, and that even if she had been angry at first all women calmed down as soon as it was over. And if she didn't calm down? Well, then, what would it matter? At least he would have had her once! But the other voice was stronger and more convincing. This voice blamed him for even trying when he knew that she was not ready and did not want it. What an ugly and joyless coupling it would have been if he had succeeded, humiliating to both of them. Nothing would have been achieved, never again would he be able to pass those afternoons in her arms, those extraordinary, childish, unfulfilled hours when they lay innocently, their bodies entwined in a brotherly passionless intimacy, and when he was obliged to be content with the light caresses that were all that this woman, so strangely ignorant of what was meant by love, would allow him.

It was incredible that Adrienne could permit those endless fondling caresses, light wandering kisses, contact between their hands, legs and bodies, and still remain cool and unaroused while he was bursting with desire, as full of tension as a tightly drawn bow-string. Up until now this strange anomaly had charged him with power and pleasure until after he had left her as dusk fell, intoxicated but not disappointed, giddy with the effort to control himself, but happy too, always happy. But on this day he was sad and depressed. Something had spoilt the magic for him and he could think only of how he could regain that strange paradise where, unlike Eden, the fruit of knowledge was not to be plucked.

※

By the early afternoon on the next day Balint was already to be found sitting at a table in front of the Hotel New York in the King Matyas Square. He had chosen a place on the sidewalk where he had a good view of everything that took place in the square. To give a reason for being there, he had ordered a cup of coffee that remained untasted on the table in front of him. The weather was sunny but even so the spring warmth had hardly begun and there was no one else at the other tables. Balint waited for a long time until he saw Adrienne approaching. He rose hurriedly and went to meet her.

Addy seemed as relaxed and gay as if nothing unusual had happened between them.

'Do you have to start calling on people at once?' asked Balint. 'Couldn't we take a stroll first? The weather's so beautiful!'

Adrienne agreed. 'We could go to the top of the Hazsongard,' she said. 'The view from there is marvellous. I often walk there. Shall we?'

The Hazsongard was the old cemetery of the town. The unusual name, which had no meaning of its own, was thought to have come from the German word *Hasengarten*, – a place where hares were to be found in abundance – and in time what had formerly been a place for hunting was found to be conveniently close to the town and so suitable as a burial place. A steep road, paved with cobblestones, led up a hill just outside the town. On both sides could be seen many tombstones, mostly old and neglected, as well as an occasional elaborate mausoleum erected by a prosperous family to house their dead in suitable dignity.

Adrienne and Balint did not speak as they climbed to the top. Finally they arrived at the far end of the burial ground and found a place to sit on the flat top of an old tomb. Up on the hillside the wind was cold and strong.

Adrienne had not exaggerated when she had said that the view was marvellous. From where they sat they could look down on the roofs of the town below and the lines of the old walls, which could only occasionally be discerned from close to, could easily be traced from here, the battlements and little defence towers clearly defining the medieval town and separating it from the more recent suburbs. The sunlight gave an ethereal glow to the old stones of the church walls and steeples. On the other side of the town the Citadel Hill rose dramatically from the faintly blue mists which shrouded the course of the Szamos river and its little tributary, the Nadas. Above, the peaks of the Gyalu mountains gleamed pale lilac above the yellow streaks of the rivers now swollen by melting snow and, far to the north east, the Tarcsa hills could be discerned rising from the valley.

'It is beautiful here, isn't it?' said Addy.

For a while Balint did not reply. He just sat there beside her, gazing at the panorama spread out before them. When he did

PART THREE

finally speak he did not look at her but looked steadily in front of him. He needed all the control he could muster to keep his tone light and gently mocking.

'You know, Addy,' he said as if he were joking, 'I've thought a lot about you, and I've made an important discovery!'

'And what is it?'

'That you are a dangerous impostor!'

'Well, really! I've never had that compliment before!'

'It's true! You talk about love as if you know all about it, while the truth is you know nothing at all, less than nothing. You've really no idea what it's all about! There are teachers, you know,' he went on lightly so as to soften the harshness of what he was saying, 'who talk about icebergs, or the sea, or the jungle, without ever having been outside the four walls of their study. They've learned all they know from books. You are like them,' he added slowly and deliberately. 'This is very dangerous for those who must listen to such teachers. It can be misleading. And you, you of all people! Why, everything about you, your lips, smile, hair, walk, it all contributes to the swindle! Yes, swindle! Everything about you tells the world that you are a woman when the reality is that you are nothing but an ignorant little girl who knows nothing at all of what she is talking about. Everything about you is false, nothing is what it seems, nothing. This is surely what the Greeks had in mind when they invented the Sphinx, half woman, half ... half monster – *un monstre*, as the French say so descriptively. And you are something even more strange, a sphinx who doesn't even know the answer to her own questions. Oh, what a danger you are to us modern wanderers!'

A deep blush spread slowly over Adrienne's ivory skin. Never before had anyone detected the sexual deficiency which for so long had made her feel set apart from other women. When some of her female friends confided their problems to her the only result was that she was made to feel different from them, poorer, lonelier, ashamed – and for this reason she had never told anyone of her own difficulties and confusions. Indeed she had done all she could to hide her misery from the world. Knowing that she was blushing, and hoping to prevent Balint from realizing it, she put up her hand as if she needed to hold on to her hat against the strength of the wind but in reality to shade her face from him, so that he could not see her expression.

'A yellow-eyed monster!' he went on. 'It sounds dreadful, doesn't it? But that's what I'm going to call you from now on; the

Yellow-Eyed Monster! In memory of this afternoon.'

Adrienne understood at once that he was not referring to that afternoon but to their meeting the day before. Balint's tiger pounce made her angry even now when she thought about it, but this feeling lasted only an instant, for she immediately consoled herself by assuming that everything that Balint had just said had been intended to justify himself, not to attack her. That must have been what was in his mind, she said to herself, when he said that she was different from women with experience in matters of love. Yet, inexperienced and innocent as she was, she still had an uneasy feeling that other women in love would not have been offended or repulsed him as she had. Refusing to admit this, even to herself, she raised her head defiantly as if to ward off further attack. Balint, however, changed the subject.

'Do you see? The willows are already green and the birches are coming into bud? They're all golden as if covered in a gauze veil, and in a week's time they'll be in leaf.'

'Yes! Yes, it is lovely!' Adrienne spoke with added eagerness, thankful to be talking of something else.

'Springtime awakes! It's like Wedekind's play. Did you ever read it?'

Adrienne admitted that she had and found it interesting but strange. So with relief on both sides they slipped into an easy discussion about books and plays and writers which lasted until they started to descend the hill once again. The wind grew stronger and, as they battled against it, the lines of Adrienne's legs were clearly visible through the serge of her skirt. With the material fluttering in the wind behind her Balint was once again reminded of Diana the Huntress in the Louvre, whose stride and bearing were nothing if not victorious.

On the following day they again went for a walk in the afternoon and it was not until three more days had passed that Adrienne allowed Balint to visit her again at her home. And then it was only because Parliament had been recalled and Balint would have to go back to Budapest on the night train. It would be his last evening at Kolozsvar.

'All right, you can come,' said Addy, and went on with severe emphasis, 'but only if you promise: as we were before. You understand?'

When Balint arrived and was shown into Adrienne's sitting-room, he found her as usual half sitting, half lying on the pile of cushions in front of the fire. He sank down beside her and it seemed to him that today she received his kisses with more response than before, as if she were tacitly trying to tell him that she wanted to be forgiven. Though no words passed her lips she seemed to say: Even if I can't give you more at least I can give you this with all my heart! But please don't ask for more! They remained for a long time, mouth to mouth and body to body, barely speaking apart from an occasional endearment, never a sentence or question that had to be answered. Adrienne's wavy hair fell in disorder round her shoulders until they had to pull apart so that she could sit up and pin her rebellious mane back into place. As she did so Balint leant back, away from her, his eyes drinking in the beauty of her slim waist and the line of her arms as they curved above her head.

The door from the bedroom door opened. Pal Uzdy came in, silently, his slow measured steps making no sound as he walked slowly to the fireplace. There he turned stiffly, straightened up his long thin body and without any polite hesitation or greeting, said: 'What are you doing here in the dark?'

'Talking!' said Addy defiantly.

'So! So! Indeed! That's very good. Of course! Of course!' Uzdy spoke slowly and deliberately, pausing between each repeated word, a smile of mockery on his cadaverous face. As he spoke it was clear that his eyes were taking in the pile of cushions strewn on the floor, some of which showed clearly by their disarray that they had been lain upon for a considerable time.

'Artistic subjects, of course! The arts ... culture. Very absorbing, I know. It's a pity I don't understand such things. Anyway I have not time for them. I arrived from Almasko this instant, and I've a great deal to do!'

Uzdy now turned to Abady and, looking down at him from his great height, said: 'I didn't know you were here, otherwise I wouldn't have dared ...'

At these words he laughed softly and pulled at his long moustaches. Standing there by the fireplace, his body lit from behind by the leaping flames of the fire, he could well have been taken for a devil, long thin legs outlined in red fluttering reflections of light, long thin form towering to an unearthly height. His feet were pressed closely together so that his body gave the impression that it swayed slightly with the uncertain outline of a disembodied apparition. Slowly he looked from his wife to Balint and then back to his wife again. His right hand, Balint noticed, was hidden under his coat, just where he kept the little Browning pistol that he had pulled out in the Casino when he had shot at the light bulb above Kamuthy's head. Balint wondered if he were about to draw it now and shoot him. Whatever he does, I won't even speak! thought Balint, and laughed to show Uzdy that he was not afraid.

'Everything's ready at Almasko, Adrienne. If you so wish we could move back next week,' Uzdy said to his wife.

'Whenever you like!' she replied. 'One day's notice is enough for me.'

Uzdy turned to Balint. 'Would you care to join us? They tell me you like shooting and you'll find some excellent roebuck in my woods. I don't know much about it myself but they tell me there's good sport to be found there. If it would amuse you?' Then without any apparent reason he burst out laughing before going on: 'Roebuck! Yes, roebuck! It's only a sort of game, of course, but some people like it.'

'You're most kind, but I have to go to Budapest tonight. There's a sitting of the House.'

'Of course! Of course! Parliament, politics ... Very important, politics! Well, perhaps when you come back? You will be coming back, will you not, sooner or later? Then perhaps you will do me, do *us* the honour? That's right, isn't it, Adrienne? He must do *us* the honour, both of us. Even if our place cannot compare with Denestornya, at least we can offer you a hearty welcome, an old-fashioned Hungarian welcome. Right?'

'I will come with pleasure as soon as I return,' said Balint. 'And I'll bring my new Schonauer rifle, if I may?'

'That won't be necessary. I have several excellent guns. I don't often shoot for sport but I like shooting at targets! You can use any of my guns ... anything of mine, can't he, Adrienne? As you please. Bring your own if you wish.'

'Naturally!' said Adrienne drily, ashamed of her husband's strange, sneering manner, so superficially polite, so laden with menace.

'Very well, then I'll count on your coming! And don't think I don't mean it; this is not just a conventional invitation, don't think that! Send a wire to our post box at Nagyalma and a carriage will meet the train at Hunyad. That's our station.'

'I'll let you know as soon as I get back!'

'Very well, then. *Au revoir* – until we meet again.'

Uzdy stepped forward, leaned down over his wife, took her face

PART THREE

between his long fingers and kissed her swiftly and unexpectedly on the forehead.

'Don't move!' he said. 'Please stay! *Au revoir.*' He walked swiftly to the door, opened it, said '*au revoir*' again without looking round and went out, closing the door behind him so quietly that they could hardly hear the click of the lock.

Adrienne and Balint looked at each other in silence. For some moments they did not move. Balint sensed that Adrienne had been deeply affected by her husband's mocking ambiguous phrases. What had Uzdy meant by that invitation? Did he have some sinister ulterior motive, a shooting accident perhaps? After all such things happened. Guns did go off unexpectedly through someone's 'carelessness'! These thoughts were soon chased from his mind by Adrienne who came to him, buried her face in his shoulder and held him tightly to her. He noticed that she was crying, soundlessly, but with sobs that racked her whole body. For a long time she continued, holding him ever more tightly as she fought to control the tears she could not stop. She went on so long that Balint began to be worried not only about her but also because if they did not soon separate the maid would come in to light the lamps and would find them in each other's arms. However, it was not possible to push her away and so they remained for a long time, Adrienne pressing herself ever closer to him as if in his arms she was seeking a refuge from life.

'Addy, my darling Addy!' he repeated over and over again, stroking her hair, her neck, her arms, as one does to a child crying for protection from some nameless horror. Even though Adrienne's whole body, from shoulders right down to her legs was pressed deeply into his, her full breasts crushed against his chest, he felt no desire other than the burning wish to help, calm and console her and bring her back to the world. He prayed that she would understand him, trust him, realize once and for all that he was her friend, for ever on her side against the whole world. For a long, long time they remained entwined together in the chaste embrace of orphans, brother and sister, abandoned and having only each other for comfort.

'Forgive me! Forgive me!' She put up her hands to arrange her hair which had once again fallen about her shoulders with some strands, wet from her tears, clinging to her face. 'I am very ashamed... I've never...'

Balint was very moved. He did not know what to say, how to reply, so he took her hand and kissed it, saying:

'Addy! My little monster! My darling Addy!'

Adrienne managed a mirthless gallant little smile.

'Yes,' she said. 'You are right! You have to leave tonight?'

'I must, alas! This has been marvellous, hasn't it?'

'Yes.' She spoke so low he could hardly hear, and they embraced calmly as if they really were brother and sister.

Balint got up and went slowly to the door. Then he looked back at Adrienne who had not moved from where she sat among the cushions. The fire had died down and gave hardly any light so that he could barely see her as she waved him goodbye before letting her hand fall resignedly to her lap.

While putting on his coat Abady saw that his right shoulder was wet from her tears.

He walked home slowly, making a wide detour so as not to get there too quickly. As he slowly placed one foot in front of another he was surprised to realize how deeply touched he had been by Addy's distress and how now he felt only compassion and tenderness.

The street lamps shed pools of light in the mists of evening, iridescent, shining, as if filtered through a web of tears.

PART FOUR

Chapter One

IN THE MIDDLE OF THE CARNIVAL SEASON, Laszlo Gyeroffy had found himself appointed to the much sought-after and respected post of *elotancos* – leading dancer and organizer of all the balls, public and private, that were given in Budapest during the social season. Every hostess giving a dance for her daughter would consult the leading dancer on all aspects of her party and rely upon him to see that everything was carried out properly. It was his skill, energy, unflagging attention to detail, good humour, tact, high spirits and knowledge of the sequence of the quadrille with its many complicated steps and formations that made a success or failure of the party; and as *elotancos* he also had to lead each dance. Everything depended on him, on his ideas, his stamina, his knowledge of music and authority over the gypsy musicians and, no less important, his iron control over those young men who seemed reluctant to dance and who, not infrequently, had to be practically ordered on to the floor. When the *elotancos* knew his job, there were no wallflowers and everyone enjoyed themselves. No one doubted the importance of the position and there were few who did not envy the man appointed to the post.

Laszlo had succeeded to the post when his predecessor, Ede Illesvary, had become engaged in the middle of January and resigned. Although Laszlo had been Illesvary's assistant, this in itself was not enough to ensure his succession, and he would not have been chosen had not something occurred which added to his social prestige just at the critical moment. Until then Laszlo had been thought of merely as one of a crowd of well-born younger dancers, related of course, to the Kollonichs and the Szent-Gyorgyis, sort of an 'extra', one who carried a spear in the battle scene but who only got a featured part when some girl needed a partner for the garland dance. To be considered for appointment as leading dancer something more was needed, some demonstration of authority, of standing, of exceptional social poise.

Laszlo achieved this almost by chance. One evening towards the end of January a gypsy party was being held in one of the private rooms at the Casino where Laszlo's cousin, Peter Kollonich, used to go with Kristof Zalamery and some other rich young men. Laszlo was invited because no one was better than that 'good Laci' in keeping the gypsy band up to the mark until the special guests — two new little dancers from the Orfeum — could get away from the theatre after the evening's performance.

On this particular evening the host was Zalamery, who was much richer than most of the others and who loved to entertain his friends with plenty of champagne and brandy served in huge goblets. As well as his cousin Peter, Laszlo found Fredi Wülffenstein there. When the girls finally arrived they danced, either with each other or solo, while the men drank and watched them, or else told gossipy tales of the *demi-monde* while sipping their wine and moving flirtatiously from one man to another.

Laszlo was bored. He did not know many of the men in this group, and even those he saw only occasionally, and he did not know who or what they were talking about. More and more he felt himself an outsider; so, to anaesthetize himself, he began to drink more heavily than usual. After a while he glanced at his watch and found that it was already past two o'clock. Since he had come back from Simonvasar he had attended the Academy of Music with unfailing regularity, not only from ambition to become a great musician himself, but also to prove himself worthy of Klara's love. 'I must be there by eight!' he said to himself, realizing, as he looked round the darkened room where the girls were reclining on divans whispering and giggling with the young men, that it would be easy to slip away unnoticed.

To get his coat, which had been left in the cloakroom at the foot of the main staircase, Laszlo had to cross the open courtyard. As he did so, the cold night air struck him and he realized that he had drunk far more than was good for him.

With considerable effort he managed to steady himself and control his legs which were showing a disconcerting tendency to stagger under him. A cold light rain was falling steadily and, seeing that he would get soaked to the skin if he walked home, he asked the cloakroom attendant to fetch him a hired car. There were none, he was told, they had all been taken, though no doubt they would return later. Laszlo told the man that he would be in one of the public rooms upstairs and asked to be informed when a car was available.

The big rooms on the first floor were all empty, the chandeliers dimmed to half their brilliance. Walking through them Laszlo saw that light was coming from the card-room at the top of a secondary stair and realized that the usual chemmy session was probably still going strong. He went up to see, as he had several times before, not to play, as he was quite indifferent to the game, but simply to stand behind the players and watch, for it was better than remaining in the public rooms to be bored by the endless talk of politics, horses or farming. Sometimes he had stood by the *chemin de fer* table for an hour. The play was always high and huge sums would change hands each evening.

There were nine men seated round the table. Laszlo stationed himself opposite Ernest Szent-Gyorgyi, whom everyone called Neszti. He loved to watch this magnificent-looking man, who much resembled his second cousin, Laszlo's Uncle Antal. They had the same tall, lean greyhound figure, the same finely modelled aquiline nose and cold grey eyes. In one respect only did they differ: while Antal's iron-grey moustaches were clipped close in the English fashion, Neszti's were long and jet-black, and curved in a thin line on each side of his mouth giving a haughty air of disdain to the otherwise noble lines of the face. Apart from the closely shaven bluish line of the jaw Neszti's skin was as pale as an ancient parchment, perhaps because nowadays he lived most of his life after dark, rarely being seen outside his house during the daytime. This ivory colour was spread evenly over his cheeks, forehead and the bald crown of his head where the skin shone like polished marble. Neszti Szent-Gyorgyi was immensely rich. He had never married and at this time must have been about fifty. It was said of him that he enjoyed life so fully that it would have taken a hundred years for any ordinary man to do as much as he had in his first half-century. Every pleasure that a rich man could buy had been his and he had exploited to the full advantages of excellent health, good looks and high social position.

In India he had hunted tiger and in the Sudan he had stalked lions. He rode to hounds in England, Ireland and France as well as in his own country. He kept a steam yacht on the Riviera and his racehorses were famous all over Europe. Many beautiful women had been in love with him and given themselves to him, but none had been able to tie him down, though he had fought duels to defend their honour considering this just another form of sport that was an essential part of the turmoil and confusion of life.

Through all these dangers – on safari, in the hunting field, in the gymnasiums and quiet meadows where sabre slashes had settled affairs of honour – Neszti had coolly passed unscathed, perhaps because no matter what he did his aristocratic heart never beat faster in passion nor paused in fear. Nothing seemed to touch him or ruffle the gentlemanly disdain with which he treated all who came near him. In his way he was the beau ideal of the *fin de siècle* man of the world. He had become the recognized authority on all that concerned the behaviour of a gentleman, and his judgement, cold and laconic, was never questioned. Sometimes he did not even have to open his mouth, his monocle spoke in his place. This little glass disc seemed to have its own language, as if Neszti had developed an extra organ of communication. He wore the rimless eyeglass attached to an almost invisible silken thread, and when he put it up to his eye he could express an infinite variety of opinion merely by varying the gesture: comic surprise, irony, increased interest or incipient boredom, appreciation for a woman's beauty or reprimand for a man's presumption. If, while someone was speaking to him he let the monocle drop by a deft movement of the eyebrow alone it would mean, as often as not: 'This subject is now closed!' or 'What an ass you are!' And no one was ever in doubt as to what was meant, whether it were approval or contempt or a whole range of subtle nuances in between. His timing was inimitable and it was widely recognized that Neszti's monocle was as much the symbol of his sway as was the sceptre of kings.

At the oval table brightly lit by a green-shaded lamp Szent-Gyorgyi, Odon ('Donci') Illesvary, younger brother to Ede Illesvary who had just resigned as leading dancer; Janos Rosgonyi, a short, tubby little man who was a famous breeder of race-horses; and the millionaire Zeno Arzenovics from Bacska constituted the hard core of big gamblers. With them were five others who played for smaller stakes but who occasionally initiated a modest bank or combined to share a stake when the play was high. These more modest players held back from the nerve-racking battles played by the first four whose initial bets would often run into thousands of crowns.

The lowest stakes were played by Gedeon Pray, but no one minded as they all knew that he was completely ruined and so they forgave the fact that he never pushed forward a chip worth more than a hundred crowns, and then only if the *taille* had come to him. And he only bet against the others if he seemed to be on a winning streak and if his opponents were on a run of bad luck.

No banknotes ever appeared on the table. The big players all made deposits with the Club Steward and collected whatever chips they needed on this security. Those who had made no deposit merely signed IOUs – for every club member had the right to ask for credit up to a limit of five thousand crowns –

which had to be settled within forty-eight hours.

Laszlo sat in silence, still feeling as much a stranger here as he had with the young men revelling in their private room. Though he was not interested in the game it was still agreeable to be in company and to watch the play undisturbed. Indeed he was more at ease in the card-room than he had been downstairs. There he had been made to feel on sufferance, barely even treated as an equal, not even as another guest but rather on the same level as the bandleader or drummer, whose presence was tolerated as a tiresome necessity. In the past, prepared for this treatment by his orphaned childhood and his homelessness, he had become resigned, accepting that it was his natural destiny, but since he had held Klara in his arms in the angle of her little room in Simonvasar he felt quite different. Now, whenever some young blood filled with thoughtless goodwill spoke patronizingly to him, Laszlo felt himself swelling with resentment and rebellion. Earlier that evening, for example, when someone had said lightly: 'Oh, yes, come too, if you wish!' and then had asked him to play the violin or get the music-hall girls to dance, just as if he were the major-domo or hired organizer of their revels, he had felt it was insufferable and that he would no longer put up with it. It was not worthy of him and certainly not worthy of the man that Klara, before all others, had chosen for herself and to whom she had offered her mouth. Ah, the memory of that kiss! Her mouth had been warm and generous and reminiscent of sun-drenched fruit and the mere thought of it made him giddy. That memory was shut in his heart as if he carried with him in secret the world's biggest diamond, a jewel so precious, so rare, so imbued with pre-eminent magic powers that whosoever carried it in his breast should pass first wherever he went. Sitting quietly at the chemmy table Laszlo, inflamed by the excess of brandy and champagne that he had felt forced to swallow earlier in the evening, felt his blood run hotly within him, clammering for this royal command to be obeyed. As he sat impassively beside the excitable Illesvary, silent and modest for all to see, within him boiled a turmoil of resentment and proud determination. The 'shoe' of gleaming mahogany now passed to Zeno Arzenovics. Before dealing he pushed out the entire pile of chips in front of him, which consisted of five hundred- and one thousand-crown pieces, and said: '*Faites vos jeux!*' He looked around expectantly, turning his head in every direction while his pointed beak of a nose, which curved out so acutely from his profile that everyone called him the 'Black Cockatoo', a sobriquet all the more appropriate since his thickly pomaded hair rose from his forehead like a crest of black feathers – seemed to dominate the table. For a while no one spoke. Arzenovics looked around expectantly, his cold prune-black eyes disdainfully seeking someone to meet his challenge. He played to the gallery, sure of his reputation as a famous gambler and hoping to astonish and horrify the usual group of anonymous watchers standing in the shadow behind the players' chairs. Even at this late hour there was no letting up. Arzenovics had to live up to his fame, which is why he always played the highest stakes, never accepted a partner and never retired from the game. Even had he wished he could now not have played in any other way. His principles were too well known, as he had so often expounded the wisdom of his methods to groups of awed and deferential onlookers.

Slowly some of the players pushed forward little piles of chips until there were some twelve thousand crowns on the table. The banker drew a nine.

'The bank will be twenty-four!' said Zeno. He pulled back the first pile of chips and built them into two neat stacks in front of him. Leaning forward, he shifted his cigar to the corner of his mouth and said: 'Twenty-four, who wants it?'

In front of Donci Illesvary only a solitary five hundred-crown piece remained, the forlorn relic of an evening of continual loss. Donci thought that if he won now he would break even; but if not, well, he could always touch his brother for another loan, as he had so often before. He knocked on the table to show that he would meet the stake.

Zeno drew a nine, winning again, and Donci gestured to the Steward to bring him an IOU to sign.

From then on the Ponte – those playing against the bank – placed ever smaller bets: eight thousand, five, three, and finally only one or two thousand, and that unwillingly, but they had to go on for it was considered dishonourable to withdraw from play just because a great gambler was on a winning streak. At a certain point they started putting up higher stakes again, for everyone felt that the run would soon come to an end. But it didn't: Arzenovics won eighteen times in a row. Now the betting slowed down. Everyone had been bled white.

'*Pour faire marcher le jeu*! – to keep the game going', said Neszti Szent-Gyorgyi, and pushed two thousand-crown chips forward with his long well-groomed fingers. He was the only player. Zeno won again.

'Nineteen times ... I counted!' said Pray nervously. 'This

man'll kill us all!' He was the only one to complain, though throughout the evening he had only occasionally risked a hundred-crown chip, and even that he had usually withdrawn before play started. He said this, however, because he liked to give the impression that he played just as high as the others and that he too had lost heavily.

At this moment the party was joined by Fredi Wülffenstein, who had been in one of the lower rooms. Despite the thick carpeting the sound of Fredi's heavy tread on the stairs could be heard in the card-room. He walked like this because he believed it was how society people moved in England. He was drunk and his elbows were spread wide. He stopped behind the chair in which Laszlo was sitting.

Arzenovics gathered his chips together. Once again he pushed a pile of them out in front of him and leaning forwards so that his handsome, rather flushed, face was fully in the light, said: 'Four thousand, who wants it?'

At this point Wülffenstein pushed roughly at Laszlo's shoulder and said: 'Get up! I want to sit here!' The words were an order, flung out arrogantly, without a 'please' or 'by-your-leave', as an ill-bred master might address his valet.

Gyeroffy was enraged. How dare this man speak to me like that! he thought. Who on earth does he think he is? Nothing would have induced Laszlo to get up. Anything, anything but that! It flashed through his mind, however, that he only had the right to stay where he was if he were playing; otherwise etiquette demanded that he give up his place. Sliding his chair forward, he rapped on the table and said: '*Banco!*'

Everyone looked up surprised, so unexpected was it that Laszlo, of all people, should enter the game... and for such high stakes. But that simple word *banco* inspired respect, even admiration. Even Wülffenstein was brought to a halt.

Arzenovics dealt. Laszlo neatly placed his two cards one on top of the other and waited until the banker spoke. When the latter said '*Je donne!*' he flashed them quickly, as he had seen Count Neszti do so often, not spreading them slowly as did hesitant, inexperienced players. His score was six, and he therefore said coolly: '*Non!*' Arzenovics had the same.

'*En cartes!*' said someone correctly but unnecessarily. Laszlo, as he had seen the others do, threw his cards nonchalantly and accurately into the wide leather receptacle in the centre of the table, that dish so oddly named the *panier* merely because in all forms of baccarat every expression had to be French. The cards were dealt again. Again it was the bank that won.

'My credit, please!' called Laszlo to the Steward, who quickly brought forward a tray of chips and a paper for Laszlo's signature. He signed and pushed four thousand-crown chips across the table to Arzenovics.

'Do you want your revenge? You have the right, *droit de suite*,' said Zeno.

'Well then, get up!' said Wülffenstein from behind him. 'I told you already I want to sit here!'

Gyeroffy glanced back over his shoulder; calmly, but between clenched teeth, he said: 'I'll stay where I am!'

'But I asked before! You weren't even in the game then! This place belongs to me!'

'No one has the right to a seat until he has said *Passe le main*. That is the rule. You didn't say it. Neither did Gyeroffy, but he entered the game before you.'

Wülffenstein did not reply for, as Neszti Szent-Gyorgyi spoke, he let the monocle drop from his eye and this, as everyone knew, was a final ruling that could not be contested. Fredi moved over to the other side of the room and sat down with an offended air. Laszlo, on the other hand was delighted to receive support from such an unexpected and exalted source. He decided to go on playing in spite of his previous intention to quit the game. He still had two five hundred-crown chips left from the five thousand float for which he had signed. With these he could call a bank from time to time and if only one turned up then he could repay the Steward at once and he would be no worse off. And if he lost he could always take the five thousand he owed from the seven thousand he had put aside when he had paid his debts at the time he came of age. It would be a blow but one that he could take without undue strain.

Zeno lost the next *coup* and if Laszlo had quit then he would have won back all that he previously lost. This flashed through his mind, though not a sign could be told from his expression. He continued playing, his face as impassive as if he played every night of his life. The iron self-control that he had learned so painfully now stood him in good stead; not a twitch of an eyelid indicated either joy at winning or pain at losses he could not afford. He spoke calmly, casually, deliberately, and with a practised air.

After a while he got the bank, though this was just the moment when luck seemed to pass to the *ponte*.

'*Contrepasse!*' said someone just as unnecessarily as before.

PART FOUR

Laszlo's bank now won three times running and if he had stopped his total losses would only have been some five hundred crowns. He could easily have got up at this point, for the servants were already announcing that the carriages were at the door and no one would think any the worse of a player who quitted the table at that moment, even if he were on a winning streak. However Laszlo did nothing of the sort. He pushed two thousand-crown chips onto the table and immediately lost them. This left him with two thousand five hundred crowns. He went on. He placed bets, won, lost, won again and suddenly he was in luck to the point that he was twenty-five thousand crowns up. A few moments later he had lost it all. Still he did not stop, but sat where he was, playing, sometimes high, sometimes low. It was relaxing, agreeable, entertaining if not particularly exciting. The chips seemed to represent only numbers, not values. It was a game, nothing more. One pushed forward some brightly coloured chips and sometimes they stayed where they were and sometimes a great many were pushed back in front of one. Someone dealt. One lost, one won. The chips were moved to where they belonged, that was all. Another deal, another win, another loss. Why stop? If one was in luck the chips piled up in front of one; if out of luck one signed another chit. Everyone was equal, only luck decided the game. Rank was nothing, riches were meaningless. One won, one lost. The only thing that mattered was style. It was like a play in the theatre. Everyone's part was already written for him and one only had to do what the author had decided. How agreeable it was! And almost for the first time in his life Laszlo felt that he was accepted by the others as an equal ... without reservations.

When Laszlo finally got up from the table – and he only did so because it was five o'clock in the morning and everyone wanted to go home – he was fifteen hundred crowns down on the evening. He had lost all his winnings with the same lack of interest with which he had acquired them. He was happy and at ease, so much so that he would have sat on indefinitely, pushing out chips and raking them in. The idea that those little coloured discs represented more money than he could ever possible afford, seemed so unreal that it did not even occur to him. Correcting his IOU from five thousand crowns to fifteen hundred he left the room and walked slowly down the stairs.

Outside the Casino the rain had stopped and a light frost covered the pavement with minute crystal needles that glimmered softly under his feet. Laszlo made his way home with a light step.

He was filled with an unusual sense of freshness and, though the air was cold he took off his hat and walked bareheaded. The fumes of alcohol which had so befuddled him in the supper-room had evaporated long before and it was with a clear head and a newfound sense of freedom that he strolled homewards along the dark streets where occasional lamps and the faint glow of dawn in the sky barely outlined the surrounding buildings.

Laszlo slept well into the afternoon. After dressing himself he tried to work on a musical score but he found it impossible to concentrate. His mind was elsewhere and the crotchets and quavers swam before his eyes. He could think of nothing but what had happened the previous evening. Finally he pushed the music away realizing that all such effort would be fruitless. It's a day lost, he thought, but he would work again tomorrow.

In the early evening he went back to the Casino to settle his debts and, as he was already in the club, he decided to dine there. As Laszlo entered the dining-room he could at once sense that something was different. A place was immediately found for him and he was eagerly asked to join some men already seated at a table. They greeted him warmly and asked his opinion in a way that had never happened before. When he spoke they listened and when they addressed him it was with a new air of attention, almost of respect. For the first time he felt appreciated, accepted. Of course they all knew that he had played high the previous night, and they knew, though Laszlo did not, what Count Neszti, in his nasal voice, had said of him before he too had put on his coat and gone home: 'Young Gyeroffy plays well. *Il a un excellent style!* I have rarely seen such stylish performance from a beginner.' Szent-Gyorgyi's praise set the seal on Laszlo's social success, but it was in reality only the official accolade, the public recognition, the putting into words what was now generally thought and accepted.

The real truth was that Laszlo had shown himself to be a gambler as the others were, and in that world the gambler was the true master, the hero whom everyone respected. And how should it be otherwise? The man who can say the little word *banco* and thereby risk thousands of crowns ... what gesture can be more lordly than that? *Banco!* Everything was in this one word – superiority, will power, calmness, the capacity to make a quick decision, courage and, of course, contempt for the vileness of mere money. And the more that this little word could be uttered with indifferent abandon, with carelessness and style, the more the speaker was obviously a superior being. *Banco!* If the player loses he pushes away his lost chips with a light wave of his hands and calls over his shoulder for a cigarette, or summons the waiter to bring him a glass of brandy as if nothing of the slightest importance had happened. It is the same if he wins, the same indifference, the same calm, no smiles, no bragging, no sign of pleasure, no unnecessary exclamations ... only those ritual, liturgical phrases: '*Je donne ... Non ... Faites vos jeux ... Les cartes passent.*' And all these said with an expressionless, stony face, like a priest saying the mass: '*Dominus vobiscum.*'

The gambler was also a lord in other ways. He lived well. It was of no importance if his dinner cost a hundred and twenty crowns and each bottle of claret another sixty or seventy. And what if he invited others to dine with him? What did the cost matter to a man who, an hour later, might win or lose tens of thousands of the same meaningless filthy lucre? And this every night of his life! Not even the richest of millionaires lived like a gambler. How long this might last was another matter; but while it did the gambler was the real king, and no one in the clubs was more admired and looked up to than he.

Of course no one ever put such thoughts into words, but everyone felt them. Even the most crotchety of the old gentlemen who snoozed away every afternoon in the deepest of leather armchairs and who complained unceasingly of the 'dreadful prodigality' of modern youth, knew that the luxury of the clubs of those days – the excellent cooking, the service, the comfort to which they were all deeply attached – was only made possible by the high stakes played nightly in the gaming-rooms upstairs, and not at all by their own more modest games of whist or bezique.

Laszlo felt completely at ease. He had never known such easy acceptance, such camaraderie, and at once ordered himself a bottle of champagne, which he would rarely have done at any other time. And he savoured with the expertise of an experienced *bon viveur* the goblet of Zalamery's own special Armagnac when the latter, previously so standoffish and superior, suggested that Laszlo might like to try it and give his opinion. When later they all moved automatically upstairs he needed no coaxing to join in the game. It all seemed so natural, the only thing to do, and the fact that the Steward immediately brought out a chit for Laszlo to sign showed the others that he had already settled the previous night's losses. This was immediately noticed – and enhanced his newly won reputation.

It was these events which led to Laszlo's appointment as *elotancos* – which, to everyone's dismay was about to become vacant right in the middle of the Carnival season – for the post was only offered to a man whose social prestige was beyond reproach and who apparently had the means to afford it. The possession of means was vitally important for it cost the dance leader a great deal of money. He had to have a carriage always available, for he must always be the first to arrive. He had to be impeccably dressed for all occasions – and for this several well-cut dress suits and at least two changes of shirts every night were needed (for who could tolerate a dancer whose boiled shirt was limp with sweat?), buttonholes for picnics and private parties had to be bought daily and his hand had always to be in his pocket providing champagne and tips for the band-leaders and gypsy musicians. Laszlo might have thought twice about accepting the position if he had not become a regular gambler but, even though he was by no means always on a winning streak, and indeed his losses normally left him slightly out of pocket, money was no longer important to him. The few thousand crowns that he had kept in reserve so as not to have always to go running to his estate manager in the middle of winter each time that he might have need of something extra, were soon gone. He had formerly made the acquaintance of some complaisant money-lenders who now gave him credit because he had paid them off without bargaining when he came of age. Presumably they had somehow discovered what properties he owned and what his expectations were, for now that he needed money again they gave it to him without demur, though still charging exhorbitant rates of interest. When he won at cards he had plenty of money, and spent it freely, and when he lost he borrowed enough to pay his debts and leave him enough to carry on as before.

Laszlo was a great success as dance leader for he was exceptionally good at the job. He could bring any party to life, invented new figures for the quadrille and even his innovations to the traditional movements of the cotillion, which many of the young people disliked, were so fresh and amusing that this old dance became the high spot of each evening. He introduced new csárdáses and the gypsies never played as well as they did for him. With deference and understanding he delighted all the dowagers, not only the prominent hostesses and great ladies whose balls were famous and with whom he spent every afternoon discussing the details of the evening's entertainment, but also those forlorn mothers who wearily attended every dance in their efforts to marry off their not very attractive and often by no means well-dowered daughters. For these ladies, who were used to spending entire nights by the buffet in sad resignation, or gently snoring in a quiet alcove, he had a special word of gentle encouragement which would send them back to the ballroom with head held high and a new lightness in their step. He was deservedly popular.

Since the shooting party he had not seen Klara. He had been asked to Simonvasar for Christmas but he had not gone, feeling that his aunt had only invited him with reluctance. She had written '*Come to us if you have nothing better to do . . .*' which did not seem encouraging, and he sensed that she had only sent the invitation as a matter of form. Also, he could not forget his own sense of outrage and his hurt feelings when she had so cruelly ordered him to leave by the next train. He had answered her letter casually, saying in a somewhat offhand manner that he would probably have to go back to Transylvania during the holidays as he had business to attend to. As it happened he had not gone anywhere, but had stayed in Budapest alone. He had regretted later that he had not accepted, but it had been too late to change his mind. And so Christmas Eve was spent in his sordid little apartment sitting alone at his window by a tiny tree he had bought, and thinking about all those other Christmases when he had been with his Kollonich cousins.

Naturally it was the picture of Klara that he had conjured up and thought about; Klara as a child, Klara as a schoolgirl, Klara as a young woman still unawakened. He saw her with white socks and flat-heeled shoes, her hair streaming over her shoulders. He saw her in pigtails, long-legged and skinny, but with huge shining eyes, radiant in a white lace dress standing under the towering, brightly lit Christmas tree. It was so vivid that he could not bear the memory and had got up from the window seat, turned off the lights in the shabby little room, and lit one tiny candle on the artificial shop-bought tree that he placed on the drawing board that served as his work table. As one candle burned out he lit another and, gazing into its minute flame, tried to make his lonely Christmas Eve last as long as possible. In this way he nursed his sorrow and transformed the Holy Night of joy into an agonized vigil of self-torment.

Near the tree he had placed a teapot and a bottle of rum so that he could get himself drunk, for if he drank enough he knew that he would be able to sleep and so forget. But when the last candle had burned out and he was forced once again to turn on the lights, there was still some rum in the bottle. With uncertain fingers he poured all that remained into the last of the tea, swilled it down and went to bed. He slept until noon, heavily and without dreaming, and when he went back into the little sitting-room he found that the electric light was still burning and that the room was filled with the stifling smell of burnt candle-wax.

For Laszlo Christmas Eve had been the darkest moment of this sorrowful period. Later, with the new-found self-confidence that he learned at the gaming tables, with his appointment as *elotancos* and his growing social success, he began once again to feel the elation with which he had returned from Simonvasar filled with the knowledge that he was loved by Klara. Of course he no longer went to the Academy of Music; there was no time, for if he was to sleep at all he could not get up before midday, and in the afternoons there were too many visits to pay and too much to organize. He told himself that once Carnival was over he would go back into seclusion, as he had done the previous autumn, and then he would be able to catch up with his studies. Until then it would be impossible. In the meantime he was living a wonderful life and soon, very soon, the Kollonich family would arrive, Klara with them, and he would be able to lay at her silk-clad feet every flower, every melody, every dance and every new social success that he had achieved since they had last met. In the middle of February she and her mother would be back from Paris where they had gone to buy clothes. In a few days he would see her again.

Suddenly they had arrived. There was to be a ball in the evening, a so-called 'picnic-dance' in the lower rooms of the Casino. Laszlo stood at the entrance to the smaller of the drawing-rooms to greet the mothers and daughters and their escorts, for on such occasions the *elotancos* acted as host. At first he did his job automatically, almost formally, for all his attention was riveted on the great doors which opened on to the street. He held himself as straight as he knew how so as to show to the best advantage the new tail-suit he had recently ordered from England, that suit which moulded his shoulders so well, and the snow-white waistcoat which emphasized the slimness of his waist. Indeed he looked at his best, very slim and tall, closely shaven, his wavy brown hair impeccably brushed, a saffron yellow carnation on the silk of his broad lapel, a figure worthy to greet a princess!

There was such a crowd in the entrance hall that he could no longer see the doors. Even so he knew at once when Klara arrived. He could not see her, but he knew she was there and his heart beat faster. In a few seconds there she was, moving serenely in the wake of her mother, and to Laszlo it was as if the room were suddenly filled with a light of dazzling brilliance in the centre of which stood Klara. It was as if all this glitter emanated from somewhere inside her pale shoulders, irradiating her white tulle balldress in much the same way that Virgin saints are portrayed as the centre of flickering golden flames that make everything around them fade to dull insignificance. The diamond at the centre was Klara, with her full mouth and smiling eyes, and no one, no one but she, existed in the whole wide world.

The princess swept forward and patted Laszlo's face with two white-gloved fingers.

'Laci! My dear nephew, how manly you have become!' she said, though her eyes remained cold, and she moved on, accepting as her due the homage with which she was greeted by those already assembled in the drawing-room. Laszlo took Klara's hand, so soft that it seemed to melt in his palm. She smiled, but did not speak, and he knew only from the gentle pressure of her seemingly boneless fingers, that she too was filled with remembrance of their last sweet moments together. Then, as she moved on in the wake of her mother, a wave of happiness rushed through Laszlo's whole being. Swiftly he strode over to the entrance of the ballroom and called to the musicians to strike up a waltz. Seeing his cousin Magda Szent-Gyorgyi nearby he seized her by the arm, rushed her on to the deserted floor, and immediately whirled her in an elaborate reverse across the highly polished golden parquet. In a moment they were joined by other couples and the ball had begun. But for Laszlo there was only one thought: 'She is here! At last she is here, here!' And every time they turned to the rhythm of the music the beat seemed to echo: 'Here! Here! Here!'

It was now the height of the season, and balls to which 'everyone' went were held nightly. Laszlo saw Klara every day, though always in a crowd of people, beneath huge brightly-lit chandeliers and surrounded by a multitude of other young girls all dressed in the colours of spring flowers. They were never alone and could never exchange two words that were not overheard by others, although at the supper which always followed the quadrille Laszlo would invariably sit on Klara's right. Since he had become the dance leader Laszlo never asked any girl to partner him for the quadrille, for, as he had explained to everyone, in directing the complicated movements of that dance the *elotancos* was bound constantly to leave his partner and this was hardly fair to any girl unlucky enough to be chosen by him! Laszlo made this announcement so dogmatically that everyone saw the logic of his argument and believed it to be the truth. It was not, of course. The real reason was that the quadrille and the supper that followed it were traditionally linked and a young man was expected automatically to escort his quadrille partner to the supper-room and sit with her. Laszlo wanted to remain free so that when Klara sat down he would be able to join her party without having to bring another girl with whom he would have to talk and gossip and flirt. Though Klara and he never discussed this manoeuvre it was perfectly clear between them that Klara would see to it that her own partner sat on her left and that she would keep the chair on her right for Laszlo. It was an unwritten law and it worked perfectly.

For both Klara and Laszlo the last two hectic weeks of Carnival passed as swiftly and as fleetingly as a dream.

During Lent, even though there were no public balls, Budapest society remained in their town houses and amused themselves with luncheons and small, informal evening parties. Most of the great houses were known for their political allegiances and in these would be received principally those whose politics matched those of the host and hostess. Sometimes the men would retire in little groups discussing party tactics, but in those houses where the head of the family was a party leader, or who hoped to be the next party leader, the hostess and her daughters would also take an active part in the discussions, especially with those whose loyalty was suspect or whom they hoped to recruit to their side – for who could contradict or give the lie to opinions, however half-baked, if they issued from lovely red lips and were accompanied by glances from smiling eyes that hinted at promises far removed from the world of politics?

All this passed Laszlo by, for he saw only the social side of these daily gatherings. No one bothered him with politics, for everyone knew that though he was a popular man-about-town, an elegant dancer and one of their own kind, he was not a figure cut out for law-making or party disputes. He was also rather silent, but no one thought any the worse of him because he did not talk about politics. As a result he enjoyed himself as he never had before, for he could see Klara every day, talk to her, even if others were with them, and delight in watching whatever she did whether walking about, standing, or sitting and eating ice-cream.

Gyeroffy was now invited out every night, not only to *soirées* and receptions but also to dinner parties – something that had rarely happened to him in the past. So much was he in demand that for the first time in his life he had to carry a pocket diary of his engagements.

At some houses the fashion was for musical evenings, at which either professional singers from the Opera or famous musicians would be engaged to perform or the singer or pianist would be a gifted society amateur. Among those the most frequently asked to sing was the beautiful Fanny Beredy. When Fanny was going to perform she would bring her own accompanist, a little shrivelled-up old maid who slipped in unnoticed by a side door and who, when Fanny was ready, was to be found already seated at the piano like a small heap of crumpled black chiffon.

One night the old lady sent word at the last moment that she was ill and could not come. If Laszlo had not at once offered to take her place Fanny's performance would have had to be cancelled; and so it happened that by coming to her rescue he found himself unexpectedly admitted to her intimate circle. Throughout the Carnival season they had often met, but it had always been casually, as slight acquaintances in the same social group. He had kissed her hand, exchanged greetings, and they had occasionally danced together – but they had never come closer. When they talked, Fanny would look at him with a faintly mocking smile in those huge slanting eyes which so reminded him of a beautiful Siamese cat, but she would never call him to her or press him to stay if he started to move away from the group in which they found themselves. On the contrary she had always been the first to insist that he returned to his duties. Only from afar had she followed him with half-closed, seemingly sleepy eyes.

'I'm indeed fortunate to accompany you again, Countess!' said Gyeroffy as they moved towards the piano. 'I would do it no matter when, with the greatest of pleasure!'

'I am sure you are far too busy . . .' she paused, '. . . with other more important things!' and she laughed, a deep, throaty laugh which underlined the ambiguity of her words. Laszlo wondered what she had meant. Was she referring to his love for Klara or to the endless preoccupations that went with his position as leading dancer? Or could she have been referring to the fact that despite having received formal invitations he had never appeared at her house but only dropped visiting cards without coming in to pay a call? Strictly, of course, this had been mildly impolite on his part, but Fanny was too much a woman of the world to take offence. She had a deep knowledge of men and she knew that if a man were deeply in love he was better left alone. After all one only had to wait; keep in touch, but wait. That was the wisest policy, and perhaps when the time was ripe, then...? Fanny was sure that things would not go smoothly for Klara and Laszlo. If she waited – and if she still wanted him – maybe then. She would see.

As soon as Fanny started to sing, her warmth, musicianship and the beauty of her voice enchanted Laszlo as much as it had at Simonvasar. Her understanding of the music was sublime, her phrasing exquisite and she gave herself so totally to what she was doing that after a while Laszlo felt that she could have been the Muse Euterpe herself. When Fanny stopped singing he sensed that the music had created a special bond between them, and he wondered if the beautiful Countess Beredy felt the same.

'If you're free on Wednesday, Gyeroffy, do come to dinner! I always have a small party on Wednesday evenings. Just a few friends. Interesting, intelligent people. Do come ... if you're not doing anything else.'

Laszlo consulted his diary. 'Wednesday. Yes, I'm free on Wednesday.'

'Well, come then! Half-past eight. Black tie, not evening dress; it's only a small party.' Fanny spoke quite simply, in a cool manner quite devoid of coquetry. She then turned and walked over to where her audience were still gathered. The men crowded round her offering their congratulations, though to most of them this was merely a form of homage offered to her beauty rather than true appreciation of her singing. Fanny accepted their praise with a gracious smile. She did not look back to where Laszlo still stood beside the piano.

Laszlo moved over to rejoin Klara.

'How beautifully she sings!' he said enthusiastically as he sat down next to her.

'I hate that cat!' said Klara, but Laszlo did not hear what she said for the music still thundered in his head and he could think of nothing else.

Chapter Two

THE FOLLOWING WEDNESDAY Gyeroffy drove up to the old fortress of Buda, to the ancient town house of the Beredy family. This was an exquisite small palace built during the reign of the Empress Maria Theresia for a rich merchant's family and later converted into an aristocrat's town house by joining many small rooms together to make big ones. After mounting a rather narrow stairway the guests had to pass through a long gallery that overlooked the courtyard to reach a superb drawing-room whose windows opened over the fortifications of the old town. This is where Fanny always received her guests, and where Laszlo, for the first time, made the acquaintance of her husband.

Count Beredy never went out in society though he was often absent from home on business. He gave the impression of being an elderly man though in fact he was only about twenty years older than his young wife. He was broad, fat and moved slowly and heavily. What hair he still possessed was dyed reddish blond, as were the few bristles between nose and mouth that passed for a moustache. He was a man of few words and had a disconcerting habit of looking at whoever he might be talking to with a fixed stare. He had lips so thin that his mouth resembled a mere incision on the skin, and his plump fingers were covered in valuable rings, as if he felt the need to prove his wealth by a display of enormous diamonds.

At Fanny's dinner there were only two other women present, both poor relations of the hostess. One was a pretty but insipid young woman while the other was an older spinster lady who must once have been good-looking. Both were dull and boring, but both made a great show of their love of music for the sake of the rich cousin who invited them to her house. They were only distant relations, but Fanny had picked them out because they were always free when she needed other women at her table and because they would never pose any threat of competition to the hostess. They laughed when they should, smiled incessantly, never interfered or criticized, 'adored' music and occasionally were heard to say 'Wonderful!' or 'Splendid!' at suitable intervals during the performance. In the cast-lists of historical dramas they would have figured as First Lady and Second Lady; and if they had names no one remembered them.

The male guests were more interesting and each in his way distinguished or important. The principal among them, the first day that Laszlo went to dinner, was old Count Karoly Szelepcsenyi, an ex-minister, privy counsellor and friend of the Emperor, for whom he had often acted as a personal envoy. He possessed numerous decorations of which the most sought-after was the Order of the Golden Fleece and, as this must be worn at all times, its miniature golden emblem was pinned to the lapel of his dinner jacket. He sat on Fanny's right. He was about sixty years old, but his fair hair and blond beard were only touched with grey at the temples. He was powerfully built, with wide shoulders and the chest of an athlete. There was not an ounce of fat on him and it was said that to keep trim he worked with a fencing master for at least an hour a day. It was said that his *garconnière* was like a museum, filled not only with the masterpieces of the past but also with paintings and bronzes by modern artists, most of them now famous but who were unknown when Count Karoly had bought their works. Very few people had actually seen the collection, except for certain ladies who never spoke of it. He was, in fact, a real collector who bought for his own pleasure and not as a socially competitive gesture. His love of music was equally eclectic. In the sixties he had championed Wagner and he was now enthusiastic about the music of Richard Strauss and Ravel.

On Fanny's left was seated Count Alfons Devereux, descendant of the English soldier of fortune who had run through the traitorous Wallenstein and who had been rewarded for that, and for the devastation he had caused in the Thirty Years War, by an over-generous grant of land in Hungary. Just as his ancestor had been known for his fatal accuracy with the lance, so the present Devereux – Fonzi to his friends – could kill with his tongue. He was about forty and had started life as a diplomat, though he had soon abandoned this career, perhaps because his superiors had not appreciated the deadly accuracy of his wit. Also present was a poet, Gyorgy Solymar, then quite unknown to the general public, partly because his work appeared only in privately printed limited editions, but also because he wrote in several other languages as well as in Hungarian. In French he would write in the style of Verlaine, while in German he would write in the style of Rilke. He was a talented dilettante rather than a dedicated poet, but this perhaps made him more acceptable in society than if he had been a real master.

PART FOUR

There were two other guests as well as Laszlo. One was Tamas d'Orly, great grandson of the Baron d'Orly who had emigrated from France during the revolution and married into a rich Hungarian family. D'Orly had no known occupation, but he played the piano beautifully, executing at sight the most difficult of pieces with ease and fluency. If his playing seemed slightly mechanical and lacking in poetry, he was always reliable and his knowledge of music was extensive and cultivated. Often he would sit at the piano and play soft roulades and impromptu pieces of his own while the others talked.

The other was Imre Warday.

Szelepcsenyi, Devereux, Solymar and d'Orly often came to see Fanny in the afternoons, though usually on different days. Each entertained her after their own fashion. The ex-minister would talk about new trends in art; Devereux would recount the latest society scandal; d'Orly discussed music and Solymar would clothe his admiration for the lovely countess in panegyrics of elegantly chosen words. Only Warday never came in the afternoons. He crossed the Beredy threshold once a week and that only for the Wednesday dinners. That he was not encouraged to come at other times was quite understandable as he never seemed to have anything to say. This handsome young aristocrat was in truth extremely boring. True, he was also exceptionally good-looking, well-groomed, healthy and possessed of a wonderful figure; but he would stand about gazing with dull eyes that seemed to have been brushed into his face in faded water-colours, clearly quite unable to follow the rapid, sparkling witty converse that was going on all around him. If he laughed at some lightning joke it was always too late and because he had seen others laughing and realized that mirth was expected of him; and he could not join in the discussions on music or art because he knew nothing of these subjects. There was, as it happened, one subject on which he could have uttered, and this was farming. He was of the few young landowners who had been to the Agricultural Academy at Ovar. Mealybugs, Italian locusts, diseases of wheat and corn, artificial manure and gluten content of cereals were all subjects on which he could have discoursed for hours – but as such matters were taboo in the intellectual artistic atmosphere of Fanny's salon he held his peace and said nothing. People sometimes wondered why Fanny invited this dull young man to her house when all the other guests were so witty and amusing.

Fanny's dinner parties were perfect in every respect. The house reflected the personality of its mistress. The drawing-room was painted pale grey with grey silk damask on the walls, and it was filled with comfortable modern sofas and chairs heaped with sugar-pink silk cushions. The rest of the furniture was of different styles, but each piece was in exquisite taste and of impeccable workmanship. The room was welcoming and obviously lived-in. The walls of the long gallery were panelled in wood that had also been painted grey and were lined with wide divans covered in a vivid, poison-green brocade. These too were strewn with a multitude of cushions, lemon-yellow and black, so that the guests could recline in comfort to listen to Fanny's singing – for it was here that she gave her recitals. When she stood in the soft light, with her back to the dove-grey walls, her red-gold hair looked like an aureole of flame round her beautiful, enraptured face. It was the perfect setting for her very individual style of beauty.

The dining-room was the best of the backgrounds that Fanny had created for herself. Psychologically it was totally in keeping with its function. The walls were covered with cloth so dark that it was difficult to tell whether it was black or grey or red, and the ceiling was painted the same colour. Only the dining table was brightly lit, with two many-branched candelabra and powerful electric lights so shaded that away from the table the room was in deep shadow. The brilliant light picked out the faces of the guests, enhanced the flower arrangements and was reflected from every facet of the highly polished silver, the cut-glass crystal goblets, the snow-white china plates decorated only with gold, the sculpted salt-cellars, fruit-bowls and, above all, from the gold and the silver of the cutlery. Fanny's table service was unique. It had been made in France in the most advanced rococo taste, every piece bearing the stamp of Juste-Aurel Meissonier. Every knife and fork and spoon was as heavy as a small cudgel and each piece was slightly different from the others, all of them masterpieces in their own right. Fanny had made her husband buy it for her for a sum so huge that even he had blenched when it was mentioned to him. But they had been on their honeymoon and he was still in love with her, so he had complied. It was supposed to have been made for the Pompadour. However it was not the beauty of the objects with which the table was furnished, nor the excellence of the food and wine, nor the rarity and heavy scent of the imported flowers which ensured the perfection of Fanny's dinners. It was rather the strange contrast between the glittering pageant laid out on the table and the cool mysterious darkness that

PART FOUR

surrounded the island of sophistication in the centre.

Laszlo felt this keenly as soon as he was seated near the spinster cousins. For him this contrast represented the triumph of a pleasure-seeking society, symbolized by the fact that mankind should be brilliantly lit while around was outer darkness. He shivered as he took his place, his face to the world but his back to a murky shadow that held who knew what untold terrors. The guests were served in total silence and the servants were all but invisible. A dish would appear at Laszlo's side, only to disappear again as if unheld by human hand. In front was everything that was good and beautiful. There was pleasure for every sense, for the eyes, the taste, the nose; every object was perfect in itself; the flowers a triumph of nature; the crystal and silver the work of dedicated masters; the virginal whiteness of the starched linen cloth and above all the pale pink roses, heavy with scent and denuded of their leaves, seemed to blush in maidenly shame to find themselves set down among the *chefs d'œuvre* of man's art. Opposite him in even more provocative nudity, the bare flesh of Fanny's arms, her neck and shoulders and the faint swelling of her breasts from which at any moment the silk of her dress might fall to reveal the voluptuous promise beneath. And yet, thought Laszlo, behind all this lay the uncertainty of real life; bleak, cold, cruel, unrelenting and evil. In front was every pleasure that man could invent: food to be savoured with knowledge, wine to drive one to ecstasy, beauty, colour, light and the rosy temptation of woman's flesh to make one forget everything, especially the merciless advance of death which lurked in the shadows behind them. The feast had been prepared so knowingly that it seemed to Laszlo that everyone present ate and drank more voraciously than usual and chatted with more hectic vivacity, as if they were driven to enjoy themselves while there was still time.

When dinner was over they moved back to the gallery where coffee had been laid out with several different kinds of brandy and liqueur, Turkish and Russian cigarettes and boxes of Havana cigars. The lively conversation which had not flagged throughout the dinner still continued, if anything even livelier now after the stimulus of the feast. After a while it was no longer even inhibited by the presence of the host, for as soon as Count Beredy had finished his cigar he stood up, took his wife's hand ceremoniously, brushing it with his strange frog-like mouth, and walked silently out of the room with a wave of farewell to his guests. This was an established part of the evening's programme; Fanny's husband never remained with the party after dinner. No one asked where he went, indeed no one cared, least of all Fanny. Everyone became slightly merrier as soon as he had gone, and later d'Orly played some Grieg. He played extremely well but Fanny did not sing.

The time passed swiftly. When the clock above the fireplace struck twelve, Warday got up, checked the time with his own watch and stepped over to Fanny.

'I really must go now, Countess,' he said rather awkwardly as he bent over her hand. She nodded to him and he left the room after brief farewells to the others.

Laszlo too rose to his feet. He took Warday's departure for a sign that it was now time to leave, even though none of the others had moved. Countess Fanny held him back for a moment., saying: 'I hope we'll see you again next Wednesday?'

'I'm not quite sure,' said Laszlo hesitantly, thinking that he might be able to see Klara that day and not wanting to tie himself down. 'I can't promise . . .'

'You don't have to. Come if you can and we'll be pleased to see you, but if not it doesn't matter. There's no formality in this house. But do come if you're free.' At this point she gave him her hand, and her fine fingers held his for a fraction longer than was necessary. Then she turned abruptly to her neighbour, Szelepcsenyi, and went on: 'What were you telling me, Carlo, about that new painter? The Italian? Segantini, did you say he was called? Is he really very good?'

Laszlo put on his coat quickly at the top of the stairs. He wanted to catch up with Warday so that they could walk down together as far as the Land Bridge, but when he reached the door there was no sign of him either outside the house or in the street, though he could see down its full length. There was no one about. It was as if the earth had swallowed him up. He must have walked very quickly, thought Laszlo since he had not heard the sound of a carriage.

So Laszlo walked alone down from the old fortress quarter of Buda and when he reached the Disz Square he was passed by several carriages probably taking home the other guests from Count Beredy's house . . .

✦

Laszlo now went to Fanny's every Wednesday. Not only were the parties relaxed and amusing but also he found himself accepted by the others on equal terms. He was able to go regularly because on that day the Kollonichs did not receive and did not accept other engagements. It was their day for staying at home. Sometimes at Fanny's he would play the piano. He would sit down at the instrument and play when he felt like it because the atmosphere was so free of protocol and so friendly that he realized that this was what was expected of guests in the Beredy house. Old Szelepcsenyi made all sorts of flattering remarks about his compositions, even when he played the most modern and daring of them, and this added to his ease and pleasure. It was wonderful to feel that he belonged to a group where he was so appreciated.

March and April went by for Laszlo in a sort of dream. He saw Klara almost every day but always in company as they were never allowed to be alone together. Even when he went to the Kollonich Palais for a family meal, Peter and Niki were always present and so, usually, was Magda Szent-Gyorgyi or some other friend or relative; and the princess' watchful eye saw to it that they had no chance of talking in private. They had to be always on their guard, watching what they said and where they went. Despite the restrictions imposed on them, both Klara and Laszlo found a certain delight in all the obstacles they were forced to overcome. After all, they were together most of the time, whether sitting in one of the drawing-rooms, walking with the others around the shops or, as spring came, playing tennis. Laszlo was always at her side, making harmless conversation with an expressionless face, and sometimes, when no one could hear, slipping in an allusion to their love that both would treasure for days. These allusions were made in a sort of code, which only they could understand, and to anyone else the phrases would seem ordinary and without any special meaning, as one day when the whole group stopped to gaze into a shop window and Klara said, apparently quite innocently: 'I still think chintz-covers are the prettiest. I have them in my room at home!' and Laszlo knew that she was thinking of the first and only time they kissed. It was for both of them a wonderful time, filled with magic and expectation. It did not matter if they had to wait for the fulfilment of their love, because that was certain, not perhaps tomorrow, or the day after, but one day soon.

Laszlo felt all this with a sort of sensuous languorousness. Everything was wonderful. He sometimes won quite large sums at cards and was able to pay back a large part, though not all, of what he had borrowed from the money-lenders. He had, of course, to keep some back for he still had a lot of expenses, and this wonderful life was not cheap.

Klara felt the same. For her too this was a time of magic and joy. The wordless pact that bound them together was pure pleasure to her, as was Laszlo's continual presence and the knowledge that everything he did was for her sake. She cherished the way he looked at her with the eyes of a faithful watchdog, the manner in which he arranged a thousand little unperceived attentions that floated round her like a cloud of incense, just as the scent she used would clothe her young girl's body with the mystery of womanhood. As a woman she did not think of this period of waiting in the same sort of mystical poetic way that Laszlo did; she was far too down-to-earth for that. She had laid her plans and she waited with determination for the moment when she could make them a reality. At the end of May she would come of age and so she could afford to wait. There would be little point in trying to get her own way now, for it would only lead to lengthy scenes with her father and an icy reception from her stepmother. This would last for months and would poison her life, and it was always possible that she might not be able to summon up enough courage to survive the ordeal. And what if she were forced into submission? It was unthinkable. As Mama Agnes had arranged her whole life until now it would not be easy to face her day after day as a rebellious daughter. No, it was far better to keep everything for one big final battle which would last only for a day and from which she was bound to emerge victorious. One day must take care of everything, must make them accept what she wanted above anything in this life. She dreaded it, but she was determined to see it through.

Klara had planned everything as she lay in her little white schoolgirl's bed at Simonvasar. A few days after she had officially come of age she would tell her parents, quite suddenly when they were not expecting anything and so would not have had any opportunity to formulate their objections; she had worked out her own arguments long ago. Her plan was this: one day after lunch, just when her father was finishing his cigar, she would come up to him and stand ceremoniously in front of his chair. She would have already seen to it that Peter had taken Niki away somewhere, so that she would be alone with her parents. Then she would tell them that she had decided to marry Laszlo, that she loved him and would accept no one else as long as she lived. She would then ask for their blessing. It wouldn't be easy, though perhaps her father would be more ready to give in than her step-mother. It was certain that Mama Agnes would fight hard against the match, but what could she say except that he wasn't grand enough for her? Well, she knew he wasn't a great match, but that was not what she wanted. She did not need parade and splendour; she only wanted a modest life with the man she loved. They could hardly use the argument that Laszlo was neither Austrian nor of a ducal family but merely an obscure Hungarian noble, because wasn't that exactly what Aunt Agnes Gyeroffy had been before she became the Princess Kollonich? Her stepmother could not deny her own origins and, in front of her husband who was no snob himself, was not likely to rake up the story of her plots with the Princess Montorio and her ambition to be accepted in the Vienna Olympus! If they asked Klara to wait, she would say that she was now of age and that she had the right to make up her own mind. All she asked, begged for, was their blessing ... but, if they withheld it, she would marry him just the same. If they asked what she and Laszlo would live on, she would reply that he had a small estate and that she would sell the jewels she had inherited from her mother. This would hurt her father who had always been proud of the diamond necklace, the ruby clasps and everything that had been her mother's. Though these trinkets had always been kept in her father's safe, he was far too much a man of honour not to hand them over when she asked. Had he not always told her, 'All these are yours, all yours'.

Klara had been through all this over and over again and always she ended up thinking only of Laszlo. She saw his tall figure, with the long lean face on which his slanting eyebrows nearly met and which gave him such a mysterious appearance. She saw the slim body, the tapering artist's hands and imagined his arms around her holding her as he had in that single magic embrace at Simonvasar when they had first opened their hearts to each other. She could feel his hands wandering over her body, lightly caressing her thighs, her breasts, her neck and arms. All this she would give him, all this would be his to do with what he liked. A restless trembling overcame her as she lay motionless in her little bed wondering how she would have the courage to yield herself. All her bones seemed to dissolve into jelly, until at last she surrendered to the over-riding need to sleep.

In the morning, when she awoke, she would find her pillow cradled in her arms as if she had slept all night in the embrace of her lover.

Chapter Three

WHEN MAY ARRIVED social life in Budapest once more became busy and animated, not only because of the races and balls, both private and public, but also because of the new session of Parliament. In political circles all interest now centred upon the nature of the Address with which the old opposition parties, who now had an overall majority in the House, would attack and condemn the policies that had been followed during the time of Count Tisza's undisputed rule.

Public support for the opposition was strong but, though the rank and file were vociferous and confident in their condemnation of Vienna and triumphantly brandished patriotic slogans, their leaders were becoming increasingly dismayed by the fact that no progress had been made to resolve the government crisis.

This was the situation when Balint Abady arrived in the capital. Balint took his seat in Parliament every day. At the first session he attended they were arguing about the Address and this continued for the whole of the first two days. Although tempted to sympathize with the opposition's point-of-view by what Slawata had revealed to him about the secret plans being formed in the Belvedere Palais in Vienna, the nonsense, hot air and chauvinistic posturings revealed by the Address and the speeches in its support drove him right back to his faith in Tisza and to the old monarch.

In the House the different parties were still seated as they had been in the winter after the elections, but the atmosphere was not at all the same. In the seats occupied by the victorious opposition, the camaraderie and friendliness, the mutual congratulations and warm hand-shakes that had united the different factions of which it was formed, had completely evaporated. Now the members looked bitter and cross, and the conflict of interest between each section had made them all as wary of each other as they had been before their victory at the polls. The divisions were there for all to see, for each group kept itself apart from the others. Balint was disgusted by the insincerity and triviality of it all.

The first two days were excessively dull. Platitude followed platitude and each mindless patriotic slogan was greeted with predictable cheers or jeers depending on which side was addressing the house. On the third day, however, it was the turn of the ethnic minorities to express their points of view, the first opportunity that they had ever had. From the centre of their little group Tivadar Mihalyi rose and, in excellent Hungarian, opposed the Address. In measured tones, with moderation and diplomacy, he explained that the minorities he represented could not accept the Address as in their opinion it did not deal with the real evils that bedevilled the progress and prosperity of Hungary. He proposed to present a totally different Address which would concentrate upon internal problems rather than those provoked by the constitutional relationship with the Austrian monarchy. In Tivadar's Address the emphasis would be on electoral reform, which would ensure that government in Hungary truly represented all those of Hungarian nationality regardless of ethnic origin. This would naturally entail the re-drawing of electoral boundaries, and revision of the nationality laws which had never been accepted by the minorities he represented. Tivadar spoke quietly in measured tones and simple straightforward phrases. Everything he proposed was moderate and reasonable – and above all he reiterated, time after time, that the minorities were an essential part of Hungary and the Hungarian political system, and that all they asked was that they should be recognized as such. When Tivadar sat down, Balint was surprised to note that this first speech by the minorities' leader caused little stir in the House and was barely applauded. Of course, he reflected, everyone here is only interested in continuing the battle with Tisza. No matter how important any other subject was they would pay attention only when the ex-Minister President rose to speak – and he noted that quite a number of the members had left the Chamber while Tivadar Mihalyi was on his feet and returned only when he sat down. Among those present only one thing counted, and that was the total destruction of Tisza no matter what the battle cost, no matter how much blood was spilt, no matter if all Hungary perished! No one paused to reflect that Tisza had already been defeated in the elections and had left office months before in January.

Bedlam broke out as soon as Tisza rose to speak. Ferenc Kossuth did all he could to quiet the members of his party, hoping that they at least would behave with the dignity required of those who claimed to be fit to rule a modern European nation. The noise died slowly and at last Tisza was able to speak.

'As one who has resigned as Minister-President I no longer have the constitutional right to direct the proceedings of the House...' he started.

'Too right! Sit down! Get out of here, you old fool!' The shouts arose from all sides, but Tisza remained on his feet, tall and erect, his dark-clad figure standing broad-shouldered and defiant against the red velvet that covered the ministerial benches. Tisza held his left hand behind his hip, as if he were taking up the stance of one about to fight a duel. When he started to speak he stabbed the air with his right index finger to underline what he was saying. Though he was backed by the members of his own party he gave the impression of being alone – completely, utterly alone.

Despite shouts of 'He's inciting the peasants against us!' he continued impassively, quoting figures and statistics to back up his argument, and for more than an hour he went on just as if he were speaking to an assembly of reasonable politicians ready to discuss what was best for their country. Despite innumerable interruptions Tisza kept on his feet until, with his virile, accusing voice, he came to the end of his argument. Then he sat down.

'He's a cheeky bastard for someone nobody wants!' one red-faced 'patriot' shouted. This was going too far and the new Minister-President Justh was obliged to give the man an official reprimand; not that this made much impression, for immediately three or four others jumped up from the rows of the 1848 Party crying: 'Cheeky bastard! Cheeky bastard! What about reprimands all round?' and the uproar grew so loud that the assembly had to be suspended.

The House quickly emptied, its members congregating in small groups in the corridors, each surrounding a party leader hoping to catch a phrase or two that they would repeat as their own in the club bars, in small party meetings and in talking to political journalists. In this way the back-benchers hoped to curry favour with the general public.

No one gave a thought to Tivadar Mihalyi's speech. The only subject thought worth discussing was Tisza, who was accused of every treachery, from intriguing with Austrians to destroy the liberty of Hungary, to plotting with disloyal Hungarians to break with Austria. The attitude of the Croatians was also a disappointment to the others. Before the House met everyone had imagined, and the newspapers had predicted, that they would vote for the Address. No one had thought that they would do the opposite. Such was the general political naïvety, and the disappointment at what had actually happened, that they at once assumed that they were the victims of conspiracy. They saw enemies everywhere, not realizing that all nations were governed by their own interests and that the skill with which these were grasped and developed was the true basis of a nation's peace and prosperity. From this distrust of anyone who did not agree with them sprang the divisions within their own ranks which would lead, eventually, to the disintegration of the ruling Croatian party. No one present at this disastrous session of the Budapest Parliament foresaw that with the defection of the Croatian party the way would be opened up for the pan-Serb coalition that would eventually succeed in depriving Hungary of the provinces beyond the Drava river.

The Transylvanian lawyer, Zsigmond Boros, summed up the general reaction, saying: 'We have to admit that our noble and patriotic Address, in the face of the united and prejudiced opposition of Tisza, the Croatians and the smaller minorities, has now no chance of being received either sympathetically or objectively by the Throne! That's the trouble. Only that. It is they who have spoiled everything. If it hadn't been for them, the King would certainly have yielded. Of course he would! The King's only too anxious to expand the army. It's his passion. Only *this* lot have spoiled it all!'

Balint listened sadly for a few moments and then turned away. As he did so he caught a glimpse of the small group of Romanians who were gathered in a dark corner, among them the lawyer Timisan. He went over and greeted them, shaking hands. Timisan, just as he had been on the train, was pleasant and seemed in a good humour, though his smile was mocking and cynical. The others, to whom he presented Balint, were cold, silent and suspicious, and Balint felt that he was being watched, doubted and judged. He started to speak about one of Tisza's commercial points that affected Transylvania, thinking that it might form a common bond of interest, but they answered him only with polite phrases that showed clearly their distrust of him. After about fifteen minutes the bell rang summoning the members back into the House. Frustrated but somewhat relieved, Balint moved away.

As he went back to his seat he passed close to Wülffenstein, who spoke to him.

'How could you speak to those barbarians? It simply isn't done! My Hungarian blood boils at the mere sight of them!'

Abady felt the veins in his forehead swelling with anger. 'I do as I see fit! Do you object?' he said fiercely to Fredi, who did not have a drop of Hungarian blood in him.

'No! No! Of course not! I only thought...' said Wülffenstein, quickly sliding down in his seat with hunched shoulders, his black and white suit in stark contrast to the red of the benches.

Later on at the Casino – and at every other political meeting-place – the view so succinctly expressed by Zsigmond Boros was rehearsed over and over again. There were minor variations, but the theme remained the same. No one spoke of anything else. In the great world outside Hungary events were taking place that would change all their lives: the uprising in Russia, the dispute over Crete, the Kaiser Wilhelm's ill-timed visit to Tangier, the revelation of Germany's plans to expand its navy – but such matters were of no importance to the members of the Hungarian Parliament. Even events closer to home, such as the rabble-rousing speech of an Austrian politician in Salzburg urging revolt among the German-speaking minorities in northern Hungary, or the anonymous pamphlet, which appeared in Vienna and revealed the total unpreparedness of the Austro-Hungarian forces compared with those of the other European powers, went unnoticed in Budapest. Naturally, when Apponyi made a speech in favour of Dezso Banffy's proposal to limit the demand for Hungarian commands in the army to using Hungarian only in regimental matters, everyone listened and discussed it as if their very lives depended on it.

Chapter Four

AS FAR AS MOST of the upper classes were concerned, politics were of little importance, for there were plenty of other things that interested them more.

There were, for instance, the spring racing season, partridge shooting in late summer, deer-culling in September and pheasant shoots as winter approached. It was, of course, necessary to know when Parliament was to assemble, when important party meetings were to take place or which day had been set aside for the annual general meeting of the Casino, for these days would not be available for such essential events as race-meetings or grand social receptions. And, after the Budapest races, the Derby season in Vienna would follow, and so many people would be away at that time that it would be useless to make plans for a time when 'nobody' would be in the Budapest.

PART FOUR

Now, at the beginning of May, the social season was at its peak. The greatest event was the King's Cup race, which many people came from Vienna to attend, especially the great Austrian breeders and stud-owners and many of the rich young men about town. Among these last Montorio had already arrived so as to attend the great race and also the big ball to be given afterwards at the Park Club. He encountered the Kollonich party at the races and immediately engaged Klara for the cotillion. As he spoke the girl detected an unusually determined ring in his voice and took this as a warning that she must be careful.

Before leaving for Budapest the prince had decided that the matter of his marriage could wait no longer. He had to know where he stood. He wanted to get married and he knew that his mother approved of the Kollonich girl. It would be a good match; he liked Klara and her ample dowry. Everything seemed to be set fair and yet somehow the matter had dragged on. It was possible that the girl was not willing, and if that were so he would look elsewhere. He decided he must get the affair settled one way or the other on the first night of his visit to Budapest. He was confident that he only had to ask to be accepted, for had not his mother shown him the Princess Kollonich's letters in which she had hinted strongly that this was so? Such a handsome young man, Princess Agnes had said, so nice, so attractive!

Laszlo Gyeroffy was also at the races. When Klara walked down with Magda Szent-Gyorgyi and some other girls to the paddock where the glossy-coated thoroughbreds were being walked round before being saddled up, Laszlo joined them. They leaned together on the white-painted wooden rails.

Although Klara gave the impression that she was engrossed in her race programme, Laszlo sensed that she wanted to tell him something important, and was only studying the names of the horses with such intensity because she was waiting until the other girls' attention was distracted. When Magda started a heated argument about the identity of one of the horses, Klara turned quickly to him and said in a low voice: 'I have to have supper tonight with Montorio. Come and sit on my right and as soon as we can get up ask me at once for the supper-csárdás. It's vitally important! I think he wants to ask me something...' She broke off and turned to the others, joining in their discussion about the bay mare. Later they all strolled slowly back to the grandstand.

The supper was given in one of the ground-floor rooms of the Park Club. The night was warm and the windows on to the garden were all open. Klara chose a table far away from the band. She sat down with Montorio and three other couples who were her usual companions. With Laszlo there were nine at the table, and because of Montorio's presence, they all spoke either in German or English. They were all very lively, led by Klara who was in high good humour, wickedly vivacious and provoking, flirting with all the young men in turn and keeping everyone so amused that the conversation remained general. She was determined that this should be so as she dreaded giving Montorio the chance to talk quietly to her alone. Her female intuition had told her that sometime that evening he would ask her to marry him, and this she was determined to avoid. It would be too awkward if he insisted on a definite answer and she was forced to prevaricate; somehow, therefore, he must not be given any opportunity to speak.

Gaily, and unusually loudly for her, she teased Magda, who was sitting opposite her across the table with Imre Warday. Her normally soft eyes glittered and her beautiful lips curled with amusement as she kept up a stream of high-spirited mockery of the others. The music could hardly be heard at this end of the room and Klara kept them all laughing and joking until the supper was over. They all thought they had never had such a good time and Warday was especially pleased that Klara seemed to have singled him out. Only Montorio was more silent than usual.

When the time came for the supper-csárdás, Laszlo went over to the band-leader to tell him to take the musicians up to the ballroom. As he did so the other couples also rose and moved away. Klara stood up and started to pull on her gloves.

'*Wollen wir nicht ein bischen in den Garten* – wouldn't you like a little turn in the garden?' said Montorio in a low voice, and added: '*Es ist so schwül hier* – it's so crowded in here.'

'*Ich finde nicht!*' said Klara, shaking her head.

'*Nur ein Moment. Ich möchte Sie etwas wichtiges fragen* – only for a moment. I have something important to ask you!'

This was serious.

For an instant Klara's ocean-grey eyes seemed to darken. She hesitated. Looking up at his face, though at his mouth and the thin line of neat moustache rather than into his eyes, she realized that she hated him because he had found the way to an intimacy from which she shrank. Then she spoke:

'*Es wäre zwecklos* – there would be no point,' she said slowly but with unmistakable emphasis.

PART FOUR

'*So?* . . .' said Montorio, straightening up stiffly. '*So . . . So . . . So . . . Vollkommen* – so that's it, then!'

Laszlo rejoined them at this moment. Klara put her arm though his and together they hurried away, as if in flight through the hall, up the stairs and into the ballroom where the slow opening in the csárdás was already beginning. Montorio stood motionless where he was. After a few moments he was alone in the supper-room. He passed his hand over his elegantly balding forehead and then, with an air of deliberate calm, he took out his cigarette-case and lit a cigarette before walking slowly towards the darkened entrance hall, threading his way through the rush of waiters who were busy clearing up the plates, and surreptitiously swilling down what remained of the champagne.

In the oval drawing-room which opened off the hall were some of the older ladies, gossiping together before going up to watch the dancing. Seeing Montorio by the doorway Princess Agnes detached herself from the group with whom she was talking and came towards him. Wearing her most proprietorial smile she said: 'How lucky I am. I was just going to look for you! Could you come to us tomorrow at midday? A small luncheon, *en famille*, just ourselves!'

The young man replied coldly: 'Thank you, Princess. You are most kind, but I shall be returning to Vienna on the morning train.' His eyes were angry. Why had this woman made such a fool of him? If it hadn't been for her letters he would never have made this humiliating attempt!

He bowed stiffly and moved on; not towards the stairs but straight to the main door and out into the open. Princess Agnes watched as he disappeared into the darkness outside.

<hr>

It was nearly three o'clock when the Kollonich carriage was driven up to the portico in front of the Park Club entrance. It was a beautiful carriage hung elegantly on eight-fold springs, so elegant indeed that only the French word *équipage* could describe it. There were only two or three others to compare with it in the whole of Budapest. It was drawn by two large bay horses, perfectly matched and as perfectly groomed, their coats shining and when, as now, they stood still their hind legs were stretched out behind them like horses in equestrian statues. They were so carefully trained that they would stand motionless, without even the smallest movement of their neatly docked tails, for as long as the coachmen wished.

Most people had already switched to automobiles but the Princess Kollonich was so proud of her carriage and beautifully matched pairs of horses that she did not want to part with them. Their perfection had been a labour of love only achieved after many years' study and careful preparation and, after all, anyone with enough money could own an expensive motor. A perfect *équipage* was only for those who understood such matters and to whom tradition and style were more important than the latest fashion. And why should anyone struggle to arrive more quickly when there was nothing to hurry for?

The two grooms jumped down and hurried forward to take their places on each side of the Park Club doorway. They bowed deeply as the princess and Klara, both wrapped in furs, moved slowly down the steps. One of them took Klara's flowers from a footman who had followed them out, while the other hastened forward to open the carriage door and let down the folding steps. When the ladies were seated and a rug placed over their knees, the steps were folded up again, the doors firmly closed and the grooms jumped back to their places. The carriage moved slowly off, its rubber wheels making no sound on the pavement. The only noise to be heard was the 'clip-clop' of the horses' hoofs as the carriage made its slow way back to town with the two ladies inside sitting in silence. Both lay back against the silken upholstery with tightly compressed lips.

The princess was pursuing the train of thought that had begun the moment that Montorio had so icily taken his leave of her.

What had happened? Something *must* have happened. Montorio had danced the quadrille with Klara so he must have had supper with her. He must have proposed at the table and been refused. That must be it! Nothing else would explain that angry glint in his eyes. This girl! This stupid, stubborn girl who could give up the chance of a husband who had everything, good looks, money, health, high rank. To refuse such a *parti*, she must be mad! Unless there was someone else? But who? Of course! She must have been blind! For Laci, that little nobody, Laci, her own despised nephew! It must be. Hadn't they sat together at supper throughout the whole Carnival? How naïve they must be if they thought that no one would notice!

These had been Princess Agnes's first thoughts as she watched Montorio leave the club. After he had gone she went up to the ballroom and, as she had expected, there she found that Klara and Laszlo were dancing together, It was clear that they had eyes only for each other and that Klara was totally absorbed in her partner.

Now the princess found herself obliged to hide her thoughts and sit down with other mothers who were watching the dancing. To these she smiled and made polite conversation, to others she waved with friendly condescension and she chatted languidly with the elderly gentlemen whose families had forced them to attend the ball. No one must notice anything was wrong, and it was especially important to her that her sister Elise, the wife of Antal Szent-Gyorgyi, should not see her agitation. Elise was sitting beside her, calm and benign, but even she, with her great position, would not understand her sister's distress. Elise was luckier than she was. She, too, had made a brilliant marriage but it had been a love-match and it had made her very happy. Szent-Gyorgyi was very different from Kollonich – the 'good Louis, as she used deprecatingly to speak of her husband – for his manner was so autocratic, scornful and proud that everyone was afraid of him and his wife had been immediately accepted not only because of his unassailable social position but also because he expected it. On the other hand Kollonich was so good-natured that he noticed nothing, not even that his wife had had to struggle to be accepted into the top ranks of Hungarian society. He had been no help to her. How she had to work and plan and fight to get where she now was! And now Klara had to ruin it all and make a fool of her! It was unbearable and a sense of irritation kept sweeping over her in such waves that she had to struggle hard to control herself and maintain that calm, regal air that she always adopted when in the presence of others.

More and more she noticed little details which annoyed and irritated her. She saw that Klara was wearing a yellow carnation pinned to her dress. It was obviously Laci's flower. He always wore yellow carnations and had them made up in corsages for his partners. So she had only to pick out one of those! How easy, but how despicable to give oneself away like that! How stupid! Did the girl have no pride?

And then she thought of her letters to Montorio's mother in which she had written her flattering praises of the son in such terms that they could equally be read either as the reaction of the whole family or that of Klara in particular. Of course the Montorios must have taken these letters as assurance of Klara's complaisance; but even if they had Montorio himself need not have been so stupidly maladroit. What on earth had he thought he was doing to arrive in the morning and propose the same evening with no preparation, no subtlety, no courting? Why couldn't he have consulted her, asked her advice, got her to prepare the ground? What a fool he had been! Well, the damage was done now and no doubt he was already blaming her, pretending that he had been misled! She was sure he was dimwitted enough to do just that!

These thoughts led her swiftly to an even more disconcerting idea. The next day Montorio would be home in Vienna and would report all this at once to his mother, who no doubt would think of her in the same way as the son so obviously now did. And, of course, the result would be that the next time they met the Princess Visconti-Montorio, backed by the pride of her Bourbon-Modena blood, would snub the Princess Kollonich, as she had before, wrinkling her nose at her from the oh-so-desirable height of the 'Olympus'. It was insufferable! It was all Klara's fault, and it hurt!

How it hurt! All the more so because, being no fool, she knew that there was more than a little truth in what they might think. She knew that she had misled the Montorios, even if she had done it from the best motives, fully believing in her ability to carry it all off. They had every right to feel aggrieved and cross. Of course she would have succeeded if Montorio had not rushed everything, as stupid young men were so apt to do.

The supper-csárdás came to an end and was replaced by a waltz. Klara and Laszlo continued dancing together, the girl's waist melting into her lover's arms. Both had their eyes almost closed like sleep-walkers. This, thought the princess, is too much. It was unbearable, indecent! She waited until the music stopped, and then waved to her stepdaughter:

'My sweet, let's go home! I'm very tired today!'

My sweet! Klara knew that phrase of old: the princess always used it when she was angry about something. Could she have guessed that she had turned down Montorio?

'Why, of course, Mama! Let's go,' she replied good-humouredly, for her conscience was not clear. They descended the stairs and put on their wraps without speaking. Both maintained the silence as they sat together in the carriage.

As the majestic *équipage* wended its way slowly back to the Kollonich Palais all the fragmentary thoughts that had tormented the princess in the brightly-lit rooms of the Park Club returned with redoubled force. Clip-clop! Clip-clop! the horses' hoofs resounded on the uneven surface of the streets like hammer-blows on the coffin of her ambitions. Clip-clop! Clip-clop! The sound was unendurable. It seemed as if they would never reach home.

The princess's thoughts went back to her youth when the Gyeroffy sisters, Agnes and her younger sister, Elise, first moved to Budapest from Transylvania. Their father, Count Tamas Gyeroffy, had just been elected a member of Parliament. The girls were chaperoned by their mother. Both were beautiful, well-educated – they even spoke English, which was rare in those days – and excellent dancers; yet they were not popular, not at all the success they had been so sure would be theirs when they came to the capital.

In Transylvania they had been among the first wherever they went, but here they were treated as unwelcome intruders of no importance, almost as 'foreigners'. The Budapest dowagers, if they spoke to them at all, did so condescendingly with a patronizing air they did nothing to hide. It had been a deeply humiliating experience and it had lasted the whole of their first Carnival season. Later came a stroke of good luck. At Balatonfured Agnes had met Louis Kollonich, who was still in mourning for his first wife. The 'good Louis' had fallen in love with her, abandoned his mourning and proposed to her four days later. She had accepted him. And why not? Of course she had not been in love with the chubby-faced widower, but she could not resist the opportunity of becoming the Princess Kollonich and queening it over all those snooty girls in Budapest who had looked down their noses at her when she first arrived. She imagined that this marriage, like a magic wand, would waft her instantly to the highest peaks. But, and this was Agnes's second great disappointment, somehow the magic wand had not worked. Although she became Princess Kollonich – after quite a short engagement – many of the dowagers and their daughters still continued to hold aloof and regard her *de haut en bas*. Some even went so far as to make sly and spiteful allusions to her Transylvanian birth. 'Lots of bears where you come from, aren't there? Anything else? Really?'

They made great play in finding it difficult to pronounce her name, even though it was of ancient Hungarian origin. '*Was ist das für ein Name* – What sort of a name is that?' They had been horrid, and she had never forgotten it. She knew that the fault was partly her own. She had developed such an inferiority complex, such a deep conviction that these Hungarian aristocrats really were her superiors, and that she herself was inferior and second-rate, that she antagonized everyone by her air of grandeur. She had adopted quite consciously a proud and disdainful manner, her head held high, one or two fingers held out when they came to greet her; but inside she was quaking with terror and lack of confidence, unsure of herself, praying that someone would be nice to her, and she would be exaggeratedly pleased if anyone was.

This had been the real reason why her acceptance had come so slowly, for it was not until more than ten years had passed – ten years of struggle, hard work and humiliation – that she had begun to feel secure. During these years the Princess Agnes had thought of little but the battle for social recognition and, because she felt that she had been judged and disliked without valid reason, her whole conception of life – and especially society life – had been soured and coloured by the conviction that nothing, nothing in the world, mattered so much as social success. And at last success came, and she realized that the battle had been won. But, as with mountain-climbers, one reaches one peak only to discover that there is another, even higher, behind it. For the Princess Agnes, though she might have become the uncrowned queen of Budapest society, there was now an even greater obstacle to be surmounted. The next step was to be accepted at court.

If once she obtained social recognition by the 'Olympus' in Vienna she would be fully revenged on the ladies who had caused her such misery in Budapest: for then it would be they who could be treated as provincial upstarts! This would be her ultimate trump-card, and once played she would take precedence over them all in the most exclusive, rank-conscious group in the whole world. She, the despised Transylvanian, would be so far above them that she would at long last be able to relax knowing that all her ambitions had been achieved. And she could have done it! The Montorio marriage would have been the master-key to all those doors that had been shut to her for so long.

And now it was all over, finished! Why? Because her two-faced nephew Laci, that devious little nobody, had come sniffing round Klara and turned her head. He was a cunning little trouble-maker; that was the word for him – trouble-maker. He had taken advantage of the hospitality and the protection she had offered the unprotected orphan; and this is how he had repaid her endless kindness. Why, she had treated little Laci as if he had been her own son ever since, at the age of eighteen months, he had been abandoned by his mother, Julie Ladossa, the depraved woman who had left her brother and run off with an adventurer.

Clip-clop! Clip-clop! All her painful memories surged upwards until she felt her head would burst.

Julie! That scheming whore, Julie Ladossa! As the name came into her head the whole sad, disreputable scandal – the one great tragedy of her family – came back to her.

One day Julie had driven away from Szamos-Kozard in her pony-trap, with God knows who, and three days later they had found her husband, Agnes's brother, poor Mihaly Gyeroffy, dead in the woods, shot by his own gun after carefully arranging it to look like an accident. That at least had had style, and that had been Agnes's only consolation. Now the Princess reflected that Laci, the son of that shameless creature, took entirely after his mother. He looked like her, with those strange eyebrows which nearly met in the middle; and it was from her that he inherited his talent for music for had it not been her hated sister-in-law's artistic tendencies that had fanned her wickedness and irresponsibility? The Princess thought only of Laci's eyebrows as recalling his mother's looks, as indeed they did, but the truth was that no one could mistake him for anything but a Gyeroffy. If he resembled anyone it was his aunts Agnes and Elise and, indeed, he was far more like herself than her own sons by the 'good Louis'. But at this moment she only felt that she hated him, that he was ungrateful and disrespectful. He had carried off her little Klara, her own Klara, when she would willingly have arranged for him a good marriage with a substantial dowry that would have kept him in comfort!

Perhaps, after all, everything was not lost. Perhaps it was nothing more than a passing fancy on Klara's part. Perhaps things could still be fixed and there had only been some minor little disagreement between Klara and the prince? Though deep down she did not believe this, Princess Agnes decided she would do what she could to retrieve the situation. In the morning she would send for Klara and have it out with her.

The carriage arrived at the covered portico of the Kollonich Palais. After the footman had opened the carriage doors and let down the steps, he had first to remove the long basket of flowers that lay on the carriage floor at the ladies' feet – this was Klara's cotillion prize, and it was filled with multi-coloured little bouquets that represented the homage of the young men to their partners. On top, larger and showier than all the others, lay Laszlo's bunch of saffron-coloured carnations from which Klara, at the ball, had picked a flower to pin on her corsage as a sign for all to see of her bondage to Laci. At the sight of it Princess Agnes could easily have lost her temper and exploded with rage. Mercifully, there were many steps to mount before arriving at the door and so she had time to control herself sufficiently to say goodnight calmly and dispassionately to her errant stepdaughter. She even kissed her on the forehead, as she always did at this moment, before turning away and moving slowly in the direction of her apartments. She was careful not to say anything about the next day lest something in her voice should betray her anger.

It was nearly twelve o'clock the next morning when Klara's maid, Ilus, came to her and said: 'Her Grace would like to see you, my Lady!' The girl spoke timidly and then stood back against the doorway to let Klara pass.

Alarmed, Klara, accompanied by the girl, went towards her stepmother's rooms. She was sure that the princess would now demand an explanation and the moment so long dreaded, when she would have to tell the truth about her feelings, would now be forced upon her. She had thought about it most of the night, lying awake filled with anxiety and wondering how she would explain herself. She regretted now that she had not told her stepmother everything months before, voluntarily revealing what was in her heart. Of course she had always imagined that it would be she who would choose the moment, never thinking that one day she would be summoned to account for herself as if she were a criminal arraigned before a court of justice, or a child accused of petty theft. Face to face with her stepmother, what could she say? Perhaps she could avoid the subject altogether? No, that would never be possible. Mama Agnes was far too direct and once a subject was raised between them there would be no getting away from it. Very well then, if there had to be a battle there would be a battle, and even though at a disadvantage she would fight to the last for the right to remain true to her own feelings and faithful to the man she loved. All she had to do was to remain steadfast. It would not be easy because Mama Agnes would never understand – and if she did not understand she would not forgive either. But perhaps all was not lost. After all, Papa loved her, and when his first rage was over things always got better!

Klara was excited, but feeling she needed a few moments to get herself fully under control before she was subjected to the princess' questioning, she turned to the maid and said: 'Ilus, why are you always so sad these days?' She did not know why she had said this. It had not occurred to her before but as she spoke she realized that it was true and that for some time the girl had not been her normal carefree self. How odd that she should only have noticed it when she was in trouble herself.

The little maid glanced briefly up at her mistress and then lowered her eyes and said shyly: 'I'm not, my lady, truly I'm not!' but her eyes contradicted her denial. 'People are wicked!' she added unexpectedly.

Klara was startled and, feeling a sudden rush of kinship for the girl, said: 'Are you in love, Ilus?'

'Oh, no! How could I be? Oh, no! Not *that*, my lady!' The girl blushed and her eyes looked even sadder.

Klara put her hand up to the girl's face and gently stroked it, feeling how good it was to have a friend who shared her longing and her distress. It made her feel stronger merely to know that someone else was suffering. Straightening up Klara pulled herself together and walked boldly towards the door of her stepmother's apartments.

The Princess Agnes's bedroom in Budapest was much the same as her room in the country, the only difference being that whereas at Simonvasar everything was gold in colour, here it was all pink. Here too a sofa stood at the foot of the bed and from it the Princess would administer justice. She was seated on it now, looking stern.

'Sit down, my dear,' she said, pointing to a chair opposite her, 'I want to ask you something.' Klara sat down and waited. After a few moments' silence the Princess said directly: 'What happened yesterday between you and Montorio?'

'Nothing,' replied Klara. 'Nothing really...!'

Princess Agnes raised one eyebrow in obvious disbelief. Narrowing her eyes she waited silently for Klara to say something more, knowing that if she said nothing the girl was sure to go on.

'...only that after supper he asked me to go with him into the garden and I didn't want to.'

'And?'

The girl twisted her fingers together nervously. 'That's all... only that also... well, it might not have been proper...'

Princess Agnes shrugged her shoulders and for a moment there was a hint of an ironic smile on her lips. 'Was that the only reason? Really?' The coldness in her voice showed her contempt for an obvious lie.

'Yes, and because I didn't want...'

'What didn't you want?'

'Nothing! I just didn't feel like it!'

There was silence again, the princess remaining, if possible, almost more rigidly immobile than before.

'It's not like you, Klara, to be so stubborn, yes, stubborn and unco-operative – not with me! After all, I am your mother, if not in nature in every other way.'

Klara blushed. This allusion to their relationship bothered her because it was true that Mama Agnes had always been to her everything that a mother should be. Even her real mother, whom she had never known, could not have been kinder.

'I'll tell you what happened,' she said. 'After supper he suggested ... well, I felt that if I went out with him he would propose. I felt it would encourage him, and so I didn't ... '

'Did he give you any hint?'

Klara hesitated for a moment. She did not know whether she should tell the truth or not but hating to lie she said: 'Yes. He said he wanted to ask me something important and I replied that there would be no point. I said that it would be useless!' Now it was out, and there would be no going back. With a determined look on her face she looked straight into her stepmother's eyes.

'You said that? You dared to say that? You little fool, do you realize that you've thrown away all your chances? Why, in God's name?' The princess's well-tended hands clenched into fists. She was so angry she nearly jumped up from the sofa. In a moment, however, she recovered her self control, and then laughed mirthlessly.

'Why? I hardly need to ask when the whole town knows that you're in love with that little Laci! Such folly! And all just because of little Laci, of all people!' She laughed scornfully.

Hearing this mocking laughter, and listening to Princess Agnes' patronizing words, Klara made up her mind. She stood up, faced her stepmother and said, calmly and firmly: 'It's true! I have decided to marry him. It's settled.' With deeper emphasis, the catch in her throat showing how much her whole being longed for love and sympathy and help, she went on: 'You see, we love each other!'

'I knew you had a crush on him. I guessed that a long time ago! But what about him? All the world knows that he's Fanny Beredy's lover! What a little hypocrite he is, carrying on like that while pretending to come courting you! Why, he hasn't even enough *conduite* to do it discreetly!'

'Countess Beredy?'

'Who else? He dines there every Wednesday and goes calling in the afternoons. Everyone knows all about it, except you, my poor little Klara!'

The girl stood very straight in front of her stepmother.

'No! No! No! It's not true. I know him and I know all about it. He's been there a few times but it's not like that! He's not involved with Fanny Beredy at all. He doesn't love anyone but me and he's loved me for years and years. He's always loved me, I know! And he's true to me. What you say is all a lie!'

'My dear girl, I don't listen to gossip. I know all about it from a most reliable source. Old Szelepcsenyi told me. He knows what goes on in that house if anyone does. He's an intimate friend of Fanny's. You can rely on anything he says.'

'It's not true! Everyone's against Laszlo!'

'Szelepcsenyi didn't tell me out of spite. He thought Laszlo had all the luck!'

'It's all nasty wicked slander, yes, slander. They've just invented it.'

'Invented it? That's quite enough!' said Princess Agnes, interrupting her and getting up at the same time. 'Don't you dare speak to me in that tone! We'll go and see your father immediately and you can tell him what you have done and why. And I hope you'll behave to him in a calmer manner than you have to me!' With this she swept out of the room like a battleship in full sail. Klara followed.

Louis Kollonich was in his smoking-room. He was walking up and down with a dead cigar in his mouth and repeatedly looking at his watch. It was past the hour when luncheon was usually served and he was both hungry and impatient.

As soon as Princess Agnes and Klara entered the room, he said: '*Na! Wird denn niemals serviert* – What! Shall we never be served?' When he was out of temper he always spoke in German.

His wife did not answer at once but sat down.

'*Lieber* Louis,' she said formally. 'Klara has something to say to you. Yesterday she turned down Montorio whom you had selected for her!'

'*Was ist das für ein Blödsinn* – what is all this nonsense?' he shouted at his daughter.

Klara kept her head. She was defiant, but she spoke calmly and bravely. She said that she did not love Montorio and would not marry him. Her own life and happiness was at stake, she said, and she would only marry for love. If not, she would not marry at all. She knew she would never be happy again if she married Montorio... and that is why she had refused him.

'*Na, Meinetwegen*– does no one think of me? And are they never going to serve lunch?' was all that her father answered. Princess Agnes did not move.

'That is not all,' she said, and turning to Klara, she went on gently: 'My dear, you had better tell your father what you told me. You owe it to him...'

'*Aber was ist denn noch* – now what is it?' asked Kollonich, by now thoroughly incensed and impatient to get all this talk done with so that he could get to table. He started to walk up and down the room again.

It was difficult to talk properly to someone who would not keep still, but Klara managed to speak firmly and stick to her guns – though she was afraid that she would not be able to remain adamant for long. She told her father that she was in love and that she was loved in return and that her only hope of happiness lay in marriage with the man she loved. In two weeks' time, she reminded them, she would come of age and be free to decide her own fate, but all the same she begged them for their consent. After all, it was her future that was at stake, her life and no one else's! Much of this was delaying tactics as, for some reason she could not quite explain to herself, she hesitated before telling him that it was Laszlo she loved.

'*Na, und wer ist der glückliche Jüngling* – and who is the happy man?'

The good Louis stopped suddenly in his tracks and stared hard at his daughter's face. Klara looked him straight in the eyes.

'Laszlo Gyeroffy!'

'*Wa-a-as? Der Laci! Dieser Kartenspieler* – that gambler. *Nicht um der Welt!* – Never!' shouted Kollonich even more angrily than before spinning round the room in his fury and pouring out a stream of abuse. '*So ein Lump* – what a scoundrel!' he cried, telling Klara that he would have no gambler marrying into his family, to spend her fortune and then come to him to have his debts paid! How could she think of such a nobody? He shouted at her until Klara felt she could bear no more and sank into a chair crying into the cushions on the armrest. '*Hat er die Impertinenz?*' he yelled in her ear, 'Has he dared to propose?'

Klara shook her head. 'No, he hasn't! But he's only waiting for a sign from me. He wouldn't dream of it until...'

PART FOUR

'Well, that's one good thing, at least,' said her father, still walking up and down and snorting with rage like a steam engine. Klara burst into loud sobs and, because Kollonich never could stand the sight of a woman in tears, he stopped walking about and came over to her, putting his hand gently on her shoulder.

'*Na! Na! Na!* Don't cry! I wouldn't mind if he weren't such a gambler but, God in heaven, a gambler!' and rage came over him again. '*Werden wir niemals essen?*' he shouted at his wife. 'Will luncheon never be served?'

The princess pressed a bell on the table beside her. Szabo the butler came in almost at once.

'Serve luncheon immediately!' she said.

'The first course is already on the sideboard, your Grace.' Szabo bowed and disappeared.

'Thank God!' said the prince, and started at once for the door not even pausing for his wife to precede him. As they walked swiftly through the great reception rooms, Klara surreptitiously wiped her eyes so as not to show anyone else that she had been crying.

There were no guests that day and so the only others at table were her brothers, Niki and Peter. They could not fail to notice that some drama had been going on and Niki, always mischievous, did his best to find out what it was. Peter, who had a kind heart and loved his sister, tactfully started to talk to their father about shooting and quickly captured his attention. Without delay Prince Louis started telling them, for the third time, how a few days before he had finally killed the great roebuck they had so often stalked in vain. And in a few minutes he had regained his normal good humour, aided, no doubt, by the excellence of the jellied *fogas* pâté, filled with smoked ham and flavoured with truffles, and his favourite *Tournedos Rossini* which followed it.

After lunch Klara went to her room. She washed her eyes and started to think, and the more she thought the calmer she became. The matter was by no means hopeless. Her father had had his tantrum and had made it clear that it was Laszlo's gambling to which he had so strong an objection. If she could prove that Laszlo had given it up — and given it up for her sake — then surely they could no longer object to him. Of course it was always said that gambling was such an overriding passion that nothing could ever be done about it, but if he gave it up that would show them all that he was worthy of her. As for that wicked tale about him and Fanny Beredy, this would be proof that that was false too because he was true to her and to her alone. The solution to all their

329

problems lay in Laszlo giving up cards ... and showing the world that he did it for her!

Klara sat down at her little writing table and quickly wrote a note in her square slanting handwriting: *'I've told them! It was quite dreadful! Try to get near me as if by chance at the races tomorrow, but keep away 'til then. I'll find a way to tell you there!'*

Then she underlined 'told' and 'chance' before going to the bell and pressing it gently so that its ring would not be too loud. In a few moments Ilus opened the door and asked: 'You rang, my Lady?'

'Close the door ... quickly now! Did anyone see you come in here?'

'No, my Lady, there was no one in the passage.'

'Ilus, this is very important! Take this letter – and don't tell anybody – do you promise?' The girl nodded. Klara went on hurriedly: 'I trust you, but you must take care!' and then, whispering, 'Give this letter to Count Gyeroffy, only to him, into his own hands, do you understand? Only to him, and no one must see you. Maybe he'll be at home now, 1B Museum Street. It's either the third or fourth floor, I can't remember which, but someone will tell you. You will do it, won't you?'

'Of course, my lady, with pleasure.'

'Take care, Ilus. No one must see you!'

'Don't worry, my lady, I'll do it straight away.'

'Hurry then. It's very important!' Suddenly Klara felt overwhelmed by hope and gratitude and she rose, put her arms round the girl's waist and kissed her as she would a sister. The little maid, however, drew back in shame as if she were unworthy of such confidence.

'Don't, my lady, please don't!' she said, and slipped quickly and silently out of the room.

The King's Cup was the most important event of the whole racing season. Everybody would be there, everybody had to be there; every woman with any pretence to being in Society wore her prettiest and most expensive clothes, and everyone was determined to be seen by everyone else. The grandstands and private boxes were crammed and the public enclosures were full. The crowds came because the races offered such a variety of entertainment – the sight of rich, fashionable, smartly-dressed society people in the private enclosures, the chance of spectacular wins at the tote, the excitement of a closely-fought finish and, above all,

PART FOUR

the exhilarating feeling that they were all part of Budapest's most brilliant social event.

The procession of carriages bringing the spectators to the Park Club was in itself a spectacle not to be missed. On the narrow road that turned off the Tokolyi Avenue just after the railway station and passed by the poor quarter of Szazhaz – the slums had not then been cleared away – hundreds of horse-drawn vehicles wended their way to the race-course. There were smart two-in-hands drawn by high-stepping trotters, four-horse English coaches driven by their owners with eight people seated on the roof together with a liveried coachman whose only function on that day was to blow lustily on his coaching horn, Hungarian *Jukkers* with four or five horses in the traces all decorated with multi-coloured tassels and, whatever the carriage, there was always a great deal of whip-cracking and noise. In the open carriages the ladies would sit with lace-covered hats; and when one of the rare automobiles entered the procession, with its rattling engine-noise and stinking exhaust fumes it seemed as if even the horses turned up their noses, sensing, perhaps, that these horrible new-fangled machines had been sent to destroy them.

The principal grandstand was the last to fill up, for the most fashionable people always tried to be the last to arrive. Row upon row of seats were gradually being occupied in what looked from afar like a gigantic sloping flower arrangement, where the ladies' dresses blossomed in a hundred different shades of pink, blue, red, lilac and white, punctuated only by the shiny black cylinders of the men's top hats. Even the lawns in front of the stands were covered with a mass of people, radiating colour, life and happiness as they moved about slowly and leisurely in the bright sunshine.

Laszlo Gyeroffy arrived early. He went immediately up to the top of the grandstand from where he could most easily watch for the arrival of the Kollonich family. He was even more carefully dressed than usual, in a new iron-grey morning coat and a double-breasted butter-coloured waistcoat. As a daring innovation he had put on a pair of pin-striped trousers which, though not yet generally worn, would be permissible on this occasion when new fashions were expected and accepted without criticism, however bizarre they might seem. They were pressed to knife-sharp creases and with them he wore a highly-polished pair of box-leather shoes with beige-coloured insets. In his lapel, as always, he wore the yellow carnation that had become the symbol of his love for Klara.

Laszlo stood very straight. The long line of his fashionably cut coat showed his slim figure at its best and more than one woman looked at him with desire in her eyes.

He, however, did not look at anybody for his eyes were fixed on the entrance gates through which streamed the crowd of race-goers who spread out over the lawns, greeted friends and looked for places to sit. From his eagle's nest Laszlo could see everything that went on beneath him. Now the proud and supremely self-confident ladies of high society and rich banking circles, and most of the lovely girls who attended the balls at the Casino and Park Club were already there. He caught a glimpse of Neszti Szent-Gyorgyi who had brought with him a famous Belgian *grande cocotte*, at that time established as his official mistress. She was seated just beyond the members' enclosure, her chair pushed slightly in front of the others as if she were the queen of Turf society. Kristof Zalamery appeared for a moment, escorting the two little *danseuses* from the Orfeum, but they soon disappeared among the crowds below. A little later Countess Beredy could be seen at the centre of a little group composed of her nieces, d'Orly, Devereux and old Szelepcsenyi. Fanny could be seen instructing her entourage to find some chairs and place them close to the rails.

The slender thoroughbreds entered for the first race had already paraded in front of the judges' box when Laszlo saw his aunt arrive with Klara. They passed slowly towards the grandstand, pausing to greet friends before finding their places below him. The princess chose a seat with the other dowagers while Klara sat with a group of young people in the first row.

Laszlo did not move; he wanted to wait until his aunt decided to walk down to the saddling enclosure, or stroll across the members' lawn surrounded by their friends, or became in some way sufficiently preoccupied that she would not notice when he staged his 'chance' meeting with Klara. He felt sure that this was what Klara had meant by the word, for she would not be at ease if she were still under the stern eye of her stepmother.

He had to wait until well after the second race. All this time the princess sat without moving, just ten paces away and slightly behind Klara. Then, as the public was beginning to move towards the saddling-up enclosure before the King's Cup race, Laszlo saw the Archduke's equerry step towards the princess, bow to her and murmur some message in her ear. Immediately she stood up and, accompanied by two other ladies, moved slowly

PART FOUR

and graciously towards an inner staircase. She had been summoned to the Royal Box. Now was the time to go to Klara and speak to her alone.

It was not easy to reach her against the stream of racegoers who were now milling about trying to find good places before the next race. It was not easy either to avoid acquaintances who tried to greet him as he pushed his way against the crowd, sometime jumping over seats when the narrow aisles were too full of people trying to come up just as he wanted to go down. At last he made it and found himself beside her. Klara made room for him on the bench beside her. They sat very close to each other, so close that Laszlo felt himself in an ecstasy of delight, intoxicated by the heady scent of Parma violets with which she seemed to be surrounded.

Klara spoke softly and rapidly, looking not at him but straight ahead. She spoke urgently, but took care that no one who saw them together – for they were surrounded by friends and acquaintances – would notice anything unusual.

'I told them yesterday. It was dreadful, but that doesn't matter. You have to promise me something...'

'Anything!'

'That you won't gamble any more. For my sake!'

'Of course. Whatever you say ... anything ... everything!' whispered Laszlo.

Now she looked straight into his eyes.

'Promise me!' she said and offered him her narrow hand hoping that anyone who saw would take it that they were shaking hands to seal a wager.

Laszlo understood at once that he could now answer out loud.

'I promise!' he said, rather pompously, and squeezed her hand.

Klara was flooded with joy and relief, all the confidence that had deserted her after the terrible interview with her parents restored by those two simple words. Once again she saw their marriage as certain; in a few months she would stand before her father and say: 'See, Laszlo isn't gambling any more. He has given it up for me and this is the greatest proof of his worth! And he'll never do it again, never ever again!' And, as these thoughts came to her she also exulted that it had been she who had saved him, this very minute, from certain destruction. Ever since the previous day's talk with her father, when she had been deeply influenced by his passionate denunciation of gamblers and gambling, she had been forced to recognize the facts and admit to herself that for Laszlo gambling could become a fatal obsession; and in recognizing this she had decided that it would be she, and she alone, who would save him. Now she had done it. He was saved... and the feeling was wonderful.

For a moment she allowed herself to look at him. Then she saw her younger brother Niki a few steps away. He was looking at them, obviously watching them; and of course this would all be reported back to the princess. It was the moment to send Laszlo on his way.

'We've been seen!' she said softly, and then went on in a loud confident voice, 'Now hurry off to the tote and put this on for me.' and, opening her little silken purse, she took out some coins and handed them to him. 'Here are ten crowns. Do hurry!'

It was all so natural, or seemed so, and it was equally natural that Laszlo should lean towards her as he took the coins from her hand and that this should give him the opportunity to whisper: 'Can I sit beside you tonight?'

'Yes, of course. Now I don't mind anymore,' she said softly, her lips scarcely moving because she was so happy and thankful and so relieved, and because she loved him all the more for those two little words which rang so loudly in her heart. She had his oath and in her thundered triumphantly the knowledge that he was hers, now and forever. Her ocean-grey eyes sparkled as she watched him leave the stand and walk across the lawn below.

'Which did you choose?' asked a girl who sat behind her. 'Not Patience, I hope, she's everyone's favourite! You won't win a sou!'

'I won't tell you,' said Klara, turning round. 'No! No! It's a secret, my very own secret!' And she laughed wickedly, but so full of joy was she, joy, triumph and sheer happiness, that her laughter was as soft and voluptuous as the cooing of a dove.

———

Gyeroffy hurried through the mass of people on the lawn propelled by a superstitious compulsion that he must, no matter what, put Klara's money on a horse. When he reached the betting counter he could hardly get to the clerk so thick was the crowd waiting to place their bets, and when he did get to the front and push forward his ten crowns his mind was a blank and he could not remember the name of a single horse that was running. 'Which horse, please?' asked the clerk impatiently. Laszlo could think of nothing. He had not even looked at his programme, indeed he seemed to have lost it. A number, quickly, he thought to himself, any number! 'Nine!' he said swiftly, without thinking; and then it suddenly crossed his mind that he had chosen right since the nine was a winning number at chemmy and baccarat and would bring him luck. He picked up the ticket and put it in the pocket of his waistcoat.

When Laszlo left the tote counter he decided not to go back to the grandstand, as he knew that if he did he would be drawn back to Klara. Instead he remained on the lawn from where he could just see the horses moving at a slow canter towards the start. Because of the dense crowd, all that he could see was the flash of racing colours above the undulating sea of black top hats. For the first time he became interested in the race and so started to look for a place from which he would be able to watch properly. He hardly noticed where he was going until his way was suddenly barred by the frothy green lace of a lady's parasol.

'Stop at once!' said a merry female voice. 'So you don't even notice me any more?' It was Fanny Beredy, surrounded by her nieces and faithful band of admirers. Greetings and laughter followed, with Laszlo being teased for his sudden interest in the races. Realizing that he must know on which horse he had placed Klara's bet, he asked the others to let him see a programme. 'Since when have you been interested in horses?' asked Fanny. 'You haven't actually bet on one, have you?'

'I have!'

'You? Backing the horses now?' The remark sounded like a mild rebuke, inferring that cards were quite enough.

'Just this once.'

'Which one, may one ask?' said d'Orly.

'Number nine.'

'That will get nowhere! The Festetic filly's bound to win hands down!'

Laszlo's heart missed a beat.

Fanny noticed that a cloud passed over Laszlo's face at this last remark and she turned towards him, concerned. 'Did you bet a lot?'

'Oh, no! Only a trifle! Just my life!' And he said it so lightly, with a soft laugh, that they all took it for a joke and laughed. But Fanny looked sharply at him, paused, and then asked him to give her a chair to stand on so that she could have a clear view of the race. Szelepcsenyi handed Fanny his race-glasses.

There was a sudden hush of excitement as the starting bell rang. Through the glasses Fanny could see the race clearly until the horses reached the first turn and were hidden by other spectators. After a few seconds there was a sudden surge of shouting from the public stands, a thundering roar as the crowd took up the name of the leader. Closer and closer it came, the noise ever louder, though all that could be distinguished was 'Pa-a-a-, Pa-a-a-', only that. All at once, in tearing speed, the horses were past Fanny's little group and the race was over. In front, several lengths ahead of the field, the wonder filly Patience, her jockey carrying the golden Festetic colours, flew effortlessly past the finish.

'Trouble?' whispered Fanny as Laszlo reached up to help her descend from her chair.

'No! No! I only risked ten crowns. It's nothing but a farce really.' Though he smiled as he spoke, Fanny did not entirely believe him and pressed his hand a little longer than was necessary out of sympathy.

In the grandstand everyone now stood up to look for some refreshment. The princess, who had returned to her place just before the race began, moved down beside Klara.

'Look there!' she said, her face rigid with disapproval, and as she pointed to where Countess Beredy was surrounded by her little court. Laszlo was helping Fanny get down from her chair, and this was the moment when Klara's lover was looking up into Fanny's lovely smiling face.

In Klara's heart something tightened and all her doubts flooded back, just as her stepmother had intended. In an instant the girl had chased her fears away, but the radiant sense of joy which had until then filled her whole being had fled, never to return.

On the evening of the King's Cup Race a grand ball was always given at the Park Club, and as this was the pinnacle of the spring season everyone felt it their duty to be there. As well as those families with debutante daughters and the young men who attended every dance as religiously as if they were going to work, the King's Cup ball was also graced by the younger married couples, by leading political figures, by the principal owners of racing stables, by members of the court, ladies-in-waiting and equerries, and all those elderly country aristocrats who contributed to the organization of the 'Gentlemen's Ball', as this event had come to be called. This year the Archduke and Archduchess were also to be present with two of their daughters, and they had brought two royal princes from Germany as their guests. There were so many people that every room at the club was filled with people. The invitations bore the magic legend 'Decorations', indicating that royalty would be present, and so all the married women wore tiaras and every man who was able to wore dress uniform just as if he had received an invitation to court. The great oval ballroom had all the air of a reception at Schönbrunn or the Hofburg.

For once Balint also decided to attend. Since he had been in Budapest for the parliamentary sessions he had accepted invitations only to a few private dinners and on those evenings when there were no debates he either dined quietly at the Casino or went to a bachelor party with gypsy musicians and girls from the *demi-monde*. But though he tried hard to find pleasure in the political struggles and in carousing with other young men at the tsigane parties, the truth was that he could raise only fleeting interest in the *cocottes* while the debates, with their endless trivial argument and the substitution of political slogans for constructive proposals, bored him to death. It seemed that no one would ever put forward any positive plan to solve the country's problems. All they did was to repeat, over and over again, what had been said before.

Perhaps the underlying reason for Balint's disillusion lay in the fact that he was depressed and inwardly perturbed. He seemed to have lost his way. If he were really to have an effective role in what was happening rather than remaining forever a spectator, then he wondered if perhaps he should choose a leader and follow faithfully wherever he might lead. As it was he felt he was an outsider, set apart from the others, forever wondering what line he should take. Surely it was both senseless and somewhat absurd for someone so new to politics to set himself apart as he had done. During this last session this feeling had become stronger and stronger, until it was clear that no matter how hard he tried to discuss things with other members, whatever their political allegiances, he was answered only by a repetition of their party's official policies which had already appeared in print a hundred times over. Politicians with party ties would shy away from him if he ever tried to discuss seriously what they really thought. Each man with whom he talked assumed at once that he was a secret envoy from one of the parties to which they themselves did not belong. This was extremely frustrating, though now Balint was starting to realize that it was natural and inevitable. A man who tried to see every side of every problem, who bent over backwards to take a fair and equitable view, was a suspect animal in the world of politics. What, to most politicians, could be more equivocal and therefore not to be trusted, than someone who admitted that those with contrary opinions might possibly also be right? *Audiatur et altera pars* (which might be translated as 'There are two sides to every question') held no attraction for committed party members for whom their own party's programme was no less than Revealed Truth, while that of their opponents was just as inevitably the work of the Devil. We are right and they are wrong, and that was that!

Thus it was, is now and ever shall be! And in the Hungary of the first decade of the twentieth century it was even more true than it was in other countries and at other times. To the generation that grew up in the years following the 1867 Compromise, the feeling of isolation that stemmed from Austria's dominant role in the Dual Monarchy together with the long years of peace, taught them to ignore any events that occurred outside the country. Since, until recently, the same Government had remained for time in office, the Opposition had never had the chance of experiencing the realities of government and instead had concentrated all its efforts in increasingly unrealistic criticism. In its turn, the Government saw in the Opposition only an irresponsible enemy who must at all costs be crushed. In these circumstances Balint began to wonder if he might not be better employed by allying himself to some party from whose ranks he could contribute more effectively to political reform. In particular, he was anxious that some attention should be paid to the problems and economy of Transylvania.

This, thought Balint, was where his mission lay. He had been much influenced by an article which had recently come out in a distinguished English publication, the *Contemporary Review*. It was written by a Romanian, one Draginesco who, in undisguised hatred of the Hungarians, put the entire blame for the present stagnation of the Hungarians on the repressive and arrogant administration in Budapest. Balint wondered if there was any connection between the publication of this article and the increasingly active agitation from the ranks of the Transylvanian-Romanians.

It was true that Mihaly had spoken with moderation in the debate on the Address, but had he not said: 'We who are members of the Hungarian political system'? Could there be a link between the emergence of minority representation in Parliament and the plotting of extremists in the province itself? And, if there were, was this not something of vital importance that the Government should take seriously?

It was such things as this that occupied Balint's mind as he was being driven to the ball. He arrived at the Park Club late. Inside the entrance the committee of the Club was grouped around Laszlo who, as representative of the sponsors, was acting as host for the evening. Behind them stood two footmen holding brightly-lit candelabra, for a telephone message from the Palace had just been received announcing that the royal party was already on its way, and custom dictated that the royal guests should be greeted at the door by the committee and escorted up the stairs with all the ritual of candle-light and court procedure.

Seeing his cousin, Balint was reminded of the rumours that Laszlo had become a reckless and fanatical gambler. When he had heard this he had decided to find an opportunity for having a serious talk with him and, if necessary, to speak to him severely, even harshly, on the dangers of such a life. This was something from which Laszlo must be saved, and he believed that because of their long-standing friendship he was the only person who could rescue his cousin. Until now no occasion had presented itself, for Laszlo was always so busy and in such a hurry that when they had met there had been no chance of an intimate talk. Seeing him now, Balint went up at once and he said: 'I've something very important to discuss with you. It's urgent. When can I see you? We'll need a little time.'

'Anytime!' said Laszlo.

'Anytime is never!' laughed Balint. 'Will you be at the Casino tomorrow afternoon?'

'Of course. I lunch there every day.'

'Well then, tomorrow at two I'll be there. We'll have to find a quiet corner where we won't be interrupted.'

'Of course!' Laszlo replied with a distracted air, for all his attention was directed at the entrance where the royals were expected. 'Of course, splendid!' he repeateded absent-mindedly.

Something is the matter, thought Balint, noticing that instead of his usual open and cheerful expression Laszlo looked serious and withdrawn. He turned away and went up the stairs.

Balint assumed that Laszlo was worried about his mounting debts but in this he was wrong, for Laszlo, who had just had a run of good luck, owed little to the money-lenders and was not being pressed for what he did owe. What had caused Laszlo to frown and look unusually serious was that he had heard indirectly that a big dinner had been given that evening at the Kollonich Palais and that he, though a close relative and a normally welcome guest, had been left out. He now realized that Peter and Niki, whom he had seen at the races, had been careful not to mention it in front of him. This clearly showed that his aunt had declared war and that the whole family knew it. All his old resentment came flooding back, and it was in a cloud of bitterness that he found himself having to stand at the door of the Park Club and force himself to attend to his duties. In vain he tried to convince himself that Klara would stand firm and be true to him and that together they would win through, but he was constantly returning to the superstitious thought that the horse on which he had staked Klara's ten crowns as a symbol of their ultimate victory had come nowhere. It was a bad omen!

Many people were crowded on the wide gallery of the main staircase, not, however, to watch the arrival of the royal party but rather to catch a glimpse of Burian, the Finance Minister of the Dual Monarchy who had that day arrived from Vienna. As the king's personal representative he had come for discussions with the coalition government, and it was rumoured that this represented the crown's final effort to achieve reconciliation. Not that Burian gave anything away. Even those who managed to talk with him questioned him in vain for he was a reserved, silent man whose bland expression revealed nothing, even though his short-sighted eyes twinkled merrily enough behind his pince-nez. In contrast to this non-committal and soft-spoken man, General Geza Fejervary was standing not far away talking loudly to a group of pretty women who had immediately surrounded him on his arrival. Fejervary's unexpected presence had caused a sensation, for though he claimed that he had put in an appearance solely to please his granddaughters, no one believed that this was the whole truth. Boisterously he laughed and joked with the beauties who crowded around him, his tall figure towering above them.

The general was an imposing figure with a eagle's beak of a nose above a white hussar's moustache and a wide manly chest which was shown to its best advantage in his court uniform of white cloth faced with gold lace. Among his many medals was displayed the little cross of the Order of Maria Theresia, which as a young captain he had won at the battle of Custozza. *This* is a man, said the glances of the women who surrounded him, and they brought into play all their feminine wiles and obvious admiration for the overpowering maleness of his presence, laughing and flirting and ogling the old general, in the hopes of getting him to reveal what he must know of Burian's mission.

The rumour had gone around that the general had been designated by the king to play an important role in this new effort at negotiation and so Balint at once decided to join the group around him. Though catching only occasional phrases from what was being said, Balint heard enough to catch the drift. One of the beauties, flashing her eyes boldly, was being more direct than all the others. She was saying that the ruler would have no alternative but to make concessions and accept the Hungarian point of view. Political arguments flowed from her lovely petal-shaped mouth and she ended by saying once again: 'There is no other way! The King must give in!'

The old general laughed loudly: 'Really? Really? You think that?' he said. 'What if something else is planned, something quite different? Ha-ha-ha! Quite different from what they expect!' And he stuck out his mighty chest even further and twirled his white moustache with an air of triumph, his whole being infused with the confident spirit of one who has never lost a battle. Balint thought that he must have been like this when leading his men to victory, and it was with a sudden pang that he heard the general, supremely confident of his own invincibility, let out a roar of mocking, victorious laughter. Balint's heart constricted. What did this confidence mean? What new, unexpected, violent solution was being brewed up in Vienna? What it could be he could not imagine, but that there was something was certain; Fejervary's whole bearing was proof to anyone with eyes to see. Was it to this that Slawata had referred when he had written '... *something quite different to anything the Hungarians expect is now being prepared.*'? What could it be? New elections controlled by the army? An attempt to impose absolute rule, putting aside the ancient constitution which Franz-Josef had sworn a coronation oath to preserve? Neither seemed probable. Such measures were unthinkable, yet the self-satisfied laughter of the old military man had made an impression that was hard to erase.

It was Balint's fate that evening that he could not escape from politics. Even when he asked Fanny Beredy to dance and then have supper with him and they joined several other ladies at a table near the buffet, the talk was all about politics. He was amazed to see how passionately these elegant ladies argued. They were all supporters of the conservative opposition. Many of them were extraordinarily well-informed, putting forward their views with well-reasoned arguments and sophisticated political acumen just as if they were lawyers arguing a case in court. Dry paragraphs of party views flowed from their rosy lips with astonishing precision and their desirable bare shoulders heaved with the vehemence of their arguments. In their hair, at their ears, and round their necks, diamonds sparkled as if to add hundreds of new arguments to their talk. They were all militant patriots, dedicated to and obsessed by the rightness of their cause, all of them the more sure of themselves because one of the more influential newspapers had just published a leading article eulogizing the political acuteness of the Hungarian ladies and the importance of their role in the national struggle. This had given these society ladies much pleasure. 'At last the press gives us proper recognition!' said one lovely blonde, as she bit into a strawberry with her snow-white teeth. Though this statement only underlined the general feeling at the time, Balint found it worrying. To change the subject he turned to Fanny and asked about Laszlo.

'I hear my cousin Gyeroffy often comes to see you these days?' he said.

'Yes. He's a sweet boy and an excellent musician. We all like him a lot.'

'Is it true that he's gambling heavily?'

'Yes,' she smiled, 'passionately.'

After a slight hesitation Balint said: 'I rarely see him nowadays, though today we've met several times. Has he been losing a great deal?'

Fanny looked straight at him, her pussycat smile even more inscrutable than usual.

'I don't think so. My friend Devereux, who is a great gossip and knows everything, would certainly have told me if he had. No! As far as I know he's on a winning streak at the moment.'

'But I'm sure he has something on his mind. He's worried about something, I can see it in his face ... you don't know him as I do.'

There was a flash of interest in her eyes, though she quickly dropped her eyelids to conceal it.

'Yes, I've noticed it too.' And she went on calmly, 'However, you're wrong about the reason. It's not money. He's much too reckless to count the cost or be worried about that!' Her eyes narrowed to slits, long diagonal lines that swept obliquely upwards, and her mouth spread in a smile as if she were savouring the taste of honey. 'Love!' she went on. 'That'll be it! Love! Perhaps something's gone wrong.'

'Klara?'

'Of course!'

'Does she love him?'

Fanny shrugged her beautiful shoulders.

'A young girl like that? What does she know about love?' Fanny spoke scornfully. 'The choice isn't hers anyway. She'll marry whoever is chosen for her. She may protest a bit, but in the end she'll do whatever Agnes decides. And Agnes, as you know, is a terrible snob!'

'That's what I thought, too.'

'There you are, you see! As far as Agnes is concerned, our good Laszlo is nobody – *Niemand*. She wouldn't care if one of us eloped with the chauffeur, but her daughter will only marry the man *she* chooses!'

The thought seemed to give Fanny pleasure, though for what reason only she could tell, and she adjusted the lace shoulder-straps which, as they often did, had slid down her bare arms.

The Gentlemen's Ball always finished early. After being on parade from noon most of the guests were tired and disinclined to dance until dawn. By three o'clock in the morning everyone had gone and Laszlo, who had to remain to say goodbye to the last guests, decided to go on to the Casino.

On arrival he found that the gamblers were still playing. As always on the night of the big race, the room was crowded and the play was higher even than usual. Bets of many thousands of crowns were being laid on the table and the atmosphere was fraught with ill-feeling. There were so many onlookers that it was not easy for Gyeroffy to get near the table. When he finally managed this a place was at once offered to him, as it was an unwritten law that room should always be found for a gambler as famous as Laszlo.

Laszlo refused the offer. 'No, thank you,' he said. 'I'm not staying.' For a few moments he stood there watching the play, then turned and left the room.

'He must have a girl waiting for him!' said somebody, for in that world *la bonne fortune* (an amorous rendezvous) was considered the only valid excuse for not joining in a game.

Laszlo went slowly down the stairs, through the halls of the Casino, hesitating as he went as if it were physically difficult for him to leave this sacred place. He then had himself driven to those cheap furnished lodgings which he had rented when he first came to Budapest to study and which he had never changed.

He went to bed, but did not sleep as it was a long time since Laszlo had come home so early. As he lay stiffly on the narrow bed he seemed to become more and more awake. The day's events went round and round in his head. Klara... his promise, ah, that he had to keep and would keep. It would be vile not to do so! But what about the ball? She must have understood that he couldn't get near her as he had been commanded to partner one of the young archduchesses in the quadrille, an honour that no one could refuse. He recalled seeing Klara supping with Warday not far from the royal table where he sat. They had been chatting vivaciously enough. No doubt that dimwitted farmer had been entertaining her with tales of muck-spreading and ergot in the wheat, thought Laszlo bitterly. Or had Klara been teasing him as she had Montorio two days before? Oh Klara! Klara! He had been dying to dance with her but his duties as *elotancos*, especially with the royals present, meant that he had been occupied the entire evening and it had seemed he would never even get close to her. Even when, just after the last figure of the quadrille, he had managed to get near her with his specially large saffron-coloured bouquet, she was already being so inundated with the favours brought to her by others that he couldn't even exchange a word with her, not a single word! How could the Kollonichs leave him out of one of their big dinners when they had always before insisted he must be there? It was obvious that this had been done on purpose so that they should not have a chance to speak to each other. Would this always be the same? It would be dreadful if there should never be an end to it!

Laszlo felt that he must find a way to communicate directly with her, but how? It wouldn't be possible through Peter; he'd never go against his mother. Niki was out of the question; he was no friend to Laszlo. Then Laszlo remembered the little maid who had brought Klara's letter. What was her name, Ilus Varga? Was that what the concierge had said when he brought up the letter after telling the girl that she could not go up to Laszlo's flat as he had given orders not to be disturbed? He would write a line to her to give a message to her mistress that she must find a way to see him.

By noon the Casino was already full to overflowing. Even the great glass-covered veranda was packed with people. After their lunch Balint and Laszlo went into the empty billiard-room.

At once Balint started off severely. Laszlo must be out of his mind, he said. If he went on like this he would be ruined, and then nothing would save him from a shameful life of depravity. Already it was obvious that he was spending far more than his respectable but by no means large fortune could provide, and if he went on gambling, everything he had would disappear. It was madness, sheer madness!

Laszlo listened to him and smiled, conscious that in a moment or two he would demolish all his cousin's arguments with a single word.

'Now you must swear not to gamble anymore!' said Balint. 'Promise me!' and he put his hand on Laszlo's shoulder in a gesture of sympathetic entreaty.

'I have nothing to promise,' replied Laszlo, 'as I don't gamble any more!'

'Not possible? Since when?'

Laszlo laughed awkwardly. 'As it happens, only since yesterday. Last night, this morning, I didn't join the game. I promised somebody!'

'Who? When?'

'Somebody . . . somebody who is even dearer to me than you, yes, even dearer than you!'

Balint realized that it must be Klara of whom he spoke.

'So much the better then. It's a pity it came so late, but no matter! I'm very glad, and I'm sure you'll keep your promise. But look here, my dear fellow, stop this stupid life at once. If you go home now, immediately, it'll be all the easier to make the break. It's a dreadful habit and very hard to resist.'

'Don't worry, I can do it!'

'You'd better,' said Balint grimly. 'Habit is strong and when everyone around you . . . Look! The Burian talks will end today – they're quite futile anyway, or so I hear – and the House will be adjourned. I'll go with you to Transylvania tomorrow. We'll travel together. I'd be happy to do it!'

'No! I can't leave yet. You must understand. Not yet, not while they are still here. At the end of the season, when everyone goes. In ten or twelve days. Then I'll go.'

'Better to go at once, while your mind is still made up. I'm really very worried about you.'

'It's impossible! I can't leave now because of something quite different. But immediately afterwards, then I'll go. I swear it.'

They got up and shook hands. Laszlo, in mock reverence, clicked his heels and gave a military salute.

'This is how I will announce myself. *Melde gehorsamst* – reporting for duty, Sir!' And with this he turned around and hurried away.

Three days went by during which Laszlo hardly saw Klara, and when he did it was always in a crowd where they would have been watched. The princess, guarding her stepdaughter like a detective on duty, was never far away from her. Three days, three bad days, during which Laszlo heard that they had been to some gathering in the woods on the Margit Island or spent an evening at a country-house not far from the city, excursions from which Aunt Agnes had been careful to arrange his exclusion.

It was more than Laszlo could bear. Somehow he would have to get word to Klara to meet him or he thought he would die of agony and frustration. If only he knew where she was and what they all were doing, then at least he might be able to catch a glimpse of her.

On the fourth morning he awoke early, still tormented by the thoughts that had kept him awake so late the night before. How to do it? How? If he wrote to Klara, the letter was sure to be intercepted by her mother, for Princess Agnes was capable of any act, however mean, to ensure that her commands were obeyed. Then again he remembered the little maid, Ilus. She was a good girl, even if she always seemed so sad. He was sure she would do anything for her mistress so if he could send a message through the maid, then it stood a chance of reaching Klara. Nobody would bother about a maidservant's letters.

He got up at once and went to his desk. As usual he had no writing paper, so he took out one of his visiting cards and wrote a few words on the back: '*Dear Ilus, Come to see me today. I'll be at home all afternoon.* Please *come!*' Only this, nothing more.

As Laszlo never had any envelopes either, he dressed hurriedly and went down to ask the concierge's wife if she could give him one. It was large and rough, but it would have to do. Slipping into it the card, he wrote on the outside the maid's name and addressed it merely to the Kollonich Palais.

Then, still unshaven, he hurried to Kalvin Square. It was about ten o'clock. Not wanting to go up to the house where he would be recognized he handed the letter to a street porter.

'Do I wait for an answer?' asked the old man when Laszlo

PART FOUR

had told him what he wanted and put some coins in his hand.

'No answer. But you must give it to her personally, into her own hands, you understand!'

'Yes, sir. Just as you wish, sir!'

It had been a bad mistake to send a street porter. If Laszlo had sent his message by post it would have arrived the same afternoon at the latest. As it was, the whole operation drew unnecessary attention to itself. Firstly, it was unusual for a maid-servant to receive letters by special delivery. What sort of person was it, anyone might wonder, who would spend money having a letter carried 50 yards just for a servant? It certainly wasn't any relation. A member of her family, someone of her own kind, would never lay out forty cents for something that normally cost eight; not only that, they wouldn't be in such a hurry. A stranger then? But who could it be? It was very odd and out of the ordinary.

The porter was a conspicuous figure who always wore a red beret. This would have attracted little notice in a block of apartments with several floors and many different tenants. There he could have entered quite freely. But it was no means the case when he presented himself at the covered portico of the grand town house of the princely Kollonich family. There he was prevented from entering the mansion by a liveried door-keeper, a huge man with a bushy beard who wore an intimidating quantity of gold braid and who peremptorily demanded where the man thought he was going and asked him to state his name and the name of the person to whom he was delivering the letter. The Kollonich door-keeper was not only powerfully built but was also filled with a sense of his own importance.

The porter, an honest and conscientious fellow, explained his mission and insisted that he had been instructed to hand the letter only to the person to whom it was addressed. This started an argument which, brief though it was, at once brought a footman running out, for the door-keeper had a stentorian voice and this undignified noise could be heard inside the house.

'Well? Who's it for?' shouted the doorman, 'Ilus Varga? No you can't go up. If you want an answer you can wait outside on the sidewalk. What? No answer? Then move along! I don't want any hanging about outside this house, thank you very much!'

There was nothing that the porter could do but hand over the letter and move on before he caused any more trouble.

The footman came down the steps to where the doorman stood.

There he was joined by a serving-man in a baize apron and hands covered in brass polish who had been cleaning the fittings of the inner doors. 'Who's this for?' they both asked. 'Ilus?' The doorman handed over the envelope and both the other men handled it trying to establish what it contained. All that they could determine was that a little rectangular disc seemed to be inside. It certainly wasn't money and therefore must be a visiting card which meant that it had been sent by a gentleman despite the poor quality of the envelope. 'Ilus must be doing all right!' chuckled one of them, as they stood round the doorman.

At this moment the butler Szabo, who was doing the rounds of the house, came down the steps.

'What's all this going on here?' he asked sternly, gesturing to the under-servant in the baize apron to get back in the house and carry on with his work. The footman, to explain why he had left his post at the foot of the main staircase in the hall – and because he was terrified of the butler – started to gabble incoherently:

'Well, you see, sir, a letter arrived, for Ilus Varga . . . a street porter . . . he wanted to come in . . . a porter . . .' he hesitated. 'Just a porter . . . therefore . . .' he tailed off lamely.

'Where is it? Give it to me!' and, as the footman handed it over, Szabo went on, 'I'll take care of this!' Slipping the letter into his breast pocket he turned and went back up the steps.

In a few moments all was back to normal. The lackey was polishing the brasses, the footman was back yawning at the foot of the great staircase, and the doorman went back to his place standing with splayed legs and chest thrown out to dazzle the passers-by with the importance of the house in front of which he stood.

The princess was just going from her bedroom to her dressing room to get out of her morning negligé and put on her afternoon dress when Fräulein Schulze, her German maid, came in.

'Your Grace! The butler Szabo begs your Grace's pardon and asks the favour of a short audience.'

'Now?' said Princess Agnes, surprised because such a request was unusual.

The household arrangements of the Kollonich Palais were performed so automatically and smoothly that something exceptional must have arisen if she had to be consulted at this hour.

'Let him come in,' she said, sitting down by her writing desk – for one must always be seated when interviewing servants.

Fräulein Schulze, whose corsetted figure had all the rigidity of a sergeant-major, went out as soon as Szabo entered the room. He stood respectfully near the door.

From head to toe the butler's whole body seemed to epitomize that of an honourable man. The expression of his face was never less than stony; not a muscle of his handsome classical features moved to reveal the smallest emotion. He was scrupulously clean and always closely shaven. With his exceptional height and the bearing of a great English statesman, no one would have thought that he was born a simple peasant boy somewhere in the country of Feher.

The butler stood erect, his mouth closed, calm and without stiffness, waiting to be spoken to.

'Well, Szabo, what is the matter?' demanded the princess who, when speaking to any of her servants, used the family names only of the butler, the chef and Fräulein Schulze; the last because she came from a better family.

'Your Grace,' said the face of stone, 'I beg pardon of your Grace for this inconvenience, but something has happened which affects the reputation and good name of this princely household.' Szabo spoke ponderously, giving equal emphasis to each word.

'What is it?' asked the Princess, surprised.

'There is a young maidservant, the Duchess Klara's maid – her name is Ilona Varga, or something like that. She is not, I beg your Grace's pardon, worthy to be employed in such a noble house.'

'Really? Ilus?'

'Yes, your Grace. I hesitated for some time before reporting the matter to your Grace, but now, because the good name of such a high ranking household is at stake I feel obliged to bring the matter to your Grace's notice.'

'What is it? Is she having some disreputable love-affair?'

Szabo paused. He seemed to be having difficulty in bringing himself to speak of such indecent matters. At last he got it out: 'She is pregnant, your Grace!' He bowed slightly, with downcast eyes, and then went on with even greater deference of manner: 'I beg your Grace's pardon, but I felt it my duty to dare to inform your Grace.'

'Well! And . . . since when, may I ask? Who is responsible?'

The butler sighed sadly and made some uncertain gesture with his hands: 'I have had my suspicions for some time, but how can one be sure of such things? However, today a street porter brought her a letter . . . to this house! That really is going too far, your Grace!'

He brought out the grey, wrinkled envelope and placed it on a table near where the princess was sitting.

'Do you imagine that I wish to read a maidservant's letters?' said Princess Agnes coldly, but before saying any more she looked up at him and realized from his expression, sad but emphatic, knowing but respectful, that there was something here, something special, that must be revealed. She reached for the envelope, opened it, and a little visiting card fell out on to the table: Laszlo's card, engraved on one side with his name and title and, on the other, in the hand-writing she knew so well, the message: '*Dear Ilus, Come to see me today . . .*'

Agnes was filled with a dreadful anger. This Laci! Now he was trifling with serving wenches! Dirty, disreputable, perverted lout, to give Klara's maid a child! And, as these thoughts rushed through her head, she realized that she didn't believe a word of it and this must only be a way of trying to get a message to her step-daughter. But what a chance this offered! She *would* believe it, it was fuel to her anger against him, fuel that could fan the flames of her wrath at his presumption and justify her hatred of her nephew.

The butler waited without moving. Not a muscle of his face twitched. He did not look at his mistress but only at the carpet beneath his feet. There was nothing for him to do. It was not his place to influence the princess, any more than it was to show that he was aware of her emotion. That would never do. It was an unwritten law that servants were not permitted to notice their employer's feelings. He was there merely to pass on information, nothing more. He must not utter another syllable. He had said enough to accomplish his duty and now his role was merely to await orders and then to carry them out. He would do what he was told, to the last letter. That was his role. Thus far and no further. Until the princess spoke he must remain silent and for that he would wait as long as necessary.

The princess rang the bell on her desk and, in an instant, her maid appeared.

'*Liebe Schulze*! Bring me the employment card of . . .' She looked up enquiringly at Szabo.

'Ilona Varga,' he said.

'*Also von diese Varga. Sofort* – at once!'

The elderly German maid hurried away. She returned in a few moments.

The princess then issued her orders: Ilona Varga was to be paid a month's wages and thrown out of the house immediately. In ten minutes she must be out in the street.

The two upper servants bowed their acknowledgement of their instructions and the princess rose and started to move towards her dressing-room. At the door she turned. 'Make sure the girl speaks to nobody before she leaves the house. Absolutely no one, do you understand? This is an order, Szabo! No one!'

The butler made a low bow, showing that the command was perfectly clear and that he would ensure that it was faithfully carried out. He did not speak. What it is to employ someone one can trust, thought the princess ... and the thought almost made her cheerful again.

When the door had closed behind her Szabo picked up Laszlo's card, slipped it back in the envelope and replaced it in his pocket. If ever the girl demanded maintenance for her child no doubt it would come in handy! Then he followed the lady's maid out of the room.

<hr />

Together Szabo and Fräulein Schulze went to look for Ilus. First they went straight through the second courtyard to the door of the great kitchen where Fräulein Schulze looked in and asked the maids who were busy washing up if anyone had seen Ilus. 'She's gone to the drying room,' said one of them as they crowded round the door eager to know why the 'Miss' and the great Mr Szabo were looking for a young maidservant. They had sensed at once that something was up, so they stayed in a group by the door to watch and listen.

Just at that moment the girl came back, carrying in her right hand two clothes-hangers on which were hung a couple of Klara's delicate, frothy muslin summer dresses. She held them high and well away from her lest one of the ruffles should be creased or the hem pick up some dust from the tiled floor. She walked lightly, almost tripping as she came.

Szabo stood back as Fräulein Schulze advanced upon the girl.

'You get out of this house at once! Do you hear me? Out! This very instant!' shouted Schulze furiously.

'What is it? What's the matter?' cried Ilus, frightened by the woman's angry tone.

'Out of here? No buts and ifs! Here's your card and your month's wages. Off with you. At once, I say!'

'What? Me? Just like that?' Ilus paused when she saw that Szabo was standing in the background and then she cried out to him: 'This is your doing. I know it. It's you ... you, Mr Szabo!' and then, her voice growing every more strident: 'You do this to me and now, now you ... you...' She could say no more, so strong was her shame and consternation. She staggered slightly and leant against the wall for support, still automatically holding Klara's dresses away from her so that they should not spoil.

At the noise the cook and the kitchen-boy came to see what was going on in the passage and the chef appeared from the door of his room. Seeing that the eyes of so many people were on her Ilus got hold of herself so that they should not gloat over her disgrace. Her courageous, proud little peasant spirit rebelled and gave her strength. She straightened up, raised her head and said to the German Fräulein: 'All right! Let's go!' and started to move away. Schulze too turned on her heel and left, the girl following behind her. As Ilus passed Szabo, who had not moved from his place in the background, she stopped for a moment.

'God will punish you for this, Mr Szabo!' she said, and then went on, still holding high Klara's beautiful dresses, dresses of such lightness and elegance, featherlight garments seemingly woven of the stuff that dreams are made of, scented and glittering. So went the little maid along the dark dusty corridor holding dreams – someone else's dreams – on her outstretched arm.

'That was nicely done! You are a clever fellow,' laughed the overweight chef, taking Szabo's arm. 'First you get her with child and then you have her thrown out! Very clever!' He went back into his room from which his chuckles could be heard for some little time.

When the two women reached Ilus's room, Fräulein Schulze took Klara's dresses and putting down Ilus's employment card and her money, said: 'Pack! Straight away, mind you!' and left the girl alone in her room.

Ilus packed hurriedly. It was quickly done for she had few possessions, and it would have been finished even sooner if the child in her womb had not moved inside her, that child conceived without joy and for which Mr Szabo was now having her thrown out.

When she was ready she stepped out into the corridor, her modest little wicker bag in her hand, thinking that at least she should go to the Lady Klara to say goodbye; but beyond the service stair, at a bend in the corridor, her way was barred by the hated Fräulein standing like the implacable guardian at the Gates of Paradise. Schulze hated all the other servants; Szabo, the chef, everyone, but most of all she hated all those pretty young maids – and most of them were pretty – that Szabo treated as his private harem. Joyless and sour herself, it was from the depths of her frustrated spinsterhood that she had conceived a loathing of those 'depraved creatures' with whom the butler took his pleasure. She well knew everything that happened in the house, but she was not powerful enough to quarrel with Szabo, whose position was impregnable, and so had to content herself with rejoicing when he arranged to have dismissed the ones he got into trouble.

'I only wanted to kiss her Ladyship's hand!' said Ilus sadly.

'She won't see you. She won't receive a little whore like you – *so eine Hüre!* Little bitch, out of here at once!' Schulze's long gaunt arm pointed back down the stairs.

Ilus turned back, descended the service stairway whose boards creaked under her little feet from the whitening powder used to clean them, passed through the two courtyards and found herself in the street. Until then she remained calm, but now alone in the bustle of the great city, the enormity of the blow that had come without warning was suddenly so dreadful that she could hardly stand.

She took a few aimless steps away from the house. Now she realized how tired she was and felt the weight of her motherhood. She would have to find somewhere to sit down, to rest and ponder what she should do.

Across the road was the garden of the Museum, so she crossed over and found a bench to sit on.

What could she do? Where could she go?

Some children were playing near to where she sat. Uniformed nannies and nursery-maids were pushing perambulators or leading well-dressed toddlers. The children were all fat and healthy and well fed and the sight of them filled little Ilus with a sense of her own grief – her own baby would most likely be swathed only in rags. Perhaps it would have been better to follow Mr Szabo's cynical suggestion that she found out some backstreet 'midwife' who knew what to do in such cases. Then she wouldn't have had any of this worry and trouble. But she hadn't wanted to and couldn't bring herself to do it...

But now what could she do, to whom could she turn? She couldn't look for work in her condition – no one would have her. Perhaps she could find a protector, a pimp; though she knew of the existence of such people only by hearsay and had never met one. She was a country girl who had come straight from her parents' cottage to service in the great house of Simonvasar, for at home there were so many mouths to feed that she had had to go out to work as soon as she was old enough.

Should she go home to her mother, go home to show her shame with a bastard child in her belly, to be the laughing stock of the village and to be driven away again for conceiving a child by some 'foreigner', as the people at home thought of all who were not born and bred in the district? And what about that lad who would soon return from his military service with whom she had held hands, and to whom she had pledged herself on the evening before he had signed up and gone away to serve his time with the 44th Infantry? The thought that he should return to find her like this, fallen and despised by all, was unbearable. He, too, would despise her, turn away from her and spit upon her. No! She would rather die than suffer such disgrace.

So she sat on the bench and pondered, not crying but just staring silently in front of her; seeing nothing.

Surely the Lady Klara would take pity on her? But that hateful 'Miss' had said she wouldn't see her, as if she too despised her and found her unclean, unfit to enter a lady's presence. Yet the Lady Klara had always been so kind and considerate. Even last week she had kissed her when she had handed her the letter to deliver, but then of course she didn't know about the child.

Laszlo Gyeroffy! Perhaps he could help. Yes, she would go to him. If Count Laszlo asked it of her, perhaps for *his* sake . . . ?

Ilus pulled herself upright. Picking up the wicker bag, she started off. Count Laszlo lived somewhere thereabouts, quite near. Of course! She remembered it was in Museum Street. She prayed she would find him at home.

Laszlo was walking up and down his little sitting-room. He had been doing so for more than an hour, waiting impatiently for Ilus to come to him in answer to his message. He was rehearsing to himself what he would tell her and how he would make her learn by heart, word by word, what she was to say to Klara, that life was impossible, that he could not go on like this and that Klara must find a way. Perhaps she could send Ilus back the following morning, to tell him what her plans were for the day, where he would be able to find her.

The doorbell rang. Laszlo went quickly to see who was there and indeed it was Ilus for whom he had been waiting so impatiently. As he ushered her into the living-room, he wondered for a brief moment why she was carrying a travelling bag.

Ilus was out of breath after climbing the three flights of stairs to Laszlo's rooms. It really was too much for her and she staggered, panting, to support herself on the end of the piano.

'Sit down, please,' said Laszlo. 'Rest a moment.' And though she tried to protest he made her sit down in an armchair facing the window. Then he noticed the desperation in her face.

'What is the matter? Is something wrong?' he asked.

'Forgive me, please forgive me!' stammered Ilus uncertainly. She was still feeling giddy from the climb.

'I'm so glad you could come,' went on Laszlo. 'I've been waiting for you!' He started to outline to Ilus his plan to see Klara and what we wanted the girl to say. He spoke very quickly and passionately. 'You do know, my dear girl, that Klara and I ... well, we love each other?'

The girl nodded. Of course she knew, that was why she had come to him. She still said nothing but just nodded.

'I haven't been able to see her for days, and it's unbearable, impossible to live like this. Four days without seeing her and I can't sleep or think. I can't stand it. Therefore I want her to know that if this goes on I'll die. It can't go on! It can't! Four days is an eternity! And you must tell her as I don't dare to write – my letter would never reach her – but a message by word of mouth ... you could take it. Will you do it? You must have many opportunities – while you're helping her dress, perhaps?'

Ilus had kept on trying to interrupt but Laszlo had not noticed. She raised her little hand, which was covered with needlepricks, but nothing would stop him, he just went on, trying in broken sentences, to explain himself. As he went on Ilus slowly began to understand that even Count Laszlo, to whom she had come for help, could not approach the Lady Klara either. This was dreadful; her last hope had vanished and so, her heart constricted with grief, she broke out in great heaving sobs.

Laszlo was just saying '... so that's why I sent the card.' when he saw that she was crying bitterly. He broke off and looked at Ilus in wonder.

'What is wrong? Tell me! Why are you crying like this!'

'I ... I ... I've been sent away, thrown out!' sobbed Ilus.

'You? When? How? Why?'

'An hour ago. Like a dog, thrown out on the street. That's why I've come to you.'

355

'But what happened? Why?'

The girl wiped her eyes with her little crumpled handkerchief. She blushed deeply and hesitated for a moment. Then she said: 'I'm going to have a baby.'

'You? For Heaven's sake!' Laszlo was taken aback.

'Yes, and because of it, and because I wouldn't have an abortion as Mr Szabo wanted, so that it wouldn't be known and be talked about, so that the masters shouldn't hear about it, he's had me thrown out! It's him. I'm sure of it.' And she started to tell her sad story, somewhat confusedly but sufficiently clearly for Laszlo to understand the essential points, of how Szabo had pursued her, pestered her, even though she had tried to explain that she was a good girl, not like that at all, betrothed to a soldier; but how nothing had stopped him. How powerful Mr Szabo was, how well-in with the masters, how he had threatened her with dismissal and finally how he had forced her despite all her entreaties. She was only a girl from a poor family with many brothers and sisters and now she was sent away because no one who got on the wrong side of Mr Szabo was ever allowed to stay. He was a very strong man and it would be terribly humiliating for her if she went back to her village, sent home like this in disgrace. And how could she go back to her mother when it would make so much trouble for her, when they already had difficulty finding food for them all?

Laszlo listened to the girl's story in silence. He was sure that every word she said was true for he remembered how, when he had been at Simonvasar for the pheasant shooting in November, he had seen the girl struggling in the butler's arms at the turn of the service stairs and afterwards had heard the sound of a scuffle in a room above his. Now, as he looked at the crumpled figure of the girl huddled miserably in the armchair in front of him, he could see clearly the signs of her pregnancy. His heart went out to her in compassion and he took her hand and stroked it.

'How can I help?' he asked.

'I thought, perhaps, my Lady Klara ... maybe she could do something for me? Put in a word for me if ... I know I don't deserve it, but out of pity, perhaps something?'

'Klara? But haven't you asked her? If she were told what that evil man had done to you – not quite as you've told me, of course, but still something of it. I know it's difficult to speak of such things.'

'I wanted to. I tried, but they told me she wouldn't receive me. I know she thinks I'm vile.'

PART FOUR

Ilus fell silent. The young man got up and, for a moment or two, walked up and down the room. Then he went to the window and looked out.

The foliage of the trees in the Museum garden moved slightly in the spring breeze. It was fresh, cool, young and green. Spring. Leaf beneath leaf gleamed even more brightly in the afternoon sunshine than did the cream-painted façade of the building behind. There, just beyond the wavy green line of the tree-tops, one could see the upper part of the Kollonich Palais. That, too, shone in the sunlight, and even its slate roof had a golden glitter. Only the two of us, thought Laszlo, this poor girl and I, only we are condemned to live in the shadows of this glorious world.

'Tell me,' he said, 'did you get that visiting card I sent you this morning?'

'Visiting card? No! I didn't receive anything.'

'That's odd.'

Laszlo began to suspect that the answer might well be here. Perhaps the card had fallen into the wrong hands. If the wrong person had got hold of it that could explain the storm that had broken over the girl's innocent head. Laszlo shivered at the thought of what must have happened if his Aunt Agnes had been shown his card and assumed that he was the father of Ilus's child. The girl must have been thrown out because they believed that she was involved with him. He felt he was greatly in her debt.

'And you never saw Klara?'

'They said...'

Perhaps, thought Laszlo, it was better that Klara knew nothing of all this – her youth and purity must remain unsullied by such a sordid little tale.

'I just thought,' went on Ilus, sticking to her original plan, 'that if your Lordship could put in a kind word for me with my Lady Klara so that... just until I can find another place...'

Gyeroffy turned round, exasperated.

'Don't you understand? They won't let me see her either. Didn't you hear what I was telling you?'

Ilus got up. With great humility, all her timidity returned, she said: 'Oh, please! Please forgive me, I didn't know. Forgive me.' She turned at once and started for the door.

Laszlo ran after her, caught her arm and pulled her back. 'It's you who should forgive me,' he said. 'This is something you couldn't understand. Please sit down again and we'll talk for a little. Tell me,' and he paused in delicacy, blushing at what was he going to say, 'how many months... I mean when... how long before...?'

The girl answered composedly. She was closer to nature than he and did not blush to discuss such matters: 'I'm six months gone. There's still three more to come, the most difficult ones.'

'All right. I think I know what I can do. I know the head of the maternity ward in the hospital. He goes to the Casino about this time each day. I'll go to see him and he will arrange to take you in as one of the charity cases.'

'To the hospital? I won't go there!' cried the girl. 'Not there with all the bad women! Never! I'd rather it was the Danube!' Nothing could move her from this. Stubbornly she repeated. 'Not there! Not with the bad women!' No matter what Laszlo said she merely repeated over and over again: 'No! No! Not there!'

'What will become of you then?' asked Laszlo, dismayed and discouraged. 'I can't take you back to the Kollonich house. Would you rather go home to the country?'

Ilus raised both hands in a gesture of panic, as if she saw something dreadful before her. The idea of returning to her village where her betrothed would shortly be back from his military service, to stand before him carrying in her belly this bastard child conceived among strangers, to wait there trying to hide her condition, always ashamed, forever sitting in the back pew at church so that no one could stare at her, to be the laughing stock of the village and of all the other girls who, if they got pregnant it was always by their known sweethearts who married them as soon as they returned on leave or left the army. No! Not home, not for all the world! As she had been well brought up she did not explain all this to Laszlo, but merely said: 'I have an aunt in Veszprem: her husband works in a factory. I could see if she would take me in. She might because they are very poor.' Automatically she began to look in her purse, her worn, grubby little purse, already thinking of how little money she had and if it would be enough for them.

'That is an excellent plan, excellent. Look! I'll gladly help you.'

Laszlo immediately felt somewhat relieved and he took two thousand-crown notes from his pocket-book – for a gambler always carried at least four or five thousand crowns on him. 'Take these!' he said. 'Perhaps it will be enough for your expenses... for them to take you in?'

'That's far too much!' cried Ilus, moved. 'One will be plenty, more than enough. I don't need any more! Really I don't!'

PART FOUR

Despite Laszlo's protests she absolutely refused to take more than one note from him and as she accepted this she suddenly bent down and kissed his hand. Two hot tears dropped on to the note as she started to fold it.

'Your Lordship is far too kind. Thank you ever so much! God bless your Lordship!'

Laszlo led her towards the door. She bent down and picked up her wicker case. As she crossed the threshold she straightened her back and turned to him and again said: 'May God bless your Lordship's kindness!'

The latch fell into place behind her.

The young man stayed for a moment behind the door listening to the sound of her footsteps as she descended the stone stair. Slowly they faded away. Now she had reached the second floor, now the first... and finally nothing was to be heard. She had gone.

───※───

Laszlo was deeply upset by the little maid's misfortune. The injustice meted out to poor Ilus made him understand for the first time that life was as cruel to others as it was to him. Until now he had had no idea of the practical horrors that faced ordinary people. His own world had been an artificial one where the pains and sorrows and loneliness, however harrowing, had been cerebral and emotional. Though Laszlo reflected that the degree of pain suffered must be subjective, he had never until now known someone who did not know from one day to another where his next meal would come from nor where he would lay his head that night; never met an unfortunate girl like this young unwed mother who did not know where her baby would be born. All this was new to him and he found it shocking and totally unexpected. He had never grasped that for thousands of people this was a daily reality, a misery that lasted their whole lives. Even now, he did not think of the multitudes whose experience of life was continual unhappiness and uncertainty; on the contrary he saw only a single reality where tyranny had been merciless and unjust.

He was filled with rage as he stood silently in the middle of the room.

The sun now began to set, its rays just visible over the roofs of the museum. It was time to go to the Park Club, where it was possible that he might see Klara from a distance, even perhaps get a chance to exchange a few words with her.

Laszlo rushed downstairs and flung himself into the hired four-wheeler which waited outside his door from noon each day.

He told the driver to take him to Stefania Street. Klara and her family were nowhere to be seen. Laszlo went through all the rooms several times, as well as searching the gardens and even the grotto. They were not there.

Later he drove back to the Casino, changed into evening dress and dined. He was in a bad mood, depressed and unhappy, and to cheer himself up he drank a bottle of champagne. After dinner he had himself driven once again to the Park Club hoping that the Kollonich party might come in to dance, for on the evenings when no official ball was planned there would be music and dancing in one of the big reception rooms. On these occasions Laszlo would take over the organization and add a quadrille or garland dance to the usual waltzes or foxtrots. This evening, however, he did not feel in the mood and contented himself with drinking a couple of glasses of brandy in a forlorn attempt to cheer himself up. Time went by, and it became increasingly clear that Klara would not appear.

Just before midnight Niki Kollonich came in. Laszlo, as casually as possible, said: 'Aunt Agnes and the others aren't coming tonight?'

'No. They went for a picnic on the river – all the way to Estergom and back. It was delightful, but they're all so fagged out they can hardly stand!' replied Niki, laughing with malicious pleasure at the thought of their tiredness, and giving Laszlo the impression that he was also laughing at him. Finding it difficult to hide his disappointment Laszlo turned away, and grabbing a girl who scarcely knew him, waltzed off as quickly as he could. When the music stopped and he had escorted his partner back to her chair, he decided he could not stand it any more and would not stay. He turned to one of the young men who always helped him and said:

'I've got a headache. Please carry on without me!'

He called for his carriage and drove back to the Casino, where he went straight up to the baccarat-room, the only place where he felt at home. Every night, after the dancing had finished, he had always, without fail, come back here for a while before going home to bed. That fatal card-room was somehow soothing and attracted him even though he was no longer interested in playing. Indeed, the frustration that he felt by holding to his promise and merely standing there gave him an almost masochistic delight. It was true that on some nights there would have been little pleasure to be gained from joining in the play, for as dawn approached the only players left would be those bad losers who, anxious to pass on their bad luck would depart in a hurry the moment they had had a couple of wins. On such nights they had tried to draw him in, but since he had made his promise to Klara, he had resisted, saying that it was too late. This evening it was different, for it was only shortly after midnight and the game was in full swing with all the great gamblers there in full force; Neszti Szent-Gyorgyi, Arzenovics, Zalamery and the others. Enormous banks were called and huge bets staked.

Laszlo did not go near the table but sat down on a couch far from the rest of the company and ordered some supper and champagne and a decanter of brandy, determined somehow to get himself sufficiently drunk to dull the thoughts that so tormented him.

The room was dark apart from shaded lights over the chemmy table, but to Laszlo it was soothing to be there and to hear from afar the murmur of the familiar liturgical phrases ... *je donne* ... *passe le main* ... Eight! ... *coup de giro* ... which, with the soft rattle of the chips, were like a comforting melody or the soft echo of a rustling brook. His scorn and sorrow were not removed, but the faint, rhythmic sounds had all the effect of a mother's lullaby.

Laszlo ate his supper quietly and into every glass of champagne he poured even larger doses of brandy, but though he emptied each glass almost as soon as he had refilled it, filled it again and drunk again, it did not work. On the contrary the alcohol seemed only to bring home ever more clearly the sorrows of the last few days, while memories of that day's awful events only increased his bitterness and resentment.

That poor little maid! That pathetic Ilus Varga, to be ill-treated to the point of being thrown on the streets in her condition. What cruelty! And no one, not even Klara, had had pity on her! Not even Klara! How could it be that Klara had refused to see her and had permitted her dismissal? There must be some explanation. Perhaps she had not dared to speak up in the girl's defence and that was why she had shut herself in her room and refused to see her. Or perhaps she didn't mind? It would be terrible if she didn't mind, if she were too heartless to care, for this would mean that he had been completely deceived in his idea of her.

It was a hateful thought; and it opened a deeper wound in his diminishing self-confidence than anything else that had occurred to him, a wound through which even more poisonous thoughts found their way to his by now drink-sodden brain. Did Klara really mind as much as he did that they had not seen each other for four days? If she did, surely she would have found a way to see him, or at least get word to him? Or had she submitted to her family's pressure and abandoned him as she had little Ilus? It was impossible, unthinkable; but the thought, like a snake's venom in the bloodstream, was not so easily removed. Desperately he tried to convince himself that he was wrong and that it was absurd even to think such things, but the nagging doubt could not be suppressed. Sitting alone on the sofa at the end of the room, he straightened up and shook his head as if the movement of denial itself would waft away the agony. Then he thought she could have sent a message by Magda Szent-Gyorgyi. He had seen her once . . . or was it several times? No, only once.

On the evening of the King's Cup ball she hadn't even come over and asked for him when it was the Ladies' Choice part of the cotillion. No, that was not right, she had asked him and they had danced together, but she hadn't spoken a single word to him, not one. Why hadn't she said anything then? Later, from his seat beside the dull little archduchess, he had watched her laughing and joking with the even duller Warday, and as far as he could see she had had a wonderful time with that boring fellow. Could she be in love with Warday? That's an absurd idea, the better voice within cried out; but the other voice, the serpent-like voice of doubt, merely whispered insidiously: Who knows? Why not?

So as somehow to get away from his self-torturing, introspective dialogue, Laszlo got up and moved slowly over to the card-table. Near Arzenovics there was an empty chair and pulling it slightly away from the table, Laszlo sat down, putting his glass, now filled with neat brandy, on a small table beside him. Thinking that it might distract his thoughts, he called for a float of twenty hundred-crown chips, deciding that he would place just an occasional side bet to keep himself amused.

'Won't you join us?' asked Wülffenstein who, since Laszlo started gambling, had quite changed towards him and now courted his friendship.

'Not today,' said Laszlo, and to soften the effect of a curt refusal, he explained: 'You see, today I have a superstitious feeling – a presentiment – that I should only bet on the side!'

Occasionally, therefore, he threw in a chip or two. It was an excellent narcotic as he had to pay attention and at least notice if he won or lost. Gradually he became calmer and, as he did so, his little store of chips vanished from the table in front of him. Then, after several big 'hits', a big bank came up which the *ponte* could not quite cover.

PART FOUR

'Two more thousand will do it!' said the banker, confident of his luck. This was just the sum the Laszlo had lost. It's fate, he thought, if I win this I'll break even. So he spoke up: '*Je reste.*'

Cards were dealt and the banker won. Laszlo signalled to the steward to bring him the rest of his credit. After a short time this, too, had gone and then he ordered a further five thousand crowns' worth of chips for which someone willingly offered to countersign. From this float he continued to play, throwing in a chip here and there when an occasion arose – but now his bets were rarely less than five hundred or a thousand.

I'm not breaking my promise, Laszlo said to himself reassuringly; after all, I'm not touching the cards, only betting as one does at the races!

But nothing went right. The five thousand soon disappeared, and so did another, and now Laszlo, as he never had before, started 'chasing his money'. Previously he had always taken his wins and his losses calmly and philosophically, unmoved by either good or bad luck; but now he became stubbornly determined to win, recklessly plunging, because of the bitterness in his soul – or perhaps because the quantity of alcohol that he had put away had removed all sense of moderation. He would win it back, he would!

When Laszlo's losses had nearly reached fifteen thousand crowns, Pray called across the table:

'Your presentiment has hardly been a lucky one tonight, friend Laszlo!' he said, winking slyly, for there was nothing he liked more than teasing the other players and turning the knife in their wounds. Laszlo did not reply, but poured himself another large glass of brandy which he drank down at once. Outwardly he appeared in perfect control, but inside he was not himself. What stupidity, he was thinking, to stay out of the game, losing money on other men's bet! No one can win like this, making side bets on the bad luck of others: only the man who holds the bank can win. This was idiotic, quite idiotic...

Well, he'd join the game properly. Just this once, he'd explain to Klara, just this once. He'd explain it so that she'd understand...

Laszlo asked for more credit and changed the few thousands he had in his pocket as well. When the cards came his way he called out: '*Passe le main!*'

As he did so he was shaken by the overpowering thought that he should desist, that this was something he must not do. But the magic words had been spoken and once said, no one should back out. If he got up now the others would laugh at him – and his fifteen thousand crowns would be gone forever.

It was four in the morning when Laszlo joined the game, and at this hour even the most faithful of the onlookers who had passed an agreeable evening being horrified at the scale of the high play in front of them, were beginning to drift away and make for their beds. They left well satisfied, knowing that they would have plenty to talk about in the morning, deploring, with great indignation, what the world was coming to. Naturally they disapproved; it sounded better that way.

Laszlo played deliberately, paying great attention to whoever seemed to have the run of the cards and where the *taille* was leading. He had never watched the game with such care and in less than half an hour he had won back all his previous losses and some ten thousand crowns more. He then rose and left the table without a word.

That night Laszlo walked home as dawn was breaking filled with a sense of triumph as he told himself he had defied Fate and crushed that infamous goddess. He would show them, he said to himself, with all the arrogance born of a skinful of brandy, he would show them!

As he walked he thought also of his broken promise to Klara. Well, Klara was just worried about him. She was as timid and fearful as women were so apt to be; that was the only reason she had exacted that tiresome little promise. There was nothing to fear – women never understood these things. He would explain that anyone who really knew how to play had nothing to fear. And that he, Laszlo, did know, was proved by what had happened that night.

He would explain, and Klara would see reason. Of course she would see reason, even if she worried a little; and it didn't matter much if a girl worried a little over one...

Klara had spent the four days since the King's Cup Race in a frame of mind quite different from Laszlo's. She, too, was deeply upset by their separation and, as they had seen each other daily for several months, she missed his presence beside her. However, since her childhood she had become accustomed to having her life ruled by other people and accepted that it was they who decided what she did each day, who escorted her when she went out, watched over her and protected her. It was obvious to Klara that her stepmother was determined to keep her away from any

PART FOUR

chance of meeting Laszlo, and so the excursions and picnics, the visits to country houses, and indeed all those plans that were kept secret from her until the last minute so that she could not send word to Laszlo, merely made her smile in pity. All this trouble that Mama Agnes took, all this cunning lavished on secret telephone calls and private little messages. It was all so futile! What did it matter if she didn't see Laszlo for a few days or even a few weeks? After all he had given up gambling and one day, be it sooner or later, she would stand before her father and confront him with the fact. And then, whatever had gone before, she would have won. For Klara, Laszlo's promise was like a buried treasure whose whereabouts only she knew, for only she knew of its existence, and, as a result, no one could steal it from her. This knowledge kept Klara calm and happy and so, while she docilely followed Princess Kollonich to all these elaborately planned expeditions, she did so with a secret smile and almost pitied her as she dutifully did what she was told.

The fate of the little maid, which had so affected Laszlo, hardly touched Klara at all since she never knew what had happened. One day she was dressed by Fräulein Schulze and when Klara asked where Ilus was the German maid replied casually: '*Sie müsste nach Hause gehen* – she had to go home.' And Klara, who knew so little about the girl who had served her daily for so many years, assumed that her parents had sent for her. It did not seem very nice of the girl to leave without saying goodbye, thought Klara, but then she dismissed the idea, reflecting that perhaps someone had died and that the girl had had to leave in a hurry. She did not worry about it, thinking that sooner or later she would be back.

At noon on the day when Laszlo had gone home at dawn euphoric as only a successful gambler can be, the Lubiansky girls and Fredi Wülffenstein came to luncheon at the Kollonichs'.

During a lull in the conversation Niki turned to Wülffenstein and asked: 'Is it true that they played higher than ever at the Casino last night?'

Fredi's crooked little mouth pouted and he replied only with an odd sound like 'Pfuh! Pfuh!' because he prided himself on being as English as possible and knew that things that went on in London clubs were not supposed to be spoken of in front of ladies.

'Do you gamble too, Count Fredi?' asked Princess Agnes with a disapproving air. Wülffenstein shrugged his padded shoulders and gestured uncertainly.

'Of course he does,' said Niki, as mischief-making as ever, 'only he doesn't like to admit it!' and, despite a forbidding look from Peter, he went on: 'I met several people at the Korso today who'd been to the Casino and watched. They said the game was terrific! Oh, I know all about it all right! You lost a little, but Laszlo Gyeroffy was cleaned out. They say he went down forty thousand!'

Mama Agnes looked at Klara but said nothing.

'Are you coming to the races today?' Peter asked the Lubiansky girls, who were sitting across the table from him. He did this on purpose to change the subject as he noticed that his sister had suddenly gone pale and that her lips were compressed into a tight line of pain.

'Oh, yes, of course!' chirped both the girls in unison. 'We've heard it'll be terribly interesting today, though we don't really know much about it.' And they both simultaneously swept into monologues about when they'd leave, how they'd go and who they'd go with, for they had been taught at an early age that only country bumpkins confined their answers to 'yes' or 'no', while well-brought-up girls chattered on to show how intelligent they were. Klara was grateful to them as it meant that there was no more talk of the previous night's chemmy game.

As soon as the meal was over Louis Kollonich retired, as he always did, his smoking-room. After she had talked to the Lubiansky girls for moment in the drawing-room, Klara joined him. She sat down on the arm the sofa in front of her father and said, a little awkwardly: 'May I ask you something important, Papa?'

'And what is this important thing, my darling?' Kollonich was always in a good mood as soon as he had lit his first cigar.

Klara blushed and hesitated a moment before speaking.

'Last time ... when we had a talk here ... well, afterwards I made Laszlo promise not to gamble any more, and ...'

'Once a gambler, always a gambler!' interjected her father.

'But he did promise. He gave me his word, and now Niki says ... but he's never liked Laszlo ... no never ... and I don't believe, can't believe ... People are so awful, so wicked, they say anything, and it's often just talk. I'm sure there's some mistake, or someone's lying. I don't believe anybody except you, Papa, because I know that you ... Only if you said it ...'

'How should *I* know? I never go to the baccarat-room; as you know I only play tarot, or low stakes, and rarely after midnight!'

'That's just it. I wanted to ask you if, just once, when Laszlo might be there, when you've finished your game . . . Couldn't you just look in and see if it's true? Please go and see, and then I'd know if it's true or not. Because I can't believe it, not after he promised, I can't!' Klara's face was as white as death and her eyes were filled with desperation.

'*Na! Na! Na!* Don't get so excited. I'll go and look and then we shall know!'

Kollonich reached out and tapped his daughter's knee soothingly. Suddenly she bent down, picked up his hand and kissed it, and then she leant over and kissed him on the forehead above his little pug-shaped nose.

'Thank you! Oh, thank you! And you'll do it soon, won't you, Papa?'

Kollonich nodded: 'The sooner the better!' he said.

At the door Klara turned. 'You won't tell anyone, will you? It'll be just between us . . . no one else?'

Kollonich understood at once that she didn't want her stepmother to know.

'*Na ja! Na ja!* Just between us, *natürlich!*' and he gave a wink as he smiled back at his daughter.

That evening another dance was given at the Park Club, one of the last of the season.

The Kollonich carriage rolled majestically out of the inner courtyard of their great town house soon after eleven o'clock. Inside were Princess Agnes and Klara. They were a little late because Klara had taken longer than usual over getting ready. For once the princess said nothing, though on other occasions she would not have missed the opportunity for a nagging remark if Klara kept her waiting even for a few moments. Today she knew that Klara was upset and worried, and maybe the delay had been caused by Klara's pondering over what she had heard about Laszlo that morning. She realized that what Niki had let fall had been a great disappointment to her and knowing her stepdaughter's character so well, she thought it wiser to leave her alone with her thoughts. A single acid reference to 'that Laci' and Klara would fly angrily to his defence. Accordingly she sat beside her in silence and didn't interrupt Klara's train of thought with a single word.

Ever since lunch Klara had been tortured by confusion and doubt. Was it possible that he had promised her, given his solemn word, and still gambled? It couldn't be a complete lie, for surely even her brother wouldn't dare? She didn't want to believe any of it and so searched her mind for a reasonable explanation, but no explanation seemed reasonable or acceptable. She remembered her stepmother's words, 'that two-timing Laci' – could that really be true too? What about the story of Laszlo and Fanny Beredy? When Mama Agnes had told her of it she had rejected the tale with all the calm conviction and moral superiority of someone sure of her ground. Now Klara began to wonder, and no matter how hard she tried to suppress her growing doubts, they surfaced again and again in the form of a heart-breaking possibility.

From the moment that Niki had let drop those mischief-making words at lunch Klara had tormented herself, though she had said nothing to anyone else for that would have been too humiliating. All afternoon she had been with others, either paying calls or having tea at Gerbeaud's. At dinner she had made a great effort to appear natural and unconcerned, but these nagging thoughts had never left her. Afterwards, when dressing for the ball, she had decided that she would purposely make them leave late for, if they arrived as early as they usually did, Laszlo would have a chance of speaking to her before her father had a chance to find out the truth. Before talking to him she had to know whether or not he had broken his word to her. No doubt Mama Agnes would be cross but this was worth risking and, indeed, she hardly cared. The only important thing was that they should arrive when Laszlo was so completely taken up with organizing the ball that he would not have time to see her and deny everything before she knew whether he were lying or not. The fear that he might lie to her hurt her most, for that would be the most terrible thing that could happen. Nothing would be worse than that! To be doubly sure that he had no opportunity, she decided to arrange matters so that he would be unable to sit next to her at supper.

It turned out just as she planned, though Klara found herself obliged to do it rather more obviously than she would have wished. When the last figure of the cotillion had come to an end, Gyeroffy had been standing just behind her and so it was impossible that he had not noticed that she had led her partner from one table to another until she had found one that had just two places unoccupied, leaving no room for Laszlo to join them. She had to do this in a rush, for she was afraid that someone would have noticed. In reality nobody did except Laszlo who, with growing astonishment and pain, saw what was happening and understood what she was doing. What made it worse was that it

PART FOUR

was Warday who was seated on Klara's right.

Laszlo stood behind her for a few moments and Klara knew it, every nerve in her body signalling that he was there, trembling with surprise, disappointment and indignation. She forced herself not to turn round and give him a smile of encouragement and consolation as if it were merely an unlucky chance that things had turned out; but she did not do so. Instead she slowly pulled off her long gloves and placed them carefully on the table beside her. But all her attention was fixed on listening until she was sure Laszlo was no longer there.

At last – it had seemed like eternity – she heard the young man's footsteps as he moved away. Then she felt that something between them had been torn apart.

It was already daylight when the ball came to an end. Laszlo, by dint of his office, had to remain until all the guests had left, but Klara went home early. Filled with gloom, hatred and spite, Laszlo danced almost to breaking point, so as to tire himself out, and when dawn was breaking, drank a great deal to help him sleep – and indeed he did sleep, in a deep, dreamless slumber that lasted until the afternoon.

When he finally awoke he was filled with the sense of having suffered some great calamity. Slowly he went over in his mind all that had happened on the previous evening and then he was suddenly struck, as with a sledgehammer, by the realization that Klara had deliberately avoided him, coldly, icily, cruelly avoided him. She had intentionally broken the tacit agreement that they had had since the beginning of the Carnival season, that they should always sit together at supper; and now she had shown that she didn't even want him at her side but preferred to sit by Warday, of all people. She had shown him that it was Warday she wanted near her, Warday! She had therefore broken the understanding that, though never put into words, had been such a strong link between them. Of course this had to mean that everything was finished, that it was all over!

After what seemed like hours of self-doubt, and while more and more demons of jealousy and speculation had chased themselves round and round in the darkening room, Laszlo got up and dressed and went to the Casino.

It was dinner-time when he arrived and he sat down at a crowded table between Arzenovics and Zalamery. When these two, after coffee and several glasses of liqueur, went straight up to the baccarat-room, he went with them.

This time Laszlo did not wait to be asked but sat down immediately at the table and joined the game. From the start he played very high indeed, for should his banks prove disastrous and his loses huge it would somehow be a vengeance on Klara for breaking this agreement. That he himself was breaking his solemn word never for a moment crossed his mind. Though Laszlo had had plenty of wine at dinner and had continued to drink steadily all evening, he felt completely sober, stone cold sober. The only effect the wine had had on him was to deepen his resentment until his body seemed aflame with it. Once again, at the card-table, he felt this same strange sixth sense which told him when to say '*Banco!*' and when to pull out. He bet very high and, apparently, wildly, but his winnings piled up in front of him umtil he was surrounded by gleaming little walls of chips.

No one noticed the passing of time.

The Steward came round at one o'clock with the players' signed chits. Some were settled at once in cash, others by the return of winning chips, while the big gamblers, if they were on a losing streak, had their debts added to their running accounts. The game went on undisturbed.

The boards on the landing outside the card-room creaked. Someone was coming up. Laszlo, who was sitting opposite the doorway, looked up: it was Louis Kollonich!

He came straight over to and stood with the onlookers directly in front of Laszlo. He stood there in silence, puffing at the Havana cigar that drooped from his mouth.

What does *he* want here, why has he come, he who was never seen in the gaming-room? Of course, it was obvious! He had come to spy, stalking Laszlo as if he were a rogue deer, sent probably by Aunt Agnes – or could it have been Klara? That idea filled Laszlo with dismay and horror. Could Klara really have gone so far as to involve her parents in the sacred pact between them, using her father to bear witness against him so that she would have cause and justification for abandoning him for Warday? Well, if that was what she wanted, here goes!

The pack reached Laszlo. With both hands he quickly pushed all his chips to the centre of the table, the carefully built piles of iridescent mother-of-pearl spilling in profusion over the baize cloth.

'The bank is twenty thousand!' he said. '*Faites vos jeux!*'

About twelve thousand was put on the table. Laszlo dealt

deliberately, slowly. He looked at his own card with apparent calm: it was a five. '*Je donne!*' he said dryly. His opponent replied: '*Non!*' Laszlo took a card, glanced at it, saw that it was a three, and spread his hand upon the table: eight! Picking up the remaining cards, Laszlo raked in his winnings with the small ivory rake and again uttered the cool, formal phrase: '*Faites vos jeux!*' All this was done with an absolutely straight face, without a flutter of the eyelids, wooden-faced, wooden-voiced, under control, as he had seen Neszti Szent-Gyorgyi do it so often. Since his Uncle Louis was so good as to come to the chemmy game and so descend to spying on him, he might at least be given his money's worth!

Old Louis stood there for only a few minutes, looking quietly at the scene with his tiny pig-like eyes. Then he turned and walked slowly back to the doors. The stairs creaked as he went down. He had gone.

As this was happening Laszlo dealt another *coup*, which he lost. In correct order he paid each winner, for his sense of discipline never wavered, and then leaned back in his chair racked by a pain so terrible and implacable that he almost fainted from dizziness. It's all over now: everything is finished! he said to himself. Suddenly a veil of cobwebs was spun over his eyes so that he could hardly see what was going on in front of him; everything, the table, the players' faces, the room itself, disappeared into a fog of nothingness. For a long time he sat without moving until, when the pack returned to him, he pushed it away mechanically, murmuring: '*Passe le main!*' Then he got up and left the table.

As Laszlo moved towards the door, reeling unsteadily, someone behind him said: 'Gyeroffy's drunk as a lord!' but he himself heard nothing. Somehow he reached the stairs and, clinging for support to the banister rail, slowly managed to get down, carried by his feet alone, for he knew not what he did. At the bottom of the stairs someone helped him into his cloak and hat and from there he walked out into the night like a somnambulist, unconscious of what he was doing or where he was going. For hours he walked the streets aimlessly, walking, walking, walking. He felt like an empty husk ... and inside the shell of his brain and body and spirit there was nothing, no thought, no feeling, no life, no pain.

At dawn he found himself wandering in the Nepliget, the People's Park, with no idea how he came to be there. He was terribly tired, and his thin patent-leather evening shoes were filthy and split. After a while the first tram came rumbling by, its lamps still lit. Laszlo boarded it and went home.

Chapter Five

A WEEK LATER, to mark the end of the season, the Lubianskys gave an evening party in the garden of their villa.

This was carefully planned: firstly, so that no one could say that the Lubianskys did not return hospitality – for they and their family were always invited everywhere – and secondly, because it would not then cost so much in champagne and food as many people would have already left for the country not waiting for the last of the races. Everyone was invited, as they should be, whether known to be still in Budapest or not, but the cost to the host and hostess would be far less than if they had given their party earlier in the season.

Countess Beredy, contrary to her usual custom, arrived early and alone. Tonight she had left her usual court behind; indeed, she had ordered them not to attend, telling them that there was no reason for them to come as it would be too utterly boring. She had to go for manners' sake, but said she wouldn't be staying long, and so all of them, since they knew how to behave and were far too well bred not to take a hint when one was offered them, kept away. Not one of them therefore – not old Szelepcsenyi, nor Devereux, nor d'Orly, and especially not her pet poet Gyorgy Solimar, who hated parties anyway – offered to escort her. Fanny, as she had planned, came by herself.

She had a special reason.

That afternoon a telegram had arrived from Simonvasar from Warday announcing that he had asked Klara to marry him and that she had accepted. Fanny had suggested this to him when, five days before, she had brought their affair to an end.

Fanny had given Warday his marching orders in the kindest and most elegant fashion.

They had been in the young man's bachelor apartment in Dobrentey Street. Fanny had just got dressed and, hat in hand, was almost ready to leave when she turned to Warday. He was smoking a cigarette on the rumpled bed, a silk dressing-gown partly covering his naked body as he lay on the silk cushions enjoying a well-earned rest.

PART FOUR

'Why don't you marry Klara Kollonich?' she asked suddenly, as if it were the most natural thing in the world.

'I? Marry Klara?' said the young man, taken aback.

'Yes, why not? It would be rather a clever move. She's a very good catch, and she likes you. You seem to like her too, so why not?'

'But, darling Fanny, I love you, really I do, and I don't even think of anyone else!'

'Not now, I know, but you didn't think this thing between us would last for ever, did you, my sweet?'

Imre sat up.

'But, darling Fanny...'

She walked over to him and lightly stroked his face until her fingers reached his chin and she gave him a little pinch as one does a child.

'You're very sweet and it's been very good between us, but you see,' and, she added, smiling down at him, 'the rule is to stop eating when you're still hungry. And as for young Klara, the right moment has come.'

Fanny's wide-set eyes, as knowing and wise as a cat's, narrowed until they seemed even longer than usual. She was thinking of the previous day when the always well-informed Devereux had told her that Laszlo's affair with Klara had evidently come to an end, for Laszlo had been going round the town for days with a dark scowl on his face while the Kollonichs had left for the country unexpectedly early.

She did not know any more, but this was enough. If Gyeroffy's love for Klara had met with a definite reverse, then that was the time for her to get rid of Warday. So, after a few moments, she started again: 'If I were you I'd get out my car and drive over to Simonvasar tomorrow. It won't look suspicious as it's only slightly out of your way to Baranya. Arrive about midday and stay to lunch. Then you'll see how the land lies.'

'But, Fanny, I don't know that ... Of course she's a nice girl and I like her all right, but does she like me?'

Fanny shrugged her shoulders and she rarely looked as beautiful as she did at that moment.

'Men are such fools in these matters! Let me tell you. Do it now, *c'est le moment psychologique*,' and she went on in the same vein as she put on her hat, looked at her reflection in the mirror, and pulled on her gloves. Then, standing erect in the middle of the room, she offered him her beautiful mouth with its arched lips:

'Kiss me,' she said, 'and we'll remain good friends!'

Warday did exactly what she had suggested. The afternoon his telegram arrived Fanny realized at once that the Kollonichs would certainly have wired the news to the Lubianskys, as they were neighbours and intimate friends, and also, of course to Countess Szent-Gyorgyi who would be at the Lubianskys party that night with her daughter Magda. With so many people in the know it would soon become general knowledge, and Fanny wanted to be on the spot when Gyeroffy heard the news. Oh, yes, it was essential that she should be there. He was such a strange one, so hot-headed and unpredictable that... well, she certainly must be there.

This was why Fanny Beredy turned up at such an unusual hour at that evening's garden party.

The Lubiansky villa was a substantial modern house in a newly fashionable quarter of Budapest. The front door was reached by mounting a shallow flight of steps which led directly from the street entrance and opened into the large entrance hall. Here Fanny took off her wraps. The hall ran right through the house and was dimly lit, perhaps so as to enhance the effect of the brilliant lanterns in the garden beyond.

As soon as Fanny greeted her host and hostess, they asked if she had heard of the engagement and at once began to discuss the affair in detail with her – not out of maliciousness, however, for Countess Beredy had always been so discreet, and had never shown herself in public with her lovers, that she had never been the victim of general gossip. The fact that Warday had been a regular guest at her Wednesday dinners had passed unnoticed and so had provoked no spiteful rumours. Fanny listened calmly, showing little interest in the news that the others found so engrossing.

'It's so unexpected, my dear; so surprising! No one noticed that he was paying any attention to her! And it isn't as if Klara's doing very well for herself, for her fiancé has only a very modest fortune and doesn't come from a grand family at all. We all thought she'd marry Montorio, or someone like that from Vienna. It must be a love-match, it must be! There's no other reason for Klara – who's so pretty, rich and well born – to throw herself away on such a second-rate and dull young man!'

Fanny listened to these effusions with an air of mild boredom. She carefully refrained from uttering a word in defence of her former lover. Instead she nodded, smiled, agreed with everything that was said, ate ice-cream and fanned herself; but out of the corner of her eye she kept watch on the wide steps down which more and more guests were entering the brilliantly-lit gardens. Time went by and just as Fanny was beginning to worry that Gyeroffy might not be coming, he suddenly appeared at the door.

The moment she saw him she was sure that he had already heard the news. There was a strange light in his wide-set eyes and his mouth was drawn and set as if he were clenching his teeth. With his head held high and standing very straight in his impeccably-cut evening clothes, he walked slowly and somewhat mechanically towards the circle surrounding his hostess and, bowing ceremoniously, kissed the ladies' hands in greeting.

One of the guests immediately said: 'Have you heard about Klara's engagement?'

'Of course! She's my cousin!' replied Gyeroffy, trying hard to make his smile seem spontaneous. 'I got a wire this afternoon.' He then bowed and went to the other end of the terrace where the young people were dancing.

Fanny did not follow, though her eyes never left him. That is good, she thought, let him dance. She would stay where he was, near the buffet, with the older ladies. If Gyeroffy was dancing, no harm could come to him and she would not have to worry until the time came for him to leave. That was when she would have to contrive to be at hand. In the meantime she leaned back in the comfortable garden chair she had chosen, the very picture of a lazy, beautiful society woman, slightly sleepy and apparently giving all her attention to the conversation that was going on around her. No one looking at her half-closed eyes could have guessed how intently she was watching what was happening at the other end of the terrace.

After the uncertainty of waiting for death, the certainly of death itself – that is what Laszlo felt when he that afternoon received Klara's telegram: 'AT NOON TODAY I BECAME ENGAGED TO WARDAY. KLARA.' That was all, and was Klara's only answer to the letter he had sent to Simonvasar four days before. It had been a bad letter, long and rambling, full of awkward, confused attempts at explaining and excusing himself. It was full of such phrases as 'I didn't think it was so serious ... please don't judge me until you know everything ... please think about it ... after all, it isn't such a big thing when everything's considered ...' and full, too, of half-expressed suspicions that Klara had been removed to the country against her will. He used far too many unnecessary words, begging and beseeching her, which, though they might have had their effect if used face to face when she would have been convinced by his sincerity and despair, on paper seemed no more than empty phrases. Had he written simply, just a few words expressing deep humility from the depths of his heart, it might have had some effect. But nothing is more difficult than to write what one does not know how to say; and Laszlo could not even put his feelings into words. To cap it all he made a further mistake. Having no writing paper at home he wrote on National Casino club paper, and the letter heading, itself symbolizing to Klara his gambling and broken promises, screamed up at her before she even began to read.

Laszlo never knew what had really happened; nor did anyone else. On the morning that Papa Louis told his daughter that Laszlo had been gambling before his own eyes – apparently recklessly and for huge sums – Klara begged that they should leave at once for the country. She did this for her own sake so as to have no chance of ever again setting eyes on the man who had so deceived her. Never ever again! She was now prepared to believe him capable of the vilest deception, even of having betrayed her with Countess Beredy – for that story was surely no more than the truth, and no doubt the two of them had discussed her and even laughed about her. No! She never wanted to see him again and decided to raise such a wall between them that a meeting would become impossible.

Laszlo knew none of this, but he sensed most of it, and now the engagement to Warday was the last straw on his load of bitterness and self-reproach. If Klara had married Montorio it would have been bad enough, but at least she would have chosen a famous name and a great fortune, neither of which Laszlo could have provided. But this? Warday? Warday was no better than himself either financially or socially; and so, even if Klara had only accepted him out of anger and disappointment, the fact that the Kollonich clan had approved meant that if he, Laszlo, had not been so stupid and weak, they would in time have accepted him too. He himself, he realized, had been the cause of his own downfall, for he had gambled away his only chance of happiness and, in the midst of all his other reasons for misery, this thought was the most painful.

Now he had nobody, nobody in the entire world. He was completely, utterly alone, and there no longer seemed any reason for living.

PART FOUR

It was a hot night and as the concrete terrace was not the best surface for dancing, it was only one o'clock when most of the young people settled down in chairs or on the grass to listen to the gypsy band who were playing old Hungarian songs and modern sentimental ballads, 'swoon-music' as these were beginning to be called.

Laszlo sat down with the other young people. From where Fanny was placed he was in profile, but she could see him well. He had pushed his chair slightly back from the group with which he was sitting and did not join in their chatter. Occasionally he would raise a hand to beat time with the music as if he were enjoying it, but Fanny noticed that when one of the waiters offered him a tray of large glasses filled with punch he waved the man away and did not drink. When Fanny saw this her heart missed a beat.

She knew, for she had watched him, just how much Laszlo usually drank and she had decided that once she had made him hers she would get him to give it up. There was something sinister and tragic in the fact that he did not now even try to find solace in wine.

It was as if he knew that that night he was faced with an all-important decision and must keep alive his sorrow so as to have enough strength to exercise judgment on himself. Apart from Fanny's deep knowledge of men her love for Laszlo gave her an instinctive, almost telepathic understanding of what was going on in his mind. She knew that this night she must stay with him and watch over him.

Some of the older ladies were already beginning to nod with sleep when a few young couples started to demand a csárdás. During the slight commotion this caused Fanny saw Gyeroffy get up and move, not in the direction of the dancing but towards the house. She realized he was about to leave and that she must somehow get near the door before he did. Slowly, so as not to attract notice, she rose and left the hostess's circle and, as she was closer to the house than Laszlo was, she managed to get into the hall before him. When Laszlo came in from the garden she was already standing in front of a mirror apparently adjusting her stole. When he was close to her she turned and spoke to him: 'Are you leaving, too?'

Laszlo started slightly: he had been too wrapped in his own thoughts to notice her presence.

'Yes, I've had enough.'

'Then would you help me find a carriage? There's a hackney stand just close to the house.'

'Of course!'

Wrapping her head and face in her lace shawl Fanny looked at the young man's reflection in the mirror. He stood quite close but was looking, not at her, but at an arrangement of artificial flowers that stood on the table beneath the mirror. They were well-made and colourful, but old and dusty; for the Lubianskys had thought it hardly worth-while to spend money on renewing them when the hall was always left in semi-darkness.

'Look at these! Look, they might be real. From a distance they look like flowers, but close to you can see what they really are: paper, nothing but torn paper!' and he began to laugh, quietly and bitterly.

Fanny put her hand on his arm and squeezed it sympathetically. 'Come, my dear, let's leave now,' She spoke with almost sisterly compassion.

They left the house and together walked slowly the short distance to Lovolde Square where there was a hackney carriage stand. The pavement was almost in darkness for the thick foliage of the horse-chestnut trees which lined the street cut out most of the light from the street-lamps. This pleased Fanny because it meant that no one would recognize her and when they reached the rank it was she who opened the door of the first carriage, got in and sat down.

'Come on,' she said to Laszlo, who obeyed without uttering a word. When he was seated and had closed the door she leant out of the window and called to the driver: 'Museum Street!'

Laszlo made no sign that he had heard. As the one-horse carriage moved slowly along the dark twisting streets of the Elisabeth district on its way back to the centre of the city, Fanny's hand searched for Laszlo's in the darkness and held it gently as if she shared his suffering. It was the very lightest of contact, a mere touch of the fingertips. She said nothing until much later, when they had almost arrived at Laszlo's lodgings, when she murmured: 'I'll stay with you tonight.'

The night porter opened the door sleepily and together, side by side as if they had been strolling in the Korso, they went up the three flights together.

They entered the apartment without a word. They did not put any lights on for the glow of the street-lighting below was enough for them.

PART FOUR

Laszlo still did not speak. He might have been alone. He sat down on the shabby divan near the wall and buried his face in his hands. Overcome by fatigue, he stayed there without moving for some time, his heart beating so slowly that he felt that at any moment it would stop — and how wonderful it would be if it did!

Laszlo noticed nothing of what was going on around him. Time went by; he had no idea how much, and all at once he felt two cool arms round his neck, a soft woman's body pressed against his hot lips covering his neck with fluttering, comforting kisses. Then silky hands caressed his head and pulled it down to naked velvety shoulders, a mouth searched for his, a tiny tongue inserted itself between his lips, and scented breath perfumed his own breathing. Slowly the purple darkness of desire wiped out the pain, dulling his misery like that legendary potion which makes a man oblivious to everything but love and passion...

At the first light of dawn Fanny awoke to find herself kissing the hand of the young man beside her. Dazed with gratitude she kept her eyes closed, happy to feel that his other hand was gently caressing her relaxed body, moving with delicate care over the skin of her thighs, arms, breasts. After a while she looked up at him. He was half-lying, half-sitting on the bed beside her, the upper part of his body raised against the pillows and his head was held high and turned towards the window. Laszlo was gazing out into the dim grey of early morning, his eyes, filled with despair, were wide open and his mouth was contorted with pain. And though his hand was stroking Fanny's body, his movements were automatic, unconscious. His spirit was not there. It was far, far away ... at Simonvasar.

PART FIVE

Chapter One

Denestornya. Village. County of Torda-Aranyos. Gyeres District. Inhabitants: 1,737: Prot. 1,730; Rom. Cath. 5: Jews 2. Castle and park of Counts Abady. District Post and Telegraph.
　　　　　　　　　– This much is told us by the *County Guide*.

THE CASTLE STOOD on the edge of the Keresztes grasslands which form the principal plateau of central Transylvania. It was sited on a small eminence seventy feet or so above the Aranyos plain, the first of a group of small hills which rise gradually to the south, eventually becoming the low mountain chain which runs from Torda to Kocsard. The original fortress must have been constructed about the time of Bela III, for the lowest vaults, like those of the church nearby, date from the twelfth century. Whoever chose this site chose well. The low rise on which the castle stood was made of smooth-surfaced clay soil enriched with layers of marl. The eastern face was steep, that to the north sloped gently downwards, as did the western side where the village had grown up under the protection of the fortress above it. When the castle was first built it must have been almost inaccessible due to the marshlands created by the flooding of the river below. Over the centuries, however, the flooding had receded, for now the land was covered in a rich layer of fertile soil. The top of the little hill was entirely covered by the castle. The only open approach was from the south but here there had been dug a deep moat which was once protected by palings and outer fortifications, the outline of whose foundations, since covered over, were now visible only when looked down on from the hills behind.

　Over the years the original outer ramparts had all disappeared, leaving only the main building to which had been added, at different times and in different styles, a series of later wings. The long rectangle of the main building was closed at each corner by massive stone towers which presumably had been added as a defence against the first cannon. Where the outer walls had stood, later Abadys, freed from the threat of siege, had planted flowerbeds and lawns.

　The last of the medieval defensive outworks, the tower over

PART FIVE

the gatehouse, had stood as late as the eighteenth century when the father of that Abady who had become Governor of Transylvania, pulled it down because the arch and drawbridge below had not been wide enough to allow his imposing new coach to pass. At first they tried to widen the narrow gateway, but in so doing the structure was weakened, dangerous cracks appeared in its masonry and the whole structure had to be demolished, leaving an empty space where once the great gatehouse had marked the entrance from the moat to the castle's defended outer courts.

Here Count Denes Abady built a horseshoe shaped forecourt, on the right of which he erected stables for thirty-two horses, while on the left there was a covered riding-school. In the apex of the horseshoe curve that joined these two buildings was an imposing gateway to the inner court through which could pass the largest carriages with all the parade of outriders and postillions. Over the doorway gigantic titans of carved stone lifted boulders menacingly as if they were always ready to hurl these down on anyone bold enough to venture that way; while towering above these giants was the figure of Atlas bearing the globe upon his back. On each side of the new great entrance were carriage-houses, tack-rooms, baking ovens to make enough bread for a hundred persons, a laundry furnished with a cauldron large enough to hold the dirty linen of a small town, and apartments for the equerries, footmen, coachmen, porters, grooms and huntsmen. The horseshoe court was built in rococo style between the years from 1748 and 1751, as an inscription over the door arch tells all those who pass below. The parapet, which half-hid the low curving roofs, was decorated on the outer side by large ornamental vases while on the inside, five metres apart, were placed statues of ancient gods and mythological figures, each with their traditional attributes and all writhing and twisting as if in ceaseless movement.

The Count Abady who created all this grandeur and fantasy had clearly been a great builder, for it was he who had also created the great stair with its stone treads, carved marble balustrade and stuccoed ceiling. And it was he who had also replaced the simple conical roofs of the four stone towers with elaborate double cupolas.

When the gatehouse had been removed the two long wings which had formed the side of the original inner court of the medieval castle had been left like legs attached to a seated body. Fifty odd years after the rococo court had been built these two wings were re-faced in the neo-classical style of the Empire period, while, even more recently, Balint Abady's maternal grandfather had added a Gothic Revival veranda to the western side of the medieval walls from which he could enjoy the truly majestic view across the Keresztes grasslands, up to the big cleft above Torda and finally to where, high in the sky, hung the snow-clad peaks of the Carpathian Mountains.

So, with time, the great house grew and was transformed and spread itself with new shapes and new outlines that were swiftly clothed with the patina of years, so that when one looked at it from afar, from the valley of the Aranyos or from the hills even further away, the old castle with its long façades, cupola-capped towers and spreading wings and outbuildings, seemed to have sprung naturally from the promontory on which it stood, to have grown of itself from the clay below, unhelped by the touch of human hand. All around it, on the rising hills behind and in the spreading parkland in front, vast groves of trees, some standing on their own while others spread like great forests, seemed like soft green cushions on which the castle of Denestornya reclined at its ease, as if it had sat there for all eternity and could never have been otherwise.

Balint Abady did not return home until the first days of June. After leaving Budapest he had gone straight to Kolozsvar and remained there to attend to his estate business, even though nearly everyone he knew there had already left the town for the country. After his prolonged absence in the capital there was a great deal that needed Balint's attention.

First of all there was much that had to be discussed with his mother. Then there were consultations with Azbej and with the new forestry manager, with whom he had to make a contract before the man went up to the mountains. The first problem to be settled was where the new manager should be based and, though in all the discussions in Countess Roza's presence Azbej supported Balint's ideas with enthusiasm – and his zeal was not faked because he was determined to keep Balint so embroiled in the management of the mountain forests that he would have no time to investigate matters nearer home – a new complication arose since the old forest superintendent, Nyiresy, adopted a policy of passive resistance and non-cooperation. As a result, matters were so delayed that it was ten days before Balint could send his new manager to the mountains and himself follow his mother to Denestornya, arriving late at night in pouring rain.

PART FIVE

The next day Balint awoke soon after sunrise to find that it was a beautiful morning. The windows of his room in one of the round towers faced east and through the louvred shutters horizontal rays of sunlight filtered through the room's semi-darkness and picked out the gilded bronzes on the commode opposite as might the glow of firelight. Outside a nightingale sang in almost crazed ecstasy.

Balint jumped out of bed and went to the window. With one movement he flung open both shutters and the sunlight was so brilliant that for a moment he stepped back, reeling.

The sun was already high above the farthest hilltops beyond the Maros. These hills looked so ethereal that they might have been formed only of vapour and mist, that same pale cobalt-blue mist that rose from the river valley and spread over the surrounding countryside, softening the outlines of the poplar plantations, and rising until even the lines of the far horizon were blurred and uncertain. The river Maros itself could not be seen; it was too far away and its banks too thickly wooded. In the far distance the silver-grey leaves of the poplars shone with a creamy whiteness in the early morning sun while nearer to the house the Canadian maples, giant trees whose trunks glowed pale lilac, cast long shadows over the cropped grassland of the park and over the newly-mown lawns. These shadows held none of the harsh shade of the forest but were dim, hazy and bluish in colour, hardly darker than the grass beneath.

Balint stood at the window watching the light spreading slowly between the groves of trees, lighting up the paler leaves of a shrub, catching the white glow of a may-tree's blossom which was like the lace of a girl's summer dress, bringing colour to the lilac flowers, and delving eagerly and inexorably to uncover the secrets of the forest undergrowth. As the sunlight grew stronger so the carmine of the Japanese cherry-trees flamed into glowing colour until it was as if the whole of nature blushed with joy and love, quivering with delight at the sweet secrets of spring. It was there in the song of the nightingales and the antiphonal chorus of all the other song-birds who called triumphantly from the clumps of jasmine, from the ivy-coloured walls, from the pastel fronds of the little groups of trimmed thuja and, above all, from the great horse-chestnut trees whose branches were now richly covered with white and pink flowers.

Balint dressed quickly and went out, stopping for a moment on the north terrace to take a new look at the parkland in front of him before starting down the hill to follow the avenue of tall Hungarian oaks whose stately branches were almost as dense as those of cypresses. On both sides the grass was filled with crowsfoot and dotted with the golden stars of buttercups. All the way down the slope from the castle's corner tower to the avenue below there were thickets of lilac bushes, now so heavy with scented flower panicles that hardly any leaves were to be seen. And everywhere the nightingales were singing, only falling silent for a moment as Balint passed the bushes in which they were concealed and then starting up again as if unable to contain their joy.

The young man reached the bank of the millstream near where the outer wooden palisades had once stood. He crossed over what was still called the Painted Bridge, even though every vestige of colour had long since disappeared, to the place where the wide path divided and led either to the left or the right, while ahead the view stretched across the park interrupted only by the clumps of poplars, limes or horse-chestnuts. In this part of the park the grass was quite tall, thick and heavy with dew. It was filled with the feathery white heads of seeding dandelions, with golden cowslips, bluebells, waving stalks of wild oats and the trembling sprays of meadow-grass, each bearing at its extremity a dew drop that sparkled in the sun. So heavy was the dew that the grasslands, as far as the eye could see, were covered with a delicate shining liquid haze.

For Balint this pageant of wild flowers was something new since, during his long years at school, at the university and later when he was always abroad serving as a diplomat, he had never managed to get home before the end of June and so had never before seen the ancient park in all the bloom of early summer. The radiance of this early morning, when spring was just merging into summer, was so inviting that Balint left the path and started to walk across the meadow. The grass was high and so wet that it was almost like walking through a stream, and each time that his knees touched the spears of grass and wild oats a tiny shower would fall before the blades straightened up as if proud that they had been brushed by the legs of the master.

After a while Balint, soaked to the knees, reached the avenue of lime trees which bordered the far side of the meadow and was immediately filled with memories of his childhood. This was where he had been taught to ride when very young, in the old avenue that had been planted so long ago. It was almost two hundred years since the Abady of those times had laid out three wide *allées* which fanned out, star-shaped, from where the predecessor of the Painted Bridge crossed the millstream a little higher up than the later bridge and thus directly in front of the castle façade. At the beginning of the nineteenth century, when the fashion for informal 'English' gardens was spreading all over Europe, Balint's grandfather had had the central avenue cut down so as to plant the lawns directly below where the castle stood. He wanted to have the view from the terrace as open and informal as possible, with a wide view to the distant plantations; for it was well understood that in English landscaping all straight lines were forbidden. Even so, the avenue that remained was still between five and six hundred metres long and, as the earth between the lines of trees was a soft loam, it was there that the Groom of the Stables, as the castle's head *écuyer* was called, would put the boy on his tiny pony and gallop him up and down, ten, twenty, thirty times until he no longer fell off.

Lord, how many times I fell! thought Balint as he gazed once more along the familiar grass-covered *allée* and remembered those frisky mischievous little ponies with minds of their own who were all the more wilful for being overfed and under-exercised. He recalled Croque-en-bouche, his first pony, who always shied at that gnarled old tree in front of him and then bucked, especially when Balint was being made to ride without stirrups and with just a blanket strapped on in the place of a saddle. And, at that huge lime-tree with the split trunk, his second pony had always stopped in her tracks and refused to budge until given a sharp reminder by his instructor's long-lashed hunting crop.

Balint wandered slowly down the centre of the *allée* where the branches of the old trees had long since met to form a leafy vault. Over his head the foliage murmured as a light breeze touched the tops of the trees, though down below nothing moved and Balint was left undisturbed with his memories of childhood. How long the avenue had then seemed, especially when he had been given his first horse, a reliable old stallion called Gambia and had been allowed to canter the whole length on his own, free at last of the *écuyer* and the leading rein!

Today it was only a few moments before he reached the end of the planted line of trees where flowed a branch of the Aranyos river which had artificially been diverted below the mill-reach many years before. He went on until he found himself opposite a sizeable island called the Big Wood – Nagyberek – which had always held a special mystery and attraction for him, as it was a wild and untamed and exciting place quite different from the trim lawns, weeded paths and carefully pruned flowering hedges of the gardens that clustered round the castle terrace. Here he would wander for hours fancying himself an explorer in an undiscovered wilderness and here he would play at Cowboys and Indians all by himself – he, of course, was always an Indian – crawling invisibly on hands and knees in the waist-high hemlock, spying on bands of marauding braves or fleeing from his pursuers. Here he would climb a branch to ambush his chief enemy or shoot arrows at the hated paleface; just as he had read in the pages of James Fenimore Cooper.

Just to walk once again in this once so familiar spot brought all these old memories crowding back.

Crossing the great meadow, Balint went to find the thickets on the other side which bordered the meandering twists and turns of the river's main stream and here and there grew in the swamps and bogs created each time the river flooded and over-flowed its banks.

The hundred-acre hay meadow was the farthest one could see from the castle terrace before the dense plantations of trees closed the open vista with a mass of impenetrable growth. These were mostly of black pine, planted some thirty years before by Balint's father not, however, as standing timber to be felled later, but rather as decoration and cover for the deer. At their roots more lilac bushes had been placed and these too were now in full bloom beneath the rose-coloured trunks of the pines and the deep green, almost black sheen of the clusters of pine needles above. The pines too, seemed to be in bloom, for the tips of all their branches were covered with tiny dark-red embryonic cones, though these could only be distinguished from close at hand.

So magical and mysterious, so still and yet so full of resurgent life, did the meadow seem that Balint stopped for a moment to contemplate its mystery, and wonder at the fact that even the distances did not seem real and stable and fixed. The park seemed to have no end but to continue for ever into the distance as if it comprised the whole world and the whole world was the park of Denestornya and nothing else. As Balint stood there, motionless, rapt in a new sense of delight and exaltation, seven fallow deer appeared slowly from a group of pines. They were wading knee-high through the morning haze, two does with their fawns and three young females, and if they saw Balint they did not take any notice of him but just walked quietly and sedately on until, after a few moments, they disappeared again into the shadow of the trees. Their sudden appearance in the distance in front of him, and just as sudden disappearance a moment or two later contributed strongly to Balint's sense of wonder and enchantment.

He pulled himself together and went on. And, suddenly, it seemed Adrienne were walking at his side.

He could almost see her, striding with long steps next to him, her head held high over her thin girlish neck and her dark hair fluttering around her face in a mass of unruly curls, just as he had seen her that time at Mezo-Varjas when together they had chased a runaway farmhorse. The image was so clear: Adrienne, walking beside him, holding herself very straight with her wide-open, topaz-coloured eyes looking unwaveringly ahead of her as she walked, silently and forever at his side...

Balint stopped abruptly, shaking his head to rid himself of her image and mentally shouting No! No!, as if the words, even unspoken, could dispel her ghostly presence. Then, quickening his pace, he hurried towards the trees remembering that somewhere thereabouts was an ancient poplar, one of the most venerable of all the trees in the park, and that it stood on the edge of a small clearing. In a few moments he had found it. This king among trees was still alive; though one of its great side branches had fallen, presumably blown down in some April storm. Even so, the fallen branch was covered in sticky buds about to burst into leaf.

Balint went up to the tree, touched its bark as if saluting an old acquaintance. 'So, my friend, you are still all right – even if they have roughed you up a bit!' said Balint out loud as he sat down on the broken stump and looked around the little clearing.

This was where he had come when he had been allowed to ride beyond the limits of the lime *allée*. It was here that he would play at camping in the wild, dismounting and hitching the reins to the stub of a branch. Properly tethered, no rustler could steal his faithful steed. He would have liked to loosen the girth as well, for he knew that this was one of the first rules when resting during a trek, but at that time he hadn't had the strength to do it by himself.

Balint sat there for a long time. All around him was infinite peace, and, strangely, for the air was alive with the song of birds, a feeling of infinite silence, the more tangible for the melodies that filled his ears. There seemed to be hundreds of different calls, of which he could distinguish only the *si-si-si* of the blackbirds, the chirping of the blue tits as they fluttered from branch to branch around him, the harsher notes of the golden orioles as they swooped low over the clearing with their distinctive swaying flight, the twittering of the sparrows that massed in the reed thickets by the river edge, and, through it all, the varied cries of shrikes as they perched on the trees' branches watching for the insects or small lizards that would be their next meal. In the distance he could still hear the calls of the nightingales from the trees and shrubs nearer the castle, and all these sounds, so varied and yet so harmonious, somehow underlined and heightened the general sense of untouched virginal silence.

The trees had too many leaves, the thickets too many weeds; there were too many flowers in the grass and, as if nature could not contain its own richness, the air was filled with ethereal wisps of white fluff carrying the seeds from the almost invisible flowers of the poplar trees. High in the branches of the great poplar above Balint's head a pair of wild doves started to coo and, to the young man below, the sound was the purest expression of love and happiness.

How wonderful it all is! How lovely! thought Balint as he surrendered himself totally to enjoying the richness and splendour around him. It was a pity no one else was there to see it, no one with whom he could share his own sense of euphoria. At once Adrienne's face floated before him, saying: 'What about me? I'm here! I'd understand!'

Balint got up, annoyed with himself, irritated that even here he was pursued by an obsession from which he had tried so hard to free himself. 'I don't want this!' he muttered as he got up and entered the thicket, leaving the clearing that had conjured up the memory of Adrienne.

Why was he doing this to himself, Balint wondered, why was he for ever thinking of a woman who, after all, was still only half awakened and so complex? It was madness. He had far better things to do, his work and his mission to aid others. One day he would get married – of course, he would have to – and then he'd found a home and a family and carry on his work tranquilly and in peace. Why stir up a tempest when there was no need, no reason? Why?

Balint had been walking so swiftly along the narrow path that, angry as he was, he had noticed nothing of where he was going and what was all around him. Here it was almost completely dark, for overhead the branches of the trees were so thick that not a ray of sunshine penetrated beneath. The willow-shoots were four or five times the height of a man and were tightly intertwined with the thick-leaved elders and other forest shrubs and, as if that were not enough, the branches were hung with creepers of many different kinds, while valerian and hemlock, angelica and a host of other plants rose from the forest floor to mingle with the lichen-covered branches of the trees. Hidden in all this riot of vegetation were thorns that scratched, burrs that attached themselves to whatever brushed against them, wild hops that festooned shrub and tree alike tying fantastic cat's cradles of creeping tendrils. Everywhere there were flowers, some tiny and budlike, as yet unopened, others, like the convolvulus, huge but insubstantial, hanging from above like motionless butterflies floating freely in the air. Across the path spread treacherous bramble shoots covered with thorns but carrying also the latent promise of a summer harvest.

In many places the vegetation was so thick that Balint could pass only with difficulty even though he tried to follow the old path. Away from the track it would have been impossible. The main stream of the river was close at hand and a dim light was just visible through the dense foliage.

Soon he came to a boggy patch thickly grown with weeds and canes. At every step the ground squelched under his feet. He still could not see the river which was hidden by the high wall of last year's growth of rushes. Just when he felt he would never arrive at his goal he found himself on the river bank walking over a strand of pebbles that had washed up on the inner curve of the river while, on the other side, the water's flow had cut a vertical line in the soft earth. An old tree-trunk lay half-buried in the stones.

Balint stopped beside it. Surely the shallow ford he had so often used in the past must be somewhere hereabouts. It was this way that he had ridden when taking the short-cut to Maros-Szilvas to visit Dinora. He knew the way well, having so often done it on the darkest of moonless nights. Perhaps that would be the answer ... to visit little Dinora and start again with her. After all she had invited him! In Budapest he had not been so tormented by memories of Adrienne: There the thought of her had sometimes come to him, but not so insistently, so intrusively, as here in Transylvania. Dinora was so sweet and no one knew better than he how soft her skin was, how tantalizing her scent and with her he would never feel that sense of revulsion which so often came to him when making love to girls in the capital. Little Dinora.

He thought of Nitwit. Well, he didn't matter; and anyway Dinora had said that it was now over and, even if it that were not true, he still wouldn't matter, for Dinora had never been exactly exclusive.

Balint turned in the direction of home. It was already past eight o'clock and he would have to hurry if he wanted to be back in time to have breakfast with his mother. He had wandered a long way from the house.

Thinking now more calmly and more prosaically, Balint again went over what he had just decided, and again he thought how sensible it would be to take up once again with Dinora; sensible, and clever. Then that inner critic who never slumbered for long but who was always alert to danger, spoke up saying: And don't go to Almasko lest you start again with Addy! It was no use. His other self, reckless and contrary, at once found a hypocritical answer: But I promised Pal Uzdy to go. It doesn't matter about Adrienne, but her husband would find it strangely discourteous if I didn't! Anyhow there would be no chance to be alone with her, what with the husband and mother-in-law always about.

And so Balint struggled with his conscience, a battle between desire and common sense; but he reached no conclusion for just then he met the stud-groom and two lads coming back from the gallops in the eastern part of the estate. They had been exercising their three mounts and were now headed back towards the avenue of lime-trees and the stables. Balint beckoned them over to him.

'The old ford in the copse? Is it still passable?'

The stud-groom dismounted. 'It was washed away by last year's flooding, your Lordship, but we'll find another if your Lordship wishes it.'

'Indeed? Washed away, was it? Well, it isn't urgent, but you might as well put it in hand when you have time. Yes, do it when you can!'

Balint stroked the glossy neck of the stud-groom's horse and they walked back together. On their way they passed the road that led to the paddock where the brood mares were kept. Balint longed to see them followed by their new foals, but did not turn that way as he knew how upset his mother would be if he had not waited until she could show them to him herself. Her stud farms were Roza Abady's greatest joy, and it was with love and pride that she would show off her beautiful horses and explain her breeding strategy. Balint knew that this would be one of the first things his mother would want to do now that he had come home; and so he hurried back through the avenue of tall pyramid-shaped oaks to reach his room and change quickly so as not to arrive in his mother's presence all wet and muddy from his early walk.

Washing and changing his sodden clothes took longer than he had expected and by the time he had got ready and gone upstairs to his mother's sitting-room he found her already seated at the breakfast table in the window.

Countess Roza was always served an ample Transylvanian breakfast. On the table were cold meats, smoked bacon, scones, sweet buns and other cakes, butter, honey in jars and honey in combs, whatever fruit was in season and, of course, coffee with buffalo milk. Though she tasted everything she ate only the strawberries and drank copious cups of coffee. Despite this it was a rule of the house that everything should be done in the way that it always had been and so Mrs Baczo saw to it that every day there was enough on the table to feed at least ten people.

After greeting his mother and kissing her hand, Balint sat down to eat. His long walk he was as hungry as a wolf and the sight of her son making a hearty breakfast rejoiced Countess Roza's heart. From time to time she dipped a strawberry in the sugar on her plate, but it was only much later that she put it in her mouth.

This morning Countess Roza's slightly protuberant grey eyes held a roguish gleam. Every day of her life, the countess's first act before breakfast, was to go down to the stables when the horses came back from their early work-out. She would inspect each one carefully, examine its tendons, order treatment if she felt it were necessary and cross-question the stud-groom and the lads on the morning's exercise. In their turn, to interest and amuse their beloved employer, they would recount what they had seen while out on the gallops, what deer, hares or gamebirds had come their way. This morning they had reported the interesting fact that they had met Count Abady at the Painted Bridge and that his Lordship had enquired if the ford over the Aranyos was still passable.

Countess Roza guessed at once what this meant, for she knew that when her son was still at the university he had always used the ford when going to visit Dinora. She knew that he used to go at night, steeling out furtively in the vain hope that these visits were a secret shared only by the two lovers themselves. She had never said a word on the subject to her son, but, privately, she had rejoiced. Since the death of Count Tamas, her own life had been arid and joyless and so it was a special pleasure to her to know that her son had become a man.

The knowledge did nothing to change Countess Abady's deep-rooted conviction that women were divided into two classes: there were decent women such as herself who never looked at any man except their husbands; and then there were ... others. These she always referred to as 'Those'; and among 'Those' Countess Roza placed all women regardless of class, background, or degree of licentiousness, who were not as chaste as herself. Quite indiscriminately she would include not only ladies who gave way from time to time to a mild flirtatiousness of manner, but also those who loved to tease men without satisfying them, women who fell deeply in love with men to whom they were not married and remained faithful to them; women who were fickle and promiscuous and often changed their lovers; famous courtesans who were kept by a great nobleman, and streetwalkers who plied their trade in the unlit alleys of the slums. To Countess Roza, whose whole life had been spent protected and infinitely remote from reality, all such persons fell equally into the category of 'Those'. Not that this bleak and uncomprehending judgement affected her manners or behaviour. She never allowed her opinion of such matters to affect in any way her comportment to those ladies whose way of life was anathema to her. She was never critical, cold or impolite. She said nothing to show her disapproval; and if they were in the same rank of society they would be received in her house and they would not be gossiped about behind their backs. For the countess it was a fact of life that some women were made born like that and so couldn't help being what they were. They were not guilty or criminal, they were just, well, different; and, as such, she accepted their existence uncritically, with good humour, if without understanding. And what she heard she kept to herself, acting always as if she knew nothing of such matters.

When Balint had first taken up with Dinora, Roza's attitude underwent a subtle change and, when such things were discussed, to her previous amused but unconcerned smile was added another expression, one of pride. She took joy and a certain consolation in the knowledge of her son's conquests. It was in some mysterious way a compensation for the loss of her own sex-life, non-existent since the death of her adored husband. It was as if her son were now vicariously taking revenge on life for her; and as if, in him, metamorphosed into the shape of a young man, she had at last been reborn. And since, for Countess Roza, all such women belonged to a quite separate race of beings, she worried no more about her son being involved with such a person than she would have been had he taken up racing or played in international polo matches; in a way it was for her just another form of sport, and so completely harmless.

Dinora had been the first but, naturally, during his years as a diplomat, there had been others. When Balint came home on leave to Denestornya, letters had come, written in women's flowing hands, firstly from Vienna and later from abroad. Countess Roza always knew when such letters were delivered, for the morning's mail was first brought to her, and great was her pleasure when, just occasionally, she managed to catch a glimpse of the addresses on Balint's outgoing letters. Alas, it did not happen often!

Countess Roza did not admit even to herself that she yearned for this information or that when, apparently quite casually, she would say to the footman: 'If Count Balint has some letters for the post, I'll have some too,' it was only a ruse to find out to whom he was writing. Usually, however, the man came to ask for her letters first or else the whole manoeuvre would be for nothing, for on that day Balint had written only business letters or to some male friend. On the few occasions when she managed to find out a name, however, she would do all she could to turn the conversation so that that name should appear to come up naturally, and then she could ask in the ordinary course of conversation for details of the lady's age, looks, situation in life – all very discreetly, of course.

When she felt that she had enough to go on she would try to fit it all together, just as if she were making a mosaic or tackling a jigsaw puzzle, until, in her own mind, all the pieces were in their right places. Then she would store away the information with secret glee as if she were making a catalogue of Balint's successes. She was innocently convinced that no one, especially not Balint, had noticed her preoccupation and her stratagems. As far as Balint was concerned she was right. It had never occurred to him that such information was important to her, or indeed that it was any of her business. The housekeepers Baczo and Tothy, on the other hand, were by no means deceived, for in front of them

Countess Roza never minced her words or tried to hide her thoughts. Though the countess had never asked a direct question on such matters, they knew how much she loved all information of that sort. They sat with her daily, watched her closely, and knew better than anyone what sort of news their mistress craved.

Since the beginning of the Carnival season they had become aware that Balint had taken to visiting Adrienne, that he went there every afternoon and often stayed a long time, even well into the evening, that the lamps were not lit in Adrienne's sitting-room until late (that is when Balint was there), and that they often sat alone in the dark. All this information they gleaned in various ways through the upper-servant network. Since Adrienne's maid was faithful to her and did not gossip about her mistress, they had managed to insinuate themselves into the confidence of Count Uzdy's cook by means of offering recipes for preserves or sharing secrets about the ingredients of the famous Denestornya pies.

What they heard in this way they would let drop, piecemeal, as they sat drinking coffee with Countess Roza after dinner. Having once or twice mentioned Count Balint's visits to Countess Uzdy they never again spoke his name but concentrated only on telling tales about Adrienne. Dissembling their malice they would tell only of the 'shocking' things they had heard about Countess Uzdy: how she would go skating in the evening but never at midday as respectable ladies did; how she would never dance a respectable csárdás, liked to go for walks in the cemetery and, when she was at home – oh, horror! – she would sit on the floor like a gypsy, yes, really, like a gypsy, a nomad gypsy. Oh dear, whatever next? It was of such things that they would talk, lamenting with gusto these depraved habits. And they took care never to involve Countess Roza in their discussions but merely gossiped in front of her, shaking their heads at each other in sad disapproval and, when they really wanted to underline a point that seemed especially depraved, they would take their knitting needles and stab their skeins of wool for all the world as if they were doing a wicked woman to death.

The picture of Adrienne that Countess Roza received in this way was most disquieting. She seemed to be amongst the most vicious and dissolute of 'Those' in Kolozsvar, indeed in the whole province; and for this reason Balint's attachment to her became a constant source of worry and distress. The instinct of a mother had already told her that of all Balint's affairs this was likely to become the most serious, which is why she had been so pleased to hear that Balint wanted the ford leading to Maros-Szilvas to be repaired. This could only mean that he was once again thinking of Dinora and, if that were so, she would no longer have to worry about Adrienne.

Balint ate his breakfast with zest. He was obviously in a good humour, and his mother sat in pleased silence looking at him fondly. Then she said: 'I'm glad you've such a hearty appetite. It's good to see you make a good breakfast!'

'Uhmmm...' Balint could not reply properly because he had just taken a large mouthful of bread and butter and honey. So it was not until he had managed to get it down that he was able to say: 'I've been for a long walk!' And he took another bite.

'Really?' said his mother, still pretending to know nothing. 'Already? Where did you go so early? When did you start?'

'At dawn. I went as far as the Aranyos. I had only thought of going to the avenue but everything was so beautiful that I just went on until I reached the river.'

'Where? At Fox Meadow, or where we find the mushrooms?'

'Neither. First I went to visit the old poplar in the clearing, and from there I went on to the old ford.'

'They tell me it's been washed away in the spring floods. Such a pity, it used to be rather convenient if I had to send Azbej or somebody to Lelbanya,' said Countess Roza. 'You know, it's much shorter than going all the way by the Hadrev bridge. For you, too, if you want to visit your constituency in summer – not by carriage, of course, but on horseback.' she added shrewdly.

'Of course. I suppose it wouldn't be more than twenty or twenty-five kilometres that way,' Balint agreed. But he didn't mention Maros-Szilvas as his mother had hoped he would.

Countess Roza tried another tack.

'I've had three new horses brought on for you,' she said. 'Don't worry, they've been well trained so you can go where you like with them. One of them is Fenyes, who you may remember from last year. The other two are Borostyan and Perdits. You won't know them as they only came into training a few months ago, but they've all been well schooled and are ready for you.'

'That's wonderful! I'll try them out tomorrow.'

'All three could do with rather more work than the usual morning exercise. A few long rides in the country – they need muscling.' She started to explain what sort of training she had in mind and what would be the effect of slow work at a walk and a trot and what would be gained by a sustained canter over measured distances, and how these two types of training should be employed alternatively. This was a subject she always liked to discuss, and today it gave her a double pleasure, firstly because she really knew what she was talking about, and secondly because she felt that if she went into such detail her son would not notice what she was in fact urging him to do.

She was still discussing her ideas about the breeding and schooling of horses when they walked together to the paddocks which were now bathed in warm resplendent sunshine.

Chapter Two

A FEW DAYS WENT BY, quiet days during which Balint would go out riding at dawn, breakfast with his mother before accompanying her on her morning walk, take a short nap before lunch, sit with her chatting after the midday meal and, later, either go to look at distant parts of the Denestornya park and estate, or drive to visit the stud farm's summer pastures or inspect the cattle sheds. Countess Roza wanted to discuss her ideas for improving the gardens: flower beds here, shrubs or red-flowering chestnuts there, perhaps something yellow just there against that dark green and, if the gardeners could have enough of them ready in the spring, there were those new canna lilies. They were all little things they talked about but, small though they were, they were important to her; and so Balint listened, gave his ideas, and gradually became more interested himself. Yet, though these days were quiet and devoted to such simple matters as where to plant next year's annuals, Balint was not at peace with himself.

His caution and his desire for Adrienne continued to wage a civil war inside him; and for the moment it was the caution which had the upper hand. No! He would not go to Almasko. Yes! He would go to Maros-Szilvas; he would spend the night there and go on to Lelbanya and, on the way back, he would again stop at Dinora's place. On the outward journey they would come to an understanding; and on his return they would consummate it! It was all so simple. The matter was settled and that would bring an end to this endless agitation.

When he told his mother of his plans – though not everything

PART FIVE

they involved — she was overjoyed and agreed to all his suggestions, especially that he should take her dear horses with him to Lelbanya. The only stipulation she made was that they were not be stalled at some dirty inn, but rather that Balint should put them up at some friend's stables, or even his cowsheds, which were sure to be clean and free of infection.

After an ample mid-morning snack he rode off with one of the stable-lads in attendance. He went over the bridge, across the Big Wood, crossed the river by the newly repaired ford, rode slowly across the great meadow on the other side of the Aranyos which was part of the Denestornya estate and which was so often flooded in spring, and along the acacia avenue towards the railway embankment. The going was good, for the ground had dried out, but it was still soft and elastic and had not yet hardened as it would in the course of the summer.

From the Aranyos they cantered gently across the fields until they reached the railroad. Riding on the sandy verge of the main road, they reached Maros-Szilvas in just over an hour.

A few hundred yards across cornfields still brightly green with the unripe harvest Balint could see the hedge that marked the limits of the Abonyi gardens. There on the right at the corner of the field was the old lime tree to which Balint had so often tethered his horse when he rode over stealthily in the late evenings. From there he had crept through the garden to find the way to Dinora's bedroom window, that window which had been unusually high off the ground that he had had to leap up, catch hold of the sill, and pull himself up against the limewashed wall of the building. Only then was it possible to crawl through the window and each time, he remembered with a smile, his clothes had been smeared with white powder. Despite the intensity of his young love, the memory today evoked only a faint smile of self-mockery.

The closer he found himself to their house the less he felt like visiting the Abonyis. It was far too early, he told himself. They had made good time and the horses were still so fresh — why, it was barely past midday! It would be far better to press on. If they stopped now there would be lunch, and then coffee, and then they'd ask him to stay on and chat and it would be dark before he got to Lelbanya, too late to accomplish anything of what he was going there for! Then he would have to find stabling for the horses and make sure of good fodder and clean bedding, and all this would take time. Far better do the journey in one go and, later, on the way home perhaps, well, then he could stay as long as he liked.

Spurring his horse to a trot he reached the village in a few moments. On the left were the peasants' houses and on the right the long high wall that surrounded the Abonyi manor-house. On the top, just where the wall took such a bend there was a vine-covered summer-house. How many times he had sat there with Dinora, covering her face with his kisses!

He was not sure, but looking up it seemed as if maybe there was the white gleam of a woman's dress to be seen through the arbour's thick veil of foliage. Perhaps Dinora was sitting there now? Quickening the pace of his horse Balint trotted swiftly through the village, looking neither to right nor left and hoping that he had not been spotted. He slowed down only when the village had been left far behind.

After passing through Maros-Ludas they had to climb a long steep ridge, from the summit of which several small paths led down to the little mining town. When travelling on the high plateau one always went along the tops of the ridges, whether on foot or on horseback, for the winding valley roads took much longer. Half way up Balint and the groom dismounted and led their horses by hand.

As they moved slowly up the hill a man came towards them from one of the paths from the ridge. He was on foot and his short spare figure could be seen from afar silhouetted against the sky. He was dressed in town clothes and he too walked slowly, but as if tired from having come a long way.

When Balint arrived at the top of the ridge he paused for a moment to admire the view, which to him was poignantly beautiful. Down below could be seen the meandering course of the Maros river. From where Balint stood it was as clear as if drawn on a map. Across the valley the rolling hillsides were covered with forest trees while on this side of the river the bare cliffs of yellow clay were cleft by innumerable steep ravines washed out by rain and wind.

The foot-traveller reached the main road just as Balint was about to remount his horse. 'Hey! Hey! Stop!' he called to Abady, who already had one foot in the stirrup. Balint turned round in surprise.

'Don't you recognize me?' cried the stranger. 'Andras Jopal! But perhaps you don't want to know me anymore?'

It was not easy to recognize the former tutor to the Laczok boys in this travel-worn stranger. Jopal, formerly so spruce and

PART FIVE

dapper, was unshaven, with several days' growth of beard on his face. His clothes were torn and filthy, the soles of his boots were flapping against the uppers and his bare toes could be seen through the slits on both sides. But his face was so unusual, with its wide cheekbones, square jaw and the staring eyes of a fanatic, that Balint would have recognized him without any introduction. His first impulse was to shake hands with the man, but then he remembered the insults which had been shouted after him when he had left old Minya's house the previous September, which had been all the thanks he had received for his well-intentioned offer to aid Jopal to develop his ideas for a flying machine.

Rather coldly he said: 'What can I do for you?'

'I was on my way to find you at Denestornya. I'm in luck to run across you here.'

'To find me?' asked Balint, astonished.

'Yes, indeed. I owe you something, and I wished to repay my debts, as I have all the others, all of them!'

'What debt? You don't owe me anything.'

'Indeed I do! I offended your Lordship, stupidly. I only realized it afterwards and I wouldn't like you to remember me only by that. What I owe you is an apology. So now I must ask your Lordship's forgiveness.'

'With all my heart, please say nothing more about it!' said Balint and offered Jopal his hand. To prove that he bore the man no grudge he called to his groom to bring him food from the saddle-bags.

'Take something too,' he said to the lad, and to Jopal: 'Let's go and sit down over there.' They sat down together on the grassy slope that bordered the road.

'Won't you join me!' said Abady, unwrapping the parcel of bacon, bread and salami.

'With pleasure. Thank you!' said Jopal, and for a few moments they ate in silence.

'How is your great-uncle, old Gal?'

'Poor man, he died three weeks ago.'

'I'm sorry. If I'd known I'd have come to the funeral. That'll be a great loss for you, surely?' said Balint, looking sadly at Jopal's torn clothes and ruined shoes.

'That's of no account. It doesn't matter anymore. I'm finished anyway!' Abady looked at him enquiringly, trying to fathom what the man meant. With a sudden burst of anger, Jopal went on: 'Didn't you hear? It's all so meaningless! This April, Santos-

Dumont flew in Paris, from the lawns of the Château de Bagatelle. And he did it with my machine, with my machine, I tell you; with my machine exactly. It was the same, or almost the same. So my work's finished. It's the end of everything I've ever worked for. I built my life on it. And could have done it, if I'd had the money for the proper equipment. I was ready in the autumn; I could have flown then, before everyone else, but I didn't have the money! If I had, then all the glory and fame and wealth would have been mine, mine! Everything for which Santos and the Wright Brothers are now suing each other! Mine!'

Balint suddenly remembered having seen a copy of the French review *L'Illustration* with photographs of Santos-Dumont when he succeeded in taking up his machine for two or three hundred yards a few feet from the ground. So the problem of flying had at last been solved. He was sorry now that he had forgotten the Transylvanian inventor and the theories he had expounded in the yard of old Minya Gal's house. He felt deeply sorry for the man beside him.

'If only I hadn't been so pig-headed and stupid! If I'd accepted your offer...' Jopal's face was contorted with misery. His lips curved back from his prominent teeth and his eyes narrowed with pain. For a moment he seemed close to tears, but then he straightened up and said: 'If my uncle had died a few months ago and I'd had his little legacy in the autumn, perhaps I could have done it!' He tightened his hand into a fist and banged it down on his knee: 'But what for, I ask you, what for?' Then he laughed bitterly and went on: 'So what did I do? I paid my debts, all of them, every penny that I'd begged and borrowed for my invention. I paid them all back. Only your Lordship remained and now I've done that too and so I can be on my way!'

He laughed again, folded his knife and replaced it in his pocket, and got up.

Balint remained where he was.

'Don't go,' he said. 'With your abilities you shouldn't despair. I'm sure there are other problems to be solved with which you could prove yourself. There's so much to be done.'

Jopal struck the air with his closed fist. 'I don't want anything to do with it!' he said. 'Goodbye!' and, turning swiftly on his heel, he went off down the hill. When he had gone about twenty paces he turned back and called: 'The violin! My uncle left it to your Lordship. You can collect it from the house. It's there with the girl Julis. She'll give it to you!'

PART FIVE

Then he hurried away and soon left the road and took a little goat-path which seemed to lead down towards the river Maros. In a few moments he had disappeared below the cliffs.

Balint and his groom were soon mounted and on their way. After a while they found themselves on a soft grassy lane which led them, still on a high ridge, deeper into the rolling grassland country where it was rare for any small hills to rise above the general level of the prairie. All around them was a sea of rolling grassland whose faint ridges were like the swell of a petrified ocean on the crest of which they were no more than tiny Lilliputian figures. The air was dry and clean. In the far distance to the north could be seen, like a distant shore across the ocean, cloud-grey in colour, the peaks of the snow-covered Besztercey mountains. There, slightly to the left were the Cibles, three peaks shining white and sparkling from the fresh snow with which they had been covered since the last rains.

At last Lelbanya could be seen a little way off, and now they had to leave the track and make their way down from the grassland prairie to where, in a cleft in the hills, stood the little town on its salt-flaked bank of clay and, beside it, the dark lake, now almost covered by the reeds and canes from which the townsfolk earned their living. Though invisible from where Balint was riding, the surface of the lake was dotted with wild duck and moorhens whose broods were brought up in safety in the cover of the reeds.

At Lelbanya, following his mother's instructions, Balint stabled his horses in the innkeeper's own cowshed.

When he had done this he visited the Co-operative Society, which was still housed in the town-hall, inspected the books, conferred with the bookkeeper who was a retired employee of the railways and an excellent man, Tobias Batta by name, and walked with him and the notary up to the Abady house. This had been repaired by Azbej, who was doing his utmost to keep in with Count Balint and who, by tact and persuasion, had obtained possession of two rooms which were to house the Co-operative.

In the evening Balint dined alone in the inn and afterwards received the leading citizens of the town who, hearing of his arrival had called to pay their respects and to take a glass of wine with him.

There was quite a gathering: the mayor, the notary, the physician, the chemist, the two priests and everyone else of any importance. Even the old knight, Balazs Borcse, condescended to put in an appearance. This was remarkable, indeed almost unheard-of since Borcse was so proud of being a Borcse of Lesser- and Greater-Borcsey, that he felt it beneath him to mingle with such lowly-born persons as made up the society of Lelbanya. When one bore such a name, he had been heard to say, one could not make friends with just anyone, even if they were your neighbours. The old man was as poor as the proverbial church mouse and this fact alone made him all the more arrogant and careful of his dignity. His decaying manor house stood on the crest of a little hillock near the town. It was a small, dilapidated, ancient dwelling with three or four plum trees and a crab apple in front. It was surrounded by some twenty acres of barren goat pasture, and here the old man lived without even one servant to wait upon him. He rarely saw anybody and he had never married, presumably because he had never found any woman worthy of bearing his great name.

Old Borcse owed money to every one in the town, to the grocery store, to the innkeeper, butcher, miller, tailor, shoemaker and even to the mayor and the chemist, who had from time to time advanced him small sums that had never been repaid. No one minded, however. They even gave the old man their respect. On important feast days he would be sent presents, a sack or two of corn-flour, a lamb or sucking pig, fruit and vegetables in summer, and in winter, cabbages or a pint or two of plum brandy. All this out of respect.

The recipient of these charitable acts took it all as no more than his due, since he firmly believed he was the social superior of all those who sent him presents and that therefore it *was* no more than his due. His conviction was so strong that it communicated itself to all around him until they had all come to believe that the old man really was some kind of superior being to whom homage must be paid. There was a rumour that he had been one of those revolutionaries who had taken up arms against the Habsburgs in 1848, though he had never allowed anyone to mention this in his presence. Anyhow, why talk about it? He was a Borcse of Lesser- and Greater-Borcsey, and that should be enough for anyone.

So when the old revolutionary descended from his eyrie and came into the inn parlour a great commotion started, with everyone jumping up and offering him their seats. A place was found for him, as was his due, in the seat of honour directly in front of Count Abady.

Balint had heard of him before when he had first come to Lelbanya at the time of his election as Member of Parliament. He had sent a message to the old man asking if he could call upon him but the reply had been that he never received anyone who supported the 1867 Compromise (and who was therefore presumed to collaborate with the hated Austrian tyranny). Today, however, he had put in an appearance; and even Balint felt that he had been honoured.

The old knight strutted in clutching in one hand a long oak walking-stick. He was a slight old man seemingly made only of skin and bones, and though he must have been well over seventy his hair and moustache were still black. He wore grey trousers which were covered with stains and from which it appeared that all colour had been drained by the application of some acid. His boots were worn and old and none too clean. He went straight over to Abady, shook hands with him, but with no one else, and sat down. Then he nodded his head graciously to the others as if indicating that they too could now be seated. When everyone was in their place and had resumed a respectful silence, old Borcse lifted a forefinger and said: 'Well? And what is the news from Budapest?'

Balint gave an outline of recent events, explaining what the Burian talks had been about and how futile they had proved, and giving a brief résumé of the various solutions that had been put forward. At first Balint was listened to in silence, but gradually his audience began to get more animated and express their own opinions, some even quite belligerently.

Most of what they said merely echoed what they had read in the columns of the opposition newspapers, quoting, perhaps unintentionally, the most sonorous phrases from the previous days' leading articles. The loudest spoken was the Armenian butcher, Kirkocsa, who sat at the end of the long table with sleeves rolled up, thick neck bulging from an unbuttoned shirt-collar, and smote the table with his great fist each time he opened his mouth. The quietest was the Romanian priest, who sat at the other end of the table without ever opening his mouth, though his moustaches seemed to be hiding what could have been a discreet smile of amusement. As one hour and then another went by, the atmosphere became more and more heated. The chemist and the miller argued so bitterly that they almost fell to blows, though neither of them had really had a chance to justify their opinions, since they were constantly interrupted either by the butcher, who bellowed like a bull bison, or by the physician, who screamed in a high falsetto. Everyone had long forgotten that the reason for the gathering was to greet their Member of Parliament and hear what *he* had to say, and so they all spoke at once saying what they would have done had they themselves been the party leaders. Time went by and the wine bottles were emptied. The smoke-filled room was filled with noise, and everyone was enjoying himself.

'We shouldn't pay the taxes!' they shouted. 'We don't need more soldiers! Give the arms to the people . . . and we'll march to Vienna!'

Borcse lifted his hand. Everyone fell silent.

'The Old Hangman should be kicked out of the Hofburg – and that'd be an end of it!' said the old revolutionary and rapped his stick on the floor.

This unexpected intervention had a most surprising effect. Suddenly the whole gathering calmed down. No one spoke, and for a moment all that could be heard was an occasional cough or clearing of the throat. The Emperor Franz-Josef commanded such general respect that they were as shocked by this remark as if old Borcse had blasphemed in church. Few of them had realized that he was still thinking of the terrible reprisals taken after the 1848 uprising in Hungary when the Emperor, then a very young man, had ordered some of the rebellious Hungarian generals to be hanged rather than shot. Balint alone understood; he made as if to get up. No one spoke. They were all pretending that they had heard nothing.

Then the mayor turned to Balint and asked: 'Will your Lordship be staying with us long?'

In a few moments everyone rose and started to take his leave.

The next morning Abady was kept busy with visits from his constituents, who came to ask his advice or present some request or petition. Among his visitors were several of those who had been present the previous evening and, even if they thought every minister an unscrupulous scoundrel and despised anyone who even spoke to such persons, they still wanted Abady to approach them and arrange for their petitions to be accepted, real life being a thing apart from politics. And, as before, each request ended with the words: 'It only needs a word from your Lordship!'

This went on well into the afternoon. At six o'clock the last petitioner left and he was free to get away. He decided to visit the Miloths and so, ordering his man to saddle up, he left the inn and together they took the road back up to the grassland plateau. Balint knew, of course, that Adrienne would not be there but thought, as he was so near, that if they heard that he'd been to Lelbanya and not ridden over they would think that last September he had come only to see Adrienne.

When they reached the ridge above the town they rode first to the north and then shortly afterwards turned to the north-west. In half an hour they could see Mezo-Varjas in the valley below. Balint stopped for a moment as from where they were they could already see the whole Miloth estate and manor house as well as the village nearby.

✦

Riding into the stable yard they had hardly dismounted and handed over their horses to the Miloths' grooms when a voice could be heard from somewhere inside the barn. It was old Rattle, as usual shouting a stream of complaint at his servants.

'You idiots! A guest arrives and no one tells me! I'll beat the daylights out of you all!' and he came bustling out crying, 'Where are you, my dear chap, where are you?' as he peered out among the lilac bushes that surrounded the barn doors. Then he turned back to face the interior of the barn, waving his arms furiously. 'Asses! Idiots! Pig-headed brutes!' but, seeing Balint, he came forward open-armed: 'How nice of you to visit us! What a pleasure! I *am* glad you came!'

When they reached the house even the normally sour Countess Miloth seemed pleased to see him, as well as her younger daughters, while Mlle Morin managed a weak smile and became almost cheerful.

Nevertheless nothing was the same as when he had last been there.

After dinner the girls went into a corner to whisper together while Countess Miloth and the French governess sat down to their needlework in silence. Only old Miloth was in his element having someone in the house to whom he could retell his stories of Garibaldi and the campaigns that unified Italy. He was so fully in his stride when Countess Miloth rose to say goodnight and left the room accompanied by the others, that he never paused or drew breath except to make sure that Balint did not leave too.

The two men remained together for a long time. The old soldier paced up and down the room laughing loudly at his own tales and describing with wide gestures and arms flung out the oddnesses of Italian behaviour and how he himself had got tangled up in the macaroni that had been hung out to dry, had been thrown from his mule on the slopes of Vesuvius; and, most hilarious of all, how once Garibaldi had scolded him in mistake for someone else! Old Rattle had not had such a good time for many a day.

Balint listened to it all with pleasure. He liked the old man and he liked, too, the fact that his tales were good-natured and humorous. Hearing him run on was like listening to a stream of light-hearted melody, flowing and unstoppable. All Balint had to do was occasionally to interject a word or two, such as 'Bravo!' or 'How amusing – fascinating – embarrassing – amazing!' or whatever adjective seemed most appropriate, and Rattle would at once embark on another tale, full of simple humour and good fun. For the first time Balint was able to observe the old man and so he remarked, as he never had before, that Rattle had the same golden eyes as Adrienne, a sort of glowing amber, and for some reason this came with a shock of surprise, for it had never occurred to him that there might be any resemblance between his Adrienne and the faintly ridiculous Akos Miloth. But the discovery of the likeness between them endeared old Rattle to him and so he listened once again to his much-told tales with affection and emotion.

Finally they went to their rooms.

Balint had just taken off his jacket and was unbuttoning his waistcoat when he heard a faint knock at the door of his room. He looked at the door-handle but it did not turn and Balint thought that perhaps he had been mistaken. There was another knock, so Balint opened the door and looked out.

It was Judith.

'Can I come in for a moment?' she asked and slipped into the dimly-lit guest-room.

The young man quickly put on his jacket again.

'There's nothing to be upset about!' said the young girl hurriedly. 'I just wanted to ask a favour of you. Don't worry, it isn't much, really it isn't!'

'Well, what can I do for you?' Balint tried to look serious and conceal his amusement at what he took to be some little girl's prank.

'Look, AB, the thing is . . . well, you see, they all treat me like a child, as if I ought to be ashamed of it. But I'm watched all the time . . . controlled . . . and, well, it isn't very much but could you just take this letter and post it, anywhere'll do, just put it in a postbox. Will you do it? Please! It'd be a great favour. You will do it, won't you?'

PART FIVE

They stood facing each other near the bed. The single candle that Balint had put down on the table lit Judith's face, passionate, determined, desperately waiting for his reply.

'A letter? In secret so that your parents won't know?'

'Yes! Please take it, please!' and she handed him a long narrow but thick envelope.

Balint's face clouded over. It occurred to him at once that the letter could only be for that scoundrel Wickwitz. After a moment's reflection he said: 'Forgive me, Judith, but no! You're asking me something I can't do!' And his voice was even colder than his words.

'I see! You really won't?'

'No.'

Judith stepped back, hatred in her eyes, her lips pulled back from her even white teeth: 'I understand. So you're on their side, are you, with all the rest of them, with my mother and Adrienne? I ought to have known better than to have asked you, of all people. I see now that it was you who put Adrienne against him, because you hate him, don't you? Oh, I've known that for a long time, I've seen it in your eyes. You're the one who's responsible for this horrible mess. First you persuaded Adrienne and then she got at my mother. I see it all now; you might as well admit it!'

Abady was very angry. Looking her straight in the eyes, he said icily: 'I didn't have to! It wasn't necessary, but if it had been, I certainly would have!'

They looked at each other for a moment. Then Judith tossed her head and left the room.

Balint was annoyed with himself for letting his last words slip from him. If he hadn't been so angry he would never have done so.

Why say such things, why he asked himself. He lay awake for some time thinking over what had just happened.

No one came to wake him in the morning, to rap on the shutters and get him out of bed. In consequence he slept late and it was nearly ten o'clock before he was dressed. He breakfasted alone on the vine-covered veranda. Everything was calm. No one bothered him and no one hurried him. It was all very different from the last time he had been there! Balint began to regret that he had come.

Eventually old Rattle came in from the fields. He was an assiduous farmer who every day from dawn until midday made the rounds of his property. He went everywhere and, as he used to say, he would put everything in order, a process which consisted mainly of scolding everyone he met. Today he returned to the house so soaked in sweat that the back of his homespun jacket was wet to the touch. He was in the high good humour that sprung from consciousness of a job well done. He shook hands with Balint and greeted him effusively: 'How are you, my dear chap? Did those idiots give you breakfast? Did they bring you any bacon? It wasn't 'off', was it? Janos, where the devil are you hiding?' he called out suddenly.

Balint assured him that everything had been done just as it should be and that his breakfast had been excellent. He asked if they could go to see the mares and their foals and then have a look at the Miloth breeding stables.

Rattle agreed, much pleased to be asked. His horses were all large, handsome and strong, big-boned animals showing all the best signs of the old Transylvanian breed though with a special touch of class, for Rattle's father, Ferenc Miloth, had been one of the first of his compatriots to bring in thoroughbred stallions from England. The first one that he had imported was called Jason and his portrait hung in the drawing-room.

When they returned from the paddocks they went to the stables where Rattle explained everything passionately. Balint noticed that the boxes were none too clean and that the horses they contained, though beautiful, had been carelessly groomed. None of this seemed to be noticed by Rattle, but then he lived surrounded by disorder, perhaps because he never ceased to shout and scold whether or not there was any reason.

As they strolled back to the house they met the two girls. Margit, as always, was bright and smiling, but Judith looked cold and withdrawn. The two men walked on and Balint, glancing back, saw that the girls had turned into the stableyard.

After lunch Balint started for home. Once again they climbed up to the grassy prairies to the crest of the ridge that led to the south. It was a cloudy day and it was perhaps as a result of this that Balint felt strangely depressed.

When they reached Maros-Ludas and were walking their horses side by side the groom suddenly broke his silence and spoke to his master:

'If your Lordship has no objection I'd like to stop for a moment at the post office.'

'Why?' asked Balint.

'One of the young ladies asked me to post a letter at the first post box we came to!' replied the young man as he took from an inner pocket the same thick envelope that Judith had tried to give Balint the night before.

'There's no point in stopping now,' said Balint. 'Give it to me and I'll post it myself at Maros-Szilvas.'

He took the letter from the lad and put it in his own pocket, thinking that it was insufferably cheeky of Judith to use his servant to smuggle out her clandestine correspondence. He was extremely angry, and became even angrier when he reflected that if Judith's parents came to hear about the letter they would think that he had been the girl's accomplice.

Balint broke into a smart trot, though he knew that this could only be kept up until they came to the next steep climb up to the plateau again. By the time they had to reduce their speed to a walk Balint's anger had subsided and he began to wonder why he had so abruptly and eagerly taken charge of the letter. It was nothing to do with him and it was always far better not to meddle in other people's affairs. He wondered what he should do with it. Burn it? Hardly that, for he had no right. If he sent it back to Judith it would probably fall into her mother's hands and then the girl would get into trouble. Post it? Not that either, because then he would be guilty of helping that loathsome Wickwitz with whatever he was now up to. He pondered the matter all the time they were climbing upwards. As they reached the top the solution came to him; he would pass the letter on to Adrienne and then she could decide the best course. He would go to Almasko as soon as he could and get rid of this embarrassing burden. That would be the best, indeed the only solution. Balint was immensely pleased with himself at the thought that he had found a way out of this latest predicament. It was always satisfying to find a suitable answer to a difficult question and Balint now felt such a sense of happiness that he whistled cheerfully as he rode along the next stretch of the way. The tune was Toselli's 'Serenade', then very much in fashion.

The garden of Dinora Malhuysen, Countess Abonyi, was hidden behind the long wall that bordered the road. Inside the gates a winding avenue of thickly planted bay trees led to the house, which was a high one-storey building built in the Biedermeier style. At the front was a long covered veranda whose roof was supported by brick pillars. Here cane garden chairs had been placed, and, from one of those, Dinora jumped up, obviously pleased, indeed delighted, that Balint had arrived.

'How nice that you've come!' she cried, running down the steps to greet him and holding out both hands joyously. They went back up the steps hand in hand and sat down next to each other in the comfortable, white-painted chairs.

'I didn't think you'd come! You rode past the other day, didn't you – the day before yesterday it was, surely? But you didn't stop. I saw you from the summer house.'

'I was in a great hurry. I was already late.' lied Balint.

'It doesn't matter. Everything's all right now that you *have* come!' And Dinora jumped up again, kneeled coquettishly on the cane seat next to Balint and kissed him suddenly on the mouth. Then she laughed: 'That's your punishment for avoiding me, Little Boy, naughty Little Boy!' She turned away and sat down again where she had been before.

'How bold you are!' said Balint. 'That was foolhardy, anybody could have seen us!' But he was laughing too.

'Oh, there's no one here. Tihamer's having a siesta in his room. He's having an early nap now as he's going to Budapest on the night train. Can you sleep in the afternoon? I can't, and anyhow why sleep so much? It's a waste of time...' and she chattered on, twittering merrily about a host of trivialities.

This was the moment, thought Balint, when he should speak to her and suggest that they come to an understanding. Why, even tonight, or tomorrow? Clearly there would be no difficulties, but somehow the words did not get spoken.

To lead up to the subject, he asked: 'What's the news about Wickwitz?'

'Nitwit? I don't know. Yes, I do. He's somewhere near Kolozsvar, shacking up with a fat Armenian widow, they tell me! Very fat, ugh! You can imagine what she looks like in bed!' She raised her hands in disgust and crinkled up her little nose. 'Yes, a widow lady, it seems, and she's called something like Bogdan Lazar. What a pretty name!'

'She isn't fat!' remarked Balint.

'You know her, then?'

'I met her at some charity do, a bazaar or something. She's much too good for Nitwit! She's dark – rather beautiful, I should say.'

'Of course! I know who you mean, I've seen her too. Do you fancy her, Little Boy?'

To tease, Balint paused for quite a long time and then, rather mysteriously and with a serious expression, he said: 'I'm not sure ... who knows?'

Dinora fell for this, completely believing him, and at once started to ask how anybody could possibly make love to such a creature, who probably had hairy legs and no doubt gave off the oddest odour when she got over-heated. How could Balint think of such a person, she demanded, he who was so fastidious? Jumping up and walking about, Dinora got quite excited trying to disgust Balint at the idea of Mme Lazar's charms.

Balint watched her with an amused smile, thinking that it wasn't fair to allow her to get so upset. He really shouldn't tease her so, he thought, and anyway, this was the moment to strike and tell her why he'd come. Accordingly he grabbed her arm and pulled her down on to the cane sofa beside him. 'Stop it!' he said. 'That's enough now!'

Dinora looked up at him, both surprised and hopeful, thinking that now he would start to hold her in his arms, caress her and kiss her and ask for love. All this she read from the expression on his face, for she had seen it before, long ago when they had been lovers.

During the brief moment that elapsed since she fell into his arms the voice of Balint's conscience spoke to him again, saying, Wait! Not now! Do it when you come back from Almasko. You can't go there straight from another woman's bed, it would not be right. Indeed it would be downright distasteful! So, instead of begging for Dinora's love, he merely said: 'You make me dizzy, spinning about like that!' He tried to laugh convincingly so that she should think he had only been making a joke of it all. For a fraction of a second a worried look passed over her face, as if she had sensed her former lover's thoughts and had found there something new – something dangerous and unexpected.

'I only wanted to demonstrate what a fat woman looked like with no clothes on...'

※

A little later Tihamer Abonyi came out of his room. He made every effort to make Balint feel at home and welcomed him effusively. The conversation was about nothing in particular, and at dusk, just before Dinora's husband had to leave for Aranyos-Gyeres to catch the Budapest train, Balint called for his horses and rode home.

※

Early next morning, when Countess Roza went to visit the stables, she spoke to the groom who had accompanied her son to Lelbanya.

'Where did you stop to rest the horses?'

'We went all in one go, my lady,' said the boy. 'But on the way back from Mezo-Varjas...'

'Ah, so you went there too?'

'Yes, my lady, we slept there the day before yesterday. But coming back we stopped at Szilvas. I gave them their feed there, and I rubbed them down before we saddled up again.'

'So you were there for some little time?'

'We arrived about four, and didn't leave until nearly eight, my lady.'

'You didn't have any trouble with the horses? They stood up to it all right?'

Countess Roza then walked over to look for herself, feeling the horses' backs to see if there was any soreness, and running her hands over their tendons. She then left the stables well satisfied. What she had heard was good.

As she walked back to the house to have breakfast with her son, a tiny roguish smile, almost invisible, might have been discerned on her round little face.

Chapter Three

THE YELLOW BRICSKA, Count Uzdy's travelling carriage which had been sent to the station to collect Balint, turned at great speed into the forecourt of the castle of Almasko, tore round the central lawn, and came to an abrupt halt in front of the main entrance.

On the steps was standing Uzdy's butler, a grey-haired man with wide powerful shoulders, a short beard and clipped moustaches. His eyebrows were long and bushy and below them his eyes were large and unusually sad. He bowed correctly and stepped forward to offer his arm to Abady as he descended from the high-slung carriage. For a second Balint availed himself of the man's aid and was astonished, when he touched the butler's arm, to notice that the old man's muscles were as hard as steel. As the butler preceded him up the steps the carriage moved on as swiftly as it arrived; presumably the luggage would be taken off somewhere else.

'The Countess will receive your Lordship in the salon,' said the butler in a lugubrious monotone and, leading the way across the oval hall, silently opened a pair of double doors. Balint went through and the doors were closed as silently as they had been opened.

The salon was a long room, oval like the entrance hall but much larger. The shutters were all closed, even those of the floor-length french windows which, presumably opened on to the castle's garden front. Balint needed a few moments for his eyes to become adjusted to the gloom. The ceiling was high and covered with baroque stucco-work. The walls were painted a cold grey and the furniture, mostly heavy sofas and armchairs dating from the 1860s, was covered in tobacco-coloured cord. There were one or two old family portraits hung sparsely on the otherwise bare walls. There did not seem to be anything personal in the room and the general impression was stern and cold with every object carefully, symmetrically, and severely in its place.

Balint walked up and down for a little, waiting, his heart beating strongly in eager anticipation of Adrienne's appearance. What would she say and how would she look in that curiously impersonal room? As he strolled over to the windows for the third time he was surprised, for he had not heard anyone enter, to hear a voice behind him. 'Count Abady, how nice of you to come!'

It was Clémence Absolon, mother to Pali Uzdy and widow of his father Domokos, a thin elderly lady who stood very straight. She was the image of her son, but an old, female version, and it was clear that she must once have been very beautiful. She wore a grey dress, buttoned up high to the chin where a narrow white collar emphasized the severity of her appearance. On her abundant white hair was pinned a little lace widow's cap. Countess Clémence walked with a curious stamping tread as if she had to force her body to move. A cold, distant smile hovered uncertainly on her thin lips. She seemed distant and unapproachable.

Seating herself in the centre of the principal sofa in the room Countess Clémence waved her guest to an armchair opposite. Her manner was formal and ceremonious.

'Pray sit! Tea will be brought presently. I hope you had an uneventful journey?'

'Excellent, thank you, Countess,' said Balint, and, as his hostess remained silent for a moment and it seemed polite to keep some sort of conversation going, he started to tell how the Uzdy *bricska* which had been sent to meet him at Banffy-Hunyad had taken all the hills and valleys at such speed that it might have been one of the new automobiles.

'My son likes to travel swiftly. That is why our carriage horses are all American trotters. My son says they are the best!'

Here was another topic. It was good for ten minutes, during which they discussed all the advantages and disadvantages of using American trotters. They then got on to their breeding. Balint began to wonder if Adrienne would ever come in.

The old butler brought in tea, placing the tray on a table by his mistress, and vanished as silently as he had come.

Now they talked about tea, whether China or Indian were preferable, or maybe Ceylon, and how nowadays in Transylvania more and more houses were serving tea instead of the traditional coffee with whipped cream. This was good for another fifteen minutes.

'When did you get back from Budapest?' The countess's languid question revived the conversation which, by now, was beginning to falter. Abady recounted the latest political moves in the capital, explaining the different problems and any solutions that had been proposed. He spoke disinterestedly, as befitted conversation on such matters in good society. This was a useful subject for it could be made to last a long as anyone wished. The old lady sat bolt upright, unyielding and severe, listening to what her guest said and occasionally, out of good manners and not because the answer would be of any interest to her, she would ask a question – for keeping a conversation going was the duty of a well-bred hostess.

From time to time she took a delicate sip at her tea.

At last Balint heard a door being opened behind him. He started and then relaxed again. They were not Addy's footsteps that he could hear, though they were obviously those of a woman. At the same time he could tell that a child had entered the room as well: it was the English nanny with Adrienne's little daughter. They went straight over to Countess Clémence. The child did not open her mouth but the nurse, speaking in English, said: 'It's time for our walk now, if your Ladyship agrees?'

Balint now saw Adrienne's daughter for the first time. She was a strange-looking child who in no way resembled her mother. The girl's face showed neither joy nor sadness; her expression was closed as if she must hide her thoughts, her complexion was pale and her big brown eyes seemed to look around without seeing what was in front of them.

'Very well,' said Countess Clémence, also in English, 'you can go out now!' She looked at the clock. 'Walk for an hour and a half at the edge of the woods. I'll join you later.'

The nanny and the little girl turned away and left the room without another word. The girl did not hop about, or jump or skip, as other children of her age would have done, but walked out sedately, politely. In a moment they were gone.

'You were telling me about the latest talks with Burian?'

So the widowed countess and Abady went on making desultory conversation, both choosing their words carefully, though neither was in the least interested in what the other was saying.

When another half hour had passed, Countess Clémence rose from her seat 'Shall we go into the garden?' she asked.

They left the room, crossed the oval entrance hall and went out on to the forecourt through the castle's main entrance. Once outside they turned left and walked round to the side of the house which faced over the valley. The house had seemed, from the entrance court to be only one storey high, but Balint soon saw that as it was built on a steep slope the façade looking over the valley had two floors and it was only from that side that one could see the house properly.

It was a pretty building in the baroque style with, in the centre, an enormous covered balcony that stretched the full length of the salon within. The balcony had tall columns which supported the half-cupola domed roof above and was itself supported on vaulted pillars beneath which a doorway led to the rooms below.

Gazing past the balcony he saw that another wing had been built jutting out at right angles from the main building and extending even further out from the hillside. This wing was entirely unexpected. Its lower walls were of rough undressed stone, the upper part of red brick, and the whole edifice had the air of a defensive redoubt. The roof was made of flat shingles, jutting well beyond the line of the walls with, as is to be found in Swiss chalets, an elaborate cornice of carved wood. At the far end a tower built of wood obviously housed a staircase, for none of its windows were on the same level. On the lower floor of this wing all the windows were heavily barred. The wing itself jutted out so far over the slope on which the house was built that at its farthest end it was three storeys high and seemed completely out of proportion to the beautiful old house to which it was attached.

'My poor husband built that wing,' explained Countess Clémence. 'He fell in love with the alpine style when we visited the Tyrol together. I often think it should be pulled down, but my son seems to have got used to it.'

They descended a steep, well-kept path to a lawn so well seeded and maintained that no sign of a weed was to be seen. Here and there were planted groups of thuja, dwarf juniper or pyramid-shaped biota, and the paths were edged by well-trimmed box. Everything was neat and tidy, but it was strange to see a garden with no flowers and no flowering shrubs either. Below the lawns the park stretched down to the north and was closed by great groups of fine old oak trees. Above the leafy crowns of the park oaks the valley could be seen continuing, interrupted only by little forest-covered hills, to the foot of the steep cliffs on which stood the giant ruins of the old fortress of Almas, for the sight of whose lonely towers Balint always searched when his train emerged from the Sztana tunnel. From the distant railway line one could see what looked like two index fingers rising from the forest. Once he had thought it must be the Uzdy house itself, but standing now at Almasko, Balint realized that those two shining vertical lines were in reality formed by the two sides of the ruined keep between which the connecting walls had crumbled.

Balint and the old lady walked on through a grove of beech trees to an orchard that was planted with the new dwarf apple trees. The fruit trees were set in rows with military precision, each in its circles of well-hoed earth and each having a band of sticky grease round its trunk as a protection against destructive insects.

At the foot of the twentieth tree in the first row a woman was kneeling. She had her back to them and was wearing a wide-brimmed straw hat on her head. Her dress was protected by a yellow canvas apron. She seemed to be busy doing something at the roots of the tree. At her side a flat basket lay on the grass. Countess Clémence led Balint towards her.

When only a few steps away the old lady called out: 'Adrienne! A guest has arrived!'

Adrienne turned, still on her knees, to see who had called to her. Balint was struck with wonder, for here before him was another Addy, different from the others he already knew. The yellow apron reached up to her neck and fell in narrow pleats to the waist. Below the tight belt it emphasized the lines and movements of her thighs as far as her bent knees. The late afternoon sun shone slanting down on to her face under the brim of the same sort of straw hat as was worn by the peasant-women of the Kalotaszeg, a flat hat like a saucer without a crown and which was kept on by a ribbon tied under the chin. With this thin body-clinging canvas covering and the floating disc of a hat, under which dark curls framed her face, she looked to Balint like a Tanagra figurine come to life.

Adrienne looked up. She was a striking figure, her pale oval face framed by a starling red ribbon like a shining, laughing mask of ivory, her amber eyes smiling and her lips as red as the ribbon tied under her chin.

'Ah, AB, it's you! I thought . . .' but she stopped and did not finish the sentence, her face clouding over as if she had suddenly remembered where she was. She stood up, threw her secateurs into the basket and brushed the earth from the apron which covered her knees. 'Look how dirty I am! I can't possibly shake hands!'

As they moved back towards the house the first to speak was Countess Clémence: 'My daughter-in-law is a great gardener, really a great gardener. She takes care of all the fruit trees and makes herself very useful.' This might have sounded like praise if the tone had not been so condescending.

'I only started last year,' said Adrienne somewhat deprecatingly. 'I've still got a lot to learn, but it amuses me, and gives me something to do.'

They walked slowly, the old lady in the middle, Balint on her right and Adrienne on her left. When they reached the grove of beeches Countess Clémence turned to Balint and said: 'I must hand you over to my daughter-in-law now. So, until dinner, I'll say *au revoir*.'

'Where is Pali?' asked Adrienne.

'In his room, I expect. He does his accounts at this time and he hasn't come down yet,' said Countess Clémence before turning away and marching along the path through the trees with her distinctive stamping tread.

The two younger people stood watching in silence as the dark upright figure went on its way and was finally lost to sight among the soft shiny new leaves of the beech trees.

When she could no longer be seen Balint and Adrienne also left the orchard and followed the path through the wood.

For a few moments they walked together, side by side without speaking.

Under the century-old trees last year's fallen leaves made a soft carpet underfoot. When they reached a twist in the path Adrienne stopped, looked swiftly around her, and then offered her mouth to be kissed. Their embrace lasted only a brief second but never before had Addy kissed him with such fervour and such abandon. Not, however, that this wild kiss was a kiss of love or surrender; rather it was an act of revenge or defiance, as if it gave her some savage satisfaction quite unconnected with him. After a second or two she pushed him away and walked on, her head held high, and her close-knit brows giving a serious and somewhat sad expression to her face. As they stepped out of the shadow of the trees into the sunlight of the meadow she turned once more towards him. 'It's so good that you came, AB. You don't know how good it is!'

They started to mount the winding path to the terrace.

'That awful wing jutting out there!' said Balint. 'It completely spoils the lovely old baroque house.'

'It was my father-in-law. He did it. Of course it's hideous, but, you know,' and Addy lowered her voice even though no one could possibly have overheard what she was saying, 'you know that he was mad, and later ... I'm sure you've heard...' She broke off without saying the words that in that house were taboo.

Balint did know. Many years before he had been told by his mother that Domokos Uzdy had died insane in his own house where his wife had kept him locked away in secret so as not to let the outside world know about it.

'Yes, I did hear.'

'That – er – butler ... you've seen him already, old Maier, was his keeper, his nurse. They brought him from somewhere, I don't know where, and afterwards, well, he just stayed on.' For a little while she did not speak, then, with a little dry laugh, she said: 'He might be needed again some time!' and the bitterness in her voice made him realize that she was thinking that it would be for her.

When they arrived at the base of the solid Swiss wing a footman was just carrying a tea-tray down the stairs which led from the wooden gallery above.

'Which room is Count Abady in?' Adrienne asked the man. Before he could reply a voice was heard coming from a window high above their head. It was Pali Uzdy, saying: 'My mother has put him in the main guest room upstairs. That's his room!' and he laughed meaninglessly before going on: 'I'll welcome him, too, of course, but I'm still busy. In the meantime look after him, entertain him, take him for a walk!' The mirthless laughter went on for a moment above them.

It was disconcerting to hear that disembodied voice coming out of the air above their heads. The invisible presence of Count

PART FIVE

Uzdy, disquietingly and in some way menacing too, was everywhere around them, next to them, between them...

Adrienne and Balint sat down on a bench at the foot of the vaulted pillars that held up the covered balcony outside the salon. They sat where they could be seen from every angle and they talked of nothing but trivialities, so strongly did they both have the feeling that they were being watched by invisible eyes, and overheard by invisible ears, from every barred window in the fortress wing and from behind every shutter of the great house above.

❦

Dinner was served at eight o'clock in the big dining-room. The table was immense and they were seated far away from each other. The room was lit by paraffin lamps hanging from the ceiling. Countess Clémence made polite conversation when she had to, Adrienne barely spoke, and it was Pali Uzdy who kept everything going and led the talk in the direction he wished. It was the same after dinner in the oval drawing-room. The shutters, of course, remained closed, as they had been in the afternoon, and outside the wind had got up and could be heard howling round the house. Afterwards Balint could not recall what they had talked about: all he could remember was the flickering of the table lamps which had thrown agitated shadows on the high carved plaster of the ceiling and that his host had suggested that Balint should go out after roebuck at dawn with one of the forest guards. The man would call him early, said Pali, and went on: 'They tell me there are some fine buck in my woods. I don't know anything about it myself as I don't shoot game, but if it would give you pleasure I should be very pleased. It's high time some of them were shot!'

Abady said he had not brought his guns.

'That doesn't matter! There's everything here you could possibly need. A Schonauer? A repeater? Or would you rather try a Mauser?' Then, seeing that Balint looked puzzled, he said: 'I do a lot of target shooting. That's why I only have high precision weapons. We can try that too, tomorrow if you wish ... naturally, of course, of course!'

Once again he went into peals of his strange, meaningless laughter until the sides of his long moustaches were pulled apart like two giant inverted commas.

Balint did not really enjoy shooting but thought it would be churlish to refuse.

❦

Dawn was just breaking when Abady was called in the morning. The forest guard took him out past the upper forecourt until, some way further on, they left the road and took to the woods walking a long way between carefully tended parcels of woodland, each marked at the corners with little whitewashed posts bearing boards marked with a number. Balint noticed at once how well-looked-after the Uzdy plantations were and thought that this was how things ought to be in his own forests.

After an hour and a half they emerged from the trees just where the whole of the slope below them had been cleared.

'Careful now!' whispered the guard. 'This is where we'll find them.' He moved on silently through the undergrowth at the edge of the trees. Just as he had said, in front of them a small herd of deer were grazing in the centre of the clearing, their reddish fur gleaming dully in the morning sunlight. At last the guard pointed to a fine roebuck that was reaching up to nibble the leaves on a spreading oak tree.

'Take that one, your Lordship! That's a fine beast for you!'

It was an easy shot, barely a hundred yards, and the buck fell at once, cleanly killed by Balint's shot. The man went down the slope to pick up the kill and Balint sat down at the edge of the trees to wait until he returned. Then they started back.

Balint knew that his mother owned some forests somewhere thereabouts and asked the man if he knew where they were.

'Pity your Lordship didn't mention it a bit earlier! Just there, where your Lordship shot the buck – across the valley the top of the ridge is the boundary between the Uzdy lands and your Lordship's. I could have taken you there. It's on the way to Hunyad when we go on foot.'

They walked briskly on and, at the last crest before the house, they met Adrienne. She looked fresh and blooming with health and good spirits, her generous mouth smiling widely as she inspected Balint's kill.

'Poor roebuck!' she said. 'But perhaps it's better to die like that, suddenly, cleanly. He might have been torn to pieces by wolves or caught in some poacher's snare. Are you tired, AB?' she asked suddenly. 'If not, I know a beautiful spot from which one can see into the far, far distance!'

The guard left them to take the buck back to be skinned and they walked, upwards again, into the woods on the opposite side to that from which they had come. The path was narrow and winding and they had hardly taken a hundred paces before they stopped and kissed. After that they kissed and held each other tightly every thirty or so steps until they reached the top and emerged from the trees. In front of them was a superb view over wave after wave of forest until, dominating the whole scene, on a high crest, stood the ruins of the old fortress. Balint noticed none of this, for he was drunk with the nectar of Adrienne's kisses and with the joy of holding her body tightly pressed to his. They did not sit but remained there for a long time, holding each other as if their very lives depended on it, as if they had both quaffed a potion that rendered them oblivious to everything except each other.

At midday Farkas and Adam Alvinczy arrived. They drove over in their own carriage because Farkas had a house at Magyarokerek which was only ten kilometres from Banffy-Hunyad. Even their presence did nothing to bring life to the cold and formal atmosphere of the Uzdy household and indeed, in some ways it had the opposite effect for both young men had been brought up in the rowdy school of Uncle Ambrus and now found themselves constrained in the presence of the dowager Countess, Adrienne and Pali Uzdy, none of whom would have appreciated their usual coarse speech and bad language. As a result they were awkward and stiffly formal, especially the younger, Adam, whom Adrienne jokingly called Adam Adamovich because he was in love with her and tried to hid the fact by adopting an even stiffer bearing than did his elder brother.

As a result the Alvinczy boys were unusually silent both during luncheon and afterwards, leaving Uzdy to keep the conversation going. This he did, in his habitual inconsequent fashion, while Adam and Farkas sat tongue-tied only occasionally contributing some inane triviality. Uzdy was in his element. As an exceptionally well-read man, cultivated and erudite, he chose his topics today only from the latest scientific researches and discoveries and, when it was obvious that the others did not have the smallest notion of what he was talking about, he would turn to one or other of them and put a question to them only to dismiss the answer with contemptuous mockery barely veiled by a veneer of good manners. In this same way he would wittily mix up details of the latest advances in electrical or astronomical research, until his audience was even more bewildered than before. Balint felt at once that Uzdy was showing off, though it certainly was not for his benefit, nor for that of the Alvinczys. For his wife then? Ah, that was it.

It was as if behind every clever phrase rang the words: 'See! This is me, this is how *I* am, your husband! Your beaux are nothing but country dullards, blockheads – look at me, only at me!'

Adrienne's face gave nothing away, her eyes quite expressionless under half-closed lids. Countess Clémence, too, was stonily entrenched behind the wall of her inexorable politeness.

The large figure of the butler, Maier, served them in silence in the shuttered dining-room. Later, when they sat in the gloomy shade of the salon whose shutters also were still closed, he would from time to time glide silently into the room to bring coffee or to empty the ashtrays and then just as silently and unobtrusively leave it again. He appeared to ignore everyone in the room, but Balint noticed that from time to time he would raise his large sad eyes and glance at his master. Uzdy went on talking wittily but nervously well into the afternoon.

All at once he got up and suggested they go out pigeon-shooting.

'That's a real sport!' he said. 'I have an excellent field for it; just like in Monte Carlo. Does everyone agree? Yes? Well then, let's go!'

Countess Clémence withdrew to her own rooms, but Addy walked down with them.

'I assume you breed them yourself?' said Adam Alvinczy as they started off.

'Pigeons? Certainly not, not one! We shoot only at clay pigeons. I wouldn't slaughter a living animal. Why should I? They don't harm anyone. People, yes. That would be different; but animals, never!' and, turning back towards the rest of them he seemed to be weighing them up, measuring their capacities and perhaps their characters, with his wide-set, slanting Tartar eyes. Then, tossing back his head and straightening his narrow shoulders, he turned and led the way down the hillside to a small valley. Targets had been set up in front of a patch of bare clay where part of the steep hillside had slipped. Some way away in the meadow, in front of the landslide, throwing machines had been placed in a fan-shaped formation, with wooden planks for the guns to stand on, and, where the path came to an end, there were tables with ammunition boxes, pistol-holders, a selection of rifles, two benches to sit on, and a small telescope on a stand.

'Here we are! This is it!' cried the host. 'It's splendid, isn't it? I practise here every afternoon. Well, my friends, choose your guns, please! They're all here!'

PART FIVE

The visitors went over to the tables at the stands and were surprised to see only sporting rifles, no shotguns. 'It's more fun with these,' said Uzdy from behind them. 'I never shoot with anything else. You'll see! This is the real sport, I assure you. Now go on, take your pick, choose what you like. If you want to you can try them out at the fifty- and hundred-metre targets.'

Adrienne sat down silently on one of the benches. The guests took a few shots at the targets and they shot well, for in those days in Transylvania target-shooting was a popular sport.

'Well done! You'll do! Let's start!' shouted Uzdy excitedly as he checked the results through his telescope. A young peasant lad, who had been waiting for a sign from his master, now slipped down into the trench behind the clay-pigeon machines, so that all they could see of him was the top of his head and his hands when he inserted the discs into the throwing machine.

Uzdy himself was the first.

'Ready!' he called, and a disc flew up. Uzdy fired and the clay pigeon was shattered before their eyes. The others followed, but with little success. Out of five throws Adam achieved only one hit: the others did not even do as well as this. Only Uzdy never missed. One by one the others gave up, but there was no stopping Adrienne's husband, who became more and more animated, jumping up and down on the wooden platform and finally discarding his hat and jacket. Moving his body frenetically and waving his long arms in their shirt-sleeves he looked like some giant long-legged spider, over-excited, almost out of control. All Uzdy's normal restraint disappeared, as if the shooting had liberated something in his soul which was normally hidden only by the man's delicately balanced self-control. The sun started to set and still he did not stop. He shouted new orders, sometimes having two discs shot up at the same time – and when he did this he invariably managed to hit both. He was an exceptional shot who took aim as if by instinct rather than by conscious skill. His appearance was frightening, with his elongated figure and satanic head etched black against that yellow hillside whose sulphurous hue was now emphasized by the rays of the setting sun.

Adrienne and the three guests watched in silence, only occasionally interjecting a 'Bravo!' or 'Well shot!' out of mere politeness. They wondered if Uzdy would ever stop and, indeed he did not do so until Maier appeared from somewhere and touched his master on the shoulder, and said quietly: 'It's time to dress, my Lord. Dinner will be served in fifteen minutes.'

After dinner Balint saw that the french windows onto the terrace had been opened for the first time since he had arrived at Almasko. The previous evening, of course, had been a windy night, but today all was still and the full moon shone with a clear milky radiance.

Adrienne led Balint and Adam Alvinczy outside to some chairs beside the stone balustrade. They talked quietly and slowly, using few words, and now it was Adam who spoke while Balint, who sat a little farther away from Adrienne, merely listened without taking in much of what the other was saying. Inside the house it was the elder Alvinczy's turn to exchange platitudes with their host and his mother, while Count Uzdy himself sat hunched up in a large wing armchair and seemed to do nothing but gaze directly at one of the table-lamps. One might have thought that perhaps he was overtired after his exertions that afternoon at the pigeon shoot, but close inspection of his eyes showed that he was possessed by some strange and secret agitation, and that he might have been seeking the solution to his problems in the flame behind its glass shade. Occasionally his facial muscles would give a twitch, sometimes the corners of his mouth were pulled back as if he were about to laugh or take a bite at something; then he would blink and slowly lean his head back against the upholstery of the chair, remaining motionless for a long time. Balint could see him well from where he sat outside the room.

Adrienne was also silent, though not with the tranquillity of mutual repose as when she and Balint would sit together in silence for hours at a time. Now her silence was hostile, like that of someone alone in an alien world. Her manner was unpropitiatory and antagonistic to those around her and the few words she spoke were hard and dismissive; and though she sometimes made a joke of what was being said, teasing Adam Adamovich and laughing at his attempts to entertain her, she was not natural and her laughter seemed artificial and forced.

Uzdy suddenly rose and left the salon, returning in a few moments with a silken shawl which he brought out to Adrienne.

'This is so that you wouldn't catch cold!' he said.

'Thank you, but it isn't cold tonight. I don't need it,' she said, protesting, as he tried to put it round her shoulders. But despite her protests her husband still wrapped the shawl round her before turning and making his way back to the drawing-room. Did Balint imagine it, or had Uzdy given him a mocking glance as he passed?

PART FIVE

It was such a little thing that Balint was not sure he had not been mistaken, and nothing else out of the ordinary was to happen before they all went to bed a little later. When the old lady got up from her accustomed place on the sofa the others all rose too, and those on the balcony came back into the room to say goodnight. They all left the drawing-room together and while the two Alvinczys were escorted by the butler to their rooms on the lower floor, Countess Clémence went directly to her apartments on the left of the oval entrance hall.

Adrienne, Uzdy and Balint went to the doors on the right, where Balint's room was to be found at the beginning of the corridor leading to the Uzdy's private wing. They stopped outside Balint's door for a moment and said goodnight. Then Uzdy put his arm round his wife and led her away. Balint watched them until they had disappeared round the corner.

Balint turned down the light as soon as he got into bed, but he couldn't sleep. It was hot in the room so he got up, went over to the windows and threw open the shutters.

Before him there was a beautiful view; or rather half a beautiful view, for everything to the left was cut off by the protruding wing and the wooden tower with its staircase at the far end. The windows were all dark, with no sign of light apart from that of the moon shining outside. Not a sound was to be heard.

The young man leaned out of the window thinking that though the view before him was exceptionally beautiful, it was in some mysterious way gloomy; though perhaps this was due the cold brightness of the moonlight. Round the house were low irregular hills covered with the black outlines of oak trees; closer to Balint the lawns and flowerless gardens were black too and only in the distance, seemingly just an inch away from the vertical line of the projecting tower, could be seen the twin ghostly outlines of the ruined fortress across the valley, shining now not with the brilliance of sunlight that had illuminated them as he looked from the train, but with a vapoury, ghostly iridescence that seemed fraught with forebodings of a tragic destiny.

Balint remained there for a long time, gazing out into the night and trying not to allow his memory of how Adrienne looked that evening to haunt his memory. Her face had been set in cold, hostile lines, not only for everyone else but also, and this he did not understand, for him as well. Since the Alvinczys had arrived she had made a point of devoting herself to Adam Adamovich rather than to him whom she had treated with a coquetry that was both cold and contrived. It had hurt; it was humiliating and, after those kisses in the forest that morning, utterly incomprehensible. Balint became filled with doubts and began to wonder if it were possible that in reality Adrienne was one of those calculating women who planned their conquests with cunning but with ultimate frigidity. Could she be one of those who carried on with several men at the same time, taking pleasure from making them suffer and only happy when she could laugh at their enslavement? Women like that can never really love, reflected Balint as he leaned on the cold window-sill, all they can do is rejoice when they know they are causing torment.

As he was thinking about the enigma of Adrienne the silence was interrupted by the sound of wooden boards creaking. The sound came from the staircase in the tower and from where he stood Balint could see the faint light of a candle held by someone slowly ascending the stairway within. For a moment there would be a glow at one dark barred aperture, then nothing, then again it would appear at a window farther up. At the topmost window it disappeared altogether.

Balint's heart constricted. Uzdy was going to his wife.

Everything that had previously mystified him was now made clear. Clear, why Adrienne's mirth had been so false and hard; clear, why she had made that flight to the covered balcony after dinner, and why she had tried to reject the wrap brought by her husband; clear, her terrified face when she said goodnight in the corridor. And, just as distinctly, Balint had seen in Adrienne's face that evening the same agonized expression as when he himself had nearly raped her at Kolozsvar. How had he not recognized it earlier? Balint now realized that all evening she had felt nothing but loathing for everyone and everything around her because she knew, in advance, what was in store for her later.

Balint struck the window-sill with his clenched fist.

On his lips there was a little trickle of blood as he bit hard not to cry his own agony aloud to the lonely night.

The following morning it had been arranged that he should again go shooting in the woods. He did not want to go and would willingly have cancelled it had he not planned with Adrienne that they should meet in the forest as if by chance, so that he would be able to give her Judith's letter when no one else could see him do it.

This morning Balint also wanted to see his mother's oak forests, so what had been planned as a morning's deer stalk was transformed into an early walk through the woods. He asked the Almasko forest guard to guide him to the ridge he had spoken of the previous day whence he could, it seemed, have a good view of his family's property. Walking briskly it took them about three hours, and any deer that they sighted on the way were allowed to go free. The strenuous exercise and the radiant morning combined to restore his composure, so that although his face clouded when, as they neared home, he saw Adrienne approaching, he was quickly able to get himself under control. It was important to him that she should notice nothing when they met. When the guard had left them and they were once again alone in the shade of the great trees, he tried to kiss her, but Addy stepped back and put her fingertips to his lips.

'No! Please, no!' She spoke so low that he hardly heard her words, and as she spoke a shudder passed right down through her body starting at the shoulders. Balint's heart missed a beat and he felt full of pity and compassion for her, for he had realized that with that involuntary movement her body had cried out to him: 'Don't touch me, I'm unclean!' She used the same gesture, an arm uplifted, that lepers used to protect others from their touch; and so he at once took her hand, gently and firmly and held it until she had understood that it was merely out of sympathy and not the first movement of an attempt to kiss her. They moved slowly along the path, holding hands like two young children. They did not speak and their footfalls on the grass-covered path made no sound. The woodbirds, finches and siskins, flitted from branch to branch in the trees, and filled the air with their song.

When they came to a small clearing they sat down. Balint was afraid that Addy would object if he put his arms around her. Before that he must put her at her ease and make her forget what had happened during the night. When she did sit down he pointedly did not sit close to her but found a place where he was just out of reach. Then he handed her Judith's thick envelope.

After a brief hesitation, Adrienne, seeing that the crumpled envelope was already half open, pulled the letter out. Four pages were covered with Judith's emphatic square letters. Adrienne read attentively what her sister had written, slowly taking it all in. Then, still holding the letter, she said: 'Poor Judith! Poor, poor girl!' For a long time she said nothing more but just sat there wrapped in her own thoughts. Balint waited, saying nothing. At last Addy spoke: 'You know, this is really all my fault. Yes, really, don't be surprised! I'm at the bottom of it all. All this unhappy affair is my doing. Not directly, of course, but she's heard me say many of the things she writes in this letter: "*I will save you. That's my vocation, to sacrifice everything to save a man from himself.*" That might have been me, a hundred years ago before I knew ... I used to say things like that! Listen to this: "*No matter how guilty the world thinks you, I care nothing as long as you are true to me.*" These were my ideas, and when I was a girl I used to proclaim them proudly, thinking that it was all so true and so beautiful. Now it's all been manna for poor little Judith...'

She paused for a while, her brows knitted in thought. Then she went on: 'But she goes even further: "*Even if you've done wrong, if you believe yourself guilty...*" She keeps using phrases like that. I don't quite understand, has Wickwitz something on his conscience, has he done something wrong, something wicked?'

'It's possible!' said Balint grimly.

'Do you know anything about it?'

Balint hesitated; but he had to answer. 'Yes I do! But I can't say anything about it as I was told in confidence. I'm sorry, but I can't tell you.'

'Not even me...?'

It was hard not to give in, but Balint's sense of honour prevailed. 'Not even you!'

Curiosity unleashed the eternal female in Adrienne. She slid over to Balint and took his hand. 'You must give me some idea! At least say something. Not everything, of course, but just what sort of thing. Is it horses ... or women? What is it? Surely you can tell me that?'

'It's money! A sordid, ugly affair. Very nasty indeed, but don't ask me to tell you more!'

'I could have guessed as much. The man has a horrid laugh.'

At midday the guests gathered in the drawing-room before lunch. Uzdy came in with a big pile of newspapers. He seemed in high good humour, a triumphant glitter in his narrow black eyes.

'News from Budapest,' he said. 'Most interesting!' He spoke slowly, choosing his words with care. 'There is a new government! Now all you politicians, which one of you can guess who's the new Minister-President?'

The Alvinczys suggested Kossuth, then Andrassy, and finally Wlassits.

Uzdy shook his head and laughed. Then he turned to Abady.

PART FIVE

'Haven't you anything to say? You keep silent but you're the only one here who ought to know. I'm only a modest member of the Upper House, but you are a Member of Parliament, an elected legislator, a professional. Well? Won't you give us the benefit of your opinion? What's your guess? We're all waiting for you?'

'Geza Fejervary?'

'Bravo! *Alle Ehre, alle Respekt, alle Ehre* – quite right, my congratulations!' and Uzdy bowed, swinging his arms and letting the upper part of his body dangle loosely as if it had been broken at the waist. 'Well said, indeed! There's clear sight for you! Congratulations! *Respekt!*' At this point Adrienne came in and Uzdy turned to her at once: 'I've just put all your followers to the test. Our friend Abady was the victor; he's a genius!'

Countess Clémence now came in. Her presence had a calming effect on her son and, though the conversation was still about Budapest politics, it proceeded in a quiet and gentlemanlike manner. Everyone deplored the nomination of a government by the Crown without any elective justification. Why, it was little else than a return to absolutism, and there had not been anything like that since 1848! This continued throughout the meal.

Seeing Adrienne once again beside her husband, Balint was haunted by the memory of what he had discovered the previous night. It was made all the worse by Uzdy's air of triumphant possession, by the way he flaunted his ownership of her in front of the guests. He would lean over and fondle her arm during the meal, caress her shoulders when they rose to leave the table, and all these things he did, not with the tender air of a man in love with his wife but rather as if he needed always to remind himself – and everyone else – that she was his, just as a dog belongs to its master. Balint shuddered every time Uzdy touched her and convinced himself that the husband knew this and redoubled his efforts to demonstrate his rights in consequence. It was unbearable, intolerable!

As soon as lunch was over Balint asked if he could have a carriage to take him to the station. He used the formation of the new government as a pretext, saying that he would be urgently needed in Budapest as there would certainly be an emergency meeting of the House. No doubt a telegram was already waiting for him at his house at Kolozsvar. He must go at once, by the very next train.

Balint felt badly about leaving so abruptly, especially as it meant that he would not be able to see Adrienne alone before he left. He wanted so much to say a few tender words to her, words that would tell her how much he felt for her and how he understood the horror of her life. But anything was better than staying in that dreadful house and having to be a witness, every minute of the day, to a situation he hated; and nothing would be worse than staying and making polite conversation, keeping a straight face, and pretending to notice nothing when all the time he had murder in his heart. He was sure that Adrienne understood why her friend was leaving so suddenly, and indeed, when he took his leave she did not urge him to stay on – though there had been sorrow in her golden eyes and an unspoken demand for his pity. When she said goodbye, her lips had opened slightly as if she were offering them to be kissed. It was just as Balint had taught her on the cushions in the Uzdy villa, but that was all...

'Never! Never again!' said Balint out loud to himself as Uzdy's fast American trotters whisked the yellow-wheeled *bricska* out of the forecourt. 'I'll never set foot in that house again!'

Chapter Four

THE ROYAL DECREE appointing the Fejervary government caused general consternation. All over the country people were stunned and apprehensive. No one believed that such a thing was possible since, for more than half a century, they had felt secure in the knowledge that they were living in a democratic parliamentary era. What had just happened was the negation of their civil rights, while that feeling of security had been suddenly and unexpectedly shattered. Those now in power issued communiqués that stated categorically that there would be no changes other than those essential for carrying on the business of government, and that nothing, again excepting only what was necessary, would affect any man's constitutional rights. No one believed a word of it and the government's explanations were not even thought worth considering. At first some people imagined that all this must be the outcome of some nefarious plot by Tisza; but this theory was soon seen to hold no water since Tisza publicly condemned the appointment of the new government and declared himself opposed to the new cabinet. He even refused to see any member of his own party who showed signs of sympathy with this unconstitutional move. Not for years had a political event been so universally condemned.

PART FIVE

The annual meeting of the Kolozsvar constituent assembly was held in an atmosphere of the general resentment which verged on an uneasy spirit of revolt.

The hall was packed tightly. Every member who could possibly attend had done so and behind them, the galleries reserved for the general public were overflowing, largely with university students. It was soon clear that the public's intention was to cheer any spokesman who opposed the new government and to shout down anyone who dared to speak in its favour. Everyone was aware that a proposition had been made that all provincial and municipal employees should refuse to obey orders from the central government. That Hungarian non-violent resistance. call it passive disobedience or what you will, had its birth at the Kolozsvar assembly was proved by the fact that the date of the meeting had been long established and therefore preceded any of the discussions in other parts of Hungary. Everyone was wondering how the president of the Assembly, the mayor Szvacsina, would proceed. Would he agree to discussing the motion for civil disobedience or not? No one knew what would happen, and it was because of this uncertainty that the radical Professor Korosi, with his colleagues the author of the motion, had not only organized the presence in the hall of all the university students, but also arranged for the streets outside to be filled with peasant youths who would march up and down, cheering and booing, to make it perfectly clear to the ruling classes who formed the majority of those attending that they really meant business. From time to time someone went out onto the balcony to speak to these young men, bolster up their interest and prevent them from returning home out of boredom.

Inside the dark hall, under the larger-than-life portrait of the Emperor Franz-Josef, the financial secretary of the assembly read out the details and figures of the annual expenditure, fully aware that no one was interested and that no one was listening. Not a single voice was raised; not a single criticism, lest any unnecessary discussion might be started which would distract the assembly before the real business began. Everyone tacitly understood this, so that when the mayor asked if the assembly passed the accounts there were impatient cries of 'Aye! Aye! Aye!'

From the back of the hall several voices were heard calling out: 'Korosi! Korosi!'

'Dr Korosi asks to be heard. Silence, please!' said the presiding mayor. He then leaned back, his thin, tired-looking form reclining in the presidential chair and his long fingers folded as if he knew that for some time now he would have nothing to do and so could relax.

Dr Korosi rose to speak. In front of him sat the real heads of the opposition in Kolozsvar, Professor Apathy and his close colleagues, who clustered round him as if they were his bodyguards. This group stared ahead of them at the benches opposite where Tisza's supporters sat. They, too, were largely composed of university professors for in Kolozsvar, as almost everywhere else, the seat of learning was also the seat of political strife. Korosi addressed his remarks directly to them, not, as protocol demanded, to the president of the assembly. He was a tall man, fat and broad; and he spoke the dialect of the great Hungarian plain where he was born. His words flowed, a constant stream of familiar slogans and platitudes: 'The accursed Austrians ... the camarilla of Vienna ... traitors! Gaolers! Lackeys! Henchmen! ... Lajos Kossuth and the Honour of Hungary ... the martyrs of Arad ... Haynau and Bach ... soldiery and army intrigues ... Hungarian sword-tassels ... the language of command ... independent national customs ... independence of the banks ... Rakoczi and Bocskai ...', and so on. Korosi left nothing out. Everything that could inflame public opinion was included and thumped home with all the superficially seductive argument of the professional theologian. His strongest arguments and bitterest accusations were hurled directly at those sitting on the benches opposite; but, though he clearly expected an uproar of protest, he was listened to with calm, smiling acquiescence. At last he read the proposition whereby provincial and municipal administrations should forbid their employees to obey the orders of the central government, should stop the enrolment of army volunteers and should withhold payment of all tax-monies to the finance ministry.

When at last he had finished, Korosi mopped his tousled forehead. Huge cheering broke out from all parts of the assembly hall and one of his colleagues rushed out on to the balcony to signal to the crowd below that the time had come when everyone should shout aloud to let the town aristocrats know that the people were behind the opposition.

Within the hall the mayor raised his hand for silence and asked if anyone wished to add to the proposal now before the assembly. He spoke calmly, in a non-committal voice.

There was silence. Apathy and his band of parliamentary coalitionists looked over to where sat the little gynaecological

professor who was the spokesman of the official government
party. They all thought that he would rise and in his well-known,
sarcastic, razor-sharp tones, begin to protest. But he did not
move, merely gazing back with an ironic smile on his face, silent
and inscrutable.

'Professor Dr Korosi's proposal is unanimously accepted,' the
mayor declared pompously.

The opposition and their followers were taken by surprise.
They had not expected things to go smoothly, and indeed had
been prepared for battle, noise and disturbance. The assembly
cheered the mayor and council and cries of 'Long live the Mayor'
went up all round. 'Long live Szvacsina! Long live the Council!'
They smiled and bowed, glad that for once they had been cheered
and were popular; on all previous occasions the careful discipline
of the Tisza party members had meant that the opposition had
normally been forced into unpopular and rowdy behaviour: and
for once this had not happened. It was extraordinary but the
Tisza party had also declared itself against this 'government by
lackeys' and so their policy of resistance was for once not only accepted but also popular! And so they started to sing that revolutionary song 'Lajos Kossuth sent a message...' to remind them of
the great days of Hungarian opposition to Habsburg tyranny.

The triumphant opposition members now left the hall to join
the mob gathered outside. This had now been increased by
groups of ordinary strollers and loiterers as well as by the gypsies
and stall-holders from the market who had all gathered round
to see the fun. The streets and pavements were covered with people. Korosi climbed on to a bench in the central part of the
square, where each morning vegetable stalls would be set up, so
as to broadcast what had happened in a spirited and patriotic
speech. As soon as he had finished another man, bull-necked with
long arms and dressed in Hungarian national costume, jumped
up on the bench opposite: 'People of Kolozsvar!' he shouted, 'I salute this patriotic town in the name of the Szekler people from
the Maros who on this sacred day...'

It was Janko Cseresznyes – Cherrytree – the unscrupulous demagogue who had been used by Azbej in engineering Abady's
election and had made such a good thing of it for himself. He happened to be in Kolozsvar that morning by sheer chance, having
come into the pig market to purchase thirty young piglets for a
firm in Torda. Having done what he came for, he had wandered
into the centre of town and, seeing a mass of people all gathered

together, could not resist the temptation to play some part in whatever was going on. Accordingly he adopted the role of an envoy from the Szeklers living by the Maros river. As such he could address the crowd to his heart's content.

'We, the Szekler people who taught the Russians such a lesson in '48; we, who chased the entire Austrian army to the very gates of hell, we are determined to fight to the end, offering our blood, our lives...'

Professor Dr Korosi and his friends waited for Cherrytree to come to an end but, seeing that he had no intention of stopping, gave up and went home to lunch. Janko went on, his huge voice carrying to the far end of the square, reciting endless promises of good things to come: 'They talk of "independent customs" but if I was in power I'd see that we got a good price for everything we sell. And, what's more, what we buy we'd buy cheap! That's what I'd do!'

'Bless you! Well said!' shouted the mob.

'And I'd lift all the taxes! Yes, sir! I'd wipe them all out!'

'That's rubbish!' cried someone from the crowd. 'You can't run a state without them!'

'I would! And I'd get enough money from the customs for the country not to need taxes. What do they want so much money for anyway? Only to make our boys into Austrian soldiers!'

'Hear! Hear!'

Then he started on foreign affairs. 'The Russians thought they'd teach the Japs a good lesson, and look what happened! They're finished! Well then, why does the Austrian Emperor need so many soldiers? Why does he want Hungarian boys to be bossed about in a foreign language – in German! – by foreign officers who are nothing but henchmen of the Austrian monarchy? Enslaving our good simple Hungarian lads, laughing at them and boasting of their own superiority...'

It was at this moment that an open carriage was driven towards the mob where Cseresznyes was speaking. It slowed down and finally stopped as the road was blocked. 'Hop! Hop! Move along there!' cried the coachman, but no one moved and some of the men in the crowd started to grumble menacingly. In the carriage sat a tall dark-haired lady and next to her was an officer in a blue uniform tunic: it was Mme Bogdan Lazar, who had been born Sara Donogan, and Egon Wickwitz.

Cherrytree saw them. 'Look there!' he shouted. 'The sacred assembly of the good Hungarian people is menaced by the army!'

PART FIVE

and he pointed to the uniformed figure of Baron Egon.

Many faces were turned towards the carriage, ugly, menacing faces that surrounded it completely. The coachman began to get alarmed and Wickwitz put his hand on his sword, ready to draw if he should have to, for the 'Kaiser's Rock – the King's uniform' – must never be desecrated. All the same, he did not move. Mme Lazar, on the other hand, leapt to her feet, threw back the carriage veil which protected her from dust on the road, and drew herself up to her full height.

'What is all this nonsense?' she cried in a commanding voice. 'Isn't a Hungarian hussar respected any more? Shame on you all!' Then, recognizing the speaker on the bench, she shouted directly at him: 'And as for you, Cherrytree, you scoundrel, you'd do better to account to me for that money I gave you to buy calves with last week instead of playing the fool here! Be off with you!'

'I kiss your hands, Gracious lady,' said Cherrytree, jumping down from the bench. 'Why, I was on my way to find your Ladyship. That's why I'm here.'

'That's all right then!' She turned to the crowd. 'And now, my friends, please let me by. I still have much to do.'

Many of the people in the square knew Mme Lazar. She was generally respected and known to be a clever and industrious woman who managed her own estates. She was often to be seen mingling with the crowd at the hay auctions or in the market place, and she always had a good word for everyone she met.

Some men came forward at once and saw to it that a way was cleared for her carriage.

For nearly two months Wickwitz had been dancing attendance on the attractive Armenian widow. Mme Lazar was a good-natured woman who accepted the bad with the good, and saw through Wickwitz at once. Many men had come chasing her and she never despised or ignored the good things of life. She was tall and desirable, handsome and strong, with a small head and long limbs. Her skin was brown and healthy, over her red lips there was a faint line of velvety down which extended also along the line of her jaw. She radiated health and strength and her large eyes glowed like black diamonds behind thick lustrous lashes, so lustrous indeed that they could have been brushed in with charcoal.

Her husband had died ten years before, and since then she

had managed her estates better than most men would have done. Her son was at the same school as young Zoltan Miloth.

She was both desirable and rich. She owed more than two thousand acres close to Kolozsvar, and Wickwitz was sure that she also had a respectable balance in the bank. It would be a sensible move to marry her, he thought; it looked as if nothing would be easier as he had already been accepted as her lover. And as for the matter with Judith ... well, that was really very complicated and he thought that maybe there he had bitten off more than he could chew! It was for this reason that he had written the girl a letter full of sad resignation, giving up honourably all that he had ever asked of her and filled with such phrases as '*and anyhow I'm not worthy*' and '*It would be dishonourable of me, and unscrupulous, if I were to ask you to share my disreputable life*'. It was a good letter. It was full of romance and honourable regret and it left him free to look elsewhere, while not entirely breaking everything off between them. *Mann kann ja nicht wissen* – who knows? He had this letter delivered by young Zoltan Miloth and the boy had brought back a brief note which had merely said: 'I'm desperate! I can't write now, but I will soon. Wait for me! I love you!' Nothing more.

Wickwitz had a whole sheaf of letters from Judith and these he had kept by him. Now, seated in the open carriage with Mme Lazar, he pondered over the nature of his relationship with the widow. It was true that she was very kind to him, exceptionally so – and generous – but it seemed to him that she did not take their friendship very seriously. It seemed that she quite realistically took the situation for granted as a simple, obvious, natural arrangement which could hardly be bettered and which could last indefinitely without any change. Perhaps she would be content to go on for ever like this? That would never do, not in his situation! The thing to do would be to throw a good scare into her, make her jealous, wave a few of his other possibilities in front of her, show her that there was someone else, younger too, who was prepared to be his wife. I've got to speed things up, he said to himself in sporting terms, for he rarely thought in any others, and so he would use Judith as a 'running mate' – as in racing they call the horse who will never win but who will keep his stable-mate going until that last effort is needed to be first at the finish. If Mme Lazar realized that she was in danger of losing her soldier lover then it shouldn't be difficult to steer matters in the right direction. Perhaps she herself might even suggest marriage. Nothing would be better than that. Nothing.

PART FIVE

After they had had lunch and were sitting sipping their coffee in Mme Lazar's cool sitting-room, Wickwitz broached the subject.

'Dearest Sara,' he said, his eyes swimming with sadness. 'I'd like to ask your advice about something very delicate. In confidence of course, because one shouldn't really talk about such matters.'

From the sofa where she was reclining, leisurely smoking a cigarette, Sara looked up from under her heavy eye-lashes: 'What sort of matter?'

'I've got some trouble on my hands. There's a girl who ... who ... well, I can't help it, says she's in love with me and I don't know what to do.'

'Who is she, this girl?' asked Sara, though she knew, and had done for some time, all about Baron Egon's pursuit of the Miloth girl. She knew about it because young Zoltan, who had often read the letters he had carried between them, had boasted to Mme Lazar's son about the matter and he, thinking she would want to know everything about someone who called upon her regularly, had recounted what he had been told to his mother. Where is all this leading to now, she wondered?

Wickwitz told his tale, little bit by little bit. It was his own version, of course. He explained how he had felt sorry for the girl, indeed so sorry for her that he'd even considered marrying her out of pity. Just that, out of pity, because she was so desperately unhappy.

Sara shrugged a generous shoulder. 'There's no reason to rush into anything, especially marriage. She'll get over it in time. All girls have some unhappy love affairs when they're young, but no one ever died of it!'

Egon insisted: 'But this isn't quite so ordinary. In fact, it's an extreme case! Look, *meine Liebe*, these are the letters I've been getting!' and he brought out a packet from his inner pocket. 'I always carry them with me,' he said untruthfully, 'as I'm afraid to leave them lying about in my hotel room. Have a look at one or two of them, and you'll see what I mean!'

Sara took the letters and started to read. When she had finished one she placed it in her lap and took up another. She read for a long time, with great attention, and when she had finished the last one, she turned to him and said: 'Poor girl! She really is very smitten!'

'Didn't I tell you? You see how serious it is?' replied Wickwitz, triumphantly thinking that his plan had worked. And he suddenly broke into a peal of that strangely ugly barking laughter which transformed his otherwise handsome if melancholy features into an ugly satyr's mask.

The woman watched him as attentively as she had read the letters. She took shrewd note of his laughter. Then she said: 'I think you were right: the best thing would be to marry the girl!'

This was quite the wrong answer and Wickwitz, shattered, did not know how to proceed. His plan hadn't worked. For a moment he looked at her dully and then, though not very convincingly, he said faintly: 'But, Sara, I love you, only you!' He reached out to take her hand and looked up with infinite sadness in his great calf-like eyes.

'Ah, well, that doesn't really matter, does it?' She laughed lightly. 'These things aren't very important for people like you and me. But, since you've asked, that's what I think you ought to do!'

'Have I done anything to offend you?' asked Wickwitz putting on his saddest expression.

'Absolutely not! On the contrary, I feel flattered that you have confided in me and, naturally, for the present, and until you're married, you'll always be welcome here! As always – on the same terms. These things really are so unimportant. It makes no difference at all.' and she allowed Baron Egon to start kissing her arm all the way to the shoulder.

Later on, before he left, Wickwitz asked her to let him have back Judith's letters, but she did not hand them over.

'I'll keep them here for you!' she said in a decided manner that brooked no denial. 'They are much too dangerous' – she almost said 'valuable' – 'to keep in a hotel room!' She went to her desk and locked them in a drawer. 'This is a much better place!'

Thus did Wickwitz's plans go awry; worse, in fact, than even he knew, for when his carriage drove away and she waved him goodbye from the window he was quite unaware that she was thinking: 'An agreeable animal, but, oh dear, what a scoundrel! And stupid! Even stupider than I thought. Imagine trying to trick me with all that talk about marrying the girl! And as for letting me see everything she's written to him, it's despicable! That poor girl! I'm glad I've kept her letters.' Stretching voluptuously she got up, dressed, selected a sunshade and went out to oversee the afternoon milking.

PART FIVE

Wickwitz was angry. As soon as he got home he counted what money he had left: only a few hundred crowns. He took a look at the banker's promissory notes and saw that in February the prolongation of Dinora's draft had cost him eight hundred and thirty crowns, in May the same. Meanwhile he had to live. There had been Carnival. That had taken a lot. Money just disappeared and he could not go on as he had. Something had to be done, and done immediately. His only remaining chance was Judith: they would just have to elope, for there was no other means of being sure of her. But for this, too, he would need money. The only way would be to cash Countess Abonyi's drafts; he could think of nothing else.

A day or two later he went to Vasarhely to see Soma Weissfeld the banker. But Baron Weissfeld would not co-operate even when shown Dinora's signatures. In fact he refused even to discuss the matter. 'We can't take these into consideration,' he said. 'We did it originally only because you told us the Countess would repay the drafts when she had sold her crops. Since then we've agreed to delay the repayment, but the matter is not straight and aboveboard, so I am afraid...'

In vain did Wickwitz try to intimidate the banker by glaring at him menacingly; but the latter held his ground and, far from becoming immediately submissive, himself took the offensive. 'Should Count Abonyi get to hear of all this, what would be the effect, do you think?'

There was obviously nothing doing here.

Back in Kolozsvar Wickwitz found a café-restaurant near the railway station which he had heard was frequented by commission agents. After giving the head-waiter a good tip he asked if the man knew where he could borrow some money. As a result of what he was told he took a train to Varad and there, at the Privatbank Blau, which was obviously more of a money-lending shop than a real bank, he obtained nine thousand crowns on the promise of repaying twelve thousand in six month's time. It was expensive, but he had to have the money. What was worse, however, was that now he had to countersign the drafts himself, with his own name. He knew that this was dangerous, for everything that he had borrowed previously had been in Dinora's name and had been covered by her signature. Until now there had been no proof that he had been involved and so, if it came to it, he could have denied all knowledge of the transactions. No one would have blamed him, or even accused him, for his word would have been quite enough, since in matters where a woman was involved it was the accepted thing that one knew nothing. Discretion was the privilege of a gentleman. But now that he had himself signed the Privatbank's drafts the matter was quite different, and much more serious. He had just six months to arrange everything and that meant that he would have to move quickly. It was lucky that before going to Nagy-Varad he had given young Zoltan a beautifully phrased sentimental letter for Judith in which he had renewed the link that he had so recently severed and asked if they could not meet somewhere in secret.

The girl's reply arrived a fortnight later. It came in a thick envelope which also enclosed the letter which Abady had given to Adrienne and which she had sent back to her sister. Judith had written the first letter when she had received that from Wickwitz saying goodbye to her. Of course it was no longer important to either of them but Judith still sent it on to him as a sort of self-justification, telling him of its history and how it had been given to AB's groom, intercepted by AB and then ... but there really was no need to go into all these details because eventually she had got it back. Now she wrote with love and devotion: *'Of course I'll join you whenever you ask. I trust you with my life.'* She told him how carefully she was guarded, so it would be impossible to see her now, but that if the family came to Kolozsvar as they usually did at this time of year, then no doubt something could be arranged.

Chapter Five

A BADY DID NOT RETURN to Budapest, for it hardly seemed worth-while to make the journey for a single session which had been called only for the House to consider – and, of course, pass – a motion calling upon all national and provincial assemblies to civil obedience.

Every day a different province, county or district would turn against the nominated government, now mockingly known as the *Darabont* – Bodyguard or Lackey Government – which was a play on words since Fejervary had previously commanded the Darabont Guard and the word *darabont* (though only in Transylvania) had a secondary and derogatory sense, for in most great aristocratic houses in that province it was the name used for a kind of inferior lackey or man-of-all-work, ever at the beck and call of his masters. And the word Bodyguard, of course, at once

PART FIVE

conjured up pictures of the monarch's own Household.

Kristoffy, who was Minister of the Interior in the 'Bodyguard' government, at once proclaimed a universal suffrage measure in an attempt to win popular support. The opposition political leaders countered with a new slogan: 'The Will of the People must be the basis of the Constitution, not its destruction!' This soon became the rallying cry of all the opposition parties. It was a good phrase and expressed what everyone felt, especially at a moment when there was a general feeling that this was not the time for inter-party feuds or for war between the right and left. Everywhere could be sensed a universal fear that the independence of Hungary, as guaranteed in the 1867 Compromise, was itself threatened, that their hard-won liberties were being secretly undermined and menaced by subversive hostile forces working towards undisputed dominance by Vienna. Even independents like Abady, who were convinced of the rightness of many of the Austrian proposals – such as those for the armies of the Dual Monarchy – and who had despised the mindless obstructions and flag-waving of the anti-Vienna lobby, now docilely fell into line with everyone who opposed the 'lackeys'. Abady realized that many people had now sensed what Slawata had already revealed to him of the plans being laid by the Heir in the Belvedere Palais.

The government declared null and void the civil disobedience motions passed by all the provincial assemblies, and those sheriffs who had supported these motions were dismissed and others appointed in their place. In Transylvania, the first General Assembly called to inaugurate the new officials was to be held in the Maros-Torda district, at Vasarhely.

For several weeks in advance plans were being laid, not only there but also all over the country, to prevent such inaugurations being effective. At Vasarhely the town was filled to overflowing the day before the assembly was due to be held. There was a grim, serious look on everyone's face. The main square was packed with people and every table on the pavement in front of the Transylvania Café was crowded. There was not a place to be found and it was difficult even to thread one's way from one table to another. At one of the marble-topped tables sat the great Samuel Barra, who had been the idol of the county ever since, the year before, he had led all the obstructionists and in particular had dared to oppose Ferenc Kossuth after the latter had suggested reconciliation between the parties. He had also taken a leading part in the controversy concerning the use of Hungarian as the language of command in the army. Barra was a dark, stocky, broad-shouldered man with a short beard and shining, dome-like forehead. He had large, dull-coloured eyes set under bushy eyebrows, but everyone who looked at him normally noticed only his enormous mouth which seemed to have become overdeveloped perhaps by the tremendous number of words that were constantly emerging from it. His lips were thick and the muscles round the mouth so exceptionally powerful that he could transform himself into a human loudspeaker at will.

Even now, though he was merely chatting with a group of his admirers, when he opened his mouth everything he said could be heard as far away as if he were talking into a megaphone. Around him sat his supporters in a tightly knit group. On his right was Ordung, the suspended prefect who was doing his best to play the martyr's part; his deputy, Bela Varju, who was a member of parliament; the older Bartokfay, who loved to recount how much better things had been in the 'Great Days of Yore'; and chubby, baby-faced Isti Kamuthy. The last two had both been unsuccessful candidates at the last elections and were now all the more fired with public zeal as they hoped to be elected next time round, always providing, of course, that there should be a change of government. Their leader at this moment was saying little, merely replying to the soft-spoken arguments of the lawyer, Zsigmond Boros, who could easily and elegantly explain, in persuasive, flowery speeches, the most complicated legal problems. It was he who was taking the lead in their talk and he did so as by right, being one of the members for Vasarhely who was now in the heart of his own constituency. Also present was Joska Kendy, his pipe clenched between his teeth, and Uncle Ambrus, both of whom remained silent. Though this was expected of Joska, who hardly ever opened his mouth, it was unusual for Uncle Ambrus. Ambrus was normally louder and more vociferous than most, but today he was keeping quiet only occasionally belching out a rude word or two with a grin of good humour and doing his best to maintain his role as an uncouth but well-meaning and ultimately guileless good fellow. He had put on an innocent face, like a new-born babe, and every now and then whispered something to the two younger Alvinczys, Zoltan and Akos, who were seated on each side of him. These two disappeared alternately every fifteen minutes or so. All around the supporters of the local leaders sat and talked and walked about and were pleased that all these great and important people had turned up for the assembly. Near to the edge of the pavement sat two so-called neutrals, Jeno Laczok and Soma Weissfeld, who were doing their best to look like patriots and thereby atone for having previously sat on the fence.

Abady remained at Barra's table for nearly an hour. The talk was of general matters, nobody mentioning the next day's assembly. The party leaders were careful to avoid the subject, even though everyone already knew what their plan was. It was an excellent plan, and, as everyone already knew it, was a well-kept secret. As soon as the notary acting as president opened the assembly, Bela Varju was to stand up and, before the notary was able even to start making his official statement, propose the suspension of the notary. If this were accepted – as it certainly would be – then the notary would automatically have to give place to the President of the Chancery Court, who was Bartokfay's younger brother, and he in turn (as had already been plotted) would at once announce that the Assembly did not recognize or accept the government nominee as prefect. This would mean that the president of the chancery court would at once be suspended: but then would be automatically succeeded by Gakffy, the Chief Justice, thereby ensuring that for many months to come, the provincial government would be headed by someone opposed to the government in the capital.

It was well thought out; and it was perfectly legal. The only worry was that, as everywhere else, there were dissensions in the province; and no one was quite sure how long it would be before they rose again to the surface. Though it was more than fifty years since the counties of Torda and Marosszek had been united in one administrative unit, the people of the former stronghold of the Szeklers in the Maros valley never wanted the same things as those of the northern part of the district. It was certain, therefore, that the Szekler party would want something different from what was being generally planned, if only to underline their independence, and that they too were plotting some 'secret' move. Being another 'secret', everyone knew it too. The Szekler move was almost identical to the majority plan, except that their refusal to recognize the government-appointed prefect, even though he had been nominated by the king, was to be based on the fact that he was a 'foreigner'. Though both sides wanted, to all intents and purposes, exactly the same thing, they wanted it in different ways, and each was prepared to stab the other in the back if thereby they could get their own way. The two parties even adopted different names: the Suspension Party and the Decree Party.

Everyone was well aware of what was going on, but no one was prepared to talk about it. At his table on the sidewalk in front of the café Dr Boros was discoursing elegantly on various non-controversial legal matters and everyone was paying attention to him. At last there was an interruption.

An unusual four-horse carriage drove up; unusual because instead of the conventional carriage horses it was driven by four stocky little mountain ponies with short strong legs, long tails and thick shaggy manes.

The coachman, and the man on the box, were dressed in long linen dust-coats and wore the high cylindrical hats of the Upper Maros. A tall man got up heavily from the rear seat of the low-slung carriage: it was Miklos Absolon, political leader of the Upper Maros region. The crowd around the coffee-house did not notice his arrival until he tried to make his way towards where everyone was sitting. Then they all jumped up and made way for him, though they knew that he was a trouble-maker and had only come in order to laugh at them and stir up what mischief he could.

Absolon immediately made for the table where the party leaders were sitting. He had a severe limp as a result of a twisted left leg that ended in a stump. He walked always with a short crutch held tightly to his thigh and now he made his way swiftly and noisily to the table where Barra was seated.

His progress was as relentless and unstoppable as that of an express train and on arrival they all rose and asked him to sit with them. 'Good evening to you all!' he said, and sat down, though without going so far as to shake anyone's hand.

'Give me a chair for my leg!' he demanded of his neighbour, the Chief Justice Galffy, who immediately surrendered his own. When Absolon was settled he put his crutch on the table and turned to Barra. 'Well, Samu, so you've come to see the fun!' he said in a rasping voice.

Barra, instead of replying with one of the well-turned phrases of which he was such a master, merely replied, in a careful, non-committal manner: 'Yes, here I am!'

Balint could see old Absolon well, for his face was lit up by the lamps of the coffee-house in front of him. He looked remarkably like his nephew Pali Uzdy, with the same stylized Tartar head, slanting back eyes and wide cheekbones. His hair, too grew from a widow's peak which was now visible as he had pushed back from his forehead the little fur-trimmed cap he always wore. This cap was from Asia, a Kirgiz cap as worn by the Gobi tribesmen

PART FIVE

in the Altai mountains, and its fur lining stood up in twin triangles on each side of his head. He was tall, though not so thin and spindly as his nephew, and he had wide muscular shoulders.

Abady was fascinated to see him. He had heard that twenty years before, during the '80s, Miklos Absolon had travelled widely in the more remote parts of Central Asia. He had had many adventures and seen many strange things, and would talk endlessly and wittily about them; though he had never written down his experiences or made any effort to publish them. As a result many people assumed that he had made it all up and that he was an habitual mythomaniac whose tales were all lies and so, though they would egg him on to recount his 'adventures', it was all nothing more than a tease and they would mock him behind his back. Balint had always thought it was probable that Absolon was telling the truth, and this feeling had been reinforced when he had met an old Russian in Stockholm who had travelled with Prsevalskij and who had asked Balint how Absolon was and if he had ever published the story of his time in Tibet. The old man had said that what Absolon had to tell would have been of world interest, and he told Balint how Absolon, when trying to escape from Lhasa, which he had entered disguised as a pilgrim, had been caught at the Tibetan frontier and had his leg broken, and how his eventual escape had been a miracle of cunning and endurance.

In Transylvania, however, no one believed a word of these old stories and so, as soon as the old traveller had seated himself at Barra's table on the Vasarhely sidewalk, someone asked, with an innocent face: 'Is your leg hurting you?'

'Naturally. Hasn't the political weather changed?' replied the Absolon with a short rasping laugh.

'Thinth when are you wounded?' lisped young Kamuthy.

The older man looked up sharply: he knew well he was being mocked but, in his turn, he laughed at those who tried to make fun of him, knowing, as they did not, that everything he said was true.

'When visiting the Dalai Lama!' he replied. This was just the sort of answer for which they had hoped. Some of his listeners laughed and others nudged each other in satisfied appreciation.

The old traveller looked around and saw Abady whom he did not immediately recognize. 'Who are you?' he called out. Someone explained: 'Ah, Tamas's son! He was a good friend of mine. I'm pleased to see you!' Then he turned to the lawyer and said:

'I interrupted your discourse. Please go on. I should like to learn something new!' Boros then went back to his dissertation on common law. Absolon listened quietly for a long time as the lawyer spoke carefully and mellifluously. From time to time he nodded as if in agreement. Then he took out a short black cigar, bit it firmly with his white teeth and spat out the end.

'That's very interesting, very good!' he said. 'We need laws. Everyone needs laws, even in the desert! There, if someone steals a woman he can redeem himself with two sheep, though, of course, if he steals something valuable, a camel for instance, then he's hanged without mercy!'

Zsigmond Boros went pale with anger. Icily, from behind his carefully trimmed spade-shaped beard, he said: 'I don't see the connection.'

'Perhaps there is none!' replied Absolon, laughing heartily.

'But, since we were speaking about the law . . .'

There was some whispering in the background and someone sniggered sensing that Absolon's apparently innocent remark might be more mischievous than it sounded, for most people had heard some rumours that Boros was in difficulties concerning a legacy from some deceased female client. However, the lawyer merely looked coldly at Absolon for a moment or two before resuming his legal discourse.

While this was happening at the coffee-house a private closed carriage, with its glass windows tightly shut, entered the square from the road that came from the mountains. It was driven by an elderly coachman and was pulled by two horses who were obviously tired after a long drive.

As soon as the carriage stopped one of its windows was let down just a crack and a young man went up to it and spoke to whoever was inside. In a moment he was replaced by another, both presumably making their reports to the person, still invisible, who was seated within. Then the Chief Justice was called to the carriage window. A minute or two later, he came back to the café table and spoke to Abady.

'Countess Sarmasaghy would like a word with you,' whispered Galffy,. 'She's in the carriage over there.' Balint found this very tiresome, but there was nothing to be done but obey.

From the darkness of the carriage a little shrivelled hand reached out to him. 'Get in!' said a thin, piping voice; and talon-like fingers drew him into the carriage. As soon as he was seated she ordered the coachman to drive on.

'I need to have you with me, nephew Balint, my young friend, because I have to go to a public restaurant and a lady of my age and standing could not possibly go there unaccompanied!'

The tired horses were now trotting very slowly. Old Lizinka complained: 'It's terrible how much I've got to do. I'm quite exhausted. I've spoken to dozens of people. I have to if I'm going to prevent that old no-good Absolon having his way!'

'Where are we going?' asked Balint.

'Just to the edge of the town. There is some sort of an inn where it seems I shall find that good-for-nothing nephew of mine, Tamas Laczok. I've got to speak to him. Why? Because of this ridiculous assembly, of course. They tell me he's on good terms with the chief engineer of the railways and I want him to help me persuade the man to vote with us – for Suspension.'

The old woman sighed deeply as she explained to her nephew how much work you had to do if you took up a cause. It was almost more than she could do, but no one would ever say that she, Lizinka Sarmasaghy, had given up easily!

Finally they arrived at a small restaurant in a garden on the outskirts of the town. Little tables covered with red cloth were placed in the shade of acacia trees. In the middle there was a long table at which sat a group of young men, students and agriculturists from the University of Kolozsvar, arguing in loud voices. Nearby, alone, sat Tamas Laczok the railway builder.

Balint recognized him at once for he looked exactly like his brother, Jeno, the Lord of Var-Siklod, though not quite so fat. He had the same short body, bald head and inscrutable oriental face. Aunt Lizinka went swiftly over to him, saying: 'Good evening, dear Tamas! How are you, my dear boy? It is an age since I've seen you and you haven't changed a bit, not a bit! I am lucky to have found you.' and she ran on, tapping his cheeks and pressing a wet kiss on his forehead. Then she introduced Balint, sat down, and started talking politics. She talked so much, and so swiftly – producing a seemingly endless stream of political argument backed by quotations of common law – that no one, should they have wanted to, could possibly have stopped the flow. As it was, Tamas Laczok just sat back calmly with the bland expression on his face of one who understands nothing of what is being said to him, taking sips from his tankard of beer and rolling one cigarette after another, licking them as the Spaniards do, and smoking quietly. He just let Lizinka talk without himself saying a word. Finally she begged him to use his influence with the chief engineer so as to be sure he voted in the right way. When at length she paused, hoping for a reply he looked up and replied, in French: '*Ma chère tante, vous avez eu la bonté de tant radoter sur mon compte* – as you have been so kind as to spread evil gossip about me – I can see no reason why I should do you the smallest favour.'

Lizinka protested but to no avail. Tamas merely shook his head and repeated: *Mais oui, ma chère tante, c'est ainsi, c'est ainsi* – that's how it is!'

Lizinka at last realized that she would get nowhere with him and jumped up screeching: '*Tu es un cochon*'! *Tu as été un cochon! Tu sera toujours un cochon* – You're a pig, always have been and always will be!' and ran out of the garden faster than anyone would have thought possible for such a frail old lady. In her rage she completely forgot Abady, who only recovered from his surprise after she had jumped back into her carriage and been driven away.

'Believe me, I have nothing to do with all this,' he said to Laczok apologetically. 'When she asked me to bring her here I had no idea...'

'I'm very glad she did!' said Tamas, laughing. 'At least it gave me the chance to tell the old witch what I thought of her! Stay and have a drink! Then I'll be able to exchange a few words with at least one of my cousins. Since I came back all the others have been avoiding me like the plague!'

Balint stayed on and was pleased to discover how agreeable and interesting this strange character really was. Tamas was obviously delighted to have someone to talk to and to whom he could relate some of his varied experiences. He talked of his time in Paris where, at the age of forty, he had finally qualified as an engineer; of Algiers, where he had had a contract to build a railway, and build it he did despite having his superior killed by wild Arab tribes before his very eyes; how they had begged him to stay on there, at an unimaginably high salary. 'But who in hell wants to stay there,' he said, 'who in hell?'

While Balint was listening to Tamas's tales he noticed that the two younger Alvinczys had joined the group of students at the long table. They seemed to be issuing some sort of orders, though Balint could catch only an occasional phrase: 'Be quiet to begin with. Don't start until I raise my hand! Understand, only when I raise my hand!' They leaned forward and continued to whisper among themselves. Tamas Laczok was still in full swing. Now he was saying: '... no matter what anyone says, home is best, if only so as to annoy my beloved brother!' He then explained how Jeno Laczok had formed a company with Soma Weissfeld, the banker, to exploit the Laczok forests in Gyergyo. These forests belonged equally to the two brothers, and Tamas was convinced that the others had done this so as to deprive him of his rightful income. It didn't matter much, he said, as at least now he could earn his own living; but from time to time he would write to them demanding statements; and then they had to set to and scribble away preparing accounts, balance-sheets, statements of profit and loss and goodness knows what else as well. 'Of course I never look at them!' he said. 'But just think how cross they must be! It's great fun!'

The students all now got up from their table and started to leave. Balint was almost sure he heard Akos Alvinczy saying to one of the other young men: 'The eggs will be handed out in the morning, at least ten each...'

Ten eggs each? thought Abady. Some breakfast that'll be! But Laczok was still telling his tales and Balint soon forgot all that he had overheard at the next table.

⁂

The town hall of Vasarhely was already packed to overflowing long before ten o'clock when the Assembly was due to be officially opened. This was because a rumour had spread among the members of the Suspension Party that that wicked fellow, the notary-in-chief, had planned to shut the doors at nine-thirty and install the government's prefect while the hall was still half empty. A rumour had also reached the Decree Party that their opponents were plotting to barricade the entrances so that they alone would be in place when any decision was reached. All the official delegates therefore came early, well before the appointed time, and they were joined by a band of thirty or forty university students who, bear-led by the two young Alvinczys, forced their way up the stairs and into the hall before the policeman on duty could do anything to stop them. Some took their seats in the public gallery where Aunt Lizinka presided like some wicked fairy – though she thought of herself rather as some Guardian Angel of the Resistance – while the majority crowded together at the back of the hall facing the platform where the president would sit surrounded by his officers-of-state.

The platform was empty: none of the officials had yet arrived.

The two parties took their places on opposite sides of the hall. On the right was the great Samuel Barra, the older Bartokfay, Varju, Isti Kamuthy, Uncle Ambrus and the Alvinczys. All these sat in the front row. On the left, Miklos Absolon sat by himself, as if enthroned, and behind him were ranged all the delegates from the Maros and Gorgeny districts, a nameless and faceless mob who listened only to their beloved leader. Many people were moving about, greeting friends, arguing and joking among themselves. Everybody was in a good mood, happily and merrily looking forward to the morning's great battle, which they all expected to provide great fun for them all, and talking about the latest news from Budapest. Meanwhile, behind the door leading to the presidential platform, the officials were busy conferring among themselves and with others as to how to have the students removed, since the notary-in-chief refused to open the meeting if they remained in the hall. They also discussed who should be allowed to speak first, Barra or the spokesman for the Decree Party. After much talk they decided that the first speaker should be Barra, for he had guaranteed that the students would keep quiet, at least while he was on his feet. At last, towards eleven o'clock, the door opened and Bartokfay, the president of the chancery court, and the assistant notaries came in and took their places on the platform. Then the notary-in-chief, Beno Peter Balog, entered, sat down in the presidential chair and rang the bell. Everyone sat down, silent and eager with anticipation.

'I hereby declare open this session of the County General Assembly,' he said in an official tone. He went on to have the minutes read and announced the names of the absentees. This non-controversial business being brought to an end, he then started: 'The Minister of the Interior has sent an order...' but he was not allowed to go on for at these words bedlam broke out. From all sides there were cries of 'Shame on you! There is no minister! Villains! Shame!'

One of the officials tried to read out the rules of assembly, but no one could hear what he said.

Then Barra rose to speak, and for a moment the hubbub subsided. Then all at once it started again, for the door behind the president's chair had opened and a tall thin man with a deathly pale face entered the hall. It was the government nominee. He had his hand on his heart and few people could see, behind his thick-lensed glasses, the scared expression in his eyes. The president rose once again and tried to read something from a paper in his hand.

From all sides there was a confused roar of shouting: 'Down with him! *Absug* – away with you! Traitor!' Then Uncle Ambrus nudged Zoltan Alvinczy who at once raised a hand in the air. From the back of the hall eggs started to fly, well-aimed eggs – for the students had obviously had much practice – which were chiefly directed at the schoolteacher-turned-Prefect. He ducked as well as he could but almost at once was struck on the forehead and yolk ran down all over his face. He dived for shelter under the presidential table while a crowd collected round the platform with raised fists and menacing shouts. As soon as he could the poor man crawled out and fled through the door at the back, swiftly followed by the notary-in-chief who had been howled down as soon as he tried to protest.

The hall was filled with people milling in all directions. Some were still shouting abuse but most of them were now overcome with uncontrollable laughter, among them Uncle Ambrus, whose laugh was louder than anyone's. In his deep bass-baritone voice, between gusts of mirth, he was calling out: 'Well done, lads! That was well done indeed! We Hungarians'll show 'em!'

All around arguments broke out. No one knew if the newly-named Prefect had had time to take the oath or not, or, if he had, whether it was valid. They cursed the notary-in-chief, calling him a traitor, and furiously discussed what should be done with such a monster.

Balint, who had arrived late and so had only been able to find a place near the doors, glanced at his watch. It was barely half-past eleven: the whole meeting had lasted only twenty minutes. If he went at once he would be able to catch the one o'clock train, he thought. So he turned and left the hall.

Although Balint had shouted with the others and even raised his fists in the air, and laughed at the comicality of the scene when the prefect had been pelted with eggs and taken refuge under the table, a great sadness descended on him as he went down the stairs and out into the street. He thought only of the fact that an innocent man had been humiliated, and that it was callous and distasteful that everyone should think the whole affair a tremendous joke and nothing more.

Within the hour Balint was at the station. He was early and no one was on the platform, so he went into the restaurant, which was empty but for one man sitting at a table: it was Aurel Timisan.

Balint went up to him and greeted him. Then he sat down and asked if he too was travelling to Kocsard.

'Not today,' said the old Romanian delegate. 'I'm going up to my constituency. I'm only here to change trains.' Then, quite softly but with overtones of ironic pleasure, he asked: 'And is your Lordship pleased with today's assembly?'

Balint shrugged his shoulders and made a non-committal reply.

'I don't imagine that it will end here, as they all seem to think,' said Timisan. 'This sort of thing merely strengthens the government in its determination to impose reform. I don't suppose *seine kaiserliche und königliche Majestät* will find the present situation any joking matter either. Of course,' Timisan went on modestly, his large whey-coloured eyes full of suppressed humour as he gazed at Balint, 'I'm only a simple Romanian countryman, a mere pamphleteer, so I really know nothing about it, but I wonder, just the same...?'

'You're thinking of universal suffrage?'

'Among other things, yes. That would strike a severe blow at all this resistance. Indeed it might upset the whole apple cart!'

'But Parliament won't pass anything this government puts forward, no matter what it is!'

'Naturally! That goes without saying!' Timisan nodded his agreement and again something of an enigmatic smile lurked under his thick white moustaches. 'What do you suppose will happen if the ruler imposes a secret ballot? Could the government be selected by such a system? What will our fine resistance leaders do then? I don't understand these things, you know, I'm just wondering...'

Balint recalled that something of this sort had been hinted at in Slawata's letter and it was suddenly clear to him that the old Romanian deputy must know something he did not. He tried to find out what it was; but Timisan was not giving anything away and remained as politely inscrutable as before.

Chapter Six

IN AUGUST Laszlo Gyeroffy returned to Transylvania. He did not go willingly, but he finally gave in to Fanny Beredy's entreaties that he go and put his affairs in order. It was she who had finally convinced him that the time had come when he must do something to settle his debts which, though he had occasionally been able to repay a small part of his borrowings from his winnings at cards, had been mounting steadily, not the least because the high interest charged by the money-lending sharks was designed to ensure that no one, if possible, ever escaped their clutches. As soon as he arrived Laszlo went to see his former guardian, his cousin Stanislo. Laszlo owned a one-third share of the

Gyeroffy forest holdings which amounted in all to something over eight thousand Hungarian acres,† and he wanted to get Stanislo to release his share so that he could sell the land and the standing timber. His guardian would not hear of it, explaining that the license for exploiting the forest was for the total acreage which could not and should not be split up. That was his opinion and therefore his answer was No! A definite, irrevocable No! Laszlo did not know what to do, for he had no other way of raising money to pay his debts. As a result, he was in an extremely bad mood, more bitter and resentful than he had habitually become since Klara's marriage. Only late at night when he had had a lot to drink was he able partially to escape from his sorrow and self-reproaches.

For some days he stayed in a hotel, drinking in the evening and going out to carouse the night away with the local gypsy girls. He seldom got up before the afternoon. One day Balint met him by chance in the street in Kolozsvar.

'Why are you destroying yourself, keeping away from us all and drinking alone?' asked Balint. 'Come back with me now, to Denestornya!' And though Gyeroffy, who nowadays seemed all too ready to take offence or pick a quarrel, merely grunted ungraciously and said: 'Leave me alone, I can take care of myself!' In fact he did as Balint had suggested.

Countess Roza was delighted to see her nephew once again. She loved to show people round Denestornya, to take them to see her horses and her gardens; and now, as Balint had told her of Laszlo's sad and disappointed love for Klara, she made herself especially kind and indulgent to the nephew she had not seen for some time, going out of her way to be sure that he had everything he needed. She even ordered wine for dinner, which was by no means her custom.

Early one morning, when Laszlo had been there for some days, Gazsi Kadacsay ('Crazy'), whose home was not far away, arrived at the castle. He was on his way to Brasso to rejoin his regiment and was travelling alone with three horses, one of which he rode while leading the other two. 'Just like the wild Cossacks, my frrriends!' he said, rolling his r's proudly, 'Like the Tarrrtarrrs!' Although Gazsi's two pack animals could have carried far heavier loads he travelled only with an old army sack containing a couple of ragged shirts, a crumpled civilian suit, a razor and a toothbrush, not only because he was totally unpretentious but also because he loved to shock people by dressing unconventionally. He

† Equivalent to over eleven thousand English acres. – Trans.

arrived at Denestornya clad only in an officer's tunic which lacked several buttons, stained khaki riding breeches, boots with tassels of gold braid and a red hussar's cap.

After dinner was over Countess Roza stayed in the yellow drawing-room, which she always used as an office, to interview the lawyer Azbej; and the three young men retired to the library. This was a circular room in the tower above Balint's own suite. All round the walls and even between the windows were fitted bookcases made of teak and fitted with doors of mirror-glass. These were full of all the volumes collected by generations of Abadys and, as they could not hold all the books, more cases had been built above them, also fitted with looking-glass doors. Above these, even more books were piled up, almost hiding the stone busts of the Seven Wise Men which had been placed there to look down on the baize-covered round table in the centre of the room.

While Baron Gazsi was looking into the bookcases, Laszlo and Balint sat at the centre table under the green-shaded hanging lamp. Their talk soon deteriorated into an argument, which began when Laszlo once again started grumbling about his treatment by his cousin Stanislo. His bitterness and resentment so overcame him that soon he was saying that there was nothing left for him but to sell up, move right away from Transylvania and leave all this misery behind him. What, he asked rhetorically, was there for him in that forgotten little province? He'd do better to go elsewhere, anywhere, where he could live his own life free of responsibilities anywhere, even abroad, where he could get right away from this trivial life.

Balint's hackles rose. All that Laszlo said was directly contrary to everything that he had been brought up to believe was important. Balint lived by that creed of duty that had first been instilled in him by his boyhood talks with his grandfather and by his grandfather's example, and later by his mother's entreaties and the letters from her which had finally induced him to give up being a diplomat and return home to look after the Abady inheritance.

'Go abroad! Never! That is something you really shouldn't do. To desert your own country is unthinkable!'

'Why not? What do I owe to this rotten society here?'

Balint jumped up angrily, the veins swelling on his forehead. 'What would you be anywhere else? Nobody! Your name would mean nothing: you'd just be a number on a passport. How dare you waste your inheritance, dissipate everything that is yours by birth! You never made your own fortune. It's not yours to throw away. You have a duty here, a duty to the community that raised you and gave you all these advantages!'

'What should I do?' said Laszlo scornfully. 'Go into politics like you?'

'All life is politics; and I don't mean just party politics. It is politics when I keep order on the estates and run the family properties. It's all politics. When we help the well-being of the people in the villages and in the mountains, when we try to promote culture, it's still politics, I say, and you can't run away from it!'

Baron Gazsi joined them at the table: 'That's interesting, what you're saying, very interesting,' said Gazsi, poking forward his woodpecker nose.

'It is as I say. The only thing that gives us any moral right to the fortunes that we inherit is a sense of duty. Our parentage binds us to it and it's an obligation that none of us can escape!'

Laszlo laughed offensively. 'Well I don't have the same *Ahnenstolz* – pride of race, as you, my friend!'

'Why speak so scornfully of *Ahnenstolz*? What do you mean by the word? If you just take it as meaning that you can name your ancestors because they are recorded in the archives, and that those archives have been preserved, then you're a fool. But when capacity is proved through several generations, is tested, refined and polished by experience, then don't you think we have a right and a duty to use our capacities for the ends for which they have been developed? Fox-hounds are better at chasing a fox than pinchers and they've got better noses than a bulldogs! The Hungarian nobility has ruled their country, and served it, for centuries. They know their job, whether it's in service to the community, to the provincial administration, to the church, or in government. And they serve freely – *in honoris causa!*'

'What an unselfish lot!' said Laszlo ironically.

'Not at all. Nobody is unselfish. Nobody ever was. But they've learnt to recognize what is for the public good and to fit it to their own advantage, too. This insight has been bred into us; just as military discipline has been bred into the Prussian Junker, and commercial trading into the Jews and Armenians. It's not by chance that until now almost every great national leader has sprung form this rank of society, for leaders must know how to lead. 'Leadership is *our* responsibility and we should not lightly avoid it until such time as all our people develop some sense of social responsibility themselves, as our Saxons seem to have done.'

It was at this point that Balint noticed that his mother was in the room, standing near the door. She must have been there for some little time, for he could see from her smile that she had heard and approved everything he had just been saying.

Countess Roza came further into the room and went over to where Laszlo was sitting. She caressed his hair lightly with her chubby little hand.

'I'd like to show you something, boys,' she said, and she went with her little tripping walk back into the drawing-room to her writing desk. From it she took an old, frayed, yellow exercise book, which had obviously been much used. Bringing it back with her she sat down, placed it on the table under the light and started to read:

> *I know that I am placing a great burden on you when I command you to deal with everything personally. You must realize that our agents, and our tenants, see only what is to their own advantage or what is to yours. I expect more than this from you. The patriarchal relationship that has existed for centuries between the landowner and the people of this village did not end when the serfs were liberated. You must still take the lead, help people, take care of them, especially all those who are not as privileged as you in matters of fortune and education. Thlnk of them as your children, the village people and the people who serve you in the house. You must be severe, but above all you must be just and understanding. This is your duty in life . . .*

Countess Roza looked at Balint, her eyes shining with emotion and pride. Then she read on:

> *. . . this is the tradition of our family. Your father abided by it and was faithful to it, as was my father. My wish is that you should be too and so should my son.*

All three young men were deeply moved listening to Countess Abady as she read them the last instructions of her long dead husband. Laszlo bent down and kissed the old lady's hand. Then she got up and said: 'I think tea will be ready now, and the stewed fruit!'

They all returned to the drawing-room.

'I'm sorry I got so cross,' said Balint to Laszlo when he said goodnight at the door of his room.

'And I am sorry I was so churlish!' said Laszlo. 'I am afraid that I offended you.' Then, as he slipped into his room, he added softly: 'But you see I am really very unhappy.'

A few moments later, as he was undressing, Laszlo heard

someone tap at his door. He called out for whoever it was to come in. The door was opened by the hairy little lawyer, Azbej. Bowing very low and excusing him himself, Azbej immediately started off in his usual obsequious manner. 'It's just that I heard that your Lordship ... that Count Stanislo Gyeroffy ... that your Lordship was unable to convince the noble Count Stanislo ... well, if your Lordship would honour me with his confidence, perhaps *I* could do something to make his Lordship see reason. If I were to explain what is involved...' and he quoted from the law books and from judgments in similar cases, going on, 'then naturally his Lordship would have to withdraw his objections. I must explain to your Lordship that though I am a lawyer I do not practise generally. I merely look after the interests of the noble Countess. I do not work for anyone else. My life is dedicated to her Ladyship's interests. But I thought that as your Lordship is a relation of her Ladyship ... perhaps I could be of assistance ... as a favour naturally ... nothing else.'

Gyeroffy was thrilled and delighted by the little lawyer, despite his plethora of lordships and ladyships, and readily signed the paper that Azbej put in front of him authorizing the lawyer to take complete charge of Laszlo's affairs. The authority had no limits and gave Azbej full power of attorney, but this signified nothing to Laszlo.

Chapter Seven

Dear AB,
 I want to ask a favour of you which I can't ask of anyone else. Would you please buy me a little Browning revolver, you know the sort you can put in your pocket. I seem to remember that I've seen them in Emil Schuster's shop in Kolozsvar; also a box or two of ammunition. Can you get it to me here at Almasko, but secretly so that no one knows. Will you do it? I want to surprise Pali Uzdy!!!
 Yours sincerely Ad.
 P.S. Could you get it to me within the next two or three weeks?

THE WORDS 'secretly' and 'surprise' were underlined twice. This note arrived at the end of August.

Balint sat at the window of his room reading Addy's letter and thinking that it was a strange request. It was odd that she would want to buy a present for her husband and even odder that she should want him to do it for her; and he found himself feeling somewhat resentful. He wondered about the matter. What could have happened between husband and wife that she suddenly wanted to surprise him with a present? It had always been his impression that neither of them was much concerned to give the other pleasure by such little attentions as surprise gifts. What could have happened between them? Was it possible that something had changed in their relationship, that things were different and that at last they had become friends as well as man and wife? After five years, had they just discovered each other so that now Adrienne no longer dreaded the physical realities of married life?

Balint's heart missed a beat at this last thought and he jumped up from his seat. Of course it was possible! It always had been possible. If it were so then it would be best for all of them, and for him it would mean freedom at last from that ever-present longing for her that he had found so destructive to his peace of mind. If she were reconciled to her husband it would be easy for him to break the invisible chains that bound him to this senseless, profitless adventure. He decided that he would comply with her strange demand and buy the Browning. Then he would take it himself to Almasko so as to make sure that Adrienne knew that he had understood what the purchase of this gift symbolized. As long as he did that she would not dare to mock his love for her, even if she had become a real wife to her husband, and he searched in his mind for the right ambiguous phrases with which to address her when they next met. Try as he would, however, instead of the lofty, disinterested, ironic words for which he sought, all that he could think of sounded bitter and vengeful, as if nothing could suppress the hurt in his soul. Later on he could think of nothing at all to say, even when one Sunday morning in early September he was already seated in the train with the little automatic in his bag and, later, when the Uzdy carriage brought him from Banffy-Hunyad to Almasko his mind was as blank as ever.

When they reached Nagy-Almas the coachman turned to Balint and asked if his Lordship would mind if they stopped to pick up the priest?

An elderly white-haired monk in a Franciscan habit was waiting for them in the town square. He got into the carriage and sat next to Balint. From their conversation Balint learned that every Sunday his companion went to say mass in the castle chapel.

PART FIVE

'But I thought the Uzdys were Protestant?' remarked Balint.

'Count Pali is, and the young Countess too, but Countess Clémence is a Catholic and so are some of the servants,' said the monk, but he did not pursue the subject and soon fell silent.

Balint had hardly descended from the carriage when Adrienne walked out across the forecourt to meet him. The old butler Maier at once led the priest away and Adrienne and Balint were alone.

'Did you bring it?' Adrienne asked softly and then, rather more loudly than usual, she said: 'Let's go into the garden! I hate it indoors at this time of year!'

They sat down on the same bench where they had talked on the first day of Balint's last visit, and once again he was impressed by how gloomy the landscape seemed. Some of the beeches were already turning gold but the great oaks were still as dark as before, some of them almost black. Only in the distance the divided walls of the ruined fortress shone white in the noonday sun. Somehow conversation did not come easily to either of them; for both of them were thinking of other things. From behind one of the ground-floor windows there was the sound of a bell, and the voice of the priest could be heard intoning: *'Dominus vobiscum . . .'*

Below where Adrienne and Balint sat Pali Uzdy's tall figure appeared from the right walking along one of the lower paths in the garden. His mother was on his arm, and they walked slowly towards the beech copse and the orchard beyond.

'Doesn't the old Countess go to mass?' asked Balint, turning towards Adrienne. The sight of her face surprised him, for it seemed as if she were irradiated by some inner glow that shone through her delicate skin. Her head was held high and her big, amber-coloured eyes were wide open. It was the face of Medusa, thought Balint, beautiful and at the same time frightening. A malicious smile hovered on her full lips as she watched the pair below her, and she did not speak until they had disappeared among the trees.

'What did you ask? Ah, yes, my mother-in-law!' Adrienne laughed so mockingly that it might have been a pæan of triumph. 'You know, AB, she too is quite, quite mad! She has decided to be *en froid* with God – not on speaking terms. I promise you it's true! She's not an atheist, not in the least! On the contrary, she's a firm believer. But she became angry with God when her husband went insane and died despite all her prayers that he should be saved. She implored God, even made him some kind of vow; but

God decided to take her husband all the same and she's never forgiven him! Since those days she has never been to church and she never prays. In her bedroom the image of Christ is turned face to the wall. She has the priest brought here, as always; but it is only for Maier and some of the other servants. As for her, she wishes to show God that He is not welcome in her house because He was not obedient to her wishes.'

'It's very sad if what you say is true.'

Adrienne laughed cruelly. 'She can't bear it if anyone does anything that she herself has not decided and ordered. She didn't succeed with Almighty God, and now she's punishing Him for it!'

There were five at lunch, the three Uzdys, Balint and the priest. Before they sat down grace was said and Balint, remembering what Adrienne had told him, watched the old countess carefully. Indeed the dowager Countess Uzdy did not pray, nor join her hands, nor cross herself as the others did. She simply stood erect, her arms at her side, and stared at nothing. Her head, with its crown of thick white hair, was, if anything, held even higher than at other times.

The butler served the meal, as always in total silence.

The conversation was desultory. All Balint's attention was concentrated on watching how the Uzdys behaved towards each other.

The atmosphere was strained, and there was an uneasy sense of pain in the room that was quite different from the last time Balint had been there. Most of the conversation was being carried by Adrienne, who talked more loudly than she usually did, apparently confident that thereby she could somehow defy her mother-in-law and dominate her husband. Uzdy was different too, more subdued and more attentive to his wife, as if he were now in some way subordinate to her, and was using his position to mediate between Adrienne and his mother. All this was barely perceptible but, to Balint's heightened sensibility, it seemed painfully obvious that the relationship between husband and wife was no longer the same. It must be true then, what he had suspected and feared! This could be the only explanation. The woman in Addy had been set free at last. It must be that. It could only be that ... and yet he could still hardly believe it. When he looked into Addy's face, studied her laugh and the relaxed way she sat in her chair, he sensed that there was something else in her, something reckless and secret and determined, which called for some explanation that was not at all as simple as that he had worked out for himself. He noticed that from time to time Pali would look at him with an expression that seemed to combine mockery, condescension and – and this was the most offensive of all – something of pity.

When lunch was over Balint walked out on to the terrace with Adrienne.

'I will take you to the ruins,' said Addy. 'Then you'll see what a wonderful view there is from there.'

Uzdy started off with them, but left them as soon as they reached the lower door of the Swiss wing. 'I'm sorry not to be able to go farther with you,' he said, 'but I have to copy out the daily estate reports.' Balint looked at him enquiringly. 'You see, every day each of the estate's managers and agents brings me his report – about weather, fodder for the animals, the work done by the men we take on by the day, the milking, ploughing, maintenance, stock-breeding programme, everything that we do here. Each afternoon I collate it all into corresponding columns in a master register, and from these I work out the statistics. Of course it all makes a lot of paper-work for me, but it does mean that I know everything that is going on, even when I'm not here. This keeps everyone on their toes and afraid, and *that* is not only desirable but absolutely necessary!'

He laughed and said goodbye: 'I leave Adrienne in your charge. I know that with you she's in good hands, the best, the most expert of hands! So I know you'll take good care of her, naturally, of course!'

He started to mount the creaking stairs with slow ponderous steps. Then, from above he called out to them once more: 'Go ahead! Walk! Walk! It's very good for you, the more the better! Of course, naturally! Go on! Walk!' and his figure disappeared into the darkness of the stairway.

It took Balint and Adrienne just over half an hour to reach the ruins. They first arrived at a giant doorway hewn from the natural rock by masters of a long vanished era. A grassy road now passed that way between perpendicular stone walls over three metres high. This road led to Nagy-Almas and to get to the ancient fortress itself one had to follow a narrow path which wound its way diagonally up the steep cliffs that dominated the valley and on top of which the castle had been built. At the top was a grassy meadow which surrounded the ruins.

On their walk neither Balint nor Adrienne had felt like talking. Addy had asked him if he had brought the pistol with him and after he had confirmed that it was in his pocket they had not spoken again until they were almost in the shadow of the castle's crumbling walls. Then, when they sat down together on a fragment of old dressed stone Adrienne asked him to give it to her. Balint took from his pocket a small tooled leather case and opened it. Inside lay the little Browning and fitted beside it were two loaded cylinders and slots for reserve bullets.

'Oh, how pretty it is!' cried Adrienne, like a small child seeing a new toy for the first time. She took the weapon from its case with practised hands, for she had often shot with Uzdy's revolvers, and inspected it with a most professional air. Then she slid one of the cylinders into place and clicked back the safety-catch. 'I'll try it at once,' she said. 'I want to see what it can do!' She took aim at the trunk of a nearby oak tree, which stood some ten paces away, and fired. The bullet tore a narrow yellow wound in the tree's bark. 'It's good. Thank you so much, it was sweet of you to get it for me.'

Balint was still searching for that knowing ironic phrase which would tell Adrienne that he had understood the change in her and that no one was going to make a fool of him. The right words would not come, and though he tried to force himself to speak lightly, as if it were all a huge joke, what came out sounded hard and slightly offensive. 'And for what joyous family feast is this little present intended?'

'Present? For whom?'

'Why, for your beloved husband I presume!'

'No! No! No!' Adrienne burst out laughing. 'You thought that ... You thought ... You really believed ... for Pali Uzdy?'

'But in your letter, you wrote that you wanted to surprise him.'

When she finally managed to control her laughter Adrienne turned back to Balint. Looking straight at him she put the little weapon carefully away in its case and then said: 'I only meant it would be a surprise for him. Of course I see it could be understood differently, but I had to be rather vague. You would never have bought it for me if ... well, if I had written the truth!'

'I don't understand.'

Adrienne was now deadly serious. The pupils of her amber eyes narrowed to pinpoints as she looked out over the shining valley of the Almas and across the wooded hills to the faint bluish line of the distant mountains beyond. She leaned her chin on her closed fist forcing her mouth into a sulky, discontented line, sad and stubborn.

Then she spoke again, softly, in broken phrases, as if it were difficult for her to find the right words. 'I have decided that I will not bring any more Uzdys into the world. Why should I? They'd only be taken away from me like the first one. No! Never again! Never! Am I to be only a brood mare, a cow in calf? No! If it happens again...' She was silent for a while, and then went on slowly with great determination: 'If I can find no other way I will shoot myself.' She laughed again, even more bitterly than before and behind her bitterness Balint could sense a certain malicious delight. 'That is going to be the surprise for Uzdy that I wrote to you about!'

Balint listened to her words. He felt he had been turned to stone and he was filled with terrible foreboding and a deep pity for the girl who had been brought to this dreadful decision. His eyes filled with tears.

'Addy! My darling Addy! You must never do that! Never!'

He took her soft yielding hand in his, that hand which he had so often held before and whose fingers were so lissom they might have had no bones in them; and he stroked her arm until he wanted above all things in the world to draw her close to him. At once she stiffened and her hand tightened round his with sudden strength and violence. Then she pushed him away: 'Not that! Not now! You must not touch me now.' She got up and started to walk towards the tower, chatting light-heartedly as if she was determined to make him forget the harshness of what she had just said. They walked together in the ruins for some little time and the sun was already beginning to set when they started for home.

When they had crossed the grassy slope just below the tower they started down the rocky hillside on separate paths: Balint chose the higher, while Adrienne set off on another, slightly lower down, which soon turned a corner of the cliff-face. She was walking very close to the edge, too close, thought Balint, for there was a sharp fall on the outer side. He was just about to call out a warning to her when Adrienne suddenly flung up her arms and disappeared into the abyss, It looked as though she had jumped deliberately, for she had made no sound, not a word, not a cry of terror or surprise. No stones followed her fall.

After a moment in which he was too stunned with horror to move, Balint leapt down from the path above and scrambled across the rocks to where he had last seen her.

Crazed with anguish he looked over the edge to see Adrienne

on her feet on a grassy shelf not far below. She was wiping the palm of one of her gloves for she had muddied it when she fell. She laughed, looking guiltily up and lied: 'It's too silly, I slipped! It's lucky the ground is so soft here. No, no, I didn't hurt myself ... I didn't fall very far. The cliff's not very high. We used to jump far further in the gymnastic class. You know when I was at school I could always jump farther than any of the others, always...' And she gabbled on, making a joke of it. But Balint saw that she was very pale and did not regain her normal colour until they were almost home.

Adrienne did not come down for dinner that night.

'My daughter-in-law isn't feeling very well,' explained Countess Clémence in her cool, formal manner. Uzdy seemed worried and unusually distracted, with a deep crease between his slanting devil's eyebrows. Nevertheless, he kept the conversation going and even essayed a mild joke or two; though Balint had the impression that his perpetual sardonic smile stayed on his face only through force of habit. Twice in the course of the evening he left the drawing-room for short periods. Later a carriage could be heard being swiftly driven away from the castle, its wheels crunching over the gravel as it raced out of the forecourt. No one spoke in the drawing-room and Balint could hear the clatter of the horses' hoofs as they faded into the night. About ten o'clock everyone went to bed.

Balint lay down but could not sleep. With teeth tightly clenched he tried to sort out in his mind what he had discovered that day. Only now did he understand that what she had feared had already happened. Poor, poor Addy! How desperate and how determined she was. He saw everything clearly now. Poor Addy!

Towards midnight he again heard the sound of a carriage, this time coming back to the castle. There was the sound of whispered conversation in the passage and hurried steps. Presumably the doctor had been sent for and had just arrived. Then there was deep silence again and it was so quiet that the young man fancied he could count the seconds by the beating of his heart.

Balint was deeply distressed and worried, but there was nothing he could do.

Poor Addy! It was nearly dawn before he fell asleep and at some moment when he must still have been half awake he heard again the sound of a carriage driving swiftly away.

Despite everything that had happened Balint awoke early,

PART FIVE

though without feeling rested. Someone could be heard moving about the corridor outside his room and Balint looked to see who it was. It was Maier, the butler, with one of his underlings.

'I'll bring your Lordship's breakfast at once,' he said, and hurried away to the pantry. In a few minutes he was back with a tray.

'Is Count Uzdy up?' asked Balint, simply for something to say.

The butler's big grey eyes seemed even sadder than usual. 'His Lordship left at dawn, my Lord.'

'Left?' said Balint, astonished.

'Before dawn, my Lord. He's gone to his estate at Bihar.'

Balint hesitated. He wanted to ask after Adrienne but could not find the right words, so that it was not until Maier had almost left the room that he said: 'The young Countess . . . tell me . . . ?'

The butler answered only with a silent gesture. He raised his right hand, shrugged his shoulders to indicate that he knew nothing, and left the room.

This was terrible, thought Balint. He would be leaving that morning and it was unthinkable that he should go not knowing how she was or what had happened in the night. He had to know. He had to find some way of discovering the truth. For a few moments he thought, and then a plan began to form in his mind. He could hardly ask Countess Clémence; and even if he did she would not tell him anything. He had already tried Maier. It would be beneath his dignity to question the other servants. What, then? Indeed, why? As Balint paused, not knowing quite what to do, he was torn between his conflicting feelings for Adrienne, between the emotions of a faithful friend motivated by old acquaintance and pity, and those of the lover whose motives were far from selfless. For a moment Balint understood himself, but he soon chased away the thought, telling himself that if he had to see Adrienne it was out of pure compassion. He knew that he must see her and he knew, too, how to arrange it. He sat down at the writing table, pulled out a sheet of paper and scribbled a few words. He wrote:

I shall be leaving at midday. U. has gone away. It would be dreadful to leave without seeing you. Who knows when we shall meet again? I beg you to let me come up to you, even if it's only for a single minute – what does convention matter? *Please! I beseech you most humbly . . .*

Then he found an envelope, slipped the note into it and sealed it firmly.

465

When he had finished dressing Balint packed his bags and stepped out into the corridor. He walked up and down, apparently aimlessly, but he was waiting for Adrienne's maid, Jolan, whom he had known in Kolozsvar and who was sure, sooner or later, to pass down the corridor on her way to her mistress's rooms. At last she appeared.

'If you would be so good, please give this to the Countess, if she's well enough, of course. If her Ladyship has an answer I shall be here, I shan't move from this spot.'

The maid disappeared down the corridor. While waiting, Balint went over to one of the windows and looked out. All he could see was Countess Clémence walking in the gardens. That, at least, was a relief. The old woman was out of the way.

He had almost begun to lose hope of a reply when Jolan suddenly appeared at his side. She brought back the opened envelope on which Adrienne had scribbled in pencil: *'In half an hour'*, no more. He glanced at his watch, and continued doing so every few minutes until the half-hour had passed. Then, trying hard to walk slowly and composedly, he started towards the bend in the corridor. There was a door at the end of the wide passage and in front of this stood the maid, Jolan. When he reached it she opened the door swiftly and silently and Balint entered.

The shutters of the room had not been opened and the curtains too were drawn. The room was in almost complete darkness, a scented darkness which reminded Balint of the natural smell of almonds or carnations. It was strong but not artificial, not a manufactured perfume but rather the intimate female scent that both maddened and intoxicated, making Balint for a moment as giddy as if he had just swallowed a draught of strong liquor. After a few more moments his eyes became accustomed to the gloom and he could make out the outlines of Adrienne's bed which was set between the dim vertical rectangles of two long windows.

The bed was very low and very wide, like a huge couch. It was covered with lace which fell in festoons to the floor on every side. Against the creamy-white of the bedclothes Adrienne's loosened hair stood out like two raven-black triangles on each side of her face. Thus framed, Adrienne's head had an oriental, almost Egyptian appearance. The bedcovers were pulled up to her chin so that her face seemed to float ethereally above the cascading froth of the lace pillows.

Balint had to muster all his will-power to keep control of himself. He had commanded himself to appear cool and matter-of-fact and he realized at once how necessary this was, for Adrienne's eyes were wary, filled with a mixture of distrust, alarm, suspicion and fear that was almost menacing. So Balint spoke lightly, joked, kept his tone as natural as if he were in the presence of hundreds of other people at a ball, or chatting in drawing-rooms where wicked old ladies lurked trying to overhear something to gossip about.

'What a scare you've given us all! How could you? You must have been a little crazy!'

A little smile crossed Adrienne's face and she replied so softly that her words were like a reproachful caress: 'Would you have preferred the more final solution?'

They went on talking for a few moments, but Balint was never afterwards able to recall what was said. It took all his strength to prevent Addy from seeing the force of the desire for her that raged within him. Somehow he managed to remain outwardly calm, for if he had for one moment allowed himself to show any real concern, he knew that he could not have contained himself. He saw the outlines of her body beneath the silken sheets and, so as not to shatter the spell, he made himself mask his desire by looking at her only through half-closed eyes. He tried to read her face, understand what that strangely joyous yet troubled expression really meant. She seemed filled with some unconscious joy that he found hard to interpret. Was she perhaps conscious all the same of how beautiful she was lying there – a mixture of happiness and sorrow, infinitely desirable, infinitely unattainable, forming a picture that he would never be able to forget but which would enslave him for ever and ensure that he never again thought of abandoning his pursuit? All this was mirrored in the huge amber-coloured eyes, the pale forehead and generous red lips. It would have been better if she had never let him into the intimacy of her room to see her lying there in bed, for she must have known that nothing would give him more pleasure than to remember her like that. Behind every other conscious feeling lay the unconquerable female instinct to attract and, at the same time, to reject.

Balint's superficial calm had the effect of making Adrienne calmer too. Slowly, but without revealing the bare skin of her shoulders, she took one hand out from under the bed-clothes and held it out to him. For a moment he held it.

This was the time to leave. He bent down, his face still expressionless, to kiss her mouth. For a brief instant he saw the alarm in her eyes but this vanished at once when Balint kissed her carefully, coolly, almost like a brother. Then he went swiftly to the door and turned, speaking for once in English just as she had ended her last letter to him: 'Sincerely yours,' he said, but he said it as if the old formal letter-ending phrase symbolized eternal fidelity.

In the corridor he was dazzled by the brightness of the morning. He felt he would go blind, not, however, from the myriad reflections of the sun through the windows but from the even brighter image that would now never leave him: the image of an Egyptian face framed by unruly black curls and two huge eyes, lovely, frightened and frightening, glowing like topazes in the darkened room.

Balint got back to his room without being seen by anyone. Then he went to look for the old countess and by the time he found her he had sufficiently recovered his equilibrium to be able to chat insipidly with her until the butler announced that the carriage at the door.

Then he took his leave, leapt into Uzdy's *bricska* and was whisked rapidly away towards Banffy-Hunyad. It was only now, when he was past all danger of discovery and the American carriage horses were racing him up- and downhill, through the valleys and over the mountainous ridges, that the passion raging within him started to abate. He felt that he was flying with wide spread wings high above the world, above woods, forests, meadows, rivers, his lungs full of ozone, his blood racing. He felt that he had just quaffed an enchanted potion whose venom fanned flickering flames in his veins that burned away all sense of caution and forever freed him of that restraint which his inner voice so often told him he must obey. Now he was once again that primeval being who knows only how to follow his instincts, the predator who seeks his mate and for whom no obstacle, law or convention will be allowed to obstruct the natural course of his desire, that animal in whom passion rages unchecked and who, if need be, will kill to achieve his object.

And Balint's mind was suddenly filled with disturbing erotic fantasies.

PART SIX

Chapter One

IN THE AUTUMN OF 1905, as in other years, the social scene came slowly back to life. A few theatres opened their doors, a few concerts were announced. Among the first to return to their town houses was Countess Beredy, who had little liking for the country and even less for her husband's country house. She would never stay there a day longer than was necessary. On arrival in the capital Fanny immediately resumed her Wednesday dinners; for her court, Szelepcsenyi, d'Orly and the others, knew what was required of them and were already back in Budapest when she arrived.

Fanny now had one guest fewer, for she did not trouble to replace Warday. The ritual was the same, except that now it was Laszlo who would take his departure before the other guests, murmuring some excuse and leaving the room about half an hour before the others. He would put his coat on at the top of the staircase and then slip through a little door covered by a curtain just opposite the head of the stairs. Behind was an anteroom with doors to left and right: the left led to a servants' staircase, the right to Fanny's apartment. Laszlo would step quickly through Fanny's door and, once inside, bolt it carefully, for Fanny had given instructions that had to be obeyed most faithfully. The reason was that under no circumstance must he be seen by anyone, and if the bedroom door had not been bolted it was always possible that Fanny's maid might have wished to come in for some reason. If she did she would find him there and know for certain that Fanny had a lover.

This was unthinkable and could be very dangerous for Fanny, for though her husband had made it very plain that she was free to do as she liked and that he was not interested, this was strictly on condition that no one, not he himself, nor the servants, nor anyone else, should know of it, and if ever the smallest indication of her infidelities were to reach his ears, then he would take immediate action against her. He had made this perfectly plain several years before when they had stopped living as man and wife, and, though the subject had only been mentioned once, Fanny knew her husband well enough to realize that nothing would give him greater pleasure than to throw her out if ever she gave him the opportunity. Even now, after eight years of going their own ways, she would shudder when occasionally he looked at her with his cold reptilian eyes, his thin-lipped mouth closed tightly giving him an expression even more merciless than usual.

Accordingly, she arranged her life with great discretion. Her lovers would on visit her only on the evenings when there were dinner parties at the Beredy Palais. Most of the servants went to bed as soon as their work was finished and only the door-keeper remained on duty in his little cabin near the main entrance. When someone rang the bell he would pull a cord to open the glazed outer doors of the mansion, and so the departing guests would find their own way out. The doorman himself never saw who was leaving, nor did he know whether the guests left in a group or alone. If, when the last time the bell rang, it was only just after midnight there was nothing to suggest that anything unusual had occurred, nothing, that is, that flouted the social conventions of the day. Fanny's guests would mostly take their leave soon after eleven o'clock and her lover soon after twelve; so for an hour, just one hour, Fanny was free to make love in her wide luxurious bed with whoever was her choice of the moment. It was a wild happy hour, an hour in which she would drape herself in her most provocative negligé, for she knew well that like this she appeared infinitely more seductive than when crudely stripped naked.

Fanny took particular delight in these stolen moments, not only because of the purely sensuous pleasure of being embraced by an handsome young lover in surroundings designed just for that purpose – the huge bed, soft carpets, cunningly placed mirrors and sugar-pink lighting – but also because of the secret satisfaction of feeling that by doing this in her husband's house she was wreaking her private vengeance upon him. When, after sixty minutes of rapture, the little alarm clock sounded it's warning and her lover would dress and leave her, she would stretch herself out in triumph and go to sleep on that storm-tossed bed which had witnessed so many other illicit embraces.

When Laszlo came into her life this brief weekly meeting did not seem enough, and so they decided to find somewhere else. Laszlo's little apartment in Museum Street was not only in a large block in a district where many of their friends and acquaintances lived – which meant that Fanny might be recognized in the street or even on the stairs of the apartment house itself – but

PART SIX

was also inconveniently distant from the Beredy Palais. It was obvious to both of them that she could not visit him there and that their secret love-nest would have to be somewhere in the old quarter, close to the royal palace and close, therefore, also to Fanny's own home. Then she would be able to slip in unnoticed when everyone thought she was out for a short walk. Laszlo soon found the ideal place in a small house in one of the streets of old Buda. It had two entrances, one leading directly to the apartment and the other, on a lower level, which led to a room where a little dressmaker lived. This was perfect, for if Fanny should need an alibi no one would wonder about her visiting a local seamstress. The apartment was dingy and in need of redecoration but Fanny swiftly solved this by covering the walls with material so that it resembled a tent. The walls, curtains and covers were all hung with the same iron-grey material; and the thick carpet was of the same colour because she knew well that it set off her rosy flesh and blonde hair. It was very pretty and was in total contrast to the shabby furnished rooms where Laszlo still lived, even though he was always promising himself he would find something better.

The rent was expensive – more than four thousand crowns – but Laszlo did not care. One won at cards, or one lost. It was good if one won, but it did not really matter any more than it mattered if one lost. At this time Laszlo had plenty of money. That excellent fellow, Countess Abady's useful lawyer Azbej, had so menaced old Stanislo with legal demands to 'terminate community interest' that his ex-guardian had agreed to buy out Laszlo's interest in the Gyeroffy forest lands. This had brought in such a handsome sum that Laszlo had been able not only to pay off his debts but was also left with a tidy sum in hand. Indeed this Azbej was wonderful, even though some people said that Laszlo had sold very cheaply. This, thought Laszlo, was very possible; but still he had the money in his hands and that was the most important thing. Anyway the money lenders' interest charge would soon have swallowed up the difference. All in all, therefore, everybody was happy; Laszlo, Stanislo and also, no doubt, Azbej himself.

On Fanny's insistence Laszlo again enrolled himself at the Academy of Music, but though he attended the lectures and followed the set courses he did so without any of his former dedication. Somehow it seemed that without the stimulus of his love for Klara, for now that she was irrevocably lost to him, his passion for music had evaporated. His head no longer surged with melody as it had when every experience had at once been transformed into music, and; though his days were spent in a world of music it was always for the music of others that he lived, not for that compulsion to rise early and work, to devote all his days to study and creation. Laszlo's way of life sapped his creative energies. He would wake up late, still sleepy and half asleep. Without zest he would play his piano for an hour or two. If he had no rendezvous with Fanny that day he would go to the Casino or to the Park Club hoping to find someone who would make up a poker game, for it was too early in the season for the *chemin de fer* games in the baccarat-room to have restarted. He would stop playing only for dinner, and each evening he would drink more and more, hoping vainly that the alcohol would drive away his increasing remorse and obliterate all memory of what might have been. The drink was like an opiate, and so were the cards.

Passions ran high that year in the world of politics. One day everyone was full of hope, the next day brought despair. On a Monday the 'Guardsman' ('Lackey') government would appoint new ministers, and on the Tuesday they would resign. The new party programme would be published and within three days its authors would find themselves once more in the wilderness. There was general rejoicing when the King summoned some of the leading parliamentarians to Vienna, but dismay and anger when His Majesty merely read out to them some severe and comminatory paragraphs condemning their actions. It gradually became clear to everyone that a stalemate had been reached, from which there was no escape without one side or the other being publicly humiliated. In the middle of September the announcement of the imminent imposition by Vienna of general suffrage in Hungary inspired a huge and unprecedented demonstration of some forty thousand workers, who gathered before the Parliament building in Budapest, menacing the established order like a thundercloud.

Laszlo did not concern himself with such matters. One morning as he was walking to the academy, he encountered the workers' march on its way to the Parliament building – thousands upon thousands of silent men in dark shabby clothes, moving relentlessly in rows of eight which took up the entire street. It was quiet and peaceful and inexpressibly sinister, but, impressive though this unheard-of demonstration was, to Laszlo it meant nothing. He lived in a world of his own, clothed, indeed insulated by his music and his own internal bitterness from everything that

PART SIX

went on about him. He ignored the political discussions in the Casino, and barely noticed when people came up to him and told him ('just between us, of course') of some new political menace, or when he overhead others sounding off with treasonable intent about the need to rebel against the Emperor.

Laszlo frequently lunched or dined with the politicians, listening with disdain to their discussions and arguments. His silence was taken by them merely as aristocratic indifference to such mundane matters and as a result his social reputation remained untarnished. The truth was that his indifference sprang only from the strange mindless lassitude with which he was now imbued. It was as if he had donned the cap of forgetfulness which weighed him down like a leaden cloak.

Even his afternoons of passion with the beautiful Fanny gave him no relief. Often, when leaving their little apartment her kisses still wet upon his lips, he would pause at dusk on the embankment of the Danube. In front of him thousands of saffron-coloured strips illuminated the dark water, reflections of the lamps which lit the riverside boulevards; while above, the great dome of the Parliament building hung in the evening sky, veiled in smoke and silence, the silence of a city about to come alive when dusk fell. Laszlo would lean against the iron railings of the Margit Rakpart gazing sightlessly over the surface of the wide slowly-moving river on which gulls and other waterbirds would float, serene and calm.

Laszlo never gave a thought to the love-making he had just left behind him, never conjured up the image of the woman who had just kissed him goodbye, never tried to recall the look in her beautiful cat-like eyes or the lines of her mouth so wise in the ways of love; nor did he think of that smooth flesh clothed only in the five long strings of pearls that she never removed even at their most intimate moments. Knowing how much the glowing whiteness of those pea-sized pearls enhanced the beauty of her body and of her pink skin, Fanny would tie these long strings round her waist or neck, in festoons over her generous breasts, and even like fetters between her thighs where they glowed like an iridescent frame around the golden moss that covered the mound of Venus, underlining her nakedness by this most ephemeral of coverings. But she would never take them off. The Beredy pearls were worth a fortune and Fanny had worn them from the day her husband had offered them to her as a wedding present, and it was perhaps because of this constant contact with her skin that they remained so magically alive and glowing. But for Laszlo all these things were as if they had never been. Nothing penetrated his solitariness, nothing drove away that forlorn sense of having been abandoned in a meaningless, hopeless world. Many times he thought it would be far better just to die.

He would stand looking over the Danube for a long time before slowly making his way back to the Casino where he would take a bath, change, read the newspapers, dine and pass the rest of the evening at cards, playing always until there was no one left to play with. He was always among the last to leave the club, usually out of pocket, for the game hardly interested him any more than did that beautiful loving woman with the lithe body of a panther, who that afternoon had been driven wild with pleasure by his embraces.

Several weeks went by, weeks which for Laszlo were utterly without significance except for those unexpected moments when he would suddenly be wounded by some minor incident that provoked a sharp flash of pain. For example, one day he had gone to the upholsterer's to order some more cushions for their modest little meeting-place and suddenly found himself being shown with pride a set of new furniture which had been ordered by Imre Warday. The worst moment was when he received a beautifully engraved wedding invitation: 'Louis Kollonich, Prince of Kraguvac and Knin, and his consort Agnes, of the Counts Gyeroffy of Kis-Kapu, have pleasure in announcing that the marriage of their daughter and stepdaughter, the Duchess Klara Kollonich, will take place on October 14th...' and when, the same day, he overheard Wülffenstein and Niki Kollonich planning to go together to Simonvasar for the wedding. Then a pang went through him disturbing, for an instant but only for an instant, that thick shell of indifference in which he had so carefully encased himself.

And still the days went by, each the same as the last.

One morning towards the end of October Countess Beredy woke early. Though the windows of her room were hung with thick silken curtains, here and there a ray of early morning sun would find its way into the room and gleam softly on the gilded curves of one of the bed legs or on one of the rose-pink flowers of the brocade bed-cover.

Fanny woke with a strange feeling of unease. She felt restless and her throat was constricted by some unknown anguish. There was no reason, no cause.

PART SIX

How odd, she thought; it must be unusually early! She raised herself from the silken pillows until, supported on one elbow, she could see her tiny jewelled clock: it was only half-past six. Fanny decided to go back to sleep but, though she snuggled down among the warm silken bedclothes, sleep would not come: she could only think of Laszlo. Poor dear Laszlo, how unhappy he was! Even though she did everything in her power to cheer him up, to make him forget Klara, nothing could remove the gloom in which he was enveloped. Recently, reflected Fanny, she had been doing more than was wise or prudent.

Ten days before, on the day of Klara's wedding she had risked doing something that would have previously been unthinkable for her: she had spent the whole day with him so as to be sure that he wouldn't be alone. They had gone on an expedition to the shrine of Maria-Besnyo, leaving early in the morning on the local train as if they were making a pilgrimage. Fanny had told Laszlo that they must go early because the forests were so beautiful at that time of year and Laszlo had docilely agreed to everything she suggested. On arrival they had dutifully said a prayer at the miraculous image of the Virgin and then they had gone to an inn for luncheon, where she made sure he had plenty of wine to drink.

Afterwards they had walked in the forest, Fanny chattering away about how beautiful were the red leaves of the beeches and how the branches of hornbeam seemed to her to be the colour of lemon-peel. Deep in the woods they rested, Fanny sitting at the foot of a tree and Laszlo lying with his head in her lap. Here she made him sleep, stroking his luxuriant wavy hair as if he were a weary child to be calmed and comforted. When the day ended they returned to the inn, where Fanny ordered a good strong red wine and a flask of brandy and, though she had never liked it when Laszlo drank too much and she could smell the liquor on his breath, on this day she had made him drunk with a purpose, and it was successful.

Slowly the tense, sorrowful expression on his face relaxed and the hard line where his eyebrows met was smoothed away. It was true that Laszlo's eyes had become somewhat dull with a glassy, sightless look; but at least he had relaxed and was calm, even if he was indifferent to where he was and what he was doing. In the end he had even laughed and joked with her. Though nearly everything he said had been, perhaps, a trifle silly, and from time to time a little drop of saliva had formed at the corner of his mouth – something that would have revolted the normally fastidious

Fanny at other times or in other men – she had rejoiced and been happy that she had made her lover forget, even if only for a brief moment, the sorrows that beset him. It had not mattered that it was not she herself, nor her beauty, her love, nor her solicitude that had wrought this miracle, but merely the quantity of strongly laced red wine that she had poured into him. No, that did not matter in the least, for what really was important was that somehow she had managed to make him forget that at Simonvasar it was the day of Klara's wedding ... and of her wedding night; and when Laszlo had nearly reached a state of insensibility she could take him home to his flat in Museum Street, quietly, by hired carriage, and leave him there to sleep. After Fanny had dropped him she had had herself put down at the Gisella Square, where she had changed carriages and then been driven back to her house near the Palace.

It had been unbelievably reckless, but she felt that she had to do it because on that day she had been deadly afraid of what would happen if Laszlo had been left on his own. It had been especially daring, for if her husband, by some unlucky chance, had come to hear that she had spent the whole day alone with another man he would have been certain to take it as proof of her infidelity and he would have used such information without mercy. It was always possible that he used a private detective to follow her.

Fanny tried to recall every detail of that foolhardy excursion. Every precaution she could think of had been taken. She herself had boarded the train at the Eastern Station, Laszlo at the next stop. When they arrived at the last little station on the line they had got out and walked to the shrine across the meadows. In the forest they had been alone and in the inn she had seen no one from the city who might have recognized them. In the evening they had dined at the other inn in the village, and again there had been no one there who knew them. Afterwards they had returned to the station in the carriage that the innkeeper kept for the use of his guests. Surely she had made no mistake, for everything had been done with the utmost prudence and care? So why this anxiety, why this nagging worry?

The more Fanny thought about it and the more she tried to reassure herself that nothing could possibly have gone wrong, the more agitated she became. From time to time she glanced at the telephone by the bed, which was on a private line whose number was known only to her intimate friends and to Count Beredy. At any moment she expected it to ring, and it would be her husband,

PART SIX

gloatingly telling her that she had at last made a fatal mistake. She knew it was madness, but she could not get the thought out of her head.

The telephone rang. For a moment Fanny stared at it in deep alarm. Then, gathering up all her courage, she picked up the receiver.

'It's me, Laszlo. I'm sorry to wake you, but I'm in terrible trouble. I've lost a great deal of money, a tremendous amount. I must see you, perhaps for the last time...'

'Where are you?'

'In our flat. I've been here about two hours. I have to talk to someone, I can't stand it any more.'

'I'll be there in half an hour, my darling! Wait! I'll be there!' said Fanny and jumped out of bed to dress.

Fanny found Laszlo lying on the big divan in complete darkness. He was fully dressed, except for his collar which had torn off, and was lying on his back staring at the ceiling. Fanny sat down beside the couch and lit the discreetly shaded lamp beside the bed which had illuminated so many hours of their passionate love-making. On the table by the lamp she saw a folded sheet of writing paper which was wrinkled as if it had been crushed in someone's hand.

'My darling, what has happened? What is the matter?'

'I'm down a huge amount, eighty-six thousand crowns! Imagine! Like a fool I plunged and lost everything. Of course I don't have it, I can't raise such a sum at all, let alone straight away. This is the end. If I don't pay up by the day after tomorrow I'll be thrown out of the club, and I couldn't bear that. I won't! So I had to see you before – before I disappear for good!'

Fanny felt her heart constrict, but outwardly she remained calm. She bent down and kissed his eyes as she had done so often, like a mother with her child.

'Your skin is burning! Wait! I'll get a sponge,' She ran into the bathroom, returning almost at once with a sponge and a bowl of cold water. Then she bathed his face, which was already wet with perspiration, his eyes and his forehead.

'Is this better? Does it feel good? Are you calmer now, my darling!'

In a little while Laszlo was indeed calmer.

'Let's take all this off, she said. 'Leave it to me, you know how I love to undress you!' She laughed softly, peeling off his crumpled clothes with practised hands until he lay naked on the bed. Then she gently sponged his chest and arms and legs, dried him and wrapped him in one of his many silk dressing-gowns. All this movement, the fuss she made of him and the caresses with which she interspersed her taking off his clothes, so quietened the desperate young man that when she finished her work and lay down beside him, he was able at last to tell her what had happened the night before.

It had started with a poker session after dinner at which he had lost some three thousand crowns. This was not a huge sum but the loss annoyed him, especially as the game had come to an end at one o'clock. Then he heard that chemmy was being played in the baccarat-room upstairs, though without any of the big players. Laszlo had gone up and sat down at the table. At once he lost and soon, though he had at first only made a small bet of a hundred crowns or so he was more than four thousand down. Recalling that he had one or two hits while holding the bank, he decided to recoup his losses by calling a bank for a sum much higher than those present were accustomed to. Then a surprising thing happened. Gedeon Pray, who for once had joined the game and seemed to be on a winning streak, looked hard at Laszlo as if singling him out as his special prey and called '*Banco!*' and won the *coup*. Again he did the same thing; and again he won. Towards morning the game had turned into a duel between the two of them. Laszlo's credit had long been exceeded and he found himself signing IOUs without reckoning the cost. He ran after his money even though he knew that it was impossible that he could win back everything that he had lost. It did not matter whether he held the bank or Pray, for the latter always held fantastic cards. When Pray suggested halving the stakes or offered to accept only something agreed between the two of them, Laszlo fell into the trap, hoping thereby to win something back. And still Pray won. As dawn was breaking there were only four men left at the table. At six o'clock the Club Steward came in and the game broke up.

Everyone rose and Pray headed swiftly for the stairs. Laszlo followed him and asked: 'Could I settle in a week or two? It's a bit difficult to find such a large sum all at once...'

Gedeon looked at him coldly. Now, as he told the story to Fanny, Laszlo could well recall how his mouth had looked like that of a shark set in a bloodless, puffy face.

'I'm very sorry, but no, I can't do it! As a member of the card-room committee I have to obey the rules. No irregularities for me!'

'I see,' said Gyeroffy. 'In forty-eight hours?'

'In forty-eight hours, starting at noon today...' Pray hurried on down the stairs.

All this Laszlo related, using as few words as possible. Then he added: 'I came here straight from the Casino. I didn't dare go home; my guns are there!'

Fanny had listened attentively. Then, thoughtfully, she said: 'So we have two days to pay?'

'But how? Where will the money come from?' Reaching out for the crumpled note on the table, he read out his list of debts, how much he owed and to whom. 'I could settle the Casino account, but that of Gida Pray, never. My credit at the moneylenders is exhausted: those sharks are already at my heels and recently they've been pestering me daily. There is no way, none! Now I really am finished!'

Laszlo now gave way to despair; unable any longer to control himself he sat on the bed racked with sobs. Then he buried his head on Fanny's shoulder. Fanny stroked him gently and then pressed her body to his so that their bodies touched from her breasts to her toes, her long legs entwined with his. 'My darling,' she whispered, 'my very dear darling!'

She kissed his mouth while her hands, knowing and practised, caressed his limbs until his sobbing ceased and he was overcome by desire, searching for solace in her arms. Afterwards he fell into a deep sleep. Fanny got up from the bed and sitting quietly beside him gazed down at her sleeping lover. Her eyes again narrowed to thin slits as she fingered the magnificent pearls around her neck. For a long time she sat there quite motionless, except for the little movement of her hands as she touched the five long ropes of pearls. Finally she srood up, combed her hair and dressed. Then she took note of the losses listed on the paper beside the bed. Just before leaving she went over to the writing table, found a sheet of paper and hurriedly scribbled a few words:

I've thought of something I can try. Stay here until I return. I expect to be back by three – maybe four at the latest. In any case, wait for me!

Returning to the bed, she placed the note beside the lamp where Laszlo was sure to see it when he woke up.

Silently she glided from the room.

Within twenty minutes Fanny entered the Dorottya Street shop of the well-known jeweller Bacherach, who was famous all over

Europe for the beauty of his stones and the marvellous settings created in his workshops.

'I would like to see the director!' said Countess Beredy as she entered the showroom, which was lined by showcases of sparkling crystal filled with masterpieces of goldsmith's handiwork and with trays of shining silverware. Through a side-door discreetly concealed by a velvet curtain from the showroom there entered a chubby little old man wearing enormous horn-rimmed spectacles on his fleshy nose. It was old Bacherach himself.

'How can I serve your Ladyship?' he asked, bowing obsequiously, for though he owned three apartment houses and possessed a fortune far larger than did many of his fashionable clients, it was his pride to appear before them as simply as if he were still a humble apprentice.

'Could I speak to you in private?' asked the countess.

'I would take it as an honour,' replied Bacherach, bowing again before he ushered her through the curtained door into a tiny room which was also surrounded by glass-fronted showcases. In one corner a large safe had been built into the wall and in the centre of the room was a small desk lit by a green-shaded tablelamp. Bacherach offered Fanny the comfortable upholstered armchair which stood by the desk and seated himself on an upright cane chair that was placed opposite it.

'How can I serve your Ladyship?' he repeated.

'You remember my pearls? I had them re-strung here last year.'

'Who could forget them? They are extraordinary, unique I should say. Five identical strings! Magnificent!'

'I . . . I'm thinking perhaps of selling them. What do you think I might get for them, Mr Bacherach?'

'It's difficult to say. Of course they are extremely valuable, exceptionally so, but for that very reason it might not be so easy to find a buyer. *Es wäre Schade zie zu verschleudern* – it would be a pity to throw them away. One would have to wait to find a serious buyer. Oh, they exist all right, if not here then in Paris, or London, or the Riviera.'

'I have them with me. You can see them. What do you think then? How much could I get for them?' She reached into her blouse, took out the pearls, unfastened them and placed them in the jeweller's fat little fingers. For a moment he weighed them in his hands, shutting his eyes. Then he placed them on the green baize table top.

PART SIX

'Perhaps ... hm ... on the international market two ... two hundred and fifty thousand francs. Maybe even three hundred *wenn ein Amateur sich findet* — if one came across a real lover of such things.'

Fanny made as if she was thinking the matter over. Then she spoke again:

'Look, Mr Bacherach, I will leave my pearls with you until I make up my mind. You are quite right, it would be a crime to throw them away. I'd like you to keep them for me. But I do need rather a large sum of money at once, and so I wondered if maybe you could advance me something, just until a proper buyer can be found?'

Bacherach smiled discreetly and for a moment he closed his eyes again. 'Of course, your Ladyship, everything is possible. What figure did your Ladyship have in mind?'

'I would need eighty-six thouand crowns now.'

'Hm ... eighty-six thousand. It shall be done at once.'

'Would it be all right — if I changed my mind — if I paid you back the money ... with interest, naturally ... and then we might call off the deal?'

'Quite all right,' said the old merchant and then, rather more slowly: '... and how much time would your Ladyship need to, er, change her mind?'

'Could it be four or five months?'

'We'll say six. In the meantime I'll make enquiries in the market. If at the end of six months your Ladyship has not decided to cancel the sale I will have the right to proceed, within the price range we have already mentioned. I suggest a reserve price of twenty thousand francs if your Ladyship agrees?'

'That will be quite satisfactory. Thank you very much. Oh! And how much interest would I owe you should I decide not to sell?'

'Nothing at all, your Ladyship! I am only too happy to be of service to my clients. Would your Ladyship prefer a cheque or cash?'

'Cash, please, Mr Bacherach. When would it be convenient for me to call for it?'

'Your Ladyship can have it at once. I believe that quite a large sum has come in today.'

In a few moments he placed in Fanny's hands a large wad of new thousand-crown notes. She looked down at the pearls which still lay in a glowing pile under the lamp on the table and for a moment it hurt that she had to part with them.

Pulling herself together she turned again to the jeweller and in a calm voice asked: 'I wonder if I could telephone?'

'Of course,' said Bacherach, who immediately opened a small cubicle in the wall in which the telephone was kept. He then discreetly left the room.

When the operator answered Fanny asked for Szelepcsenyi's number and waited until, after a few moment, she heard the voice of her old friend.

'Carlo, is that you?' she asked. 'Does that little door still exist, the one onto the side-street? Yes? Then I'd like to come round now, in fifteen to twenty minutes? Would you leave it open? It would be better if I didn't have to ring ... Yes, I want to ask you something important. Thank you so much, you are a dear. In twenty minutes then, I'm coming on foot.' Then she laughed at something Szelepcsenyi said. 'Don't be silly! That's an old story!' and replaced the receiver.

Szelepcsenyi's little town house stood at the junction of Eotvos street and Szekfu street. Fanny walked past the main entrance and stopped at a little door just around the corner which yielded at once to her touch. She swiftly went inside, shut the door behind her and mounted a short stair of some ten steps. On a landing, standing in front of a tapestry that hid another doorway, Szelepcsenyi was awaiting her. Pulling back the tapestry, he opened the door and ushered Fanny into the room behind. It was the old statesman's bedroom in the middle of which stood a huge ornate bed made by Andrea Brustolon at the end of the seventeenth century and bought by Szelepcsenyi in Venice during the sixties. It was hung with cut velvet of the same period, as were the walls of the room. This background suited Szelepcsenyi who, with his wide forehead, jutting chin and closely trimmed beard himself had all the air of a Renaissance tyrant. However, he did not stop there but led Fanny on into the big drawing-room beyond. This room, so much larger than one would have thought possible from looking at the elegant exterior of the house, combined the functions of living-room with those of art gallery and museum. The walls were covered with the best works of the modern painters whose style was then coming into vogue and the ornate console tables that lined the room were covered with rare and costly examples of the work of Renaissance gold and silversmiths. On one side of the room was a giant baroque fireplace made of black and orange marble, and it was in two comfortable armchairs on each side of this that Fanny and her host sat down.

'Well, well, my little Fanion,' he said, using his old pet-name for her. 'And to what do I owe the pleasure of this visit?'

Fanny sat bolt upright, clutching hard with both hands to the elegant handbag which now held all the banknotes given to her by the jeweller. She hesitated for a while before answering: 'Someone we know lost a lot of money at the Casino last night . . .' she started.

'We needn't enquire who, need we?' said Szelepcsenyi to help her. 'Go on!'

'I have here everything that is needed to settle the debt. But, of course, I can't do it myself. Therefore I thought that, maybe, you would do it for me? Send someone round? I don't even know what the procedure is . . . but it must be settled right away.'

The old man shook his head with faint mocking disapproval. He smiled: 'Well! Well! Well! It's gone as far as that, has it?'

Despite herself Fanny felt herself blushing, a rare occurrence for her.

'He gave me this money himself, this morning.' She lied only to maintain a fiction for the sake of good form, knowing full well that Carlo would not believe a word of it. Indeed, with a smile of knowing complicity, he deftly changed direction.

'Do you know to whom the money is owed?'

'Of course, I've got it all here,' Getting up from her seat she moved over and sat on the arm of Szelepcsenyi's chair. From her bag she took out the banknotes and the list she had copied from Laszlo's. 'Here is the list. Everything's there: names, figures, everything.' and she brushed against him, catlike, provocative. 'You will do it for me, my dear, won't you? Now! It would be so sweet of you, and it's very important to me. Straight away?'

Szelepcsenyi looked sharply up at her. It was possible, indeed probable, that Fanny was doing this without Laszlo knowing anything about it. That would certainly explain why she seemed in so much of a hurry, for then she would be able to return to him and present him with a *fait accompli*. He put his arms around her shoulder and pressed her gently to him.

'It will be done at once!' he said, going over to the big Italian refectory table that he used as a writing desk. He put on his glasses and carefully copied Fanny's list onto another sheet of paper.

'Just go into the bedroom for a moment will you, my dear,' he said to Fanny. 'It is not necessary that my man should see you!'

Countess Beredy went into the adjacent room, but she did not close the doors behind her. She therefore heard Szelepcsenyi giving orders that the money should be given to the Club Steward in Count Gyeroffy's name and that a receipt and all the original IOUs should be put in an envelope and brought back immediately. The servant was told to take a hired carriage and be quick about it. When he had gone Szelepcsenyi called to Fanny: 'Fanion! Come and look at my newest acquisition!'

They went on talking and looking at the old man's treasures until the footman returned. As before, Fanny disappeared into the bedroom while the man was in the room. When Szelepcsenyi was assured that all had been done as he wished he called her back and together they checked that everything was in order. When this had been done Fanny put the envelope in her bag and, glancing in an antique mirror to be sure that before she could allow herself to be seen in the street the Countess Beredy looked her usual immaculate self, she went back through the bedroom to the landing beyond the tapestry-hung door. There she turned again to her old admirer, gave him a hug so tight that he could feel the swell of her breasts beneath the light silken dress. This was her gift to him.

'Thank you! Thank you! I thank you more than I can say!' She lifted up her head and planted a kiss right into the middle of his well-trimmed beard, for Szelepcsenyi did not bend down to her but remained standing erect, his head held high as ever. He patted her on the shoulder in a fatherly way and then stood, still motionless, at the head of the little stairway until Fanny had reached the door below.

'At your service always, my Fanion!' he said softly as she waved goodbye to him from the door.

Half an hour later, Fanny was back in the little flat near the royal palace, carrying, as well as her handbag, a large parcel in which were cold tongue, ham, a little pot of *foie gras*, two slices of coffee cake covered with whipped cream and a bottle of champagne – 'to drown his sorrows in!' she had thought when selecting these things on her way back from Szelepcsenyi's.

Laszlo was still asleep, just as she had left him. Fanny's first move was to put the champagne bottle under a cold tap and leave the water running so as to cool the wine. Then she undressed completely and slipped into a silk kimono which she selected from half a dozen others that she always kept there. Then she wound a

PART SIX

green chiffon scarf round her blonde hair, glancing into the long looking-glass to be sure that she looked her best, and went back into the darkened room where Laszlo lay asleep. Without disturbing him she pulled forward a small table and arranged on it the food she had brought in, fetching china, cutlery, glasses and a white table-cloth from the minute kitchen which opened off one side of the room. Finally she rescued the champagne from the sink and put it in a bucket with some cold water. Only when all this had been done and Fanny had checked that no detail had been forgotten, did she sit down on the bed beside Laszlo and awaken him by kissing his closed eyelids.

Laszlo smiled with pleasure when he saw the woman bending over him, but in a moment, he remembered what had happened and his eyes widened in horror as the details all came back to him.

Fanny touched his mouth with her tapering fingers.

'Don't think about ... about all that darling! Everything's going to be all right, you'll see! Look! I've brought some food, all the things you like best, and a little wine too, champagne. Now we'll have lunch together. Come along, I'm terribly hungry!' So she encouraged him, coaxed him, consoled him with light caresses, stroking his cheeks until he got up and joined her at the table. They sat on stools, facing each other, and Fanny did all she could to charm him so that the sad memories of the disastrous evening before would be obliterated and forgotten. In the dark blue kimono with the pale green chiffon scarf wound round her head, Fanny looked even more like a great cat, dark-skinned and blonde-headed, her mouth smiling with mysterious pleasure and her long eyes only half visible through her thick black eyelashes. Her pleasure sprang from the fact that Laszlo ate with a good appetite, happily quaffing the champagne from an ordinary water tumbler as they had nothing else to drink from in the flat.

When their lunch was over Fanny went back to the couch. 'Come here,' she said. 'Come close to me, and I'll tell you what I've done about that problem of yours.' She spoke proudly, thinking how adroitly she had managed everything. Laszlo lay down beside her.

'Look!' said Fanny, taking the Casino's envelope out of her bag. 'Everything has been settled. Here are your IOUs – two for five and one for three thousand. See, they've been torn across and countersigned by the club cashier! And here is something else ...' and she handed him a slip on which was written: '*I hereby certify that I have this day received from Count Laszlo Gyeroffy the sum of 73,000 crowns (that is seventy-three thousand crowns) for Mr Gedeon Pray.*'

Laszlo raised himself on his elbow, taking the little slips of paper from her and studied them carefully. He could hardly believe what he saw. It was true; the IOUs and the cashier's receipts were all there, just as she had said. Laszlo was flooded with an immense sense of relief, but then he suddenly straightened up and stared at her with wide eyes.

'This is not possible!' he said. 'How did you do it? Where did you get all this money? You? You? I can't accept this! No! Never!'

'Why not? It's only a loan ... a loan, I tell you. I found someone ready to lend it to you.'

'A loan?'

'Yes, just for a few months, to give you time to raise the money. A few months should be enough.'

'Who lent it? Who? I want to know!'

'It doesn't matter. It's enough that I know. You'll give it to me and I'll pay it back.'

'I insist on knowing who it is!' cried Laszlo, furiously. 'There's something very tricky about all this. That ... through you ... I can't possibly accept it ... and I don't believe a word of what you've said unless you tell me who! Tell me at one, who is it? Who?'

Fanny tried to lie: 'It's an old lawyer of my father's. You don't know him; he worked for my father. He's very rich!'

'His name! Tell me his name at once!' Laszlo grabbed her roughly by the shoulder and then flung her back brutally on to the bed. As he did so the kimono fell open revealing Fanny's white body against the dark blue satin. Laszlo stared at her, fascinated – the pearls! There was no sign of the pearls, either round her neck, nor over her breasts, nor wound round her waist or thighs. The pearls had gone, vanished!

It was only slowly as he looked at her with amazement that the connection came to him. Then, in stunned disbelief, he said dully: 'You sold your pearls!'

Fanny sat up. She pressed herself to him and clung to him tightly. 'No! I didn't sell them, really I didn't!' And she told quickly how she had gone to the jewellers and pawned them as she often had in the past when she needed money. That it really didn't signify – everyone did it, there was nothing to it, it was the most natural thing in the world. One could get them back any time, at a moment's notice, a few days, a few months, it was all the same. It really didn't matter at all and it meant nothing. That's all she had done. It was no sacrifice, nothing he couldn't or shouldn't accept from her. Why, it cost her nothing; wearing the things concealed by her blouse or leaving them there for a little while, it was all the same to her. And she clung to him even more fiercely.

Laszlo did not respond, either to her words or to her embrace. He stood there, quite still, his arms hanging down loosely, his whole body slack as if he were infinitely weary. He only moved his head, shaking it continuously from side to side and muttering over and over again:

'No! No! No! No!'

Fanny went on trying to cajole him. She became more eloquent in her love for him which, perhaps even now, though she did not realize it was a real love, inspired her to find the right words, the most persuasive arguments. What was done could not be undone. The debts had been settled, the money paid over and accepted. Nothing could be recalled. The only thing for him to do was to accept the fact and to forgive her – and he must get it into his head that he was not humiliated or dishonoured by what she had done – it wasn't even a favour, it was really nothing. And he would do her a favour if he would forgive her. Possibly she had been thoughtlessly impulsive but she was only a woman who didn't understand these things and who meant well. She had done it because she loved him as she had never loved anyone else and she had suddenly realized that if she lost him she would lose everything ... everything. As she said these things she was seized with the fear that she might still lose him and the panic that possessed her then gave an even more convincing ring to her arguments and a warm softness to her voice. With renewed passion, now completely real and not, as when she had first started, carefully calculated to impress and persuade him, she clung to him tightly as if she feared ever to let him go, and for the first time in her life broke into deep wracking uncontrollable sobs, her tears running down his chest as she continued to murmur incoherently, kissing his neck, his ear, his hair, hurriedly, hurriedly, as if she feared that if one word were lost she would lose him be for ever. So she talked and talked and kissed and sobbed and held him tightly to her, her warm limbs naked under the kimono enlaced with his until, involuntarily, almost unconsciously, he began to respond, stroking her body automatically and then out of habit, returning her kisses, face to face, all possibility of argument or reproach submerged in their mutual desire. Fanny sank back on to the bed, drawing him down upon her until they were both lost to the world as they came together in the deep sensuous depths of their passion.

For a short time they slept, entwined in each other's arms.

When Fanny awoke she thought at first that Laszlo was still sleeping but when she propped herself up on one elbow and looked at his face, she saw that his eyes were open. She slid one leg over his above the knee and held him as in a vice. Now at last he was really hers, her very own property who could no longer resist her and their love-making had been a pact, almost a contract by which he had accepted her sacrifice and help and admitted that what she had done for him was right. Now there was no way that he could demur or protest. She looked at him for a long time as he lay there motionless beside her, silent, his eyes still open as if he were a hundred miles away. No matter how much you fought me, she thought, you are now entirely mine, you can no longer resist or take refuge in those silly men's prejudices against which it was normally impossible to make any headway. How meaningless such things were, how stupid and full of humbug, and how irrelevant to everything that really mattered in life.

She smiled to herself at the thought of what a mad world it was – why, even now he had not thanked her for what she had done for him; he wasn't grateful. Far from it, indeed, for had he not been angry and struck her and flung her roughly on to the bed? It was not as if she had minded being manhandled, even beaten, for she had been flooded with pleasure when he had grabbled her shoulders with his two strong hands and so flung her so roughly from him. Still, it puzzled her, and she asked herself why she had done so much, and taken such risks, for a boy who did not love her and who had shown all too clearly that he only tolerated her presence and her devotion. Why, he barely even accepted what she had to offer, for did he not still love someone else, that girl who had turned from him and rejected him? It was clear that he did not, never had and never would love Fanny. Always it was that other ... no one else ...

Finally, when all these melancholy thoughts had become clear in her mind, she raised herself even higher on the pillows, still gazing down at the young man beside her, and involuntarily put her thoughts into words: 'And you don't even love me!'

It was not a question but a bare statement of fact, nothing else: a little, sad, resigned phrase that summed up all that had been going on in her mind.

Laszlo replied slowly, still looking upwards at nothing in particular. His voice too was very soft; and he seemed infinitely sad and very, very tired:

'No. I can't say I truly love you.'

Chapter Two

THE TURMOIL OF EMOTION that had overwhelmed him in Uzdy's fast carriage, after he had slipped unobserved into Adrienn's room before making his formal farewells to old Countess Uzdy, had still not evaporated when Balint arrived in the town square of Banffy-Hunyad early in September.

He drove straight to the station where the clock on the tower told him that it was not yet midday and that he had somehow to get through a two hours' wait before the next train left for Kolozsvar. What should he do with all this time on his hands? Still tormented by his thoughts he drove to the Tigris Hotel and ordered an early lunch. Though it was market day in the town and the main square was filled with a multitude of people dressed in their best finery, Balint sat alone, unable to think of anything but those last few moments in the dark room beside Adrienne's bed. Try as he would he could find no way of calming himself, and he realized that he could not yet face going back to Denestornya where he would have to talk dispassionately to his mother about Almasko and find some convincing reason as to why he had returned earlier than expected. His mother was sure to cross-question him about the visit and Balint felt quite unable to face, let alone parry, the anxious, loaded enquiries she was sure to make.

The only answer, obviously, would be not to go home at all but to go somewhere else where he would be able to get rid of all that pent-up energy and emotion in the physical tiredness which would spring from activity and hard work. Where? The mountains, of course; he would go straight to the mountains, where he always had work to do and where the outdoor life was hard and exhausting. It was true that no one was expecting him, but that hardly mattered as his tent and all his camping equipment was kept at Nyiresy's. Everything he needed, even his mountain boots and warm clothes, was there in the little room that he had had put at his disposal at the forest manager's house at Beles. And it was just as well sometimes to arrive unannounced.

He sent someone to find the forester, Honey Zutor, who, as it was market day was sure to be in the town where he was a prominent and respected citizen. In an hour or two Zutor had procured him a carriage and some adequate horses, and by four o'clock they were on the road. The carriage was laden with a good supply of smoked bacon, bread and cornmeal packed hurriedly in with blankets, flour and cheeses, especially cottage cheese for the *gyorniks*. Liquor they would obtain at Beles. The road was good, for it was much used in the autumn, and the weather was dry, even up on the normally rain-soaked meadows on top of the Csonka-Havas ridge. This was unusual on that particular watershed so the carriage passed easily. It was just after nine o'clock when they drove up to the wooden fence of the forest manager's house.

Here Balint was surprised to see, beyond the wide forecourt, that the veranda of the house was brightly lit by lanterns and a big party was in progress. Men and women were moving about and the sound of a gypsy band could be heard. Maids bustled around a long table carrying trays, and two of the younger forest guards in their formal livery were filling up the glasses from large cut-glass decanters.

Abady had the carriage stopped in front of the entrance gate. After a few moments' pause, he said: 'Zutor! Go inside and bring me my mountain boots, tent and sleeping bag. You know where they are, don't you? And don't forget my rubber washing-bowl.'

The forester knew that his master was angry because when he was in a good mood he always used his nickname, Honey. Accordingly he clicked his heels smartly and replied with formal brevity: 'As you command, my Lord!'

'I shall also need my big Tyrolean raincoat, the folding chair, the iron kettle and the case of knives and forks. Bring those too; we'll find room for them somewhere. I shall wait here.'

Zutor hesitated for a moment before asking: 'How far does your Lordship intend going? We can't get far into the mountains with the carriage.'

'Just to the bend of the road. We'll camp there for the night.'

Honey saluted without a word and turned on his heel. Annoyed though he was, Balint could not help being amused to notice how smartly the forester, rifle on his back, marched away to obey his master's orders. His broad shoulders were etched in black in

PART SIX

front of the illuminated glitter from the veranda and as he mounted the steps he stamped his feet noisily as if he were Nemesis arriving to confront old Kalman Nyiresy.

When Honey told the old manager that Count Abady was in his carriage at the door, the pipe nearly dropped from the old man's mouth. Commotion raged. The gypsies fell silent and all the guests peered outside. No matter how hard they tried they could see nothing; but Balint, from where he sat, could easily recognize some of them; the notary Gaszton Simo, the director of the sawmills and the sheriff of the Hunyad county district – all of whom he had met on his last visit – and, at one end of the table, Timbus, the Romanian *popa* from Gyurkuca.

Nyiresy got up and disappeared into the house with Zutor. Two of the *gyorniks* went with them. They were followed by three girls and Balint thought that he recognized two of them as the priest's daughters whom he had seen when he had gone up into the mountains the previous winter.

Seen from outside in the dark it was like watching a brightly-lit pantomime in the theatre. A few peasants strolled out from their tied cottages nearby to gape at the carriage and question its driver as to who could possibly be inside. The coachman, who normally earned his living as a carter, had jumped down and was pulling at the horses' ears, for it was a country superstition that this was the quickest way of freshening up a tired animal. He answered in low tones and in an instant the men bowed low to the carriage and retired to a respectful distance, whispering among themselves that something must be seriously wrong if the *mariasza* did not wish to set foot in the house of the *domnule director*, even though the much feared judge was there as well as the even more terrible and powerful notary. The Lord must be angry about something and this could mean trouble. How and why no one knew, but it would obviously only be prudent to stand on the sidelines and watch from a distance without giving any sign of whose side they might be on.

Half an hour went by, half an hour which seemed like an eternity to the spectators. Then Nyiresy reappeared on the veranda, his face red with anger behind the white beard. From the house emerged three figures, Honey and the two foresters, who hurried out to the carriage and piled in all that they could. The two *gyorniks* hoisted the rest on to their shoulders, for the Noble Count had ordered that they should accompany him.

They made camp about fifteen minutes' walk away on a

491

meadow between the road and the banks of the Szamos. Rapidly they erected the tent and started a fire and as soon as this was done Balint sent the two men and the carter away. Then he sent Honey back to the forest manager with orders that the carriage horses should be housed in the estate stables and that lodging and food should be given to the driver. Honey was also told to arrange that some mountain ponies should be collected that evening so that the party could set off for the mountains at dawn.

Balint sat in front of his tent alone. He had cut himself a sharp hazel twig to use as a spit, as he had learned in his youth, and started to roast some bacon over the camp fire in front of him.

It was a modest little fire, but even so he was reminded of the great fires the *gyorniks* had lit each evening of his trip during the winter. Looking into the flames, he thought again of Adrienne, not that he needed anything to bring her to mind for her image had not left him the entire day. So engrossed was he in his thoughts that he did not notice that the piece of bacon had long since fallen from the spit and was sizzling among the embers of the fire. He just sat there, his jaw thrust forward, his mouth open and his lips drawn back showing his anger and frustration.

After a while he heard little tripping steps over the grass and in a moment Nyiresy's two young maids stood before him, barefoot, dressed in snow-white cotton blouses, voluminous white skirts and little black bodices stretched over their breasts. '*Poftyic, mariasza* – at your service, my Lord!' they said, as they placed before him all sorts of delicacies: cold trout, venison, fried chicken and roast turkey with slices of *strudel* and cakes, all of which they had brought in two large baskets with plates and cutlery, glasses and wine. All this they laid out on a cloth on the grass in front of him and, smiling and giggling, urged his Lordship to eat.

Balint set to with gusto. He sat on the ground at the entrance of his tent using the folding chair as a table, his feast now lit by the rising moon. And he dined. The two girls served him assiduously, alternately passing through the narrow entrance of the tent to offer him selections of what they had brought. The entrance was narrow and it was no doubt because of this that from time to time, as they changed his plates or poured his wine, a hand would brush his face or a soft shoulder press gently into Balint's own. They chattered away merrily, though they spoke so quickly that Balint was unable to understand their prattle. They were young and gay and they smiled as they gazed into his face with their large shining brown eyes.

PART SIX

Later there was only one girl near him, not at his side but behind him in the tent. Then, from the shadowy interior, two naked arms crept around his shoulders, embraced him and drew him back out of the moonlight. Balint felt that he was falling softly into some deep welcoming darkness.

⁂

Dawn was breaking when he awoke. It was still dark inside the tent but a pale light found its way in through the slits between the entrance flaps and he realized that the little Romanian *fata* must thoughtfully have closed them after he had fallen asleep. As everything that had happened the night before came slowly back to him, Balint was filled with a great anger.

Firstly he was angry with himself. How could he have allowed himself to do such a thing on the very evening of that holy day when Adrienne had been so good to him! Balint could still smell that odour of rancid butter, the butter that country girls used to smooth their hair. His nose was full of it and it disgusted him, just as he was disgusted with himself. How base he was, how selfish and ignoble! How mean! Then his anger took a different direction. He thought of old Nyiresy. The decaying old lecher must have planned it. That is why he had sent over the supper and no doubt given careful instructions to the girl as to what she should do, and how she should report it all to him afterwards so that he and his cronies could laugh at him and make fun of him!

Balint jumped up and stepped out of the tent. On the road the horses were already waiting, together with three foresters. The first two were those who had been serving Nyiresy's party and the third was Krisan Gyorgye who had been sent for from his home at Toszerat. Honey himself stood a little farther away with the notary Gaszton Simo. The latter must have been watching the tent, for as soon as Balint came out he began to saunter towards him.

'Well!' he called in a familiar tone, 'and how are we the morning after? I hope the noble Count passed an agreeable night?' and he winked lasciviously. This impertinent allusion made Balint even angrier than he had been before.

'How is it, Mr Notary, that you come to be eating trout in September, in the middle of the closed season? You can be fined heavily for this, especially as you are supposed to be a responsible official. I warn you here and now that I propose to inform the authorities!'

Simo smiled in a superior, self-satisfied manner.

'Those fish were confiscated from a poacher, as the law provides. I've several witnesses to the fact, indeed as many as you like. Someone has to eat the fish once they've been caught. Anyhow, they tasted good, didn't they?' he added impudently as he twirled his moustaches with a gesture of defiance.

Balint turned away angrily and called to Honey: 'Bring my wash-basin and water!' He went back into the tent thinking what a scoundrel the notary was and how he was being mocked with that pack of lies about 'witnesses'. Of course he could and would get as many witnesses as he wanted. This was unendurable, thought Balint. Nevertheless he would have his revenge and show him who was the master. Therefore, when he stepped out of the tent he said, with an expression of frozen displeasure on his face: 'Since I last visited the mountains I have been informed that the peasants are being ruined by some unscrupulous money-lender. Do you know anything about the matter, Mr Notary?'

Gaszton Simo's small eyes glinted suspiciously. Then he forced himself to look sad and said sorrowfully: 'Indeed I'm sorry to say it's perfectly true, though I do everything I can to protect our poor people, everything possible. I try to educate them, make them understand. What's more I write all their contracts for them, but they are so stupid, they won't be helped! They are their own worse enemies. You can have no idea, Mr Deputy, how stupid they are...' and he went into lengthy tales of what he had tried to do, quoting names, dates, figures and this... and then that... He told how all his efforts were in vain because the peasants were so backward and helpless and also suspicious of 'us gentlefolk'. And all the while he looked hard at Balint, trying to learn how much this pesky meddling aristocrat knew about his own part in the matter.

While this was going on Honey had seen to it that the horses had been fully loaded.

'Goodbye, Mr Simo. We'll talk about all this some other time, without fail!' Balint said as menacingly as he could. Now in good humour, for he knew that he had thrown a good scare into that swaggering dishonest brute of a notary, Balint mounted swiftly and rode away.

The road they took was the same as when Balint had come in February. It led first to Gyalu Botira, and then along the crest of the mountains. How different it is now, thought Balint. The distant chains of mountains were barely visible through the haze produced by the heat and dust of an exceptionally dry summer. Nearer at hand were the meadows that Balint had only previously seen covered in a blanket of snow, and on them had been erected haystacks, each mounted on three wooden poles so that the autumn rains would run unimpeded beneath them. On the juniper trees the berries were already ripe, while the beech trees were turning red and yellow. Only the fir trees were the same, dark and unchanging. From the valleys below occasional wisps of fog rose gently as soon as they were reached by the rays of the morning sun.

'There'll be rain tonight,' said Honey, turning back in his saddle. 'We'll be lucky if we make good enough time to erect a shelter.'

Now Balint could see that some order had been brought to the different stands of timber. Since the new engineer had taken charge, the licence system for felling had been abolished and now all those trees that were to be cut had been carefully marked. Indiscriminate felling by individuals had been prohibited. Of course this was easy to enforce in summer, because everyone was kept occupied in the fields cutting and making hay and harvesting the corn. In winter it would be more difficult, but Balint hoped that the Viennese firm to whom he had contracted the timber would start the systematic felling that would give steady work to the mountain people. It had been a strict article of the contract that local labour must be employed and only skilled foremen were to be brought in from elsewhere.

The effect of the new management could everywhere be seen. The road along the crest of the ridge bordered the stands of timber, and Balint now saw that every two hundred metres there had been placed numbered stakes that marked the boundaries of each hundred-acre stand that was ready to be felled. It was the same system that had been so highly developed on the Uzdy property, and Balint was pleased to see that at last a beginning had been made to modernize the exploitation of the Abady forests.

When they reached the summit of the crest they were joined by old Zsukuczo who, after the fashion of the mountain people, knelt briefly in front of Abady and kissed the hem of his coat before asking where they were going. When Balint told him that they were heading for the Prislop meadows the old man took the lead, for this was in his territory. At the crossroads near Toszerat, they found waiting for them Juanye Vomului, the forest guard for the next district who was wearing a giant sheepskin cap, a wide belt studded with nails and his most elaborate national dress to underline the fact that he owned his own land and was not a cotter, or tied worker, like the other *gyorniks*. Balint's party had now increased to six, including the *mariasza* himself. About midday they arrived at their destination on the Prislop. Here they made camp.

The spot chosen by Zutor was indeed beautiful. It was a rich meadow that sloped gently down between woods of mixed beech and fir trees to the valley of Feherviz – the White Water – behind which rose the mass of the Humpleu. Above that towered the summit of the Vortup. It was here, at the heart of the Abady forests, that he had decided to build a hunting lodge. Now he started to plan where it should be sited and when he had marked the spot and returned to camp with Honey in faithful attendance, the afternoon was already drawing in. Old Zsukuczo, whose function on this trip was to find water, then asked Abady if he would like to shoot a *kapre de paduren* – a roebuck, telling him that he knew all their haunts in this part of the forest.

'But I haven't brought a gun!' said Balint.

'*Nu bai* – it doesn't matter!' said Zsukuczo with an exaggerated wink from one of his red-rimmed eyes. '*Tara bun* – look here!' and he unslung his own Werdli rifle which, as an official forest guard, he was entitled always to carry. The old poacher had looked after his gun with loving care and had indeed himself improved it, filing down the sight at the barrel's end so that a more accurate aim could be obtained. Balint agreed that he would very much like to kill a buck and, after sending Honey back to the camp, set off into the undergrowth with Zsukuczo leading the way.

There was no road or trail, not even a track, but the old poacher marched on without for an instant pausing, and found such an easy way through the dense thickets that Balint scarcely had to brush away branches in front of his face or step over a fallen log. Sometimes it seemed that the young growth of fir trees was so thick that they would not be able to go any farther, but the old man, by turning this way or that, always got through without difficulty: and, whether he was walking over moss or on a carpet of dry beech leaves, which of all substances crackled the most when walked upon, his tread was always silent and twigs never snapped under his feet though he wore hobnailed boots as large as boats.

They went on slowly and cautiously until they reached an ancient white fir. Here Zsukuczo stopped, checked the direction of the wind, and then bent down and swept clean a small patch of pine-needles. Then he knelt down facing the trunk of the old tree and, bowing his head to the ground, murmured something that sounded like a prayer. Then he traced a cross on the earth where his master was to sit, and also on the bark against which he would lean his back. When this ceremony was over he whispered: '*Poftyic mariasza!*' and crawled behind the tree.

Balint was fascinated and amused by these antics. Even if no game were conjured up it would have been worth coming all this way merely to watch Zsukuczo's peasant magic at work. He doubted if any deer would come near them here in the depth of the woods, for surely there would have been more hope of game if they had stopped at the edge of a clearing, or on some jutting rock which overlooked the sort of open space where deer liked to graze, rather than here where one could not see further than twenty paces. This was all quite ridiculous, he thought. All the same he sat down obediently so as not to offend the pride of the old *gyornik*. Behind the tree Zsukuczo was muttering some prayer or incantation and the murmuring sound was continued for about half an hour. Then a soft rustling could be heard – tip tip tip – and then a more confident step, and suddenly a doe slipped out of the thicket of low branches of fir and ground elder. She came cautiously but calmly, two fawns at her heels. She looked directly at the hunter seated under the tree, her large gentle eyes unblinking and confident, stamped twice with her forefeet and then, as he did not move, herself moved slowly forward confidently grazing all the while, her two offspring still behind her. They passed by, barely three yards from Balint, and disappeared into the undergrowth on the other side of the clearing.

Zsukuczo emerged from behind the tree looking puzzled. He seemed almost angry, demanding why the *mariasza* had not lifted his gun for the kill. 'Why? Why? The game was here, here!' Abady explained that only buck could be shot and it was forbidden to shoot does, especially when followed by their young. '*A se! A se!*' muttered the old man, nodding his head in apparent agreement while thinking to himself that these noble lords were strange animals and that you could never know what odd quirks they had in their heads. However, since Balint rewarded him with a five-crown piece, he regained his good humour at once and swiftly guided his *mariasza* through the dark woods and back to their camp.

Abady remained three days more on the Prislop, though the rain predicted by Honey started that very evening.

Even the rain seemed different. The clouds settled low over the valleys completely shrouding the mountain tops. Here, where Balint camped, one could not always see the tops of the trees and when one could the clouds formed a dense impenetrable blanket of fog only a few feet higher. The rain fell so heavily that it looked like ropes falling from the sky. Everything was soaked and even Balint's thick Austrian rain-coat was soon like a sponge. Because the expedition had been decided upon so suddenly he had only one change of clothes and two pairs of boots, one hobnailed, the other with rubber soles, and all these were drenched with water by the end of the second day. In the tent, too, though a deep ditch had been dug all round it, water flowed everywhere. By the second evening Balint had to strip to the skin and dine wrapped in a damp blanket, while his clothes were hung up near the fire in the shelter built by the *gyorniks*. He hoped they would be dry by morning. It was like a Kneipp cure, he said to himself as he huddled down into the steaming wool and laughed out loud because he was so happy. The daylight hours were spent walking, walking, walking until he exhausted himself. With Honey as his guide Balint climbed over all the neighbouring mountains, checking on the improvements made by the new forestry manager. When the whole area of the Prislop had been covered, they moved camp to the head of the Vale Saka at the base of the Vlegyasza. Here Balint stayed another three days. The rain never stopped.

Chapter Three

ON HIS LAST EVENING in the mountains Balint returned to camp in the evening to discover four men waiting to see him. They, too, came from the Retyicel district but their little settlement, Pejkoja by name, had been built in a remote corner at the northern boundary of the Abady properties, some six or seven kilometres from the village. They came to see Count Abady.

The news that the *mariasza* had refused to enter the *domnu director*'s house, despite the fact that the great judge and the all-powerful notary had been there, had spread through the mountains like wildfire. It was everywhere told that this was not

PART SIX

all but that the Lord had also interrupted the great man's feast, removed two of the *gyorniks* who were serving them and had then, to their great shame, camped barely five hundred paces away. This fascinating and important news had naturally become much embellished in the telling. It was related with great relish how the *Grofu* – the Count – had publicly upbraided the hated notary and turned his back on the judge. What sort of mighty nobleman could he be, they asked themselves, who would dare act like this with such powerful and important people? And they told how even the arrogant notary himself had risen at dawn and despite the manner in which he had been insulted the night before, waited outside his tent until the *mariasza* should awake. Not only this but, when the Count had emerged, the notary had humbled himself in full sight of all the others. Oh, it must be a mighty Lord indeed who could perform such wonders!

All this news had reached the men of Pejkoja within twenty-four hours and at once the men of the village met together to discuss what they should do, for they were in great trouble. The problem was this. The money-lender, Rusz Pantyilimon, had taken the village to court and sent the bailiffs in to collect a debt he claimed from them. If they did not pay up, all they possessed would be sold by public auction. Everyone in the village had a share in this debt, which had somehow inexplicably grown to an astronomical sum out of a simple loan of made to two villagers four years previously. The story went that the men had borrowed two hundred crowns but, simple, illiterate peasants that they were, somehow they had signed for four hundred. In six months the sum had mounted to seven hundred and, as the debt grew and grew, so the other villagers had come forward to give their guarantees for its repayment, for everything they owned was held in common and was so entered into the land registry – sixty-seven Hungarian acres of grazing land, sixteen houses and a small sawmill. All the village families therefore were forced to band together to defend their community inheritance, and this is why they were all now involved. By the time Balint came to the mountains the money lender was claiming some three thousand crowns. To repay such a sum would mean that everything they owned would have to be sold and all the families made homeless ... And all this for a paltry loan of two hundred crowns. It was the grossest injustice.

For five days the men of the village met and talked and finally decided to do what the village elder, Juon Lung aluj Maftye, advised. Juon, who was now well over sixty, had known well Balint's maternal grandfather, the elder Count Tamas, and for many years had managed all the communal property of the village, always going to Denestornya for advice as Count Abady, to whom they had formerly owed allegiance as serfs, still took a fatherly interest in everyone who lived and worked on his properties. Besides, he was also the county court judge. Old Juon Maftye therefore proposed that they should now go to the young *mariasza*, ask his help and tell him of their complaints, for there was no doubt that, just like his grandfather before him, he was a mighty man who would put all to rights.

After much discussion this proposal was accepted, though by no means unanimously. There were those among them who merely complained without themselves offering a solution; there were others who were swayed by the much respected head man and who put their faith in an approach to the young count; and there were those who declared that this was not the right way to go about it and that the only final solution was to be found 'one night'! What was to be done on that night was not specified, but everyone understood what was meant by that little phrase – *la noptye* – namely that 'one night' people should go to Rusz Pantyilimon's house ... but what they should do there – burn the records, beat the rascal to death or merely give him a good scare – was never said: such things were better not discussed.

After all the talk, however, they took Juon Maftye's advice and it was agreed that the old man himself, with two others, should seek out the *mariasza* at his camp and tell him of their troubles. The other two men who sent with him were Nikolaj Lung, who was nicknamed 'Cselmnyik' – Tiny, because he was so huge, and the headman's grandson, Kula, who had somehow scrambled himself into a little education. This last was scarcely more than a boy, but he came along not only to help his grandfather but also because he had met the *mariasza* on his visit the previous February. On their way to Balint's camp they had been joined by a fourth man, who was ironically called 'Turturika' – Little Dove. It was he who had so strongly urged *la noptye*.

It was these four men whom Balint found seated round the camp-fire. He at once offered them slices of bacon and draughts of mountain brandy and asked them to come to his tent, which stood a little way apart from the gyorniks' shelter, as soon as they had eaten. He did this because they would be able to speak more freely away from the men who came from other districts. Balint made one exception: he told Honey to be present, not only because the men of Pejkoja respected him but also because Balint, though his Romanian had greatly improved, felt it would be better to have someone by him who could translate if necessary.

The old man presented the villages' case. He spoke at length, but cogently with much detail and, after Balint had posed several questions and received their answers, Maftye explained exactly what they wanted him to do. In short, the petition to their lord was that he should intervene, summon the wicked money-lender to his presence and forbid him to do any further harm to the respectable people of Pejkoja. In exchange they offered the sum of eight hundred crowns to Rusz to settle the debt. This great sum they had managed to scrape up but further they could not go, not now or ever. Balint tried in vain to explain that in these times he no longer possessed such powers as they attributed to him and that there was no way he could force Pantyilimon to anything he did not wish. The old man did not believe him. For him the *mariasza* was all-powerful and if he did not do something it was because he did not wish it. The *Excellenciasza* Abady, his grandfather, said the old man with dignity, would not have let them down; *he* would have stood by them in their trouble! Balint was touched by their faith and in the end agreed that he would do what he could. In saying this he was swayed by the fact that the Little Dove, who had hitherto remained silent, suddenly broke angrily into the discussions, saying: 'Didn't I tell you this wouldn't be any use? There's only one answer – *la noptye*!'

What an evil face that man has, thought Balint, looking hard at the bearded Turturika. I certainly wouldn't want to be at his mercy!

In the end everyone went to sleep, and long before dawn the men from Pejkoja had disappeared back into the forest from which they came.

Abady broke camp at first light, and long before the bells of the little wooden church at Retyicel had rung their noonday peal Balint's party had arrived at the foot of the mountain on whose lower slopes the village had been built. They rode slowly through the village until they reached the last house. This was the fortress-like building that Balint had seen from the other side of the valley on his previous visit. It stood completely isolated, well away from the others. Balint's little caravan stopped outside a massive oak door which led into a courtyard in front of the main building.

Balint waited behind the others while the gyorniks, led by Krisan Gyorgye, hurried up to the front door and started knocking fiercely. From inside could be heard the furious barking of the three guard-dogs and they set up such a clamour that even Krisan had to bellow at the top of his voice for anyone to hear. Krisan stayed at the door, hammering hard against its great oak beams and shouting as if his lungs would burst. Inside the house and compound nothing stirred except the dogs. It was as if they alone inhabited the house. Nothing moved. The veranda of the house, which was visible from the road, was deserted and there was no sign of life behind the iron grills that covered all the windows.

'Perhaps this Rusz isn't at home!' said Balint to Krisan. At this moment, above the cruel line of broken glass which protected the top of the great stone outer wall, there appeared the head of a young boy.

'What do you want?' he asked timidly.

'The *mariasza* wants to see *Domnu* Rusz. Open the doors for his Lordship or I'll break them down,' shouted Krisan Gyorgye and he swung his great axe above his head and let out a stream of curses.

The boy's head disappeared and in a few seconds one of the doors was opened. Balint rode in while the dogs were kept at bay by the *gyorniks*' long staves and by having stones thrown at them. As soon as Balint reached the foot of the steps that led up to the entrance of the house a tall, narrow-shouldered man appeared on the veranda. Abady looked him over carefully. The man's face was completely hairless and covered in wrinkles like that of an old woman. He had tiny eyes and his hair was longer than was then usual. He wore a grey suit of city clothes with the tails of his shirt hanging loose from under his jacket which gave him a surprisingly broad-hipped look. At the sight of Abady he started bowing obsequiously and wringing his hands. So this is the wicked and terrible monster feared by everyone, thought Balint. So this is Rusz Pantyilimon!

'Why are you here? What do you want of me?' asked Rusz in a frightened voice.

'Rusz Pantyilimon!' said Balint sternly; 'I wish to speak with you!'

He dismounted and, going up the steps was nervously shown by Rusz into a living-room which opened off one end of the veranda. Rusz kept turning as they went, looking back suspiciously at the grim faces of the mountain men that formed Balint's band of *gyorniks*. Honey sat down on the top step and the others remained below. When Rusz saw this he realized that all was well as long as Honey stayed where he was. Then he followed Balint nervously indoors.

The men in the forecourt were still discussing the Pejkoja affair just as they had been the previous night and all through that morning's trek. Once again there was no general agreement. Zsukuczo and the two younger *gyorniks* believed that, although no one stood a chance against Rusz as long as he was supported by the notary and the *popa*, they still hoped for a miracle if the *mariasza* should intervene. Krisan Gyorgye, himself a violent man, held that *la noptye* was the only practicable solution; while Juanye Vomului remained silent. He, as a well-to-do and respectable man, had been unwise enough the previous evening to suggest that those who incurred debts ought to be man enough to settle them. This had caused such an uproar that he had shut his mouth and hardly opened it since.

The room that Balint was ushered into was small and airless. Balint sat down at once on a bench, above which hung a holy icon, and took out his notes. Speaking deliberately and dispassionately he went through the history of the affair as it had been reported to him by the village people. He then told Rusz of their offer 'which,' he said firmly, 'I find fair and reasonable!'

Pantyilimon had listened to what Balint had to say standing in front of him and shifting his weight restlessly from one long spindly leg to the other. At the same time he moved his head like a horse with the habit of 'weaving'. It was not clear whether this was the result of panic, fright or excitement, or whether it was an habitual nervous tic. When Balint had finished, he hesitated a few seconds before replying and, when he did so, seemed to have difficulty in getting out the words: 'Can't be done, please, can't be done!'

'Can't? Very well then, we must think of something else!' said Balint, forcing as much menace as he could into his tone. 'I shall hire a lawyer and fight you myself. I shall make the case my own. According to the law you have no right, no right at all, to the sum you are claiming. You are limited to receiving back the original loan plus eight per cent annual interest, not a penny more. I shall instruct my lawyers to insist that your behaviour to these people constitutes a criminal offence which, you may like to know, carries a penalty of two years' imprisonment!'

'Can't be done, please, can't be done!' was all that Rusz managed to get out as he stood squirming in front of Balint.

'Yes, it can be done! What you are doing is no less than a felony, extorting between three and four hundred per cent! How could you?'

'Please! It isn't all true and it isn't only me. Please! I have to pay dear to get money. It's very expensive!'

'And from whom do you get it, may I ask?'

The former teacher was still weaving about, but now there was a hint of a smile buried in his wrinkled face. He did not answer the question but went on: 'Expensive money, very expensive, and much losses, very much ... his Lordship not know how it is on mountain. Land register book is never in order, many men there only in grandfather's name still. People here like that; one day here, one day not here. They go away and I see no more, never. Money not paid, man gone. Cannot do anything. I pay, I lose much money. I have to ... much loss, always loss ...' And he went on in his broken Hungarian repeating the same feeble arguments and reiterating that it wasn't his money, and that as he only had a tiny profit from the whole affair there was nothing he could do.

'Well, then, go to your principals! Let them relent!' interrupted Balint.

'Can't be done, please, can't be done!'

'All right then, but I warn you of two things. The first is both for you and for your charming associates: I shall prosecute this case as if it were my own. The second is for you alone. Since I have come to the mountains I have found out how desperate these people are and how much they hate you. It is my duty to warn you of this. From now on you hold your fate in your own hands!'

Pantyilimon shrugged his shoulders: 'I know, please, bad people, bad people. Bad ... bad ...'

Balint left the room while the money-lender stood aside bowing and wringing his hands. He descended the steps rapidly, jumped on to his horse and road swiftly away followed by Honey and the *gyorniks*. The huge oak entrance gates swung to behind them and the dogs could still be heard barking as they rode swiftly down the hill, through the village and back to their road.

In the train back to Kolozsvar Balint thought over the whole affair and found himself more and more annoyed by the part that he had allowed himself to play. He had done it again. Once more he had become personally involved.

He should never have promised his help to the men of Pejkoja,

PART SIX

but weakly he had allowed himself to be carried away, first by the old man's talk of his grandfather and then by his fear of what the evil-faced Turturika might do if they all decided upon *la noptye*. So now he had got right into the middle of their fight with the money-lender and what had begun as disinterested mediation had ended in personal involvement. Now, if he did not succeed in winning the case for the people of Pejkoja, his own prestige would suffer in the eyes of the mountain people. The case would not be easy. He never doubted the identity of Rusz's silent anonymous partners. These were obviously the Romanian priest from Gyurkuca and the notary Gaszton Simo. Between them they would not miss a trick, however dishonest, to see that Rusz was exonerated. In their own world they wielded great power and they had the unutterable advantage of being always there, on the spot where they could frighten people and put pressure on them in a hundred different ways; whereas he, Balint, could only occasionally come among them. During his rare visits they put their trust in him, but if he were not there what would happen? Obviously he would have to find a lawyer who was prepared not only to accept the case but who would also be trusted by the people of the mountain.

Balint thought for a long time until at last inspiration came to him: Aurel Timisan. He was the perfect candidate; being both a lawyer and a Romanian who sat in Parliament to defend the interests of his fellow Romanians. The peasants would respect him and do as he said and he might even be able to influence the *popa* himself. Of all people surely Aurel Timisan had more chance than any of settling this affair properly – maybe even without taking it to court. He was generally known to be an honest man. Balint congratulated himself and decided to visit him as soon as possible, telling himself that the old radical was sure to agree to help, for it was entirely a question of protecting impoverished Romanians.

After several telephone calls in the morning Balint managed to make an appointment to see Timisan in the early afternoon. The old man received him in his smoking-room.

'This is an honour indeed!' said Timisan with an ironic smile under his huge white moustaches. 'His Lordship dares to visit me, who spent a year in the prison of Vac! See! There is proof, on the wall behind you!' He pointed to a large photograph in a heavy frame which portrayed a group of eight men. Balint's host was easily recognized from the great sweep of his moustaches, though of course they were then still black. Balint asked about the others and was told that they were all his fellow defendants in the famous Memorandum trial.

'And who is this?' asked Abady, pointing to a man seated at the centre of the group who had not been identified by the lawyer.

'Ah!' said Timisan. 'He was the governor of the prison. He was very good to us and so we – at least that's how we put it then decided to pay him this honour!'

The two men sat down facing each other in large armchairs that were upholstered in that Paisley-printed velveteen which was then all the vogue in well-to-do middle-class homes.

'I did not come to continue our last discussion,' said Balint, 'but I should be grateful, Mr Deputy, for your advice and help in a legal dispute in which I am interested. It concerns the welfare of a group of Romanian peasants, and therefore I am hoping that you will be interested.' He then took out his notes and told the whole story, ending up with Rusz's rejection of the offer made by the men of Pejkoja. He added that expense was no object and that he, Balint, would guarantee to see the matter through to the end.

Timisan heard him out in silence. Then he looked up; but instead of asking any question pertinent to the story Balint had related, asked: 'Tell me, why does your Lordship mind what happens to these people?'

Balint was so surprised that for a moment he did not know what to say. It was so much a part of his nature and upbringing that he should do what he could to protect those in need that he was unable, at such short notice, put his motives into words. At last he said: 'It's so appallingly unjust! This sort of thing should not be allowed. I understand, Mr Deputy, that you advise the Unita Bank, which, through the *popa* Timbus, supplies this Rusz with the money he lends out. Surely if the bank gets to know how their funds are being misused they'll issue a warning so that the money-lenders will be forced to give up this sort of extortion and we'll be able to rescue their unfortunate victims!'

Timisan explained, rather as if he were giving a public lecture, that the bank was only concerned to receive regularly the interest on the money that it lent out. If their loans were correctly amortized, what was done with the money was not their affair. Timisan spoke for some time, coolly and professionally.

'But, Mr Deputy, doesn't it shock you personally when you hear of cases like this? These are your own people, and they are being ruined. You represent them in Parliament, you speak about their "rights". Surely you will defend them?'

PART SIX

'That is politics.'

'Politics? Politics have nothing to do with this. Here we have some poor mountain people who need help!'

'That too!' The old deputy smiled. 'Just so!' He paused again and thought for a moment before going on: 'Your Lordship is full of goodwill and you honour me with your visit. You will understand that I am not often honoured by visits from Hungarian noblemen!' He laughed drily, then went on: '... and because of this I shall give your Lordship an explanation. Centuries ago this country was conquered by the swords of your ancestors and so the great Hungarian-owned estates were formed. In these days we have to find other means of getting what we want. We need a wealthy middle class and up until now this class has not existed. Most of the Romanian intellectuals like myself are the sons of poor Romanian priests who were the only ones among us who were properly educated. Do you see that picture? It is of my father, who was Dean of Pancelcseh.' He pointed to the wall where, over the souvenir of the prison of Vac, there hung an almost life-size portrait in oils of a venerable *popa* with a huge beard: it looked as if it had been copied from a photograph. Timisan went on:

'We are all equal, and we have no means. We have therefore decided that, no matter how, we must create a wealthy middle class. And that is what we are doing. Our bank furnishes the original funds and, apart form other businesses, it lends money to certain people we believe can be trusted firstly to build up their own fortunes and then to use those fortunes for political purposes. Naturally these people have to deal with – you would say exploit – poor Romanian peasants, and that is only natural because they have no one else to exploit! Were there are no victims when your marauding ancestors over-ran our country? Well, it's the same today, but the difference is that you did it on horseback and wearing coats of mail! So much for glory! Hail to the conquering hero! Perhaps it was all more picturesque in those days, more decorative, more "noble"!' and he gave an ironic note to the word "noble" before laughing wryly. 'But we are more modest. We are modern people, simple and grey and not decorative at all!' The cold, cruel glint that had lit up his eyes as he spoke now faded. 'I have never said anything like this to anyone before – and you won't hear it from anyone else. If any of you Hungarians raised the matter, we'd deny it, naturally; but then you are not likely to, for Hungarians only think in political terms!'

Timisan laughed again. It was not a pleasant sound. Then he said: 'Your Lordship will understand from what I have said that I can be of no help to you and, if you will forgive the presumption, I would advise your Lordship not to bother with such matters!'

Balint rose from his chair and shook hands automatically. He was perturbed and upset by what he had just heard. Then the old man spoke again, his voice now full of compassion, fatherly, concerned, as if he himself were moved.

'I tell you all this because I am an old man with much experience. And I am filled with pity for your goodwill, which is so very rare...' He walked to the door to show Balint out.

'Thank you for your visit,' he said.

Chapter Four

KOLOZSVAR WAS AT ITS BUSIEST in the autumn because that was the time of the hunting in the Zsuk country and of the steeple-chases which were held on three Sundays. The Hubertus Hunt met every day except Sunday, usually on the hilly grasslands that lay between the valleys of the Szamos and Fejer rivers and sometimes on the right bank of the Szamos in the country bordered by the districts of Mocs, Gyulatelek and Szuk. Those young men who did not live in country houses nearby or who did not put up in the Hubertus Hunt building itself stayed in Kolozsvar and went to the meets by train or in their own carriages. And because wherever a goodly quality of eligible young males were to be found, mothers would find some excuse to bring their unmarried daughters, so they too would come to town at this season. As a result there were plenty of dances and grand balls, evenings of gypsy music and other entertainments. The provincial capital in autumn was even gayer than it was in the Carnival season after Christmas.

Balint too went to Kolozsvar that year, encouraged by his mother even though it was a great sacrifice for her to send him away and remain alone herself in the great house of Denestornya. Countess Roza had several reasons for making this decision, among them her ambition to see Balint shine socially and take what she considered was his rightful place in Transylvanian society. Also she felt that it was important that he should have every opportunity of meeting suitable girls, one of whom might

PART SIX

perhaps take his fancy, for she knew from what she had been told by her old housekeepers that Adrienne, whom she had come more and more to distrust as a bad influence on her son, would not be coming to Kolozsvar that season.

There was also another reason. Countess Roza was immensely proud of her horses and she wanted them to be shown off and admired. She was sure that she bred the best mounts in Transylvania and she wanted everyone else to know how beautiful they were, how fast, good-natured, well-proportioned, strong, triumphant and splendid. Nevertheless, it was with a pang of regret that she made the decision to let herself be separated for eight to ten weeks from those beautiful animals whose welfare and training she supervised daily and who, every morning, she would visit and caress. She would miss them every bit as much as she would her son. So it was with tears in her slightly protuberant eyes that she stood in the horseshoe-shaped forecourt, fed lumps of sugar to the three horses she had decided to send with Balint and watched them clatter away through the great entrance gates. A dray-cart rumbled out after them laden with blankets, saddles, bandages, sacks of oats and special fodder and a hundred other things so that they should want for nothing while away from home.

Riding in hilly country was a new experience for Balint, who was not accustomed to having to spare the horses when climbing steep hillsides lest they should get winded, nor to galloping at full speed downhill so as not to let the hounds get away from him. However he soon got into the run of things by following the example of Gazsi Kadacsay, who this year was acting as gentleman whipper-in and who could race down any slope, no matter how steep or slippery, as swiftly as the wind. During the days in the hunting field Balint became much closer to many of the other young men of his own age with whom previously he had not been particularly friendly. Apart from Gazsi himself, there was Pityu Kendy and the four young Alvinczys, and with all of them new ties of friendship sprung up through their daily meetings and participation in a sport they all loved. It was a carefree life, and the hard physical effort brought with it an agreeable and languourous tiredness. The desire for Adrienne that had always overwhelmed him whenever he was alone, began to fade and, though it never left him, was no longer the feverish yearning which had so tormented him ever since his last visit to Almasko.

So passed the month of October and the first half of November. Since coming to Kolozsvar Balint had engaged a university student to give him lessons in Romanian every evening. The vital need to speak that language had been brought home to him not only by his talks with Timisan, but especially by the difficulty of communicating properly with the people in the mountains. Balint also wanted to be able to read everything that the Romanian-language newspapers said, and not merely those extracts which the Hungarian papers thought fit to reproduce. If ever he was to get to the bottom of all those complicated problems, and thereby form his own unbiased opinion, then he must know what the other side was saying. *Audiatur in altera pars.*

In mid-October Balint went again up into the mountains and this time he took with him to Pejkoja a young Romanian-speaking lawyer who, after much searching, had been found in Banffy-Hunyad. The man was well spoken of, had undertaken several similar cases and seemed in every way suitable.

The atmosphere at Pejkoja was not at all what Balint had expected. Despite the fact that old Juon Lung aluj Maftye had managed to get a small group of ten men to meet the *mariasza*, they listened sullenly to what he had to say, shrugged their shoulders with apparent indifference, and found all sorts of excuses not to sign the power of attorney which would enable the lawyer to act for them. Only one man refused openly and that was the terrible-faced Turturika, who greeted their proposals with mocking laughter.

The meeting broke up without Balint having achieved anything. Just as he was riding down the hillside thinking that the whole expedition had been nothing but a waste of time, old Juon's grandson, Kula, stepped out from behind some hazel bushes and waylaid them. Balint realized that the boy must have taken a shortcut so as to catch up with them and, thinking that probably Kula had brought a secret message from his grandfather, he let the others ride ahead so that the boy could speak to him privately. Kula jumped up onto the steep bank so that he could whisper directly into Abady's ear.

'I've come to report,' he said, 'what happened after the *mariazsa*'s last visit.' Then he told, with much detail, how one day the notary Simo had ridden into the village with two gendarmes, declared that the sawmill constituted a fire hazard and had it closed down. Further, he had call-up papers served on one of the young men of the village who had been exempted from military service because he was the only bread-winner in the family, and had renewed a charge against three farmers for some forestry

PART SIX

offence long since dropped and forgotten. He had fined Kula's grandfather for the trivial reason that he had moved his farm wagon to the left of the road rather than the right when he had met the notary's carriage on its way to Mereggyo; and he had taken several men aside and had menaced them privately with his own vengeance unless they all kept quiet about what had been going on in the village. He had told everyone that if any action was brought against Rusz Pantyilimon, he, Gaszton Simo, would personally testify that they truly owed the money. He had made it clear that his word was law as he had been appointed by the government. Finally, the notary had called up the whole village for community service on the roads just at the time of the maize harvest.

Kula explained that he had come himself to tell the *mariazsa* all this so that he would understand what had happened and would not be angry at the village people. After the notary, said Kula, the *popa* Timbus had come – but he did not tell Balint that the priest had scolded them for turning to a hated Hungarian lord for help against their own flesh and blood, saying that they had betrayed their priest and his good friend Rusz and that this he would never forgive or forget. Let them only come to him when they were in need, he had said, and then they would discover what it was to defy him! But young Kula told none of this to Balint, merely repeating a couple of times: 'The priest was here also! He too came to see us...'

Balint thanked him and gave the young man a two-crown piece.

'No! No! I didn't do this for money! Please believe me, not for a reward!' But Balint insisted and the boy finally accepted the coin before vanishing once more into the thicket of hazel bushes beside the road.

A few days later Balint went to see the chief notary for the district, for it was he who remained in charge after the sheriff had been suspended. He related what had happened up on the mountain, what Timisan had told him (without revealing his source) and, giving details of Simo's involvement, laid the whole blame on the district notary, explaining how abominably he treated the people under his jurisdiction.

The county notary listened with a cold expression on his face.

'I am unable to take any action at present, my Lord,' he said at last. 'Everything has now become a matter of politics – or at least it is treated as such either by the government or else by the people in the districts. Besides, Simo is one of the best notaries in the service. He's completely trustworthy!'

'Do you know that from your own experience?'

'From the reports of his immediate superior, the chief sheriff, who always...'

'Yes,' interrupted Balint angrily. 'He does not check on such things because he's in on all the deals himself!'

The chief notary stiffened in his seat, offended.

'It is quite natural that they should be socially acquainted. Simo comes from a very good family. His uncle is a Chamberlain and he himself only became a notary because, for private reasons he was unable to finish school. I understand that he does an excellent job and up there in the mountains, he is, shall we say, our Hungarian sentinel.'

'Hungarian sentinel?'

'Yes indeed; sentinel!'

Balint laughed in disbelief:

'Hungarian sentinel? The man who aids the bank that provides the money because he makes a profit himself? The man who sides with the money-lenders?'

'These are very grave accusations of which I would require further proof before any action could be taken. If your Lordship insists I can initiate an inquiry, but your Lordship must realize that this puts me in a most awkward situation. In the present circumstances... well, it could mean that I was risking my job because both the government and the opposition will assume I'm interfering in politics. Anything I do...' and he trailed off weakly.

This is just a waste of time, thought Balint, as the notary accompanied him to the stairs all the while explaining effusively what a difficult situation he was in. Balint left the building depressed by the fact that party politics could so impede the most disinterested and humane efforts to help those in trouble. One aspect of the affair, however, gave him a little cheer. At least it had been the villagers themselves who had refused his help so no one could accuse him of leaving them in the lurch: it was the only good point in the whole unfortunate affair.

Until the middle of November Balint would pass his days in the hunting field and his evenings, after his Romanian lessons, dining with friends and going out in society. At the weekends he went back to Denestornya.

PART SIX

On the Saturday after St Katherine's Day he found his mother in bed with a bad cold. The doctor said that she had bronchitis and for some days Countess Roza had a high temperature. When the fever subsided she was left with a persistent cough and a chest specialist announced that Countess Roza must spend the winter in a warmer climate. He always suggested natural cures and this time he proposed the Riviera. For a long time she would hear nothing of it, but Balint finally was able to persuade his mother to do what she was told. The old lady agreed, but only on her conditions, which were that Balint should go with her and that some little-known and simple resort on the Italian coast east of Genoa be chosen rather than the mondaine Côte d'Azur.

Balint guessed that this was because she had travelled there on her honeymoon with his father and had a hankering to return to a place where she had been so happy. He wrote to one of the friends he had made during his diplomatic days, an Italian now *en poste* in Vienna, and in a few days received an answer recommending Portofino, where there was an excellent little hotel with a good reputation. Soon Denestornya was in a flurry of packing and all the preparations for a long absence.

This was a cruel blow to Balint. The thought of having to go so far away from Adrienne — and for so many months — just when he had at last become so close to her, was unbearable. He knew that it was his duty to go with his mother but he could not go without seeing Adrienne once more. There was always the possibility that maybe this time, in the emotion of their imminent separation, she might, just might, yield to his entreaties. Balint dismissed the thought as soon as it came to him, for he knew in his heart that there was little hope of that unless he forced himself on her. He wrote a letter to Adrienne explaining that he had to go away on a prolonged journey and that before going he must see her, not at Almasko but somewhere where they could be alone, perhaps in Kolozsvar. It might — who knows? — be the last time they ever met. He wrote truthfully that he could not go unless he could see her first, not merely for a brief leave-taking but for several hours, just the two of them. It was a good letter, ardent and humble at the same time.

In a few days he had an answer.

Adrienne wrote that she could not go away at this time for 'they' would see through any excuse she might make. She told him that she too longed to see him before he went away and said that she could think of only one way: Balint should make his way to where the Abady forests joined the Almasko property; just in front of the clearing where he had shot the roebuck and he should be there punctually at 10 o'clock: '*I will be there, at 10 exactly and you too, no matter what the weather. This is the only solution I can think of. Next Wednesday, at 10 o'clock sharp...*'

This was not quite what Balint was hoping for, but it would have to do.

He prayed that the weather would be fine and not a day of mist and November drizzle – though, for what he was hoping, there was little to choose between the four walls of a room and the heather in the forest...

Balint was already at the appointed place long before he heard the distant sound of the Nagy-Almas town clock ring out the hour of nine o'clock. He walked down from the boundary of the Abady forest, which was on the crest that divided the valleys of Sebes-Koros and the Almas, and stood by the trunk of a huge beech tree. From there he had a clear view over the clearing at the edge of the Uzdy woods, as well as far beyond to where the path followed the line of the hills.

He was lucky. It was one of those deceptive autumn days when no one would believe that winter was so close at hand. It seemed more like a day in late summer, for many of the trees had not yet lost their leaves. Where Balint stood he was surrounded by luxuriant foliage of all colours, from pale lemon-yellows through every shade of gold to the darkest red-bronze. Balint looked at none of this but kept his eyes fixed upon the track beyond. Once some men passed along the road on their way to Banffy-Hunyad, but after them no one was to be seen. At last, in the distance, he saw Adrienne emerging from the distant trees and walking fast with long strides, her head held high.

Diana the huntress! thought Balint as the memory of his first image of her came strongly back to him. He moved forward to meet her and they kissed, his arms holding her tightly to him. He felt her lips on his, opening obediently as he had taught her, her body yielding to the pressure of his arms, though as they kissed Balint knew that her embrace was still that of an unawakened girl, virginal, ignorant, innocent of any passion or feeling other than the joy of meeting.

'Let's go deeper into the woods,' he said. 'People pass by here on the road.'

They walked back to the edge of the clearing. Abady spread his coat on the ground and they sat down.

'So you are going away?' said Addy. 'For some time?'

Though she spoke sadly Balint could see that her eyes were still sparkling with pleasure at seeing him again.

Leaning back against the slope of the hill, Balint took her in his arms. Her head sank back against his shoulder, sweetly confident, and the curls of her loose hair gently tickled his face, his ears, his moustaches, until he felt that they had a life of their own as independent as starfish in the sea. Adrienne did not speak as Balint started to tell her all that had happened.

He began in the most matter-of-fact way, recounting the details of his mother's illness and present condition, the doctor's orders and the preparations for their departure. As he spoke so his hands began to caress her, firstly at the waist and then slowly down to her knees and back. Later his fingers reached the hem of her skirt and below, to the softness of her silken stockings and, as the movement of his hands took up a slow rhythm of their own so his words became more impassioned, colourful, warmer, themselves a caress. He talked of his deep love for her, the captivity of his soul, how whenever he saw something beautiful the picture of Adrienne's face would rise up in front of him until he could see nothing but her golden eyes, raven hair and her generously curving, half-opened lips. As he spoke he would from time to time bend down and kiss those lips, fleetingly and without interrupting the flow of his words, beautiful words that sprang like sparks from the furnace of his desire, words that were transformed into a hymn of homage; and as he talked his hands, as if directed by a spirit independent of his own, found their own way, gently and carefully and ever more daringly, over Adrienne's body. As they lay together on the slope of the hillside Adrienne's skirt slid back from her knees and Balint's rhythmically caressing hands reached ever higher on the thin silk of her stockings.

Adrienne did not move but leaned back against Balint's shoulder. She seemed oblivious to everything but the gentle murmur of his voice, and the soft caresses of his hands over her body. It gave her a new and soothing feeling, something that she, who had never been fondled as a child or cherished as a woman, had not known before. Lulled, almost stunned, by Balint's melodious words and the smooth regular strokes of his caresses, Adrienne did not notice that his hands, from moving softly over her dress and stockings, had now reached the naked flesh of her thighs.

The Balint who talked in such innocent, poetic phrases was miles away from the primitive male intent only on gaining his desires. Yet as he talked, stringing together such beautiful words, Adrienne became aware of his awakening desire. All at once she got up, her back stiff, her whole body rigid. She noticed that her skirt had slid up and, swiftly pulling it down, she stared at Balint with hatred in her eyes, her whole being poised for flight. It was exactly as she had been that time on the carpet in front of the fire in her drawing-room at Kolozsvar and when they were sitting on the bench her father's garden.

Balint knew instantly that if he could not now regain her confidence then she would be for ever lost to him. Humbly, he acted as if he were offended and astonished by her sudden reaction and slowly, oh, so slowly, he coaxed her back into his arms stroking her always with quiet gentle hands, as one calms a frightened child, and telling her that if she allowed him to kiss her lips and neck, her shoulders, hands and arms, then she had nothing to fear if he touched her knees and even caressed her higher up and let him kiss her flesh there too. She must remember that he had promised that he would never demand more of her than she was ready to give and so, as a pledge of peace, he let his mouth slide up from her knee until, for a brief instant, he kissed a tiny spot of flower-petal skin above the top of her stocking. For an instant only, for Adrienne pushed him swiftly away and drew down the hem of her skirt; but as she did so she blushed like a young girl. Once more they leaned back against the soft earth and, though Balint felt his heart beating so strongly he thought it would burst, he continued his murmured litany of love until the creed of beauty with which he was always inspired whenever he found himself alone with Adrienne filled his soul with the blinding revelation that he must write down all his feelings and put them into a book. Even the title now came to him, *Beauty in Action*, and he decided there and then, that, while exiled on the shores of the Mediterranean, he would sit down and write it, pouring into his work all these feelings of love and ecstasy. After a few months he would return and lay his work at Adrienne's feet as the proof that always, even though far away, her beauty haunted every hour and every minute of his day. His sentences would march to the rhythm of her own goddess-like stride and would be alive with the sheen of her alabaster skin, the curves of her lips and the wild flutter of her hair.

Over the trees, from the valley of the Almas, the faint sound of

PART SIX

the faraway town clock told them that it was already midday. It was time for them to part and never before had they felt so close as now when they had to take leave of each other. Standing closely together at the edge of the forest they clung to each other for a long time. Then Balint fell to his knees and kissed her slowly from the waist, down her skirt and legs to her feet. Adrienne made no movement to stop him but stood there, with her knees slightly bent like the ancient statues of Greek gods, in marble immobility. To Balint her whole attitude seemed like the gift of an unspoken promise.

Eight days later Countess Abady and her son left Denestornya. When they boarded their sleeper at Kolozsvar the station was enveloped in rain and sleet. During the first part of their journey it started to snow heavily and at Banffy-Hunyad the train waited for some time while the snow-plough was fitted. During this stop Balint, who up until then had sat in his mother's compartment chatting, got up and went into the corridor. He leaned out of the window to look at the snow and also to say a mute farewell to the station that was always associated with his visits to Adrienne. Thick snow flakes were falling, covering everything with a soft carpet of white. At Almasko it must be snowing too, thought Balint as he closed the window and went back to his own compartment to get ready for bed.

Up in the mountains it had been snowing hard for two days. Almasko was already blanketed in snow, as was the whole Kalotaszeg district. The wolves started to appear.

As soon as this was known to Honey, he cut up some goat meat and poisoned it with strychnine, threaded the pieces on lengths of wire and going to the edge of the forests, tied them to low boughs of pine and juniper. He covered the whole region, making sure the poison was placed wherever the presence of wolves had been reported, in the woods beside the waterfall in the district of Szentyisora and in the country around Pejkoja; everywhere that the wolves were known to gather. That night, his work finished, Honey returned to his forester's hut in Scrind.

That night, too, a band of silent men left their houses in Pejkoja. They were all dressed alike, in felt jackets, rough peasant's boots and black sheepskin hats. Each man, as always, carried an axe and a long wooden staff. One of them also carried something else, something that hung on long wires, red and chunky, like an outsize bouquet held upside down. Without making a sound they moved quickly through the heavily falling snow with sure movements of men used to the ways of the forest.

Although it was pitch dark and the paths were covered they found their way unerringly. For a long time they walked down to the valley of the Szaka and then up to the crest of the mountain on the far side. Finally they left the forests and emerged by the peak below which Balint's caravan had formed up on leaving Rusz Pantyilimon's house. Now they had only a hundred yards or so to go.

The leader of the band, Turturika, called back: '*Moy* Kula!' he said softly. 'Go ahead with the meat and throw it in. If the dogs make no noise, rattle the door so that they can hear you. Mind you chuck the meat about so that they all get some!'

Young Kula, for it was he who had carried the poisoned bouquet, went ahead. He had agreed to do that for the others, but only that, and only because he knew that he must. When he had gone a few steps he was swallowed up in the falling snow. The rest of them remained where they were, leaning on their long sticks like shepherds on watch. Soon, though slightly muffled by the curtain of snow, they could hear the dogs barking.

The first sounds seemed to come from farther away down the hill, but then the barking came from nearer at hand, probably from the upper corner of the fortress-like compound: it was the sound of dogs fighting over something. Kula came back and joined the men who had been waiting. Soon the barking stopped, but the men from Pejkoja did not move. They waited for a long time, for the people of the mountain are patient. They had to wait, so time did not matter. After an hour had gone by, Turturika gave a few brief orders and they started off downhill. Two men with axes went to the door while the others went to that part of the wall nearest the mountain, threw a felt jacket over the jagged broken glass that was fixed along the top, and climbed over.

The next day the enquiries started. Gaszton Simo came to the village and, instead of bringing the usual two gendarmes, he came accompanied by four of them, all heavily armed. This was unheard-of and caused much comment in the village.

The great oaken doors were still intact, locked and barred. The house too seemed untouched, until one saw that smoke was seeping out of the windows darkening the walls above with dark smears of soot, and that part of the roof had caved in where the flames in the living-room had caught the beams above. The falling snow had nearly extinguished the fire, but it still smouldered

PART SIX

inside where Rusz Pantyilimon lay dead upon the floor of his room. Here everything had been smashed into small pieces, and everything that could burn had been set alight. Obviously petrol had been poured everywhere and there remained intact only one corner of the letter tray among the ashes of burnt papers and the icon on the wall in front of which the little oil lamp still glowed, protected, no doubt, by the gusts of snow that had blown in through the broken windows. All this was quickly ascertained by the notary's inspection, along with the fact that the dogs – two of whom still had pieces of wire in their mouths – had been poisoned by strychnine. That was all: nothing else. The pretty little servant boy, Rusz's slave, who had run down the hill to the village and hidden in the mill as soon as the men had entered the house could tell them nothing. He had heard a noise. He had looked out and seen some men. It was dark and the men were dark too. He saw that there were some more outside the gate so he had climbed the wall and fled. His hands had been badly cut by the glass and he had run bleeding profusely, as fast as he could and as far as he could.

That was all he knew.
'Whom did you see?'
'I don't know!'
'Didn't you recognize anyone?'
'Nobody!'
'How were they dressed?'
'I don't know!'

No matter how hard they tried or how much they threatened the lad they could get nothing else out of him. Of course it was true that he was still shaking with fright and it was always possible that even if he knew more he would never dare admit it.

'What time did all this happen?'
'I don't know. It was night.'
'All right. Early at night, or late at night?'
'I don't know. It was night. *La noptye!*'

Later at the inquest nothing more was discovered. Many people were summoned and questioned, for many people had been heard to utter threats against the hated money-lender. Every man who owed money to Rusz was a suspect and naturally this included all the men of Pejkoja. But no one knew anything, no one confessed or admitted even hearing anything. That night everyone had been at home, everyone had been asleep. The story was always the same. They were morose and sullen, shrugging

519

their shoulders. They knew nothing; they had all been at home in their beds, asleep. No one even tried telling lies or making up complicated alibis by which they might have been trapped into discovery. 'It was snowing. I was at home, asleep.'

Nothing was ever discovered.

It wasn't until a month later that Abady heard the news in a letter from Honey Zutor. Honey had been summoned for questioning. They wanted to know where he had hung the meat that was to poison the wolves. He told them in exact detail. It is true that no poisoned meat was found near Pejkoja, but then it wasn't found anywhere. It could have fallen into the snow and been long covered or it could have been dragged away and eaten somewhere else. One or two dead wolves were found; the corpses of others were no doubt deep under the snow. The only person who had been with Honey and who also knew where the meat had been placed was the forest guard Todor Paven. He was also questioned but he had returned with Honey afterwards and had spent the rest of the night with him in Scrind. Neither of them had moved from there until the next day when Rusz was already dead. Honey vouched for Todor and Todor vouched for Honey, who wrote all this to his master knowing that he would be interested in everything that affected the people in the mountains.

Balint read Honey's letter on the terrace of the hotel in Portofino. Here, sitting before the calm radiance of the blue sea below, surrounded by fruit-covered groves of orange and lemon trees, it was hard to believe in the bitter winter up in the mountains, the all-enveloping snow, silent men striding forth in a blizzard, in cruel murder and mysterious comings and goings in the all-embracing darkness. Where Balint sat everything spoke of life and joy and the resurgence of spring. He could not have chosen a place better fitted for his work. He was surrounded by everything that was beautiful. The olive trees were covered in silver-grey foliage, the gnarled trunks glowed in the sunlight, the golden fruit of the orange and lemon trees hung everywhere among shining green leaves, the fronds of great palms moved gently in the breeze, and in the bay below small sailing boats flitted to and fro under triangular lateen sails. In the distance the rocky cliffs on the other side of the bay could just be seen through a haze of heat. Here Balint need only think of what was serene and beautiful and here he could shrug off all the worries of life and work quietly in a world that was free of troubles.

PART SIX

Balint worked calmly with nothing to disturb him. Even at home there was a lull in the otherwise turbulent political life in Budapest. Kristoffy, the Minister of the Interior, had managed to break down the organized civil disobedience of the municipalities, and those noisy undisciplined meetings that had so disturbed town halls all over the country had become rarer and finally ceased altogether. The counties and districts were now ruled by government-appointed commissioners and somehow the daily work of administration was done, though no one was quite sure how. As Parliament had not met to pass the budget no taxes had been put to the vote and so little money was coming in. Men who had completed their period of military service could not be demobilized and so the next age-group was not being called up. The recall of Parliament had been indefinitely postponed. In this situation the opposition sat quietly waiting with clenched fists, praying for the day when a total collapse of law and order would call them to power. It was their only hope. Even they had now come to realize that their economic and political programme was hopelessly inadequate and would never work, no matter how much they brandished their well-worn slogans. The party leaders went on repeating themselves, and they were echoed by the newspapers they controlled; but the general public, after all the excitements of the previous summer, was content to resume normal life.

Apart from what he was able to glean from the Hungarian newspapers, which took an unconscionable time to reach him, Balint had little news from home. One day he met an old friend in Genoa who told him that Gyeroffy was still gambling heavily and also that he had again been named as *elotancos* for the autumn season. He heard a little society gossip, how the King of Bulgaria had passed through Budapest and how a grand ball had been given by the archduke in his honour. This, apparently, had been a magnificent occasion; but it was of no interest to Abady.

Apart from his work Balint wrote only to Adrienne, short, non-committal letters every two or three weeks; and she in turn sent him news of what she was doing. He knew therefore that Addy had made her usual move to Kolozsvar for the winter and that there she was chaperoning her two sisters; that Wickwitz was not there as he had been unable to get leave of absence from his regiment. Judith was apparently much calmer, and Adrienne even wrote that maybe her sister had got over all that nonsense.

Later Adrienne reported that the doctors had ordered an urgent cure for her mother, who had gone into a nursing home in Vienna. As a result the Miloth girls had also moved to the Uzdy villa where they were living in the rooms of Adrienne's daughter who had gone to Meran with her grandmother. Adrienne now spent all her days with her sisters, for the old countess had closed the main reception rooms of the villa leaving Adrienne the use only of her own drawing-room in the wing that led off the courtyard. It was tiresome for Adrienne no longer to be sure of the privacy of her own rooms, but at least it meant that they passed most of each day in each other's company. In consequence things were going much better between her and Judith. '*It was rather awkward at first,*' wrote Adrienne, '*especially for Judith, but maybe she'll stop thinking of me as her enemy! In the evening when we don't go out to a ball they both come in and talk to me while I go to bed. We talk for ages . . . and that's very good. I hope that I may be able to help heal her wounds. Maybe I'll succeed . . .*'

Their love was never mentioned in these letters; indeed they made only oblique allusion to it: Adrienne would end each letter with three letters instead of a signature: Y.E.M. And Abady would head his missives with the same cryptic initials. They stood for 'Yellow-Eyed Monster'.

Each time that Balint reached this ending to Adrienne's letters, he would think back to that day when they had walked up to the Hazsongard and he had angrily given her that name on realizing for the first time that for all her beauty she was not a real woman but only the incomplete image of one, infinitely desirable, but remote and hating the realities of love. How little progress he had made in his pursuit! Practically none, if their last day in the woods was any criterion. However perhaps it was better like that for who knew what might happen if he did become her lover? This was not something that could be a passing adventure, rather it would be a bondage for life. Perhaps, after all, it would be better to lose himself in work. He would pour his love into his writing and perhaps, possibly, if he could transform his feelings into words he would somehow manage to cauterize and burn out the yearning he felt to possess her body. As the weeks went by he consoled himself with these thoughts and became quieter, even, he fancied, free.

On 16th February a telegram arrived: 'PLEASE COME AT ONCE. Y.E.M.' No more. What could have happened? It must have been serious. Perhaps Pali Uzdy, or the mother-in-law?

PART SIX

Whatever it was, however dangerous or disastrous, Adrienne clearly thought that only he could help. He had to leave at once to go to her; he must.

The telegram had been delivered early in the morning before his mother was awake, so Balint had plenty of time to work out some untruth that his mother would accept. Only one thing seemed plausible. Parliament had unexpectedly been recalled for 19th February, in three days' time, and though there was no need for him to go, his mother would certainly believe him if he told her that he had been asked to return. It would only be for a few days, or a week, and then he would come back to bring her home.

Countess Roza listened in silence when Balint said that he had to leave at once for Budapest. Though her eyes filled with tears she said nothing to hold him back. At last she said: 'All right, I'll wait for your return. I know a few people here now so I shall not be too lonely. They'll keep me company until you come back.'

Balint left the same evening.

Chapter Five

WICKWITZ HAD TO RETURN to his regiment in the middle of October. He did not want to do so but it was forced upon him by a chain of unfortunate events. In August he received a letter from Tihamer Abonyi, Dinora's husband, begging him to come back to Maros-Szilvas for a few weeks so as to get his horses ready for the races at Vasarhely and Szuk. Abonyi wrote that he had no faith in any other trainer. When Baron Egon told Mme Bogdan Lazar that he was going to accept this invitation she was not at all pleased, thinking that it was merely his excuse for going back to Dinora. Nitwit tried to convince her that she was being stupid as he really was going there only to train racehorses, but she wouldn't believe him and threw him out.

That autumn the Miloths did not go either to Vasarhely or to Kolozsvar and this made it extremely difficult for Wickwitz to keep in touch with Judith. Occasionally he sent her a scribbled note – addressed naturally to Zoltan – just to make sure that the girl 'stayed in form'; but as letter-writing bored him and he felt he was no good at it he soon realized that he'd better look for some girl near at hand in Brasso, or his affairs would never get settled. He had heard tell of the daughter of a textile millionaire, who was going to come out that winter, so he did everything he could to scrape acquaintance. It might well have worked, for the girl clearly liked him, but her family began to notice Wickwitz's attentions and, as they had already decided that the girl should marry a cousin who had shares in the family firm, they took care to keep Baron Egon away from the house. This was serious, because Wickwitz had spent a lot of time in pursuing the girl, time that was now seen to have been wasted, and the date was not far off when Dinora's promissory notes, which he had deposited with the banker at Nagy-Varad, would expire. The Privatbank Blau, as the money-lender so pretentiously styled himself, had recently been pressing for repayment and though, this had been done with a veneer of respect, Wickwitz was quite bright enough to detect the menace behind the polite phrases. Something had to be done very soon, for Wickwitz was haunted by two little words that seemed engraved in huge black letters in his brain: '*Infam kasssiert*' – dishonourably discharged – cashiered'.

At the end of January Wickwitz was at his wits end and wrote a letter to Judith, who was now in Kolozsvar, which completely revived the girl's now somewhat faded feelings for him. Adrienne had been right when she wrote to Balint that Judith seemed calmer and more at ease. This had come about because it was now some time since she had last seen the Austrian baron and, as her infatuation was largely based on the sacrifices that she would make to save that unhappy man, it needed the constant reminder of his presence to keep her love alive. Judith's feeling for Egon Wickwitz was based on the belief that she alone could save that great but unfortunate man, who was the soul of honesty but in trouble through no fault of his own other than his helplessness when faced by the world's duplicity. She it was who could keep him from eternal damnation, and so she loved him. Now, however, it seemed that for several months Wickwitz had no longer been threatened, and so the self-sacrificing element in Judith's love had had nothing on which to feed. Without a battle to fight on his behalf her love had lost its heroic character. She remained true to him, but she was prepared to wait calmly for whatever the future might bring. This was how she felt; and so, deprived of the urgency and opposition that had made her so rebellious and determined, she had gradually learned once again how to laugh and joke and be merry.

In this new letter Wickwitz reverted to the trick that had been so successful when he first wooed her. Then the lie had been that he could have had Dodo Gyalakuthy if he had not fallen in love with Judith and felt it dishonourable to go on pursuing the heiress. Now he used the textile manufacturer's daughter. He wrote that he had only begun that pursuit so as to free himself from his 'obsession' with Judith, an obsession that was not fair to her. But it was no good, there was no way he could rid himself of his deep love for her and therefore it was better that he should, must, kill himself and be done with it. He could not live without her and he could not bear to share his life with anyone else. In a few days his shame would be public knowledge, so that it was better that he should shoot himself now – it was the only solution. There was, of course, one other possibility, but he hardly dared mention it and wasn't even sure he wanted it: it was that Judith should elope with him at once. However, he would never ask for such a sacrifice. He would rather choose death! For once it was a well-written letter, and it was written well because Wickwitz penned the words with very little hope and with real despair in his heart.

When Zoltan gave his sister Wickwitz's letter she answered it at once, getting her brother to address the envelope and post it. She wrote: '*I do want to save you. Come for me. From here it wlll be easy for us to run away together.*'

Three days later Wickwitz' reply arrived, full of humble gratitude ... and a carefully worked out plan. '*We will go to Graz,*' he wrote, '*and there we'll be married in church. No civil wedding is necessary in Austria!*' His mother would find them a priest. In a few days he would get leave and come for her.

Margit Miloth, who was sharing a room with her sister on the nursery floor of the Uzdy villa, noticed a change in Judith when she received Wickwitz's first letter. She said nothing and she asked no questions but merely watched and saw Judith's attempts to conceal her agitation and her sudden increase of nervousness. She also saw Zoltan hand over the second letter and again watched her sister carefully and noted where Judith hid it when she went to bed. Later, when Judith was asleep she got up, took the letter quietly from its hiding place and hurried down the servants' staircase and along the passage to Adrienne's apartments. In her long white nightgown she flitted down the dark corridor like a benevolent ghost.

Adrienne was in bed, reading. Margit sat down beside her and together they read Baron Egon's letter. The next day Adrienne sent the telegram to Balint to call him back from Portofino.

Abady arrived in Budapest the evening before Parliament was due to reassemble. He decided not to go on to Kolozsvar until the next afternoon so that he would be able to attend the morning session. He knew from the newspapers that he had bought on his journey that this time there would be no adjournment but that Parliament would almost at once be dissolved by royal decree. This was contrary to all law and custom for it was part of the constitution that Parliament could not be dissolved until the budget had first been passed. Balint saw the whole manoeuvre as a violent step which would widen the rift between the Crown and Parliament and could lead to open rebellion. Anxiously, he went straight to the Casino so as to hear the latest news. The great hall and all the public rooms were filled with a large crowd all talking excitedly, even though this new move had come as no surprise to the people in the capital for, just as it had been at the beginning of the crisis, everyone already thought they knew what the government was planning and what the coalition party's answer would be.

As it had been a few months before, so it was now, and everyone in the Casino had their own ideas of what was going to happen on the following day. They wandered from group to group noisily broadcasting their views. The only thing upon which everyone agreed was that a period of dictatorial rule had started and would continue into the foreseeable future. What should be done? There were worried faces on all sides. Everyone had a different theory. No doubt, swore some of those arguing in the Casino, their leaders would come up with some clever, hitherto unthought-of solution, politically adroit and unassailable. As they waited for definite news the arguments raged. One idea, which made everyone laugh gleefully, was put forward by a well-known Budapest lawyer renowned for his wit; and this had at once been been headlined in the newspapers. It was beautiful, it was simple and it put everyone in a roar. Briefly it was that all Members of Parliament should at once resign their seats and all elected official resign their positions. Thus there would be no speaker, no officials of the house, not even a sergeant-at-arms to whom the royal decree would be handed.

'What a tremendous joke that'd be!' shouted Wülffenstein. 'Fancy General Nyiri running about in all directions, paper in hand, and no one there to give it to! Why, he couldn't even call a meeting as the house-rules state you have to have forty members for that.'

'Pity they hadn't thought of this before. It's a bit late now!' said someone else.

So they waited and talked until word came from the party leaders: everyone was to be at the parliament building and in their seats by half-past nine at the latest. Nothing else; but it was enough.

In the morning all entrances to Parliament Square were blocked by police. No one could pass without showing his official papers. The square itself presented an alarming, sinister sight. Everywhere there were soldiers, national guards with their rifles stacked in neat pyramids, and Colonel Fabritius, their commander, standing in front of them. Right in the centre there was a squadron of hussars, mounted but at ease. Behind the police cordons waited groups of silent, grey-clad working men, not many but certainly a few hundred. More of them were collected farther back in Alkotmany Street, and a man in the crowd called out that the workers had been summoned by the government itself. There were a few newspaper men in the square and these cheered the better-known deputies as they arrived. All the elected members hurried inside, where they collected in groups whispering among themselves.

Bells sounded to announce that the House was in session and everyone went swiftly to his place. The official notary started reading something, gabbling in a low voice. Then Rakovszky, the vice-chairman, took the stand.

Rakovszky was heard in dead silence. He said that the session had been called to receive the King's message. General Nyiri, the plenipotentiary Royal Commissioner, had announced that he would expect the people's elected representatives to attend him at eleven o'clock at the royal palace, when he would read out the royal decree dissolving Parliament. Rakovszky now added his own remarks to the official statement, raising fine points of the legality of such a procedure. It seemed that the royal message was not to be handed to him by the Minister-President but by two army officers, and that it would be in a sealed envelope. Since, he said, it was customary for such documents to be presented to the House by the Minister-President, he advised that the Parliament should not accept the envelope but that it should be handed back at once to the appointed officers. This was the formula decided on by the party leaders at the previous evening's meeting. It was a revolutionary decision because it would mean that, after all the fuss, nothing would have happened. It would be a fact that Parliament had been called into session . . . but dissolved? No one would have any knowledge of that, either officially or legally. Those unfamiliar with parliamentary procedure were somewhat bemused by this solution and it took a few moments for Rakovszky's words to sink in. However, so strong was the feeling that they must act in strict accordance with the law, and that this only was important, that general approval was soon given to the proposal.

The chairman of the assembly now quickly suggested that the house should meet again two days later, on 21 February. Everyone knew that this would never happen, for the army had already been ordered to occupy the Parliament building and at that moment the soldiers were pouring into the ground floor and were already coming up the stairs that led to the chamber. This was disregarded, for everyone felt that they must stand on their own legal rights and proceed accordingly. At this point one of the sergeants-at-arms rushed in and shouted: 'They're coming! They're already in the corridor!'

At once there was a general uproar, the chairman rose, closed the session and hurried off the platform. Everyone made for the exits, jostling each other in their hurry to get away.

Then through the lower door a stout uniformed officer stalked in. It was Colonel Fabritius. All those heading for that exit turned and rushed towards whatever other escape from the chamber they could find. As they did so the colonel mounted the podium and read out the royal decree of dissolution, but the only people to hear him were the journalists in the press gallery. As soon as he had finished the chamber was occupied by armed soldiers.

In the corridors the fleeing members found that soldiers had been posted everywhere. They were all from the National Guard of Budapest. It was a tragic and shameful sight – an armed military occupation of Parliament, the ancient citadel of Hungary's independence. The soldiers stood shoulder to shoulder facing the entrances to the chamber, like a dark wall shutting out even the grey morning light from the windows behind them.

Balint, who scorned the idea of running away, was one of the last to leave the chamber. He walked slowly and sadly towards the main stairway but stopped when Bela Varju came running towards him.

'They've closed the entrance. No one can get out that way!' he called from a distance.

'Perhaps we can go through the common rooms?' suggested Abady and together they quickly disappeared through one of the doors. Once inside Balint glanced back and saw that they had only just been in time, for he could already see the backs of soldiers lined up outside the wide glass doors through which they had just slipped.

Balint was quicker than Varju, who was now somewhat out of breath. He turned at the exit on the other side of the room and, for the first time seeing the comic side of it all, called back: 'Hurry up, my friend, we don't want to find our coats again in the Vienna prison-house!'

───

Balint's train did not leave until two o'clock, so he went first to lunch at the Casino. There the atmosphere was one of unrelieved gloom. One or two people were conferring in low tones, but they fell silent if anyone came near them. Even at the long communal table the events of that morning were hardly mentioned. Shoulders were shrugged but everyone kept their opinions to themselves. Fredi Wülffenstein, normally so ebullient, never once talked of how his Hungarian blood was boiling. It was the realization that no one knew any longer what the future would bring that deadened everyone's spirits. Secretly there were many who began to wonder if they had not been wrong in making those demands about the army and the laws which had brought them into direct confrontation with the monarch.

───

Laszlo Gyeroffy was travelling on the same train. Though Balint and he greeted one another and sat together in the same compartment, Balint sensed at once that the warmth had gone out of their friendship.

'Are you going home to Kozard?' enquired Balint.

'No, I'm getting off at Varad,' To ward off any further questioning from his cousin, Laszlo added: 'I have some business there.' Then he turned away and pretended to look out of the window.

Neither of them spoke again for some time. Laszlo was thinking about the Carnival season which had just ended. Once again he had been named as *elotancos* and there had been no diminution in his position in society. On the contrary this year he had reached the pinnacle of social success at the archducal ball when he had dined at the same table as the King of Bulgaria, opened the ball with the Queen and spent the entire evening surrounded by Imperial and Royal Highnesses and their Majesties themselves. Despite all this public glory Laszlo himself sensed that this year his prestige had been somehow diminished. He was no longer interested in his job as leading dancer, and he neglected it. During the picnic dances at the Casino he would sometimes disappear for an hour or more, going up to the gaming tables and more than once returning drunk, and angry that his assistant had sent a message asking for him.

He knew that he had been remiss, but even so he had resented it when, three days before, one of the town's great hostesses had asked Niki Kollonich and Gyuri Warday, Imre's younger brother, to organize her ball rather than he, the official *elotancos*. Accordingly he had thrown up the job, giving it out that he was obliged to return to Transylvania. This was the reason for his being on the same train as Balint. Of course, he reflected, it was just as well that he would no longer have to bear all those extra expenses. Neither could he continue to postpone settling the question of Fanny's pearls. Somehow he had to find the money to redeem them, for he felt he could no longer bear the shame of being indebted to a woman. It was as bad as being kept!

As they sat face to face in the railway carriage, Balint was closely studying his cousin's face. It had grown hard, with a bitter line to the mouth, and he had developed a vertical furrow where his eyebrows met. Laszlo's eyes were both watery and inflamed and Balint knew at once that he must have been sitting up late and presumably gambling as heavily as before. Well, he thought, I'll try and make him see reason. So, as tactfully as he could he introduced the subjects. Laszlo shrugged his shoulders and his replies were barely polite. This made Balint so angry that he began to say openly everything that was in his mind. His words were cruel and wounding. Finally, enraged, he said: 'You're quite mad! If you go on like this you'll end up bankrupt and dishonoured!'

Gyeroffy got up, the bitter line of his mouth even more marked than before: 'I am already bankrupt and dishonoured!' he said quietly. Then he left the compartment.

Laszlo did not return until the train reached Nagy-Varad. While his bags were being collected he came over to his cousin and said: 'Thank you for caring what becomes of me. But don't bother any more. I'm a hopeless case!'

Before Balint could reply, Laszlo had disappeared.

When he arrived in Kolozsvar Balint went straight to his apartment in his mother's house in Farkas Street. It was already late in the evening. He found waiting for him a note from Adrienne: '*Come to tea tomorrow at half-past four. Turn up unexpectedly. There will be several people there. I'll tell you more later.*'

Adrienne wrote in English and the word 'unexpectedly' was underlined.

Balint arrived the next day at five. In Adrienne's big drawing-room he found a number of men grouped round each woman present. Judith was in one corner with three young men talking to her, and Margit was at the other end of the room with two of the Alvinczys. The two Laczok girls were there, also surrounded by young men, and Adrienne was near the fireplace, not this time sitting on the pile of cushions on the floor but in an armchair, with Adam Alvinczy on one side and Pityu Kendy on the other. Balint went over to join them. Everybody wanted to hear about the marvels of the Riviera and Kamuthy demanded the latest news from Budapest. While dutifully telling everyone what they wanted to hear Balint was straining every nerve, searching for some sign which would explain why Adrienne had called him home. He looked carefully at everyone in turn but he could see nothing out of the ordinary, either in their faces or in their bearing. Everyone looked exactly as they always did and though he fancied that he caught a flash of hostility in Judith's eyes when he shook hands with her, it disappeared immediately and she went on chatting with her friends. All this continued for some little time.

When the lamps were brought in Adrienne got up so that the servant could reach the pedestal behind her chair. She moved over to the french window which overlooked the Szamos and gazed out into the twilight. Balint stood beside her.

'Look hard at that bridge!' murmured Addy softly without turning towards him. She pointed with her chin towards it and then rejoined the others in the room.

Balint stayed where he was studying the little wooden bridge which spanned the river about ten paces from the house. On the garden side, there was a flimsy gate made of canes which was obviously nailed into place. A few planks were missing from the bridge and the wooden parapet was broken in several places. It was clear that it had not been in use for many years. Across the bridge there was a path through the park which followed the banks of the river.

When Balint rejoined the others Adrienne turned to him and said: 'I nearly forgot! I've still got a book of yours. It was most interesting, thank you so much.' And she picked up a little paper-back Tauchnitz volume from her desk and handed it to him. Balint glanced at the title. The book certainly wasn't his; he had never even heard of it.

He put it in his pocket and, as he did so, realized that something had been slipped between the leaves. A letter? Though filled with excitement, his reply was cool and blandly devoid of emotion:

'It's good, isn't it? Nothing out of the ordinary, but very well written, I thought. I'm glad you liked it.'

'Oh, yes. A good read...'

Abady continued to make conversation for a little while longer. Then he took his leave and hurried home. Only when he had reached his own room and closed the door behind him did he take out the book and find Adrienne's letter.

At one o'clock tonight you must find your way over the bridge. If there is a light behind the french window come straight in. If there isn't, don't! It's very important, but I have to be seen to go to bed because of my sisters. Don't get any wrong ideas, it's all about Wickwitz! You are my only friend, I can't speak about this to anyone else or at any other time. We are in great trouble.

Adrienne had wondered for a long time what to do, and this seemed the only way of getting her news to Balint without being detected. Ever since the incident of the clandestine letter at Mezo-Varjas, Judith had thought of Balint as her sworn enemy and the fact that at the Uzdy villa the three sisters shared Adrienne's only sitting-room meant that it would be impossible to take Balint on one side and consult him without her sisters being present. If she asked Abady to call in the morning, Judith would get to know of it even if she didn't catch a glimpse of him from the windows of her room which looked over the forecourt of the villa. If they went walking together in the town, just the two of them, this would be certain to arouse Judith's suspicions, for all this season the three sisters had been everywhere in a group and some acquaintance was sure to see them together and so Judith was sure to hear about it later. None of these things was possible. Adrienne knew her sister well and realized that if it came to Judith's notice that Adrienne was asking Balint's advice, then the girl was quite capable of taking fright and fleeing immediately to Wickwitz, maybe even to his regiment at Brasso. Up until now Judith had had no reason to suspect that she had been carefully watched by her eldest sister for, although the girls had been entrusted to Adrienne's care by their mother, Adrienne had cunningly arranged their lives so that it seemed to them that they were doing exactly what they themselves wanted. In fact, Judith never went out in the mornings without either Mlle Morin or Margit being with her and from lunchtime until sometimes quite late at night, the three sisters were always together.

The only time that Adrienne would be able to talk to Balint unobserved would be in the middle of the night. Luckily she had discovered that though the little cane gate was nailed into place, the nails were so rusty that it was easily opened. And it could be closed again just as easily. Adrienne checked it again when her sisters had briefly left the room to change.

All the same she was not completely happy about this midnight rendezvous. She wondered how she should receive Balint. Every night her sisters remained with her while she undressed and went to bed, and they often then stayed on chatting until it was late. They would think it odd if she suddenly decided to do something different. Obviously she would have to keep to their nightly routine, but should she get up and dress again after the girls had gone to their own room? It would be rather complicated. Perhaps she should just put on a wrap so as to give the signal for Balint to come in ... but then she realized that this would not do either. A wrap would be quite wrong, it might open, for such silken garments were difficult to keep closed, and the last thing she wanted to do was show him a bare knee or shoulder, which he might wrongly take as an invitation. Adrienne shuddered at the thought of being misunderstood. All in all, it would be best to be already in bed when he arrived. Balint had already been in her room at Almasko, and she could easily pull the bedclothes well up as she had done then.

There was just a slight click as Balint opened the french window as silently as he could. Then she heard the door close again. Slow, careful steps, just audible on the floor-boards, and in a moment he was framed in the doorway to her room, the candlestick in his hand. Swiftly he put it down on a side-table, took off his hat and coat, threw them over a chair and came towards the bed. He kissed Adrienne's forehead as would a brother.

Balint could just see that Adrienne was looking up at him with frightened hostility, but, seeing that the young man's manner was quiet and composed, the hostility slowly died from her expression and she relaxed. He sat down in a chair at the foot of the bed.

'What is it? What has happened? I'm glad you sent for me. Naturally I came at once,' he said softly.

Adrienne replied in the same low tones. She told him all about Wickwitz's letter and about her anxiety because Judith had been placed in her care. She had no one, she said, whom she could trust to help or give her advice, who would let her know if Wickwitz arrived in town and who, away from the Uzdy house, would be able to keep an eye out and tell her when she had to be particularly watchful. She felt completely helpless, and there was Judith's good name to think of.

Adrienne told her tale as dispassionately as if she were asking legal advice in some lawyer's office and not lying in her scented bedroom. Because she was speaking only in whispers, Balint left the chair he had chosen and came and sat beside her on the bed. As she talked Balint lowered himself down until he was reclining beside her, his head supported on one elbow, his left ear close to her mouth. Now they could talk so quietly that no one near at hand would have been able to hear a word of what they were saying. Consciously subduing his desire, he calmly and matter-of-factly answered all her questions, calmed her fears and agreed to keep watch in town and let her know the moment that Wickwitz arrived in Kolozsvar. In the meantime he would try to think out some plan.

The whole time that Balint was with Adrienne half of his brain was searching for a way to making sure that one day soon, perhaps even tomorrow, she would let him again visit her during the night. Then, or later, perhaps Addy would feel desire welling up in her and, even if it were the merest spark on her side, the moment would be ripe.

He was glad that at Portofino he had already written some sixty pages of the treatise that he had first envisaged when lying in her arms. Now he turned the subject of their conversation to this, saylng that he must read it to her and that their only chance would be if he were able to come to her secretly in the night. He explained at length that it was so important for him to read what he had written out loud, for only in that way could he be sure of the quality of what he had written. Eventually Adrienne said that he could come again on the following evening. Happy with this promise he went no further that night and, even when he kissed her farewell, he did so gently, without any rash sign of passion, so

PART SIX

that she should not be alarmed or frightened into telling him not to come again. When he gave her his last kiss, he made it only slightly deeper than before and held her only just a little more tightly. No more. His inner voice told him that it would have been folly to risk losing the ground he had only just regained.

Life can be very bizarre, he said to himself as he walked briskly home down the path that followed the river bank in the park. If anyone knew where I had been they'd never believe that I am not that woman's lover! And God knows if I ever will be!

Chapter Six

LASZLO GYEROFFY ARRIVED IN KOLOZSVAR shortly after Balint. He came from Varad and was even more bitter and disillusioned than before. The reason he had been to Varad was to see a money-lender, a certain Blau, who called himself a private banker. This was the same Blau who held Countess Abonyi's promissory notes which had been countersigned by Wickwitz. Laszlo had been trying desperately to raise the sum of eighty-six thousand crowns so as to be able to redeem Fanny's pearls. At first he had hoped that a good run of luck at the gaming table would put him in funds but somehow it had not turned out quite as he had expected. Most of what he won was apt to disappear the next evening and if there was anything left this too was soon spent. First Laszlo had tried to touch the money-lenders he knew in Budapest. They all refused, making various excuses but without revealing the real reason, namely that they had all heard tell that Laszlo was not only plunging deeply at the gaming tables but also drinking far too much. An acquaintance from Behar had let drop that he knew this useful fellow in Varad and that had been the 'business' for which Laszlo had gone there.

The visit was hopelessly unsuccessful. Laszlo never wanted to go near the man again; indeed he had run from his office in flight.

At the start of their discussion the self-styled banker announced that it was not his practice to lend money on a single guarantee and asked Laszlo if it was not possible for him to find, among his large acquaintance, some friend who would add his signature and so vouch for him. Then he began to ask questions as to who Laszlo's friends were in Transylvanian high society. At first it seemed to Laszlo that the money-lender merely wanted to find out about his family connections, so he replied quite openly and truthfully, especially as this Mr Blau had an educated manner and played to perfection the part of the sympathetic financier. Blau had used this approach as a cover for what he really wanted to find out. Recently he had become increasingly worried by the matter of the Abonyi-Wickwitz loan. Now he regretted having been induced to have anything do with extending Dinora's notes of hand, for he had had no reply from several letters addressed to the countess, and it had also proved impossible to pin down Baron Egon. He had been wondering whether he should take Dinora to court or whether he should denounce Wickwitz to his superior officer. Both procedures were bound to be difficult and unpleasant, both would bring much publicity; and too much publicity was always undesirable in his business. Action of that drastic sort should only be taken as a last resort, and so, when this Count Gyeroffy came to see him, he thought that fate had provided him with the solution. The noble Count might perhaps be so good as to intervene discreetly and explain to this rich lady that she really must pay; and, as for the officer, tell him what a scandal there would be if the matter became public knowledge.

So, after quite a series of flattering remarks about what a great gentleman his Lordship obviously was, he took out Dinora's notes and showed them to him. Laszlo's reaction was not at all what he had expected. Gyeroffy stared down at Wickwitz's signatures petrified with horror, his mind suddenly flooded with the awful realization that the matter of Fanny's pearls put him, Laszlo, on the same plane as Nitwit. He too was nothing less than a scoundrel who allowed himself to be kept by a woman. Now he suddenly saw how far he had sunk and he meant it for himself, every bit as much as for Wickwitz, when he softly and angrily repeated: 'What a scoundrel! What a vile scoundrel!'

'What are you saying? Do you mean the Countess's signature is a forgery?' cried Blau, horrified. Laszlo made no reply but seized his hat and ran from the house like a madman.

―――

Two days went by, two days during which nothing happened. Then Fate, that dramatist without mercy, decided that now was the time to enact the tragedy which would crush poor Judith.

In the dining-room of the hotel in Kolozsvar the gypsy musicians, led by the great Laji Pongracz, were playing late and everyone was there, drinking heavily. It was well after midnight.

PART SIX

Several tables were occupied by people from the town, another by a group of agricultural students from Monostor. The famous Laji was playing, not to them, of course, but to the principal table where Uncle Ambrus sat with his group of young followers: the Alvinczys, Joska and Pityu Kendy, Isti Kamuthy and, as a non-paying member of the band, old Daniel Kendy too. They were listening to the music, quaffing champagne, talking loudly and sometimes singing the words of the tunes Laji played. The men at the other tables did not mind because they knew that Laji always played his best on such occasions, and now they could listen to him for nothing. So they sat there quietly without trying to become involved, for if they did they knew that Uncle Ambrus would take the band into a private room, and if that happened they might as well all go home.

So the music went on. Song followed song.

Laszlo was there too; sitting between Adam Alvinczy and the puffy-cheeked Kamuthy. He sat stiffly upright because he had drunk a great deal.

Then Wickwitz entered the room.

He had come from Brasso by the late evening express and was in uniform. It had been a long and tiresome journey and he was deeply worried by the precarious position in which he found himself. It was really beyond bearing, he thought! Dinora – silly goose – had written several letters asking him to explain what Blau's increasingly pressing demands could possibly mean: she couldn't make head nor tail of it all, she said. Then, too, that monster Blau was himself becoming more and more menacing; and even the colonel – *so ein Kerl* – what a fellow he was! – had been decidedly sticky about granting him leave just when he most needed it. It was all beyond bearing, intolerable! The need to scribble all these lies to Dinora and Blau – and all the time desperate with fear that everything would come out into the open before he could get his leave and scamper off with Judith. Then, he prayed and hoped, her family would come to the rescue for their daughter's sake, and settle this odious matter for him once and for all.

He felt like a stag at bay, surrounded by angry keepers and barking dogs, hemmed in, caught in a trap with no way of escape. Even Wickwitz's nerves, usually as insensitive as a coil of ship's rope, were beginning to fray, so he decided, on arriving at the hotel, that an hour or two with the gypsies and a few glasses of champagne would do no harm and would help him to see the world in a better light in the morning. The following day he would send a message to Judith and the day after, at dawn, they would be on their way to Austria. Just a day and a half and he would be safe. Nothing untoward, surely, would happen in such a short time. Wickwitz had already written to Varad saying that everything would be settled in two week's time – and, of course, in two weeks he could truly be master of his fate.

Seeing Uncle Ambrus seated there he went up, clicked his heels in the classical military fashion and sat down modestly at the end of the table. However he did not stay there for almost at once Laszlo Gyeroffy called out to him loudly: 'Come over here, my good namesake! Come here, where I can see you!'

Wickwitz had no idea why Laszlo should call him his namesake, but knowing that there was no point in arguing with a drunk, got up and went over and sat down where Gyeroffy indicated. He put his sword between his knees and ordered a small bottle of champagne.

'Why a small one?' interrupted Gyeroffy. 'Why economize? People like us don't have to economize. Others maybe, but not us! Why should we? A big bottle for my *alter ego* – my other self, my brother, he that bears the same name as I!'

Champagne was brought. The music played. Uncle Ambrus burst into song from time to time, his huge bass-baritone filling the room, and at times he shouted, always louder than the others. After several verses the gypsies played a new song and it was time for everyone to drink another toast.

'To your special health, Nitwit, my very dear *alter ego*,' said Laszlo once again. 'And as for you, you should drink only to me, not to the others. The others ... they're different from us, very different ... but you and I belong together!' The words may have sounded friendly but Laszlo's tone of voice certainly was not, nor was the mocking laughter which followed his words; indeed it was filled with anger and hostility. They touched glasses and drank to each other. This happened several times and each time Gyeroffy said more or less the same words, and each time the sarcasm and the latent desire to pick a quarrel became more and more evident. However Baron Egon was a peaceful man by nature and submitted with all the calm of some great mastiff dog to the incomprehensible hints about himself and Gyeroffy being in some way the same. He only thought that Laszlo was extremely drunk and did not really know what he was saying.

It was true that Laszlo was drinking heavily.

PART SIX

'Do you know why we are brothers?' he asked at last, leaning across the table towards Wickwitz. 'Don't you really know? Well, I'll whisper it to you! Come on, lean forward. Let me speak into your ear!' Wickwitz obeyed meekly. 'We are brothers,' murmured Laszlo, 'because I am just as infamous a villain as you are! That's why!'

Wickwitz was surprised, but he merely leaned back in his chair, waved a hand and said: 'All right! All right! You've had an awful lot to drink!'

'No way "All right! All right!" It's the truth.' Gyeroffy was now shouting. 'It's nothing but the truth! You are a scoundrel! Oh yes, I know all about you, all about you, I say!'

'Steady on,' said the officer calmly. 'Careful what you say. I won't accept this, not here in a public place.'

'And why should I be careful? What can't you accept this here in a public place? You don't have to pretend with me! It's just as I say: you're a scoundrel too and I know it!'

It flashed across Wickwitz's mind that all this was very inconvenient because he would be obliged now to make it an affair of honour and more time would be lost before he would be able to get away. As he hesitated the other went on, shouting more and more loudly:

'Just one word, that'll be enough! Blau! You understand. Blau! Blau! Blau!' Then Laszlo stood up and screamed: 'And me too, me too! Scoundrel! Scoundrel! Scoundrel! Base, vile scoundrel!' and he beat the table with his fists, was full of rage, as much against himself as against Nitwit, hating everyone, hating himself, desiring only to strike so hard that he too would be annihilated by his own blows. A glass overturned on the table in front of him and a plate clattered to the floor. Laszlo's neighbours jumped up and grabbed him, pulling him back from the table. Everyone rose and tried to calm him and shut him up. They all talked at once.

'God damn it! Don't be such an ass!' bellowed Ambrus Kendy at Laszlo; and to Nitwit, who was already on his feet with his hand on his sword, he roared: 'You, too, don't you be idiotic either. Can't you see he's dead drunk!' Uncle Ambrus, who knew what he was doing, tried to stop the quarrel before it got too serious. Anyway, he hated to have his drinking bouts disturbed.

Baron Egon did not even hear Uncle Ambrus. Laszlo, though reeling and held back by the others across the table, was still shouting: 'Blau! Scoundrel! Blau! Blau!' until his legs gave way beneath him and he fell back into the arms of Akos Alvinczy and Isti Kamuthy. All Wickwitz could think of was that Gyeroffy knew everything about him, and that therefore he would have to kill him, right now in this very room, before he was able to say more. But the table was between them and several of the young men had come round and were holding him back too. There was nothing he could do at that moment. If he drew his sword they would all surround him and stop him at once. So he drew himself up as straight as he knew how, clicked his spurs together, bowed to the assembled company in front of him, turned and, making his way slowly through the other tables where everyone was sitting in stunned, frightened silence, left the hall.

The next day at noon an infantry captain and a senior lieutenant waited on Gyeroffy. Wickwitz, who knew his Army Regulations, was aware that as an officer on active service he was obliged, if publicly insulted, to ask only other officers to act as his seconds. This was just as well, for soldiers don't ask questions, don't intervene in such affairs and certainly require no explanation. For them the *Tatbestand* – the cause of offense, was enough. Wickwitz had reported what had happened to divisional level, which in turn sent back an order that the commanding office of the infantry regiment stationed at Kolozsvar should select seconds in this affair. The colonel, as it happened was on leave, but the second-in-command, one Lieutenant-Colonel Zdratutschek, was in charge during the colonel's absence. Wickwitz went to see him and explained the insult offered to him, and which was serious chiefly because he had been in uniform at the time and that therefore it was the 'Kaiser's Rock' – the official dress of the emperor's service, which had suffered the insult. This was a good argument with Zdratutschek who became red with rage, named two officers at once and told them, off the record, that they must insist on the most severe conditions. '*Dieser magyarischer Rebellen-bagage* – these rubbishy Hungarian rebels,' he shouted, 'must be taught a lesson! We'll show them!' For Wickwitz this support was not an unmixed blessing for the irate lieutenant-colonel ordered him to shut himself up and see no civilians until the duel had been fought, which meant that he couldn't see Judith. This was annoying, but Wickwitz hoped that he would be able to deal with Gyeroffy that afternoon and so be free to contact Judith in the evening.

However, things did not go anything like as smoothly as

PART SIX

everyone expected. Gyeroffy's seconds, Major Bogacsy, the assessor at the county court, and Joska Kendy, found that Wickwitz's conditions were far too harsh to be acceptable. Three shots, the first from twenty-five paces, the second from twenty paces, and the third from fifteen paces, and, should there still be no definite result, a fight with heavy cavalry sabres until one or the other was disabled – and this without bandages. Despite the fact that Gyeroffy had no objections, his seconds refused to accept these proposals for, as the arch-expert Bogacsy stated, the duelling code prescribed that such murderous conditions were to be allowed only when the offence had included actual bodily harm. This is what the Code Duverger said, and the Code being his bible, the major was not going to budge an inch. 'Gyeroffy has no say in the matter,' he declared and that was an end of it. Instead, Major Bogacsy demanded that a Court of Honour be convened to decide how the duel should be conducted. This time it was the turn of the soldiers to object. They said that they would submit to no authority that was not military. More discussion followed, for this last demand was not acceptable to the civilians. Major Bogacsy resigned his place, as he was a soldier on retired pay, and was replaced by Uncle Ambrus, who declared that there was only one kind of honour, that everyone knew what it was and that he, Ambrus Kendy would not yield, even to Almighty God himself.

Three days passed, three long days for all concerned.

The whole town was buzzing with the news of the affair of the impending duel. Everyone talked of it, discussed it and had their own views on the rights and wrongs of the affair. In the coffee-houses and on the streets people talked of nothing else. Even the students at the university took up the cause.

The subject was no longer what sort of satisfaction Wickwitz was entitled to demand from Gyeroffy, but rather how monstrous it was of the military to browbeat respectable civilian gentlemen and refuse to accept their age-old code of honour. Daily Uncle Ambrus could be heard in the Casino castigating the *soldatesca* – the soldiery, to everyone within earshot. The club was packed and the big drawing-room was full from noon until late at night. The older men sat round the fireplace, among them Sandor Kendy, Daniel, Stanislo Gyeroffy, Laszlo's former guardian, Count Adam Alvinczy, father of the young Alvinczy quartet, old Rattle Miloth and, of course, Uncle Ambrus. All these were of one mind, and they were supported by Tihamer Abonyi and Major Bogacsy who, since he had to retire as a second, became even more passionately involved in the case never stopping for a moment to expound the issues involved and taking the opportunity to give everyone a good lecture on how these things had to be done. Chubby-faced Kamuthy was another who seemed to think of nothing else and he, and the others who were present on the fatal evening, explained it all to each other over and over again. Only Joska Kendy kept his mouth shut, nodding occasionally as he drew on his pipe.

Balint, too, spent most of his time at the Casino, not because he much wanted to take part in all these passionate discussions but because he needed to know what was going on so that he could report it all to Adrienne.

Gyeroffy himself was not to be seen. He shut himself up in his hotel room and refused to see anyone except his seconds. Even these only received curt answers to their questions and absolutely no explanation as to why he had called Wickwitz a 'scoundrel'. In vain, too, did they ask him what he had meant by the word blau – blue, which they hadn't even realized was a proper name. Gyeroffy refused to reply and made it perfectly clear that he just wanted to be left alone. As soon as they had gone he took his brandy bottle out of the wardrobe and drank deeply.

Finally, on the afternoon of the fourth day it seemed that some sort of agreement had been reached between the soldiers and Laszlo's seconds. It was not completely satisfactory but seemed to give hope of a solution. The officer-in-charge let it be known that he would agree, though not officially, to the substitution of a Weapons Commission for the Court of Honour demanded by Gyeroffy's seconds. It was emphasized that the army officers would not consider themselves bound to accept any decision reached by such a commission. They would, nevertheless, receive official instructions in accordance with such a commission's findings. The colonel accepted this compromise not because he liked it but as a result of a message from the divisional general saying that, in view of the growing unrest in the town, an immediate solution must be found and the matter put to rest. Accordingly, it was arranged for the Weapons Commission to meet at half-past two so that at three or just after the duel could take place.

Wickwitz had been spending his time exclusively with his army friends. On the first day after the challenge he had been worried lest Gyeroffy had let out what he knew of the Dinora-Blau affair and would not therefore be obliged to fight. However, seeing that his seconds remained as cordial and friendly as when they were

PART SIX

first appointed, he became calm again for it was clear that Gyeroffy must have kept his mouth shut. When midday came on the fourth day of waiting and they told him to be ready to fight at three o'clock, he was not merely relieved but also overjoyed. *Na, endlich* – at last, well, at dawn the next morning, he would elope with Judith; up and away! Quickly he scribbled a few lines to her: '*Tomorrow morning I'll be at the station before five. I'll be in the second-class waiting-room.*' Then he thought he ought to add some endearing, eager phrase, for he knew that girls appreciated that sort of thing; but though he pondered for some time he could think of nothing more eloquent than '*ewig dein* – forever yours', that would have to do! He added these two words at the end, put the note in an envelope and sent it with one of the hotel pages to Zoltan at his school. He knew the boy would somehow get it to his sister.

The Weapons Commission met in the Casino and consisted of the elder Count Adam Alvinczy and Tihamer Abonyi, who had proposed his services with such insistence – for he was much attached to Wickwitz – that he managed to get appointed. Crookface Kendy presided. Just before half-past two they retired to the library together with Gyeroffy's seconds. The anteroom outside was also closed to other members so that no one could overhear the discussions inside.

By the time the commission had already been in session for a quarter of an hour, everyone in the club was eagerly watching the inner doors of the library. Instead it was the entrance doors from the street which opened.

Baron Egon's seconds entered the Casino in full uniform, looking stiff and unhappy, their shakos in their hands. They asked where Gyeroffy's seconds were to be found. At once they were ushered through the smoking-room and into the library beyond. The doors closed behind them. Everyone wondered what could have happened. What was this? What did they want, barging in here?

There was another surprise. Baron Gazsi Kadacsay was now standing in the outer hall. He did not come in but remained with his shako on his head, pacing up and down. He, too, was in full uniform. It was amazing, unheard-of: Gazsi, who was always so careless of his appearance, here in the club, freshly shaven and dressed to the nines. They tried to question him, pouring out into the entrance hall and begging him to come in and tell them what was going on. 'Why are *you* here? Why don't you come in?

543

Whatever are you doing in uniform? Is the King expected? When did you arrive? Where have you come from? From your regiment? From Brasso? Are you on duty?' The questions poured out, but they received no answer.

Gazsi was by no means his usual light-hearted self. He stood there unusually serious, and replied as shortly as possible to all the questions with which he was plied. When at last someone asked about the duel, enquiring if he had been sent to Kolozsvar in connection with Nitwit's challenge, Gazsi turned away, and seeing Balint Abady across the room, went over and drew him towards the staircase.

'Thank heavens you're here, my friend. For God's sake talk to me about something, anything, and get me away from these lunatics. What a bunch of fools!'

They did not get far because at this moment the two officers came down. Baron Gazsi stood to attention, Wickwitz's seconds joined him for a brief moment and stood one on each side of him; then all three saluted, turned and marched smartly out of the building.

Everyone rushed to the smoking-room where they found the members of the Weapons Commission just coming out of the library. But their curiosity was not to be satisfied. No matter how hard they tried they could get no proper answers to their questions. Crookface merely grunted in a negative way; Alvinczy shrugged his shoulders. Uncle Ambrus swore at everyone telling them all to go to hell. Then, with Joska Kendy, he left the building and everyone assumed that they were going to see Gyeroffy. Abonyi muttered: 'The duel is postponed!' and hurried away without explanation.

Baron Gazsi and the two officers drove at once to Wickwitz's hotel. They found him waiting for them in the passage.

'*Servus Kadacsay! Bist auch hier? Also was ist* – You here too? What's up then?' he asked as he showed the way to his room. '*So nehmt's doch Platz!* – find yourselves a seat' he said, sitting down himself and offering them all chairs. Then he looked up into their faces and said no more.

No one sat; the three men just looked down at him, their expressions grim and set. They stood there, stiffly, their shakos still on their heads, and looked at him in silence. Wickwitz shuddered, his spine tingling. He rose from his seat.

'*Oberleutnant Baron Egon von Wickwitz!*' the captain spoke in

PART SIX

German, 'a legal complaint has been lodged against you; therefore we are obliged to withdraw as your appointed seconds. Lieutenant Kadacsay will inform you further!'

The two men saluted and left the room without shaking hands. Baron Egon sank back on to the sofa. Gazsi took off his shako and pulled up a chair beside him. It was clear that he did not relish the task he had before him. He smoothed his short-cut hair a couple of times and, his head held sideways like a raven, he looked at the man beside him.

'*Na also, was hast Du mir zu sagen* – well then, what have you to say to me?' asked Wickwitz in a low voice.

Kadacsay opened one of the braided buttons on his loose hussar's jacket and took out an official-looking paper from an inner pocket. He handed it over without saying a word. It read:

> *Auf Anzeige der Privatbank Blau und Comp. Grosswardein, ist gegen Oberleutnant Baron Egon von Wickwitz das Ehrengerechtliche-Verfahren eingeleitet worden. Gennanter Oberleutnant hat – following information laid by Blau and Co., private bankers and assayers, proceedings have been taken against Lieutenant Baron Egon von Wickwitz. The said Lieutenant must . . .*

Though these terrible words seemed to swim before his eyes Wickwitz was still able to try and lie his way out of it: 'There must be some mistake,' he murmured in a low voice.

Gazsi inclined his head, his whole demeanour showing that he doubted if any mistake had been made. For a moment neither of them spoke.

'*Hast du noch etwas zu sagen* – haven't you anything else to tell me?' asked Wickwitz at last.

Now Kadacsay replied instantly, though very slowly and with special emphasis: 'The colonel entrusted me with a private message to be passed by word of mouth only. It is this: the commanding officer of your regiment informs you that should the signatures on Countess Dinora Malhuysen-Abonyi's promissory notes be forgeries, then you are to proceed at once to Brasso and report to regimental headquarters. But if those signatures are really your own . . .'

'If they are?'

'If they are genuine . . . if you signed those papers . . . then it were best . . . if only for the honour of the regiment that . . .' and Gazsi got up and placed a revolver on the table, '. . . that you should use this at once! That is the colonel's message.'

The dark hair over Wickwitz's low forehead seemed to fall even lower over his brows. His large cows' eyes were almost closed:

'So? So? So that's it, is it?' He repeated the words several times more.

Kadacsay picked up his shako. When he reached the door he turned: 'These things are easier if done quickly!' he said lightly. 'Shall I close the door behind me?'

Baron Egon got up, straightening his fine athlete's figure to its full height. 'I'll close it myself!' he said in a hard and determined voice.

Gazsi hesitated a moment. Then he turned back. 'Goodbye, my friend!' he said putting out his hand which Wickwitz took in his hand and grasped strongly. For some seconds they remained hands clasped and silent. Then Kadacsay slipped quickly out.

Egon was alone. He walked up and down the room, once, twice, three times... and at the fifth turn he suddenly broke into peels of hard, ugly laughter. He rang the bell; and when the servant came in he asked the man to bring him a railway time-table. There was an outgoing train at six o'clock. This was extremely handy, for at that hour he was unlikely to encounter anyone he knew at the station. He looked at his watch: it was ten to five. Wickwitz quickly changed into shooting clothes. Then he packed all his civilian clothes into the smaller of his two suitcases. The larger he left where it was. His uniforms he hung neatly in the wardrobe. Then he picked up his sword with its gilded hilt and looked at it, remembering what a joy it had been when he had first been entitled to wear it. Then he put it carefully into the wardrobe. He looked around the room. On the table lay the revolver, the gift of his excellent colonel. Egon smiled ironically to himself, his moustaches curling with amusement. That present is far too good to leave behind! he thought, as he slipped the weapon into his pocket. Then he rang the bell again and ordered a carriage to be brought to the door.

'I shall be away for a day or two,' he said. 'Most of my things are still in the room. Please see that it's kept for me until I return!'

When they announced that the carriage was waiting Wickwitz looked around the room to check that he had forgotten nothing. He had everything he needed. He was driven to the station where he calmly boarded the six o'clock train and left. He had completely forgotten the message he had sent to Judith that morning. It had never even entered his head.

PART SIX

By dawn the next day he was over the Romanian border.

Kadacsay walked back slowly, stopping briefly every so often as if he were expecting someone to come hastening after him. At last he reached the Casino. He had not really wanted to come back, for he dreaded having people coming up to him asking questions, but he felt himself obliged to do so because he had told the hotel concierge to telephone him there 'should anything happen'.

The Casino was humming like an upturned beehive. The only thing that everyone knew for certain, and this they had got from Alvinczy at once, was that no duel would take place and that Nitwit had been ordered back to his regiment. When Uncle Ambrus returned he had said it was because of some questionable dealings that touched the Austrian baron's honour.

As soon as Kadacsay came in he was besieged with questions, but he replied so rudely that the others soon left him alone. Disappointed, they said to each other that really this Gazsi was getting above himself! Why, he was behaving just like an Austrian, a lackey of the Emperor in Vienna! It was the sort of thing that showed how much they needed Hungarian words of command and sword tassels in national colours! It was obvious. Everything would then be different. As it was, as soon as anyone put on the imperial uniform they didn't want to have anything more to do with their old friends!

Joska Kendy was sitting with this group so Gazsi was unable to run to the shelter of his old hero. Therefore he went to look for Abady with whom he had become far more friendly since his visit to Denestornya. He needed someone to talk to with whom there would be no need to discuss what had just happened in Wickwitz's hotel room. He wanted to have someone to sit with until that telephone call came for him. Balint and he settled down in the empty reading room where no one was expected to talk. For some time Gazsi did not open his mouth and there was a long silence between them. Then Balint said: 'It was Dinora's promissory notes, I suppose?'

Baron Gazsi nodded. Still he said nothing. They waited until it was already after half-past six. Then they went to the telephone and were put through to Wickwitz' hotel. Kadacsay asked for the hall porter and when he came on the line, said:

'Please go at once to Lieutenant Wickwitz's room. What? He left the hotel? When? An hour ago. All right, thank you.'

'You'd better come with me,' said Gazsi, after a moment's

thought. 'I'm not sure I can cope with this on my own!'

Both men hurried over to the hotel.

'He only took his overnight bag – the small one,' said the porter. 'He didn't say where he was going. It must have been about six o'clock: there are three trains around then, going to different places, of course. No, he didn't pay his bill, he said he'd be back in a day or two!' They asked for the key and went up.

The room was in perfect order. Gazsi looked down at the table. The revolver was nowhere to be seen. He went over to the wardrobe and opened it: inside there were all Wickwitz's army things, tunics, blouses, braided satin waistcoats, parade trousers, officer's caps, two pairs of hussar's boots with their woods in place, and even his sword: not a trace of plain-clothes, no civilian suits, no shirts, no under-linen, no shoes!

Gazsi felt sick and he was so shocked that he went quite pale: 'Come on!' he said, 'let's get out of here!'

They left the hotel and wandered about the narrow streets of the old town. As they did so Gazsi told the whole story to Balint. Now it was obvious that Nitwit had run away, but before Gazsi took any further action Balint said that they must get definite proof of what had happened; they only had the word of the hotel porter that he'd gone to catch a train.

They went together to the station and questioned the porters. Yes, one of them remembered the gentleman; he had put his luggage on the train to the frontier. 'Yes, he definitely went on that train. I know the Lieutenant well, I've often carried his bags.'

Kadacsay went to see the stationmaster who confirmed that they had sold a half-price officer's ticket, second class, for the six o'clock train that afternoon. Kadacsay and Balint walked back together to the town centre. They walked slowly along while they discussed what action should be taken. Someone had to be told that Wickwitz had bolted, but who? The Hussar regiment at Brasso would not thank them if the news had first been reported to the local infantry garrison. They didn't like to send a wire, for that was too public; and a letter would take too long.

Finally Gazsi decided he would return himself to Brasso on the night express. There they would know what was to be done.

Chapter Seven

As soon as Balint reached home after his long walk with Gazsi that evening he sent a note to Adrienne. He wrote: '*W. decamped this afternoon. Tell you all tonight.*' That night at his usual time he let himself in through the window of Adrienne's sitting-room and told her in detail everything that had transpired during the day. They talked for a long time, relieved at the way everything had turned out, for surely Judith would now see how worthless was the man on whom she had pinned her hopes. Of course it would be dreadful for her when she found out the whole truth, and so Adrienne planned next morning to tell her only what was absolutely necessary, letting it out bit by bit as Balint reported it to her. She felt it would be easier for Judith if she were to learn the truth gradually, but always as soon as Balint brought any more news, just in case Judith might hear something elsewhere.

The clock of the Monostor tower had just chimed out the quarter after three when Balint was about to let himself out.

It was a bright moonlit night. Even so, outside the windows of Adrienne's rooms the shadow of the house was so dense that it was difficult to see anything before the little gate which led to the bridge. Balint's hand was already on the handle of the french window when he suddenly stopped. In front of him he had seen the dark outline of a woman walking quickly towards the bridge. It was Judith. Swiftly she passed to the other side and took the path beside the river bank. For a moment Balint hesitated, wondering if he ought not to go back and tell Adrienne, but there would be no time for that if he were to follow the girl to prevent her doing something foolish. Quickly he slipped out and went after her.

It was easy to follow her along the moonlit road, even though from time to time he lost sight of her for a moment in the shadow of the trees. She was in a great hurry, walking so fast that even Balint was pushed to keep up with her. When they reached the outskirts of the town Judith headed straight towards the railway line, slipping quickly into the station as soon as she arrived.

The station was dimly lit and Balint had to look furtively around for a while until he discovered her sitting alone in the second-class waiting room. There she was, hunched on a bench by the wall and clutching a small overnight case on her lap, waiting.

Keeping discreetly out of sight Balint, wondered what he should do next. Should he speak to her? But if he did, what could he say? He would have to explain how he came to be here, disclosing that he had followed her from the villa and therefore revealing too that he had been with Adrienne. That was clearly impossible. He decided to wait and see what transpired and, as he stood there, began to piece together what must have happened. He was filled with pity for the poor girl who did not know that the man she loved so much had already left the previous day without giving her a thought. Here she was, at dawn the day after he had bolted, waiting, waiting, waiting for him to come so that they could escape together to Austria to what she thought would be infinite bliss.

Poor, poor Judith . . . to be waiting for Wickwitz!

What could he possibly do? Should he go to her and tell her the truth? She would never believe him and was sure to assume that he had made it all up, and God knows what she would do then! It was a pity that he had no way to warn Adrienne of what was happening, but it *was already* after four and if he were to return to the villa, he would have to do so on foot, for at that early hour there were no fiacres available and it would soon be dawn and someone was sure to see him. Best, perhaps, to stay where he was and speak to Judith only after the express to Budapest, which was to have taken Judith and Wickwitz on the first stage of their journey to Graz, had already left. Then he would not have to explain anything for the facts would speak for themselves: and what hideous, vile facts they were!

Slowly the station came to life. A locomotive could be heard shunting in the marshalling yards. Then there was a plaintive whistle and a goods train rumbled slowly by the sooty windows of the station. Some lamps were waved at the end of the platform and a market train came slowly to a halt, from which third-class passengers emerged carrying heavy loads on their shoulders.

Then dawn came, and dim light began to filter on to the platform. The carriages for the Budapest train were shunted in and a few sleepy passengers began to arrive. Soon the platform was crowded.

Bells rang in the waiting rooms and a porter started shouting: 'Nagy-Varad, Puspokladany, Szolkok, Budapest!' in a slurred voice, and people began boarding the train. Balint watched Judith from a distance. She did not move but, as time went by, she obviously became more and more restless. Her hands were clenched nervously on the handles of the bag on her lap. When the second bell sounded she came out on to the platform, brushing by Balint without seeing him, her eyes searching down the length of the platform. She looked into the train and then into the first-class waiting room. Finally Balint could stand it no longer. He stepped over to her and touched her arm. The girl started violently.

'Judith! The man you're looking for left yesterday!' he said.

Judith stared at him, eyes wide open as if she had seen a ghost, her mouth distorted with hatred.

'You? You here? Everywhere it's you!'

Balint repeated what he had just said.

'Who? What are you saying? Left yesterday?'

The carriage doors were being slammed shut. There was a blast from the locomotive's whistle and the train started to move. The girl looked wildly around her, then she ran forward a few steps but the train gathered speed and moved off down the track. Her hopes vanished as she looked vainly after the disappearing train and her knees gave way under her. She would have fallen if Abady had not quickly put his arms round her waist and supported her.

'Come with me,' he said. 'There's no point in standing about!'

He led her swiftly out of the station and into a one-horse carriage which he found waiting there. 'To the Monostor road. I'll tell you where later,' said Abady to the driver.

Until now Judith had let herself be led without seeming to notice what was happening. The shaking of the carriage soon brought her to her senses. When she saw who it was sitting beside her, she shrank back into the corner of the carriage, her eyes filled with fright like a wild bird caught in a trap. She stared into Abady's face with a look of surprise and loathing and as they drove her gaze never wavered, so hard was she looking at him. Petrified, unable to speak, she just stared at him as the carriage rumbled slowly down the long road to the Uzdy villa. Twice Abady tried to explain that he himself had just been going to catch that train when he had chanced to see her, but he faltered, unable to continue, faced with the look in those wide-open eyes.

When at last the carriage stopped in front of the wrought-iron gates of the Uzdy villa, Judith was still staring at him in silence.

Balint did not know what to do next. It was only now that they had reached the girl's home that he realized how awkward it would be if he were to be caught bringing home one of the Miloth girls at dawn. How could he possibly smuggle her into the house without being seen by the servants, who must at that time be stirring?

To be discovered now would provoke God knows what gossip!

He need not have worried, thanks to Margit's quickness in grasping what had happened. Margit had woken just as dawn was breaking. She saw at once that Judith's bed was empty. She had dressed quickly and run down to Adrienne who had told her of the dramatic turn in the story, of the duel between Laszlo and Wickwitz and how Wickwitz had left town suddenly. Sensibly Margit did not enquire how Adrienne knew all this, but she quickly realized though she had not herself seen it, that Zoltan, who had come to see them in the morning, must had brought a message for Judith and that Judith must have tried to follow their prepared plan and slipped away to the station in the night. It was there that they must look for her.

As Adrienne was dressing hurriedly Margit went to find the Uzdy doorman and sent him to find a fiacre, and she was therefore waiting for it to arrive when the one-horse carriage bringing Abady and Judith drew up before the gates. She ran out, helped her sister out of the carriage, kissed her swiftly and led her into the house without saying a word.

All this was done so rapidly that none of the Uzdy servants were aware that anything untoward had happened to Judith. So resolutely and sensibly did Margit act that neither then nor ever afterwards did anyone in the house except Adrienne and Margit – nor anyone in the great world outside – ever hear even a whisper of Judith's attempted escape.

If Judith Miloth was spared the town's gossip, poor little Dinora Abonyi was not, and her part in the Wickwitz débâcle was quickly the talk of Kolozsvar.

Outside the family the only people to know the truth – Abady, Gyeroffy and Kadacsay – kept their mouths shut and said nothing. And yet, within the space of two weeks everyone knew all about Dinora and her promissory notes.

Aunt Lizinka's overheated and airless drawing-room was the *Solfatara* – the sulphurous volcano – from which most of the poison gas was distributed abroad. Recently the old Countess Sarmasaghy had occupied herself principally with the so-called 'Tulip Drive'. This was the new craze from Budapest where a number of grand society ladies had started a movement to buy only Hungarian-made articles. Though everyone convinced themselves that thereby they were striking a body-blow at the industries of Austria, and the capital rang with patriotic speeches

PART SIX

and fervent leading articles in praise of the movement, the fact remained that it had little practical effect. Shopkeepers cunningly pretended that all their fabrics were made in Hungary, whether or not the silk was really manufactured at Lyons and woollens and linen in Austria. In Transylvania the vogue did not catch on as it did in the capital, for everyone had always bought their rich trousseaus and grand dresses in Vienna as things were cheaper there than in Budapest, and they were not going to change just because someone in Budapest said they should. In the past, Aunt Lizinka had done the same. However, learning that her archenemy Miklos Absolon bought his boots from Goisern, his suit-lengths from Tyrol and his sporting guns from Springer, she threw herself into the Tulip Drive principally so that she could accuse him publicly of being a traitor to his country.

The Wickwitz affair came as a godsend to Aunt Lizinka, who promptly dropped the hopeless cause of the Tulip Drive for the infinitely more delectable task of stirring the cauldron of local scandal. She applied herself to this with tremendous energy, serving up daily to the old ladies who frequented the Sarmasaghy drawing-room new slices of scandal-cake, each more titillating than the last and new draughts of witches' brew strong enough and shocking enough to go to anyone's head. Lizinka made the very most of such a tasty affair and stirred up the biggest storm she could: a storm in a teacup it might be, but a tempest to those who lived in a teacup – and poor little Dinora drowned in it. It was not long before Aunt Lizinka had ferreted out all the facts, and everything she discovered she immediately broadcast using an assumed moral indignation to mask her enjoyment of such lurid and sordid details. She became a sort of dirt volcano whose daily eruptions splattered all within reach. Apart from the central figures, Wickwitz, Dinora and poor Tihamer Abonyi, there were plenty of others who suffered from Lizinka's gossip factory. Jeno Laczok and his banker friend Baron Soma Weissfeld were given a good smear as it had been their establishment that had first accepted Dinora's notes when presented by the Austrian baron: 'What a disreputable action by a bank, my dears, downright shady I call it to accept such things'; Laszlo Gyeroffy: 'my precious nephew, you know, the reckless gambler'; young Dodo Gyalakuthy, because Wickwitz had once pursued her; Baron Gazsi, because he was Wickwitz's companion in arms; Abady: 'Remember how *he* used to run after that little whore!'; and even Miklos Absolon, though all she could think up to say about him was: 'I can't say anything now, but you'll all soon find out that that old liar is mixed up in it too!' Everyone came in for their share of Lizinka's brand of innuendo and self-righteous condemnation.

Abonyi, though much against his will for he owed his social position to his wife, found himself obliged by convention to sue for divorce and, when this was granted, retired sadly to his own property in the Vas district where he counted for nothing.

Poor little Dinora was socially ostracized and cut by everyone. She found herself with a mountain of debts, but she somehow managed to survive and remain cheerful, for being possessed of very little brain she never really understood what had happened to her.

In every great upheaval there is always someone who comes out a winner: and this time it was Kristof Azbej, Countess Roza Abady's cunning little man of business.

A few days after the Wickwitz affair had set the town by the ears, Azbej received a telegram from Gyeroffy asking him tersely to come to see him at Kozard.

As Countess Roza was still at Portofino, Azbej was free to do as he wished. He replied that he would obey at once. At the station at Iklod a carriage was waiting for him which took him swiftly to Laszlo's manor-house at Kozard. As he drove, Azbej had a careful look at the fields beside the road: they were loam-rich meadows which bordered the river. On arrival an untidily dressed youth led Azbej into the house. From a small entrance hall a staircase without a hand rail led to the low first-floor rooms under the sloping roof. The walls were only whitewashed for the Kozard manor-house had not been finished when Laszlo's father had shot himself and the big reception rooms on the ground floor had not even been plastered for decoration. Laszlo had therefore installed himself upstairs, as his parents had before him. Here everything gave the impression of being temporary, even improvised, the furniture placed at random with no attempt at order or convenience. Laszlo's bed, which stood in one corner of the long room, was unmade and the remains of the previous day's meal were still on a tray together with a half-empty bottle of plum brandy.

When the little hedgehog-like attorney waddled into the room he found Laszlo pacing up and down impatiently. Laszlo stopped briefly to shake hands and then at once started again to walk up and down as he had done for several days.

'Here I am...' said the lawyer, and pushing aside a pile of

clothes from the chair on which they had been thrown, he sat down without further ceremony, '... at your Lordship's service.'

The young man did not answer at once but continued marching up and down the room. Then he stopped and said in a stern voice: 'I need eighty-six thousand crowns... at once!'

'Ah,' said the attorney with a sigh, 'that is a very large sum, a very large sum indeed!'

'I know. I've tried every way I can think of but I can't raise it. I don't understand these things. That is why I sent for you.'

The fat little attorney closed his bulging, prune-shaped eyes.

'How large is the estate?' he asked, his lips hardly moving behind his untrimmed beard.

'The cultivated part is eight hundred acres.'

'Is it mortgaged?'

'Yes. For sixty thousand.'

'I see! I see!' repeated Azbej, seemingly deep in thought. After a long pause he said: 'When do you need the money?'

'I've told you already. Now! At once!' cried Gyeroffy. 'I can't wait. I can't stand it any more!'

'Excuse me. Please...' said Azbej apologetically. 'I don't quite know... if your Lordship would permit me, perhaps I could just have a look round, and then ... then maybe I could think up some solution to your Lordship's problem.' Bowing obsequiously, he backed out of the room.

In an hour he was back, still bowing as obsequiously as before. He sat down and now the words poured from him.

He was ready to help, he said. His only object, naturally, was to be of service for he was after all only a servant, a servant of the Count's family and, as Count Gyeroffy was a member of the Noble Family he served, therefore, and only because of this and to please the noble Count, he would seek a way to make himself useful. Then he recounted all the difficulties there were in raising money, listing the various obstacles and delays there would be in trying to raise such a sum from the banks. Even though this might eventually produce results there were bound to be delays for all the necessary discussions, searches and legal formalities, not to speak of the expenses involved. Some other solution must be sought, either leasing the estate or pre-selling that year's crops or a part of them. Yet even the whole would not raise the sum needed, and tenants were always reluctant to pay in advance even if an eager tenant could be found at such short notice. This was the sort of thing which could never be done in a hurry and anyway he would never recommend it for he had only his Lordship's best interests at heart. No! That sort of solution could never be hurried, indeed he wouldn't even consider it!

'Well then, why are you telling me all this?' asked Laszlo angrily.

For a few moments Azbej looked at him without expression, seemingly bewildered and helpless. Then, as if he had suddenly seen the light, he opened wide his eyes so that they protruded more than ever and cried: 'I have it! I'll do it myself, even though it'll be a sacrifice! I'll lease the whole property myself, come what may. I'll pay you what you need!'

The very same day the contract was drawn up and signed and Azbej became Laszlo's tenant, paying ten years' rent in advance. As it was to be paid all at once it was only reasonable – was it not? – that he should set the rent at five crowns an acre. That made forty thousand crowns. For a further fifty thousand crowns or thereabouts he bought all the agricultural machinery, though, as God was his witness it was worth barely half that sum, but he did not care for his only desire was to be of help. The next day he handed Laszlo three savings-bank books from Kolozsvar worth eighty-seven thousand crowns in all and three new banknotes of a thousand crowns each.

'I am very happy,' said the little attorney on taking his leave, 'to be of service to your Lordship in this way. Should your Lordship find some other solution at a later date, naturally I will withdraw and we can cancel the arrangement.'

In this way Laszlo raised enough to redeem Countess Beredy's pearls. The next day he went to Budapest by the midday train, thinking that with such a large sum in his pockets it was wiser to travel by day.

Chapter Eight

ADRIENNE SAT AT HER DESK but she was not writing. Instead she looked out over the garden which, though leafless was now free of the winter snow, to the rickety wooden bridge over which ten days before Judith had made her escape from the house and which Balint had used each time he came to see her.

He had been there only last night...

Because of Judith, Adrienne had still only been able to see

PART SIX

Balint at night. If she so much as heard his name Judith's face became contorted with terror as if it had been he who had been the sole cause of her terrible disappointment. Most of the day the girl would wander about pathetically, answering mechanically any questions put to her. She would only come to life if Balint were mentioned, and then it was as if the sound of his name was a torment to her. Consequently Adrienne could not allow Balint to visit her during the day as long as her sisters remained at the Uzdy villa; and for the moment there was no question of their leaving, for Countess Miloth was still in the sanatorium.

All the same, thought Adrienne, these night visits must stop, and not only because of the risks involved.

Four days before, when Balint had just let himself in through the drawing-room window, Uzdy had arrived unexpectedly from the country. Luckily they had heard the clatter of horses' hoofs from the courtyard and there had just been time for Balint to slip back into the darkness of the drawing-room and hide himself behind the door to Adrienne's room, holding himself rigidly motionless lest the parquet should give a creak under his weight, and for Adrienne to replace the candle on the table by the bed, when Uzdy entered her room still in his hat and travelling coat.

'You're still awake? At this hour? Why is that?' he asked from the door that led from the passage.

'My sisters have only just left me.'

'Of course. Yes, of course.' Uzdy's little eyes looked around the room, apparently searching for something. His glance fell on the little Browning on the lower shelf of the bedside table.

'You have a revolver? Since when?'

Adrienne did not answer. With the bedclothes pulled up to her chin she merely stared at him. Uzdy laughed.

'That's good! Very clever! Out here, so far from the town, anybody could cross the mill stream, a burglar, anybody!' He walked up and down for a minute or two, taking long strides with his extra-long legs. Then he abruptly stopped by the drawing-room door, opened it and peered into the darkness of the room beyond. He seemed to be listening. It was only for an instant but to Adrienne it seemed like an eternity. Her heart was beating strongly, but she did not move or speak.

Uzdy closed the door.

'You are right to be prepared,' he said. 'Anyone could get in from there. Would you like a wire fence by the river? Or perhaps a wolf-trap? What? A trap, eh? That'd be good, very good!

557

What?' He laughed again, though for what reason it was not clear. Towering above her, his laughter seemed to come from the ceiling. Still Adrienne said nothing. He went on: 'Well, I'll be going now. You just sleep ... sleep ... sleep.' He threw his head back and, seemingly even taller than ever, he turned to go. At the door he looked back, and with no expression on his satanic features, said '*Au revoir!*' and left the room as quickly as he had come.

At noon on the following day Uzdy left again for the country.

That night Abady had come again and told her how he had stood, scarcely daring to breathe, behind the open door and they had both laughed about it regardless of the danger they had been in. Neither of them minded, for neither was afraid for their lives.

But, thought Adrienne, now it was not because of the danger that these stolen meetings would have to stop. What was life? That signified nothing ... but there was something else.

On their last night together something had happened that had frightened her. A strange new feeling had flooded over her and filled her woman's body. She knew not what, but it had frightened her. It was something altogether new, and came without warning.

Until now she had always remained calm when Balint was caressing her. It had been agreeable, soothing, so soothing that sometimes she had fallen asleep in his arms just like a child. Those hands that stroked her body, that glided so gently over her skin, the lips that strayed from her mouth, always kissing so gently, gently, and then returning to take possession of her lips for longer than before, had given her merely a sense of agreeable languor, so that this unnoticed conquest to which she had yielded more and more territory had not disturbed her and indeed had hardly meant more than when they dined at the same table or danced together at the public balls, But last night, as their farewell kiss came to an end, Adrienne had felt overwhelmed by a sudden and unexpected weakness. From somewhere deep inside her there came an altogether new feeling which threatened to overcome any strength she had, to sweep away all control, all will power so that her very bones seemed to melt in the radiance of some magic daze. Somehow she had managed to recover herself sufficiently to push him away, suddenly, almost rudely, saying: 'Go! Go now!' It was an order: 'Go! Go!'

Balint looked down at her for a long time, and she was still not sure whether there had not been just the shadow of a smile upon his face.

PART SIX

'May I come tomorrow?'
'Tomorrow, yes! But now you must go!'
It was of this that Adrienne was now thinking.

For a long time she pondered, wondering if she should write to tell him not to come any more. Should she write that she did not want to yield to him and become his lover, his mistress? That this was something that she couldn't, wouldn't do? Should she tell him all the thoughts that had obsessed her the whole morning, that she had pondered over a hundred times? She did not know how to write such things, and yet she could hardly put him off without giving some reason. Her courageous nature was such that she had always been prepared to face anything, and now what she would have liked most in the world was to open her heart and tell him face to face, when he came to her that evening, everything that was in her mind. But for once she was afraid, afraid of herself, afraid that she would not have the strength to resist him and afraid that his searching, caressing hands, his mouth, his eyes, his very presence beside her, would overcome her will and soothe her anxieties as they so often had before until she became bewitched into acquiescence. She was afraid that at this meeting, which she planned to be their last, her sorrow at parting would so shake her determination that now, just when they should part, she would no longer be able to resist him and they would at long last be joined for ever together.

And so she would have to write.

After a long time she took up her pen and started, and when she had started she wrote hurriedly, finding the right words with great difficulty and often scratching them out and starting again. Luncheon was announced long before she had finished, but still she did not move. Margit came into fetch her, but still she did not get up. 'You go in,' she said. 'Sit down, start without me. I'll join you later, perhaps, but don't disturb me now!' And she went on writing, the words pouring from her helter-skelter, just as they came from her heart, muddled, haphazard, desperate.

When she had finished she felt dizzy. Nevertheless she folded the sheets and put them in an envelope and rang for her maid. When the woman came she found Adrienne standing erect, apparently quite calm.

'Please take this at once and be sure that you give it only to him. To nobody else, you understand?'

The elderly, grey-haired Jolan curtsied and left the room and then, and only then did Adrienne dissolve in tears.

My dearest,

I have changed my mind Don't come to me tonight! Or any other night. Never again! Never! This is a dreadful word I know, but the whole thing is impossible. I didn't realize it until last night. I didn't know. It was so good, so beautiful. Do understand. I know that you love me and I, too, love you, every day more and more and more, if that is possible, and I now know what it is to love, I know that ... one day, sooner or later ... the thing will happen and we will become true lovers. But now that is impossible, so impossible that if it ever happened I would have to kill myself. Please don't be angry with me! Just think of what would follow. Think how impossible everything would be! I am that man's wife, his possession, What could happen then? That I ... with you ... and him. Even now it is terrible with him. You know it. You've felt it and you have understood even better than if I had ever spoken about it ... But if I became yours, then afterwards ... if with you and then afterwards ...? No! Never! Never that, I would rather die! There would be no other way for me. You would say that I should divorce. If I could have I'd have done it long before you came into my life. But I can't! He clings to me, pinions me, holds me down — he will never let me go, never release me and if I breathed a word of all this to him he would kill me. Me, and you too, or anyone else. You know what he's like. I don't have to explain. He would kill in cold blood, and enjoy it, laughing as he did so. I can't let all this happen, start all this off, bring about this, this nothing! Just think where it would lead us. Only to death, and what use would that be?

We must part. We must, there is no other way, no other way at all. You must go abroad. Please, I beg you! Don't even try to see me again, not after this. Perhaps later, when we are both calmer — but, until then, no! I could never refuse you if I saw you again. I know it now and freely admit it. If you came I would yield at once ... and it would be the end of me. I would die ... I would have to. ... after that I could only face death. Please have pity on me! I never meant to do you any harm I know now what I've done to you, so have pity on me, I beg you. If you could forget me, it would be the best for you. If this is to be our final goodbye it would be best for both of us. Try it, please try it! Perhaps it will be easier for you than for me, perhaps? I only had you, nothing else. It will be so difficult for me, still I do beseech you to go away and wherever you go remember me and keep me in your heart knowing that I shall love you always and knowing that you didn't kill me because I came to love you ...

I know that you'll be strong enough to do this and I thank you from the bottom of my heart for the sacrifice that you will make for my sake, a sacrifice I believe is just as great as mine. Know that I am filled with

PART SIX

gratitude for having known your love and that I kiss your mouth as you have taught me and that I shall for ever be lying in your arms and listening to the beautiful things that you tell me and that you write for me and that I kiss you and that I am always . . . and forever . . . yours . . . and yours alone . . . But don't kill me, I beg you . . . don't kill me . . .

Two days later Balint was back in Portofino. He went there straight from Budapest without stopping except to change trains, hardly noticing the changing landscapes, the continuous rumbling of the carriages, the discomfort of two sleepless nights and two endless days. Everything was unreal to him compared with the throbbing of the pain he was feeling and the feverish visions conjured up by his imagination. He knew then that Adrienne had glimpsed something she had never before imagined or experienced and that from it she had recoiled in terror.

It was this last troubled look in Adrienne's eyes that Balint saw most often in his mind as he fled away, back to the Riviera. He read and re-read Adrienne's letter a hundred times and always he came to the same conclusion, that what he was doing was right and that there was no alternative but to do what she asked of him.

He had to obey her, give her up, go far away from where she was, disappear from her life. Poor, poor Addy! She had been right; there was no other way open to them.

At last, after driving along roads bordered by orange groves and gardens filled with spring flowers, azaleas and camellias, he arrived at the little hotel beside the bay. The colour of the sea was as blue as a picture postcard, and all around him nature seemed to mock his anguish by displays of healthy, luxuriant growth, as if telling him that the world was indifferent to his pain and, no matter who fell by the wayside, life still renewed itself annually and eternally.

Countess Roza received him in her room. She had been angry that he had stayed away so long, making her wait three whole weeks for his return and she was sure that the excuses he made in his one short letter were nothing more than awkward pretexts to conceal a truth he did not want to reveal. As she was getting ready to receive her son she decided to each him a lesson and at every sound outside the room she glared balefully at the door with a carefully prepared expression of disapproval. When, however, the door finally opened and her son appeared, everything was changed in an instant. With one glance she saw in the tenseness of the young man's face the expression of one who had been in hell. Countess Roza had never seen her son like this before. Looking at him, she knew at once that this was a man in torment and all her thoughts of his neglect of her vanished as if they had never been. She was flooded by a mother's anxiety, ran to the door to greet him, lay her head on his shoulder, her tiny hands holding him closely to her, so moved that all she could say was: 'My little one... my son... my own little boy...'

On their way back they stopped for two or three days at Milan, Verona and Venice; and wherever they went, to museums, palaces, picture galleries, to churches and in their hotel at mealtimes, Countess Abady discreetly studied her son. She asked no questions and she knew no details, apart from the fact that he had stayed longer than planned at Kolozsvar – and from the reports of the two housekeepers who had not failed to tell their mistress not only who was staying in town but also the fact that – Lord preserve them! – Count Balint seldom came home before dawn. Countess Roza had built up a picture for herself, a picture of what had been happening. She, of course, knew no details and mostly was far from the truth; but of one thing she was certain and that was that it was Adrienne, that wicked, wicked Adrienne, who was the reason for her son's desperate unhappiness. It was she, that selfish, depraved, wicked woman, who had caused this terrible change in her beloved son; and the heart of the tyrannical old chatelaine of Denestornya was filled with hatred and the desire for vengeance on the creature who was responsible.

They arrived at Budapest at the end of March and there they parted, Countess Roza travelling on alone to Transylvania. Not for a moment did the old lady try to persuade her son to come with her. Not a word did she utter. Let him stay in Budapest, she had no need of him at home. She would go back to Denestornya, and later, when spring came, he would join her there. 'Until then, my darling, you stay here and enjoy yourself. I'll be all right. Don't mind me!' and she travelled on home alone, something she had never done before.

The political atmosphere was quite different from what it had been when Balint had left Budapest in February. Now, by a sudden volte-face, the leaders of the Andrassy and people's parties had to accept what they had so often and so publicly rejected. A pact had been made and a new ministry formed. Apart from the three portfolios reserved for nomination by the king – these were the positions of Minister of War, Minister of Croatian Affairs, and the sovereign's personal representative, the Minister *a latere* – the cabinet was to consist of three members of the 1848 Party and three members of the 1867 Party, all of whom had voted for the universal suffrage measure. Thus everyone who had opposed the liberalization of voting rights would be excluded.

However, matters did not turn out quite as everyone had feared. That same afternoon Kossuth called a meeting of the central committee of the coalition parties so that he could present and explain the projected agreement.

No one expected what was to follow.

The leaders of the Constitution party and of the People's Party both announced that they too accepted Kristoffy's universal suffrage measure.

For a moment there was consternation, until everyone present grasped that though it had been a great sacrifice for these astute politicians suddenly to agree to something they believed dangerous and against the national interest, they had taken this course so as to exclude from office those time-servers who were prepared to ignore the will of the people provided they could be seen to bend the knee to the Emperor. They agreed also so that if the universal suffrage became a reality the running of the state would still be in their own experienced hands. The mood changed immediately. The skies had cleared and now, suddenly everyone ran about in joy and ecstasy shouting that victory had come, that everything they had always wanted was now theirs. Victory! Victory! At last! Never mind if there were no separate army, no Hungarian words of command, no sword-tassels in national colours, never mind if the economic union with Austria remained as strong as ever with no independence for the banks or customs: these issues, of course, were merely postponed. Everyone agreed that a clever formula had been found which upheld the rule of law. Everything was now legal again and so everyone's face was saved, though no one would have admitted it.

Flags were hoisted all over town and speeches were made to the gathering crowds from the balcony of every party headquarters. The politicians shouted their triumph and the populace roared their approval. El Dorado, the Promised Land, call it what you will, had that day been found in Budapest.

Balint himself was relieved that at least some solution had been found to that dangerous and unhealthy situation which had threatened the stability of the state. His own position was not affected, for Ordung, the sheriff who had been suspended and who was now Prefect of Maros-Torda, did not want any change of member. Ordung had realized that it would not be easy to oppose Abady and so he decided to concentrate all his efforts on the northern part of the district, where until now old Miklos Absolon had held absolute sway. In this he had been supported by Aunt Lizinka, who never let drop her enmity for Absolon and who now came forward as the self-appointed figurehead of the new order. Balint she protected and approved of because, on the eve of the assembly at Vasarhely, he had been her escort when she had tried to enlist that no-good Tamas Laczok, and also because he had shouted 'Scum!' at the rioters in the egg battle.

At the same Balint was not happy. There were two things that disturbed him. The first was a phrase in a recent letter from Slawata who wrote: *'Was wird bei dieser Lösung mit der Wehrbarkeit der Monarchie – what effect will all this have on the defence structure of the Dual Monarchy? It is dangerous to keep on postponing bringing our armies up to date. We alone will come too late into the arms race. Everyone else is hard at it, but we remain idle . . .'*

Balint tried to chase away the thoughts that these words provoked, saying to himself that surely their only enemy was Russia and that she was too preoccupied with recovering from the shameful disaster of the war with Japan, with controlling the latent revolutionary movements, with the recurrent mutinies in the army and the recent re-emergence of pogroms against the Jews, to pose any threat to Austria-Hungary? It would take a long time for Russia to recover her strength, though it was true that, as she had been repulsed in the Far East, it was likely that she would next turn her attention to the Balkans. However, there was time enough to start thinking about that.

The other matter was more personal. As soon as he arrived back in the capital he asked about Laszlo Gyeroffy and, unhappily, the man he asked was Niki Kollonich.

Niki laughed maliciously: 'Haven't you heard? Don't you know about it?' he said, with obvious enjoyment. 'You won't see him at the Casino any more! His gambling went too far, but they allowed him to resign, thank God. He was lucky to escape being thrown out!'

'You seem pretty pleased about it!' Balint rounded on him angrily.

'Not at all,' the other said hurriedly. 'I only meant that it was just as well for the rest of us, for his family. It would have been very awkward if there had been a scandal and he'd been thrown out publicly. It was all hushed up.'

Balint went round at once to the apartment house in Museum Street where Laszlo had had his flat. By the entrance door he found a sign posted: FOR RENT. FURNISHED ROOMS WITH PRIVATE ENTRANCE. THIRD FLOOR. He went in search of the hall-porter, who confirmed that, two weeks before, Count Gyeroffy had given up his flat, packed up all his possessions and left.

'Did he leave an address?'

'No, but I believe he went back to Transylvania. I don't really know.'

Chapter Nine

BEFORE GYEROFFY WENT TO VARAD, and afterwards to Kolozsvar where he had the unfortunate encounter with Wickwitz, he had promised Fanny Beredy to remain in Transylvania only for two or three days before returning to go with her, and the rest of her court, Szelepscenyi, d'Orly, Solymar, Devereux and the two nieces, to Milan to hear a new Puccini opera. Fanny hoped that the trip might help wean her lover away from his foolish wasteful life and she had also thought how wonderful it would be to travel together, to stay in the same hotels, spend the nights in each other's arms, and do so many things that were impossible for them in Budapest where their every move was sure to be seen by someone they knew. When a week had gone by and Laszlo had not returned, she sent him a telegram: no reply. She sent him another and another. Still no reply. Fanny was deeply hurt and, telling herself that her lover needed to be taught a lesson, she swallowed her disappointment and left for Italy with the others.

Gyeroffy got back to Budapest the day after Fanny had left. He arrived late in the evening. In the depressed and self-tormenting mood that he had been unable to shake off since his discovery of Wickwitz's perfidy and unscrupulous behaviour, nothing would have induced him to remain alone in his cold little furnished apartment. The mere thought of it filled him with repulsion.

All the time in the train from Transylvania, during which he had felt impelled to reassure himself every few minutes that the great wad of banknotes was still safely in the inner pocket of his jacket, for that large sum of money was the sacred ransom by which he would redeem Fanny's pearls and his own honour, he had been obsessed by the thought that he himself was no better than Wickwitz. You are a scoundrel, he said to himself, just like Nitwit. By what right did you insult him when you are just as guilty as he is? And, as the train rumbled on he kept on repeating to himself to the rhythm of the train's movement: You're as bad as he is ... as bad as he is ... as bad as he is ... as bad as he is ...

He had to go out. But where? He went to the Casino, his legs seemingly finding their own way with no conscious direction from his head. He just dashed out, unchanged, only pausing long enough to throw some cold water on his face and wash his hands. On the way he kept on touching the packet in his pocket, that sacred packet which must not be lost as it represented all that he had left in the world. When that had gone there would be no more!

It was midnight when he walked up the Casino steps.

A ball was in progress in the great ground-floor rooms. Carnival had lasted longer than usual that year and the huge building resounded with the music of the band. As Laszlo walked through the hall they were just carrying into the ballroom the cotillion favours, those little delicate nosegays of flowers, and the sight pierced Laszlo's heart sharply. All this life was finished for him now. Never again would he set foot here, immaculately dressed, to lead the dancing. Here, too, he had failed. He almost ran to the stairs so as to escape the sounds of music and gaiety that came from the ballroom. In the hall there were a number of little groups of men discussing politics, arguing and making statements. Laszlo hurried past and disappeared up the stairs.

In the big card-room on the first floor poker was being played for small stakes. Gyeroffy decided not to join in but had a small table brought close to the play and told them to serve his dinner there. He ordered a bottle of absinthe, the most potent of the waters of Lethe, hoping that thereby he could drown the self-accusatory feelings that gnawed at his heart. Time went by and some of the onlookers from the big game at the baccarat-room upstairs came down and told how play was higher than ever upstairs, with astronomical sums being won and lost. Laszlo automatically felt his inner pocket to be sure that the packet of money

PART SIX

was still in its place. He went on drinking in silence, talking to no one. Later on someone else came in and told everyone that the Black Cockatoo, the Croatian millionaire Arzenovics, was 'losing his shirt' upstairs. It seemed that he had had the most amazing run of bad luck. A little later someone else put their head round the door and said the same thing.

Laszlo got up and went into the little anteroom from which led the stair up to the baccarat-room. He paused, listening. From above nothing could be heard except the soft chink of counters and the occasional phrase: '*Je donne... Non! Les cartes passent.*'

He stood there for a long time his fingers just touching his jacket where he could feel the wad of money in the inside pocket.

Then slowly, as if drawn by a magnet, automatically, he started up the stairs.

For a while Laszlo watched the play, standing mesmerized behind the seated gamblers. There were never less than twenty or thirty thousand crowns on the table. Donci Illesvary, young Rosgonyi, Wülffenstein and Gedeon Pray were all there and whether they bet high or low they always won. Stacks of chips were ranged in front of Neszti Szent-Gyorgyi and across the table from him sat Zeno Arzenovics; but no one was standing near Zeno, for onlookers don't like to stay too close to a loser. All those not playing were grouped behind Szent-Gyorgyi across the table: it was as if everyone were laying siege to the rich man from Bacska who, his elbows spread wide on the baize-covered table and seated between two empty chairs, stood his ground with a stony, expressionless face. Each time he lost he calmly noted the sum on a slip of paper by his side. The only sign that these continual losses were becoming a serious matter even for him was the chewed-up state of the cigar in his mouth. 'Sixteen! *Banco!*' He lost again. 'Twenty-four! *Banco!*' That went too. And so it went on. Arzenovics did not win once; but one of the others at the table won twenty-eight times running, and most of what he won had been lost by the Black Cockatoo.

A little voice inside Laszlo said: 'You could win all you need on a single hand!' but Gyeroffy did not move. The voice went on: 'Try it! The money's on the table: you've only got to grab it! You can stake ten or fifteen thousand, that's all you need, and there's plenty in your pocket. Remember Napoleon's '*La victoire est aux gros bataillons!*' But Laszlo stood fast, not moving, only his hand fingering his waistcoat pocket. Then Pray, who was sitting next to the empty chair on Arzenovic's right, won nine times running. 'You idiot!' muttered Laszlo's little voice. 'If you'd joined in as I suggested a lot of that would be yours. Go on! Join in! Just with the four thousand that's your own, if you must, but at least with that...'

At this moment the Steward came round to see if anyone needed more chips or wanted to cash in their winnings.

'Here! Bring me a float!' said Laszlo as he passed, and sat down in the empty place between Zeno and Pray. It was considered lucky to sit on the right of a big loser. When the *taille* came in front of him Laszlo uttered those decisive words: *'Passe le main!'* Some time went by before the cards came his way again. They remained for a long time on the other side of the table. In the meantime Laszlo ordered his bottle of absinthe to be brought up to him and, feeling a chill of fear run down his spine, took several large swigs to chase away the unwelcome feeling. The pack came round to him at last. Zeno, on his left, won a single coup. Laszlo put two thousand crowns on the table. He won. He won four more times and when the fifth time came he lost but, even though he had not halved, some twenty thousand remained on the table in front of him, for his last bank had not been matched.

Now Laszlo was flooded with a strange sense of liberation, his conscious mind hardly registering what was going on around him. He felt as if he were floating in a great sea, on the crest of waves that themselves were merely the surface of profound unknown depths. He was like a man who, after days thirsting in a waterless desert, could at last plunge his body in a cool mountain stream. In this instant he was almost happy, freed of the nagging thoughts and self-reproaches that had recently so haunted his imagination. Now he thought of nothing but the game, the *esprit de taille* – the way the cards were running. This was the only thing of importance in the world: for this one had to know if one really wanted to win.

Laszlo no longer played with the elegant disdain which has so won Neszti Szent-Gyorgyi's admiration when he had started playing eighteen months before. At that time everything had seemed unreal, the chips signifying only numbers, not money; for then all that mattered was that he should be accepted as an equal among them, accepted and respected. But later, firstly when he had lost Klara by breaking his word to her and even more so since the day when Fanny had paid his debts by pawning her pearls, Laszlo had played with a fierce intensity, intent only upon winning. Win! Win! At all costs he must, must win... and, as a

PART SIX

result, he played with intense determination, his nerves stretched ever tauter by the knowledge of his mounting losses and rapidly approaching ruin.

The time had come when any heavy loss would mean disaster.

The game continued for a long time as fast and furious as when Laszlo had first come in to watch. Now that he was playing the pile of chips in front of him sometimes grew and sometimes dwindled almost to nothing. At nearly half-past four the run of the cards changed. Arzenovics suddenly began to hold better cards, winning outright several times running. Gyeroffy, still on his right, started to swim with the bank, though by no means betting high. In a few moments he was losing heavily. A chill ran down his spine. Now he was really in deep water, for he was playing with money that was not his. He knew that he must not do this, must not run after his money, but if he did not, what was he to do? Somehow he had to win back what he had lost. Twice more he tried to come to the surface, like a man drowning; and twice more he sank to the depths, losing all he had staked. The Black Cockatoo still held the bank, but Laszlo sat back in his chair, the world darkening around him.

He closed his eyes, but fiery circles danced before him and he came to his senses only when the Steward announced that five o'clock had struck and everyone else started to get up and leave.

'How much do I owe, please?' said Laszlo as he got up from his chair beside Zeno.

'Wait a moment, I'll just add up! Seventy-two, yes, that's it.'

'Thank you, I just wanted to know.' said Laszlo, and walked slowly to the door and down the stairs. He fingered the thick wad of notes in his pocket to pay. He had eighty-six thousand. It was there, still there...

It was daylight when Laszlo walked home. Market carts were rumbling through the streets and the refuse collectors' bells tinkled as they stopped in front of one house after another.

───※───

Laszlo slept until the late afternoon. Then, lying in the darkened room, he took stock of his position and passed judgement on himself. He sentenced himself to social death. From this, he realized, there was no escape. The choice was simple – public disgrace or secret shame. Either he would be thrown out of the Casino for not paying his debts, and out of society, too, of course, or else he could pay his debts and forget about redeeming Fanny's pearls, thereby living a lie, living without honour, no better than that Wickwitz whom he had publicly insulted for doing precisely the same! He had to choose one of these alternatives; there was nothing else open to him. It would be terrible to live on, shunned by everyone and branded as a fool and a defaulter, but it would be even more terrible to have to live with his secret shame if he did not honour his debt to Fanny. The first would be more bearable, for all his worldly ambitions had crumbled to dust anyhow during the last year. He said to himself that everything had to come to an end sooner or later, and that if social ruin was to be his fate it was better that it should come of his own free will and by his own decision.

He sat for a long time at the desk he had placed in the window and where once he had worked so hard upon his music and with such a will. Now it was covered in dust, unused for many months, and on it was the packet of banknotes, worth more than he had lost the previous night, which was to be the ransom for Fanny's pearls, wrapped in brown paper and tied with thread, untouched. And so it should remain. This was her money, not his, and if he were to use a cent of it he would be a thief as well. That he would not do.

Now that his mind was at last made up he felt a calm indifference spread over him, as if he were making plans not for himself but for someone long since forgotten.

For the next two days Laszlo was extremely busy. First of all he went to the jeweller's in the Dorottya Street where he was told that Mr Bacherach had gone away for a few days but was expected back soon: at two o'clock on the day after next he would, no doubt of it, be back in the shop. Then he went up to the old quarter near the royal palace, to the house in Donath Street, gave his notice, paid for the last quarter's rent and sold his furniture, naturally for far less than it was worth. Then he packed up all Fanny's things – her silken wraps, kimonos, cosmetics, slippers, everything he could find that belonged to her – and had it all posted to the Beredy Palais. Then he arranged for his piano to be sent to Kozard.

It took Laszlo two days to get all this done. On the second day he gave up the Museum Street flat. He removed all his clothes from the cupboards and carefully packed them in his trunk and suitcases. As he did so he became aware of the new grey morning coat which he had worn only on the day of the King's Cup race and never again since. It was lying on his bed, the striped trousers beside it and on the floor the black and beige shoes with their wooden lasts in place. It was as though the corpse of his former life lay there on the bed, empty, inert, disembowelled. He

PART SIX

folded everything carefully and as he picked up the waistcoat, a little betting slip fell to the floor from the breast pocket; the number nine looked reproachfully up at him from the threadbare carpet. He picked it up. It had been the tote ticket for that ill-omened bet, the bet he had lost. His superstitious words came back to him; suddenly ringing in his head he could hear his reply when Fanny had asked him how much he had risked: 'Not much! Only my life!' How true that had been! He thought about it for a few moments, then slipped the little paper back into the pocket from which it had fallen and packed the whole suit as if it had never meant anything to him. He felt no excitement or emotion of any sort: he might have been packing away the life and memories of someone he did not know.

A little before midday, the telephone rang. It was the secretary of the Casino reminding him that precisely at noon that day the forty-eight hours' delay would be up and that if Count Gyeroffy's debts had not by then been settled, his name would be posted on the blackboard.

'Thank you! I understand,' said Laszlo, and rang off.

So his name would be on the board, which wasn't black even though they called it so. In fact it was a large rectangle of smooth green felt in a frame two metres wide. On it, fastened only by a drawing pin, would be a little slip of paper with a name written on it, nothing more, but everyone knew what it meant ... if the person whose name appeared there had not settled his losses within one week he would automatically be scratched from the list of members. Laszlo had once seen there such a name, though now he could not recall whose it was. It hardly mattered, for now it would be his, pilloried there for all to see – Count Laszlo Gyeroffy – just that, no more. It would remain there for a week and then it would disappear ... for ever.

The telephone rang again. This time it was Neszti Szent-Gyorgyi's butler saying that his master would like to see Count Gyeroffy at once if that were possible. Laszlo automatically replied that he would, only later wondering why he had been summoned and regretting that he had not refused to go. However, he had said he would and he could hardly back out of it now. Therefore he picked up his hat and gloves and went out, but not before putting the packet of money in his pocket, for Mr Bacherach would be in his shop at two o'clock.

Count Neszti lived quite close by in a house surrounded by a garden in Horanszky Street. It was a strange house and everything inside bore the imprint of its owner's tastes. The floors were covered with the skins of lions and tigers, shot of course by Count Neszti himself, and the walls were closely patterned by the stuffed heads of more wild game also slaughtered by the owner of the house. Under these trophies, low bookcases contained every issue of the stud book and on the chimney-shelf were arranged a multitude of great cups and trophies which his horses had won all over the world during the past three decades. When Laszlo came in he found Count Neszti seated in a deep armchair, the remains of his breakfast on a table beside him. He was smoking a pipe because he liked it, and because he believed that every pleasure should be indulged even if it were not the fashion.

'Come along in,' he said in his usual swift monotone. He gestured Laszlo towards a chair. 'Sit down, I want to ask you something.' He put up his monocle. 'Did you know that your name has been posted on the blackboard?'

'I know.'

'Well? Can you settle ... or not?'

Laszlo hesitated for a moment, his elbow pressed tightly against the wad in his pocket.

'No,' he said. 'I can't.' He looked Szent-Gyorgyi firmly in the face. Count Neszti let his eye-glass drop. He lifted a hand to his face and twirled his long drooping moustaches. Not a muscle moved, his features might have been carved from granite.

'So you can't! I thought as much.' He, too, paused for a moment. Then he passed a hand over the smooth marble-like surface of his bald skull before asking: 'How much is it altogether?'

'Seventy-two thousand on word of honour and five thousand signed for.'

'And what do you intend to do about it?' said Count Neszti with ice in his voice. Laszlo continued to look the older man in the eye, but he did not answer or move, only his fingers imperceptibly caressed the money in his pocket.

There was silence for a few minutes. Then Szent-Gyorgyi put his monocle once more to his eye and, his words clipped hard like the clanking of a rusty cog-wheel, he said: 'I shall settle the debt. For your part you will immediately inform the Casino of your resignation as a member. I will arrange that this is accepted without query. You will do this in writing. There is paper on the table.' and he pointed with the stem of his pipe to a writing desk that stood in front of the window.

Gyeroffy did as he was told. He walked over to the desk and

when he had finished writing and handed the paper to his host, he tried to stammer out his thanks, saying that naturally as soon as he could he . . . Count Neszti interrupted him: 'I care nothing for all that! And please do not thank me. I am not doing this for you but because I do not like to see disgrace fall on someone bearing a noble name like yours. That is the only reason.' The monocle dropped from his eye: for Count Neszti the matter was settled, the case finished and there was nothing more to be said. He did not put out his hand when Laszlo rose to say goodbye and the latter knew that his punishment had started.

What would he have thought if he'd known that the money was in my pocket all the time, thought Laszlo, smiling in cynical self-mockery as he found his way out through the garden to the street.

When Laszlo arrived at the jewellers he was told that Mr Bacherach was in the shop and would be with him in a moment. Then he was shown into the room lined with showcases where Fanny had arranged to pawn her pearls. He sat down in the same armchair that had been offered to the Countess Beredy. After a short wait the fat bespectacled little jeweller came in and asked who it was that he had the honour to serve. Laszlo gave his name.

'And how can I serve your Lordship?' asked Bacherach, seating himself at the chair behind the table.

'Before leaving for Italy Countess Beredy entrusted me with the sum which you had advanced her on the security of her pearls. Eighty-six thousand crowns, was it not?'

'That is so,' said Bacherach, counting the banknotes that Gyeroffy had placed on the table. When he had finished he said: 'What does her Ladyship wish me to do with the pearls?'

'The Countess would like you to keep them in safe custody until she returns. Then she will send round for them. In the meantime, however, please give me a paper confirming that the Countess's account has been settled and that the pearls are at her disposal any time she might wish to collect them. Naturally the paper will mention only Countess Beredy's name. Mine should not appear.'

A discreet smile hovered for a moment over the merchant's fat face. Then he bowed slightly, rose, and said: 'Certainly, your Lordship. It will be done at once!' He hurried out of the room and in a few minutes was back with a letter, which he signed in Laszlo's presence before putting on the firm's official stamp and handing it over.

Laszlo went straight to the post office and sent off Bacherach's receipt to Fanny by registered letter.

With the words 'It is finished' ringing in his head, Laszlo stepped out, head held high, and walked briskly home. As he passed the Casino, on the other side of the street, he looked across defiantly thinking that at last he had rejoined the ranks of the just.

Back in his little apartment, which was now empty of nearly all his things, he looked around to make sure that nothing had been forgotten. From the wall he took down a hand-coloured photograph of his father that he had brought from Kozard and laid it in a suitcase that had not yet been closed. Then he thought he must write some line to Fanny for good manners required at least that. He had no writing paper so he took a visiting card from his case and wrote on it: '*Thank you for everthing!*' It was enough. It said all that was necessary. Then he addressed it to the Beredy Palais so that she would find it on her return.

Now it was nearly dark. Laszlo looked at his watch and saw that it was already after five. He had decided to take the six o'clock train, hoping that he would see no one that he knew and so would be able to travel alone. He called down to the hall porter to carry down his luggage and summon a carriage and, while waiting, went over to the window embrasure.

The trees in the Museum garden were still bare. Above them the sloping slate roof of the Kollonich Palais could be clearly seen rising high above the corner of Sandor Street, the long elegant lines emphasized by the copper ribbing that had been placed every few metres and now glowed in the light of the street-lamps. The roof was cluttered with many chimneys which could only be seen from high up and far away. Laszlo gazed at that enchanted house, now for ever beyond his reach, and he thought back to the evening when he had returned from Simonvasar delirious with happiness and how on that evening he had stood at the same window and looked for a long time at the same distant roofs. Then the boulevards had been illuminated with a thousand brilliant lights, lights that were set in long straight rows and had seemed like the symbol of his triumph. Funeral torches now! he thought grimly. Down below the brakes of a tram screeched like an animal in pain...

Chapter Ten

AFTER KOSSUTH'S AND ANDRASSY'S NEGOTIATIONS with the King's representatives a new coalition government had been formed under the leadership of Dr Wekerle. Then in the first week of May there was a general election. A large majority was won by the candidates of the 1848 Party and, along with other members of the old opposition, the liberal party of Count Tisza was practically wiped out, only a few of his old supporters obtaining seats as independent members. The representatives of the ethnic minorities increased their numbers to twenty-four, but this signified little in a house of four hundred and fify-three seats. Among the successful candidates from Transylvania was Uncle Ambrus, old Bartokfay, Farkas Alvinczy, Bela Varju, Dr Szigmond Boros, who was appointed a junior minister, and young Kamuthy, who just managed to scrape in a few weeks later as a result of a controverted election which had to be re-held.

Parliament reassembled in a cheerful mood. After the Royal Decree announcing that the new Parliament's first duty was to work out and put into effect a programme of universal suffrage, the Speaker's opening address, which spoke of the 'sovereignty of the people' had no more effect than the distant rumbling of a thunder storm that had passed. Peace had been declared: now it was time to get down to work to catch up and complete all the essential business of government which had been so neglected during the unconstitutional period of Fejervary's government. There were national commercial agreements to be ratified, defence and other national estimates to be voted and, in the counties and districts, order had to be restored and the confusion resulting from the 'Guardsman' government's appointment of unacceptable officials, cleaned up: for it was essential that these unpopular 'lackeys' should be weeded out, like tares among the corn. Joska Kendy, who now became Prefect in Kukullo, set about the task with undisguised delight and vigour, so much so that his zeal rivalled even that of Ordung in Maros-Torda, who was now busy finishing off his old enemy, Beno Peter Balog.

Balint saw something of this unscrupulous settling of old scores when he went to Lelbanya. There someone had slandered the honest notary Daniel Kovacs who had served the little town so long and so unselfishly and who had been so helpful with the starting of Abady's altruistic schemes for the co-operative and cultural centre. It took him a week of hard work in Kovac's defence before the matter was settled and he could return to the capital.

In Budapest Balint attended the sitting of Parliament though he was in a depressed mood and found it difficult, however hard he tried, to work up much interest in the proceedings. He also tried to get on with the book he had started in Portofino, but inspiration was lacking. It was as if the spring that had spurred him on had broken when he had to give up Adrienne. 'Beauty in Action' had been his theme and now, though he tried hard to convince himself that there was beauty in his renunciation of her, perhaps even heroism, he could not rid himself of the disconcerting thought that maybe after all he might subconsciously have been acting from caution, from a desire to escape his responsibilities. Surely it could not be that. Adrienne had written those agonized and agonizing words *'Don't kill me . . . I beseech you . . . don't kill me . . . !'* What could he have done but obey?

When Isti Kamuthy was finally elected, second time round, he came to the capital to take his seat. One of the first people he saw in Budapest was Balint, and he at once told him how he had travelled in the same train as the Miloths, for old Rattle was going to Baden where his wife now was, while Adrienne and her sisters were going to stay at the Lido in Venice in two days' time.

'I expect you know that Judith ith a little touched in the head,' he lisped. 'They didn't thay a word on the whole trip, though I did my betht to make agreeable converthathon!'

Balint did not reply, but turned on his heel and walked away. He did not want to hear any more; he did not want to discover, even by chance, where they were staying. He had promised himself that he would not see Adrienne again and if he knew where she was it would not be easy to keep that promise; so he decided that for the next few days he would not eat out except in the Casino club dining-room.

That very evening his resolve was broken.

In the centre of town it was stiflingly hot, unbearably so. Accordingly, Balint had himself driven out to the Wampetics Restaurant near the Zoological Gardens. After looking round he told himself that it was so full of people also trying to escape the heat that there would be no point in staying there. He walked across the road and into the City Park. Here, at the Lake Restaurant, it was just the same: throngs of people and the only table free was so near the band that he would be deafened. He decided it would be better to go to Gerbeaud, for though it was much more expensive it was sure to be less crowded...

He saw them as soon as he came in. There, sitting on the left, was the whole Miloth family group. Luckily Rattle and Judith were sitting with their backs to him and could not see him.

It looked as if Margit had not noticed his arrival either. Even Adrienne, though she was facing him, had not looked in his direction and so was unaware of his presence. She was talking to Isti Kamuthy and Joska Kendy and she looked unnaturally pale. Balint decided to place himself so far away from them that they would be unlikely to see him, and also so that, if by chance they did, there would be so many tables between him and them that he could either wave a greeting from a distance or else pretend that he was so pre-occupied with his own affairs that he had not noticed they were there.

He sat down near the lattice-work screen that divided the restaurant from the garden. In the distance he could just see Adrienne's wide-brimmed Florentine straw hat under which her hair seemed even more raven-hued than ever. Occasionally he caught a glimpse of her lips as she conversed with her companions, and once or twice he saw her whole face; but when a fat man sitting near Abady leant forward to shovel more food into his mouth, then Adrienne was once again hidden from view. It was enough, however, to know that she was there even though separated from him by table after table of total strangers. He felt a sort of misterious warmth creep over him.

All at once the crowd in the restaurant started to thin out and Balint's fat neighbour got up and left. Now he could see Addy unimpeded, and now, too, something sang in his heart: Adrienne was looking straight at him, her gaze fixed as if she were trying to say something to him from afar. Her lips moved. After a little while the Miloth party rose and started to move away along the central pathway between the crowded tables. Rattle led the way followed by the two younger girls, Kamuthy and Joska. Adrienne lingered behind the others, apparently engaged in pulling on her gloves. She paused, and as she did so she turned towards Balint, summoning him to come to her.

In an instant he was at her side.

'Tomorrow. Room 23 ... the King Istvan Hotel ... four

o'clock.' It was an order issued so quickly that he barely heard it, her voice barely more than a whisper, feverish and desperate. It was hardly out of her mouth before she had turned and rejoined the others. Balint returned to his own table, his heart racing so hard he thought it would pound its way out of his chest.

Abady found his way to the little old-fashioned hotel where only people from the country stayed, and promptly at four o'clock he knocked on her door and went in.

Addy came forward to meet him, her expression unusually solemn and serious. She did not let him put his arms round her or kiss her cheek but pushed him away with a single imperious finger. She did not even use the familiar form when addressing him. They sat down in two chairs near the window.

'I wanted to see you for just a moment. We haven't got long. The girls have gone shopping with Mlle Morin and they'll be back soon. Did you know? We are going to Venice. We are all very worried about Judith. Since ... well, you know all about that. Since then she's been like someone in a trance, like a sleepwalker. And sometimes she gets so muddled, not often and luckily only those who know her well seem to notice. The doctors told us to try a change of scene, to get her away from all the places that remind her of what's happened. My mother's still away ill and Father cannot get away for long as there's the whole place to run. That is why I am going with them. It wasn't easy to arrange, I can tell you, but in the end I managed it!'

They were silent for a few minutes. Balint trembled with expectancy. He was sure that something else was coming, something that Adrienne had not yet allowed herself to say, but which was fully thought-out, definite and serious. When she spoke at last her voice was cool, with no trace of excitement.

'We are planning to stay at least four weeks, possibly five. At Almasko they have agreed to that ...' Adrienne's onyx-coloured eyes opened very wide. She looked straight into Balint's face and very slowly she said: 'So we have one month. That's all, one month, a whole month ... if you would care to join me ...?'

'Addy! My darling Addy!'

Even now she did not allow him to come any closer to her.

'Not now! No! Later, in Venice. We'll have four weeks together. It's not much, I know, but four whole weeks ... and after that – well, after that it's over!'

'What do you mean, over? Surely you don't mean what you

said up there... that you would...?'

'What does that matter to you? Why should you care?' Addy laughed a new laugh he had never heard, like the deep cooing of doves, a laugh that sprang from some deep, unknown joy. 'Why should you care? Four weeks together ... why should you care what comes after that?'

She rose from her chair, moving her fingers in the air in front of her face as if she were counting.

'You'd better go now. The others will be back any minute and it wouldn't be good if Judith saw you.' He put his arms round her to say goodbye, and she gave him a swift, absent-minded kiss her, thoughts obviously far away. Then she pushed him out of the door.

Abady arrived in Venice in the early afternoon. The sun was shining brightly when he stepped into a gondola and gave the directions of a little-known hotel behind the San Marco Square to which few foreigners ever discovered. At seven o'clock the same evening he went to the Ponte Canonica, just as they had planned in their letters. It was easy for Adrienne to find her way there through the little backstreets where no one would see and recognize her. She was staying in the Danieli Hotel in the old Palazzo Dandolo on the Riva, though she was the only one of her party to do so. Her sisters and Mlle Morin were installed in one of the huge palace hotels on the Lido where Adrienne joined them each day, bathing with them, eating her meals with them, and then returning to Venice in the late afternoon or evening. 'It'll be better like that,' she had said to Margit. 'I can't sleep out here with the roaring of the sea in my ears. Anyhow it's better for Judith if I'm not always before her eyes.'

She wondered afterwards if it might not have been better to have given only one reason – two was perhaps protesting too much – but Margit, cleverer and brighter than the others, had merely replied unconcernedly: 'You're right! I've noticed that she's still rather resentful of you. Far better not to be around all the time.' However, when Adrienne moved out of their hotel and had boarded the launch that would take her to the Danieli, Margit walked slowly back from the quay. As she did so little secret smile played round the corners of her mouth.

The Ponte Canonica is only just behind St Mark's and can be reached either through the basilica itself or by way of a narrow street behind the hotel. It is a bridge of white marble, arched in the centre, with shallow flights of steps leading down to the canal. Balint had his gondola tied up on the side by the little church so that he would be able from afar to see Adrienne as she came to their rendezvous.

The seven o'clock chimes from the nearby Campanile had just sounded when she appeared in the distance, her distinctive walk as elegant as ever. The lines of Adrienne's long legs were clearly etched beneath the thin green silk of her spring dress. Balint did not wait to greet her but returned swiftly to his gondola. In a few minutes she had joined him.

Their gondolier, one Riccardo Lobetti, did not have to be told that Balint and Adrienne's meeting was a romantic tryst. He knew it instinctively and so off he went only asking where he should go when they were well away from the meeting place and were gliding down a lonely stretch of canal bordered by high walls.

'To the Lagoon!' ordered Balint.

The slight splash made by the single oar made a slow gentle rhythm behind them and the long craft swayed slightly at each movement. They glided through deserted canals where the low tide had revealed festoons of river moss that covered the foundations of the tall houses on each side. All around it was quiet with no sound other than the soft swishing of Riccardo's long oar just behind their little curtain-hung cabin. Only sometimes, as they approached the junction with another canal did they hear the long-drawn-out call of the gondolier '*Saa . . . aa . . . i.i.i . . .!*' and from around a corner the answering cry from another as yet unseen boatsman. Their gondola glided on, so skilfully handled by their own invisible oarsman that they never even touched another boat, or the sides of the canals, not even when the passageway was at its narrowest and they met huge heavily-laden barges. No sound, no touch; everything passed as silently as in a dream. To Balint and Adrienne, seated side by side under the flimsy canvas tent of the gondola's tiny cabin, it was like a God-given dream of unexpected ecstasy.

They leant back on the soft cushions, their hands clasped, not speaking, not moving, almost in a trance, as slowly their little craft emerged from the haunted shadows of the canal into the shining radiance of the lagoon itself where the horizon seemed to be at an infinite distance, the late afternoon sun glistening in a thousand reflections on the smooth waters over which they floated. Everything was marvellously pale, in iridescent shades of grey and pearl, with only the faintest hints of the softer shades of

PART SIX

the rainbow. The sky was greyish-blue and the waters bluish-grey, so alike that it was difficult to tell where one began and the other ended. Everything melted into everything else, fusing all they could see into one uncertain, vaporous abstraction. Far in the distance there was what might have been the outlines of an island with, in front of it, other smaller islands identifiable only by the unexpectedly dramatic vertical lines of black cypress trees which looked like distant exclamation marks on a faded parchment.

There was nothing around them but water. Nothing else. Water, only water; and it was as if they were utterly alone in a world of their own, floating over the waters of the lagoon just as their minds floated over the mystery of their love. Adrienne took off her wide-brimmed straw hat and, holding it in her right hand, nestled her left shoulder into Balint's. However, when he bent down to kiss her, she demurred gently but firmly, with a gesture that somehow was not really denying him but only waiting for the right moment. Her brows came together, her eyes looked at something far, far away. She was thinking. Balint sensed that she was remembering all those things that had happened to them both in the past and had now led to this moment when, as they lay in each other's arms, they both knew that very soon their love would be fulfilled. Adrienne went over in her mind all she could remember of the turbulent course of their meetings and she knew that they were now approaching the great turning point in their mutual fate, a turning point that she both ached for and yet feared. They were on the threshold of something ineffably wonderful ... and yet, reviewing in her mind all that had happened in the past, Adrienne was suddenly overcome by a feeling of bleak uncertainty, of terror at the thought of the unknown future. Balint felt it too. Looking at Adrienne's pensive face, he recalled the terrible words of the letter she had written admitting the reality of her love for him but begging him to leave her alone because of what the consummation of their love would force her to do.

He wondered if she still felt the same way. Was she still obsessed by that terrible decision? Was she really prepared to sacrifice her life to pay for these few weeks of happiness? And would he, knowing this, accept the gift of her body? Her soul was already his, so why should he pay such a price to possess her body as well? Because that was what all this amounted to, what it all meant. If they were to have this month of happiness together and then Addy killed herself, it would be far more terrible than dying himself. He could never live on if he carried with him the knowledge that he had allowed it. It would be as if he'd committed murder.

Obsessed and confused by these thoughts Balint knew that now, somehow, all this must be made clear and that he had to extract a promise from her that she would never do anything as terrible as she had threatened. Her ear was close to his mouth, so close that he didn't have to bend down when he whispered: 'May I come to you tonight?'

'After midnight. Before that there are people in the hall...'

Balint squeezed her fingers. He paused for a moment and then said, very softly: 'If... if we should... if it happened, would it mean what you wrote?'

She did not answer and he had to repeat the question. Then she replied in broken uncertain phrases: 'Why should you care? Don't ask me that. Don't think about it.'

'Look, Addy, this cannot be. Things aren't like that...' and he started to say in simple words all that had been torturing him ever since he had her letter. He spoke for a long time, repeating himself over and over again, saying that to make love to her knowing what price had to be paid was unthinkable, cruel and wrong. At that price, never! He spoke warmly, begging her, saying over and over again: 'Not at that price! Not at that price!'

Adrienne did not reply. She only shook her head to show that her mind was made up. He felt her soft curls brushing his face. Finally, when he had talked for a long, long time she said: 'I couldn't live on like that. You, and the other... But it isn't a sacrifice for me, I've thought about it so often.' So Balint started again: but all that Adrienne would say was: 'I can't divorce, you know that. So don't wish me to live. I couldn't...'

They were floating far out in the lagoon. Darkness had fallen and already the lamps were being lit on the three-legged water beacons. Riccardo somehow sensed what was required of him and turned his gondola back towards the town. In the darkness of their little cabin Balint's voice was hoarse with emotion and grief: 'But then I couldn't go on living either! There would be nothing left! I, too... You can be sure of that.'

Adrienne sat up abruptly and, looking hard into Balint's face, cried: 'No! No! That's not the same at all! That you, who love life ... That's not for you!'

'What else would be there for me? What choice would I have?' Balint really meant what he said, though subconsciously he also hoped that maybe this at least would break Adrienne's resolution. But all she now said was: 'That is something I can't accept. Very

PART SIX

well then, there is only one solution. Go away! Leave! Then there'll be nothing to torture ourselves about!'

'There is no other way?'

Once again there was silence between them as they sat together surrounded by the darkness of the night, feeling that endless sadness had spread over the murmuring waters. This was the end. Definitely, finally, for ever, the end. As the gondola edged its way into the narrow entrance of the little canal and dark shadows of great palaces close round them, Balint said: 'I'm too late to catch the night express. Can I come and talk to you, just the way we always have . . . and tomorrow, in the morning, I'll go away.'

'All right. Just as we always have . . .'

❦

When Balint went to Adrienne that night there were no lights in her room. She had purposely not allowed the lamps to be lit for she had cried for a long time and did not want him to see this in her face. It was not completely dark, for the light from the lamps that illuminated the quay outside cast a faint glow through the soft folds of the white net curtains and it was reflected from the ceiling on to the bed like the first light of dawn. The room was heavy with the mingled scent of the woman and that strange aroma from the lagoon, composed equally of the salt of the ocean and the decay of the city.

Balint sat down beside her, leaning against the cushions behind her head. They started to talk, but not coherently, both of them uttering short broken phrases that had no beginning and no end. Their faces came ever closer to each other, their mouths not just touching as they whispered to each other sad words of farewell, goodbye . . . goodbye . . . goodbye. As they did so, from time to time their lips met in a tender kiss, a caress that was sorrowful rather than passionate. And slowly, for Adrienne, it was as if her mouth, her hands, her hair and skin, had a separate life, totally independent of her will. She herself felt that she was dreaming and around her head the thick black curls fell tumbling over her face released by some magic power from the tight coils and knots into which she had bound them earlier that evening. Like Medusa's snakes, the curls of Adrienne's unruly hair moved mysteriously over her face, covering her eyes, her mouth and having a life of their own, leading her of their own volition to madness and abandon. Her fingers, long, slender and searching along his back, his neck, pressed him to her as if she needed to be reassured that he really was there, and all the while her wide, swelling lips kissed Balint's face and hands, kissed the curls that fell between their mouths like a curtain, and even kissed the air. In Adrienne that great, latent force of nature, so long suppressed, was now at long last set free so that she was totally possessed by that joy of life which Balint had seen in her so long ago at the skating rink. Now her back was arching, as it had then, and her legs moving rhythmically, her arms flung wide until, a little later, softly, so softly that he hardly heard her words she asked, in wonder: 'What am I feeling? What is this? What is this?' with the astonishment of one who, for the first time experiences a marvel whose existence until then was unimagined.

The young man leaned above her, his approaching fulfilment pulsating through him like great waves of intoxicating fever. Now there was nothing left of the hunter, the coarse human stalking its mate; these had been wiped out by the terrible reality of a primeval, eternal emotion that had swept over him with the inexorable force of a tropical storm. In one tiny corner of his conscious mind, however, there still lurked the memory of their talk that afternoon, the knowledge that in four weeks' time all this joy must be paid for … Gently, but urgently, he whispered in her ear: 'Do you want to? Now?' fully aware to what he was committing them both. And when Addy did not answer in words, but flung her arms around him, drawing him down upon her, opening wide her mouth to receive his ardent kisses, surely she knew it too?'

For a long time they lay together in each other's arms, and from outside the room could be heard a faint rustling sound, which might have been the night breeze in the trees of some distant garden or the soft movements of the waters of the lagoon but which to them sounded like the beating of the wings of fate, that fate which had now and for all time chained them to one another.

From far away in the distance could be heard the soft notes of a tenor voice singing a late-night serenade to his beloved. The white folds of the voluminous net curtains moved in the early morning breeze, and outside the sky began to lighten with the approach of dawn. Adrienne, who had been lying wide-awake in Balint's arms, said: 'It's time for you to go!'

'Already? But it's still dark!'

'It's time, and I want to be alone. I have to think.' Adrienne's amber-coloured eyes were serious. She was asking, beseeching, but she was also giving an order.

PART SIX

'We'll meet this afternoon? At the same place as yesterday? We'll meet there again?'
'Yes. But be there at six, I shall be free by then.'

This time Balint waited in the gondola to be sure that no one witnessed their meeting. Before him on the bench lay a huge bouquet of dark red roses, but when Adrienne had arrived he did not give them to her, indeed he did not even mention them. As she stepped into the boat he rose and kissed her hand as he always did, but today with even a touch more formality and respect than before: and when she sat down beside him his first words were not of love but were a simple question, spoken softly, asking if she would like to visit the church of Santa Maria dei Miracoli. He explained that it was very close to where they were now, and was a miracle of beauty made out of white marble by Pietro Lombardi. He spoke so quietly and in such a matter-of-fact way, allowing no trace of triumph of possession to colour his voice or manner, that there was nothing to remind Addy of what had passed between them only a few hours before. In this way he helped her to pass through what could have been for her an awkward moment after holding him off for so long. Even later on Balint did not speak of their night together: only the bunch of red roses spoke for him. There it lay, almost at her feet, paying homage to her with that great splash of red, the colour of passion, the huge blossoms wide open to symbolize the ripeness of fulfilment.

Only later, as they floated gently back, did he murmur in her ear: 'May I . . . like yesterday?'

And so the days passed, each as dreamlike as the last. Sometimes they visited a church, or looked for a little-known picture that hung halfconcealed on the dark walls of some neglected *Scuola*, but mostly, unlike the tourists who never tired of sight-seeing, they remained in their gondola, floating down obscure canals and always, in the end, out on to the great expanse of the lagoon, lying there in each others arms in sweet exhaustion, fingers entwined while they were still in town, kissing with joy and abandon as soon as they were away from the shore. They always had the same gondolier. From his post behind their cabin, their faithful Riccardo plied his oar so slowly and silently that it seemed that the gondola was propelled by no human hand. Each day, they would go even further from the city, until it seemed that they were the only two people in the whole wide world and that they would float on for all eternity, surrounded only by the mother-of-pearl waters of the lagoon and the faint rainbow iridescence of the late afternoon sky. Time stood still and nothing was real except their love, only their love.

Never again had either of them made the slightest allusion to what they had so long discussed on their first day together. Both were aware, all too aware, of what the future might hold, but by tacit mutual understanding, they pushed aside such thoughts as if they never had been and never would be.

Adrienne passed her mornings on the Lido beach where the sun beat down ferociously, very different from the soft radiance of the afternoon light over the lagoon. She and her sisters used to swim for hours together as all of them had been strong swimmers since the days they had splashed about in the great lake at home and been taught to swim when still young children. They felt quite at home in the water and now, in Venice, they bathed separately, Adrienne consciously taking herself a little way off from her sisters for she had noticed that Judith's face still hardened if she came near. It was quite enough to be with them at lunch or sit with them in the hotel lounge in the early afternoon when Mlle Morin went upstairs to take a nap. In the mornings she swam alone, energetically and with great long strokes and almost savage pleasure, just as she did when she walked, or skated or danced.

Often Adrienne swam a long way out to sea, where the waters were dark and deep and far bluer than closer inshore. When she returned after swimming far out she would often stop for a moment as soon as she arrived in shallow water where she could stand with the little waves just below her knees. Sometimes she would stand there for a long time, quite motionless, and then, the water running off the black swimsuit which clung wet and shining to the lines of her body, she was like some polished marble statue.

She stood there, oblivious of the many men who eyed her from the shore. She never even noticed their looks. For her only one man existed, and he would be waiting for her later in the gondola by the quay under the Ponte Canonica. So she would stand there just gazing out to sea, looking towards the far horizon, head held high, brows knitted as if she were thinking hard.

Where she stood, the waves flowed over her feet and legs and were yellowy-green in colour, for here it was shallow and the golden sand beneath could be seen through the translucent water. Only farther out, where the deep waters started, did the sea become dark and mysterious.

PART SIX

There were no ships to be seen except, very occasionally in the far distance, they could glimpse the sails of fishing boats going towards the shores of Istria where the catches were unusually rich for the Adriatic. One little boat was always there, riding at anchor. It was the boat of the life-guard placed there by the authorities to make sure no one swam out too far or got into difficulties out of reach of the shore. Outside the limits of where most people swam there were dangerous currents against which even the most experienced of swimmers were powerless. Once taken by one of these no one could get back without help. Adrienne often looked out towards that little boat, anchored there so far from the shore.

She seemed thoughtful, as if weighing up something in her mind...

Chapter Eleven

ON THE SECOND SATURDAY IN JULY, Riccardo Lobetti, the gondolier, who had hardly ever opened his mouth when he was with them as if he knew and understood that they wanted to be alone with their love, suddenly made them a proposition, volubly and excitedly crying: '*Domani sera, la festa del Redentore. Una bellissima festa. Magnifica! Aaah... magnifica...*'

The great feast of the Redeemer, the most famous of the Venetian Carnivals, was to take place the following evening. Riccardo wanted them to see it from his gondola.

'*Bisogna vederla! Bisogna vederla! Gran' festa!* – You must see it, it's a great festival' he said, waving his hands in the air to emphasize what an important occasion this was. They accepted at once.

About ten o'clock Riccardo arrived at the Palazzo Dandolo, where he picked up Adrienne and rowed her to the Piazzetta where Balint was waiting. Lobetti, who normally wore a grey linen garment, none too clean and much worn, was now clad in all his finery; a bright red silk shirt, white and yellow striped cotton trousers, and round his waist a magnificent broad green cummerbund with golden tassels. He was resplendent, and his gondola was the same. In the place of the canvas-covered cabin he had constructed a great sea-shell of basket-work covered all over with flowers, and flowers also decorated the length of the gunwales right up to the high curved prow from whose top hung a lighted oil-lamp.

'*Per la donna* – for the lady!' repeated Lobetti several times, bowing deeply when they congratulated him. They moved off slowly towards the Giudecca.

There were some lights visible in the distance, but the moment that they had rounded the point of the Dogana they were greeted by a marvellous and unexpected sight.

The great stretch of water, three hundred yards across, between the Zattere and the three islands of the Giudecca, was spanned by a temporary bridge festooned with electrical bulbs in the form of arches and pillars of fire. On one side the great Palladian church of the Redentore was a blaze of light and everywhere there were boats, thousands of them, covering the water as far as they could see. The state barges of the old patrician families had been brought out; every gondola in Venice seemed to be there and all were covered with flowers glowing in the light of baroque lanterns. Here also were the long barges normally used for transporting seaweed or wood or reeds across lagoons, the broad market boats that supplied the markets all through the week, little *sandali* and other rowing boats, all packed with people in festive clothes. Everyone mingled together, the richest beside the poorest, the lavish beside the meagre. One thing they had in common: all were decorated and everywhere people were laughing and happy. Some of the smaller craft, like Riccardo's gondola, carried a bower of flowers, while the large barges had tables laid with food and drink and were peopled with handsome young men and pretty girls. The boys played guitars and mouth-organs and caressed the girls, who in their turn laughed and sang and giggled and kissed the boys and hid their faces in their brightly coloured shawls, those *scialli* which were an essential part of Venice's traditional costume. Every boat was packed with as many people as could crowd aboard and everywhere was laughter and happiness.

In the centre of this vast crowd of boats was the largest of them all, the 'Serenata', which rose in the water high above all the others and was hung with delicate paper lanterns. On board all the singers were in theatrical costume and on the deck Balint and Adrienne could just see the faces of Harlequin and Columbine dancing a pantomime, though they could not get close enough to make out what the others were doing.

Behind them many other gondolas were being rowed as swiftly as their gondoliers were able, everyone wanting to be right at the heart of this great concourse of boats. In front of them there were so many craft that Balint and Adrienne could not see the surface of the water and, looking back to the Dogana, they saw that it was now the same behind them as well. It was a world of boats, nothing but boats, stretching across the waters as if the world were made of nothing else.

Then, from behind the gleaming temporary bridge, the fireworks began.

To Balint and Adrienne this was almost more dreamlike and unreal than had been their solitary excursions across the lagoon each evening. In the sky the myriad stars of exploding flame made the night sky seem even darker and more remote and, though the spectators were nearly blinded by the brightness of these lightning flashes of brilliance, to those standing behind, everyone in front of them became mere shadows, dark silhouettes rather than real living people. So it happened that for Balint and Adrienne, though they were surrounded by life and light and noise and the whole pulsating festive crown, it was still as if they alone existed and were real.

It was their last carefree evening together.

The next morning, as on every other of their stay on the Lido, the younger Miloth girls went swimming while Mlle Morin remained in the shade of the beach cabin.

A little later, Margit, who was coming in from a long swim, heard shouting, not as might be expected from the shore but farther out to sea. She put her feet to the ground and stood up. She could not see much as the sea came up to her shoulders. All she could make out was that the noise came from the loud-hailer on the guard-boat. Margit realized at once that someone must be in difficulties as the guard-boat was no longer at anchor and stationary, but was being rowed frenziedly out to sea by the two guards.

Margit looked around, her eyes searching for Judith, who should have been close behind her: she was nowhere to be seen.

Instinctively, she knew the alarm was for her sister, who must have swum too far out to sea, to the undertow and the fatal offshore currents. From where she was standing on tiptoe, the sea coming up to her shoulders, all Margit could see was a tiny speck that from time appeared above the waves. She was certain it was Judith and at once struck out as fast as she could towards that little speck, her strong young arms cutting the water in a powerful crawl. She thought of nothing but how to save Judith and, as her head was half under water, she head nothing more of the commotion on the beach and did not see that a motor-launch was being hurriedly pushed out into the shallow water.

Margit had to work hard to make headway against the waves. Water splashed over her but she battled on, using all her strength so as to get there as quickly as possible. She never heard the launch race past her and it was already returning to shore when she suddenly found herself being hauled on board. It was just in time, for she was now so tired that she too was at breaking point and had to be lifted out of the water by the strong arms of the beach guards.

Judith was lying like a corpse in the middle of the boat. Margit crouched by her, panting. At this moment the ambulance boat arrived alongside and Judith was lifted into it. Artificial respiration was started at once as the hospital launch sped towards the shore.

Judith was still not breathing when she was carried onto the beach. They laid her down and once again tried to pump life into her unconscious body.

At this moment Adrienne arrived on the beach. Seeing the tumult and confusion in front of the hotel beach cabins she asked someone what had happened.

'*Una donna ungherese e morta!*' was the reply.

She thought of Judith immediately and ran towards the crowd, pushing people aside in urgent haste.

There, on the golden sand, surrounded by a crowd of onlookers eager to gaze at the detail of disaster, lay Judith, quite naked, for her swimming costume had been ripped off her, her little girlish breasts bare to the sky, her ribs and pelvis bones pathetically outlined through the naked flesh of her young body. Three burly life-guards were still desperately trying to bring her back to life.

Just as Adrienne got near, Judith opened her eyes; but in them there was no expression, no sign that she knew where she was or what had happened to her. Then she closed them again, but already her breathing was regular and so the guards flung a wrap over her, put her on a stretcher and carried her to the hotel. There Judith fell into a deep sleep.

Young Margit too was still a little confused and had to be helped to her room. Though she protested vigorously, her legs would not carry her and she had unwillingly to agree. Mlle Morin, who, at the sight of Judith's unconscious form, had cried: '*Oh, mon dieu! Oh, cette pauvre enfant!*' and collapsed in a faint to the ground, was picked up by the largest of the beach guards, thrown across his hefty shoulders like some broken old doll, and carried upstairs.

PART SIX

Margit was soon herself again. After lunch she started to search among Judith's things and found hidden in her underclothes a bulky envelope which, she could tell from the postmark, had been forwarded from Mezo-Varjas and must have arrived the previous day. In the envelope was a bundle of letters tied with a ribbon and with it a letter in an unknown hand which read:

Dear Countess Judith,
I have learned that a certain Baron W. has left the country suddenly as a result of some unpleasant scandal. This person at one time used to stay in my house. Once, though whether it was to gain my confidence or out of sheer bravado, he showed me the enclosed letters. Thinking that if he showed them to me he was quite capable of showing them to other people too, I took them from him and kept them in a safe place. When the scandal broke I wondered for a long time what I should do with them. First I thought they should be burnt, but then I thought you might be worried thinking they were still in Baron W.'s hands and that he might – for he would be quite capable of such a thing – use them to blackmail either you or your family. So finally I thought it best to send them back to you so that you would know that there was no such danger. Please believe me when I tell you that no one else knows of their existence and no one, apart from myself, ever saw them while they were in my house.
Sara Bogdan

Margit and Adrienne read this together. So this was the explanation! Poor Judith. What had happened that morning was obviously no accident, no unlucky accident due to recklessness.

Judith had wanted to die, and this well-meaning letter was the last death-thrust to her already wounded and grieving heart. Before she had learned what had happened to her letters she had believed firmly that everything that had taken place was the result of bad luck and the malice of other people. In her eyes her lover, that handsome young officer, had committed only one fault, and that was that he had not told her about his need to run away and that he had left her alone in Kolozsvar instead of taking her with him.

All had been a terrible shock and it had been enough to kill her confidence in the man and his declarations of love for her. But now this, this was sheer ignominy – and the knowledge that he had actually shown those letters, in which she had bared her heart, to another woman and had allowed that other woman to keep them, that was enough, her sisters realized at once, to make her try to kill herself that morning...

Later in the afternoon, when Judith woke up, they saw that she was not quite normal, that her manner was strange, disconnected, uninterested. Dutifully she drank the beef broth they gave her to drink. She even sipped a little brandy, but when the doctor came to examine her, she merely mouthed an odd sort of dumb laughter, as if she did not know where she was nor what was required of her.

Adrienne started to tell all this to Balint when, a little later, they met at the foot of the bridge where Lobetti always brought their gondola. As they floated away from their trysting place she told him every detail and, when she had come to the end of her tale, she slid down into his arms, seeking consolation and forgetfulness.

In the days that followed Judith recovered physically. Already on the morning after the 'accident' she was up and about in their suite, eating her food with appetite, but there was no improvement mentally. She had lost that hard, determined reserve that had been so marked in Transylvania and in the first weeks in Venice. Then, though somewhat stiff with the others and always distrustful of Adrienne, she had been full of strength, will-power and resolution. Now she was like a sick child, weak and needing constant guidance. She laughed without reason, and when she spoke there was something peculiar about her speech, for her words came out unnaturally slowly and she talked in a slovenly and drooling manner, little drops of saliva falling from the corners of her mouth.

The day of the accident Adrienne wrote to her father to tell him what had occurred, describing everything as if it really had all just been an unfortunate accident which had ended well. However, a few days later she found herself obliged to write again, admitting that Judith's state was giving them cause for alarm, and that the mental specialist they had consulted had ordered them to take her somewhere quiet, either to the country or to a sanatorium. Something had to be done at once, and so Adrienne wrote to ask what she should do.

As she wrote this second letter to her father Adrienne knew that this meant the end of her stay, the end of those enchanted weeks of unexpected bliss and happiness, the end of everything...

After a few days a letter came from her mother, but it contained nothing but complaints. Then old Rattle wrote to say that he was

PART SIX

too busy to come himself and so had asked his son-in-law, Pali Uzdy, to send out the old butler, Maier, who used to be a male nurse and who could speak German. No doubt if Uzdy could spare him, his presence would be a great help to Adrienne.

One evening while they were waiting for an answer from home, Riccardo rowed Balint and Adrienne farther than they had ever been before, southwards towards the salt-swept fishing town of Chioggia. It was already dusk when they started, for Adrienne now felt she had to stay on much later at the Lido.

In silence they floated over the calm waters, leaning closely against each other and holding each other tight, both too overwhelmed by their approaching separation to speak.

For once the weather was cloudy, and when they went far out, so far out that they could hardly see any sign of the shore they told Riccardo to stop rowing and just let them glide as the current took them. They stayed like this for a long time. Here the lagoon was at its widest and loneliest. There were no other boats to be seen and, as dusk slowly fell, the faint lines of the distant shores disappeared until they could no longer distinguish the horizon from the darkening sky above. Now all was a uniform greyness, empty, cold and lifeless.

Both of them felt that they were surrounded by a void, an empty space that had nothing above and nothing below, no sound, no colour, no past and no future, and that they glided disembodied over a nothingness that had no beginning and no end.

That night they returned very late having hardly exchanged a word the whole time they were together.

The next afternoon Adrienne arrived at their meeting exactly at the hour they had arranged. Without a word she handed Balint a telegram which read: 'ARRIVING TOMORROW AT MIDDAY – UZDY'. That was all. He gave it back looking at her enquiringly. Without a trace of emotion Adrienne, in a cold voice, said: 'You must leave here tomorrow!'

They sat in the gondola slightly apart from each other, but as soon as they emerged from the narrow dark canal and were well away from the city they fell hungrily into each other's arms.

When they parted later at the quay she turned to him and said: 'Come to me later ... just once more ... to say goodbye.' And she hastened away in the dark.

In Adrienne's dimly-lit room they made love as they never had before.

In the last weeks, since they had first come together and all Adrienne's latent femininity had been awakened, an ever-increasing frenzy of passion had seized her every time she lay in Balint's arms. That wild joy of life that Balint had so often sensed in her but never before aroused, now so overwhelmed her that Adrienne had given herself without reserve and, in realizing to the full the satisfaction of her own nature so she had been able to make it the same for her lover. When, exhausted and spent, they had fallen asleep, it had been as if they were but one person. And if, from time to time in the course of those delirious nights, the Angel of Death was beating his wings above them, they had turned away consciously refusing to think of the future...

On this last night they did not sleep. Without uttering a word, they clung to each other desperately, kissing, biting each other's flesh, tearing at each other trying to suffocate in their overwhelming search for oblivion. It seemed that all that was left to them was to seek death from exhaustion, as if now the only fulfilment was to be found in killing the other with the urgency of their love.

When dawn broke Balint lifted himself up onto his elbow. Now, for the first time he spoke:

'What is going to happen, when . . . ?'

They looked into each other's eyes for a long time, seriously, not very close, almost at arm's length apart. He did not have to say more, for Adrienne knew at once what he had meant. The look in his eyes was enough. It said, as clearly as if he had pronounced the words out loud: If you decide to die, I shall too. I must know and I demand an answer, straight, clear, unequivocal...

As she looked up at him, into those wide, questioning eyes, she thought for a moment of all those plans she had made when they had not been together. Her original plan was now unthinkable. As soon as Balint had left she had decided to swim out to sea, carefully keeping out of the sight of the lifeguard in his boat, until she was wafted away for ever by those currents whose force no one could ever overcome. It would seem like bad luck and unlucky chance. But that was now impossible, for Judith had thought of the same thing, got there first as it were, and so spoiled her carefully thought-out plan. No one could do that now, for they had posted a double guard; besides which the memory of Judith lying there naked on the sand being looked at pruriently by all those people filled her with horror. No! That way was no longer open to her. Of course, she reflected, she still had the little

PART SIX

Browning; but she could not use that either, not here in Venice. Everyone would know at once that she had killed herself on purpose and Uzdy would soon find out how she had acquired the weapon and then as sure as anything on this earth he would search out Balint and kill him.

Abady's eyes were still on her, demanding an answer.

Adrienne looked back at him, and then, very slowly, she said: 'I will try to go on living. Maybe I'll succeed, even if we never see each other again...'

Now it was nearly daylight.

Adrienne sat on the side of the bed, still in her torn, thin nightdress. She did not move, but leant back on her elbows, her head thrown back and her eyes tightly closed.

Balint was already dressed. He was standing face to the wall. Then he turned back towards her and fell at her feet, burying his face in her lap and sobbing as if his heart would break. His whole body was so racked with sobs that his back heaved and shook as he pressed his face ever deeper into her lap, into the smooth curves of her half-naked thighs. Deep groans broke from him and he cried ever harder as if he would never stop. He was like a child in the grip of an unknown horror, a nightmare that could never be told in words, clinging to his mother's knees and clasping her as strongly as if he would never let go. His hands clutched at her body, at her bare flesh, not in desire but as a drowning man clutches at anything that comes his way. Through these racking sobs which so tore his throat that she could hardly distinguish what he was trying to say, through the waves of pain that both were feeling, came only one word, repeated over and over again: 'Addy... Addy... Addy...'

Adrienne gently stroked his head, not caring that her nightdress was torn, not noticing the ever-brightening light of the morning sun, regardless of her bare breasts, feeling no shame at the revelation of her torn and bruised and naked flesh. She felt nothing but sorrow, a dreadful, suffocating sorrow and pity.

Somehow she managed to find the strength to try and calm him, hushing him as one would a frightened child, vainly trying to lift his head, caressing his tousled hair as if he were her son, and all the while her hands, gentle and motherly, softly stroked his head as she tried to utter some words of comfort:

'My darling ... my own darling. You mustn't ... no, you mustn't... My very own... my darling... no, you mustn't...'

As Balint reeled out of Adrienne's room the hotel was coming to life. He staggered out, not looking back, banging into the doorpost as he went, like a man mortally wounded and unconscious of his surroundings.

Adrienne rose from the bed and walked slowly to the window. From far, far away she thought she could hear music, but it sounded like a funeral march or the sad songs that accompany the dead to their last resting place. Perhaps it was only the echo of some distant siren. Her heart throbbed, beating unevenly as if it were about to stop for ever.

Adrienne just stood there by the window, looking fixedly into a distance that for her did not exist. She never touched the curtains but just stood there, alone, staring into nothing, her nightdress in shreds and in front, where Balint had buried his head, it clung to her thighs wet with his tears, and cold to the touch, for from outside the open window the early morning breeze had just begun.

The voluminous folds of the fine white netting floated around her, veiling her face, her dishevelled, unruly hair, her naked shoulders, until she was entirely covered.

She might have been wrapped in a shroud . . .

ALSO AVAILABLE FROM ARCADIA BOOKS

Eddy: The Life of Edward Sackville-West
Michael De-la-Noy

Heir to Knole and a peerage, novelist, discerning critic and brilliant pianist, the intimate of Bloomsbury writers and painters, Edward Sackville-West was born with the proverbial silver spoon in his mouth. Through diaries and previously unpublished letters, we see a life dogged a chronic ill-health and a masochistic psychological make-up.

'Nobody can fail to respect the skill and industry which De-la-Noy has devoted to bringing Eddy Sackville-West back to life in this elegant and sympathetic biography' – *Sunday Times*

The Tangier Diaries 1962-1979
John Hopkins

American novelist Hopkins arrived in Tangier at the age of twenty-four and ended up spending almost two decades in Morocco, mixing with a wide cast of characters, Paul and Jane Bowles, William Burroughs, David Herbert and Malcolm Forbes among them.

'Hopkins writes as powerfully of place as of people, capturing the steamy bustle of the Kasbah market and the awesome mystery of the Sahara'
– Michael Arditti, *Daily Mail*

Doubtful Partners
John Haylock

The latest novel from the author of *Eastern Exchange* is a light-hearted look at the barriers and frustrations in close attachments – especially those doubtful partnerships in which communication is entirely physical.

'If there is one thing to bring out the candid in Haylock, it is the ins and outs of intimate intercourse' – *The Times*

Eastern Exchange
John Haylock

'For those with a fascination for eccentric lives, Haylock's book is a little gem, the record of an extraordinarily interesting life'
– Ian Buruma, *Sunday Telegraph*

ALSO AVAILABLE FROM ARCADIA BOOKS

When Memory Dies
A. Sivanandan

A three-generational saga of a Sri Lankan family's search for coherence and continuity in a country broken by colonial occupation and riven by ethnic wars. *Winner of the Sagittarius Prize 1998* and *shortlisted for the Commonwealth Writers Prize 1998*

'Haunting ... with an immense tenderness. The extraordinary poetic tact of this book makes it unforgettable' – John Berger, *Guardian*

The Last Kabbalist of Lisbon
Richard Zimler

A literary mystery set among secret Jews living in Lisbon in 1506 when, during Passover celebrations, some two thousand Jewish inhabitants were murdered in a pogrom. THE INTERNATIONAL BESTSELLER.

'Remarkable erudition and compelling imagination, an American Umberto Eco' – Francis King, *Spectator*

Night Letters
Robert Dessaix

Every night for twenty nights in a hotel room in Venice, a man recently diagnosed with HIV writes a letter home to a friend. He describes not only the kaleidoscopic journey he has just made from Switzerland across northern Italy to Venice, but reflects on questions of mortality, seduction and the search for paradise.

'Dessaix writes with great elegance, with passion, compassion, and sly wit. Literally a wonderful book' – John Banville

Double Act
Fiona Pitt-Kethley

'This poetry collection reads like it's been written by a sexually charged Philip Larkin. Both witty and scathing, it avoids the tender eroticism often employed when discussing sex and instead goes straight for the jugular' – *D*i*tour Magazine*

ALSO AVAILABLE FROM ARCADIA BOOKS

Tomorrow
Elisabeth Russell Taylor

In August 1960, a number of ill-assorted guests gather at a small hotel on the Danish island of Møn. Among them is Elisabeth Danziger, whose happy memories of growing up in a brilliant and gifted family are overshadowed by darker ones, over which she struggles to achieve control.

'A memorable and poignant novel made all the more heartbreaking by the quiet dignity of its central character and the restraint of its telling' – Shena Mackay

Present Fears
Elisabeth Russell Taylor

'It is hard to pinpoint what makes these stories so unsettling. Their worlds – some border territory between genteel suburbia and dreamland – are imagined with an eerie thoroughness. The inhabitants are all out of kilter, and terrifyingly fragile; spinsterish middle-agers paralysed by sexual fear; anxious children in the centre of parental power games. Russell Taylor's abrupt, elegantly engineered anticlimaxes leave the reader with the disquieting feeling of waiting for the other shoe to fall' – Sam Leith, *Observer*

Isabelle
John Berger and Nella Bielski

A compelling recreation of the life of Isabelle Eberhardt.

'A tantalizing enigma, Berger and Bielski's filmic approach is appropriate to her literally dramatic life, and the symmetry of the imagery is an indication of the artistry of this work' – *Observer*

Fear of Mirrors
Tariq Ali

Lovers want to know the truth, but they do not always want to tell it. For some East Germans, the fall of Communism was like the end of a long and painful love affair; free to tell the truth at last, they found they no longer wanted to hear it.

'When Ali's imagination goes wild he is superb' – *New Statesman*

ALSO AVAILABLE FROM ARCADIA BOOKS

Time Exposure
Brodrick Haldane
in conversation with Roddy Martine

For almost six decades Brodrick Haldane moved among the rich and the famous, photographing everybody who was anybody, including the Queen Mother, Bernard Shaw, the Aga Khan and Margaret, Duchess of Argyll. *Time Exposure* is a witty and charming portrait of an age peopled by extraordinary characters.

'The original society paparazzo, snapping the Duke of Windsor and Wallis Simpson in exile, Charlie Chaplin and a youthful JFK' – *Sunday Times*

False Light
Peter Sheldon
Foreword by Francis King

Karl is a handsome adolescent in Vienna between the wars. He has every advantage, but all is not as it seems in a situation full of political tensions and erotic undercurrents.

'An absorbing read' – Sebastian Beaumont, *Gay Times*

Eurydice in the Underworld
Kathy Acker

The last work of new fiction Acker published before her death from breast cancer in late 1997, *Eurydice* is Acker's response to her diagnosis. Its 'raw truth is shot through with surprising lyricism and tenderness' – *Observer*. The collection also includes Acker classics such as 'Lust', 'Algeria' and 'Immoral', on the banning in Germany of *Blood and Guts in High School*.

'Kathy Acker's writing is virtuoso, maddening, crazy, so sexy, so painful, and beaten out of a wild heart that nothing can tame. Acker is a landmark writer' – Jeanette Winterson

ARCADIA BOOKS

are available from all good bookshops
or direct from the publishers at 15–16 Nassau Street, London W1N 7RE.
Write for a free catalogue.